Index to Vital Data

in

Local Newspapers

of

Sonoma County

California

Volume 11
1916-1918

Sonoma County Genealogical Society, Inc.

HERITAGE BOOKS
2012

HERITAGE BOOKS

AN IMPRINT OF HERITAGE BOOKS, INC.

Books, CDs, and more—Worldwide

For our listing of thousands of titles see our website
at
www.HeritageBooks.com

Published 2012 by
HERITAGE BOOKS, INC.
Publishing Division
100 Railroad Ave. #104
Westminster, Maryland 21157

International Standard Book Numbers
Paperbound: 978-0-7884-5455-4
Clothbound: 978-0-7884-9275-4

Contents

Index to Vital Data in Newspapers

Sonoma County, California

1916-1918: Volume XI

The indexing of Sonoma County newspapers was undertaken to help fill in the gaps in some of the early records in Sonoma County. The first volume, which covers the period from 1854 through 1875 was published early in 2001.[1] Nine additional volumes have been published between that time and the present, covering the period through 1915.

The present volume contains an index of surnames found in those papers published in Sonoma County between 1916 and 1918 and contains more than 14,500 entries. Other volumes are planned for the future. Some of the entries include residents from the surrounding counties of Marin, Napa, Solano, Lake, and Mendocino. This volume is unique in that letters from soldiers, many serving in other than the US army (British, Canadian, French and Italian) are included.

Newspapers indexed

CR   *Cloverdale Review*

GT   *Guerneville Times and Russian River Advertiser*

HT   *Healdsburg Tribune*

PA   *Petaluma Argus*

PC   *Petaluma Daily Courier*

PD   *Press Democrat*

SIT   *Sonoma Index Tribune*

SRR   *Santa Rosa Republican*

ST   *Sebastopol Times*

Other newspapers published during this time period

Other newspapers were published during this period, but no copies of them could be located. They include the *Cloverdale Enterprise, News (Schellville), Santa Rosa Herald, Santa Rosa News, Sonoma County Herald, Sonoma Expositor Forum, Sotoyome Scimitar,* and *West Coast Mountaineer.*

---

[1]Sonoma County Genealogy Society, *Index to Vital Data in Newspapers, Sonoma County, California, 1854-1875: Volume I* (Bowie, Md.: Heritage Books, 2001).

Microfilm copies of the newspapers may be found at these libraries

Library	Newspaper Code
Sonoma County Library Annex 3rd and E Streets Santa Rosa, CA 95404 707-545-0831 ext. 562	GT, PD, SIT, SRR, ST
Healdsburg Museum 221 Matheson Street Healdsburg, CA 95448 707-431-3325	HT
Healdsburg Public Library Piper and Center Streets Healdsburg, CA 95448 707-433-3772	HT, RRA
Petaluma Public Library 100 Fairgrounds Drive Petaluma, CA 94952 707-763-9801	PA, PC
Sonoma State Library 1801 E. Cotati Ave. Rohnert Park, CA 94928 707-664-2161	PD, SRR

Aids to interpreting the data

This eleventh volume contains more than 14,500 entries. There were many typographical errors in these early papers, and although every effort has been made to ensure the accuracy of the names, the reader will note variations in spelling of both surnames and given names. If the name you are researching does not appear where you expect it to be, consider variant spellings. Just as may be found in other early vital records—birth, death, marriage, and the like—newspapers also include errors of fact or transcription. Some microfilms of the early papers are difficult to read, and while our abstractors did their best, some inaccuracies may have occurred among the people who dealt with the material to make this volume possible. The serious researcher is always encouraged to go to the original source if at all possible, and to check other local sources if they exist. In particular, consider variations in spelling or spacing in surnames and given names, as well as possible initials, which may occur in the various sources. You may suspect missing or misplaced letters, but the data is entered as it was found in the original records. We have not attempted to make a decision about which form is correct or commonly used; that is up to the individual researcher.

Be aware that a particular type of record, i.e., a marriage record, may contain the names of persons other than the bride and groom, such as the minister or parents. A death record may also include the names of other family members. In some cases, an item may refer only to the son, daughter, or infant of a person. When that happens, (son), (dau), or (infant) may appear following the given name of the parent. Occasionally, a birth or a marriage announcement is listed years after the event. These births and marriages usually did not take place in Sonoma County, but occurred elsewhere in the state or country.

In order to conserve space we have used some standard abbreviations:

Code	Type of Record
b.	Birth record. The entry will almost always be under the name of the father, as the child's name is seldom given in the newspaper. Birth records were first recorded in Sonoma County in 1871.
d.	Death record. Some of the names listed may be family members as well as the deceased. Deaths were first recorded in Sonoma County in 1871.
m.	Marriage record. Marriages were first recorded in 1847.
p.	Probate record. In many cases this is the only indication of a person's death in Sonoma County.
o.	Other record. This may be a divorce, or any other type of record giving some genealogical information about the individual.
s.	The article appears in a supplement to the newspaper of that date.

Comments

In some cases, the last column in the chart contains comments. These may include the name of a cemetery if known, a location mentioned in the item, special circumstances, where additional information can be found, and the like. A list of Sonoma County cemeteries follows, as does a map of the county and a list of Sonoma County place names. *Place names which do not include a state abbreviation should be assumed to be in California and are often in Sonoma County.*

Towns and Villages in Sonoma County

Historical information on towns and villages in Sonoma County is reprinted here from *The Sonoma Searcher.*[2]

SONOMA COUNTY TOWNS
AND VILLAGES: VINTAGE 1890

America is ten miles north of Santa Rosa; including the immediate vicinity; it has a population of 250. It is more widely known as Mark West Springs. It has a hotel and post office and is a resort for tourists and invalids. A stage line affords communication with Santa Rosa.

Bloomfield is a thriving community at the head of Big Valley, twelve miles north of Petaluma. The population is about 350. The village has a full complement of stores, churches and societies; a good hotel is maintained. It has communication by stage with Petaluma. It is growing and offers inducements to settlers.

Bodega is eighteen miles north of Petaluma, and located on Bodega Bay in the midst of a fine dairy country from which, with the fishing business, it derives its support. It boasts of a hotel, post office and express office.

Clairville is located twenty-three miles northwest from Santa Rosa on the line of the S. F. & N. P. R. R. It is in the midst of a farming and vine growing district. There are several wineries in the immediate neighborhood. It has a population of 150. Skaggs' Springs are six miles distant from this point with which communication is maintained by stage.

Cloverdale is fourth in point of wealth and population amongst the towns of Sonoma County. It is the present terminus of the San Francisco and North Pacific Railroad, and is distant thirty-three miles northwest of Santa Rosa and eighty-four miles from San Francisco. It is in the midst of a large and productive region, and is the center of trade for the wool interest and extensive hop fields of this part of the country. The climate here is more bracing than in the southern portion of Sonoma, and is especially adapted to the growth of the hardier varieties of fruits. The population is about 1,400 and is steadily growing. The leading denominations have places of worship with good congregations. All the leading secret and fraternal orders and societies have flourishing organizations. Hotel accommodations are good. The town is amply supplied with water furnished by the Cloverdale Water Company. Real estate is low, and the opportunities offered to the settler are unexcelled by those of other places. Stages leave here for Ukiah, Mendocino City, Eureka and other points on the North Coast, and for all points in Lake County and northern Napa. A railroad will, in a few months, connect it with Ukiah, Mendocino County. The Cloverdale *Reveille* ably advocates the interest of the community. It is published weekly.

Cozzens. A small burg located a few miles distant from Healdsburg. It has a population of 150 and is surrounded by a prosperous farming and wine growing community. A saw mill is located here and a general merchandise store supplies the needed requirements of the village.

---

[2]"Sonoma County Towns and Villages: Vintage 1890," *The Sonoma Searcher*, volume 23 (June 1996): 52; reprinted from *Illustrated History of Sonoma County* (Chicago: Lewis Publishing, 1889), pp. 168-170.

Duncan's Mills is located thirty miles north from Petaluma. It has communication with San Francisco by the North Pacific Coast Railroad. It is supported by important lumber, dairy and stock raising interests. The Duncan's Mill's Land and Lumber Company saw mills are located here. The population is about 250. The surrounding country is noted for its romantic and picturesque scenery, and abundance of game and fish. It is a favorite resort for the tourist, the sportsman and for camping parties during the summer months. Stages leave here for all points in Mendocino and Humboldt counties.

Fisherman's Bay is located on the coast above Fort Ross. A population of 200 is supported by the farming interest and employment at the saw and shingle mills which are located here.

Fisk's Mills is a small village of about 150 population, in Salt Point Township, distant about twelve miles north of Fort Ross. Communication is had with Duncan's Mills by stage.

Forestville is distant twelve miles northwest of Santa Rosa, on the S. F. & N. P. R. R. Large quantities of tan-bark are shipped from this point. A rustic chair factory is located here. The business community consists of a hotel, blacksmith shops and two general merchandise stores. The surrounding country is devoted to farming.

Fort Ross is a small settlement forty-two miles north of Petaluma. It contains many reminders of the early days when a Russian colony was located here. It is one of the oldest settlements on the northern coast of California. The population is about 130, who are principally engaged in stock raising and farming. It is connected with Duncan's Mills by stage.

Freestone is on the line of the North Pacific Coast Railroad. The population is about 175, supported by the dairying and farming carried on in the vicinity.

Fulton. An ambitious and growing village on the line of the S. F. & N. P. R. R., four miles from Santa Rosa, is surrounded by a rich agricultural district. Considerable fruit is raised here. The population is 200, dependent upon the fruit and farming interests of the vicinity. From this place a branch of the S. F. & N. P. R. R. extends to Guerneville.

Geyser Springs is located sixteen miles from Cloverdale, from which place they are reached by stage. It is a noted health and pleasure resort. The numerous mineral springs in the vicinity are the chief attraction.

Guerneville. The progressive and prosperous town of Guerneville is situated in the midst of a large lumber producing district, and is surrounded by forests of redwood; a branch of the S. F. & N. P. R. R. has its terminus at this point. The town derived its name from one of its pioneer residents who is engaged in the large milling interests of the town. There are four extensive lumber mills located in the town, employing a large number of men. The present population is variously estimated at from 750 to 900. As the forests are being cleared off the land is put under cultivation, producing fine crops of vegetables and cereals, and a large yield of fruit. The Korbel mills located about three miles up the Russian River, are the most extensive lumber mills in the county. Considerable attention has of late been paid to the vine, and many acres have been set out. In addition to the lumber mills, there is also a box factory and shingle mill in active operation. The prospects of this town are very bright. Its rapid growth and prosperity are assured.

Kellogg. A summer resort, sixteen miles from Santa Rosa, with which it is connected by stage.

Lakeside is a thriving and growing village, twenty-two miles southeast of Santa Rosa. There are large farming, dairy and stock raising interests in the vicinity; the population is about 150.

Litton Springs. A noted health and pleasure resort, four miles from Healdsburg, on the S. F. & N. P. R. R. The water of the mineral springs located here is bottled and finds a market all over the State. The Litton Springs College is located at this point. The country in the neighborhood is rich and productive, and inviting to settlement.

Mark West is on the line of the S. F. & N. P. R. R. six miles north of Santa Rosa. The leading interests of the vicinity are farming, fruit and vine growing. The population is about 100. The surrounding country is rich and fertile and excellently adapted to the growth of vines and fruit.

Occidental. This growing and prosperous town is located on the line of the North Pacific Coast Railroad, about thirty miles north of Petaluma. Farming, fruit growing and lumber manufacturing are the principal industries in which the inhabitants are engaged. The population is 225.

Penn's Grove is a small settlement five miles north of Petaluma on the line of the S. F. & N. P. R. R. It is in the midst of a large vine growing and wine producing district. The population is 125.

Timber Cove is forty-five miles north of Petaluma, and has a population of 160. The occupation of the residents is mainly farming, stock raising, and dairying. It is known by the Post Office Department as Seaview.

Skaggs' Springs. Has long been noted as a health and pleasure resort, twenty-nine miles distant from Santa Rosa. A stage connects it with Clairville, six miles distant. The population is about 115, who are principally engaged in wool raising.

Smith's Ranch, or more generally known as Bodega Roads, is twenty-five miles north of Petaluma, and is on the line of the North Pacific Coast Railroad. The people of the surrounding country are principally engaged in dairying and farming, from which their support is chiefly derived. The population is about 250.

Stony Point. Is located seven miles north of Petaluma in the midst of a large fruit, dairy and farming region. The population is about 200, including those residing in the immediate vicinity.

Valley Ford is one of the prosperous communities of Sonoma. It is on the line of the North Pacific Coast R. R., eighteen miles north of Petaluma. It boasts of a flouring mill. The population is about 250. It is supported by the large dairying, farming, and stock raising interest by which it is surrounded.

Windsor is another of the large and thrifty villages of Sonoma County. It is ten miles northwest of Santa Rosa, in the midst of a large farming and fruit growing section. There are many vineyards in the neighborhood and several nurseries. It has a population of 400. The village boasts of a brick manufactory, several fruit-drying establishments, and other industries of minor importance.

———————

Other Sonoma County Towns and Townships

Alexander Valley
Altruria
Analy Township
Annapolis
Asti
Bennett Valley
Bodega Corners
Bodega Township
Cloverdale Township
Donahue
Dry Creek
El Verano
Elmore
Forestville Station
Geysers
Geyserville
Glen Ellen
Green Valley
Healdsburg
Kenwood

Knights Valley
Lakeville
Lewis
Liberty
Llano
Los Guilicos
Lytton
Markham
Matanzas
Mendocino Township
Ocean Township
Petaluma
Petaluma Township
Pocket Canyon
Redwood Township
Rincon
Rincon Valley
Rio Nido
Roblar
Russian River Township

Salt Point Township
San Antonio
San Luis/Louis
Santa Rosa
Santa Rosa Township
Schellville
Sea View
Sebastopol
Soda Rock
Sonoma
Sonoma Township
Stewarts Point
Table Mountain
Two Rock
Vallejo Township
Washington
Washington Township
West Windsor

Sonoma County, California Townships

Map — Circa 1896-1897

Cemeteries of Sonoma County
Jeremy Dwight Nichols

Cyrus Alexander Family
John Anderson Ranch
Annapolis Church
Appleseed Farm
Asti Family
Baha'i
Beeson
Benitz Ranch
Bennett Valley
Bloomfield
Bodega Bay
Bodega Town Calvary
Walter Brain Ranch
Branscomb
Buckeye Creek Ranch
Burbank
Campbell
Canfield
Catron Family
Chanate
Chapel of the Chimes
Cheney
William Churchman Ranch
Cloverdale
Cooper Ranch
Crane Ranch
Cunningham Ranch
Curry
Druids
Duncans Mills
Eldridge
Elim Grove
Evergreen
Faught
Fisk Ranch
Fisk Mill
Forestville
Fort Ross
Fulton

Geyserville
Gilliam
Green Valley
Hall
Harper
Charlie Haupt Ranch
Healdsburg Oak Mound
Healdsburg Old
Holliday Ranch
Howie Ranch
Joy Ranch
Knipp and Stengel Ranch
Koger-Bice
Kricke Ranch
La Vala's Crossing
Liberty
Jack London Ranch
Long Family Ranch
Los Alamos
Lynch Ranch
Macedonia M.E. Church
Manzanita
Mason
McPeak
Mt. Olive
Neils Island
Nobels Ranch
Nun Canyon
Oak Hill
Jasper O'Farrell Ranch
Olivet
Otis Ranch
Charles Patton Ranch
Petaluma Calvary
Petaluma Cypress Hill
Peterson Ranch
Pine Flat
Pioneer
Pleasant Hills

Preston
Pritchett
Pythian
Redwood Memorial Gardens
Ruoff-Thomas
St. Catherine
St. Francis Solano
St. Teresa
Santa Rosa Calvary
Santa Rosa Memorial Park
Santa Rosa Memorial Park, Shiloh Road Addition
Santa Rosa Rural
Seaview
Sebastopol Memorial Lawn
Sharp Cemetery
Shiloh
Skaggs
Sky Farm
Slattery Ranch
Sonoma Mission
Sonoma Mountain
Sonoma Valley
Spring Hill
Steele Family
Del Stewart Ranch
Stewarts Point
Thompson Family
Pearl Trosper Ranch
Two Rock Church
Upper Dry Creek
Vallejo Home
Vallejo Ranch
Valley Ford
Walker Ranch
Warneke Ranch
Mark West
Young Family

Acknowledgments

This project was prepared using a four-step process. First, microfilms of the early newspapers were read and the information was abstracted onto prepared forms. Next, the information on the forms was entered into table format by data entry persons using their own hardware and software. The data were then sent online to a person who acted as the central data collector. Finally, camera-ready copy was prepared and proofread against the abstracted information.

Persons contributing to this effort included the following:

Project Coordinator
Audrey Herman

Abstractors
Shirley Flick
Audrey Herman
Muriel Morrow

Data Entry
Anna Conley
Lois Nimmo

Proof Readers
Doris Dickenson
Audrey Herman

Camera-Ready Copy
Carmen Finley

Column Headings

To conserve space, some column headings are not written out completely. The information is given in eight columns, as follows:

(1)   Surname, including some alternative spellings when used elsewhere

(2)   Given Name, may include relationship to the individual listed

(3)   Type of record - b.=birth; d.=death; m.=marriage; p.=probate; o.=other (includes letters written by World War I soldiers)

(4)   Newspaper Code - see Introduction page v

(5)   Date of newspaper

(6)   Page of newspaper listing

(7)   Column of newspaper listing

(8)   Comments - 5:1 means page 5 column 1

A

(1) Surname	(2) Given Name	(3)	(4)	(5) Date	(6) Pg	(7) Col	(8) Comments
Abbey	Alfred	d.	HT	30 Mar. 1916	8	5	Mountain View, Oakland
Abbott	George	d.	PD	23 Nov. 1917	3	2	also 24 Nov., 8:5; 27 Nov., 2:2
Abbott	George	d.	SRR	23 Nov. 1917	5	4	also 8:1; 26 Nov., 2:4
Abderhalden	Jacob (son of)	d.	PC	10 Apr. 1917	5	5	
Abeel	David K.	o.	ST	3 May 1918	2	4	
Aberhalden	Jacob	b.	PC	7 Mar. 1917	5	6	
Ables	Thomas J.	d.	PA	17 Dec. 1917	4	3	Tomales; also 18 Dec., 13:4; 19 Dec., 8:3
Ables	Thomas J.	d.	PC	18 Dec. 1917	5	3	also 19 Dec., 5:3
Abraio	Clara	m.	PA	3 Dec. 1918	5	1	also 9 Dec., 2:2
Abrams	Sherman	m.	PD	2 Mar. 1917	8	2	
Abramsky	Sarah Jane	d.	PD	4 July 1916	2	1	
Abramsky	Sarah Jane	d.	SRR	5 July 1916	5	1	I.O.O.F. Cemetery
Abrio	Clara J.	m.	PC	10 Dec. 1918	3	4	
Abru	Sophie	d.	PA	22 July 1918	5	1	also 24 July, 4:5
Abru	Sophie	d.	PC	23 July 1918	1	2	
Ackerman	Charles	b.	HT	25 Apr. 1918	3	2	
Ackerman	Charles J.	m.	PD	11 Aug. 1917	2	3	
Ackerman	Charles J.	m.	SRR	11 Aug. 1917	6	1	
Ackerman	Charles J.	m.	PC	12 Aug. 1917	1	4	
Ackerman	O. B., Mrs.	d.	PC	24 Feb. 1917	1	6	
Acorne	Melville	m.	PA	4 June 1917	4	7	also 8 June, 5:6
Acorne	Melville	m.	PC	10 June 1917	5	4	
Acuse	Sophie	d.	PD	23 July 1918	6	1	
Adams	Adam C.	d.	ST	15 Nov. 1918	1	4	
Adams	Adam Crawford	d.	CR	15 Nov. 1918	8	1	
Adams	Adam Crawford	d.	PD	16 Nov. 1918	1	7	
Adams	Albert	o.	PA	7 July 1917	6	1	
Adams	Albert	o.	PC	8 July 1917	5	5	
Adams	Bob	o.	PA	21 Nov. 1918	8	3	
Adams	Clara	m.	PD	22 Nov. 1916	2	2	
Adams	Clara V.	m.	SRR	21 Nov. 1916	7	4	
Adams	Clare A.	o.	PA	14 June 1917	1	6	
Adams	Claude Milton	m.	PA	20 June 1918	8	3	
Adams	Claude Milton	m.	PC	20 June 1918	1	4	also 21 June, 4:3
Adams	Clement S.	o.	PD	15 Sept. 1917	3	1	also 16 Sept., 3:3
Adams	Clement S.	o.	SRR	22 Sept. 1917	5	4	

(1) Surname	(2) Given Name	(3)	(4)	(5) Date	(6) Pg	(7) Col	(8) Comments
Adams	Darwin C.	m.	PD	28 May 1916	3	1	
Adams	Elizabeth Ada	d.	PA	30 Dec. 1918	5	3	Cypress Hill; also 31 Dec., 5:3
Adams	Elizabeth Ada	d.	PC	31 Dec. 1918	5	4	
Adams	Hannah	d.	SRR	31 Jan. 1917	5	1	
Adams	J. W.	d.	SRR	23 May 1917	1	2	
Adams	J. W.	d.	PD	24 May 1917	6	2	
Adams	James C.	d.	PC	3 June 1916	6	2	
Adams	Ken	o.	PD	17 Dec. 1918	2	4	
Adams	Ross	b.	PD	22 Dec. 1918	3	1	
Adams	William	d.	PD	12 Jan. 1918	4	2	
Adams	William	d.	PC	13 Jan. 1918	1	2	Duncan Mills
Adamson	Forrest	b.	PC	25 Apr. 1918	4	4	
Aggenson	Carrie	m.	PA	5 Sept. 1918	3	3	
Aggeson	Carrie K.	m.	PD	5 Sept. 1918	2	3	also 5 Sept., 2:5
Aggio	Pietro	d.	PD	8 Dec. 1918	8	3	France
Agnew	Elizabeth J.	m.	PC	11 Aug. 1918	3	2	
Agnew	Elizabeth J.	m.	PA	9 Aug. 1918	8	5	
Agren	Arthur Louis	m.	PD	22 Sept. 1916	5	1	
Agren	Arthur Louis	m.	SRR	22 Sept. 1916	2	4	
Agren	Arthur Louis	m.	PC	23 Sept. 1916	6	3	
Agrio	Pietro	d.	PC	10 Dec. 1918	3	3	
Aguar	Jose Martin	d.	PA	12 Jan. 1916	4	4	Calvary Cemetery; also 13 Jan., 5:4
Aguar	Jose Martin	d.	PC	12 Jan. 1916	5	5	Calvary Cemetery;also 14 Jan., 4:4
Aguar	Jose Martin	d.	PA	18 Dec. 1916	6	4	Calvary Cemetery; also 19 Dec., 4:6
Aguar	Jose/John Martin	d.	PC	19 Dec. 1916	8	4	Calvary Cemetery; also 20 Dec., 8:3
Ahern	George	m.	SRR	18 Aug. 1917	6	5	
Ahern	George	m.	PC	19 Aug. 1917	3	2	
Ahern	George F.	m.	SRR	15 Sept. 1917	6	2	
Ahern	George F.	m.	PD	16 Sept. 1917	2	5	
Ahl	Harry J.	o.	PD	17 Apr. 1917	7	1	
Ahl	Harry L.	o.	SRR	30 Oct. 1917	7	3	also 8:3
Ahl	Kate	o.	PD	17 Apr. 1917	7	1	
Ahl	Kinlay	o.	PD	6 Mar. 1918	2	1	
Ahl	Kinley	o.	PD	4 June 1918	7	1	
Ahl	Ruby	m.	SRR	19 Dec. 1916	2	3	also 20 Dec., 7:4
Ahl	Ruby	m.	PD	20 Dec. 1916	2	5	also 21 Dec., 2:5
Ainslie	Joseph	d.	PD	21 Jan. 1916	8	1	Poiint Arena Cemetery

(1) Surname	(2) Given Name	(3)	(4)	(5) Date	(6) Pg	(7) Col	(8) Comments
Ainsworth	H.	d.	ST	16 Dec. 1916	7	4	
Ainsworth	Henry	d.	PC	13 Dec. 1916	3	3	Cloverdale; also 16 Dec., 4:4
Ainsworth	Henry	d.	PD	13 Dec. 1916	3	3	also 16 Dec., 2:5
Ainsworth	Henry	d.	SRR	9 Dec. 1916	7	2	Cloverdale,; also 12 Dec., 10:4; 15 Dec., 10:3
Albertini	Theodore	d.	SRR	13 Dec. 1917	3	2	
Albertoni	D.	b.	PC	21 Sept. 1916	5	4	
Albertoni	J.	d.	PC	24 Mar. 1918	8	4	
Albertoni	Theodore	d.	PC	12 Dec. 1917	8	4	
Alberts	Matthew	d.	PA	27 Apr. 1916	8	3	Cypress Hill; also 28 Apr., 2:7, 8:5; 1 May, 5:5
Alberts	Matthew	d.	PC	27 Apr. 1916	1	5	Cypress Hill; also 28 Apr., 5:2; 2 May, 6:3
Albertson	Mrs.	d.	HT	14 Dec. 1916	6	3	
Albertson	Nellie	d.	PD	10 Dec. 1916	5	2	
Albertson	Nellie Ozier	d.	SRR	9 Dec. 1916	3	1	
Albini	Alice Amelia	d.	PA	31 Mar. 1917	6	3	Tomales
Albini	Alice Amelia	d.	PC	31 Mar. 1917	4	2	Tomales; also 3 Apr., 8:3; 4 Apr., 4:3
Albini	Domenico	o.	PD	9 Apr. 1918	3	3	
Albini	Ersillio	o.	PD	9 Apr. 1918	3	3	
Alcorn	Ada Catherine	m.	PA	7 Feb. 1916	7	5	
Alden	Priscella B.	m.	PD	1 Aug. 1916	3	3	
Alden	Priscilla	m.	PA	31 May 1916	3	3	
Alden	Priscilla B.	m.	PC	2 Aug. 1916	2	1	
Alderman	William	m.	PA	6 Apr. 1918	3	3	
Alderman	William	m.	PC	6 Apr. 1918	5	2	
Alderson	Earl	d.	ST	27 Dec. 1918	1	2	
Alderson	Morland Earl	d.	ST	27 May 1916	2	4	
Alexander	Archibald	m.	PA	30 Mar. 1916	1	4	
Alexander	John	o.	PC	16 Dec. 1917	1	3	
Alexander	John	o.	PC	27 Oct. 1918	2	2	
Alexander	Joseph	d.	PC	6 Apr. 1918	1	5	
Alexander	Joseph	d.	PD	6 Apr. 1918	6	1	Rural Cemetery; also 7 Apr., 4:2; 9 Apr., 3:3
Alexander	Lawrence	d.	HT	20 Oct. 1916	1	1	Oak Mound Cemetery
Alexander	Lawrence	d.	SRR	25 Oct. 1916	3	2	
Alexander	Lawrence	d.	PD	26 Oct. 1916	6	1	
Alexander	Lawrence	d.	PC	27 Oct. 1916	2	2	
Alexander	Selma	m.	SRR	2 Feb. 1916	10	6	

(1) Surname	(2) Given Name	(3)	(4)	(5) Date	(6) Pg	(7) Col	(8) Comments
Alexander	Selma	m.	PD	3 Feb. 1916	3	3	
Alfanso	Joseph	m.	SIT	27 Apr. 1918	2	5	
Alfonso	Joseph	m.	PA	4 Apr. 1918	4	5	
Alford	Charles	d.	PC	6 Nov. 1918	2	2	France
Alkire	Clara Ella	m.	PC	4 Apr. 1918	8	4	
Alkiro	Cora K.	m.	PD	5 Apr. 1918	3	3	
Allegrini	Francis	d.	CR	13 Apr. 1917	1	3	
Allegrini	Francis Julius	d.	SRR	5 Apr. 1917	10	2	Cloverdale; also 7 Apr., 5:5, 10:3; 18 Apr., 8:2
Allegrini	Francis Julius	d.	PD	6 Apr. 1917	4	3	Cloverdale; also 8:5; 8 Apr., 5:2
Allegrini	Frank	d.	PA	5 Apr. 1917	4	5	
Allen	Alice Elizabeth	m.	PA	15 Dec. 1916	4	1	also 16 Dec., 4:5
Allen	Alice Elizabeth	m.	PC	16 Dec. 1917	5	3	
Allen	Anna Martha	d.	PC	2 Mar. 1918	4	2	
Allen	Carena	d.	PA	11 Oct. 1917	8	3	Cypress Hill; also 12 Oct., 4:1; 13 Oct., 4:4
Allen	Carena	d.	PD	12 Oct. 1917	8	4	
Allen	Carl G.	b.	PA	21 Sept. 1918	1	5	
Allen	Corena	d.	PC	11 Oct. 1917	4	3	Cypress Hill; also 13 Oct., 3:3; 14 Oct., 6:4
Allen	Elizabeth	d.	PD	27 Dec. 1916	8	2	also 30 Dec., 5:2
Allen	Ethel	m.	PD	3 Aug. 1917	2	1	
Allen	Ethel	m.	SRR	3 Aug. 1917	3	2	
Allen	Francis Erskine	d.	PA	29 Apr. 1916	1	3	also 1 May, 2:6
Allen	Francis Erskine (Frank)	d.	PC	29 Apr. 1916	1	2	cremation; also 30 Apr., 5:4, 8:4
Allen	J. Finley	m.	PC	16 Mar. 1918	6	4	
Allen	Jerry	d.	PA	16 Oct. 1918	8	3	
Allen	Jerry	d.	PD	16 Oct. 1918	3	1	
Allen	Jerry	d.	PC	17 Oct. 1918	3	4	
Allen	Jim	m.	PD	10 Dec. 1916	5	2	also 17 Dec., 3:5
Allen	Jim	m.	SRR	16 Dec. 1916	10	3	
Allen	Jim	m.	PC	17 Dec. 1916	5	5	
Allen	Jim	m.	PA	28 Oct. 1916	5	1	portrait; also 16 Dec., 4:1
Allen	Jim	b.	PA	29 Sept. 1917	8	1	
Allen	John Findley	m.	PA	15 Mar. 1918	4	3	
Allen	John Rittenhouse	d.	SIT	19 Oct. 1918	1	5	
Allen	Mary	d.	PA	24 Dec. 1917	5	3&4	Calvary Cemetery; also 26 Dec., 8:3
Allen	Mary	d.	PC	25 Dec. 1917	1	5	Calvary Cemetery; also 4:2; 27 Dec., 8:5

(1) Surname	(2) Given Name	(3)	(4)	(5) Date	(6) Pg	(7) Col	(8) Comments
Allen	Nancy Maria	d.	PA	10 Apr. 1918	8	5	
Allen	Thomas E.	m.	PC	25 Oct. 1918	2	2	
Allenberg	Selma	d.	PC	15 Oct. 1918	5	3	
Alletti	Joe	o.	PA	28 Sept. 1918	4	4	
Alley	L. S.	m.	PD	2 Feb. 1916	8	5	Henry, IL
Alley	Leona	m.	SRR	30 June 1916	8	5	
Alliette	Joseph	o.	PC	29 Sept. 1918	8	3	
Allman	Henry	d.	PC	12 July 1918	1	3	France
Allman	Henry	d.	PD	12 July 1918	1	6	France
Allman	Henry	d.	HT	18 July 1918	1	3	
Alloggi	Lucienne	m.	PA	11 Apr. 1917	6	3	also 27 Apr., 5:3
Alloggi	Lucienne	m.	PC	13 Apr. 1917	5	3	also 27 Apr., 5:3
Almada	Manuel T.	d.	PC	8 Dec. 1918	4	4	Calvary Cemetery; also 12 Dec., 4:4; 14 Dec., 3:2
Almada	Manuel T.	d.	PA	9 Dec. 1918	8	5	Calvary Cemetery; also 13 Dec., 4:1
Alphon	Dr.	d.	SIT	10 Feb. 1917	1	2	
Alphon	Dr.	d.	PC	14 Feb. 1917	3	3	
Alphonse	Joseph	m.	PC	6 Apr. 1918	3	4	
Alten	Anna Martha	d.	PA	2 Mar. 1918	8	2	Odd Fellows Cemetery, Santa Rosa
Alten	Anna Martha	d.	PD	2 Mar. 1918	4	2	I.O.O.F. Cemetery
Alten	Anna Martha	d.	ST	8 Mar. 1918	8	1	
Altenreuther	Leo	b.	PA	10 Sept. 1917	4	7	also 8:5
Altenreuther	Leo C.	m.	PC	29 Oct. 1916	5	2	also 22 Nov., 4:2
Altenreuther	Leopold	m.	PD	22 Nov. 1916	3	2	
Altenreuther	Leopold	m.	SRR	22 Nov. 1916	5	2	
Altheer	Ben	m.	PA	29 Jan. 1916	8	7	
Althenreuther	Leopold C.	m.	PA	21 Nov. 1916	5	3	also 22 Nov., 8:6
Alther	B.	b.	PC	21 Feb. 1917	5	2	
Alton	Mr., & Mrs.	o.	PD	18 Nov. 1917	8	2	adoption
Alvarado	Winifred	o.	HT	7 Mar. 1918	1	3	adoption
Alvarez	Joe	m.	ST	30 Nov. 1917	4	3	
Alvernaz	Manuel	b.	PA	18 May 1917	5	6	
Alves	F. Sidney	d.	PC	5 Apr. 1918	8	5	
Alves	Frank Sydney	d.	ST	5 Apr. 1918	1	3	
Alves	Gladys	d.	PA	8 Jan. 1916	4	3	
Alves	Joseph	d.	PD	16 July 1918	5	5	Holy Cross, San Francisco; also 17 July, 4:2; 18 July, 8:1; 19 July, 3:3
Alves	Sidney	d.	PD	4 Apr. 1918	8	2	

(1) Surname	(2) Given Name	(3)	(4)	(5) Date	(6) Pg	(7) Col	(8) Comments
Alves	Sydney	m.	ST	11 May 1917	3	5	also 4:3
Amaral	Agnes	d.	ST	17 Feb. 1917	1	1	
Ambjornson	Flora A.	d.	ST	20 Feb. 1916	3	6	
Ameral	Anthony	m.	PC	31 Oct. 1917	3	2	also 3 Nov., 5:3
Ames	Alden T.	d.	PA	21 Dec. 1916	5	5	
Ames	Fred Forrest	d.	ST	26 Oct. 1917	1	5	
Ames	Frederick F.	d.	SRR	25 Oct. 1917	8	6	also 26 Oct., 1:5
Ames	Frederick F.	d.	PC	26 Oct. 1917	1	4	
Ames	John	d.	SRR	5 June 1916	8	1	
Ames	John A.	d.	PC	7 June 1916	3	2	
Ames	John S.	d.	PD	7 June 1916	7	5	Masonic Cemetery, Sebastopol
Ames	John S.	d.	HT	8 June 1916	5	3	
Ames	John S.	d.	ST	10 June 1916	1	2	
Amick	Virginia R.	d.	PC	9 Oct. 1917	6	4	Odd Fellows, S.F.
Amundsen	A. O.	o.	ST	19 July 1918	1	3	
Amundson	A. O.	o.	ST	8 Mar. 1918	1	1	
Andersdon	P. C.	m.	PC	19 Oct. 1916	3	3	
Andersen	Anna I.	m.	PC	20 May 1916	6	2	
Andersen	Erick	b.	PD	13 May 1916	5	1	
Andersen	Louise	m.	SRR	21 Sept. 1916	6	6	
Anderson	A.	m.	PD	29 Sept. 1917	8	2	
Anderson	A. M.	b.	PA	14 Sept. 1917	4	4	
Anderson	Alexander	d.	PA	18 Jan. 1917	4	1	also 20 Jan., 5:1
Anderson	Alexander	d.	PC	18 Jan. 1917	1	4	also 20 Jan., 3:6; 21 Jan., 4:3
Anderson	Alexander	d.	SRR	18 Jan. 1917	8	1	
Anderson	Andrew	m.	PC	17 Mar. 1917	5	5	
Anderson	Annie	d.	PD	19 June 1917	1	6	Odd Fellows Cemetery; also 20 June, 4;3
Anderson	Annie	d.	SRR	19 June 1917	5	6	I.O.O.F. Cemetery; also 8:1; 21 June, 8:6
Anderson	Annie/Anna Rose	d.	PC	20 June 1917	2	3	also 23 June, 3:2
Anderson	Arthur	m.	PA	24 Mar. 1916	7	3	
Anderson	Arthur	m.	PC	24 Mar. 1916	3	3	
Anderson	Ashbey	m.	PD	12 Oct. 1917	6	3	
Anderson	B. A.	b.	PA	27 May 1916	1	2	
Anderson	Catherine	d.	PD	10 Feb. 1916	2	5	
Anderson	Catherine	d.	PC	12 Feb. 1916	5	3	Cypress Hill
Anderson	Catherine	d.	PA	9 Feb. 1916	5	3	Cypress Hill; also 6:4; 11 Feb., 4:4
Anderson	Catherine	d.	PC	9 Feb. 1916	1	4	

(1) Surname	(2) Given Name	(3)	(4)	(5) Date	(6) Pg	(7) Col	(8) Comments
Anderson	Charles E.	d.	PC	6 Dec. 1918	6	4	France
Anderson	Clarence A.	o.	PA	9 May 1918	7	3	
Anderson	D. J.	b.	PC	5 Dec. 1917	5	5	
Anderson	David M.	o.	PD	29 May 1918	8	2	
Anderson	Elizabeth W.	m.	PD	10 Sept. 1916	3	2	
Anderson	Ellis R.	m.	PD	27 June 1916	7	5	
Anderson	Ensign B.	d.	PA	1 Apr. 1918	6	4	Cypress Hill; also 2 Apr., 4:6, 4:3, 5:7; 3 Apr., 5:2
Anderson	Ensign B.	d.	PC	2 Apr. 1918	5	2	also 4 Apr., 4:3; 5 Apr., 2:2; 6 Apr., 4:4
Anderson	Erick (dau of)	b& d	PC	14 May 1916	5	3	
Anderson	Frances	o.	SRR	20 Aug. 1917	8	6	
Anderson	Frances	o.	PD	21 Aug. 1917	7	5	
Anderson	Francie	o.	PD	18 Apr. 1917	2	5	
Anderson	Frank B.	o.	SRR	19 Nov. 1917	8	5	
Anderson	Frank B.	o.	PC	7 Nov. 1916	2	3	
Anderson	Frank B.	o.	PD	7 Nov. 1916	5	2	
Anderson	Frederick A.	d.	PC	9 Jan. 1917	4	3	Woodlawn Cemetery, S.F.
Anderson	Gladys	o.	PC	21 Mar. 1916	1	3	portrait
Anderson	Hazel	p.	PD	18 Dec. 1918	8	3	also 19 Dec., 3:1; 20 Dec., 5:1; 21 Dec., 5:1; 23 Dec., 9:1; 24 Dec., 8:1
Anderson	Hazel Lenora	d.	PD	18 June 1918	4	2	I.O.O.F. Cemetery
Anderson	I. J.	b.	PA	4 Dec. 1917	4	3	
Anderson	J.	m.	SRR	26 May 1917	10	6	
Anderson	J. W.	b.	PA	24 May 1918	4	7	
Anderson	Jacob	d.	PC	18 May 1917	4	3	cremation
Anderson	John A.	m.	SRR	4 May 1917	8	6	
Anderson	John A.	m.	PD	5 May 1917	5	3	also 27 May, 6:5
Anderson	John Alfred	d.	PA	11 Aug. 1916	6	4	Benecia; also 12 Aug., 8:4; 15 Aug., 7:5
Anderson	John Alfred	d.	PC	11 Aug. 1916	1	4	Benicia
Anderson	John F.	m.	PD	21 May 1916	10	2	
Anderson	John L.	m.	SRR	2 May 1917	8	5	
Anderson	Josephine	d.	PD	17 May 1918	3	4	I.O.O.F. Cemetery, also 4:2
Anderson	K. H. B.	d.	PD	25 Jan. 1918	4	3	
Anderson	Leland Gale	o.	PC	22 Nov. 1917	3	4	
Anderson	Louis	b.	SIT	16 Feb. 1918	4	6	

(1) Surname	(2) Given Name	(3)	(4)	(5) Date	(6) Pg	(7) Col	(8) Comments
Anderson	Louisa	m.	SRR	24 Nov. 1916	10	3	
Anderson	Marguerite	m.	PD	16 Oct. 1917	5	5	
Anderson	Mary	o.	PC	7 Nov. 1916	2	3	
Anderson	Mary	o.	PD	7 Nov. 1916	5	2	
Anderson	Mary A.	o.	SRR	19 Nov. 1917	8	5	
Anderson	May Etta	m.	PD	11 Nov. 1917	8	3	
Anderson	Mr.	d.	PA	20 Jan. 1917	8	3	
Anderson	Neil C.	b.	PA	24 May 1918	4	7	
Anderson	Nellie	d.	PA	9 Oct. 1918	5	4	also 10 Oct., 4:4
Anderson	Nellie	d.	PC	9 Oct. 1918	1	3	also 10 Oct., 8:5
Anderson	Paul	b.	PA	4 Aug. 1917	4	3	aslo 8:7
Anderson	Peter C.	m.	PA	18 Oct. 1916	5	4	also 19 Oct., 6:9
Anderson	Ruth	m.	PD	26 Oct. 1918	5	1	
Anderson	Ruth	m.	PA	28 Oct. 1918	6	3	
Anderson	Ruth	m.	PA	28 Sept. 1917	4	3	also 1 Oct., 5:4
Anderson	Ruth	m.	PC	28 Sept. 1917	3	4	also 30 Sept., 6:6; 2 Oct., 6:3
Anderson	Ruth M.	m.	PA	1 Sept. 1917	2	4	
Anderson	Ruth M.	m.	PC	1 Sept. 1917	5	2	
Anderson	W. J.	b.	PC	22 May 1918	4	4	
Anderson	Walter	o.	PD	19 June 1918	3	1	also 20 June, 3:1; 21 June, 8:1
Anderson	Walter	o.	PA	17 Jan. 1918	4	3	
Anderson	Walter	o.	PD	17 Jan. 1918	1	7	
Anderson	Weston	m.	PD	26 May 1918	7	6	
Anderson	Weston	m.	PA	28 May 1918	6	3	
Anderson	Weston	o.	PD	20 Sept. 1918	6	5	
Anderson	Weston Reid	m.	PC	28 May 1918	3	4	
Anderson	William	o.	SRR	20 Aug. 1917	8	6	
Anderson	William	o.	PD	21 Aug. 1917	7	5	
Anderson	William Dwight	d.	HT	21 Mar. 1918	7	1	
Anderson	William P.	m.	SRR	22 May 1916	5	4	
Anderson	William S	o.	PD	18 Apr. 1917	2	5	
Anderson	Winslow	d.	PD	10 May 1917	7	2	
Anderton	Mary Louise	b.	PC	18 Dec. 1917	6	4	
Andreasen	J. P.	d.	PD	21 Jan. 1917	3	3	also 23 Jan., 5:2
Andreasen	James P.	d.	SRR	20 Jan. 1917	1	1	also 22 Jan., 8:3&5
Andreasen	James P.	d.	PC	21 Jan. 1917	4	1	
Andreotte	Mary	d.	SIT	16 Nov. 1918	1	5	
Andresen	Ethel	m.	PA	2 Aug. 1918	3	5	
Andrette	Mary	d.	PC	16 Nov. 1918	5	3	San Jose
Andrew	Carrie M.	o.	SRR	19 June 1917	3	6	

(1) Surname	(2) Given Name	(3)	(4)	(5) Date	(6) Pg	(7) Col	(8) Comments
Andrew	Walter	o.	SRR	19 June 1917	3	6	
Andrews	Arthur	d.	PA	15 Mar. 1917	5	4	
Andrews	Arthur	d.	SRR	15 Mar. 1917	1	3	
Andrews	Arthur	d.	PC	16 Mar. 1917	1	6	
Andrews	Arthur	d.	PD	16 Mar. 1917	8	3	
Andrews	Carrie M.	o.	PC	20 June 1917	2	2	
Andrews	L. W.	b.	SRR	8 Feb. 1016	8	1	
Andrews	L. W., Mr. & Mrs.	b.	PD	9 Feb. 1916	6	2	
Andrews	Mae	m.	PD	4 May 1917	1	2	
Andrews	Mae	m.	SRR	4 May 1917	2	4	
Andrews	Walter	o.	PC	20 June 1917	2	2	
Andrieux	Celestine	b.	SIT	21 Apr. 1917	4	1	
Andrieux	Emile	m.	PD	5 Sept. 1918	3	3	also 8 Sept., 3:4
Andrieux	Emilie	m.	SIT	7 Sept. 1918	1	7	
Angee	Della	m.	PA	5 Mar. 1917	6	6	
Angee	Della	m.	PC	6 Mar. 1917	1	5	
Angove	George	o.	SIT	27 July 1918	3	4	
Angrove	George	o.	SIT	16 Nov. 1918	1	1	also 7 Dec., 1:1
Ansell	Katherine M.	d.	SRR	22 May 1917	10	3	also 23 May, 8:3; Guerneville
Ansell	Katherine M.	d.	PD	23 May 1971	2	1	Guerneville; also 24 May, 6:4
Anthony	Florence	d.	PA	22 Aug. 1918	5	4	Newman; also 24 Aug., 8:3
Anthony	S. J., Mrs.	d.	HT	5 Oct. 1916	1	2	
Anthony	Sarah	d.	SRR	9 Oct. 1916	3	3	
Antognini	Alfred	b.	PC	1 Dec. 1917	5	5	
Antognini	G. E.	d.	PD	16 Mar. 1917	5	5	
Antoguini	Alfred	b.	PA	30 Nov. 1917	4	6	
Antonietti	Peter	d.	SRR	18 Oct. 1917	8	2	also 20 Oct., 6:3
Antonietti	Peter	d.	PD	19 Oct. 1917	4	2	
Apodaca	Fermina S.	m.	PC	17 Apr. 1917	3	3	
Apostle	Arthur	m.	PC	27 Dec. 1917	6	5	
Appleby	Ray	m.	CR	11 May 1917	1	5	
Appleton	H.	d.	PA	17 Dec. 1917	1	3	
Appleton	Horace	d.	SIT	22 Dec. 1917	1	6	
Appleton	Horatio	d.	SRR	18 Dec. 1917	8	1	
Appleton	Horatio	d.	PD	21 Dec. 1917	7	1	
Appleton	Horatio	d.	ST	21 Dec. 1917	5	2	
Aquine	Amadeo	m.	PC	17 Apr. 1917	3	3	
Archambeau	Ilene M.	m.	PC	5 Feb. 1918	5	4	
Archambeau	John	d.	SRR	30 Jan. 1917	3	1	

(1) Surname	(2) Given Name	(3)	(4)	(5) Date	(6) Pg	(7) Col	(8) Comments
Archambeau	John	d.	PC	31 Jan. 1917	1	6	
Archambeau	John	d.	PD	31 Jan. 1917	6	1	
Archbold	Reginald	m.	PD	9 June 1918	2	5	
Archer	Claude	b.	SRR	16 Oct. 1916	3	5	
Archer	Claude	b.	HT	26 Oct. 1916	6	4	
Archer	John Henry	d.	SRR	15 May 1916	8	2	
Archer	Leroy	d.	SRR	20 Sept. 1916	7	2	also 21 Sept., 8:3
Archer	Richard W.	d.	PD	16 May 1916	8	2	Shiloh Cemetery
Archer	Roy	d.	PD	22 Sept. 1916	6	6	
Archer	Roy	d.	ST	23 Sept. 1916	3	3	
Arcucci	Fortunato	d.	PD	20 Apr. 1918	7	2	
Arfsten	A. J.	d.	PD	8 May 1918	8	3	
Arfsten	Annie	m.	PD	9 Dec. 1916	2	5	
Arfsten	Arfat J.	d.	PC	7 May 1918	6	4	Cypress Hill; also 9 May, 1:3
Arfsten	Arfat Jurgen	d.	PA	6 May 1918	4	5	Cypress Hill; also 5:4; 8 May, 5:5
Arfsten	Eva N.	m.	PD	30 Jan. 1916	8	7	
Arfsten	Mr. & Mrs.	b.	PA	14 June 1916	8	1	
Arialle	Adeline T.	m.	SRR	13 Nov. 1917	7	5	
Armbruster	Louise	m.	PA	19 Apr. 1916	3	4	
Armbruster	Louise Margaret	m.	PA	17 May 1916	4	6	also 25 May, 5:5
Armbruster	Louise Margaret	m.	PC	17 May 1916	8	5	also 25 May, 1:4
Armbruster	Louise Margaret	m.	PC	19 Apr. 1916	3	3	
Armstroff	Lucille	o.	PC	25 Nov. 1918	8	2	
Armstrong	Charles	m.	PC	3 June 1916	6	2	
Armstrong	Mary	d.	PA	30 Mar. 1916	1	3	also 1 Apr., 5:4
Armstrong	Mary Elizabeth	d.	PC	31 Mar. 1916	1	4	also 2 Apr., 3:3
Armstrong	Nellie B.	d.	SRR	1 June 1917	7	4	also 4 June, 3:4
Armstrong	Nellie R.	d.	PD	2 June 1917	6	2	also 3 June, 10:3
Armstrong	Nellie R.	d.	ST	8 June 1917	1	4	
Armstrong	Sherman E.	d.	PA	9 Nov. 1918	5	5	Cypress Hill; also 8:7
Armstrong	Sherman Edwin	d.	PC	9 Nov. 1918	1	2	Cypress Hill; also 10 Nov., 2:1; 12 Nov., 3:6
Arnold	A. W.	d.	PC	1 Mar. 1916	4	3	
Arnold	Amasa	d.	SRR	1 Mar. 1916	5	2	also 2 Mar., 1:4
Arnold	Amasa W.	d.	PD	1 Mar. 1916	8	3	
Arnold	Amasa W., Mrs.	d.	PD	7 June 1917	4	3	also 6:3; 9 June, 5:2
Arnold	Camilla	d.	PD	4 Dec. 1918	4	2	also 5 Dec., 2:3, 8:3
Arnold	Julia Minnie	d.	SRR	6 June 1917	5	2	also 8 June, 4:4
Arnold	Richard	o.	SRR	9 Mar. 1916	5	3	
Aschermann	Harold C.	m.	PC	11 Sept. 1918	5	3	

(1) Surname	(2) Given Name	(3)	(4)	(5) Date	(6) Pg	(7) Col	(8) Comments
Asherman	Harold C.	m.	PA	10 Sept. 1918	5	6	
Askew	Joe R.	d.	ST	12 Feb. 1916	8	3	Camp Meeker
Askew	Joe R.	d.	SRR	19 Feb. 1916	1	6	Druids Cemetery
Aspben	Mathyas	d.	PC	25 Oct. 1918	4	4	also 27 Oct., 5:4
Aspden	Matthias	d.	PA	25 Oct. 1918	4	6	Novato
Aspden	Minni	m.	PC	7 Feb. 1916	5	3	
Aspesi	Guiseppi	m.	CR	24 June 1917	1	3	
Astand	Alphonse	d.	PA	16 July 1917	4	4	
Astand	Alphonse	d.	SRR	16 July 1917	5	1	
Astand	Alphonse	d.	PC	17 July 1917	8	3	
Astand	Alphonse	d.	ST	20 July 1917	7	3	
Asti	Augusto	d.	PD	24 Oct. 1916	6	2	
Asti	Augustus	d.	SRR	21 Oct. 1916	12	5	Calvary Cemetery
Asti	Joseph	o.	SRR	23 July 1917	4	4	
Asti	Joseph	o.	SRR	19 Mar. 1917	4	3	
Asti	Joseph	o.	PC	20 Mar. 1917	3	2	
Asti	Joseph	o.	PD	26 Mar. 1918	3	4	
Asti	Joseph	o.	SRR	28 Dec. 1917	8	2	
Asti	Joseph	o.	PD	29 Dec. 1917	2	2	
Asti	Josephine	m.	PC	21 Aug. 1918	4	3	also 22 Aug., 8:4
Asti	Josephine L.	m.	PA	21 Aug. 1918	5	4	
Asti	Josephine L.	m.	PD	21 Aug. 1918	8	3	
Asti	Julia	o.	SRR	19 Mar. 1917	4	3	
Asti	Julia	o.	PC	20 Mar. 1917	3	2	
Asti	Julia	o.	PD	26 Mar. 1918	3	4	
Asti	Julia	o.	SRR	28 Dec. 1917	8	2	
Asti	Julia	o.	PD	29 Dec. 1917	2	2	
Asti	Louis Joseph	d.	PD	10 Apr. 1917	1	2	Asti Cemetery; also 4:3
Asti	Louis Joseph	d.	SRR	10 Apr. 1917	8	2	Asti Cemetery
Atkinson	Joseph	o.	PC	14 Dec. 1917	4	4	
Atkinson	Joseph	o.	PA	19 Oct. 1916	4	6	
Atkinson	Joseph	o.	SRR	19 Oct. 1916	1	5	
Atkinson	Joseph	o.	PC	21 Oct. 1916	6	4	
Atkinson	Joseph	o.	PC	5 Apr. 1917	3	4	
Atkinson	Joseph	o.	SRR	5 Dec. 1917	8	1	
Atkinson	Joseph E.	o.	PD	20 Oct. 1916	1	7	
Atkinson	Laura	m.	SRR	7 Mar. 1917	6	3	
Atkinson	Laura	m.	PD	8 Mar. 1917	3	2	
Atkinson	Laura M.	m.	PA	2 Mar. 1917	4	3	also 5 Mar., 8:3
Atkinson	Laura M.	m.	PC	3 Mar. 1917	5	4	also 6 Mar., 3:1

(1) Surname	(2) Given Name	(3)	(4)	(5) Date	(6) Pg	(7) Col	(8) Comments
Atkinson	Sadie I.	o.	SRR	5 Dec. 1917	8	1	
Atkinson	Sadie L.	o.	PC	14 Dec. 1917	4	4	
Atkinson	Sadie L.	o.	PC	5 Apr. 1917	3	4	
Atkinson	Sarah E.	o.	PA	19 Oct. 1916	4	6	
Atkinson	Sarah L.	o.	SRR	19 Oct. 1916	1	5	
Atkinson	Sarah L.	o.	PD	20 Oct. 1916	1	7	
Atkinson	Sarah L.	o.	PC	21 Oct. 1916	6	4	
Ault	Byrd Moore	m.	HT	14 Nov. 1918	3	4	
Ault	Byrd Moore	m.	PC	16 Nov. 1918	5	2	
Austin	James S.	d.	PD	27 Oct. 1917	5	1	also 28 Oct., 4:2; 30 Oct., 3:2
Austin	James S.	d.	SRR	27 Oct. 1917	1	4	also 10:2; 29 Oct., 5:1
Austin	Leslie	m.	SRR	28 Dec. 1916	3	1	
Aver	James H.	m.	SRR	1 May 1916	8	1	
Averill	Herbert	m.	PD	27 Sept. 1916	6	1	
Avery	Annette	d.	SRR	10 Jan. 1916	5	4	cremation; also 11 Jan., 6:5
Avery	Annette A.	d.	PD	9 Jan. 1916	1	3	also 11 Jan.7:2; Oakland
Avilla	Mabel	m.	ST	30 Nov. 1917	4	3	
Ayer	James H.	m.	PD	2 May 1916	6	1	
Ayers	Ernest	m.	PC	19 June 1918	4	1	
Ayers	Laura	m.	PC	23 Nov. 1916	2	1	
Ayers	Laura	m.	SRR	27 Nov. 1916	8	4	
Ayers	Laura	m.	PD	28 Nov. 1916	2	7	
Ayers	Mabel	m.	PC	27 Sept. 1918	4	3	
Ayers	William D., Jr.	m.	PC	3 Oct. 1917	3	5	
Azaveda	William	m.	PC	6 June 1917	3	5	
Azavedo	Peter, Mrs.	d.	PC	7 Nov. 1918	8	2	
Azavedo	William	m.	PD	5 June 1917	3	3	
Azavedo	William	m.	ST	8 June 1917	1	2	

B

(1) Surname	(2) Given Name	(3)	(4)	(5) Date	(6) Pg	(7) Col	(8) Comments
Baage	Andrew Lewis	d.	PD	13 Aug. 1918	4	2	
Baagoe	A. L.	d.	PC	13 Aug. 1918	8	4	
Babbini	Antonio	m.	PD	29 Jan. 1918	2	3	
Babbini	Paul	d.	PD	30 Oct. 1918	4	2	also 7:3
Babcock	Alfred Benjamin	d.	SRR	20 Sept. 1916	3	5	Gridley
Babcock	Alfred Benjamin Franklin	d.	PD	20 Sept. 1916	8	5	Gridley; also 22 Sept., 2:3
Babcock	Emma	m.	PA	27 Aug. 1917	1	4	
Babcock	Emma	m.	PC	27 Aug. 1917	4	3	also 28 Aug., 5:2
Babcock	Emma	m.	PD	28 Aug. 1917	8	3	
Babcock	Robert	o.	PC	15 Oct. 1918	4	4	
Babcock	Robert	d.	PC	28 Nov. 1918	1	3	France
Babcock	Robert	d.	PA	29 Nov. 1918	2	3	France
Babcock	Robert C.	d.	PD	23 Nov. 1918	3	5	France
Baber	Nellie G.	m.	PD	20 Sept. 1917	8	4	
Baboni	Charles	o.	SRR	17 Apr. 1916	8	5	
Baccala	Geneva	m.	PA	26 Nov. 1918	3	5	also 29 Nov., 6:5
Baccala	Geneva	m.	PC	28 Nov. 1918	6	3	
Bachman	Hilda	o.	PA	4 Apr. 1916	6	4	
Bachman	Hilda	o.	PC	8 Apr. 1916	3	3	
Bachman	John	o.	PA	4 Apr. 1916	6	4	
Bachman	John	o.	PC	8 Apr. 1916	3	3	
Bacigalupi	Irene	m.	PD	5 May 1918	3	1	portrait
Bacigalupi	John	d.	SRR	10 Jan. 1916	8	4	Rural Cemetery; also 11 Jan., 5:3
Bacigalupi	John	d.	PD	26 Jan. 1916	5	1	
Bacigalupi	John E.	d.	PD	11 Jan. 1916	6	5	Rural Cemetery; also 12 Jan., 8:4
Bacigalupi	Nate	o.	SRR	27 Sept. 1916	3	4	
Bacigalupi	Virginia	m.	PD	20 May 1917	8	2	also 25 May, 5:2; 27 May, 7:2
Bacigalupi	Virginia	m.	PA	24 May 1917	5	2	
Bacigalupi	Virginia	m.	HT	31 May 1917	1	1	
Bacigalupi	Virginia	m.	SRR	21 May 1917	4	4	also 24 May, 8:5
Bacigliainpi	John E.	o.	PC	11 Jan. 1916	4	3	
Bacon	Charmion Butts	m.	SRR	4 Feb. 1916	3	3	also 8 Feb., 6:3; 20 Mar., 8:4
Bacon	Jay S.	m.	PA	4 Nov. 1916	4	3	
Bacon	Jay S.	m.	PC	5 Nov. 1916	7	3	
Baer	Hyman	m.	PD	4 Sept. 1918	6	4	
Baer	Mark	o.	CR	6 Dec.1918	1	5	also 27 Dec., 1:5
Baer	Markell	o.	PD	15 Sept. 1918	6	4	

(1) Surname	(2) Given Name	(3)	(4)	(5) Date	(6) Pg	(7) Col	(8) Comments
Baer	Markell	o.	PD	7 Dec. 1918	6	4	
Bagin	Edith Belle	d.	PA	13 Nov. 1916	2	5	
Bagley	Herbert	d.	SRR	10 Apr. 1917	8	2	Guerneville; also 11 Apr., 6:3; 12 Apr., 6:2
Bagley	Herbert L.	d.	PC	10 Apr. 1917	5	6	
Bagley	Herbert L.	d.	PA	11 Apr. 1917	8	1	Guerneville
Bagley	W. F.	d.	PC	25 Oct. 1916	7	3	
Bagley	Walter	d.	PD	10 Apr. 1917	4	3	Guerneville; also 12 Apr., 5:5
Bagley	Weaver	m.	HT	12 Apr. 1917	6	3	
Bagley	Weaver T.	m.	ST	7 Apr. 1917	3	2	
Bagley	William P.	d.	PD	24 Oct. 1916	8	1	portrait; also 26 Oct., 6:5
Bagley	Willm P.	d.	SRR	24 Oct. 1916	5	1	portrait
Bagucci	Filippo	b.	PA	30 Nov. 1917	4	6	
Bahr	Annie Elizabeth	d.	PA	16 Jan. 1917	5	4	also 18 Jan., 4:4
Bahrs	Anna Elizabeth	d.	PC	17 Jan. 1917	4	1	Cypress Hill; also 6:4; 19 Jan., 5:4
Bahrs	Herman	d.	PA	5 Mar. 1917	6	4	also 6 Mar., 5:5
Bahrs	Herman	d.	PC	6 Mar. 1917	2	2	Cypress Hill; also 5:4; 7 Mar., 1:3
Bailey	A. L.	b.	PA	21 Jan. 1916	4	2	also 10:3
Bailey	Al	b.	PA	8 May 1917	8	3	
Bailey	Elma	m.	PD	10 Dec. 1916	5	2	also 17 Dec., 3:5
Bailey	Elma	m.	SRR	16 Dec. 1916	10	3	
Bailey	Elma	m.	PC	17 Dec. 1916	5	5	
Bailey	Elma	m.	PA	28 Oct. 1916	5	1	also 16 Dec., 4:1
Bailey	G. H.	b.	PD	9 Nov. 1916	6	1	
Bailey	Glen	d.	PA	25 Nov. 1918	5	5	
Bailey	Glen	d.	PC	26 Nov. 1918	1	6	Forest Hill, Placer County
Bailey	Marguerite	m.	PD	17 Feb. 1918	8	2	
Bailey	Marguerite	m.	PD	23 Nov. 1917	5	4	
Bailey	Marguerite	m.	SRR	23 Nov. 1917	6	5	
Bailey	Marguerite	m.	PC	24 Nov. 1917	5	2	
Bailey	Mildred	m.	SRR	13 Aug. 1917	8	6	Rural Cemetery; also 14 Aug., 1:2
Bailey	Rosa	d.	SIT	23 Nov. 1918	3	4	Mt. Olivet, S.F.
Bailey	Thomas J.	d.	PC	9 Nov. 1916	1	2	Holy Cross, S.F.; also 11 Nov., 5:3
Bailey	W. M.	b.	SRR	24 Nov. 1917	12	2	
Baim	Hilda M.	m.	PC	14 Sept. 1916	6	4	
Baines	Leo	d.	SIT	10 June 1916	3	3	
Baines	Minnie R.	d.	PA	21 Aug. 1918	5	7	Woodland also 22 Aug., 2:3

(1) Surname	(2) Given Name	(3)	(4)	(5) Date	(6) Pg	(7) Col	(8) Comments
Baines	Sarah	d.	PC	14 Dec. 1917	8	3	
Baines	Sarah	d.	SIT	15 Dec. 1917	1	1	Mountain Cemetery
Bair	Morris	d.	PC	16 Aug. 1918	6	3	Marne, France
Bair	Morris	d.	SIT	17 Aug. 1918	1	4	France
Baker	Georgia	m.	PC	15 Aug. 1918	8	4	
Baker	Harry	d.	SRR	11 June 1917	4	3	also 12 June, 10:5
Baker	Harry	d.	PD	12 June 1917	4	3	also 6:1
Baker	Harry	d.	PC	13 June 1917	6	3	
Baker	Julia	m.	PD	6 Dec. 1916	3	3	
Baker	Julia J.	m.	PA	5 Dec. 1916	4	1	
Baker	Julia J.	m.	SRR	5 Dec. 1916	4	4	
Baker	Julia J.	m.	PC	6 Dec. 1916	4	1	
Baker	Melissa D.	d.	PD	30 Apr. 1918	4	2	also 5:3; 1 May, 7:1
Baker	Ruth	m.	SRR	6 Sept. 1917	3	5	
Baker	Ruth	m.	PD	7 Sept. 1917	5	4	
Baker	Ruth	m.	SRR	9 Aug. 1917	3	3	
Baker	Sadie	m.	PD	18 June 1916	5	2	
Baker	Sheridan W.	b.	PD	27 Sept. 1916	6	3	
Baker	Sheridan W., Jr.	b.	PD	11 July 1918	3	4	
Baldesberger	Carl	m.	SIT	26 Jan. 1918	1	2	
Baldi	A.	b.	PD	7 Jan. 1917	3	1	
Baldi	A.	b.	SRR	8 Jan. 1917	2	5	
Baldwin	Edward	d.	HT	25 July 1918	5	2	
Baldwin	Edward	d.	PD	5 Oct. 1917	8	1	
Baldwin	Edward C.	d.	PC	3 Oct. 1917	4	3	Cypress Hill
Baldwin	Edward Charles	d.	PC	5 Nov. 1917	1	1	
Baldwin	Edward Charles	d.	PA	5 Oct. 1917	8	1	
Baldwin	John	d.	PA	18 Jan. 1916	4	4	also 19 Jan., 5:6
Baldwin	John T.	d.	PC	20 Jan. 1916	4	2	Cypress Hill
Baldwin	John T.	d.	PD	20 Jan. 1916	7	1	
Baldwin	Leulla	o.	PD	12 Sept. 1918	5	2	
Baldwin	Luella	o.	PD	17 Dec. 1918	5	3	
Baldwin	Luella B.	o.	PC	17 Dec. 1918	3	3	
Baldwin	Lydia	d.	PD	10 Feb. 1918	8	2	Rural Cemetery; also 12 Feb., 4:2
Baldwin	W. H.	o.	PD	12 Sept. 1918	5	2	
Baldwin	W. H.	o.	PC	17 Dec. 1918	3	3	
Baldwin	W. H.	o.	PD	17 Dec. 1918	5	3	
Baldwin	Winnifred	d.	PD	13 Feb. 1918	6	3	
Bales	Minnie Estella	m.	PA	28 Jan. 1916	5	2	also 29 Jan., 6:4
Bales	Minnie Estelle	m.	PD	28 Jan. 1916	5	2	
Bales	Minnie Estelle	m.	PC	29 Jan. 1916	4	1	
Bales	Nettie	m.	PC	10 Mar. 1917	5	2	
Baley	Samuel	d.	SRR	23 Oct. 1916	2	2	Druids Cemetery
Baley	Samuel T.	d.	PC	22 Oct. 1916	4	3	

(1) Surname	(2) Given Name	(3)	(4)	(5) Date	(6) Pg	(7) Col	(8) Comments
Ball	Julia	m.	PC	27 Dec. 1917	6	5	
Ball	Ray	m.	SRR	19 Dec. 1916	2	3	also 20 Dec., 7:4
Ball	Raymond	m.	PD	20 Dec. 1916	2	5	also 21 Dec., 2:5
Ball	Stephanie	m.	SIT	3 Mar. 1918	4	2	
Ball	Stephianna	m.	PC	27 Feb. 1918	2	3	also 1 Mar., 5:2
Ball	William	d.	PD	7 June 1917	2	3	also 12 June, 8:2
Ball	William	d.	SRR	7 June 1917	8	6	
Ball	William, Mrs.	d.	SRR	27 Aug. 1917	6	4	
Balldisberger	Carl	o.	SIT	15 Apr. 1916	2	6	
Balldisberger	Ida	o.	SIT	15 Apr. 1916	2	6	
Ballestra	John	d.	PD	10 July 1917	3	3	also 4:3
Ballestra	John	d.	PC	11 July 1917	2	2	
Ballestra	John	d.	ST	13 July 1917	1	3	
Balletti	Charles	d.	SIT	15 June 1918	1	5	
Balm	Hilja N.	m.	PA	12 Sept. 1916	5	3	
Balsberger	Carl	o.	PA	21 Nov. 1916	6	5	
Balsberger	Carl	o.	PD	21 Nov. 1916	5	2	
Balsberger	Carl	o.	SRR	21 Nov. 1916	2	2	
Balsberger	Lea	o.	PA	21 Nov. 1916	6	5	
Balsberger	Lea	o.	PD	21 Nov. 1916	5	2	
Balsberger	Lea	o.	SRR	21 Nov. 1916	2	2	
Balsey	Edith	m.	PD	4 June 1916	9	2	also 9 June, 6:3
Balsley	Edith	m.	SRR	3 June 1916	4	3	also 8 June, 8:2
Balzari	James	m.	PC	9 July 1918	1	3	
Balzari	James A.	m.	PA	9 July 1918	5	7	
Balzari	James A.	m.	PD	9 July 1918	8	4	
Balzarini	Katherine	d.	PC	26 Jan. 1918	4	4	
Banchero	Bartholomew Thomas	d.	PD	18 Dec. 1918	1	4	Calvary Cemetery; also 19 Dec., 4:2
Bandini	May R. E.	d.	PD	5 Mar. 1918	8	3	Shiloh Cemetery; also 6 Mar., 4:2; 8 Mar., 5:4
Bandini	Robert	m.	PD	10 May 1917	5	1	
Bandini	Robert	m.	PC	11 July 1917	7	4	
Bandini	Robert M.	m.	SRR	10 May 1917	3	3	also 11 May, 1:2
Bandini	Robert, Mrs.	d.	PA	5 Mar. 1918	3	4	
Banfield	Fred	m.	PA	11 Mar. 1916	4	6	also 13 Mar., 2:3&4
Banfield	Fred	m.	SRR	11 Mar. 1916	2	2	also 13 Mar., 5:1
Banfield	Fred H.	b.	PA	23 Apr. 1917	5	3	
Banfield	S. E.	m.	PD	12 Mar. 1916	5	3	
Banfield	S. Efi	m.	PC	14 Mar. 1916	1	5	
Banisfield	Robert	m.	PD	3 Aug. 1918	2	3	
Banks	Benjamin "Buzz"	d.	PC	26 Sept. 1918	8	3	
Bannon	Mary	d.	PA	22 Jan. 1917	2	4	Calvary Cemetery; also 24 Jan., 8:4

(1) Surname	(2) Given Name	(3)	(4)	(5) Date	(6) Pg	(7) Col	(8) Comments
Bannon	Mary	d.	PC	23 Jan. 1917	3	1	Calvary Cemetery; also 6:5; 24 Jan., 3:1; 25 Jan., 2:1
Bannon	Mary	d.	SRR	23 Jan. 1917	5	2	
Bannon	Mary	d.	PD	24 Jan. 1917	2	3	
Banta	John	d.	SRR	25 July 1917	6	6	Healdsburg; also 27 July, 6:6
Banta	John Henry	d.	PD	26 July 1917	8	2	
Banta	John Henry	d.	HT	2 Aug. 1917	1	4	
Banum	Mildred	m.	CR	3 Aug. 1917	1	2	
Baptista	August "Gus"	m.	PA	24 Apr. 1918	3	4	
Barazim	Charles	m.	PD	3 July 1918	3	2	
Barazini	Charles	m.	PA	3 July 1918	4	3	
Barbara	Feliz	d.	PD	6 Dec. 1918	2	3	France
Barber	Marjorie	m.	PA	19 Jan. 1918	5	3	
Barber	Marjorie	m.	PC	20 Jan. 1918	5	3	
Barber	Matilda	d.	SRR	5 May 1917	6	3	
Barber	Walter	m.	PD	20 Feb. 1917	7	2	
Barber	Walter	m.	PD	26 Apr. 1917	6	1	
Barbera	Felix	d.	PC	6 Dec. 1918	1	4	France
Barbera	Feliz	d.	PC	13 Dec. 1918	4	3	France
Barbera	Irene	m.	SRR	29 Apr. 1916	8	5	
Barbera	Matilda	d.	PD	5 May 1917	4	3	Calvary Cemetery; also 5:4; 8 May, 2:3
Barbera	Matilda	d.	SRR	7 May 1917	4	3	
Barbere	Irene	m.	SIT	6 May 1916	5	3	
Barberi	Augustino	d.	PD	10 Feb. 1917	2	4	Calvary Cemetery; also 4:2; 11 Feb., 3:3
Barberin	Louisa	d.	SIT	26 May 1917	1	1	Mountain Cemetery
Barberin	Louise	d.	PD	27 May 1917	1	4	
Barboni	Constantino	m.	PA	14 Mar. 1918	6	3	
Barboni	Constantino	m.	PC	14 Mar. 1918	1	3	also 15 Mar., 4:2
Bargagliotti	Mary	d.	PA	26 Nov. 1917	2	4	also 27 Nov., 5:2
Bargagliotti	Mary	d.	PC	27 Nov. 1917	4	3	Italian Cemetery, S.F.; also 8:2; 28 Nov., 8:5
Bargagliotti	Rosie	m.	PA	15 Jan. 1918	5	6	
Barger	Willie E.	o.	PA	7 Nov. 1918	3	3	
Barham	John P.	o.	PC	24 Feb. 1916	4	3	
Barker	Marian Louise	m.	SRR	5 July 1917	6	3	
Barlow	Eva	d.	PA	7 Feb. 1918	8	5	paper filed after 6 Apr. 1918
Barlow	Eva	d.	PA	8 Feb. 1918	4	2	Two Rock
Barlow	Eva	d.	PC	8 Feb. 1918	6	6	Two Rock; also 9 Feb., 4:2
Barlow	Leland	o.	ST	16 Aug. 1918	8	1	

(1) Surname	(2) Given Name	(3)	(4)	(5) Date	(6) Pg	(7) Col	(8) Comments
Barlow	Louisa E.	m.	PA	31 Oct. 1917	6	5	Two Rock; also 1 Nov., 8:3; 2 Nov., 5:5; 3 Nov., 3:4
Barlow	Louise	d.	ST	2 Nov. 1917	1	5	
Barlow	Louise E.	d.	PC	1 Nov. 1917	5	5	also 3 Nov., 8:4
Barlow	Mary	m.	PA	12 Jan. 1917	6	4	
Barlow	Mary E.	m.	PD	12 Jan. 1918	3	1	also 13 Jan., 3:4
Barlow	Mary E.	m.	PC	13 Jan. 1918	1	6	
Barlow	Mary E.	m.	HT	17 Jan. 1918	3	1	
Barlow	Mary Elizabeth	m.	ST	18 Jan. 1918	1	3	
Barnard	A. F.	o.	PA	7 Jan. 1916	6	4	
Barnard	Florence G.	o.	PA	7 Jan. 1916	6	4	
Barnes	B. H.	m.	PC	13 Dec. 1918	4	4	also 17 Dec., 5:5
Barnes	Ben H.	m.	PA	13 Dec. 1918	5	2	also 16 Dec., 5:5
Barnes	Ben H.	m.	PD	13 Dec. 1918	8	3	also 15 Dec., 7:2
Barnes	Ben, Mrs.	d.	PD	1 Mar. 1916	5	2	also 4 Mar., 6:1
Barnes	Cynthia	d.	PC	1 Mar. 1916	4	5	
Barnes	Cynthia	d.	SRR	29 Feb. 1916	8	1	
Barnes	Emily	m.	PD	16 Dec. 1917	6	3	
Barnes	Florence	m.	PA	15 Feb. 1917	8	3	
Barnes	Florence	m.	SRR	15 Feb. 1917	1	3	
Barnes	Florence	m.	PC	16 Feb. 1917	8	5	
Barnes	Florence M.	m.	PD	16 Feb. 1917	8	4	
Barnes	Florence M.	m.	HT	22 Feb. 1917	3	1	
Barnes	Howard H.	m.	PD	10 Nov. 1916	8	4	
Barnes	Howard H.	m.	SRR	11 Nov. 1916	8	1	
Barnes	Howard H.	m.	PA	10 Nov. 1916	7	5	
Barnes	Lydia	d.	PD	17 June 1916	6	5	Pleasant Hill Cemetery
Barnes	Lydia	d.	ST	17 June 1916	1	4	
Barnes	Lydia	d.	PC	18 June 1916	6	5	Sebastopol
Barnes	Minnie E.	d.	PC	21 Aug. 1918	8	3	Woodland; also 23 Aug., 5:6
Barnes	Thirra	d.	PA	13 Dec. 1917	4	2	
Barnes	Thirza	d.	SRR	12 Dec. 1917	4	3	cremation; also 8:2; 14 Dec., 8:2
Barnes	Thirza	d.	PC	13 Dec. 1917	4	4	cremation
Barnes	Thirza	d.	PD	13 Dec. 1917	3	3	cremation; also 4:2; 14 Dec., 5:3; 15 Dec., 7:5
Barnett	Catherine	d.	PD	7 Dec. 1916	8	4	also 8 Dec., 6:3
Barnett	Catherine Marion	d.	SRR	6 Dec. 1916	8	5	also 9 Dec., 8:5
Barnett	Cora Eldridge	d.	PC	20 May 1917	1	3	Cypress Hill; also 22 May, 4:2
Barnett	Cora Eldridge	d.	PA	21 May 1917	5	1	Cypress Hill
Barnett	Frank	b.	PD	13 Oct. 1916	8	7	

(1) Surname	(2) Given Name	(3)	(4)	(5) Date	(6) Pg	(7) Col	(8) Comments
Barnett	Katherine	d.	PD	25 Mar. 1918	3	2	also 4:1
Barnett	Lester	b.	ST	1 June 1917	3	4	
Barnett	Lester (dau of)	d.	ST	8 June 1917	6	3	
Barnett	Marion	d.	PA	5 Dec. 1916	3	3	
Barnett	Marion L.	d.	PC	10 Dec. 1916	4	2	Sebastopol
Barnett	Marion L.	d.	ST	9 Dec. 1916	1	3	Pleasant Hill
Barnett	Marion Leroy	d.	SRR	4 Dec. 1916	6	1	Pleasant Hill Cemetery
Barnett	Marion Leroy	d.	PD	5 Dec. 1916	5	3	
Barrett	Fred	d.	PD	26 Sept. 1918	8	4	
Barrett	Fred E.	p.	PD	25 Oct. 1918	6	4	
Barrett	George	o.	PD	11 Sept. 1918	2	3	
Barrett	Jennie A.	d.	SRR	25 July 1917	8	6	
Barrett	Jennie A.	d.	PD	26 July 1917	2	2	
Barrows	Olive M.	m.	SRR	16 Oct. 1916	8	4	
Barry	George Herman	m.	PC	21 Apr. 1917	5	3	
Barry	Margaret M.	o.	PA	4 Mar. 1916	2	2	
Barry	William M.	o.	PA	4 Mar. 1916	2	2	
Barsotti	Frank	m.	SRR	27 Nov. 1916	5	4	
Bartlan	Jean	d.	PC	29 Sept. 1916	1	2	Red Bluff; also 30 Sept., 4:6
Bartlett	James	d.	SRR	4 Feb. 1916	5	2	
Bartlett	William	d.	PD	28 Sept. 1917	4	2	Bennett Valley Cemetery
Bartlett	William	d.	SRR	28 Sept. 1917	8	3	Bennett Valley Cemetery; also 29 Sept., 4:4
Bartoli	E.	b.	SRR	30 Sept. 1916	12	4	
Bartolmei	Orlando	d.	PD	10 Dec. 1918	1	5	also 8:3
Bartolomei	Louesa	d.	PD	24 Dec. 1918	4	2	Calvary Cemetery; also 5:5
Bartolomei	Victor	d.	PD	4 Aug. 1917	2	3	Calvary Cemetery; also 4:2
Bartolomei	Victor, Jr.	d.	SRR	3 Aug. 1917	8	1&2	Calvary Cemetery
Barton	Sarah	d.	SRR	24 July 1917	2	3	
Basaglia	Rose	m.	SIT	21 Apr. 1917	1	2	
Basaglia	Rose	m.	SRR	23 Apr. 1917	6	2	
Bassett	Elsie	d.	PC	23 Sept. 1917	1	5&6	Tomales; also 25 Sept., 5:4
Bassett	Elsie	d.	PA	24 Sept. 1917	8	1	Tomales
Bassett	Ralph	o.	PC	20 Sept. 1918	8	2	
Bassett	Stanislaus "Stanley"	d.	PA	21 Aug. 1917	1	4	also 22 Aug., 2:2; 6:3&5
Bassett	Stanley	d.	PC	21 Aug. 1917	1	3	Calvary Cemetery; also 22 Aug., 1:4, 6:3
Bassett	Stanley	d.	PD	21 Aug. 1917	8	2	also 23 Aug., 2:3

(1) Surname	(2) Given Name	(3)	(4)	(5) Date	(6) Pg	(7) Col	(8) Comments
Bassett	William	p.	PC	24 Jan. 1917	5	4	
Bassett	William	d.	PC	9 Jan. 1917	6	3	Tomales; also 7:4; 11 Jan., 8:2
Bassett	William D.	d.	PA	8 Jan. 1917	6	6	Tomales; also 10 Jan., 8:5
Bassett	William D.	d.	PD	9 Jan. 1917	7	5	
Bassi	R.	b.	PA	29 Aug. 1916	5	7	
Bassi	Rocco (son of)	d.	PC	26 Jan. 1918	8	3	Calvary Cemetery; also 27 Jan., 8:1
Bassi	Rocco (son of)	d.	PA	28 Jan. 1918	2	6	Calvary Cemetery
Batchelder	Agnes	d.	PD	21 Jan. 1916	6	2	Sebastopol Cemetery
Batchelder	Agnes R.	d.	SRR	20 Jan. 1916	5	3	I.O.O.F. Cemetery
Batchelor	D. W.	b.	PC	13 Dec. 1916	4	3	
Batchelor	Herbert	o.	PA	31 May 1917	4	2	
Batchelor	Herbert	o.	PC	1 June 1917	5	3	also 29 June, 3:3; 30 June, 5:3
Batchelor	Herbert	o.	PC	1 July 1917	5	3	
Batchelor	Wayne	o.	SIT	8 July 1916	1	4	also 29 July, 3:3
Batchelor	Wayne	m.	PD	1 July 1917	2	1	also 1 Aug., 8:5; 3 Aug., 2:3; 4 Aug., 8:2
Batchelor	Wayne	o.	PA	3 Aug. 1917	6	2	
Bateman	John	o.	PC	9 Dec. 1917	3	4	
Bates	Fred	m.	PD	15 Feb. 1916	5	3	
Bates	Nancy	m.	PC	11 Sept. 1917	4	4	
Bates	Nancy	m.	SIT	15 Sept. 1917	1	5	
Bates	Nancy C.	m.	SRR	8 Sept. 1917	8	5	
Batt	George Ray	d.	PD	13 Sept. 1918	8	3	
Batt	George Ray	d.	PC	14 Sept. 1918	6	4	
Batt	George Ray	d.	PD	3 Oct. 1918	3	4	
Battaglia	Dominico	o.	SRR	3 Mar. 1916	1	6	
Battaglia	Dominico	o.	PD	4 Mar. 1917	5	5	
Battaglia	Luisa	m.	ST	10 Mar. 1917	1	1	
Battaglia	Luisa	o.	SRR	3 Mar. 1916	1	6	
Battaglia	Luisa	o.	PD	4 Mar. 1917	5	5	
Battaglia	Luisa	m.	SRR	7 Mar. 1917	5	2	
Battaglia	Luisa	m.	PD	8 Mar. 1917	7	5	
Batten	Cora S.	o.	PD	21 Sept. 1917	3	4	
Batten	Cort S.	o.	SRR	21 Sept. 1917	5	5	
Batten	George M.	o.	PD	21 Sept. 1917	3	4	
Batten	George M.	o.	SRR	21 Sept. 1917	5	5	
Batten	Margaret Ann	d.	PD	3 Jan. 1918	5	5	also 4 Jan., 4:2
Batten	Margaret Ann	m.	PC	4 Jan. 1918	3	6	
Batton	Margaret Ann	d.	ST	18 Jan. 1918	4	2	
Baudroit	J. E.	o.	PD	1 Nov. 1918	3	2	
Baudroit	Julia A.	o.	PD	1 Nov. 1918	3	2	

(1) Surname	(2) Given Name	(3)	(4)	(5) Date	(6) Pg	(7) Col	(8) Comments
Bauer	B.	d.	PC	4 May 1918	1	5	
Bauer	B.	d.	PD	5 May 1918	6	5	
Bauer	Bernard B.	d.	PA	6 May 1918	4	7	
Bauer	John William	d.	PA	18 Mar. 1918	4	4	Cypress Hill; also 8:2, 4; 19 Mar., 4:5; 21 Mar., 3:4
Bauer	John William	d.	PC	19 Mar. 1918	4	2	Cypress Hill; also 6:1&4; 20 Mar., 8:2
Bauer	Valesca	m.	PD	12 Sept. 1917	3	1	
Bauer	William	d.	PD	19 Mar. 1918	5	3	also 21 Mar., 2:2
Baugh	Clive Everett	m.	PD	22 June 1918	3	4	also 25 June, 7:5
Baugh	D. G.	m.	PD	11 Oct. 1917	2	6	
Baugh	Douglas G.	m.	PD	11 Aug. 1917	6	2	
Baugh	Douglas G.	m.	SRR	11 Aug. 1917	8	5	
Baugh	Douglas Guy	m.	SRR	10 Oct. 1917	4	6	
Baugh	Douglas Guy	m.	PC	11 Oct. 1917	4	3	
Baugh	Douglas Guy	m.	PC	10 Aug. 1917	5	4	
Baugh	Guy D.	b.	PA	26 May 1916	4	1	also 27 May, 8:5
Baugh	Guy D.	b.	PC	26 May 1916	8	2	
Baugh	Robet Douglas	d.	PA	14 June 1916	4	4	Cypress Hill
Baugh	Ruby	d.	PC	3 June 1916	1	6	
Baugh	Ruby Elizabeth	d.	PA	3 June 1916	4	2	also 5 June, 5:3
Bauman	Charles H.	m.	PD	10 Apr. 1917	8	4	
Bauman	Charles H.	m.	ST	14 Apr. 1917	3	2	
Bauman	Charles H.	m.	SRR	9 Apr. 1917	4	4	
Baxman	Hattie	m.	PC	16 July 1916	1	5	
Baxman	Hattie	m.	PA	18 July 1916	3	4	
Baxter	Harriett	o.	SRR	14 Mar. 1917	5	1	
Baxter	Samuel	o.	SRR	14 Mar. 1917	5	1	
Beach	Riley	o.	PD	17 July 1917	6	4	
Beach	Riley	o.	SRR	17 July 1917	5	1	
Beach	Riley	o.	PD	20 Nov. 1918	7	6	
Beach	Rosie M.	o.	PD	17 July 1917	6	4	
Beach	Rosie M.	o.	SRR	17 July 1917	5	1	
Beach	Rosie M.	o.	PD	20 Nov. 1918	7	6	
Beahling	Herman	d.	SRR	4 Aug. 1917	6	6	
Beaks	C. H.	d.	PA	14 Oct. 1918	8	5	Sebastopol
Beal	Almatia	m.	PA	20 Dec. 1918	8	3	
Beal	Elizabeth I.	d.	PD	2 Nov. 1916	7	2	
Beal	Elizabeth Lovinda	d.	SRR	1 Nov. 1916	8	6	Rural Cemetery; also 2 Nov., 1:2; 3 Nov., 4:5
Beal	Silas	d.	SRR	23 Jan. 1917	8	4	also 26 Jan., 3:5
Beal	Silas	d.	PD	25 Jan. 1917	2	2	also 26 Jan., 8:2
Bean	Homer	b.	SRR	20 Mar. 1916	1	3	

(1) Surname	(2) Given Name	(3)	(4)	(5) Date	(6) Pg	(7) Col	(8) Comments
Bean	Norman	o.	PC	14 Apr. 1916	1	5	portrait
Bean	Wesley	m	PC	29 Aug. 1917	5	1	
Beane	Helen	d.	PD	18 Nov. 1916	8	1	also 21 Nov., 7:5
Beane	Helen Margaret	b.	PD	22 Mar. 1916	8	3	
Beane	Homer C., Jr.	b.	SRR	4 June 1917	3	1	
Beardin	Lucretia	d.	PD	9 Jan. 1917	8	8	Pleasant Hill Cemetery
Beardsley	Ada	m.	PD	25 Dec. 1917	8	1	also 27 Dec., 2:5
Beardsley	Ada	m.	SRR	26 Dec. 1917	5	5	
Beasley	Nettie	m.	PD	25 May 1918	6	3	
Beato	Antone	d.	PC	30 Nov. 1918	1	3	Calvary Cemetery
Beauchamp	William W.	d.	PA	3 Mar. 1917	6	4	
Beaulieu	C. B.	b.	CR	24 Feb. 1917	4	2	paper filed after 20 Feb. 1909
Beauregard	George B.	m.	PC	10 Mar. 1917	5	2	
Bech	George N.	m.	HT	29 Aug. 1918	8	2	
Bech	George Neils	m.	PD	27 Aug. 1918	8	3	
Beck	George N.	m.	PD	11 Apr. 1918	7	1	
Becker	Adam	d.	PC	10 Nov. 1917	5	4	Cypress Hill; also 11 Nov., 8:2
Becker	Adam	d.	PD	11 Nov. 1917	1	4	
Becker	Adam	d.	SRR	12 Nov. 1917	3	6	
Becker	Adam	d.	PA	9 Nov. 1917	8	3	Cypress Hill; also 10 Nov., 4:3
Becker	John Henry	d.	PC	10 Apr. 1918	6	5	
Becker	John Henry	d.	PD	9 Apr. 1918	4	2	also 8:2; 11 Apr., 6:5
Beckley	Cinthy	d.	PD	29 May 1918	3	4	Shiloh Cemetery
Beckley	Cynthia A.	d.	PC	23 May 1918	3	3	Shiloh Cemetery
Beckley	Joseph	m.	PD	18 Oct. 1918	7	4	
Beckley	William, Mrs.	d.	HT	30 May 1918	1	1	
Beckman	Emma	m.	SRR	23 June 1917	12	3	also 25 June, 6:1; 3 July, 6:4
Beckman	Emma	m.	PC	24 June 1917	5	4	
Beckman	Emma	m.	ST	29 June 1917	6	5	
Bedford	Elsie	m.	PD	26 May 1917	5	5	
Bedford	Elsie	m.	SRR	26 May 1917	6	1	
Bedford	Elsie	m.	PD	3 June 1917	5	1	
Bedford	Fred	o.	PD	31 Aug. 1918	2	1	
Bednognatti	child	d.	PC	15 Sept. 1917	1	6	Calvary Cemetery
Bedognatti	Ruth	d.	PA	12 Sept. 1917	5	3	Calvary Cemetery; also 14 Sept., 8:4
Bee	Sam	d.	PA	7 Dec. 1918	3	4	
Beebe	Olive	d.	SRR	20 Mar. 1916	5	3	
Beebe	Olive	d.	PD	21 Mar. 1916	6	4	also 22 Mar., 6:3
Beebe	R. Forrest	m.	SRR	23 July 1917	5	3	
Beebe	T. J.	d.	SRR	24 Apr. 1916	5	1	

(1) Surname	(2) Given Name	(3)	(4)	(5) Date	(6) Pg	(7) Col	(8) Comments
Beedle	Georgie F.	m.	SRR	8 Feb. 1917	4	3	
Beeson	Eda	m.	PD	1 Dec. 1917	2	1	also 2 Dec., 5:5
Beeson	Eda J.	m.	SRR	1 Dec. 1917	3	2	
Beeson	Eda Josephine	m.	HT	6 Dec. 1917	1	4	
Beeson	Eddie	b.	SRR	9 June 1917	6	4	
Beeson	Eddie	b.	HT	14 June 1917	3	5	
Beeson	Elva	m.	PD	30 Dec. 1916	6	2	
Beeson	Elva	m.	HT	4 Jan. 1917	1	3	
Beeson	Elva Marie	m.	SRR	30 Dec. 1916	6	3	
Beeson	Marie	m.	SRR	2 Jan. 1917	3	3	
Beeson	William	d.	SRR	7 July 1916	8	6	
Beffa	Antone, Mrs.	d.	PD	9 Nov. 1918	6	2	
Beffa	Caesar	b.	SRR	29 July 1916	4	2	
Beffa	James	b.	PA	15 Mar. 1918	4	7	also 6:6
Beffa	James	b.	PC	15 Mar. 1918	6	3	
Beffa	Jessie M.	d.	PA	8 Nov. 1918	4	1	also 9 Nov., 5:3
Beffa	Jessie M.	d.	PC	8 Nov. 1918	1	4	also 9 Nov., 5:3; 10 Nov., 4:2
Beffa	Joseph	m.	SRR	15 Jan. 1916	4	4	
Beffa	Joseph	m.	HT	20 Jan. 1916	4	1	
Beffa	Joseph Edward	m.	PC	16 Jan. 1916	1	5	
Beffa	Lillian	m.	SRR	2 Apr. 1917	5	2	
Beffa	Lillian	m.	PA	3 Apr. 1917	3	7	
Beffa	Lillian	m.	PC	3 Apr. 1917	3	5	
Beffa	Lillian	m.	ST	7 Apr. 1917	3	2	
Beffa	Tony	b.	PA	1 Nov. 1918	5	6	
Beffa	William	m.	PA	19 May 1916	8	7	
Beffa	William	m.	PC	19 May 1916	5	3	
Beffa	William	b.	PC	13 Dec. 1916	4	3	
Beggs	Frank	b.	PA	14 Jan. 1918	5	4	
Beggs	Genevieve	o.	PD	21 Mar. 1916	2	2	
Beggs	Genevieve	o.	PA	20 Mar. 1916	4	5	
Beggs	Genevieve	o.	SRR	20 Mar. 1916	8	2	
Beggs	Genevieve	o.	PA	21 Feb. 1916	1	1	
Beggs	Genevieve	o.	PC	21 Mar. 1916	8	3	
Beggs	Genevieve	o.	PA	26 Sept. 1918	2	4	
Beggs	Genevieve	o.	PC	26 Sept. 1918	1	2	
Beggs	W. P.	o.	SRR	20 Mar. 1916	8	2	
Beggs	W. P.	o.	PD	21 Mar. 1916	2	2	
Beggs	Will	o.	PC	26 Sept. 1918	1	2	
Beggs	Will P.	o.	PA	20 Mar. 1916	4	5	
Beggs	Will P.	o.	PA	26 Sept. 1918	2	4	
Beggs	William P.	o.	PA	21 Feb. 1916	1	1	
Beggs	William P.	o.	PC	21 Mar. 1916	8	3	
Begnotti	Charles	b.	PA	1 July 1916	8	4	

(1) Surname	(2) Given Name	(3)	(4)	(5) Date	(6) Pg	(7) Col	(8) Comments
Beherens	Carl	b.	PA	1 Aug. 1916	3	7	also 5:7
Behling	Herman	d.	HT	9 Aug. 1917	1	3	
Behmer	Edward	m.	PA	9 Aug. 1917	5	4	
Behmer	Edward	m.	SRR	9 Aug. 1917	1	2	
Behrens	Albert P.	b.	PA	16 Apr. 1918	5	3	
Behrens	Mary	d.	PA	5 Feb. 1917	2	3	Cypress Hill; also 6 Feb., 8:3
Behrens	Mary	d.	PC	6 Feb. 1917	4	1&5	Cypress Hill; also 7 Feb., 8:3; 9 Feb., 4:1
Behrens	Mary	d.	PD	6 Feb. 1917	5	6	
Behrens	Mary	d.	SRR	6 Feb. 1917	5	3	
Behrens	William	b.	PA	19 Feb. 1918	8	2	
Behrens	William	b.	PC	20 Feb. 1918	8	3	
Behrs	Henry	m.	PC	22 Apr. 1918	5	2	
Behrs	Mr.	m.	PC	18 May 1918	3	4	
Beilo	Mary	m.	PD	24 Aug. 1917	3	1	
Belding	Lizzie S.	d.	PC	10 June 1916	1	2	
Belinsky	Isaac	d.	SRR	12 Dec. 1917	4	1	
Belinsky	Isaac	d.	PD	13 Dec. 1917	3	1	
Bell	Albert	d.	SRR	10 Apr. 1916	8	4	
Bell	Albert	d.	PC	11 Apr. 1916	4	3	
Bell	Albert	d.	PD	12 Apr. 1916	2	4	Mt. Olive Cemetery, San Mateo
Bell	Benecia	d.	PA	21 Oct. 1918	4	5	also 8:5; 22 Oct., 8:3
Bell	Benecia	d.	PC	22 Oct. 1918	8	2	San Francisco; also 23 Oct., 5:3
Bell	Benecia	d.	PD	22 Oct. 1918	5	4	
Bell	E. R.	o.	PC	21 Aug. 1918	3	4	
Bell	John	d.	SRR	8 June 1917	6	3	also 11 June, 6:5
Bell	John	d.	PD	9 June 1917	5	3	
Bell	John	d.	HT	21 June 1917	4	3	
Bell	R. W.	d.	PD	9 Mar. 1916	5	4	
Bell	T.	o.	SRR	18 Jan. 1916	3	3	
Bell	Wilbur	d.	SRR	20 Dec. 1916	3	1	Shiloh Cemetery
Bell	Wilbur	d.	PD	21 Dec. 1916	5	5	
Bella	Mary	m.	PA	5 Sept. 1917	6	4	
Belli	Santi	b.	PA	4 Nov. 1916	8	6	
Belli	Santi	b.	PC	5 Nov. 1916	5	7	
Bello	Mary	m.	PC	24 Aug. 1917	5	5	
Bello	Mary	m.	PC	6 Sept. 1917	5	2	
Beltrami	Giacomo	d.	PA	20 June 1917	4	4	Calvary Cemetery; also 21 June, 5:5
Bemis	Samuel	d.	PD	30 June 1916	8	4	I.O.O.F. Cemetery
Benbeck	L. S.	o.	SIT	11 Aug. 1917	1	2	
Bender	Marie D.	m.	PC	5 June 1918	5	3	

(1) Surname	(2) Given Name	(3)	(4)	(5) Date	(6) Pg	(7) Col	(8) Comments
Benedetti	Gilade	d.	PD	10 Nov. 1918	4	2	
Benedict	Ruth	m.	PD	10 Nov. 1916	2	1	
Benedict	Ruth	m.	PC	11 Nov. 1916	5	1	
Benepe	Laura Bella	d.	PD	17 Mar. 1918	8	3	
Benepe	Laura Belle	d.	PC	17 Mar. 1918	1	4	Cypress Hill; also 19 Mar., 4:4
Benepe	Laura Belle	d.	PA	18 Mar. 1918	8	5	Cypress Hill
Benepe	Laura Belle	d.	ST	22 Mar. 1918	8	3	
Benham	Drury	m.	PD	13 June 1916	5	4	
Benjamin	Frank	o.	SIT	23 Mar. 1918	1	2	
Benjamin	George Washington	d.	HT	19 Dec. 1918	4	5	Beeson Cemetery
Benjamin	George Washington	d.	PD	28 Dec. 1918	6	4	
Benjamin	Maria	d.	PD	7 Nov. 1917	2	5	Bennett Valley Cemetery; also 4:2; 9 Nov., 3:4
Benjamin	Maria	d.	SRR	7 Nov. 1917	3	6	Bennett Valley Cemetery; also 8 Nov., 8:2
Benjamin	Maria	d.	PC	8 Nov. 1917	3	4	
Benn	George	o.	PA	17 Oct. 1918	2	2	2
Bennett	Eva C. or Ida	m.	PD	5 Dec. 1916	2	1	
Bennett	Joseph Albert	d.	PC	22 May 1917	2	3	cremation
Bennett	Naomi	o.	PD	12 July 1917	6	2	
Bennett	Naomi	o.	PC	13 July 1917	3	5	
Bennett	Naomi	o.	SRR	19 July 1917	8	5	
Bennett	Ralph	o.	PD	12 July 1917	6	2	
Bennett	Ralph	o.	PC	13 July 1917	3	5	
Bennett	Ralph	o.	SRR	19 July 1917	8	5	
Bennett	Susan	d.	SRR	8 Oct. 1917	8	2	cremation
Bennett	Susan	d.	PD	9 Oct. 1917	3	3	cremation
Bennett	Tryra	o.	PC	4 Apr. 1916	1	4	portrait
Bensen	Arthur W.	d.	PA	11 Dec. 1918	5	4	France
Benson	Arthur A.	d.	PA	20 Dec. 1918	8	3	France
Benson	Arthur W.	d.	PC	11 Dec. 1918	1	3	France
Benson	Arthur W.	d.	PD	12 Dec. 1918	3	2	France
Benson	August	m.	PD	2 Oct. 1917	8	4	also 3 Oct., 2:5
Benson	August	m.	SRR	2 Oct. 1917	4	5	
Benson	August	m.	HT	4 Oct. 1917	1	5	
Benson	Bertha	o.	PA	18 Jan. 1917	5	2	
Benson	Bertha J.	o.	SRR	16 Feb. 1917	4	2	also 17 Feb., 1:2
Benson	Bertha J.	o.	PA	17 Feb. 1917	1	4	
Benson	Bertha J.	o.	PA	17 Feb. 1917	6	3	
Benson	Bertha J.	o.	PC	18 Feb. 1917	8	2	
Benson	Bertha J.	o.	PD	19 Jan. 1917	5	2	
Benson	Bertha Josephine	o.	SRR	18 Jan. 1917	3	5	

(1) Surname	(2) Given Name	(3)	(4)	(5) Date	(6) Pg	(7) Col	(8) Comments
Benson	Elwin D.	b.	PA	22 Nov. 1916	8	7	
Benson	Joseph	b.	PA	17 Apr. 1918	4	3	
Benson	Lars	d.	PD	12 June 1917	5	3	
Benson	Roy D.	o.	SRR	16 Feb. 1917	4	2	also 17 Feb., 1:2
Benson	Roy D.	o.	PA	17 Feb. 1917	1	4	
Benson	Roy D.	o.	PA	17 Feb. 1917	6	3	
Benson	Roy D.	o.	PC	18 Feb. 1917	8	2	
Benson	Roy D.	o.	PD	19 Jan. 1917	5	2	
Benson	Roy Douglas	o.	SRR	18 Jan. 1917	3	5	
Benson	Roy Douglas	o.	PA	18 Jan. 1917	5	2	
Benson	Velma	m.	PC	12 Aug. 1916	4	4	also 17 Aug., 1:2
Benson	Velma I.	m.	SRR	11 Aug. 1916	5	2	also 17 Aug., 6:1
Benson	Velma L.	m.	PA	11 Aug. 1916	6	3	also 16 Aug., 4:4
Benson	Velma L.	m.	PD	11 Aug. 1916	1	3	
Bentley	Mabel S.	m.	PC	25 Apr. 1917	4	3	
Bentley	Mabel Schell	m.	PA	24 Apr. 1917	3	6	also 5:2
Bentley	Mabel Schell	m.	SRR	24 Apr. 1917	2	4	
Benton	H. B.	m.	SRR	7 Mar. 1917	6	3	
Benton	H. B.	m.	PD	8 Mar. 1917	3	2	
Benton	Henry B.	m.	PA	2 Mar. 1917	4	3	also 5 Mar., 8:3
Benton	Henry M.	m.	PC	3 Mar. 1917	5	4	also 6 Mar., 3:1
Benton	Laura M.	d.	PD	1 Mar. 1916	5	2	Eureka, NV
Berge	Phil	o.	SRR	31 Dec. 1917	8	4	
Berger	Albert	o.	PD	7 May 1918	6	5	
Berger	Clara	m.	PD	9 Apr. 1918	7	1	
Berger	Clara Lee	m.	PD	14 May 1918	8	2	also 16 May, 6:5
Berger	Fred W.	m.	SRR	19 Sept. 1917	5	1	
Berger	Fred W.	m.	PD	20 Sept. 1917	5	2	
Berger	Fred W.	m.	SRR	26 Nov. 1917	8	1	
Berger	Jane	d.	PD	20 June 1918	5	3	
Berger	Jeanette	d.	PA	5 Sept. 1916	6	4	Salem Cemetery, San Mateo
Berger	Otto	m.	PD	26 Sept. 1917	5	3	also 27 Sept., 3:4
Berger	Otto W.	m.	PA	25 Sept. 1917	4	5	
Berger	Otto W.	m.	SRR	25 Sept. 1917	4	4	also 26 Sept., 4:3
Berger	Otto W.	m.	PC	27 Sept. 1917	5	5	
Bergevin	Alexander Wickersham	o.	PC	8 Aug. 1917	1	2	
Berglund	Harvey	b.	SRR	26 Dec. 1916	6	2	
Bergstrom	Edith	d.	PA	23 Dec. 1918	3	2	also 8:4; 24 Dec., 4:5
Bergstrom	Edith W.	d.	PC	24 Dec. 1918	4	3	
Bergstrom	Edith W.	d.	PC	25 Nov. 1918	4	3	
Berman	Bertha	m.	PC	16 Aug. 1918	3	4	
Berman	Bertha	m.	PD	17 Aug. 1918	4	2	
Bernal	Candido P.	b.	PA	26 Dec. 1917	4	7	
Bernard	A., Jr.	d.	PA	26 Oct. 1918	6	4	

(1) Surname	(2) Given Name	(3)	(4)	(5) Date	(6) Pg	(7) Col	(8) Comments
Bernard	Blanche	m.	SRR	21 Dec. 1917	7	2	
Bernardi	Theodore	m.	PD	24 Mar. 1917	8	2	
Bernasconi	Ferdinand P.	m.	PC	5 Jan. 1918	4	5	
Berns	Mary Jane	d.	SRR	17 Feb. 1916	8	4	Rural Cemetery; also 21 Feb., 6:4
Berns/Berens	Mary Jane	d.	PD	18 Feb. 1916	1	5	Rural Cemetery; also 20 Feb., 12:3; 22 Feb., 3:2
Bernstein	D.	b.	PC	12 Sept. 1918	4	4	
Bernstein	David	m.	PA	13 Apr. 1917	5	5	
Berri	A.	p.	PC	2 July 1918	8	4	
Berri	Arnold	b.	PA	1 Apr. 1918	3	3	also 8:3
Berri	Arnold	m.	PA	10 Jan. 1917	4	2	
Berri	Arnold	m.	PC	11 Jan. 1917	5	3	
Berri	B.	d.	PD	13 June 1918	2	1	
Berri	B.	p.	PA	1 July 1918	5	1	
Berri	Bartolomeo	d.	PA	12 June 1918	4	5	Calvary Cemetery; also 13 June, 4:4; 14 June, 4:4
Berri	Bartolomeo	d.	PC	12 June 1918	8	3	also 13 June, 3:4; 14 June, 2:2; 15 June, 4:1, 8:2
Berry	Gladys	m.	PA	28 Apr. 1916	8	3	
Berry	Gladys	m.	PC	28 Apr. 1916	5	3	
Berry	Gladys	m.	PD	28 Apr. 1916	6	5	
Berry	Isabelle	m.	PD	18 Feb. 1917	5	4	
Berry	Isabelle	m.	SRR	19 Feb. 1917	5	4	
Berry	Roy	o.	ST	1 Nov. 1918	1	6	
Berry	Roy	o.	ST	16 Aug. 1918	1	6	
Berry	Rufus	d.	PD	7 July 1918	6	3	
Berryhill	Sarah	d.	SRR	1 June 1917	1	3	
Berryhill	Sarah A.	d.	SRR	5 May 1917	6	3	also 7 May, 8:2
Berryhill	Sarah A.	d.	HT	10 May 1917	5	4	Oak Mound Cemetery
Berryholl	F. D., Mrs.	d.	PD	6 May 1917	8	4	
Bertelsen	Thomas L.	m.	PA	26 Nov. 1918	3	5	also 29 Nov., 6:5
Bertelson	Thomas L.	m.	PC	28 Nov. 1918	6	3	
Bertina	Kate	m.	SRR	23 July 1917	5	3	
Bertini	A. (dau of)	d.	ST	28 Sept. 1917	1	1	
Bertino	Louis	d.	PD	26 Nov. 1918	1	2	also 1 Dec., 7:6
Bertino	Louis	d.	PD	28 Nov. 1918	4	2	
Bertino	Rose	m.	PD	29 Sept. 1918	2	5	
Bertola	Gerry	m.	SRR	23 Apr. 1917	6	2	
Bertolani	Angelo	d.	PD	16 Mar. 1918	8	4	also 19 Mar., 5:1
Bertolani	Victor	b.	SRR	26 Feb. 1916	10	2	
Bertoli	Garry	m.	SIT	21 Apr. 1917	1	2	

(1) Surname	(2) Given Name	(3)	(4)	(5) Date	(6) Pg	(7) Col	(8) Comments
Bertolotte	Julia	d.	SIT	16 Nov. 1918	4	7	
Berton	C. E.	b.	SRR	19 Dec. 1917	3	4	
Bertoni	August	d.	PD	24 Mar. 1916	3	3	Fulton Cemetery; also 28 Mar., 5:5
Bertoni	August	d.	SRR	24 Mar. 1916	6	4	Fulton; also 27 Mar., 8:5
Bertoni	Mary	d.	SRR	16 Dec. 1916	8	2	Calvary Cemetery
Bertossi	Guiseppi	d.	PD	26 Jan. 1916	8	2	Calvary Cemetery
Bertossi	Marie	d.	SRR	18 Dec. 1916	8	6	
Bertossi	Mary	d.	PD	16 Dec. 1916	8	2	also 19 Dec., 8:2
Bertram	Ludwig	d.	PC	22 Feb. 1916	3	2	Cypress Lawn
Bertrand	James	b.	HT	20 June 1918	2	3	
Bertrand	Myrtle J.	o.	PD	6 Oct. 1917	8	4	
Bertrend	Jean S.	o.	PD	6 Oct. 1917	8	4	
Best	Mary Ellen	d.	PD	23 Nov. 1916	8	5	Portland, OR
Best	Mary Ellen	d.	PC	24 Nov. 1916	2	2	
Betinelli	S.	b.	PA	1 Oct. 1918	5	2	also 2 Oct., 8:2
Betrami	Giacomo	d.	PC	20 June 1917	4	3	also 21 June, 5:6; 22 June, 5:5
Bettencourt	Elvira	m.	PD	16 Aug. 1916	2	3	
Bettencourt	Joseph A.	m.	PC	11 Apr. 1917	6	6	also 12 Apr., 5:2
Bettiga	Buno	m.	PD	24 Nov. 1918	6	3	
Bettinelli	A.	b.	PC	10 Mar. 1917	8	4	
Bettinelli	A.	b.	PA	9 Mar. 1917	5	5	also 8:3
Bettinelli	Philip	d.	PC	21 Dec. 1916	8	2	Calvary Cemetery; also 22 Dec., 4:2; 24 Dec., 5:5
Bettinelli	Phillip	d.	PA	21 Dec. 1916	5	3	Calvary Cemetery; also 23 Dec., 4:2
Bettinelli	Silvia	m.	PC	10 Oct. 1917	1	5	also 25 Oct., 6:3
Bettinelli	Sylvio	m.	PD	11 Oct. 1917	3	3	also 25 Oct., 8:3
Bettinelli	Sylvio	m.	PA	9 Oct. 1917	5	1	also 24 Oct., 4:4
Bettini	Joseph	b.	SRR	6 Sept. 1916	6	3	
Betts	Ethel	m.	PD	2 July 1916	2	2	
Betz	Charles A.	m.	PC	21 Sept. 1916	2	2	
Biacomini	T.	b.	PC	8 Nov. 1918	5	1	
Biaggi	Joe	d.	PA	28 Oct. 1918	5	7	Calvary Cemetery; also 8:3
Biaggi	Joseph	d.	PC	29 Oct. 1918	8	2	also 30 Oct., 8:3
Bianchi	Antonio	m.	SRR	14 May 1917	3	5	
Bianchi	Giovanni W.	m.	PD	29 Sept. 1918	2	5	
Bianchi	Joe	m.	SRR	21 Sept. 1916	5	1	
Bianchi	Pietro	d.	PD	19 Dec. 1916	8	5	also 21 Dec., 3:4
Bianchi	Severino	m.	PD	4 May 1917	2	2	also 15 May, 2:6
Bianchini	Joe	m.	PC	20 Sept. 1916	4	6	
Bianchini	Louise	m.	PA	3 Apr. 1916	4	1	

(1) Surname	(2) Given Name	(3)	(4)	(5) Date	(6) Pg	(7) Col	(8) Comments
Bick	W.	d.	PC	25 July 1916	3	4	Salem Cemetery, S.F.; also 26 July, 5:2
Bickerstaff	Florence	o.	SRR	21 Sept. 1917	8	2	
Bickerstaff	Florence	o.	PC	22 Sept. 1917	3	3	
Bickerstaff	Florence	o.	PD	4 Nov. 1917	3	3	
Bickerstaff	Florence E.	o.	PA	19 Sept. 1917	5	5	
Bickerstaff	Florence E.	o.	PD	21 Sept. 1917	3	4	
Bickerstaff	Florence E.	o.	SRR	3 Nov. 1917	1	5	
Bickerstaff	Joseph	m.	SRR	21 Dec. 1916	4	4	
Bickerstaff	Joseph	o.	PD	4 Nov. 1917	3	3	
Bickerstaff	Joseph A.	o.	PA	19 Sept. 1917	5	5	
Bickerstaff	Joseph A.	m.	PD	21 Dec. 1916	5	3	
Bickerstaff	Joseph A.	o.	PD	21 Sept. 1917	3	4	
Bickerstaff	Joseph A.	o.	SRR	21 Sept. 1917	8	2	
Bickerstaff	Joseph A.	o.	PC	22 Sept. 1917	3	3	
Bickerstaff	Joseph A.	o.	SRR	3 Nov. 1917	1	5	
Bidwell	Annie	d.	PD	10 Mar. 1918	8	1	
Bidwell	Annie E. K.	d.	ST	8 Mar. 1918	2	3	
Bidwell	Delbert W.	m.	PD	30 Dec. 1917	3	2	
Bidwell	Delbert W.	m.	SRR	31 Dec. 1917	2	3	
Bierkie	Alfred B.	m.	PD	14 May 1918	3	7	
Bierkin	Alfred R.	m.	PA	13 May 1918	5	1	
Bierkle	Alfred R.	m.	PC	14 May 1918	4	4	
Bigelow	Mary E.	m.	PD	23 Nov. 1917	8	2	
Biglow	Charles P.	d.	PD	20 Dec. 1917	2	2	
Bihn	William	b.	PA	8 Aug. 1917	5	2	
Bill	Henry	o.	ST	27 Sept. 1918	1	5	
Bill	Herbert	o.	ST	23 Aug. 1918	1	2	
Bill	Joe	d.	HT	3 Mar. 1916	5	4	
Bill	Philip, Jr.	b.	SIT	5 Feb. 1916	4	6	
Bill/Dill	John Merrill	d.	PD	25 Sept. 1918	4	2	Rural Cemetery; also 26 Sept., 6:3, 4
Billing	J.	b.	PC	12 Jan. 1917	5	1	
Billing	William Harold	d.	PA	15 Oct. 1917	5	5	also 6:2
Billing	William Harold	d.	PC	16 Oct. 1917	8	4	also 17 Oct., 3:4
Billings	Nellie I.	m.	PA	15 Mar. 1916	1	5	also 16 Mar., 4:4
Billings	Nettie Iter	m.	PD	16 Mar. 1916	3	4	
Billings	R. E.	b.	SRR	21 Feb. 1916	10	6	
Bindi	Acilli	m.	ST	10 Mar. 1917	1	1	
Bindi	Aeille	m.	PD	8 Mar. 1917	7	5	
Binel	child	d.	PC	2 Nov. 1916	5	5	Calvary Cemetery
Bingham	Alice	m.	PD	28 July 1917	3	2	
Bingham	William W.	d.	SIT	7 Sept. 1918	1	6	Lodi
Binkley	Allen Thomas	b.	PC	19 Dec. 1917	8	3	
Binkley	R. P. (son of)	d.	PA	7 Jan. 1918	8	5	

(1) Surname	(2) Given Name	(3)	(4)	(5) Date	(6) Pg	(7) Col	(8) Comments
Binkley	Ralph	m.	PD	7 Oct. 1916	2	4	
Binkley	Ralph P.	m.	HT	12 Oct. 1916	1	1	
Binkley	Ralph P.	m.	SRR	6 Oct. 1916	4	3	also 10 Oct., 3:1; 18 Oct., 3:6
Binkley	Ralph P.	m.	PC	7 Oct. 1916	5	3	also 11 Oct., 1:4; 13 Oct., 3:6
Bird	A. B., Mrs.	d.	PD	29 June 1917	5	2	
Bird	Emma L.	m.	SRR	17 May 1917	8	6	
Bird	Grace	d.	PC	24 June 1917	6	4	
Birkhofer	Oscar	m.	PC	23 Nov. 1916	2	1	
Birkhofer	Oscar	m.	PD	28 Nov. 1916	2	7	
Birkhoffer	William Oscar	b.	PD	12 Sept. 1917	8	3	
Birmingham	Mary	m.	PD	9 Sept. 1917	7	4	
Bisbee	George	o.	PD	4 Apr. 1917	3	3	
Bisbee	George	o.	PC	5 Apr. 1917	8	3	
Bisbee	George M.	b.	SRR	27 Oct. 1917	1	5	
Bish	Marie	m.	PC	5 Sept. 1917	4	2	
Bish	Rena Marie	m.	SIT	8 Sept. 1917	4	7	
Bishop	Eugene	m.	PD	17 Apr. 1917	8	5	
Bisordi	Theresa	d.	SRR	28 May 1917	8	2	Masonic Cemetery, Sebastopol; also 31 May, 4:6; 2 June, 8:5
Bisordi	Theresa	d.	PD	29 May 1917	8	4	also 30 May, 4:3; 1 June, 4:3; 2 June, 6:1
Bisordi	Theresa	d.	PA	31 May 1917	8	4	
Bixby	W. E.	o.	ST	6 Sept. 1918	1	5	also 6 Dec., 1:2
Black	Holle	m.	HT	16 Aug. 1917	4	4	
Black	Hollie A.	m.	PD	22 Aug. 1917	8	5	
Black	Marie	m.	PA	3 Oct. 1918	4	3	
Black	Marie	m.	PD	3 Oct. 1918	3	1	
Black	Marie	m.	ST	6 Oct. 1918	1	4	
Blackburn	Caroline W.	o.	PD	4 Oct. 1916	2	4	
Blackburn	Caroline W.	o.	PA	8 Sept. 1916	5	4	also 3 Oct., 1:3
Blackburn	Frank L.	o.	PD	4 Oct. 1916	2	4	
Blackburn	Frank L.	o.	PA	8 Sept. 1916	5	4	also 3 Oct., 1:3
Blackburn	Walter	d.	SRR	16 Oct. 1916	1	3	
Blackburn	Walter C.	d.	PC	17 Oct. 1916	1	6	Presidio; also 4:3; 18 Oct., 1:4
Blackburn	Walterd.	b.	PA	16 Oct. 1916	1	4	also 17 Oct., 5:3
Blackwell	Edward	d.	PA	3 Nov. 1916	8	4	
Blacques	Christobol	b.	PD	1 Jan. 1916	6	4	
Blake	Evelina	d.	PA	11 Aug. 1916	5	5	Cypress Hill; also 12 Aug., 8:6
Blake	Evelina	d.	PC	12 Aug. 1916	5	5	Cypress Hill; also 13 Aug., 6:2
Blake	Virginia Susan	d.	PD	4 Jan. 1917	5	2	

(1) Surname	(2) Given Name	(3)	(4)	(5) Date	(6) Pg	(7) Col	(8) Comments
Blake	Virginia T.	d.	SRR	2 Jan. 1917	10	2	Suisun; also 3 Jan., 3:3; 4 Jan., 2:3
Blake	Virginia T.	d.	PC	3 Jan. 1917	1	4	
Blakeley	Delma Mae	m.	PC	25 Dec. 1917	5	2	
Blakely	Delma Mae	m.	PA	24 Dec. 1917	5	1	
Blakley	Allen Thomas	d.	HT	10 Jan. 1918	1	4	
Blakley	John R.	o.	SRR	4 Oct. 1916	8	5	
Blakley	Mabel T.	o.	SRR	4 Oct. 1916	8	5	
Blakley	Thomas F.	m.	SRR	19 July 1917	8	3	
Blanchard	Miss	o.	PC	7 Mar. 1917	3	4	adoption
Blanchard	W. L.	m.	PA	15 Oct. 1917	4	3	
Blanchard	W. L.	m.	PC	16 Oct. 1917	3	4	
Blanchini	Louise	m.	SRR	5 Apr. 1916	3	4	
Blanciarini	Henry T.	m.	PA	28 Dec. 1917	4	3	
Blankenberger	Adam	d.	PA	23 Apr. 1917	5	7	
Blankenship	Lola	m.	PD	24 Aug. 1917	3	1	
Blankenship/Blank enberger	Adam	d.	PC	22 Apr. 1917	1	3	Cypress Hill; also 24 Apr., 5:4
Blazer	Lloyd	b.	HT	14 June 1917	7	1	
Blazer	Lloyd	b.	HT	3 Feb. 1917	4	3	
Bledsoe	Gladys	m.	HT	10 Jan. 1918	4	3	
Bledsoe	J. C.	d.	PA	18 June 1917	3	5	
Bledsoe	John C.	d.	PC	19 June 1917	8	4	
Bledsoe	John Carson	d.	PD	19 June 1917	3	1	Rural Cemetery; also 4:3; 21 June, 7:1
Bledsoe	John Carson	d.	SRR	19 June 1917	8	1	Rural Cemetery
Bledsoe	John Carson	d.	HT	21 June 1917	8	2	Rural Cemetery
Bledsoe	John Carson	d.	ST	22 June 1917	1	6	
Bledsoe	Lynn	d.	HT	1 Feb. 1917	3	3	Oak Mound Cemetery
Bledsoe	Lynn	d.	PD	27 Jan. 1917	3	4	
Blesdsoe	Lynn	d.	SRR	26 Jan. 1917	3	1	also 27 Jan., 10:4
Blevins	Norma	m.	SIT	28 July 1917	2	4	
Blim	Theresa	o.	PC	7 May 1918	5	4	
Block	Clara	m.	SIT	13 May 1916	1	6	
Block	Clara M.	m.	PD	18 May 1916	8	7	
Block	Herman	b.	PA	1 Apr. 1916	5	3	
Blohm	H.	b.	PA	2 Nov. 1916	4	7	
Bloom	Amertoo	b.	PA	16 June 1917	8	4	
Bloom	Solomon	d.	PC	7 Dec. 1918	2	2	
Bloom	Solomon	d.	PD	7 Dec. 1918	5	5	
Bluxome	Doris	d.	SIT	9 Nov. 1918	1	7	
Blythe	Ethel Saxe	m.	SRR	6 Jan. 1916	10	2	
Boakes	John	d.	PA	8 May 1917	5	4	
Boakes	John	d.	PD	10 May 1917	2	4	

(1) Surname	(2) Given Name	(3)	(4)	(5) Date	(6) Pg	(7) Col	(8) Comments
Boalt	Elizabeth	d.	PD	17 Feb. 1917	3	4	
Bocca	G.	d.	PD	7 June 1917	2	3	
Bocca	G.	d.	SRR	7 June 1917	6	5	
Bocca	Guiseppe	d.	PA	5 June 1917	6	4	
Bocca	Guiseppe	d.	PC	7 June 1917	3	6	
Bocca	Guiseppi	p.	SRR	12 June 1917	5	5	
Bockee	David	o.	PD	21 Feb. 1917	3	2	adoption
Bockee	David G.	o.	SRR	20 Feb. 1917	4	3	adoption
Bodwell	C. A.	d.	PD	14 Apr. 1916	5	1	
Bodwell	C. A.	d.	SRR	14 Apr. 1916	5	3	
Bodwell	Charles A.	d.	PC	13 Apr. 1916	5	4	cremation; also 15 Apr., 4:3; 16 Apr., 4:5
Body	Ben	m.	SRR	9 June 1916	8	4	
Body	Charles	b.	PD	18 Apr. 1917	2	3	
Body	Charles	b.	SRR	18 Apr. 1917	2	4	
Boggiano	Anna	o.	SRR	4 Dec. 1916	5	5	
Boggiano	Domenico	o.	SRR	4 Dec. 1916	5	5	
Bogini	John	d.	SRR	31 Mar. 1917	1	2	
Bogini	John	d.	PA	4 Apr. 1917	4	3	
Bogini	John	d.	PD	5 Apr. 1917	8	3	
Bogle	Marion	m.	PD	12 July 1918	8	2	
Bogle	Marion	m.	PC	13 July 1918	6	5	
Bogle	S. S.	m.	SRR	5 June 1916	8	3	also 10 June, 2:1
Bogle	Samuel S.	m.	PD	3 June 1916	8	3	
Bogle	Samuel Saffell	m.	SRR	24 Apr. 1916	4	4	
Bohan	Elizabeth	d.	PA	22 Nov. 1918	6	5	also 23 Nov., 5:2
Bohan	Elizabeth	d.	PD	22 Nov. 1918	3	4	Holy Cross, S. F.; also 23 Nov., 6:2; 24 Nov., 10:1
Bohan	Michael	m.	SRR	20 Sept. 1917	4	3	
Bohan	Mrs.	d.	PC	23 Nov. 1918	4	2	
Bohlin	Louis C.	m.	SRR	2 May 1916	8	1	also 4 May, 6:2
Bohlin	Louis G.	m.	PC	3 May 1916	4	4	
Bohlman	Adolph	d.	PC	7 Mar. 1918	4	5	Cypress Hill; also 5:6; 8 Mar., 4:3
Bohlmann	Adolph	d.	PA	7 Mar. 1918	6	4	
Bohz	Frank	o.	SRR	10 Mar. 1917	2	5	
Bohz	Marie	o.	SRR	10 Mar. 1917	2	5	
Boileau	Caroline	m.	PC	29 Aug. 1917	5	1	
Boin	Louisa	d.	PD	23 May 1918	5	1	San Francisco
Bois	Frank	o.	PA	10 Mar. 1917	6	6	
Bois	Marie	o.	PA	10 Mar. 1917	6	6	
Boitano	John	d.	PD	27 Dec. 1918	7	2	
Boivin	Emil	b.	PA	3 Mar. 1916	4	1	also 5:2

(1) Surname	(2) Given Name	(3)	(4)	(5) Date	(6) Pg	(7) Col	(8) Comments
Boivin	Emile	d.	PC	28 Nov. 1916	3	4&5	also 29 Nov., 8:3
Boivin	Emile Peter	d.	PA	27 Nov. 1916	8	2	Cypress Hill; also 28 Nov., 4:4
Bolano	John	d.	PA	7 Apr. 1917	8	2	also 10 Apr., 5:4
Bolham	Richard	m.	PA	19 Sept. 1917	5	7	
Bolin	Adeline	m.	PA	25 Oct. 1917	4	3	
Bolin	J. W., Mrs.	d.	SIT	25 May 1918	1	1	
Bolin	S. W.	d.	PA	16 Oct. 1918	5	3	Indianapolis, IN
Bolin	S. W.	d.	PC	18 Oct. 1918	3	4	
Bolla	Adeline	m.	PA	23 Aug. 1917	5	3	
Bolla	Adeline	m.	PD	24 Aug. 1917	3	1	
Bolla	Adeline E.	m.	PD	26 Oct. 1917	2	4	
Bolla	Esther	m.	PA	12 Sept. 1917	5	4	
Bolla	Esther	m.	PC	13 Sept. 1917	5	2	
Bolla	Esther	m.	PD	13 Sept. 1917	8	3	
Bolla	Esther	m.	SRR	13 Sept. 1917	3	5	
Bolla	Harold	o.	PA	17 Apr. 1917	5	3	
Bolla	Harold	o.	PC	19 Apr. 1917	3	2	
Bolle	Henry	d.	PA	16 July 1917	4	2	
Bolle	Henry	d.	SRR	16 July 1917	1	3	
Bolle	Henry	d.	PC	17 July 1917	1	2	also 18 July, 1:2
Bolle	Henry	d.	PD	17 July 1917	3	1	
Bolton	W. A.	o.	SRR	22 Mar. 1916	10	4	
Bolz	Frank	o.	PA	21 Feb. 1917	5	7	
Bolz	Frank	o.	SRR	21 Feb. 1917	1	6	
Bolz	Frank	o.	PC	22 Feb. 1917	5	3	
Bolz	Fred	o.	PD	22 Feb. 1917	7	4	
Bolz	Marie	o.	PA	21 Feb. 1917	5	7	
Bolz	Marie	o.	SRR	21 Feb. 1917	1	6	
Bolz	Marie	o.	PC	22 Feb. 1917	5	3	
Bolz	Marie	o.	PD	22 Feb. 1917	7	4	
Bolz	Marie	m.	PA	22 Mar. 1918	5	4	
Bolz	Marie	m.	PC	24 Mar. 1918	3	4	
Boman	Beatrice	m.	PC	10 June 1917	5	4	
Bon Omi	Angelo	b.	PA	7 Nov. 1917	5	4	
Bonar	Leslie	b.	PD	26 Jan. 1917	2	3	
Bond	Charles	d.	PD	12 Sept. 1917	2	3	
Bond	George	d.	PA	20 Nov. 1918	4	7	cremation; also 8:5; 21 Nov., 4:5; 22 Nov., 7:6
Bond	George	d.	PC	20 Nov. 1918	8	4	cremation; also 21 Nov., 6:1; 22 Nov., 4:3
Bond	George	d.	PD	21 Nov. 1918	3	4	
Bond	Louis	d.	SRR	1 Feb. 1916	3	6	

(1) Surname	(2) Given Name	(3)	(4)	(5) Date	(6) Pg	(7) Col	(8) Comments
Bond	Seth	d.	HT	10 Feb. 1916	7	3	
Bonechristiana	Tony	d.	SRR	20 Mar. 1917	8	6	
Bones	Bessie	m.	SRR	3 Feb. 1917	10	2	
Bones	Charles	o.	ST	8 Nov. 1918	2	4	
Bones	Charles M.	o.	PA	2 Sept. 1918	7	6	
Bones	Charles M., Jr.	o.	PD	29 Aug. 1918	6	2	
Bones	Charles M., Jr.	o.	PC	31 Aug. 1918	1	5	
Bones	Ella	m.	PC	4 Feb. 1917	6	2	
Bones	Hazel	m.	SRR	15 Sept. 1917	6	2	
Bones	Hazel	m.	PD	16 Sept. 1917	2	5	
Bones	Hazel	m.	SRR	18 Aug. 1917	6	5	
Bones	Hazel	m.	PC	19 Aug. 1917	3	2	
Bones	Ira Leslie	o.	PC	25 Aug. 1916	1	6	also 26 Aug., 1:5; 27 Aug., 6:4; 8 Sept., 1:1; 15 Sept., 1:5; 8 Dec., 1:3; 9 Dec., 1:5; 14 Dec., 1:3; 23 Dec., 1:4
Bones	Ira Leslie	o.	PD	8 Dec. 1916	2	1	also 9 Dec., 2:7; 12 Dec., 1:2, 1:3; 14 Dec., 6:5; 23 Dec., 5:1; 30 Dec., 1:3
Bones	John	d.	SRR	1 Sept. 1916	8	4	also 2 Sept., 4:2
Bones	John	d.	PC	2 Sept. 1916	5	5	Occidental
Bones	John	d.	ST	2 Sept. 1916	1	2	Occidental
Bones	Lesly	o.	PA	24 Aug. 1916	5	4	also 25 Aug., 3:3; 26 Aug., 6:3
Bones	R. W.	o.	PD	20 Dec. 1918	2	1	
Bones	Reuben	o.	ST	15 Nov. 1918	6	2	
Bones	Reuben	o.	PA	17 Dec. 1918	4	2	
Bones	Sarah Emily	d.	PA	1 Apr. 1916	4	5	also 3 Apr., 3:6
Bones	Sarah Emily	d.	SRR	1 Apr. 1916	5	3	
Bones	Sarah Emily	d.	PD	2 Apr. 1016	3	3	also 4 Apr., 6:4
Bonfigle	Alvise	b.	PD	15 Oct. 1916	3	2	
Bonfigli	Matilda	m.	PD	14 May 1918	7	3	also 15 May, 7:3
Bonfiglia	Alvise	b.	SRR	16 Oct. 1916	4	2	
Bonham	Joseph	m.	PA	4 Jan. 1918	8	3	
Bonham	Joseph	m.	PD	5 Jan. 1918	2	5	
Bonham	Noah S.	m.	SRR	10 Jan. 1916	1	2	
Bonham	Noah S.	m.	PD	11 Jan. 1916	5	3	
Bonomi	Angelo	b.	PC	7 Nov. 1917	4	2	
Bononi	A.	b.	PC	6 Oct. 1916	5	6	
Bontini	Tony	d.	HT	12 Sept. 1918	5	5	
Boone	Nestor W.	d.	HT	14 Nov. 1918	8	5	
Boraccio	(3 children of)	d.	SRR	13 Feb. 1917	1	3	
Borba	C. M.	o.	PC	16 Nov. 1917	2	1	

(1) Surname	(2) Given Name	(3)	(4)	(5) Date	(6) Pg	(7) Col	(8) Comments
Borba	Charles	o.	ST	6 Oct. 1918	1	5	
Borba	Louis	o.	PC	16 Nov. 1917	2	1	
Bordenave	John P.	o.	PD	4 July 1918	2	1	
Border	Lee Scott	b.	SRR	5 Jan. 1916	10	6	
Borges	Manuel	d.	PC	16 Nov. 1918	8	4	
Borgia	Frank	m.	PC	19 May 1917	4	6	
Borgo	Philip	o.	PC	1 Jan. 1918	6	4	
Borquin	Joseph	o.	PD	22 Feb. 1917	7	4	
Borquin	Lillie J.	o.	PD	22 Feb. 1917	7	4	
Bortossi	Chris/Carlo	d.	PD	30 May 1918	4	2	Calvary Cemetery; also 1 June, 4:2; 2 June, 1:6
Bosch	Frank	d.	PC	1 Dec. 1918	1	5	France
Bosch	Frank	d.	PD	1 Dec. 1918	3	5	France
Bosch	Frank	d.	SIT	30 Nov. 1918	1	3	
Bose	John E.	m.	PD	3 Sept. 1916	5	3	
Bossi	Mr. & Mrs.	b.	PA	14 Jan. 1918	5	4	
Bosso	F. L.	b.	SRR	11 Aug. 1917	8	4	
Boswell	Benjamin	d.	PD	6 Sept. 1916	2	2	
Boswell	Benjamin	d.	SRR	8 Sept. 1916	6	4	Enterprise, OR
Boswell	James H.	d.	SRR	16 Oct. 1916	4	1	also 17 Oct., 8:6
Boswell	James H.	d.	PA	17 Oct. 1916	4	1	also 18 Oct., 8:6
Boswell	James H.	d.	PC	17 Oct. 1916	1	2	
Boswell	James H.	d.	PD	18 Oct. 1916	3	2	
Bott	Ethel	m.	PD	29 June 1916	5	1	
Botts	Elizabeth	d.	SRR	17 Oct. 1916	5	2	also 18 Oct., 1:3
Botts	Elizabeth	d.	PD	18 Oct. 1916	2	2	
Botts	Elizabeth	d.	ST	21 Oct. 1916	1	4	
Botts	Ethel	m.	SRR	28 June 1916	8	5	
Botts	Ethel	m.	ST	1 July 1916	7	4	
Botts	James	d.	PD	7 July 1917	3	4	also 7 July, 4:3
Botts	Junius	d.	SRR	6 July 1917	8	2	also 7 July, 8:3; 9 July, 8:5
Bouchez	Joseph	d.	HT	25 Oct. 1917	3	2	
Bough	D. G.	m.	PA	9 Oct. 1917	5	3	
Bouk	A. R.	m.	SRR	23 July 1917	4	5	
Bouk	Alvin	m.	PD	24 July 1917	6	1	
Bourdens	Lucie	d.	HT	21 June 1917	8	2	Olive Hill Cemetery
Bourke	Frank J.	o.	PC	5 Aug. 1917	1	2	
Bourke	Patrick	d.	PA	14 Nov. 1918	1	2	Calvary Cemetery; also 5:7; 15 Nov., 5:1
Bourne	C. W.	o.	HT	15 Apr. 1918	5	4	
Bourquin	Joseph R.	o.	SRR	21 Feb. 1917	1	6	
Bourquin	Joseph R.	o.	PC	22 Feb. 1917	5	3	
Bourquin	Lillie R.	o.	SRR	21 Feb. 1917	1	6	

(1) Surname	(2) Given Name	(3)	(4)	(5) Date	(6) Pg	(7) Col	(8) Comments
Bourquin	Lillie R.	o.	PC	22 Feb. 1917	5	3	
Bower	Bertram	m.	SRR	12 Apr. 1917	8	6	
Bower	Bertram H.	m.	PD	11 Apr. 1917	8	3	also 15 Apr., 6:1
Bower	Bertram H.	m.	PC	22 Mar. 1917	5	6	
Bower	Clarence H.	m.	ST	24 Mar. 1917	1	2	
Bower	Jay	b.	SRR	17 Nov. 1916	10	3	
Bower	Richard	d.	ST	15 Apr. 1916	1	2	also 22 Apr., 1:2
Bowers	LeVern	d.	ST	29 Apr. 1916	7	5	
Bowers	Stella May	d.	SRR	24 Apr. 1916	3	4	
Bowers	Stella May	d.	PD	25 Apr. 1916	8	4	
Bowers	Stella May	d.	HT	27 Apr. 1916	4	1	
Bowler	Amos	b.	PA	21 Jan. 1916	4	3	
Bowles	Elizabeth	d.	PA	19 July 1918	5	3	also 20 July, 3:4. 4:3; 22 July, 8:5
Bowles	Elizabeth	d.	PC	20 July 1918	5	3	Cypress Hill; also 8:4; 23 July, 4:3
Bowles	Elizabeth	d.	PD	21 July 1918	8	4	
Bowles	Elizabeth	p.	PD	1 Aug. 1918	6	4	
Bowles	Ira R.	d.	PD	20 Feb. 1918	7	3	
Bowles	Ira R.	d.	PC	21 Feb. 1918	2	3	
Bowman	Alex, Mrs.	d.	PD	19 Jan. 1916	7	1	Sebastopol
Bowman	J. C.	d.	PC	16 Mar. 1917	5	4	
Bowman	William C.	d.	PD	23 Mar. 1918	6	4	also 24 Mar., 4:2
Bowman	William Charles	d.	PC	23 Mar. 1918	1	2	
Bowman/Boman	Beatrice	m.	PA	4 June 1917	4	7	also 8 June, 5:6
Bowuman	Amelia	d.	ST	22 Jan. 1916	6	4	
Box	Samuel	d.	SIT	5 May 1917	2	5	Valley Cemetery
Box	Samuel B.	d.	PC	1 May 1917	4	3	
Box	Samuel P.	d.	PD	29 Apr. 1917	6	1	
Box	Samuel P.	d.	SRR	30 Apr. 1917	5	4	
Boyd	Elizabeth	d.	PD	17 Dec. 1916	8	2	
Boyd	John	m.	PA	10 Nov. 1917	7	7	also 13 Nov., 5:5; 14 Nov., 5:3
Boyd	John	m.	PC	10 Nov. 1917	1	2	
Boyd	John	m.	PC	14 Nov. 1917	6	3	also 15 Nov., 6:4
Boyd	Leonard Russell	m.	SRR	5 July 1917	6	3	
Boyd	Mabel	m.	ST	24 June 1916	1	3	
Boyden	W. B.	d.	PC	19 Sept. 1916	6	4	
Boyden	William B.	d.	PD	17 Sept. 1916	1	3	Healdsburg
Boydeston	Grace Eloise	m.	PD	16 Aug. 1917	6	5	
Boydsen	Louise Margaret	d.	PA	5 Sept. 1917	4	5	Cypress Hill
Boydston	Grace Eloise	m.	SRR	16 Aug. 1917	8	3	
Boyer	Clayton	d.	PA	25 July 1918	8	3	Woodland; also 26 July, 4:4; 27 July, 3:3

(1) Surname	(2) Given Name	(3)	(4)	(5) Date	(6) Pg	(7) Col	(8) Comments
Boyer	Clayton	d.	PC	26 July 1918	4	3	Woodland; also 8:2; 27 July, 4:1
Boyer	Clayton	d.	PD	27 July 1918	2	2	
Boyes	Lola	m.	PA	3 Nov. 1917	4	3	
Boyes	Lola	m.	PC	3 Nov. 1917	1	3	
Boyes	Lola	m.	PD	3 Nov. 1917	8	3	
Boyes	Lola	m.	SRR	3 Nov. 1917	5	2	
Boylan	Anna	d.	PD	22 June 1918	3	3	also 4:2
Boyle	Samuel E.	m.	PC	25 Apr. 1916	3	3	
Boynton	Charles A.	d.	PD	17 June 1916	6	5	Oakland
Boynton	Charles Albert	d.	ST	17 June 1916	1	5	
Boynton	Florence	d.	SRR	24 Mar. 1917	5	3	
Boynton	Florence Dodge	d.	PA	24 Mar. 1917	6	5	
Boynton	Florence Dodge	d.	PD	24 Mar. 1917	5	2	
Boynton	Fred, Mrs.	d.	PC	24 Mar. 1917	1	2	
Boyol	Frank P.	m.	PD	1 Sept. 1916	5	3	
Boysen	Clarence C.	m.	PA	3 Nov. 1917	4	3	
Boysen	Clarence C.	m.	PC	3 Nov. 1917	1	3	
Boysen	Clarence O.	m.	PD	3 Nov. 1917	8	3	
Boysen	Louise	d.	PD	5 Sept. 1917	6	4	
Boysen	Louise M.	d.	PC	5 Sept. 1917	8	4	also 6 Sept., 8:3
Boysen	Louise Margaret	d.	SRR	4 Sept. 1917	4	2	Petaluma; also 8:5; 5 Sept., 5:3
Boysen	S. M., Mrs.	d.	PC	20 Mar. 1918	5	3	
Boysen	S. M., Sr., Mrs.	d.	PA	20 Mar. 1918	8	5	
Boysen	William H.	m.	PD	25 Feb. 1916	7	2	
Boyson	Andrew	d.	PA	19 Mar. 1917	6	2	Cypress Hill
Boyson	Clarence C.	m.	SRR	3 Nov. 1917	5	2	
Boyson	Walter	b.	PA	25 Jan. 1917	8	2	
Brackett	Ray	b.	SRR	12 Sept. 1916	8	4	
Bradbury	A. J., Mrs.	d.	HT	13 Jan. 1916	2	5	Burr Oak, Kansas
Bradbury	Philip H.	m.	SRR	6 Sept. 1917	3	5	
Bradbury	Philip H.	m.	PD	7 Sept. 1917	5	4	
Bradbury	Philip H.	m.	SRR	9 Aug. 1917	3	3	
Bradley	Donald	m.	PA	30 July 1917	4	3	
Bradley	Donald	m.	PC	31 July 1917	3	3	
Bradley	Donald	m.	PD	31 July 1917	5	1	
Bradley	Mattie A.	o.	SRR	28 Feb. 1916	8	5	
Bradley	Mattie A.	o.	HT	3 Mar. 1916	4	3	
Bradley	Quinn M.	o.	SRR	28 Feb. 1916	8	5	
Bradley	Quinn M.	o.	HT	3 Mar. 1916	4	3	
Brady	Charles H.	o.	SRR	28 Aug. 1917	4	1	
Brady	Charles H.	o.	PD	29 Aug. 1917	6	3	
Brady	Howard	b.	PA	5 Feb. 1916	3	7	also 8:1
Brady	Irene E.	o.	PC	20 Feb. 1917	3	6	

(1) Surname	(2) Given Name	(3)	(4)	(5) Date	(6) Pg	(7) Col	(8) Comments
Brady	Mary	o.	SRR	28 Aug. 1917	4	1	
Brady	Mary	o.	PD	29 Aug. 1917	6	3	
Brady	Sarah	d.	PA	5 Apr. 1916	2	2	Calvary Cemetery; also 5:3
Brady	Sarah	d.	SRR	5 Apr. 1916	8	3	
Brady	Sarah	d.	PC	8 Apr. 1916	1	5	Calvary Cemetery; also 6 Apr., 4:1; 7 Apr., 6:3
Brady	Thomas M.	o.	PC	20 Feb. 1917	3	6	
Brain	W. H.	d.	PC	23 Jan. 1917	4	2	Green Valley
Brain	W. H.	d.	PD	24 Jan. 1917	3	2	Green Valley
Brammer	Rhoda	d.	HT	6 June 1918	4	4	
Branchi	Pietro	d.	SRR	20 Dec. 1916	7	3	
Brand	August	d.	PC	26 Sept. 1918	8	3	
Brandon	Helen	d.	PC	18 Nov. 1917	8	2	also 20 Nov., 8:2
Brandon	Helen	d.	PD	18 Nov. 1917	4	2	
Brandon	Helen Adelaide	d.	PA	17 Nov. 1917	4	3	Calvary Cemetery; also 19 Nov., 5:7
Brandt	August	d.	PA	25 Sept. 1918	1	4	
Brandt	August	d.	HT	26 Sept. 1918	1	3	
Brandt	August	b.	HT	3 Aug. 1916	4	2	
Brandt	Dorothy	m.	PA	27 Aug. 1917	1	4	also 2:2
Brandt	F. G.	d.	HT	21 Nov. 1918	8	3	
Brandt	F. O.	d.	PD	22 Nov. 1918	1	3	
Branern	William	d.	HT	3 Oct. 1918	1	5	
Brannon	T. A.	d.	SRR	11 Feb. 1916	8	5	Sebastopol
Brannon	Theodore	d.	ST	12 Feb. 1916	1	7	
Brannon	Theodore A.	d.	PD	13 Feb. 1916	1	4	Sebastopol Cemetery
Brannon	Theodore A.	d.	PC	15 Feb. 1916	3	2	Sebastopol Cemetery
Bransford	William A.	d.	PD	10 Apr. 1918	5	2	
Branson	Miss	m.	SRR	2 Jan. 1917	3	1	
Branstad	Louis	m.	PA	8 June 1918	3	5	
Branstetter	Grayce	m.	PD	27 May 1917	5	4	
Brant	Dorothy F. R.	m.	PD	28 Aug. 1917	8	3	
Brant	Dorothy Ruth	m.	PC	28 Aug. 1917	5	6	also 29 Aug., 8:2
Brarens	Clarence	o.	PC	20 Nov. 1917	6	4	
Brattain	Ed	m.	PD	15 Dec. 1917	6	5	
Brattain	Ed	m.	HT	20 Dec. 1917	6	3	
Braun	Lulu	d.	PA	27 July 1918	8	4&5	Cypress Hill; also 29 July, 5:3
Braun	Lulu	d.	PC	27 July 1918	4	3	Cypress Hill; also 28 July, 3:4; 30 July, 5:3
Bravo	F.	d.	PD	4 July 1916	1	5	
Bravo	Henry	d.	PA	3 July 1916	4	3	
Bravo	Henry	d.	PC	4 July 1916	4	3	
Bravo	Peter	b.	PA	8 Aug. 1916	4	5	

(1) Surname	(2) Given Name	(3)	(4)	(5) Date	(6) Pg	(7) Col	(8) Comments
Bravo	Peter	b.	PC	8 Aug. 1916	5	2	
Bravo	Peter (son of)	d.	PA	6 Mar. 1917	5	5	
Bravo	Peter (son of)	d.	PC	7 Mar. 1917	1	4	also 9 Mar., 2:1
Bray	Mae	m.	PD	1 Aug. 1916	3	3	
Bray	Mary E.	d.	PA	19 July 1917	6	6	
Bray	William	d.	PD	1 Jan. 1916	8	2	
Brazil	Marie	m.	PA	4 Jan. 1918	5	4	
Brazil	Marie	m.	PC	5 Jan. 1918	5	6	also 9 Jan., 5:4
Brazil	Rose	m.	PA	4 Apr. 1918	4	5	
Brazil	Rose	m.	PC	6 Apr. 1918	3	4	
Brazil	Rosie Hallen	m.	SIT	27 Apr. 1918	2	5	
Breaks	Charles	o.	ST	8 Feb. 1918	7	3	
Breaks	Charles H.	d.	ST	18 Oct. 1918	1	2	
Breaks	Gent (son of)	d.	ST	25 Jan. 1918	3	3	
Breaks	Gent (son of)	d.	PC	26 Jan. 1918	1	2	
Brehan	Mr.	d.	PD	29 June 1918	3	5	
Breitenbach	Anita	m.	SIT	16 Sept. 1916	1	4	also 23 Sept., 1:1
Breitenbach	Anita	m.	PD	19 Sept. 1916	2	2	
Breitenbach	Anita	m.	SRR	9 Sept. 1916	7	4	also 10:4; 19 Sept., 8:6
Breitenbach	Dorothy	m.	PD	1 Dec. 1918	10	2	
Breitenbach	Gertrude	m.	PD	19 Sept. 1917	2	1	
Breitenbach	Gertrude	m.	SRR	19 Sept. 1917	8	1	
Breiterbach	Gertrude	m.	SIT	22 Sept. 1917	1	2	
Brenard	John	d.	ST	1 Feb. 1918	4	4	
Brenard	John	d.	PC	27 Jan. 1918	1	2	
Brenard	John	d.	PD	27 Jan. 1918	4	2	Sebastopol; also 8:3; 30 Jan., 7:2
Brenard	John	d.	HT	31 June 1918	6	2	
Brenciani	Charles	o.	PA	10 Nov. 1917	5	3	also 12 Nov., 8:6
Brenstein	David	m.	PC	12 Apr. 1917	8	3	
Brenstein	Davis	m.	SRR	11 Apr. 1917	1	5	
Bresciana	Francesco	m.	PA	7 Dec. 1916	8	7	
Brescina	F.	b.	PA	14 Sept. 1917	4	4	
Brett	Minnie M.	o.	PD	5 Sept. 1918	2	4	
Brewer	C. C.	m.	PD	27 Dec. 1917	2	2	
Brewer	Clyde	m.	PC	25 Dec. 1917	3	2	
Brewer	Clyde	m.	PA	27 Dec. 1917	4	3	
Brewer	Lucy	m.	SRR	18 July 1917	8	4	
Brewer	Lucy	m.	PC	19 July 1917	8	2	
Briano	Carrie	o.	PD	5 June 1918	2	4	
Briano	James	o.	PD	5 June 1918	2	4	
Brians	Carrie	o.	SRR	30 Oct. 1917	4	2	
Brians	James C.	o.	SRR	30 Oct. 1917	4	2	
Brickner	Horace	d.	PD	5 Jan. 1918	3	2	

(1) Surname	(2) Given Name	(3)	(4)	(5) Date	(6) Pg	(7) Col	(8) Comments
Bridge	C. R.	b.	PC	23 Apr. 1916	8	5	
Bridge	C. R.	b.	PA	24 Apr. 1916	2	6	
Bridge	Oliver Worden	d.	PC	27 Sept. 1917	8	3	Cypress Hill; also 29 Sept., 3:4; 2 Oct., 5:2
Bridge	Oliver Worden	d.	SRR	27 Sept. 1917	8	4	
Bridge	Oliver Worden	d.	PD	28 Sept. 1917	8	1	
Bridges	Minnie	m.	SIT	30 June 1917	2	4	
Bridges	Oliver Worden	d.	PA	1 Oct. 1917	7	4	
Briesenos	Reuben C.	m.	PD	10 Oct. 1916	3	1	
Briggs	Ezra	m.	PD	12 Sept. 1916	6	4	
Brinkman	Louise	m.	PD	18 Aug. 1918	10	2	
Briones	Emma	d.	PD	10 June 1917	6	1	
Briones	Emma	d.	SRR	11 June 1917	3	2	also 3:5
Briones	Emma	d.	PC	12 June 1917	2	1	
Briseno	Ruben C.	m.	SRR	9 Oct. 1916	8	2	
Brisono	R. C., Mrs.	d.	ST	27 Sept. 1918	1	2	
Brittain	Clarence	d.	SRR	16 Apr. 1917	5	3	also 17 Apr., 3:2
Brittain	Clarence	d.	PD	18 Apr. 1917	7	1	
Brittain	Geneva E.	m.	SRR	20 Mar. 1917	1	3	
Brittan	Edward	m.	SRR	15 Dec. 1917	5	6	
Britton	Catherine	d.	PA	28 Oct. 1916	3	5	
Britton	Catherine	d.	PC	28 Oct. 1916	1	4	
Britton	Catherine	d.	PD	28 Oct. 1916	3	2	
Britton	Catherine	d.	SRR	28 Oct. 1916	10	2	
Brochman	Wilhelmina	m.	SRR	19 June 1916	1	1	also 28 June, 8:4
Brockman	Rachel	m.	SRR	20 Dec. 1917	8	3	
Brockman	Wilhelmina	m.	PC	22 May 1916	6	2	
Brockman	Wilhelmina	m.	PD	28 June 1916	2	3	also 29 June, 2:3
Brockman	Willhemina	m.	PD	2 July 1916	2	2	
Brodersen	Herman C.	m.	PA	22 Jan. 1917	2	2	
Brodersen	Herman C.	m.	PC	23 Jan. 1917	7	4	
Broderson	Peter	m.	PC	10 Mar. 1918	8	2	
Broderson	T.	b.	PA	18 July 1918	8	7	
Broner	Walter J.	m.	PD	30 Jan. 1916	8	7	
Brook	Margaret	d.	HT	27 Dec. 1917	1	2	
Brooke	Emma	d.	HT	7 June 1917	5	4	
Brooks	Joseph F.	m.	PD	23 June 1916	2	5	
Brophy	James M.	d.	PD	29 May 1917	3	4	
Brothering	Joseph, Mrs.	d.	PA	3 Jan. 1918	5	1	
Brotherington	Joseph, Mrs.	d.	PC	4 Jan. 1918	5	4	also 8 Jan., 3:2
Brotherington	Joseph, Mrs.	d.	PD	4 Jan. 1918	6	4	also 13 Jan., 6:1
Brotherton	Joseph, Mrs.	d.	SIT	5 Jan. 1918	1	3	also 12 Jan., 1:4; 19 Jan., 1:3; 26 Jan., 4:4
Brotherton	Mrs.	d.	PC	26 Jan. 1918	1	4	

(1) Surname	(2) Given Name	(3)	(4)	(5) Date	(6) Pg	(7) Col	(8) Comments
Brovelli	Stefano	d.	PD	20 Oct. 1918	3	1	Calvary Cemetery; also 4:2
Brower	Mary Elmira	m.	SRR	11 Oct. 1917	8	1	
Brown	Angenette	d.	PC	13 July 1917	5	3	cremation; also 8:3; 14 July, 5:6; 15 July, 1:6
Brown	Anna C.	o.	PC	6 Oct. 1918	2	2	
Brown	Anna C.	o.	PA	7 Oct. 1918	4	3	
Brown	Antone J.	d.	PA	13 Nov. 1916	8	3	Calvary Cemetery; also 14 Nov., 4:4
Brown	Antone J.	d.	PC	14 Nov. 1916	3	4	Calvary Cemetery; also 5:4; 15 Nov., 4:5
Brown	B. C., Mrs.	d.	PA	12 July 1917	5	3	
Brown	B. C., Mrs.	d.	SRR	13 July 1917	7	3	
Brown	Ben	m.	PD	5 June 1918	6	4	
Brown	Benjamin	m.	PD	1 June 1917	6	5	
Brown	Benjamin F.	m.	SRR	31 May 1917	1	6	
Brown	Blevina Macon	d.	PD	7 Jan. 1917	10	5	
Brown	Carl J.	m.	PD	28 July 1916	6	2	
Brown	Charles A.	o.	PC	6 Oct. 1918	2	2	
Brown	Charles A.	o.	PA	7 Oct. 1918	4	3	
Brown	Dick	o.	PC	7 Dec. 1917	2	1	
Brown	Earl	d.	PA	27 Nov. 1916	4	3	
Brown	Edna L.	m.	SRR	1 Feb. 1916	5	4	
Brown	Edward H.	b.	PD	2 Oct. 1918	7	1	
Brown	Emma C.	m.	PC	29 Feb. 1916	4	4	
Brown	Emma G.	m.	PA	23 Feb. 1916	5	4	also 29 Feb., 5:3
Brown	Frances	m.	PD	23 May 1918	5	2	
Brown	Frances Leslie	m.	PA	22 May 1918	4	5	also 1 June, 4:5
Brown	Frances Leslie	m.	PC	23 May 1918	4	4	
Brown	Fred	d.	PA	24 June 1916	2	2	
Brown	Fred	d.	PC	25 June 1916	5	6	
Brown	George	o.	HT	6 Dec. 1917	1	4	
Brown	George P.	m.	PD	7 Nov. 1916	7	3	
Brown	George P.	m.	SRR	7 Nov. 1916	3	1	
Brown	George P.	m.	HT	8 Nov. 1916	1	6	
Brown	George W.	d.	PA	22 Dec. 1917	1	3	
Brown	George W.	d.	PC	23 Dec. 1917	8	2	
Brown	Harry C.	m.	SRR	22 Nov. 1917	6	6	
Brown	Helen Cecil	m.	PA	6 June 1916	4	7	
Brown	Helen Cecil	m.	PA	29 June 1916	5	2	
Brown	Helen Cecile	m.	PC	7 June 1916	5	5	also 30 June, 5:2
Brown	J.	m.	SRR	15 July 1916	12	1	
Brown	J. Wilson	m.	PD	12 July 1917	2	5	
Brown	J. Wilson	m.	SRR	12 July 1917	5	2	

(1) Surname	(2) Given Name	(3)	(4)	(5) Date	(6) Pg	(7) Col	(8) Comments
Brown	John	d.	PA	14 Aug. 1916	4	3	Cypress Hill; also 15 Aug., 4:2
Brown	John	d.	SRR	18 Aug. 1916	2	1	
Brown	John H.	d.	PD	14 Aug. 1916	6	5	
Brown	John H.	d.	PC	15 Aug. 1916	1	5	
Brown	Leila E.	d.	ST	24 May 1918	1	1	
Brown	Leila F.	d.	PD	24 May 1918	8	2	also 26 May, 5:4
Brown	Lena	m.	PC	30 June 1918	8	3	
Brown	Lena	m.	PA	1 July 1918	4	4	
Brown	Lena	m.	PC	2 July 1918	5	4	
Brown	Lena	m.	PA	15 Apr. 1918	4	3	
Brown	Lena	m.	PD	16 Apr. 1918	6	3	
Brown	Lena	m.	PC	20 Apr. 1918	5	4	
Brown	Lida E.	m.	PD	7 Sept. 1916	1	6	
Brown	Lillian	m.	SRR	31 July 1917	7	4	
Brown	Limina	d.	SRR	11 Oct. 1916	3	3	
Brown	M. C.	o.	PD	31 Oct. 1918	8	3	
Brown	M. C.	o.	PD	4 Oct. 1918	3	4	
Brown	Mary	d.	PC	9 Jan. 1918	4	4	San Francisco; also 11 Jan., 6:5
Brown	Mary E.	m.	PA	17 July 1918	6	6	
Brown	Mary E.	d.	PA	8 Jan. 1918	5	3	also 10 Jan., 6:6
Brown	Melvin	m.	SRR	24 Apr. 1917	2	4	
Brown	Mildred	m.	PA	24 June 1916	8	5	also 26 June, 5:6; 29 June, 6:5
Brown	Mildred	m.	PC	25 June 1916	5	5	also 27 June, 3:1
Brown	Nancy	d.	SRR	11 Jan. 1916	4	2	also 12 Jan., 8:3; 13 Jan., 1:2
Brown	Nancy	d.	PA	12 Jan. 1916	4	5	
Brown	Nancy	o.	PC	12 Jan. 1916	1	4	
Brown	Nancy	d.	PD	14 Jan. 1916	7	2	
Brown	R. C., Mrs.	d.	PD	13 July 1917	8	1	
Brown	Rose Magaret	m.	PA	6 Apr. 1918	3	3	
Brown	Rose Margaret	m.	PC	6 Apr. 1918	5	2	
Brown	Ruth Marfette	m.	PC	10 June 1916	8	3	also 25 June, 5:5; 27 June, 3:1
Brown	Ruth Mariette	m.	SRR	12 June 1916	1	6	
Brown	Ruth Marlette	m.	PA	9 June 1916	4	1	also 24 June, 8:5; 26 June, 5:6; 29 June, 6:5
Brown	Vernon	d.	PA	26 June 1918	1	3	
Brown	Vernon	d.	PC	26 June 1918	1	3	
Brown	Vernon	d.	PD	26 June 1918	1	6	
Brown	Vernon	d.	PD	27 June 1918	4	2	I.O.O.F. Cemetery; also 7:5; 29 June, 7:2
Brown	Walter	b.	SRR	12 June 1917	6	3	

(1) Surname	(2) Given Name	(3)	(4)	(5) Date	(6) Pg	(7) Col	(8) Comments
Brown	Walter	b.	HT	28 June 1917	1	3	
Brown	Walter M.	m.	SRR	22 Aug. 1916	3	3	
Brown	Walter M.	m.	HT	24 Aug. 1916	1	4	
Brown	William M.	m.	PC	25 Apr. 1917	4	3	
Brown	William Melvin	m.	PA	24 Apr. 1917	3	6	also 5:2
Brown	William N.	o.	PC	26 Jan. 1918	1	6	
Brown	Wilson J	m.	PD	16 May 1917	4	2	
Brown	Wilson J.	m.	PA	15 May 1917	4	6	also 25 June, 2:6; 12 July 4:4
Brown	Wilson J.	m.	SRR	15 May 1917	3	4	
Brown	Wilson J.	m.	PC	16 May 1917	5	3	
Brown	Wilson J.	m.	SRR	25 June 1917	1	4	
Brown	Wilson J.	m.	PC	12 July 1917	3	3	
Browne	Louis Anthony	o.	PA	16 May 1917	3	4	
Browning	Alice Buckley	d.	PC	3 Jan. 1917	1	3	
Browning	Allie Buckley	d.	SRR	30 Dec. 1916	12	3	
Browning	Allie Buckley	d.	SRR	2 Jan. 1917	5	2	
Brownlee	Emmaline	d.	PA	3 June 1918	4	4	Cypress Hill; also 4 June, 4:5, 5:3; 5 June, 5:1
Brownlee	Emmaline	d.	PD	5 June 1918	3	4	
Brownlee	Harriet Emiline	d.	PC	4 June 1918	4	2	Cypress Hill; also 5 June, 6:2; 6 June, 4:3; 9 June, 5:3
Brownley	Charlotte	m.	PA	8 Oct. 1917	4	5	also 9 Oct., 4:6
Brownscombe	T. F.	b.	SRR	8 Jan. 1016	6	3	
Brownscombe	T. J.	b.	PD	9 Jan. 1916	8	3	
Bruner	Harold	o.	PD	6 July 1918	7	1	also 12 July, 6:5
Bruner	Harold	o.	PD	14 Aug. 1918	5	2	also 13 Sept., 2:1
Bruner	Harold	o.	PD	17 Mar. 1918	6	3	also 30 Mar., 6:3
Bruner	Harold	o.	PD	9 Jan. 1918	3	1	
Bruner	Hazel	o.	PD	4 July 1918	7	1	
Bruner	Hazel	o.	PD	23 Mar. 1918	8	1	also 28 Mar., 8:1
Bruner	J. M., Mrs.	d.	PD	21 May 1916	6	5	
Bruner	Jennie	d.	SRR	22 May 1916	4	1	also 23 May, 4:4
Bruner	Olive	m.	PD	5 Feb. 1918	7	3	
Bruner	Olive L.	m.	PA	1 Feb. 1918	8	5	also 4 Feb., 4:5
Bruner	Olive L.	m.	PC	2 Feb. 1918	6	6	also 5 Feb., 4:3
Brunetti	G.	b.	PA	13 Jan. 1916	8	6	
Brunk	Arion	d.	PD	27 June 1917	5	3	
Brunk	Hugh D.	m.	PA	11 Aug. 1916	6	3	also 16 Aug., 4:4
Brunk	Hugh D.	m.	PD	11 Aug. 1916	1	3	also 17 Aug., 5:1
Brunk	Hugh D.	m.	SRR	11 Aug. 1916	5	2	also 17 Aug., 6:1
Brunk	Hugh D.	m.	PC	12 Aug. 1916	4	4	also 17 Aug., 1:2
Bruno	Max	d.	PA	22 Nov. 1917	5	7	

(1) Surname	(2) Given Name	(3)	(4)	(5) Date	(6) Pg	(7) Col	(8) Comments
Bruno	Max	d.	PC	23 Nov. 1917	4	1	
Bruno	Max	d.	HT	29 Nov. 1917	1	3	
Bruns	Richard	m.	SRR	8 June 1917	6	2	
Bruns	Richard	m.	PD	26 Apr. 1917	2	3	
Brunson	Frank	m.	PA	28 July 1917	5	5	
Brush	Dorothy	m.	SRR	7 Sept. 1916	1	3	portrait; also 9 Sept., 10:1; 11 Sept., 8:6
Brush	Dorothy	m.	PA	8 Sept. 1916	5	3	
Brush	Dorothy	m.	PC	8 Sept. 1916	8	3	
Brush	Dorothy Alice	m.	PD	12 Sept. 1916	8	3	
Brush	F. A.	o.	SRR	18 Mar. 1916	8	2	portrait
Brush	George M.	d.	PA	14 Aug. 1918	4	4	Cypress Hill; also 5:5; 15 Aug., 8:2
Brush	George M.	d.	PC	14 Aug. 1918	5	3	Cypress Hill; also 16 Aug., 8:3
Brush	George M.	d.	PD	15 Aug. 1918	7	1	
Brush	Henry	b.	SRR	12 June 1916	1	3	
Brush	Howard	o.	SRR	18 Mar. 1916	8	2	portrait
Brush	J. H.	o.	SRR	18 Mar. 1916	8	2	portrait
Brush	Samuel	d.	PD	29 Oct. 1918	4	2	Occidental; also 8:4
Brush	Samuel	d.	PC	30 Oct. 1918	2	2	
Brust	Al, Mrs.	d.	PC	26 May 1916	5	5	
Brust	Mabel	d.	SRR	25 May 1916	1	3	
Bryan	Hilda	o.	PA	24 Feb. 1916	1	7	
Bryan	Joseph	o.	PA	24 Feb. 1916	1	7	
Bryan	Nellie	o.	PD	26 Sept. 1918	2	4	
Bryan	Sally	d.	HT	11 Apr. 1918	2	2	
Bryan	William T.	o.	PD	26 Sept. 1918	2	4	
Bryan	William Vose	p.	PA	5 June 1917	6	5	
Bryant	Bertha	m.	PD	14 Dec. 1916	3	2	
Bryant	Bertha A.	m.	SRR	13 Dec. 1916	3	1	
Bryant	J.	m.	PC	13 Apr. 1916	2	1	
Bryant	Jay	m.	PD	12 Apr. 1916	2	3	
Bryant	Jay	m.	SRR	12 Apr. 1916	7	5	
Bryant	Minnie	d.	SRR	23 June 1916	8	2	also 24 June, 1:5
Bryce	Evaline	m.	PD	21 Dec. 1916	8	2	
Bucchi	Dora	o.	PD	20 Nov. 1917	6	3	
Bucchi	Henry	o.	PD	20 Nov. 1917	6	3	
Buchan	Ralph	o.	SIT	24 Nov. 1917	1	5	
Buchanan	Edward A.	o.	SRR	5 Nov. 1917	1	2	
Buchanan	Eugenia	o.	SRR	5 Nov. 1917	1	2	
Buchi	Dora	o.	SRR	11 Oct. 1917	4	2	
Buchi	Henry	o.	SRR	11 Oct. 1917	4	2	
Buchi	Henry, Mrs.	d.	SRR	25 May 1916	5	3	
Buchierri	Dorothy D.	m.	SRR	23 Oct. 1917	4	4	

(1) Surname	(2) Given Name	(3)	(4)	(5) Date	(6) Pg	(7) Col	(8) Comments
Buchigani	Angelo	o.	PC	20 Mar. 1918	1	4	
Buchignani	George	d.	HT	22 Feb. 1917	8	5	
Buck	Margaret	m.	ST	29 June 1917	1	1	
Buckett	Samuel	d.	PA	26 Dec. 1918	4	1	
Buckett	Samuel	d.	PC	28 Dec. 1918	3	2	also 31 Dec., 4:3
Buckett	Samuel	d.	PD	28 Dec. 1918	7	2	
Buckhalter	Jameson O'Kane	d.	PD	25 Aug. 1917	5	2	
Buckingham	Violet	o.	SRR	27 June 1916	7	3	
Buckley	Alfred	d.	ST	1 Nov. 1918	1	3	
Buckley	Alfred E.	d.	PA	26 Oct. 1918	4	6	
Buckley	Alfred E.	d.	PC	26 Oct. 1918	4	1	
Buckley	Alfred E.	d.	PD	26 Oct. 1918	7	1	
Buckman	Claire Leona	m.	SRR	31 July 1916	8	1	
Buckman	Claire Leona	m.	PC	2 Aug. 1916	5	2	
Buckman	Edward	o.	PD	24 Feb. 1918	3	3	
Buckman	Eugenia	o.	PD	24 Feb. 1918	3	3	
Buckman	H. F.	o.	SRR	27 Jan. 1916	5	1	
Buckman	H. T.	o.	PA	27 Jan. 1916	3	6	
Buckman	Mary A.	o.	PA	27 Jan. 1916	3	6	
Buckman	Mary A.	o.	SRR	27 Jan. 1916	5	1	
Buckmaster	R.	b.	SRR	15 Sept. 1916	8	5	
Buckmaster	R.	b.	PD	16 Sept. 1916	8	4	
Bucknam	Claire Leone	m.	PA	1 Aug. 1916	3	1	
Bucknam	J. B.	d.	PA	27 May 1916	5	1	
Bucknell	Bert Monroe	m.	PD	1 Jan. 1918	3	4	
Buckner	Horace	d.	PA	4 Jan. 1918	3	3	
Buckner	Horace	d.	PC	5 Jan. 1918	4	1	
Buckner	May C.	m.	PD	29 June 1916	8	4	
Buckner	May C.	m.	SRR	29 June 1916	5	3	
Bucknum	Claire Leone	m.	HT	3 Aug. 1916	3	2	
Budde	Diedrick	m.	PA	31 Aug. 1916	5	3	
Buffi	Gina	m.	SRR	11 Dec. 1916	8	4	
Buffi	Virginia	m.	PD	10 Dec. 1916	8	2	
Bufford	Lawrence	b.	PD	29 Jan. 1918	2	4	
Bugbee	Clarence	o.	SRR	24 Apr. 1916	1	2	also 28 Apr., 1:3; 19 May, 7:5
Bugbee	Grace	o.	SRR	24 Apr. 1916	1	2	also 28 Apr., 1:3; 19 May, 7:5
Buhl	Dorothy	m.	SRR	19 June 1917	3	6	
Buhl	Dorothy	m.	SRR	15 Aug. 1917	4	4	also 22 Aug., 5:2; 23 Aug., 4:4
Buhl	Dorothy	m.	PC	16 Aug. 1917	5	3	also 23 Aug., 5:4
Buhl	Dorothy	m.	PA	22 Aug. 1917	1	5	
Buhl	Dorothy I.	m.	PA	19 June 1917	3	3	
Buhl	Dorothy I.	m.	PD	19 June 1917	8	2	

(1) Surname	(2) Given Name	(3)	(4)	(5) Date	(6) Pg	(7) Col	(8) Comments
Buhl	Dorothy I.	m.	PC	20 June 1917	5	1	
Bukhofer	Oscar	m.	SRR	27 Nov. 1916	8	4	
Buletti	Catherine	m.	PD	7 Nov. 1917	5	4	also 25 Nov., 9:1
Buletti	Delphine Catherine	m.	PA	26 Nov. 1917	3	3	
Buletti	Delphine Catherine	m.	SRR	26 Nov. 1917	5	3	
Buletti	Delphine Catherine	m.	ST	30 Nov. 1917	6	3	
Buletti	Delphine Catherine	m.	PA	6 Nov. 1917	4	2	
Buletti	Emma	m.	PC	15 July 1917	6	4	
Buletti	Emma	m.	PA	1 Sept. 1917	2	3	
Buletti	Emma	m.	PC	1 Sept. 1917	8	3	also 2 Sept., 8:3
Buletti	Emma E.	m.	PA	14 July 1917	4	4	
Buletti	Emma E.	m.	PD	15 July 1917	8	3	
Buletti	John	m.	PC	8 Nov. 1917	5	2	also 24 Nov., 1:2; 27 Nov., 6:3
Bulotti	Charles F.	m.	PA	27 Apr. 1916	5	4	
Bulotti	Vergilio	d.	SIT	3 Mar. 1918	1	4	
Bundesen	Carl	m.	PC	5 Aug. 1917	5	1	also 7 Aug., 3:4 & 6
Bundesen	Carl/Karl	m.	PA	4 Aug. 1917	3	4	also 6 Aug., 4:3
Bundesen	Henry	m.	PA	1 June 1917	6	5	
Bundesen	Henry Theodore	d.	PC	23 June 1918	1	4	also 25 June, 1:4; 26 June, 4:3
Bundesen	Josie	m.	PC	29 Oct. 1918	4	4	
Bundesen	Josie	m.	PA	30 Sept. 1918	4	5	
Bundesen	Josie M.	m.	PA	28 Oct. 1918	3	3	
Bundesen	Karl	m.	PC	1 June 1917	5	4	
Bundesen	Karl	b.	PA	8 Sept. 1918	5	4	
Bundesen	William	m.	PA	18 Apr. 1916	2	4	also 29 Apr., 7:5; 1 May, 5:3
Bundesen	William	m.	PC	18 Apr. 1916	5	5	also 2 May, 3:1
Bundesen	William	b.	PC	23 Aug. 1918	4	1	
Bundeson	Henry T.	d.	PA	24 June 1918	5	1	Cypress Hill; also 8:3; 25 June, 4:1
Bundi	Acille	m.	SRR	7 Mar. 1917	5	2	
Bundschu	Francis	m.	PD	7 Jan. 1917	7	1	
Bundschu	Ralph	b.	PD	5 Nov. 1916	2	2	
Bundschu	Walter	b.	PD	5 Sept. 1918	6	2	
Burbank	David	d.	PA	20 July 1918	5	1	cremation; also 22 July, 7:6
Burbank	David	d.	PD	21 July 1918	8	3	also 23 July, 6:5
Burbank	David Ball	d.	PC	21 July 1918	3	2	cremation; also 8:3; 23 July, 8:4
Burbank	Luther	m.	PA	20 Dec. 1916	4	5	also 21 Dec., 4:4; 22 Dec., 3:1
Burbank	Luther	m.	SRR	20 Dec. 1916	1	3	also 21 Dec., 1:3; 23 Dec., 6:1
Burbank	Luther	m.	PC	21 Dec. 1916	3	2	

(1) Surname	(2) Given Name	(3)	(4)	(5) Date	(6) Pg	(7) Col	(8) Comments
Burbank	Luther	m.	PD	21 Dec. 1916	2	1	also 22 Dec., 8:2
Burbank	Luther	m.	ST	22 Dec. 1916	3	2	
Burbank	Margaret	d.	PA	25 Apr. 1916	5	3	Tomales; also 26 Apr., 6:4; 27 Apr., 7:5
Burch	James Nye	d.	PD	15 May 1918	8	4	also 17 May, 6:5
Burger	Frederick W.	m.	PD	27 Nov. 1917	7	1	
Burgess	Blandford C.	m.	PA	25 Mar. 1916	4	3	
Burgess	Eva Ruth	d.	PA	17 Dec. 1918	5	2	
Burgess	Eva Ruth	d.	PC	18 Dec. 1918	4	3	
Burgess	Eva Ruth	d.	PD	18 Dec. 1918	8	3	
Burier	Frances Marie	m.	PD	1 Dec. 1917	2	4	
Buright	Nellie	m.	PD	15 Dec. 1917	6	5	
Burke	Ben L.	b.	SRR	14 Feb. 1917	8	3	
Burke	Edmund	m.	PD	17 Sept. 1916	6	6	
Burke	Ellen	d.	PA	10 Jan. 1917	2	3	Holy Cross, S.F.
Burke	Ellen	d.	PC	10 Jan. 1917	8	5	
Burke	Evelyn	o.	SRR	5 June 1916	1	2	also 24 June, 3:1
Burke	Helen	o.	PC	27 June 1917	8	4	body moved form Calvary to Holy Cross cemetery; also 29 June, 8:4
Burke	Helen, Miss	d.	PA	26 June 1917	5	7	also 29 June, 5:5
Burke	Helen, Mrs.	d.	PA	27 June 1917	4	5	moved from Holy Cross to Calvary; also 27 June, 3:5; 29 June, 5:5
Burke	M. F.	o.	PD	28 Mar. 1918	3	3	
Burke	Mary Jane	d.	PC	5 June 1918	1	3	Lake County
Burke	Mary Jane	d.	PD	5 June 1918	3	5	Lake County; also 4:2; 6 June, 6:2
Burke	Patrick	d.	PC	15 Nov. 1918	5	2	Calvary Cemetery; also 16 Nov., 5:1; 17 Nov., 5:1
Burke	Patrick, Mrs.	d.	PC	29 June 1917	8	4	Calvary Cemetery
Burke	Walter A.	o.	SRR	5 June 1916	1	2	also 24 June, 3:1
Burler	Frances Marie	m.	ST	30 Nov. 1917	1	3	
Burmeister	C. F. D.	b.	PA	24 Nov. 1916	4	4	
Burmester	Henry L.	o.	SRR	19 Jan. 1917	1	3	
Burneson	Andrew J.	d.	PD	4 Jan. 1917	2	4	
Burneson	Andrew Jackson	d.	SRR	3 Jan. 1917	4	1	
Burneson	Andrew Jackson	d.	PC	4 Jan. 1917	3	4	Sebastopol
Burnett	Margaret B.	m.	PC	25 July 1917	4	4	
Burnett	Margaret S.	m.	PA	24 July 1917	2	2	
Burnett	Naomi G.	m.	PA	9 Sept. 1918	3	3	
Burnett	Naomi Genevieve	m.	PC	7 Sept. 1918	4	4	

(1) Surname	(2) Given Name	(3)	(4)	(5) Date	(6) Pg	(7) Col	(8) Comments
Burnetti	Albert	d.	SRR	31 July 1917	5	4	
Burnham	Arthur	b.	HT	14 Dec. 1916	1	3	
Burns	Josephine Jeanette	d.	PC	1 Sept. 1917	1	3	also 5 Sept., 8:2
Burns	Edward F., Mrs.	d.	PD	2 Sept. 1917	1	1	
Burns	Edward, Mrs.	d.	PC	1 Sept. 1917	1	3	also 5 Sept., 8:2
Burns	Edward, Mrs.	d.	SIT	8 Sept. 1917	1	6	
Burns	Gerald	d.	SRR	25 Apr. 1917	6	4	
Burns	Gerald	d.	PC	26 Apr. 1917	4	2	
Burns	Gerald	d.	PD	26 Apr. 1917	5	2	
Burns	Gerald	d.	ST	28 Apr. 1917	8	4	
Burns	Janette	de.	SIT	8 Sept. 1917	1	6	
Burns	Jeanette	d.	PA	4 Sept. 1917	5	4	
Burns	Josephine Janet	d.	PD	2 Sept. 1917	1	1	
Burns	Matilda	d.	PC	9 Jan. 1918	4	6	Guerneville
Burns	May	d.	PA	4 Sept. 1917	5	4	
Burns	Mrs. Dr.	d.	PD	30 Dec. 1917	3	2	Guerneville
Burns	Peter	p.	PC	12 Mar. 1918	1	2	
Burns	Peter	d.	PA	16 Feb. 1918	4	5	Calvary Cemetery; also 18 Feb., 5:1
Burns	Peter	d.	PC	16 Feb. 1918	4	4	Calvary Cemetery; also 17 Feb., 6:1; 19 Feb., 4:3
Burns	Peter	d.	PD	17 Feb. 1918	8	2	
Burns	Richard	m.	PD	8 June 1917	3	3	
Burns	Richard	m.	SRR	25 Apr. 1917	8	1	
Burns	Robert	d.	PD	21 Feb. 1917	1	2	also 22 Feb., 4:2; 24 Feb., 1:2
Burns	Robert	d.	ST	24 Feb. 1917	1	1	
Burns	Robert W.	d.	PA	21 Feb. 1917	2	3	
Burns	Robert W.	d.	SRR	21 Feb. 1917	2	3	also 4:3; 23 Feb., 6:5
Burns	Robert W.	d.	PC	22 Feb. 1917	4	5	
Burr	Eugene	d.	PD	18 Aug. 1917	3	1	
Burright	Nellie	m.	SRR	15 Dec. 1917	5	6	
Burright	Nellie	m.	HT	20 Dec. 1917	6	3	
Burris	Shirley	d.	PA	10 July 1916	1	3	cremation; also 12 July, 6:5
Burris	Shirley David	d.	SRR	10 July 1916	5	1	also 11 July, 7:4
Burris	Shirley David	d.	PD	11 July 1916	5	1	Oakland
Burris	Shirley Davis	d.	PC	11 July 1916	4	3	
Burroughs	Annie O'Connor	d.	HT	17 Feb. 1916	1	3	
Burroughs	Charles	o.	ST	18 Oct. 1918	1	5	
Burroughs	Charles	o.	PD	25 Nov. 1917	5	1	
Burroughs	Charles, Jr.	o.	ST	28 Dec. 1917	1	2	
Burroughs	Eva W.	d.	ST	1 Apr. 1916	1	1	
Burroughs	Eva W.	d.	PA	28 Mar. 1916	4	2	

(1) Surname	(2) Given Name	(3)	(4)	(5) Date	(6) Pg	(7) Col	(8) Comments
Burroughs	Eva W.	d.	PD	28 Mar. 1916	5	4	also 30 Mar., 5:5
Burroughs	Eva W.	d.	SRR	28 Mar. 1916	4	6	also 29 Mar., 4:3
Burroughs	Eva W.	d.	PC	29 Mar. 1916	4	1	Sebastopol; also 30 Mar., 4:1
Burroughs	Ivy	m.	PD	20 July 1918	3	4	
Burroughs	Ivy F.	m.	ST	26 July 1918	1	3	
Burrows	Myrtle P.	o.	SRR	7 Nov. 1916	5	1	
Burrows	Robert W.	o.	SRR	7 Nov. 1916	5	1	
Burt	Elizabeth	d.	PD	21 Jan. 1916	8	2	
Burt	Elizabeth	d.	SRR	21 Jan. 1916	5	2	also 22 Jan., 10:3
Burt	Elizabeth	d.	ST	22 Jan. 1916	1	6	also 29 Jan., 7:1
Burton	George	m.	PA	3 June 1918	5	5	also 5 June, 8:5; 17 June, 5:4
Burton	George	m.	PA	11 Mar. 1918	1	1	
Burton	George	m.	PC	12 Mar. 1918	5	2	
Burton	George Walter	m.	PC	9 June 1918	2	2	also 18 June, 8:2
Bush	Marie	m.	PD	6 Sept. 1917	7	5	
Busini/Buiani	John	d.	PC	7 Apr. 1917	5	6	Calvary Cemetery; also 10 Apr., 3:3 11 Apr., 8:4
Buss	Wilhelmina	d.	PD	2 Apr. 1918	6	5	
Buss	William, Mrs.	d.	PC	2 Apr. 1918	5	2	also 4 Apr., 5:1
Bussman	Fred	b.	PD	14 Dec. 1916	2	1	
Butcher	Maria	d.	SRR	10 June 1916	11	4	
Butler	Carl G.	b.	SRR	2 Oct. 1917	4	1	
Butler	Carl G.	b	PD	3 Oct. 1917	7	1	
Butler	F. M.	b.	PC	29 Nov. 1916	8	1	
Butler	George	o.	SRR	4 Oct. 1917	8	3	
Butler	George Ide	d.	PD	27 July 1918	6	5	
Butler	George W.	o.	PD	11 June 1918	6	5	
Butler	George W.	o.	SIT	27 Oct. 1917	3	2	
Butler	Grace	m.	HT	7 June 1917	5	2	
Butler	L. H.	b.	PA	28 June 1917	5	4&6	
Butler	Leah	m.	PD	30 Dec. 1917	3	2	
Butler	Leah	m.	SRR	31 Dec. 1917	2	3	
Butler	Minerva	o.	PD	11 June 1918	6	5	
Butler	Minerva	o.	SIT	27 Oct. 1917	3	2	
Butler	Minerva	o.	SRR	4 Oct. 1917	8	3	
Butler	Neal W.	d.	HT	21 Feb. 1918	1	1	
Butler	Neal W.	b.	PA	28 Feb. 1918	8	5	
Butler	Neil	d.	PA	20 Feb. 1918	5	3	
Butler	Neil W.	d.	PC	21 Feb. 1918	1	5	
Butler	Neil W.	b.	PC	27 Feb. 1918	8	2	
Butler	Neil W., Jr.	d.	ST	22 Feb. 1918	1	4	
Butler	Neil/Neal W., Jr.	d.	PD	21 Feb. 1918	8	1	also 26 Feb., 2:1

(1) Surname	(2) Given Name	(3)	(4)	(5) Date	(6) Pg	(7) Col	(8) Comments
Butler	Philip	d.	SRR	4 Oct. 1917	4	4	
Butler	Tom	d.	SIT	16 Nov. 1918	1	5	also 23 Nov., 1:3
Buttler	Wilmer	m.	PD	18 Nov. 1917	7	5	
Buttler	Wilmer	m.	SRR	19 Nov. 1917	6	6	
Button	Herbert	o.	PC	26 Feb. 1918	3	6	
Button	Herbert	o.	PC	28 Nov. 1917	1	2	
Button	Herbert	o.	PC	9 Feb. 1918	3	5	
Button	Ray	m.	PD	6 Dec. 1916	3	3	
Button	Ray	m.	SIT	9 Dec. 1916	1	6	
Button	Ray E.	m.	PA	5 Dec. 1916	4	1	
Button	Ray E.	m.	SRR	5 Dec. 1916	4	4	
Button	Ray E.	m.	PC	6 Dec. 1916	4	1	
Butts	Margaret	d.	PD	8 July 1917	4	3	
Butts	T. V.	o.	PD	30 June 1918	5	1	portrait
Butts	Thomas J.	d.	PC	25 June 1916	1	7	
Butts	Thomas J.	d.	PA	26 June 1916	2	2	
Butts	Thomas J.	d.	SRR	26 June 1916	3	3	portrait
Butz	Caroline E.	d.	SRR	25 June 1917	4	3	Rural Cemetery; also 5:5
Butz	Caroline Elizabeth	d.	PC	26 June 1917	4	6	
Butz	Carrie Hood	d.	PD	24 June 1917	2	1	also 26 June, 5:3; 27 June, 6:2
Buzzetti	Rose	d.	PD	12 June 1917	4	3	Odd Fellows Cemetery; also 15 June, 8:5
Buzzetti	Rose Lena	d.	SRR	11 June 1917	8	2	Odd Fellows Cemetery; also 12 June, 10"6; 13 June, 8:1; 14 June, 4:4
Buzzi	Rose	m.	SRR	25 Nov. 1916	4	4	
Buzzi	Rose	m.	PD	26 Nov. 1916	4	2	
Buzzini	Charles	b.	PA	14 Sept. 1916	8	6	
Buzzini	Charles (son of)	d.	PA	29 July 1918	2	5	
Buzzini	John	o.	PA	18 June 1917	5	4	
Byce	Evalina	m.	PA	18 Dec. 1916	5	3	also 20 Dec., 5:3
Byce	Evalina	m.	PC	19 Dec. 1916	8	2	also 21 Dec., 1:6
Byce	Harrison W.	o.	PC	22 May 1916	1	3	
Byce	Harrison W.	o.	PD	23 May 1916	6	5	
Byce	Harrison W.	o.	PA	24 Apr. 1916	6	7	also 22 May, 1:6
Byce	Julia	o.	PD	23 May 1916	6	5	
Byce	Julia	m.	PA	25 June 1917	2	3	
Byce	Julia Brown	m.	PC	26 June 1917	1	5	
Byce	Julia E.	o.	PC	22 May 1916	1	3	
Byce	Julia E.	o.	PA	24 Apr. 1916	6	7	also 22 May, 1:6
Byce	W. E.	o.	PA	16 Feb. 1918	3	3	
Byce	Wilbur	o.	PA	16 July 1918	7	3	

(1) Surname	(2) Given Name	(3)	(4)	(5) Date	(6) Pg	(7) Col	(8) Comments
Byce	Wilbur E.	o.	PA	8 May 1918	5	1	
Byerrum	C. H.	b.	HT	11 Apr. 1918	5	5	
Byers	Herbert	o.	HT	15 Apr. 1918	2	3	also 2 May, 4:2
Byers	Herbert	o.	HT	6 Dec. 1917	1	2	
Byington	Lewis	o.	HT	26 Sept. 1918	1	3	
Byrne	Edna Ethel	d.	PC	19 Nov. 1918	3	4	Cypress Hill
Byrne	Edyth Ethel	d.	PA	15 Nov. 1918	8	3	Cypress Hill; also 16 Nov., 4:1
Byrne	James	d.	PA	23 Nov. 1918	5	4	also 25 Nov., 4:4, 5:3; 27 Nov., 8:3
Byrne	James	d.	PC	27 Nov. 1918	5	3	Cypress Hill; also 28 Nov., 4:3
Byrne	Moore Foster	d.	PC	22 Nov. 1918	4	3	
Byrne	Thomas	d.	PA	10 Nov. 1916	4	1	also 13 Nov., 4:4
Byrne	Thomas	d.	PC	10 Nov. 1916	1	2	also 14 Nov., 3:2
Byrne	Thomas	d.	SRR	10 Nov. 1916	1	3	
Byrne	Thomas	d.	PD	14 Nov. 1916	5	3	
Byrne	Thomas	d.	PA	5 Sept. 1916	4	4	Tomales; also 6 Sept., 8:1
Byrne	Thomas J., Jr.	d.	PC	6 Sept. 1916	3	3	Tomales; also 6:1; 7 Sept., 4:3
Byrne	Wiliam Joseph	d.	PC	6 Nov. 1918	1	3	Tomales; also 4:4; 7 Nov., 5:1
Byrne	Will	d.	PA	5 Nov. 1918	4	5	also 6 Nov., 5:6
Byrne	Thomas J., Jr.	d.	PD	7 Sept. 1916	3	3	
Byron	Alice	d.	PD	10 Aug. 1916	8	1	
Byron	Alice	d.	SRR	10 Aug. 1916	5	4	
Byron	James H.	d.	PD	10 Nov. 1918	4	2	

C

(1) Surname	(2) Given Name	(3)	(4)	(5) Date	(6) Pg	(7) Col	(8) Comments
Cabanne	M.	b.	PA	31 Mar. 1916	6	6	
Cabazut	Florence	d.	PD	28 Dec. 1918	8	3	
Cacarossa/Vacarossa	Ernest Virgil	o.	PA	23 July 1918	2	7	
Cacarossa/Vacarossa	Mary Henrietta	o.	PA	23 July 1918	2	7	
Cadagan	Dennis	b.	PA	21 Mar. 1916	5	6	
Cademartori	Elvera R.	m.	PC	20 Feb. 1917	2	1	
Cademartori	Elvera Rosa	m.	PA	17 Feb. 1917	4	4	
Cader	Charles	o.	PA	5 Nov. 1918	5	5	
Cader	Israel	o.	PC	5 Nov. 1918	1	4	
Cader	J.	b.	PC	27 June 1916	8	1	
Cader	Mr. & Mrs.	b.	PA	26 June 1916	5	1	
Cadra	Margherita	m.	PA	7 Dec. 1916	8	7	
Cadwell	Elizabeth Ann	m.	PC	4 May 1916	8	2	
Cadwell	Harriet	d.	ST	6 May 1916	2	3	
Cadwell	Harriet	d.	PA	27 Apr. 1916	4	2	Cypress Hill; also 5:3; 28 Apr., 1:3
Cadwell	Harriet	d.	PD	27 Apr. 1916	2	3	
Cadwell	Harriet M.	d.	PC	27 Apr. 1916	1	3	Cypress Hill; also 28 Apr., 5:6
Cadwell	Harriet M.	d.	SRR	27 Apr. 1916	1	6	
Cahalan	James Bernard	d.	SRR	25 Mar. 1916	8	1	
Cake	Charles	b.	HT	12 Apr. 1917	8	4	
Cake	Charley	b.	SRR	9 Apr. 1917	6	4	
Cake	Homer	m.	SRR	2 Jan. 1917	3	1	
Calanchini	Emil	m.	SIT	29 Apr. 1916	5	4	
Calanchini	Emil F.	m.	PA	5 Apr. 1916	4	3	also 25 Apr., 5:3; 26 Apr., 5:3
Calanchini	Ermenegilda	o.	PC	17 Dec. 1918	1	3	
Calderwood	Sophia	d.	PD	18 May 1917	5	7	
Calderwood	Sophia	d.	SRR	18 May 1917	6	3	
Calderwood	Sophia	d.	SIT	19 May 1917	1	7	cremation
Caldwell	Elizabeth A.	m.	ST	6 May 1916	1	3	
Caldwell	Ora	m.	PD	13 Dec. 1918	3	3	
Caldwell	Ora Helena	m.	HT	7 Nov. 1916	5	3	
Calenberg	Hugo, Jr.	m.	PD	24 Apr. 1917	5	1	
Calenchini	Emil P.	m.	PC	6 Apr. 1916	6	1	
Caliano	Giani	d.	SIT	22 Jan. 1916	3	7	
Caligari	Albino	d.	PA	29 Oct. 1918	5	4	
Caligari	Albino	d.	PC	29 Oct. 1918	1	4	
Call	George H.	b.	PC	10 Dec. 1918	3	3	
Call	George H.	b.	PD	8 Dec. 1918	3	3	
Callenberg	Hugo, Jr.	m.	SRR	23 Apr. 1917	3	1	

(1) Surname	(2) Given Name	(3)	(4)	(5) Date	(6) Pg	(7) Col	(8) Comments
Callison	J. J.	o.	PD	11 July 1918	3	1	
Callison	J. J.	o.	PD	2 June 1918	2	3	
Callison	J. J.	o.	PD	28 Dec. 1918	6	1	
Calmina	Mamie C.	m.	PC	15 Nov. 1917	3	1	
Calvert	Mabel	d.	PD	25 May 1916	8	1	also 26 May, 2:3
Cambra	Manuel	b.	SRR	20 Nov. 1916	2	2	
Cameron	David Emery	d.	PC	30 June 1916	8	4	Pinole
Cameron	George H.	m.	PD	7 Sept. 1916	3	2	
Cameron	Guy	o.	PA	16 Mar. 1913	7	4	
Cameron	May	o.	PA	16 Mar. 1913	7	4	
Camm	J. R.	m.	PD	24 June 1917	2	2	
Camm	John R.	m.	PA	23 June 1917	5	3	
Camm	John R.	m.	PC	24 June 1917	4	4	
Camotta	Lawrence	b.	PA	13 Jan. 1916	8	6	
Camozzi	Louis Arnold	m.	ST	3 Aug. 1917	2	3	
Camp	Henry C.	d.	PC	25 Nov. 1918	2	2	
Campaglia	Denemic	m.	PD	20 June 1916	2	3	
Campana	Joe	m.	PC	19 Sept. 1917	4	1	
Campbell	D. L.	m.	PC	17 Mar. 1918	5	4	
Campbell	David L.	m.	PC	1 Apr. 1918	4	3	
Campbell	David L.	m.	PA	16 Mar. 1918	4	4	also 1 Apr., 5:5
Campbell	Donald	o.	SIT	30 June 1917	3	2	also 18 Aug., 4:4
Campbell	Donald	o.	SIT	22 Dec. 1917	1	5	also 26 Jan. 1918, 1:3
Campbell	Ernest	b.	SIT	31 Aug. 1918	4	3	
Campbell	Everett	o.	PD	31 Aug. 1918	6	1	
Campbell	J. Otto	b.	PD	19 June 1918	5	5	
Campbell	James	o.	PA	31 July 1918	3	6	
Campbell	James	o.	PD	31 July 1918	6	5	
Campbell	James	o.	PD	2 Nov. 1918	3	3	
Campbell	James	o.	PA	23 Apr. 1918	4	3	
Campbell	Joseph	o.	PD	23 Apr. 1918	3	5	
Campbell	Mary Ellen	m.	HT	20 Dec. 1917	1	5	
Campbell	Mollie	m.	SRR	17 Dec. 1917	5	5	also 19 Dec., 8:3
Campbell	Mollie	m.	PD	19 Dec. 1917	7	1	also 20 Dec., 6:5
Campbell	Ross	m.	SRR	8 Nov. 1917	8	1	
Campbell	Ross	m.	PD	9 Nov. 1917	5	3	
Campbell	Sarah E.	o.	PA	31 July 1918	3	6	
Campbell	Sarah E.	o.	PD	31 July 1918	6	5	
Campbell	Sarah E.	o.	PD	2 Nov. 1918	3	3	
Campbell	Sarah E.	o.	PA	23 Apr. 1918	4	3	
Campbell	Sarah E.	o.	PD	23 Apr. 1918	3	5	
Campbell	W. A.	d.	PC	6 Aug. 1916	1	1&6	cremation; also 8 Aug., 5:3
Campbell	W. A.	d.	PA	7 Aug. 1916	5	1	cremation; also 8 Aug., 5:6; 9 Aug., 8:5

(1) Surname	(2) Given Name	(3)	(4)	(5) Date	(6) Pg	(7) Col	(8) Comments
Campbell	W. A.	d.	PD	8 Aug. 1916	3	3	
Campedonica	Adolf	m.	SIT	25 Nov. 1916	1	3	
Campodonica	Adolf	m.	PD	21 Nov. 1916	6	5	
Canama	Walter	m.	PC	18 Dec. 1917	3	3	
Candelario	Francisco Canales	d.	SRR	12 June 1916	7	3	
Cane	William C.	d.	PD	18 Apr. 1917	4	3	
Canepa	Angela	d.	PA	19 Feb. 1917	5	3	Calvary Cemetery; also 21 Feb., 3:3; 6:5
Canepa	Angela	d.	PC	20 Feb. 1917	2	1	also 3:1; 21 Feb., 5:3; 22 Feb., 5:3
Canepa	Angela	d.	PD	20 Feb. 1917	8	5	
Canepa	Angela	p.	PA	21 Feb. 1917	4	5	will
Canepa	Angela	p.	PC	22 Feb. 1917	3	1	
Canepa	Angela	p.	SIT	3 Mar. 1917	1	2	
Canepa	Clementia	m.	PC	22 Oct. 1916	5	1	also 27 Oct., 3:4
Canepa	Clementina	m.	SRR	26 Oct. 1916	5	1	
Canepa	Silvio	d.	PC	1 Sept. 1918	1	5	Calvary Cemetery; also 4 Sept., 6:3; 6 Sept., 8:3
Canepa	Silvio	d.	PA	2 Sept. 1918	5	3	Calvary Cemetery; also 8:1; 4 Sept., 4:4
Canepe	A., Mrs.	d.	SRR	19 Feb. 1917	1	5	
Canesascini	Leo	d.	PD	23 Nov. 1918	1	2	France
Canevari	Don A.	m.	SRR	8 June 1916	6	1	also 24 June, 12:6
Canevari	Giovanni	d.	SRR	13 Dec. 1916	8	2	Calvary Cemetery; also 15 Dec., 10:6
Canevascini	Ella	m.	PC	3 Dec. 1916	5	4	
Canevascini	Inez	m.	PA	1 Apr. 1918	4	4	
Canevascini	Inez	m.	PC	31 Mar. 1918	1	4	also 1 Apr., 5:3; 2 Apr., 5:2
Canevascini	Leo	o.	PA	9 Nov. 1918	5	4	Ireland; also 14 Dec., 3:3
Canevascini	Samuel Leo	d.	PC	15 Dec. 1918	1	3	
Canevascini	Samuel Leo	d.	PA	22 Nov. 1918	4	4	France; also 30 Nov., 5:3
Canevascini	Samuel Leo	d.	PC	23 Nov. 1918	1	3	
Canevescini	Ella	m.	PA	4 Dec. 1916	2	5	
Canfield	Bessie	o.	SRR	29 Feb. 1916	1	2	
Canfield	William	o.	SRR	29 Feb. 1916	1	2	
Caniff	Lois	m.	ST	6 May 1916	1	5	
Caniff	Lois	m.	PC	7 May 1916	2	2	
Cannell	Jessie	d.	PD	7 Sept. 1917	8	3	
Cannell	Jessie	d.	SRR	7 Sept. 1917	6	2	
Canning	Robert	o.	SIT	11 Aug. 1917	1	1	
Cannon	Calvin	b.	PC	6 June 1917	8	4	

(1) Surname	(2) Given Name	(3)	(4)	(5) Date	(6) Pg	(7) Col	(8) Comments
Cannon	Elizabeth Catherine	d.	PA	30 Jan. 1917	5	2&4	Cypress Hill; also 31 Jan., 2:5
Cannon	Elizabeth Catherine	d.	PC	30 Jan. 1917	1	2	Calvary Cemetery; also 3:3; 31 Jan., 3:4; 1 Feb., 5:4
Canova	Dino	d.	PC	29 Sept. 1916	1	6	Calvary Cemetery; also 1 Oct., 8:5
Canoys	Dino	d.	PA	29 Sept. 1916	8	4	also 30 Sept., 5:1
Cantel	Eugene	d.	PA	8 Feb. 1918	5	2	Cypress Hill; also 9 Feb., 5:4; 11 Feb., 4:5
Cantel	Eugene	d.	PC	9 Feb. 1918	6	4	also 8:5; 12 Feb., 3:3; Cypress Hill
Cantel	Eugene	d.	PD	9 Feb. 1918	2	2	
Capell	J. E.	m.	CR	3 Mar. 1917	1	2	
Capell	J. M.	m.	PD	3 Mar. 1917	8	3	
Capella	Louise	d.	PA	17 Apr. 1916	5	2	also 18 Apr., 5:4
Capella	Louise	d.	PC	18 Apr. 1916	1	6	
Capella	Louise	d.	PC	19 Apr. 1916	8	6	
Caporgno	Petero	d.	PC	24 June 1916	8	1	
Capucci	Mary	d.	PD	9 May 1917	1	2	Calvary Cemetery; also 4:3
Capucci	Mary	d.	SRR	9 May 1917	10	3	
Caracio	Emelia	o.	PD	22 Jan. 1918	5	1	
Caracio	Ralph	o.	PD	22 Jan. 1918	5	1	
Caratti	Antonio	o.	SRR	26 July 1917	4	2	also 3 Aug., 4:3
Caratti	Antonio	o.	SRR	6 Nov. 1917	8	1	
Caratti	Domenica	o.	SRR	26 July 1917	4	2	also 3 Aug., 4:3
Caratti	Domenica	o.	SRR	6 Nov. 1917	8	1	
Carbao	Venie	b.	SRR	29 Sept. 1917	8	6	
Cardiff	Jerry	m.	SRR	20 Apr. 1916	4	3	
Cardosa	Joseph	m.	PD	26 Apr. 1918	3	1	
Cardoza	Antone	d.	PC	5 Dec. 1917	2	2	also 7 Dec., 4:1
Cardoza	Joseph S.	m.	PC	25 Apr. 1918	5	3	
Cardoza	Mary	d.	PA	28 June 1918	1	3	
Cardoza	Mary	d.	PC	28 June 1918	8	2	
Carey	Delia	m.	PC	25 Oct. 1918	2	2	
Carillo	Leo	m.	PD	16 Mar. 1916	3	4	
Carini	Constance	d.	PD	16 Sept. 1917	6	5	
Carini	John M. (dau of)	d.	SRR	17 Sept. 1917	4	4	
Carlsen	Lawrence	b.	PC	16 May 1916	8	4	
Carlsen	Martin	b.	PC	16 Feb. 1917	8	6	
Carlson	C. F.	d.	PA	8 July 1918	5	1	
Carlson	C. F.	d.	PC	9 July 1918	6	4	
Carlson	Charles W.	d.	PD	9 July 1918	8	1	
Carlson	Chris	b.	PC	2 Mar. 1917	4	2	

(1) Surname	(2) Given Name	(3)	(4)	(5) Date	(6) Pg	(7) Col	(8) Comments
Carlson	Dena Barbara	d.	PC	8 Mar. 1917	1	6	Cypress Hill; also 10 Mar, 4:4
Carlson	Dena Barbara	d.	PD	8 Mar. 1917	5	2	
Carlson	Dena Barbara	d.	PA	7 Mar. 1917	5	4	Cypress Hill; also 9 Mar., 4:5
Carlson	E., Miss	d.	SIT	26 Oct. 1918	1	7	
Carlston	Agnes F.	m.	PC	4 May 1918	5	2	
Carman	Missouri Arizona	d.	ST	21 Apr. 1917	4	5	Odd Fellows Cem.
Carmer	Arthur	o.	SIT	29 Sept. 1917	1	1	
Carmody	Fred	b.	PA	2 Nov. 1918	6	5	
Carmody	J. H.	b.	PA	9 July 1918	5	6	
Carmody	James H.	m.	PC	1 Nov. 1917	8	3	
Carmody	James H.	m.	SRR	1 Nov. 1917	1	2	
Carmody	James H.	m.	PD	2 Nov. 1917	6	5	
Carmody	James H.	m.	PA	31 Oct. 1917	8	5	
Carniglia	Amelia	d.	SRR	1 Oct. 1917	6	3	
Carniglia	Amelia	d.	PD	2 Oct. 1917	4	2	also 5:3; 3 Oct., 6:2
Carpenter	Clair W.	m.	PA	4 Apr. 1916	5	4	also 12 Apr., 5:3; 15 Apr., 4:2
Carpenter	Clair W.	m.	PC	7 Apr. 1916	6	1	also 15 Apr., 4:2; 16 Apr., 5:3
Carpenter	Elbert	o.	PC	27 Nov. 1917	1	5	
Carpenter	George	m.	SIT	7 Sept. 1918	1	7	
Carpenter	George	m.	PD	8 Sept. 1918	3	4	
Carpenter	George B.	d.	SIT	5 May 1917	1	6	
Carpenter	Henry W.	d.	PC	11 May 1916	1	4	
Carpenter	Lawrence	b.	PA	31 July 1916	6	3	
Carpenter	Lawrence	b.	PC	1 Aug. 1916	8	4	
Carpenter	Lawrence	b.	PD	2 Aug. 1916	2	2	
Carr	Beatrice	o.	PC	2 May 1917	6	1	
Carr	Beatrice	o.	SRR	30 Apr. 1917	1	5	
Carr	Genevieve	m.	PC	23 Mar. 1918	3	4	also 24 Mar., 5:4
Carr	Givendola Kathleen	d.	HT	12 Dec. 1918	8	2	
Carr	Marian Genevieve	m.	PA	23 Mar. 1918	5	4	
Carr	Minnie	o.	PA	7 Feb. 1917	5	4	
Carr	Minnie B.	o.	PC	9 Jan. 1918	2	1	
Carr	Minnie Beatrice	o.	PC	1 Dec. 1917	8	3	
Carr	Minnie Beatrice	o.	SRR	27 Sept. 1917	4	5	
Carr	Minnie Beatrice	o.	PD	28 Sept. 1917	5	3	
Carr	Minnie Beatrice	o.	SRR	30 Nov. 1917	8	2	
Carr	Minnie Beatrice	o.	SRR	7 Feb. 1917	1	2	
Carr	Minnie Beatrice	o.	PC	8 Feb. 1917	1	1	
Carr	William	o.	PC	2 May 1917	6	1	
Carr	William	o.	PC	1 Dec. 1917	8	3	
Carr	William	o.	SRR	27 Sept. 1917	4	5	

(1) Surname	(2) Given Name	(3)	(4)	(5) Date	(6) Pg	(7) Col	(8) Comments
Carr	William	o.	PD	28 Sept. 1917	5	3	
Carr	William	o.	SRR	30 Apr. 1917	1	5	
Carr	William	o.	SRR	30 Nov. 1917	8	2	
Carr	William	o.	PA	7 Feb. 1917	5	4	
Carr	William	o.	SRR	7 Feb. 1917	1	2	
Carr	William	o.	PC	8 Feb. 1917	1	1	
Carr	William	o.	PC	9 Jan. 1918	2	1	
Carrell	Ethel	o.	SRR	19 Dec. 1916	6	2	also 20 Dec., 5:4
Carrell	Jesse	o.	SRR	19 Dec. 1916	6	2	also 20 Dec., 5:4
Carriger	Jewell	m.	PC	22 Feb. 1918	2	2	
Carrillo	Lawrence	m.	PD	13 Dec. 1917	5	3	
Carrillo	Lawrence	m.	PC	15 Dec. 1917	2	1	
Carrillo	Lee A.	o.	PA	18 June 1917	5	5	
Carrillo	Lee A.	o.	SRR	18 June 1917	8	3	
Carrillo	Lee A.	o.	PC	19 June 1917	3	2	
Carrillo	Lee A.	m.	PA	15 Mar. 1916	1	5	also 16 Mar., 4:4
Carrillo	Lee A.	o.	PC	2 Mar. 1918	8	5	also 26 Mar., 3:6
Carrillo	Lee A.	o.	PD	6 Nov. 1917	5	3	
Carrillo	Lee A.	o.	SRR	6 Nov. 1917	2	3	
Carrillo	Lee A.	o.	PD	6 Oct. 1917	8	1	
Carrillo	Lee A.	o.	PC	6 Sept. 1917	8	5	also 6 Oct., 3:3; 10 Oct., 3:3; 7 Nov., 4:6
Carrillo	Lee G.	o.	PD	19 June 1917	2	3	
Carrillo	Nan	d.	PC	24 Oct. 1918	8	3	
Carrillo	Nan	d.	PD	24 Oct. 1918	4	2	Sebastopol
Carrillo	Nellie	o.	PC	6 Sept. 1917	8	5	also 6 Oct., 3:3; 10 Oct., 3:3; 7 Nov., 4:6
Carrillo	Nellie C.	o.	PC	2 Mar. 1918	8	5	also 26 Mar., 3:6
Carrillo	Nellie I.	o.	PA	18 June 1917	5	5	
Carrillo	Nellie I.	o.	SRR	18 June 1917	8	3	
Carrillo	Nellie I.	o.	PC	19 June 1917	3	2	
Carrillo	Nellie I.	o.	PD	6 Nov. 1917	5	3	
Carrillo	Nellie I.	o.	SRR	6 Nov. 1917	2	3	
Carrillo	Nellie I.	o.	PD	6 Oct. 1917	8	1	
Carrillo	Nellie R.	o.	PD	19 June 1917	2	3	
Carrington	Charles N.	o.	PD	14 Oct. 1917	8	4	also 15 Dec., 3:4; 21 Dec., 3:1
Carrington	Charles N.	o.	SRR	15 Oct. 1917	8	4	also 19 Dec., 4:4; 21 Dec., 9:5
Carrington	Charles N., Jr.	m.	SRR	24 Jan. 1916	1	2	
Carrington	Charles, Jr.	o.	PC	22 Dec. 1917	5	6	
Carrington	Nellie	o.	PD	14 Oct. 1917	8	4	also 15 Dec., 3:4; 21 Dec., 3:1
Carrington	Nellie M.	o.	SRR	15 Oct. 1917	8	4	also 19 Dec., 4:4; 21 Dec., 9:5
Carrington	Nellie V.	o.	PC	22 Dec. 1917	5	6	

(1) Surname	(2) Given Name	(3)	(4)	(5) Date	(6) Pg	(7) Col	(8) Comments
Carroll	Ether	o.	SRR	29 Nov. 1916	5	6	
Carroll	Harold	d.	SRR	24 July 1917	4	4	
Carroll	Jesse E.	o.	SRR	29 Nov. 1916	5	6	
Carroll	William Howard	d.	PA	24 July 1917	5	3	also 26 July, 4;3
Carroll	William Howard	d.	PC	25 July 1917	5	4&6	Calvary Cemetery
Carsley	Freeman	m.	SRR	18 Aug. 1916	6	1	
Carsley	Freeman	m.	PC	20 Aug. 1916	5	2	
Carson	Jessie	o.	SIT	28 Sept. 1918	3	2	
Carson	Jessie M.	o.	PD	29 Mar. 1918	3	4	
Carson	Mary E.	m.	PA	10 July 1917	5	6	
Carson	Thomas	o.	SIT	28 Sept. 1918	3	2	
Carson	Thomas R.	o.	PD	29 Mar. 1918	3	4	
Carstensen	Carsten A.	d.	SRR	9 June 1916	7	4	
Carstensen	Carstens A.	d.	PA	8 June 1916	4	5	Cypress Hill; also 9 June, 5:7; 12 June, 5:3
Carstensen	Carstens A.	d.	PC	9 June 1916	5	3	Cypress Hill; also 11 June, 8:5; 13 June, 6:3
Carstensen	Charles	b.	PC	21 June 1918	4	2	
Carstensen	Charles R.	m.	PA	12 Sept. 1916	4	3	
Carstensen	Charles R.	m.	PC	13 Sept. 1916	5	4	also 15 Sept., 4:4
Carstensen	Charles R.	m.	SRR	13 Sept. 1916	5	2	
Carter	Charles	b.	PA	15 Apr. 1916	8	5	
Carter	Charles Ray	b.	PC	18 Apr. 1916	8	1	
Carter	Constance Sylvia	d.	PA	1 Oct. 1917	8	4	
Carter	Constance Sylvia	d.	PC	2 Oct. 1917	1	4	
Carter	Henry Ford	d.	PA	18 Oct. 1917	4	6	
Carter	Henry Ford	d.	PC	19 Oct. 1917	3	3	
Carter	Howard	o.	PA	17 July 1917	2	2	
Carter	Howard	o.	PD	17 July 1917	3	1	also 7 Aug., 6:1
Carter	Howard F.	o.	SRR	16 July 1917	8	2	
Carter	Howard F.	o.	PC	18 July 1917	7	5	
Carter	Howard F.	o.	SRR	5 Sept. 1917	6	2	
Carter	Lois	m.	SRR	29 Nov. 1916	3	4	
Carter	Lois York	m.	PD	2 Dec. 1916	5	4	also 6:1
Carter	Lois York	m.	SRR	2 Dec. 1916	9	2	
Carter	Louis	o.	PA	25 July 1917	2	4	also 26 July, 7:4
Carter	M. D.	d.	SRR	12 Sept. 1917	6	4	Fortuna
Carter	Marie Jesse	o.	PC	18 July 1917	7	5	
Carter	Marie Jessie	o.	SRR	16 July 1917	8	2	
Carter	Marie Jessie	o.	PA	17 July 1917	2	2	
Carter	Marie Jessie	o.	PD	17 July 1917	3	1	also 7 Aug., 6:1
Carter	Mary Jessie	o.	SRR	5 Sept. 1917	6	2	
Carter	Thomas F.	b.	PC	20 Feb. 1918	8	3	
Carter	Thomas S.	b.	PA	19 Feb. 1918	8	2	
Carter	William D.	d.	PD	12 Sept. 1917	6	4	Eureka

(1) Surname	(2) Given Name	(3)	(4)	(5) Date	(6) Pg	(7) Col	(8) Comments
Carter	William I.	d.	PC	13 Sept. 1917	6	4	
Cartwright	Charles F.	o.	SRR	3 May 1916	1	4	
Cartwright	Charles F.	o.	PC	4 May 1916	1	2	
Cartwright	Charles F.	o.	PA	18 Apr. 1916	1	4	also 3 May, 1:6
Cartwright	Charles F.	o.	PC	19 Apr. 1916	1	2	
Cartwright	Helen	o.	PA	18 Apr. 1916	1	4	also 3 May, 1:6
Cartwright	Helen	o.	PC	19 Apr. 1916	1	2	
Cartwright	Helen M.	o.	SRR	3 May 1916	1	4	
Cartwright	Helen M.	o.	PC	4 May 1916	1	2	
Casali	Adolf	d.	SRR	15 Feb. 1916	10	2	
Casali	Adoph	d.	PD	16 Feb. 1916	7	5	Calvary Cemetery
Casarotti	Camilia	m.	PA	19 Sept. 1918	3	5	
Casarotti	Celestina	d.	PA	22 Jan. 1916	5	4	also 24 Jan., 5:1
Casarotti	Charles F.	d.	PA	31 May 1917	5	5	Calvary Cemetery; also 2 June, 5:3
Casarotti	Charles F.	d.	PC	1 June 1917	3	3	Calvary Cemetery; also 2 June, 3:5
Casarotti	Henry	d.	PA	20 Nov. 1918	4	6&7	Calvary Cemetery; also 22 Nov., 5:2
Casarotti	Henry	d.	PC	20 Nov. 1918	4	3	Calvary Cemetery; also 21 Nov., 3:3; 23 Nov., 6:3
Casarotti	Mario	m.	PA	29 Aug. 1916	8	3	
Casassa	Frank Ursula	d.	SRR	26 Dec. 1916	1	2	also 27 Dec., 8:3
Case	Clara	d.	ST	15 Apr. 1916	3	2	
Case	Clara	d.	PD	8 Apr. 1916	6	3	Odd Fellows Cemetery, Forestville
Case	Clara E.	d.	SRR	7 Apr. 1916	1	2	
Case	G. S.	m.	PA	20 Sept. 1918	5	4	
Case	J. L.	b.	ST	11 Oct. 1918	5	3	
Caseres	Francesco	m.	ST	5 July 1918	1	5	
Caseri	A.	b.	PA	10 Aug. 1916	5	5	
Caseri	A.	b.	PC	11 Aug. 1916	5	2	
Caseri	Robert A.	m.	PA	1 June 1916	6	2	
Caseri	Robert A.	m.	PC	2 June 1916	3	3	
Casper	Joseph	b.	PD	14 Jan. 1917	2	3	
Cassarotti	Americo	b.	PA	22 Nov. 1917	5	2&4	
Cassarotti	Charles	b.	PC	15 Aug. 1916	4	6	
Cassarotti	Mario	m.	PC	30 Aug. 1916	6	2	
Cassasa	Frank, Mrs.	d.	PD	27 Dec. 1916	3	4	
Cassasa	Louise	m.	PD	4 Sept. 1918	6	4	
Casse	William	m.	PC	4 Dec. 1918	1	4	
Cassin	Richard J.	m.	PD	1 Aug. 1916	3	3	
Cassoratti	Henry	d.	PD	21 Nov. 1918	3	4	
Cassorotti	Celestina	d.	PD	23 Jan. 1916	1	4	
Castagnasso	Harry	m.	SIT	6 May 1916	5	3	

(1) Surname	(2) Given Name	(3)	(4)	(5) Date	(6) Pg	(7) Col	(8) Comments
Castagnasso	Mr. & Mrs.	b.	PD	10 Feb. 1917	3	4	
Castle	Carey	d.	SRR	1 Feb. 1917	4	4	also 2 Feb., 3:3
Castle	Cary	d.	HT	8 Feb. 1917	7	5	
Castle	Mr.	d.	PA	1 Feb. 1917	4	4	
Castner	Mildred	m.	SRR	24 Aug. 1917	6	4	
Castner	Mildred E.	m.	HT	28 Dec. 1916	1	3	
Castner	Mildred E.	m.	SRR	28 Dec. 1916	3	2	
Castner	Mildred E.	m.	PD	29 Dec. 1916	6	5	
Castner	Ralph	m.	SRR	25 May 1917	6	4	
Castner	Ralph	m.	HT	31 May 1917	5	4	
Castner	Ralph W.	m.	HT	28 Dec. 1916	1	3	
Castner	Ralph W.	m.	SRR	28 Dec. 1916	3	2	
Castner	Ralph W.	m.	PD	29 Dec. 1916	6	5	
Casucci	Angelo	d.	PD	19 Nov. 1918	1	5	
Catalina	Conchetta	m.	PD	18 Nov. 1917	10	3	
Catenacci	Clara Josephine	d.	PA	24 Jan. 1917	5	7	Calvary Cemetery; also 25 Jan., 4:4
Catenacci	Clara Josephine	d.	PC	25 Jan. 1917	3	3	Calvary Cemetery; also 26 Jan., 6:1
Catenacci	John, Jr.	d.	PA	12 Sept. 1916	5	5	Calvary Cemetery; also 14 Sept., 4:2
Catenacci	John, Jr.	d.	PC	13 Sept. 1916	4	3	Calvary Cemetery
Catendo	Albert G.	m.	SRR	16 Apr. 1917	6	4	
Catendo	Albert G.	m.	PD	19 Apr. 1917	3	4	
Catherine	Mary, Sister	d.	PD	7 Aug. 1917	8	1	Calvary Cemetery; also 8 Aug., 7:3
Caughey	William	b.	PD	8 Sept. 1916	6	6	
Caughey	William	b.	PD	9 Sept. 1916	4	6	
Cavalli	Fortunato	d.	PA	23 Oct. 1916	4	6	Cypress Hill; also 25 Oct., 4:3
Cavalli	Fortunato	d.	PC	24 Oct. 1916	1	4	Calvary Cemetery; also 4:5; 25 Oct., 4:5; 26 Oct., 8:3
Cavarotti	Camilla	m.	PC	20 Sept. 1918	4	3	
Cayla	Raymond M.	m.	PC	21 Aug. 1918	4	3	also 22 Aug., 8:4
Cayla	Raymond M.	m.	PD	21 Aug. 1918	8	3	
Cayla	Raymond N.	m.	PA	21 Aug. 1918	5	4	
Cazarotti	Celetsina	o.	PC	23 Jan. 1916	5	4	
Cazarotti	Mrs. C. F.	d.	PC	25 Jan. 1916	3	2	Calvary Cemetery
Cazes	Mr. & Mrs.	b.	SIT	8 July 1916	4	2	
Cella	Dominick	b.	PA	13 Feb. 1917	5	5	
Cella	Dominick	b.	PA	18 Jan. 1916	1	3	
Cella	Domnick	b.	PC	14 Feb. 1917	5	3	
Ceregino	Joseph T.	m.	PD	26 Aug. 1917	3	5	
Cereni	Nora	m.	PA	24 Apr. 1918	4	2	also 25 Apr., 5:3
Cereni	Nora	m.	PD	26 Apr. 1918	3	1	

(1) Surname	(2) Given Name	(3)	(4)	(5) Date	(6) Pg	(7) Col	(8) Comments
Ceriale	Giovanni	d.	HT	8 Feb. 1917	3	2	Oak Mound Cemetery
Cerialle	Adeline Theresa	m.	HT	8 Nov. 1917	1	1	
Cerialle	Adeline Theresa	m.	PD	9 Nov. 1917	5	3	
Ceriallo	Giovanni	d.	SRR	2 Feb. 1917	3	3	Oak Mound Cemetery; also 5 Feb., 3:4
Cerini	Constance	d.	PA	14 Sept. 1917	4	5	Calvary Cemetery; also 15 Sept., 6:5
Cerini	Constance	d.	PC	15 Sept. 1917	1	3&4	Calvary Cemetery; also 18 Sept., 5:5
Cerini	Gracomo	d.	PA	9 Mar. 1916	3	5	
Cerini	Nora A.	m.	PC	25 Apr. 1918	5	3	
Cerletti	Lorenzo	b.	PA	8 Mar. 1916	5	4	
Chabon	G. C.	m.	SRR	21 Nov. 1916	7	4	
Chahon	G. C.	m.	PD	22 Nov. 1916	2	2	
Chakurain	Enoch E.	d.	PD	28 Sept. 1916	8	1	also 30 Sept., 5:1
Chakurian	Enoch E.	d.	PA	28 Sept. 1916	6	5	Santa Rosa
Chakurian	Enoch E.	d.	SRR	28 Sept. 1916	5	2	also 29 Sept., 6:4; 30 Sept., 4:1
Chambaud	Marie P.	d.	SRR	5 Oct. 1917	10	5	cremation; also 9 Oct., 8:2
Chambaud	Marie P.	d.	PD	7 Oct. 1917	5	2	
Chamberlain	Eva	m.	PA	17 Oct. 1916	2	4	
Chamberlain	Ralph	m.	PA	23 Aug. 1917	5	3	
Chamberlain	Ralph	m.	PD	24 Aug. 1917	3	1	
Chamberlain	Thurston R.	d.	PC	2 June 1918	1	3	
Chamberlain	Eva	m.	PC	19 Oct. 1916	3	2	
Chamberlin	Ralph M.	m.	PA	25 Oct. 1917	4	3	
Chamberlin	Ralph M.	m.	PD	26 Oct. 1917	2	4	
Chambers	Ben, Mrs.	d.	PA	30 Mar. 1916	6	4	
Chambers	Thurston R. C.	d.	PD	2 June 1918	7	3	
Champlin	Walter Leroy	d.	PC	7 Mar. 1918	4	4	
Chandler	Ella C.	d.	PA	4 Mar. 1916	5	4	also 7 Mar., 8:5
Chandler	Ella C.	o.	PC	5 Mar. 1916	4	3	
Chandler	Hattie M.	d.	PA	13 Aug. 1918	5	4	Cypress Hill; also 14 Aug., 5:5; 15 Aug., 4:1
Chandler	Hattie Marie	d.	PC	14 Aug. 1918	4	3	Cypress Hill; also 15 Aug., 8:2; 16 Aug., 8:4
Chandler	Hattie Marie	d.	PD	14 Aug. 1918	5	5	
Chandler	R. O.	d.	SRR	22 Aug. 1917	1	1	I.O.O.F. Cemetery
Chandler	Robert	m.	PC	30 June 1918	8	3	
Chandler	Robert	m.	PC	20 Apr. 1918	5	4	
Chandler	Robert C.	m.	PA	15 Apr. 1918	4	3	
Chandler	Robert C.	m.	PD	16 Apr. 1918	6	3	

(1) Surname	(2) Given Name	(3)	(4)	(5) Date	(6) Pg	(7) Col	(8) Comments
Chandler	Robert Curtis	m.	PC	2 July 1918	5	4	
Chandler	Robert Curtiss	m.	PA	1 July 1918	4	4	
Chandler	Rollo O.	d.	PD	21 Aug. 1917	4	2	also 8:1
Chandler	Rollo O.	d.	PD	22 Aug. 1917	4	2	also 23 Aug., 5:1
Chaney	Henry	m.	PC	15 June 1916	3	1	
Chapman	Edith	m.	PC	24 Mar. 1916	3	3	
Chapman	Edith	d.	PA	27 Mar. 1916	4	1	also 30 Mar., 3:4
Chapman	Edith	d.	SRR	27 Mar. 1916	1	5	
Chapman	Guy	m.	PD	2 Dec. 1917	6	3	also 18 Dec., 8:3
Chapman	Guy	m.	SRR	3 Dec. 1917	2	4	also 17 Dec., 2:3
Chapman	Helen Edith	m.	PA	24 Mar. 1916	7	3	
Chappel	F. J.	d.	PD	27 Dec. 1917	6	3	
Chappell	James Fenton	d.	SRR	26 Dec. 1917	8	1	
Charles	E. R.	d.	PD	12 Dec. 1918	6	4	
Charles	Elbert R.	d.	PA	11 Dec. 1918	4	5	Cypress Hill; also 12 Dec., 7:3; 13 Dec., 4:4
Charles	Elbert R.	d.	PC	12 Dec. 1918	8	3	also 14 Dec., 3:1
Charles	Elizabeth	d.	PC	23 Jan. 1918	6	2	
Charles	Elizabeth	d.	PD	23 Jan. 1918	6	3	
Charles	Mrs.	d.	PA	22 Jan. 1918	5	5	
Charles	Oscar	b.	PD	15 Nov. 1918	1	6	
Charles	Oscar	b.	PC	16 Nov. 1918	3	2	
Charles	Virginia	d.	PC	18 Jan. 1917	1	6	
Charmley	Gertrude	m.	PD	23 May 1918	8	1	
Chase	Ernest	m.	ST	29 June 1917	1	1	
Chase	F. J.	d.	SRR	8 June 1917	8	4	
Chase	F. J.	d.	PC	9 June 1917	1	3	also 10 June, 2.3
Chase	F. J.	d.	PD	9 June 1917	2	5	
Chase	F. J.	d.	ST	15 June 1917	1	4	
Chase	Frank J.	d.	PA	8 June 1917	1	3	
Chase	George	o.	SIT	27 Oct. 1917	2	5	
Chase	Harry	d.	PA	26 Sept. 1917	4	5	
Chase	Harry	d.	PD	26 Sept. 1917	8	1	
Chase	Harry	d.	SRR	26 Sept. 1917	4	4	
Chase	Harry	d.	HT	27 Sept. 1917	1	1	
Chase	Harry	d.	PC	27 Sept. 1917	6	4	
Chase	Harry, Jr.	d.	SIT	29 Sept. 1917	1	7	
Cheda	Ida C.	d.	PA	21 May 1917	4	3	Calvary Cemetery; also 5:4; 23 May, 4:1
Cheda	Ida C.	d.	PC	22 May 1917	3	2	Calvary Cemetery; also 5:4; 24 May, 1:4
Cheda	Ida C.	d.	SRR	22 May 1917	6	3	
Cheesewright	Joseph	d.	PA	9 Mar. 1917	4	3	cremation; also 10 Mar., 3:5
Cheesewright	Joseph	d.	PC	9 Mar. 1917	1	5	

(1) Surname	(2) Given Name	(3)	(4)	(5) Date	(6) Pg	(7) Col	(8) Comments
Chelini	Guiseppe	p.	SIT	12 Feb. 1916	1	7	
Chelini	Guiseppe	p.	PC	21 Sept. 1916	8	1	
Chelini	Joseph	d.	PC	2 Feb. 1916	3	2	
Chelini	Joseph	d.	PD	4 Feb. 1916	2	3	
Chelini	Joseph	d.	SIT	5 Feb. 1916	`	7	
Chenoweth	Hardin	b.	PC	3 Dec. 1918	6	2	
Chenoweth	Mary Edith	m.	SRR	9 May 1917	6	3	
Cheyney	Ernest	b.	SRR	9 Mar. 1916	2	1	
Chick	Edward	d.	PC	22 Dec. 1918	3	3	
Childers	Juanita	m.	PC	4 Jan. 1918	4	5	
Childlaw	Lester	o.	PD	20 Oct. 1918	2	1	
Chisholm	Annie C.	d.	PA	16 Jan. 1918	6	5	Cypress Hill; also 17 Jan., 4:6
Chisholm	Annie C.	d.	PC	16 Jan. 1918	4	3	also 8:5; 18 Jan. 4:4; Cypress Hill
Christ	Chester B.	m.	HT	3 May 1917	4	5	
Christ	Chester H.	m.	PD	2 May 1917	6	5	
Christensen	Anna B.	m.	PA	18 Sept. 1916	4	6	also 19 Sept., 4:5; 20 Sept., 7:5
Christensen	C. F.	o.	PD	10 Oct. 1916	5	5	
Christensen	Christen P.	o.	SRR	15 Sept. 1917	8	3	
Christensen	Christian F.	o.	PD	14 Feb. 1918	5	3	
Christensen	Clarence	b.	SRR	31 Aug. 1916	8	6	
Christensen	Marie	d.	PD	10 Aug. 1918	4	2	Odd Fellows Cemetery; also 8:2
Christensen	Theresa	o.	PD	10 Oct. 1916	5	5	
Christensen	Theresa	o.	PD	14 Feb. 1918	5	3	
Christensen	Therese	o.	SRR	15 Sept. 1917	8	3	
Christensen	Thor	m.	PA	8 June 1916	6	2	
Christenson	Charles R.	m.	PD	13 Sept. 1916	1	6	
Christenson	Thor	m.	SRR	8 June 1916	5	2	
Christian	A.	b.	SRR	28 Apr. 1916	1	4	
Christian	Elsie	d.	ST	18 Ma.r 1916	8	3	
Christian	H. H.	m.	PD	5 Feb. 1918	8	4	
Christiansen	Anna B.	m.	PC	20 Sept. 1916	4	1	
Christiansen	Anna Bigitte	m.	PC	17 Sept. 1916	6	2	
Christiansen	C. P.	o.	PC	14 Mar. 1918	2	1	
Christiansen	C. P.	o.	PC	5 Dec. 1917	6	4	
Christiansen	Chris	d.	PA	11 Dec. 1918	1	3	cremation; also 12 Dec., 3:7
Christiansen	Chris	d.	PC	12 Dec. 1918	3	4	
Christiansen	Clara	m.	CR	20 Apr. 1917	1	5	
Christiansen	Clara	m.	PC	21 Apr. 1917	5	3	
Christiansen	Laura	m.	PA	11 Mar. 1916	4	6	also 13 Mar., 2:3&4
Christiansen	Laura	m.	SRR	11 Mar. 1916	2	2	also 13 Mar., 5:1

(1) Surname	(2) Given Name	(3)	(4)	(5) Date	(6) Pg	(7) Col	(8) Comments
Christiansen	Martha	m.	PD	12 Mar. 1916	5	3	
Christiansen	Martha	m.	PC	14 Mar. 1916	1	5	
Christiansen	Mathilda	m.	PA	25 Apr. 1916	6	3	
Christiansen	Matilda	m.	PC	26 Apr. 1916	8	3	
Christiansen	Theresa	o.	PC	5 Dec. 1917	6	4	
Christiansen	Theresa A.	o.	PC	14 Mar. 1918	2	1	
Christiansen	Thor	m.	PC	8 June 1916	1	5	
Christianson	Matilda	m.	SRR	26 Apr. 1916	8	4	
Christie	Alfred J.	d.	PD	27 Apr. 1917	4	3	Masonic Cemetery; also 8:3
Christie	Alfred J.	d.	SRR	27 Apr. 1917	3	5	
Christie	Alfred J.	d.	PA	28 Apr. 1917	3	6	
Christie	Alfred J.	d.	PC	28 Apr. 1917	6	3	Sebastopol
Christie	Alfred J.	d.	ST	28 Apr. 1917	1	2	
Christie	Edith Ray	d.	PA	17 Apr. 1916	4	1	also 18 Apr., 1:1
Christie	Emma Edith	d.	PC	18 Apr. 1916	1	7	Cypress Hill; also 2:1; 19 Apr., 5:2
Christie	Frances	d.	PC	12 Oct. 1918	5	4	
Christie	Frances	d.	PA	7 Oct. 1918	4	3	Cypress Hill; also 8 Oct., 5:4; 10 Oct., 6:5; 11 Oct., 8:4
Christie	Frances A.	d.	ST	11 Oct. 1918	8	3	
Christie	Harry	m.	SRR	11 June 1917	8	3	
Christie	Irving	d.	PC	16 Nov. 1918	1	3	also 22 Nov., 1:3; 24 Nov., 4:1; 27 Nov., 8:3; 28 Nov., 4:4
Christie	Irving/Ivan	d.	PA	16 Nov. 1918	6	4	Mt. Olivet, San Mateo Co.; also 23 Nov., 4:1; 25 Nov., 5:3; 26 Nov., 4:4; 27 Nov., 3:4
Christy	Albert	d.	SRR	3 May 1917	6	3	
Chubb	Mary M.	d.	PA	12 Sept. 1917	1	6	
Chubb	Mary M.	d.	PC	13 Sept. 1917	5	5	
Chun	Gertie	o.	SRR	9 Oct. 1916	8	1	
Chun	Gertrude Higginson	o.	PD	10 Oct. 1916	6	1	
Chun	Tom	o.	PD	10 Oct. 1916	6	1	
Chun	Tom	o.	SRR	9 Oct. 1916	8	1	
Church	Edith M.	m.	PA	27 Dec. 1917	5	3	
Church	Lorin	d.	PD	10 Aug. 1918	8	2	
Church	Lorin K.	d.	HT	15 Aug. 1918	5	3	Marne-Aisne, France
Church	Lorin N.	d.	PA	10 Aug. 1918	5	4	France
Church	Lorin N.	d.	PC	10 Aug. 1918	1	1	France; also 11 Aug., 1:3
Church	Myrtle E.	m.	PA	28 May 1917	5	1	
Church	Myrtle E.	m.	PC	29 May 1917	8	2	
Church	Myrtle Elsie	m.	PA	11 Apr. 1917	5	3	

(1) Surname	(2) Given Name	(3)	(4)	(5) Date	(6) Pg	(7) Col	(8) Comments
Church	Viola	o.	PC	30 Mar. 1916	1	3	portrait; also 16 Apr., 4:4
Churchill	Abbie	m.	PD	6 Jan. 1918	5	4	
Churchill	Abbie	m.	PA	7 Jan. 1918	2	6	
Churchill	Abbie	m.	PC	8 Jan. 1918	6	4	
Churchill	Clara	m.	PD	2 Sept. 1917	7	3	
Churchill	Clara	m.	SRR	4 Sept. 1917	2	3	
Churchill	Clara	m.	PC	5 Sept. 1917	3	3	
Churchman	John William	m.	ST	2 Feb. 1917	3	5	
Churchman	Ruth	m.	ST	1 Mar. 1918	3	2	
Churchman	Ruth E.	m.	PC	27 Feb. 1918	2	3	
Cicala	Emilie	m.	PD	18 Oct. 1917	8	1	
Cinelli	Albert D.	d.	PC	3 Nov. 1918	5	2	France
Cinelli	Albert Dante	d.	PA	23 Oct. 1918	7	3	France
Cinelli	Catherine	o.	PC	14 Nov. 1916	3	3	
Cinelli	Elbert D.	o.	PC	14 Nov. 1916	3	3	
Civarelli	A.	b.	SRR	18 Aug. 1916	8	6	
Claasen	Inken	d.	PA	7 Feb. 1917	3	4	Cypress Hill; also 8 Feb., 2:3; 9 Feb., 4:4
Claassen	Inken	d.	PC	7 Feb. 1917	8	2	Cypress Hill; also 8 Feb., 8:5; 10 Feb., 8:3
Clanachini	Emil	m.	PD	27 Apr. 1916	4	2	
Clare	George	m.	SRR	3 Apr. 1916	1	2	
Clare	George	m.	PC	4 Apr. 1916	4	3	
Clare	George C.	m.	PA	3 Apr. 1916	4	3	
Clare	George W.	m.	PD	4 Apr. 1916	3	1	
Clark	A. J.	d.	PD	2 Mar. 1917	7	5	Rural Cemetery
Clark	Ada	m.	PD	2 Feb. 1916	8	5	
Clark	Alberta	m.	SRR	20 Jan. 1916	6	4	
Clark	Alberta	m.	HT	27 Jan. 1916	1	4	
Clark	Annie M.	d.	PA	9 July 1917	4	6	Cypress Hill
Clark	Annie M.	d.	PC	10 July 1917	4	4	Cypress Hill; also 13 July, 8:4
Clark	David, Jr.	d.	PD	6 Feb. 1918	6	2	
Clark	Elmer L.	d.	SRR	18 Dec. 1916	5	2	
Clark	Emily Jane	d.	PA	13 Aug. 1918	8	3	Cypress Hill; also 14 Aug., 5:5; 15 Aug., 5:5; 16 Aug., 4:3
Clark	Emily Jane	d.	PC	14 Aug. 1918	6	2	Cypress Hill; also 8:4; 17 Aug., 3:1
Clark	Emily Jane	d.	PD	14 Aug. 1918	8	3	
Clark	Gladys	m.	ST	11 May 1917	3	5	also 4:3
Clark	Halloveen	m.	PD	1 May 1918	5	4	
Clark	J. D.	b.	HT	20 June 1918	2	3	
Clark	James	d.	PC	14 Aug. 1918	8	3	Tomales; also 16 Aug., 8:2

(1) Surname	(2) Given Name	(3)	(4)	(5) Date	(6) Pg	(7) Col	(8) Comments
Clark	James	d.	PD	15 Aug. 1918	3	4	also 17 Aug., 3:2
Clark	John Alexander	d.	SRR	27 Feb. 1917	8	1	also 28 Feb., 8:3
Clark	John C.	d.	PD	1 May 1917	8	3	
Clark	Joseph L.	m.	PC	5 May 1916	1	2	
Clark	Leslie A.	m.	SRR	2 Jan. 1917	10	1	
Clark	Leslie D.	m.	PA	10 Dec. 1917	2	2	
Clark	Leslie D.	m.	PD	2 Dec. 1917	7	1	also 9 Dec., 7:1
Clark	Leslie D.	m.	SRR	8 Dec. 1917	4	1	
Clark	Leslie D.	m.	PC	9 Dec. 1917	5	4	
Clark	Lottie	m.	PC	22 Nov. 1916	1	4	
Clark	Lottie J. M.	m.	PA	21 Nov. 1916	4	3	
Clark	Lottie J. M.	m.	SRR	22 Nov. 1916	7	4	
Clark	Luella	m.	SRR	15 Oct. 1917	7	4	
Clark	Luella	m.	PC	16 Oct. 1917	5	3	
Clark	Mary E.	d.	PA	26 Feb. 1916	4	4	
Clark	Mary J.	m.	PC	22 Feb. 1918	6	5	
Clark	Mary J.	m.	ST	22 Feb. 1918	8	5	
Clark	Peter P.	d.	PA	13 Nov. 1916	5	3	Holy Cross, S.F.; also 14 Nov., 5:2
Clark	Peter P.	d.	PC	14 Nov. 1916	4	2	Holy Cross, S.F.
Clark	Ralph	d.	PD	20 Oct. 1918	8	4	
Clark	Robert	d.	SRR	7 June 1917	8	3	also 8 June, 8:3
Clark	Susan P.	m.	PA	8 Oct. 1918	6	5	
Clark	Thomas Ewing	d.	PD	24 Dec. 1918	2	2	
Clark	Vernon L.	o.	PA	8 June 1917	1	4	
Clark	Werner	m.	SRR	20 Dec. 1917	8	3	
Clarke	Elizabeth	m.	PA	10 Apr. 1917	2	3	
Clarke	Leslie	m.	PD	31 Dec. 1916	6	4	
Clary	Thomas	m.	PD	21 May 1916	8	2	
Clary	Thomas	m.	SRR	24 May 1916	1	4	
Clary	Thomas	b.	SRR	1 May 1917	1	3	
Clary	Thomas P.	m.	PC	30 Apr. 1916	8	5	
Clausen	Inken	d.	PD	8 Feb. 1917	3	3	
Clausen	John Wesley	d.	PC	20 Apr. 1916	1	3	
Clausen	Prince Albert	d.	HT	8 Aug. 1918	2	3	
Clay	Art	o.	PC	31 July 1918	6	4	
Clay	Arthur	o.	PC	24 Apr. 1918	3	4	also 3 May, 2:2
Clayton	Jack	d.	PA	5 Oct. 1916	5	3	Berkeley; also 11 Oct., 1:3
Clayton	John	d.	PC	5 Oct. 1916	1	3	Berkeley; also 6 Oct., 3:4; 12 Oct., 5:4
Clayton	John W.	d.	SRR	19 Apr. 1916	3	3	
Cleary	George	d.	PD	19 May 1918	4	2	also 8:4
Cleary	George	d.	PC	22 May 1918	2	1	
Cleary	George	d.	PD	2 Nov. 1918	2	6	Calvary Cemetery

(1) Surname	(2) Given Name	(3)	(4)	(5) Date	(6) Pg	(7) Col	(8) Comments
Cleary	George	d.	PC	29 Oct. 1918	5	4	
Cleary	Richard	d.	PA	14 Feb. 1917	4	5	Calvary Cemetery; also 16 Feb., 4:5
Cleary	Richard	d.	PC	14 Feb. 1917	1	2	
Cleary	Richard	d.	PC	15 Feb. 1917	8	4	
Cleland	Mary	m.	PA	22 Dec. 1916	5	3	
Cleland	Mary	m.	PC	23 Dec. 1916	8	4	
Cleland	Mary M.	m.	SRR	22 Dec. 1916	3	3	
Clemensen	Charles	d.	PA	2 Jan. 1918	8	5	also 4 Jan., 3:4
Clemensen	Charles P.	d.	PC	3 Jan. 1918	8	3&6	also 4 Jan., 8:6; 5 Jan., 4:1
Clemensen	Pauline	d.	PA	7 Feb. 1916	4	1	cremation; also 8:7; 9 Feb., 7:4
Clemensen	Pauline	d.	PC	8 Feb. 1916	4	4	Mt. Olive Cemetery; also 10 Feb., 5:5; 16 Feb., 5:4
Clement	William	b.	SIT	15 Dec. 1917	3	2	
Clements	Katherine	m.	PD	1 Sept. 1916	5	3	
Clerici	John	d.	PA	27 Oct. 1916	6	3	Carizo (Frontiere Regiment) Italian Army
Clerici	John	d.	PD	27 Oct. 1916	5	2	Italian Army
Clerkin	Phillip	o.	PC	28 July 1917	8	2	
Cleveland	William	d.	PD	9 Oct. 1917	4	2	
Clevenger	Frank	d.	PA	28 Dec. 1916	6	3	
Clewe	Helena	m.	SIT	3 June 1916	1	1	also 8 July, 1:7; 22 July, 1:6
Clewe	Helena	m.	PC	12 July 1916	5	2	
Clewe	Helena	m.	PD	16 July 1916	6	2	also 18 July, 2:4; 21 July, 6:3
Clewe	Helena	m.	PA	21 July 1916	8	3	
Clewe	Helene	m.	PC	3 June 1916	4	6	
Clewe	Helene	m.	SRR	21 July 1916	5	4	
Clewe	Helene	m.	SRR	3 June 1916	7	6	
Clewe	Maria	d.	PC	6 June 1917	1	3	7 June, 4:6
Clewe	Maria	d.	PD	7 June 1917	3	1	
Clewe	Maria	d.	SRR	7 June 1917	6	4	
Clewe	Maria	d.	SIT	9 June 1917	4	5	cremation
Clewe	Martha	d.	PA	5 June 1917	6	4	also 6 June, 2:3
Clewe	William	b.	SRR	8 Jan. 1016	5	3	
Clift	Francis	m.	PA	30 Mar. 1916	1	4	
Clinch	Henry	d.	PD	15 Nov. 1917	6	4	
Clinch	Henry W.	d.	SRR	14 Nov. 1917	8	2	
Cline	Arthur N.	m.	SRR	9 Nov. 1916	8	5	
Cline	Thomas J.	m.	PA	7 Aug. 1918	4	3	
Cline	Thomas J.	m.	PC	8 Aug. 1918	3	4	

(1) Surname	(2) Given Name	(3)	(4)	(5) Date	(6) Pg	(7) Col	(8) Comments
Cline	Thomas J.	m.	PD	8 Aug. 1918	2	3	
Cline	Tom	o.	PC	4 Dec. 1917	5	4	
Clore	Sarah	d.	SRR	25 July 1916	5	2	
Clore	Sarah C.	d.	PD	25 July 1916	5	3	
Clore	Sarah C.	d.	ST	29 July 1916	1	3	I.O.O.F. Cemetery
Clough	Julia	m.	SRR	3 Apr. 1916	1	2	
Clough	Julia	m.	PC	4 Apr. 1916	4	3	
Clough	Julia	m.	PD	4 Apr. 1916	3	1	
Clough	Julia M.	m.	PA	3 Apr. 1916	4	3	
Clover	Harold H.	m.	PA	23 July 1917	2	3	
Clubb	Herbert R.	o.	PD	1 May 1918	7	3	British Army
Cluver	Harold	b.	PA	19 June 1918	5	6	
Cluver	Harold Henry	m.	PC	24 July 1917	3	4	
Cluver	Henry, Sr.	d.	PC	29 Mar. 1918	1	2	Cypress Hill; also 30 Mar., 5:2; 31 Mar., 4:3
Cluver	Henry, Sr.	d.	PA	30 Mar. 1918	3	2	Cypress Hill
Clyma	Myrtle P.	o.	PD	1 Nov. 1918	3	2	
Clyma	Walter LeRoy	o.	PD	1 Nov. 1918	3	2	
Cnopius	Eugene	m.	PA	13 Nov. 1917	2	5	
Cnopius	Eugene	m.	PD	13 Nov. 1917	2	3	also 15 Nov., 8:3
Cnopius	Eugene B.	m.	SRR	12 Nov. 1917	8	3	also 14 Nov., 4:3
Cnopius	Eugene B.	m.	PC	13 Nov. 1917	5	2	
Cnopius	Gertrude	m.	SRR	3 June 1916	4	1	also 7 June, 8:1
Cnopius	Gertrude	m.	PD	7 June 1916	5	3	also 8 June, 5:4
Cnopius	Gertrude	m.	PC	8 June 1916	6	3	
Coates	C. A.	d.	PA	11 May 1916	5	4	
Coates	C. A.	d.	PD	11 May 1916	2	3	
Coates	C. A.	d.	SRR	11 May 1916	8	5	I.O.O.F. Cemetery; also 12 May, 5:2
Coates	E F.	o.	PD	31 Mar. 1918	3	4	
Coates	Earl	o.	PD	10 Oct. 1918	3	3	
Coates	Mary L.	d.	PA	2 Mar. 1918	4	2	
Coates	Mary L.	d.	PD	2 Mar. 1918	2	3	3 Mar., 4:2
Coats	Charles A.	d.	ST	13 May 1916	1	5	
Cobb	Clarence	b.	PA	24 Aug. 1917	5	4	also 25 Aug., 8:6
Cobb	Leslie H.	d.	PD	12 Sept. 1917	6	3	Mountain View, Oakland
Cobb	Lewis H.	d.	SRR	11 Sept. 1917	10	1	Mountain View Cemetery, Oakland
Cobb	Lewis H.	d.	PC	12 Sept. 1917	5	3	
Cobb	O. O.	d.	HT	1 Aug. 1918	1	3	
Cobb	Omar C.	b.	PA	5 Sept. 1917	5	7	also 6 Sept., 2:2
Cobb	Omar O.	d.	PA	29 July 1918	5	5	also 31 July, 3:5
Cobb	Omar O.	d.	PC	30 July 1918	4	3	

(1) Surname	(2) Given Name	(3)	(4)	(5) Date	(6) Pg	(7) Col	(8) Comments
Cobb	Omer O.	d.	PD	30 July 1918	2	5	also 31 July, 4:2
Coburn	Joseph	d.	ST	20 Dec. 1918	2	1	
Cochran	Arthur	o.	PD	6 Oct. 1918	5	2	
Cochran	Arthur F.	o.	HT	7 Mar. 1918	8	5	
Cochran	Gertrude	o.	PD	6 Oct. 1918	5	2	
Cochran	Gertrude	o.	HT	7 Mar. 1918	8	5	
Cochran	Margaret E.	d.	PC	13 Mar. 1917	3	4	also 14 Mar., 8:2
Cochrane	Ida	m.	PA	28 July 1917	8	3	
Cochrane	Ida	m.	PC	29 July 1917	5	3	
Cochrane	Margaret E.	d.	PA	12 Mar. 1917	4	3	
Cochrane	Wirter W.	m.	PA	28 July 1917	8	3	
Cochrane	Wirter W.	m.	PC	29 July 1917	5	3	
Cockrill	George	o.	PD	11 July 1918	2	3	
Cockrill	George	o.	PD	13 Apr. 1918	7	1	
Cockrill	George B.	o.	PD	14 June 1918	3	4	
Cockrill	Obe	o.	PD	22 Sept. 1918	5	1	
Cockrill	W. A.	b.	PA	24 Jan. 1916	5	2	
Cockrill	W. A.	b.	SRR	26 Jan. 1916	2	2	
Cockrum	M. M.	b.	PA	24 June 1916	4	4	
Cockrum	M. M.	b.	PC	25 June 1916	8	1	
Codding	George C.	b.	SRR	11 July 1917	8	2	
Codding	George C.	b.	PC	12 July 1917	5	6	
Codding	George C.	b.	PD	12 July 1917	3	3	
Code	Harriet M.	d.	PC	16 Apr. 1918	3	2	also 17 Apr., 5:3
Code	Harriet Melissa	d.	PA	15 Apr. 1918	4	5	Cypress Hill; also 16 Apr., 8:7
Codeni	Erminia	m.	PD	18 Oct. 1917	3	3	
Codiga	Domenico	d.	SIT	11 May 1918	3	3	
Codiga	Ed	m.	SIT	28 July 1917	2	5	
Codoni	Ermina	m.	PA	16 Oct. 1917	8	3	
Codoni	Erminia	m.	PC	17 Oct. 1917	4	2	
Cody	Louis B.	m.	PA	25 Nov. 1916	3	4	
Cody	Louis P.	m.	PC	24 Nov. 1916	4	1	
Cody	Louis P.	m.	SRR	24 Nov. 1916	10	5	
Cody	Margaret	m.	PD	3 May 1918	2	1	
Coen	M., Mrs.	d.	PA	2 Oct. 1917	5	1	
Coen	Matilda	d.	PC	3 Oct. 1917	1	2	
Coen	Melinne	d.	PD	3 Oct. 1917	6	4	
Coen	Melissa	d.	HT	4 Oct. 1917	1	4	
Coen	Ola Almira	d.	SRR	30 Aug. 1916	6	1	Olive Hill Cemetery; also 2 Sept., 6:4
Coffey	Henry	d.	SRR	3 July 1916	10	4	
Coffey	Henry	d.	PD	4 July 1916	2	5	
Coffman	Doris	m.	SRR	2 Dec. 1916	3	2	
Coffman	Doris	m.	PD	3 Dec. 1916	8	3	

(1) Surname	(2) Given Name	(3)	(4)	(5) Date	(6) Pg	(7) Col	(8) Comments
Coffman	Doris	m.	HT	7 Dec. 1916	7	4	
Coffman	Mildred	m.	HT	1 Aug. 1918	1	3	
Cohenhour	Josephine	m.	PD	2 Dec. 1917	8	2	
Cohenour	Josephine	m.	SRR	1 Dec. 1917	3	4	
Colabellas	Carlo	b.	SRR	20 Feb. 1917	2	3	
Colbroth	Mervyn	d.	PA	20 Aug. 1918	5	2	Santa Rosa; also 21 Aug., 8:5
Colbroth	Mervyn Ellsworth	d.	PC	21 Aug. 1918	4	3	
Colbroth	Mervyn Ellsworth	d.	PD	21 Aug. 1918	4	2	Odd Fellows Cemetery; also 5:2; 22 Aug, 3:3
Colbroth	Molly Belle	d.	PD	14 June 1917	3	1	Rural Cemetery; also 4:2; 16 June, 3:2
Colburn	Brewer	d.	PA	5 July 1917	4	4	Bloomfield; also 7 July, 4:5
Colburn	Brewer	d.	PC	6 July 1917	4	1	Bloomfield; also 8:4; 8 July, 5:6
Colburn	Brewer	d.	PD	6 July 1917	5	3	also 7 July, 3:5
Colburn	Brewer	d.	SRR	6 July 1917	6	6	
Colburn	Glen	o.	PC	1 July 1917	1	4	also 15 July, 1:5
Colburn	Glen D.	o.	PD	23 Nov. 1917	6	1	
Colburn	Glen P.	o.	PA	28 June 1917	8	5	
Colburn	Merle	b.	PC	3 May 1917	8	3	
Colburn	Orlin	b.	SRR	3 May 1917	6	6	
Colby	Mary H.	d.	PA	4 Sept. 1918	8	3	Cypress Hill; also 6 Sept., 5:3
Colby	Mary H.	d.	PC	5 Sept. 1918	8	4	Cypress Hill; also 6 Sept., 2:1; 7 Sept., 5:4
Colby	S. H.	m.	PC	17 Mar. 1917	4	6	
Colby	S. H.	b.	PA	21 Feb. 1918	5	2	
Cole	Alta	m.	SRR	8 Feb. 1917	8	4	
Cole	Alta	m.	PD	9 Feb. 1917	5	1	
Cole	Charles Harry	d.	ST	10 May 1918	8	3	
Cole	Harriet M.	d.	PA	6 Sept. 1916	5	3	
Cole	Leon F.	b.	PD	16 Apr. 1916	1	2	
Cole	W. E.	b.	PD	19 May 1918	8	5	
Cole	W. E.	b.	PD	24 Apr. 1917	8	1	
Cole	Willard Chester	m.	SRR	6 Jan. 1916	10	2	
Coleman	Kathleen	m.	PA	1 July 1916	1	4	also 3 July, 5:3
Coleman	Kathleen	m.	PC	2 July 1916	4	2	also 6 July, 3:1
Collicool	H. A.	b.	PD	8 Jan. 1918	3	5	
Collinel	Louise	m.	PD	29 May 1918	6	2	
Colling	Elaine Elizabeth	m.	PD	1 Jan. 1918	3	4	
Collins	F. M.	p.	PA	13 Sept. 1917	5	4	also 14 Sept., 6:3
Collins	F. M.	p.	PC	14 Sept. 1917	8	3	will
Collins	Frank M.	d.	HT	13 Sept. 1917	1	2	

(1) Surname	(2) Given Name	(3)	(4)	(5) Date	(6) Pg	(7) Col	(8) Comments
Collins	Frank M.	d.	PA	8 Sept. 1917	5	1	Cypress Hill; also 10 Sept., 8:5; 11 Sept., 4:4, 8:5; 12 Sept., 2:4; 13 Sept., 3:5, 8:5
Collins	Frank M.	d.	SRR	8 Sept. 1917	1	2	portrait; also 11 Sept., 10:2; 12 Sept., 8:1
Collins	Frank M.	d.	PC	9 Sept. 1917	1	5	Cypress Hill; also 13 Sept., 3:3
Collins	Franklin Miller	d.	PD	9 Sept. 1917	4	3	Cypress Hill; also 13 Sept., 2:1
Collins	J. B.	d.	HT	15 Nov. 1917	1	1	
Collins	J. B.	d.	PD	16 Nov. 1917	3	1	Alexander Valley Cemetery
Collison	Mrs.	d.	SRR	10 July 1916	8	4	
Collister	Vivian Eloise	m.	SRR	26 June 1917	8	4	
Collister	Vivian Eloise	m.	PC	27 June 1917	9	2	
Collister	Vivienne	m.	PD	8 May 1917	5	3	
Collister	Vivienne	m.	SRR	8 May 1917	2	3	
Collister	Vivienne	m.	PD	27 June 1917	5	3	
Colombo	Elsie	m.	PD	21 Dec. 1917	2	3	also 23 Dec., 5:4
Colombo	Katherine Elsie	m.	SRR	20 Dec. 1917	8	3	
Colombo	Oliver	m.	SRR	23 Oct. 1917	4	4	
Colombo	Romeo	m.	PA	4 June 1918	4	1	
Colombo	Romeo M.	m.	PC	4 June 1918	5	3	
Colson	Marie	d.	PD	21 Nov. 1916	4	2	
Colton	Charles W.	m.	PD	5 May 1917	5	3	
Colton	Harry	d.	PD	26 Nov. 1918	2	3	France
Colvin	Thomas Floyd	m.	SRR	23 Nov. 1917	5	1	
Colwell	Florence	m.	PD	15 Jan. 1918	3	2	
Coman	Robert G.	m.	PD	10 June 1916	5	5	
Coman	Robert G.	m.	SRR	10 June 1916	2	1	also 12 June, 6:6; 17 June, 4:1
Combs	Henry C.	m.	PD	25 Oct. 1917	3	4	
Combs	Myrtle	d.	HT	30 Oct. 1918	1	4	
Comozzi	Louis A.	m.	PD	21 July 1917	3	3	
Comozzi	Louis Arnold	m.	PA	20 July 1917	8	4	
Comozzi	Luis Arnold	m.	PC	21 July 1917	5	1	also 22 July, 5:1
Compton	Charles F.	m.	PC	24 Apr. 1918	5	2	
Compton	Emma L.	o.	SRR	1 Nov. 1917	8	6	
Compton	Harriet	d.	PD	8 May 1918	3	3	cremation
Compton	Theodore J.	o.	SRR	1 Nov. 1917	8	6	
Comstock	Hilliard	m.	PD	7 July 1918	7	3	also 14 July, 6:1
Comstock	Hilliard	o.	PD	13 Nov. 1918	2	1	also 3 Dec., 8:1
Comstock	Hilliard	o.	PC	17 Dec. 1918	5	3	
Comstock	J. Walter	o.	PC	12 May 1917	2	1	
Comstock	Leslie	m.	PC	10 Aug. 1917	5	3	

(1) Surname	(2) Given Name	(3)	(4)	(5) Date	(6) Pg	(7) Col	(8) Comments
Comstock	Leslie	m.	PD	11 Aug. 1917	3	3	
Comstock	Leslie F.	m.	PA	10 July 1917	4	3	also 8 Aug., 8:4; 10 Aug., 5:3
Comstock	Leslie F.	m.	PC	14 July 1917	8	3	
Comstock	Lois Mae	m.	PC	5 Nov. 1918	5	3	
Comstock	Ralph	o.	PC	12 May 1917	2	1	
Condiff	Harry	m.	SRR	3 June 1916	4	3	also 8 June, 8:2
Condoff	Harry	m.	PD	4 June 1916	9	2	
Condy	Albert	m.	ST	24 June 1916	1	3	
Condy	Albert	b.	SRR	16 Oct. 1917	3	2	
Conger	Henry E.	m.	SRR	25 Apr. 1916	8	5	
Conklin	Marion	d.	PA	15 Nov. 1918	5	1&6	Cypress Hill; also 7:2; 18 Nov., 5:1
Conklin	Marion	d.	PC	15 Nov. 1918	1	3	Cypress Hill; also 16 Nov., 3:2; 14 Nov., 3:6
Conley	Emery	d.	PD	11 June 1916	10	3	Pleasant Hill Cemetery
Conley	Emery	d.	SRR	12 June 1916	5	4	
Conlin	Andrew	d.	SIT	22 July 1916	1	1	
Connama	Walter J.	m.	SIT	15 Dec. 1917	2	3	
Connams	Walter J.	m.	SRR	11 Dec. 1917	7	3	
Connelly	Katherine	m.	SRR	2 Feb. 1916	5	6	
Connelly	Katherine Rose	m.	PC	2 Feb. 1916	4	1&2	also 16 Jan., 6:1
Connelly	Myrtle	m.	PD	19 Oct. 1916	6	1	
Conner	A. B.	b.	PA	25 Apr. 1918	4	2	
Conners	A. F., Mr. & Mrs.	d.	PA	12 Nov. 1918	5	5	
Conners	Naoma	m.	PD	26 Apr. 1918	6	5	
Connolley	Rose	m.	PD	2 Feb. 1916	5	4	
Connolly	M. J.	d.	PA	8 Mar. 1917	4	3	also 10 Mar., 4:5
Connolly	Martin	d.	PD	20 July 1918	6	4	
Connolly	Mary	m.	PC	1 Jan. 1918	5	3	
Connolly	Mary	m.	PD	1 Jan. 1918	3	3	
Connolly	Mary	m.	PA	29 Dec. 1917	4	2	also 31 Dec., 7:5
Connolly	Mary Virginia	m.	PC	30 Dec. 1917	4	4	
Connolly	Michael D'Arcy	d.	PC	9 Mar. 1917	1	4	Mt. Olivet, San Rafael; also 6:3; 10 Mar., 6:3; 11 Mar., 3:6
Connolly	Michael D'Arcy	d.	PD	9 Mar. 1917	1	4	
Connolly	Michael D'Arcy	d.	SRR	9 Mar. 1917	5	1	
Connors	Charles	b.	PD	9 Aug. 1918	5	2	
Connors	Emily	d.	PD	10 Nov. 1918	1	6	I.O.O.F. Cemetery; also 12 Nov., 4:2; 13 Nov., 3:2
Conrad	Charles F.	m.	PD	9 July 1916	3	4	

(1) Surname	(2) Given Name	(3)	(4)	(5) Date	(6) Pg	(7) Col	(8) Comments
Convers	Elma Juanita	d.	PA	19 May 1916	2	2	
Convers	Elma Juanita	d.	PD	19 May 1916	8	2	also 20 May, 7:4
Convers	Elma	d.	SRR	19 May 1916	5	1	also 20 May, 7:2
Converse	Bertha A.	d.	PD	25 June 1918	3	2	
Converse	Elma Juanita	d.	PC	20 May 1916	1	5	
Conway	Hannah T.	d.	PC	27 Mar. 1917	2	2	Calvary Cemetery; also 3:4; 28 Mar., 2:3
Conyers	Elma Juanita	d.	ST	20 May 1916	1	1	also 27 May, 3:2
Coode	John C.	d.	PC	1 Sept. 1918	1	3	France
Coode	John G.	d.	PA	31 Aug. 1918	5	1	France
Coogan	Carrie M.	m.	SRR	5 Nov. 1917	1	5	
Cook	Albert	d.	HT	6 Jan. 1916	10	6	
Cook	Albert Walter	d.	PD	1 Jan. 1916	2	5	Oak Mound Cemetery
Cook	Alice Emma	m.	SIT	9 Feb. 1918	1	5	
Cook	Constance	o.	PA	3 June 1918	2	1	
Cook	Fountain	p.	PC	28 Feb. 1917	2	1	
Cook	Isaac F.	p.	PA	27 Feb. 1917	5	5	
Cook	Isaac Fountain	d.	SRR	10 Feb. 1917	1	4	also 12 Feb., 8:4
Cook	Isaac Fountain	d.	PD	11 Feb. 1917	4	2	Pleasant Hill Cemetery; also 13 Feb., 7:5
Cook	Isaac Fountain	p.	PC	12 Apr. 1917	1	4	
Cook	Isaac Fountain	d.	PA	12 Feb. 1917	4	3	
Cook	Isaac Fountain	d.	HT	8 Feb. 1917	8	4	
Cook	Issac Fountain	d.	PC	11 Feb. 1917	6	3	
Cook	John, Mrs.	d.	PD	27 Apr. 1917	6	2	
Cook	John, Mrs.	d.	PC	28 Apr. 1917	6	4	
Cook	Louise	m.	PD	18 Jan. 1918	5	1	
Cook	Maggi	d.	SRR	23 Apr. 1917	6	6	
Cook	Raymond E.	b.	SRR	11 Aug. 1916	1	3	
Cook	Vrine	m.	SRR	7 Nov. 1916	3	1	
Cooke	Constance	o.	HT	6 June 1918	1	1	portrait; also 13 June, 1:4; 12 Aug, 1:2; 5 Sept., 4:1
Cooke	Constance	o.	PD	7 June 1918	6	3	portrait; also 13 June, 7:1; 27 June, 5:1
Cooke	Constance	o.	PD	17 July 1918	2	3	
Cooke	Constance	o.	PD	16 Aug. 1918	3	1	also 23 Aug., 3:1
Cooke	Constance	o.	PD	20 Dec. 1918	3	1	
Cooke	Marden	o.	PD	20 Dec. 1918	3	3	
Cooke	Marden	o.	SRR	9 Aug. 1917	6	3	
Cooke	Marden G.	o.	HT	2 Aug. 1917	3	3	
Cookson	Ruth	m.	ST	24 June 1916	1	2	
Coolbroth	Mollie Belle	d.	SRR	13 June 1917	8	1&4	
Coolbroth	Molly Belle	d.	PC	14 June 1917	1	4	also 16 June, 4:6
Cooley	Ed	d.	HT	19 July 1917	1	5	

(1) Surname	(2) Given Name	(3)	(4)	(5) Date	(6) Pg	(7) Col	(8) Comments
Cooley	Ed A.	d.	PA	16 July 1917	8	4	
Cooley	Ed A.	d.	PC	17 July 1917	1	1	
Cooley	Ed H.	d.	SRR	16 July 1917	1	1	also 8:1; 17 July, 3:4
Cooley	Edward A.	d.	PD	17 July 1917	6	1	also 19 July, 7:1
Cooley	Edward A.	d.	CR	20 July 1917	1	1	
Cooley	John	o.	CR	8 Nov. 1918	1	4	also 29 Nov., 1:2
Cooley	John L.	o.	CR	13 Apr. 1917	1	2	
Cooley	W. S.	b.	PA	23 Apr. 1918	2	6	
Cooley	W. S.	b.	PC	25 Apr. 1918	4	4	
Cooley	Walter A.	m.	PC	5 Oct. 1916	3	3	
Cooley	Walter S.	m.	SRR	4 Oct. 1916	8	4	
Cooley	Walter T.	m.	PA	4 Oct. 1916	5	3	
Coolidge	Homer	m.	HT	7 June 1917	5	2	
Coolidge	Jane	d.	PD	28 Sept. 1916	5	1	Oak Mound Cemetery
Coolidge	Jane	d.	SRR	28 Sept. 1916	6	1	
Coolidge	Jane	d.	HT	29 Sept. 1916	5	4	Oak Mound Cemetery
Coombs	Ella	m.	PA	11 Jan. 1917	8	4	
Coombs	Ella	m.	PC	11 Jan. 1918	4	5	
Coombs	Ella	m.	PD	11 Jan. 1918	2	4	
Coon	Irvine	b.	PC	21 July 1916	8	1	
Coon	Jack	d.	PA	6 Apr. 1918	7	4	
Coon	Jack	d.	PD	6 Apr. 1918	6	4	also 16 Apr., 5:1
Coon	Maggie	d.	HT	26 Apr. 1917	1	5	
Cooney	Lydia M.	m.	SRR	27 June 1917	8	2	
Coonle	George	o.	PD	10 Sept. 1918	6	4	
Cooper	Allen	d.	PC	1 Sept. 1916	5	4	
Cooper	Allen	d.	PD	31 Aug. 1916	8	5	
Cooper	Allen	d.	SRR	31 Aug. 1916	8	4	
Cooper	Bridget	d.	SIT	10 Nov. 1917	1	4	
Cooper	Charles	m.	PA	23 Apr. 1917	5	3	
Cooper	Charles	m.	PC	24 Apr. 1917	5	1	
Cooper	Charles	m.	SRR	24 Apr. 1917	5	2	
Cooper	Charles	m.	SIT	28 Apr. 1917	1	3	
Cooper	Charlotte A.	d.	PD	20 Nov. 1918	8	4	Rural Cemetery; also 21 Nov., 6:2; 22 Nov., 1:4
Cooper	Edna	d.	PC	2 June 1918	8	4	
Cooper	Edna E. Poppe	d.	PD	1 June 1918	4	2	Mountain Cemetery; also 8:3; 4 June, 7:1; 7 June, 2:1
Cooper	Edna Poppe	d.	SIT	8 June 1918	1	2	Mountain Cemetery
Cooper	Ernest	b.	PD	29 Nov. 1917	8	3	
Cooper	Ernest	b.	SRR	30 Nov. 1917	2	4	
Cooper	Ernest G.	m.	SRR	2 Jan. 1917	6	4	
Cooper	Ernest G.	m.	PD	3 Jan. 1917	5	2	

(1) Surname	(2) Given Name	(3)	(4)	(5) Date	(6) Pg	(7) Col	(8) Comments
Cooper	Goliah	m.	PD	15 Oct. 1918	3	6	
Cooper	James R.	d.	PD	23 May 1916	8	2	Shiloh Cemetery
Cooper	James R.	d.	SRR	23 May 1916	5	2	Shiloh Cemetery
Cooper	Janetta	m.	PD	13 Aug. 1918	3	3	
Cooper	John D.	d.	SRR	13 Mar. 1917	8	2	also 15 Mar., 4:3
Cooper	John D.	d.	PA	14 Mar. 1917	2	3	
Cooper	John D.	d.	PC	14 Mar. 1917	1	3	
Cooper	John D.	d.	PD	15 Mar. 1917	4	3	Rural Cemetery; also 16 Mar., 3:3
Cooper	Minnie L.	m.	SRR	8 June 1916	6	1	also 24 June, 12:6
Cooper	Pearl	m.	PA	21 Dec. 1917	1	3	
Cooper	Pearl	m.	PC	21 Dec. 1917	1	3	
Cooper	Thomas G.	d.	ST	1 Feb. 1918	4	3	
Cooper	Thomas G.	d.	PD	25 Jan. 1918	2	4	
Cooper	Thomas G.	d.	HT	31 June 1918	6	2	
Cooper	Vera	d.	SRR	13 Sept. 1916	8	5	
Cooper	Vera	d.	PD	14 Sept. 1916	2	3	
Cooper	Wallace	b.	PD	16 July 1918	7	3	
Coops	Harold	m.	PD	21 July 1918	5	3	
Coops	Harold	m.	PA	22 July 1918	4	7	
Coops	Harold	m.	SIT	27 July 1918	1	4	
Coops	Harold	m.	SIT	16 Feb. 1918	1	5	
Coops	Harold	m.	PD	19 Feb. 1918	5	3	
Cootes	Vrina	m.	PD	7 Nov. 1916	7	3	
Cootes	Vrina	m.	HT	8 Nov. 1916	1	6	
Copf	Antone	d.	PA	25 Nov. 1918	4	7	
Coppedge	Ernest Frank	m.	SRR	19 Dec. 1916	4	5	
Coppin	Claude Albert	d.	PA	11 Sept. 1916	8	5	also 13 Sept., 5:4
Coppin	Claude Albert	d.	PC	12 Sept. 1916	4	5	also 13 Sept., 4:3; 14 Sept., 4:4; Calvary
Corbit	Hazel M.	m.	PD	23 June 1916	2	5	
Corda	Elmo	o.	PC	17 Dec. 1918	1	3	
Cordova	Marcellino	d.	SRR	5 Feb. 1916	1	5	
Cordova	Marcello	d.	PD	6 Feb. 1916	6	3	also 8 Feb., 3:3-4
Cordoza	Antone	d.	ST	30 Nov. 1917	1	4	I.O.O.F. Cemetery
Cordoza	Joseph	m.	PA	24 Apr. 1918	4	2	also 25 Apr., 5:3
Cordoza	Mary	d.	HT	4 July 1918	5	4	Madera
Corey	Isabel	m.	PC	31 Oct. 1917	3	2	also 3 Nov., 5:3
Corfu	Charles	b.	PC	21 Mar. 1917	5	6	
Corippo	Ben	b.	PA	13 Nov. 1918	5	4	
Corippo	Ben	b.	PC	13 Nov. 1918	4	1	
Corippo	Ben	b.	PC	17 Apr. 1917	5	6	
Corippo	Benjamin	m.	PA	17 May 1916	6	4	also 24 May, 4:4
Corippo	Benjamin	m.	PC	17 May 1916	4	3	also 25 May, 1:3
Cornett	Ruby	m.	PC	20 Sept. 1916	8	5	

(1) Surname	(2) Given Name	(3)	(4)	(5) Date	(6) Pg	(7) Col	(8) Comments
Cornett	Ruth	m.	PC	5 May 1916	1	2	
Cornish	Matilda J.	d.	ST	14 Sept. 1917	2	2	
Cornish	Matilda J.	d.	PC	15 Sept. 1917	8	4	
Cornwall	Frank	d.	SIT	1 Sept. 1917	1	6	cremation
Cornwall	Frank	d.	PD	2 Sept. 1917	6	5	cremation
Corria	A. F.	m.	HT	23 Nov. 1916	6	4	
Costa	Giaconda	d.	PD	31 Dec. 1916	6	5	
Costello	Rose	d.	PA	24 Aug. 1918	5	5	Calvary Cemetery; also 6:4
Costello	Rose	d.	PC	25 Aug. 1918	8	2&4	Calvary Cemetery; also 27 Aug., 1:4
Costello	Rose	d.	PD	25 Aug. 1918	6	3	
Cotrell	Mark H.	d.	PD	19 Apr. 1918	6	2	
Cottle	Harold	b.	HT	13 June 1918	2	5	
Cottrell	C. C.	b.	PA	3 Jan. 1918	8	6	
Coughlin	Wiley	d.	PD	6 Jan. 1916	3	3	Oakland; also 7 Jan., 8:3; 8 Jan., 6:3
Coughran	Wiley	d.	SRR	5 Jan. 1916	10	1	cremation; also 6 Jan., 1:2; 7 Jan., 8:3
Coulter	Rachael	d.	PA	5 Apr. 1916	7	4	
Coulter	Rachel	d.	SRR	4 Apr. 1916	8	3	Rural Cemetery; also 6 Apr., 8:5
Coulter	Rachel Matilda	d.	PD	5 Apr. 1916	6	1	also 6 Apr., 7:2; 7 Apr., 5:3
Counsins	J. E.	b.	HT	11 Oct. 1917	5	3	
Courtz	Ben	b.	PA	3 May 1916	1	3&7	
Courtz	Ben	b.	PC	4 May 1916	8	5	
Courtz	Frank	b.	PA	1 May 1917	5	7	
Courtz	Frank J.	b.	PC	1 May 1917	4	4	
Cowan	Hazen	o.	SIT	11 Aug. 1917	1	1	
Cowell	L. A.	b.	PC	29 Aug. 1916	8	4	
Cowgil	Martha Washington	d.	PC	5 Feb. 1918	5	3	
Cowgill	C. G.	o.	PD	24 Feb. 1917	6	4	adoption
Cowgill	Martha Washington	d.	PA	2 Feb. 1918	6	4	
Cowgill	Martha Washington	m.	SIT	9 Feb. 1918	1	6	
Cox	Alice	o.	SRR	25 Aug. 1916	3	3	
Cox	Charles J., Jr.	o.	SRR	25 Aug. 1916	3	3	
Cox	George	m.	HT	15 June 1916	2	4	
Cox	Willard S.	m.	PA	28 May 1917	5	1	
Cox	Willard S.	m.	PC	29 May 1917	8	2	
Cox	Willard S.	m.	PA	11 Apr. 1917	5	3	
Cozad	Cora	m.	SRR	14 Feb. 1917	8	6	also 12 Mar., 2:4
Cozad	Cora	m.	PD	15 Mar. 1917	2	3	
Cozad	Lulu E.	m.	SRR	29 Mar. 1917	3	3	
Cozzens	Emma Campbell	d.	PD	17 May 1918	3	3	

(1) Surname	(2) Given Name	(3)	(4)	(5) Date	(6) Pg	(7) Col	(8) Comments
Cozzens	Emma Campbell	d.	SIT	18 May 1918	1	6	Duala, Africa; also 20 July, 1:2
Cozzens	Emma Campbell	d.	PD	21 July 1918	6	3	Africa
Cozzens	Pearl Adele	m.	PD	29 June 1916	2	5	
Cragin	C. C.	d.	PD	29 Sept. 1917	5	3	also 30 Sept., 7:3; 2 Oct., 5:4
Cragin	Charles C.	d.	PC	31 Aug. 1917	1	5	
Craig	A. J.	d.	PC	28 Mar. 1918	1	3	Odd Fellows Cemetery, Sebastopol; also 30 Mar., 4:3
Craig	A. J.	d.	PD	28 Mar. 1918	5	4	
Craig	Albert G.	d.	PA	28 Mar. 1918	7	4	Sebastopol; also 29 Mar., 8:3
Craig	Edwin A.	m.	PD	30 July 1918	7	3	
Craig	Edwin Alfred	m.	HT	1 Aug. 1918	2	3	
Craigin	C. C.	d.	SIT	1 Sept. 1917	1	7	
Cramer	Lillian	d.	PA	21 Nov. 1918	5	4	Cypress Hill; also 22 Nov., 4:1; 23 Nov., 5:3; 25 Nov., 5:4
Cramer	Lillian	d.	PC	21 Nov. 1918	1	3	Cypress Hill; also 21 Nov., 8:3; 26 Nov., 4:4
Crandall	Ida May	d.	PA	30 Dec. 1918	4	4	Redding; also 31 Dec., 2:3
Crandall	Ida May	d.	PC	31 Dec. 1918	4	2	
Crandall	Jack, Mrs.	d.	PD	31 Dec. 1918	7	1	
Crane	Eva Grace	m.	PA	15 Oct. 1917	7	5	
Crane	Eva Grace	m.	SRR	15 Oct. 1917	5	3	
Crane	Grace	m.	PD	14 Oct. 1917	8	2	
Crane	Lawrence	b.	ST	5 Apr. 1918	5	5	
Crane	Lawrence Edgar	m.	SRR	7 July 1917	8	4	
Crane	Mildred	m.	SRR	16 June 1917	10	5	
Crane	Mildred	m.	PC	17 June 1917	5	1	
Crane	Rebecca	d.	PC	19 Mar. 1918	4	4	
Crane	Susan	d.	SIT	14 Dec. 1918	1	7	
Crane	William C.	d.	ST	21 Apr. 1917	1	2	Rural Cemetery
Crane	William C.	p.	ST	21 Apr. 1917	5	4	
Cravers	Anna	m.	PD	4 July 1917	2	2	
Crawford	Calvin A.	m.	ST	6 May 1916	1	5	
Crawford	Calvin A.	m.	PC	7 May 1916	2	2	
Crawford	Charles	m.	HT	24 May 1917	1	4	
Crawford	R. F.	o.	SRR	10 Aug. 1916	1	3	
Crawford	R. F.	d.	CR	17 Feb. 1917	1	3	
Crawford	Richard F.	p.	SRR	26 Feb. 1917	8	2	
Crawford	Richard F.	d.	HT	8 Feb. 1917	1	4	
Crawford	Richard F.	d.	PA	9 Feb. 1917	3	4	also 12 Feb., 6:3

(1) Surname	(2) Given Name	(3)	(4)	(5) Date	(6) Pg	(7) Col	(8) Comments
Crawford	Richard F.	d.	PC	9 Feb. 1917	1	6	also 10 Feb., 6:6; 14 Feb., 2:2
Crawford	Richard F.	d.	PD	9 Feb. 1917	8	1	portrait; also 10 Feb., 4:1; 13 Feb., 2:1; 6 Mar., 6:1
Crawford	Richard F.	d.	SRR	9 Feb. 1917	8	1	portrait
Crawford	Roy	m.	PD	26 Mar. 1916	1	2	
Crawford	Roy	m.	PA	27 Mar. 1916	2	6	
Crawford	Roy	m.	SRR	27 Mar. 1916	3	2	
Crawford	Roy	m.	PC	28 Mar. 1916	2	1	
Crawford	Roy S.	m.	ST	1 Apr. 1916	1	2	
Crayne	Rebecca	d.	PD	17 Mar. 1918	2	4	
Crayne	Rebecca	d.	ST	22 Mar. 1918	8	6	
Crayne	Steve	b.	PD	2 Aug. 1916	7	1	
Crayne	Steve	b.	PC	3 Aug. 1916	8	3	
Creagmile	John	m.	SRR	6 Sept. 1916	6	2	
Creagmile	John C.	m.	HT	7 Sept. 1916	1	4	
Creda	Ida C.	d.	ST	25 May 1917	8	4	
Creib	Mr.	d.	SRR	27 Apr. 1917	6	5	Mountain Cemetery
Cresap	Birdie S.	m.	PC	23 Sept. 1916	3	3	
Cresap	Birdie W.	m.	PA	22 Sept. 1916	8	4	
Crispin	Alice	m.	HT	17 Jan. 1918	1	2	
Crist	Chester B.	m.	SRR	2 May 1917	8	5	
Crist	Katherine	o.	SRR	28 Mar. 1916	2	3	
Crist	Walter J.	o.	SRR	28 Mar. 1916	2	3	
Crist	Walter T.	o.	SRR	8 Dec. 1917	3	3	
Crofta/Crosta	Matteo	d.	PA	2 May 1918	5	4	Tomales; also 4 May, 2:4
Crofta/Crosta	Matteo	d.	PC	3 May 1918	5	2&3	Tomales; also 4 May, 4:2
Crohare	Pierre	o.	PD	27 June 1918	7	3	
Croman	Edward J.	d.	PD	18 Apr. 1918	6	4	I.O.O.F. Cemeetery; also 19 Apr., 4:2; 23 Apr., 4:2
Cromwell	Pierce	m.	PD	25 July 1917	3	2	
Cromwell	Pierce	m.	PC	15 Sept. 1917	6	4	also 19 Oct., 4:1
Cromwell	Pierce Ellis	m.	PA	24 July 1917	2	5	also 28 July, 2:5
Cromwell	Pierce Ellis	m.	PC	25 July 1917	3	4	
Cromwell	Ralph	o.	PC	5 Aug. 1917	1	2	
Cromwell	William	d.	PD	9 Feb. 1918	6	5	
Cronin	Patrick	d.	PA	12 Aug. 1918	4	1&5	Calvary Cemetery; also 13 Aug., 5:5; 14 Aug., 4:5
Cronin	Patrick	d.	PC	13 Aug. 1918	6	3	also 15 Aug., 8:2
Cronin	Patrick	p.	PA	14 Aug. 1918	4	1	will
Cronin	Patrick	p.	PC	15 Aug. 1918	4	3	

(1) Surname	(2) Given Name	(3)	(4)	(5) Date	(6) Pg	(7) Col	(8) Comments
Cronin	Patrick	p.	PD	15 Aug. 1918	3	3	
Crook	Ernest	b.	PA	1 Oct. 1917	5	7	
Crooke	Mrs.	d.	PC	12 Jan. 1917	1	5	Bloomfield
Cross	Elzada	m.	PD	10 Dec. 1918	5	1	
Crossfield	Rose E.	d.	SRR	28 June 1917	8	2&5	Odd Fellows, Forestville; also 30 June, 4:5
Crossfield	Rose Estelle	d.	PC	29 June 1917	1	6	
Crossfield	Rose Estelle	d.	PD	29 June 1917	2	4	Odd Fellows Cemetery; also 4:3
Crosta	Peter	d.	PC	16 Apr. 1916	4	5	
Crosta	Peter	d.	PD	16 Apr. 1916	1	2	Tomales Cemetery
Crotts	Emily Kenton	d.	ST	17 Mar. 1917	1	6	
Crotts	Mrs.	d.	SRR	19 Mar. 1917	7	4	Masonic Cemetery, Sebastopol
Crowell	Elmer H.	m.	SRR	5 May 1917	10	4	
Crowell	Elmer H.	m.	HT	10 May 1917	1	5	
Crowell	Florence Pool	m.	PD	21 Dec. 1916	5	3	
Crowell	Florence Pool	m.	SRR	21 Dec. 1916	4	4	
Crowell	M. E., Mrs.	d.	SRR	12 May 1917	6	6	
Crowell	M. I., Mrs.	d.	PD	13 May 1917	2	4	
Cruzan	Donald E.	b.	SRR	22 May 1917	3	5	
Cruzan	Donald E.	b.	PC	24 May 1917	8	4	
Cruzan	Donald E.	b.	PD	23 May 1971	6	6	
Cruzan	Donald	b.	PA	22 May 1917	5	6	
Cudahy	J.	d.	PC	3 Dec. 1918	2	2	
Culbertson	Alexander	d.	PD	5 Jan. 1918	3	3	
Cullen	Fred	b.	PA	28 Dec. 1916	8	6	
Cullen	James	d.	PC	12 Dec. 1918	3	2	
Cullen	James C.	d.	PA	11 Dec. 1918	4	4	
Cummings	Anna	d.	PD	27 Jan. 1918	8	3	
Cummings	Anna M.	d.	PC	11 Aug. 1916	4	2	Santa Rosa
Cummings	Anna M.	d.	PD	11 Aug. 1916	5	4	Calvary Cemetery; also 12 Aug., 2:2
Cummings	Anna M.	d.	SRR	11 Aug. 1916	5	4	Calvary Cemetery
Cummings	Fred	d.	PD	2 July 1918	3	4	also 3 July, 5:3; 4 July, 5:5
Cummings	Fred	d.	HT	4 July 1918	1	4	
Cummings	George	m.	HT	1 Aug. 1918	1	3	
Cummings	George	o.	HT	8 Nov. 1917	8	4	
Cummings	Gordon	d.	ST	1 Feb. 1918	1	4	
Cummings	Gordon	d.	PC	3 Feb. 1918	6	4	
Cummings	Harry K.	d.	SRR	15 June 1916	8	4	also 19 June, 5:4
Cummings	Harry K.	d.	HT	22 June 1916	7	3	
Cummings	Rose	d.	SRR	4 Dec. 1916	8	3	
Cummings	Rose	d.	PC	5 Dec. 1916	8	1	

(1) Surname	(2) Given Name	(3)	(4)	(5) Date	(6) Pg	(7) Col	(8) Comments
Cummings	Thomas, Mrs.	d.	PA	11 Aug. 1916	4	5	
Cummins	Jhilson P.	d.	PD	3 Mar. 1918	8	1	also 5 Mar., 2:4
Cundiff	J.	d.	PC	4 June 1916	8	3	
Cuneo	Tony/Antonio	m.	PC	20 Apr. 1917	5	3	also 28 Apr., 6:3; 2 May, 5:4
Cunningham	Charles J.	b.	PA	7 Oct. 1916	5	2	
Cunningham	Hugh	b.	PA	12 May 1916	5	5	
Cunningham	M. A.	d.	PA	28 Dec. 1916	5	1	France (Canadian Army)
Cunningham	M. A.	d.	PC	30 Dec. 1916	8	3	France
Cunningham	Marion	d.	PC	1 Mar. 1918	7	4	Two Rock; also 8:4; 2 Mar., 7:4; 3 Mar., 6:3
Cunningham	Marion	d.	PA	2 Mar. 1918	4	3	Two Rock
Cunningham	Mary	d.	PD	14 Feb. 1917	4	2	Bloomfield; also 5:1
Cunningham	Mary Olivia	d.	PA	14 Feb. 1917	7	3	
Cunningham	Mary Olivia	d.	SRR	14 Feb. 1917	4	2	
Cunningham	Mary Olivia	d.	PC	15 Feb. 1917	3	4	also 17 Feb., 3:2
Cunningham	Mike	d.	PA	4 Oct. 1917	5	7	Canadian Army
Cunningham	Olivia	d.	ST	17 Feb. 1917	1	2	Bloomfield
Curley	Emery	d.	PA	12 June 1916	4	5	
Currari	Joseph S.	m.	SRR	28 Sept. 1917	7	5	
Curtin	Henry N.	m.	PC	29 Nov. 1917	5	6	
Curtis	Catherine	d.	PC	5 Feb. 1918	8	4	
Curtis	Catherine	d.	PD	5 Feb. 1918	2	2	Rural Cemetery; also 4:2; 6 Feb., 5:3
Curtis	Charles C.	m.	SRR	29 Aug. 1917	6	2	
Curtis	Charley C.	m.	PD	30 Aug. 1917	8	3	
Curtis	Katharine	d.	PA	2 Feb. 1918	4	4	Santa Rosa; also 5 Feb., 4:3; 6 Feb., 7:5
Curtis	Peter L.	m.	SRR	25 Apr. 1916	8	5	
Cutter	Mary	o.	PC	22 Jan. 1916	1	3	
Cutter	Mary Carey	d.	PD	22 Jan. 1916	3	4	Mountain Cemetery
Cutter	Mary Carey	d.	SRR	22 Jan. 1916	5	1	

D

(1) Surname	(2) Given Name	(3)	(4)	(5) Date	(6) Pg	(7) Col	(8) Comments
Dabner	Frank	d.	PA	20 Nov. 1918	5	1	France; also 21 Nov., 5:1
Dabner	Frank	d.	PD	21 Nov. 1918	2	1	France
Dabner	Frank (Avilla)	d.	PC	21 Nov. 1918	1	4	France; also 22 Nov., 1:6
Dabner	Jesse	o.	PC	9 June 1918	8	4	
Dabner	Jesse	o.	PC	25 Oct. 1918	2	3	
Dado	Olivia	d.	PA	13 Dec. 1918	1	5	Calvary Cemetery; also 14 Dec., 4:7, 6:4, 8:5; 16 Dec., 4:1
Dado	Olivia	d.	PC	14 Dec. 1918	5	4	Calvary Cemetery; also 15 Dec., 5:4; 17 Dec., 5:4
Dado	Paul	o.	PA	20 Sept. 1918	5	2	
Dado	Paul	o.	PC	20 Sept. 1918	1	3	
Dafoe	E. E., Mrs.	d.	PD	4 Nov. 1916	4	4	
Dahling	H.	d.	PC	4 Aug. 1917	5	4	
Dahlman	Alba	m.	PC	25 Jan. 1916	3	1	also 6 Jan. 4:1
Dahlmann	Georgia Wilma	m.	PC	8 Sept. 1917	5	3	also 15 Sept., 5:2; 16 Sept., 1:5
Dahlman	Georgia Wilma	m.	PD	9 Sept. 1917	2	1	also 16 Sept., 3:3
Dahlmann	Alba	m.	PD	26 Jan. 1916	3	2	
Dahlmann	Alba F.	m.	PA	6 Jan. 1916	5	2	also 22 Jan., 7:4; 24 Jan., 5:4
Dahlmann	Clara	m.	PA	14 July 1917	5	3	
Dahlmann	Clara	m.	PC	15 July 1917	4	3	
Dahlmann	Georgia Wilma	m.	PA	7 Sept. 1917	5	4	also 15 Sept., 3:3
Dahlmann	Georgia Wilma	m.	SRR	8 Sept. 1917	8	5	
Dahring	Frederick S.	o.	SIT	5 Oct. 1918	2	6	
Dairdson	Adele E.	m.	PD	29 Sept. 1916	2	1	
Daito	N.	d.	PA	13 May 1918	7	3	
Daitoku	N.	d.	PD	12 May 1918	6	1	
Dake/Drake	Adah V.	m.	PD	6 Dec. 1918	1	6	also 3:1
Dakin/Deakin	Mr.	m.	SIT	7 July 1917	1	5	
Dal Pogetto	Newton	o.	SIT	19 Jan. 1918	1	4	
Dalbon	G.	d.	SIT	14 Apr. 1917	4	1	
Dalessi	Walter	o.	PC	1 Dec. 1918	3	3	
Dalessi	Walter	o.	PA	30 Nov. 1918	4	3	
Dall Pino	Guiseppe	o.	PD	9 June 1917	7	5	
Dall Pino	Mary	o.	PD	9 June 1917	7	5	
Dalos	John	b.	SRR	2 Feb. 1917	8	5	
Dalton	F. G.	m.	PC	27 Aug. 1917	3	4	also 31 Aug., 3:2; 2 Sept., 5:5

(1) Surname	(2) Given Name	(3)	(4)	(5) Date	(6) Pg	(7) Col	(8) Comments
Dalton	Graham	o.	PC	12 July 1918	2	1	
Dalton	Graham	o.	PD	13 July 1918	2	1	
Dalton	S. G.	m.	PA	1 Sept. 1917	3	5	
Dalton	S. G.	m.	PA	25 Aug. 1917	5	3	also 31 Aug., 4:4
Dalton	Thomas B.	d.	PA	14 Nov. 1916	5	4	Cypress Lawn, San Mateo; also 15 Nov., 2:4
Dalton	Thomas Benton	d.	PD	26 Nov. 1916	10	2	
Daly	James R., Jr.	m.	ST	28 Sept. 1917	1	3	
Daly	Jane	d.	SRR	19 Feb. 1917	5	4	
Daly	Jane	d.	PD	20 Feb. 1917	2	5	
Daly	Jane	d.	SRR	20 Feb. 1917	6	3	
D'Ambrogi	Cecil	d.	PA	2 Sept. 1918	4	4	Calvary Cemetery; also 4 Sept., 1:3, 5:5
D'Ambrogi	Cecil	d.	PD	4 Sept. 1918	5	3	
D'Ambrogia	Cecil	d.	PC	4 Sept. 1918	8	2&3	Calvary Cemetery; also 5 Sept., 6:5; 6 Sept., 4:4
Damcke	Otto	d.	SRR	8 July 1916	7	3	Sebastopol Masonic Cemetery
Damcke	Otto Rogers	d.	PD	8 July 1916	5	1	Masonic Cemetery; 16 yrs.
Damke	Otto, Jr.	d.	ST	15 July 1916	1	3	
Damonti	Rosalia	d.	PD	1 May 1917	1	4	also 2:1; 2 May, 2:3
Damonti	Rosalia	d.	SRR	30 Apr. 1917	6	4	
Damonti/Monti	Rosa	d.	SRR	30 Apr. 1917	6	4	
Dangers	Diedrich	o.	PA	4 Oct. 1916	5	4	
Dangers	Diedrich	o.	SRR	5 Oct. 1916	5	3	
Dangers	Hermine	o.	PA	4 Oct. 1916	5	4	
Dangers	Hermine	o.	SRR	5 Oct. 1916	5	3	
Danhausen	Meta	d.	PD	4 Aug. 1917	2	4	Calvary Cemetery; also 4:2
Daniels	Elsie K.	d.	PD	1 Dec. 1917	7	1	
Daniels	Elsie K.	d.	HT	6 Dec. 1917	3	1	
Daniels	Lloyd	d.	PC	29 May 1918	1	4	
Daniels	Lloyd	d.	PD	29 May 1918	2	4	also 6 June, 2:4
Daniels	Rosalina	d.	PA	3 July 1916	2	3	Cypress Lawn, San Mateo
Daniels	Rosaltha Miranda	d.	PC	2 July 1916	4	3	
Dankin	Henry	o.	SRR	24 Aug. 1916	8	2	
Dannhausen	Meta	d.	SRR	3 Aug. 1917	4	4	
Danugers	Diedrich	o.	PC	14 July 1916	6	3	
Danugers	Hermine	o.	PC	14 July 1916	6	3	
Darby	Floyd	m.	HT	14 June 1917	6	3	
Darden	Charles E.	d.	PD	11 Apr. 1918	2	3	Rural Cemetery; also 4:2; 13 Apr., 7:5

(1) Surname	(2) Given Name	(3)	(4)	(5) Date	(6) Pg	(7) Col	(8) Comments
Darden	Rena	m.	PA	20 Sept. 1918	5	4	
Darden	William H.	d.	PA	15 May 1918	4	1	Two Rock; also 16 May, 8:3; 17 May, 4:4, 8:3; 18 May, 4:6
Darden	William H.	d.	PC	16 May 1918	8	3	Cypress Hill; also 17 May, 4:1; 18 May, 2:2; 19 May, 8:4
Darden	William H.	d.	PD	16 May 1918	7	4	Two Rock; also 18 May, 8:3
Darling	Elvin Charles	d.	SRR	17 Mar. 1917	10	1	I.O.O.F. Cemetery; also 19 Mar., 8:3
Darling	Elvin Charles	d.	PD	18 Mar. 1917	4	3	I.O.O.F. Cemetery; also 9:3; 20 Mar., 5:2
Darling	Elvin Charles	d.	PA	19 Mar. 1917	7	4	I.O.O.F. Cemetery, Santa Rosa; also 20 Mar., 5:1
Darling	L. E.	o.	SIT	11 Aug. 1917	1	2	
Daroux	Mae	m.	PD	23 Dec. 1917	3	4	
Daroux	Mae	m.	SRR	24 Dec. 1917	9	4	
Daunt	Lozelle	m.	PA	30 Oct. 1917	4	3	
Daut	Jeanette	m.	SRR	17 June 1916	4	2	also 19 June, 4:1
Daut	Jeanette	m.	PD	31 Oct. 1916	2	3	
Davello	Antonio	m.	ST	18 Nov. 1916	1	4	
Davello	Joseph L.	m.	SRR	14 July 1917	4	3	
Davello	Tony J.	m.	PC	14 Nov. 1916	8	3	also 21 Nov., 2:2
Davi	Horace	m.	SRR	6 Dec. 1917	8	6	
David	Mr.	m.	PC	7 Feb. 1916	5	3	
Davidson	James	b.	PC	10 Oct. 1916	1	5	also 12 Oct., 4:6
Davidson	James	d.	PD	10 Oct. 1916	8	2	
Davidson	James	d.	PA	9 Oct. 1916	8	2	Cypress Hill; also 11 Oct., 1:6
Davidson	Mabel	d.	PC	3 Dec. 1918	3	4	
Davidson	V. O.	d.	PC	5 Nov. 1918	6	3	
Davies	A.	d.	PA	11 May 1916	1	5	
Davies	Albert	d.	PD	12 May 1916	2	3	
Davies	Albert	d.	ST	13 May 1916	1	5	Masonic Cemetery
Davies	Alfred	d.	PC	12 May 1916	4	3	
Davis	A. C.	b.	PD	9 Sept. 1916	4	6	
Davis	A. C.	b.	PD	8 Sept. 1916	6	6	
Davis	Alfred	o.	PC	3 July 1918	3	3	
Davis	Alfred A.	o.	PA	2 Aug. 1918	8	3	
Davis	Alfred A.	o.	PD	2 Aug. 1918	3	4	
Davis	Alice	o.	SRR	9 Oct. 1916	8	1	
Davis	Alice A.	o.	PD	19 Oct. 1916	3	4	
Davis	Alice Aitro	o.	SRR	14 July 1916	8	3	
Davis	Alice Albro	o.	SRR	18 Oct. 1916	8	4	

(1) Surname	(2) Given Name	(3)	(4)	(5) Date	(6) Pg	(7) Col	(8) Comments
Davis	Alice Albro	o.	SRR	23 Oct. 1917	10	3	
Davis	Alice Allen	o.	PD	25 Oct. 1917	7	2	
Davis	Ann	d.	SRR	7 Feb. 1916	8	6	
Davis	Ann	d.	PD	8 Feb. 1916	3	3	
Davis	August N.	o.	PD	8 Jan. 1916	6	3	
Davis	Calude H.	d.	PA	4 June 1917	5	2	Cypress Hill; also 6:4; 6 June, 5:3; 7 June, 5:7
Davis	Charles	d.	ST	9 Dec. 1916	1	5	
Davis	Charles A.	d.	PD	8 Dec. 1916	5	1	
Davis	Claude	d.	SRR	6 June 1917	5	4	
Davis	Claude	d.	PC	7 June 1917	8	2 & 5	Cypress Hill; also 8 June, 5:5; 9 June, 2:1
Davis	Claude H.	d.	PC	5 June 1917	8	3	
Davis	Claude H.	d.	PD	5 June 1917	7	2	
Davis	Donald S.	o.	ST	26 July 1918	8	1	
Davis	Elvira Evelyn	d.	PC	11 Feb. 1916	5	4	
Davis	F. M.	o.	SRR	15 May 1917	2	3	
Davis	Fabitha J	d.	SRR	26 Feb. 1917	4	6	also 8:2
Davis	Floyd	m.	SRR	1 Dec. 1916	8	5	
Davis	Floyd	m.	PC	29 Nov. 1916	5	1	
Davis	Floyd	m.	ST	9 Dec. 1916	1	2	
Davis	Floyd F.	m.	PD	28 Nov. 1916	7	3	also 30 Nov., 8:3; 2 Dec., 6:4
Davis	George	b.	PD	18 Jan. 1916	3	5	
Davis	Gladys	o.	SRR	15 May 1917	2	3	
Davis	Gladys	m.	SRR	6 June 1917	3	3	
Davis	Gladys	m.	SRR	2 Jan. 1917	6	4	
Davis	Gladys	m.	PD	3 Jan. 1917	5	2	
Davis	Gladys	o.	PD	8 Jan. 1916	6	3	
Davis	H. A.	d.	PD	13 June 1918	5	3	
Davis	Harry O.	m.	SRR	29 July 1916	10	4	
Davis	Harry O.	m.	SRR	27 Sept. 1916	5	3	
Davis	Harry O.	m.	PC	28 Sept. 1916	3	4	
Davis	Henrietta	m.	SRR	8 Nov. 1916	8	5	also 9 Nov., 2:1
Davis	Henrietta Lydia	m.	PD	9 Nov. 1916	6	4	
Davis	Horace	m.	PD	7 Dec. 1917	6	4	
Davis	Howard O.	b.	HT	20 Jan. 1916	5	3	
Davis	Joe	b.	ST	2 Nov. 1917	5	1	
Davis	Joe	o.	PA	22 Nov. 1918	3	6	also 5:4
Davis	John	o.	SRR	9 Oct. 1916	8	1	
Davis	John M.	o.	SRR	14 July 1916	8	3	
Davis	John M.	o.	SRR	18 Oct. 1916	8	4	
Davis	John M.	o.	PD	19 Oct. 1916	3	4	
Davis	John M.	o.	SRR	23 Oct. 1917	10	3	
Davis	John M.	o.	PD	25 Oct. 1917	7	2	

(1) Surname	(2) Given Name	(3)	(4)	(5) Date	(6) Pg	(7) Col	(8) Comments
Davis	Joseph	o.	PC	23 Nov. 1918	5	1	
Davis	Julius A.	d.	PA	25 Mar. 1916	5	2	Cypress Lawn, San Mateo Co.
Davis	Lottie	d.	PD	22 Feb. 1916	8	4	Rural Cemetery
Davis	Marie Louise	m.	SRR	6 Oct. 1916	4	1	
Davis	Mary	m.	PD	15 Jan. 1916	5	3	
Davis	Mary Ore	d.	PD	23 Mar. 1918	6	4	also 24 Mar., 4:2
Davis	Mary Ore	d.	PC	24 Mar. 1918	2	2	
Davis	Mary Ore	d.	ST	29 Mar. 1918	3	3	Fulton
Davis	Milton M.	m.	PD	14 Sept. 1916	3	5	
Davis	Minnie	d.	SRR	28 Feb. 1916	3	5	
Davis	Minnie	d.	PD	29 Feb. 1916	4	1	Odd Fellows Cemetery
Davis	Morrison	d.	PA	19 May 1916	4	3	
Davis	Morrison Joseph	d.	PC	18 May 1916	1	5	Calvary Cemetery; also 20 May, 8:4
Davis	Ruby	m.	HT	11 July 1918	2	2	
Davis	Susan R.	o.	PA	2 Aug. 1918	8	3	
Davis	Susan R.	o.	PD	2 Aug. 1918	3	4	
Davis	Tabitha	d.	PD	27 Feb. 1917	2	4	also 4:2
Davis	Tabitha J.	d.	ST	3 Mar. 1917	1	4	
Davis	Walter	d.	PD	19 Oct. 1916	8	3	also 20 Oct., 8:4; 21 Oct., 3:1; portrait
Davis	Walter F.	d.	PA	18 Oct. 1916	5	6	
Davis	Walter S.	d.	SRR	18 Oct. 1916	8	1	also 18 Oct., 5:2; 20 Oct., 4:4
Davis	Walter S.	d.	PC	19 Oct. 1916	8	4	
Davison	Harry Waite	d.	PC	6 July 1918	5	3	Bloomfield; also 8:4; 9 July, 4:3
Davison	Henry Waite	d.	PD	6 July 1918	8	3	Bloomfield
Davison	Henry Waite	d.	ST	12 July 1918	6	2	
Davison	Henry Walter	d.	PA	5 July 1918	5	6	Bloomfield; also 8 July, 8:4
Dawson	W.	d.	PC	7 Mar. 1918	4	4	St. Helena
Dawson	W. J. G.	d.	SIT	9 Mar. 1918	1	3	
Dawson	William	d.	PD	5 Mar. 1918	1	7	also 8:3; 6 Mar., 8:4; 7 Mar., 3:1
Dawson	William J. G.	d.	PA	5 Mar. 1918	8	3	St. Helena; also 6 Mar., 4:4; 7 Mar., 3:3
Day	Fillemore	d.	PA	27 Mar. 1916	8	2	
Day	Filmore	d.	PC	26 Mar. 1916	1	2	
Day	Laura	m.	HT	20 Oct. 1916	1	5	
Day	Laura	m.	SRR	21 Oct. 1916	7	4	
Day	Laura	m.	PD	24 Oct. 1916	5	2	
Day	Marjorie	d.	HT	10 Aug. 1916	1	6	
Day	Marjorie	d.	SRR	7 Aug. 1916	1	3	
Day	Marjorie M.	d.	PC	6 Aug. 1916	3	4	also 8 Aug., 4:1

(1) Surname	(2) Given Name	(3)	(4)	(5) Date	(6) Pg	(7) Col	(8) Comments
Day	Marjorie M.	d.	PA	7 Aug. 1916	6	4	
Day	Marjorie M.	d.	PD	8 Aug. 1916	2	1	San Francisco for cremation; also 9 Aug., 5:4
Deacon	Fred	d.	PA	22 Jan. 1916	5	1	
Deady	David	d.	PC	30 Dec. 1916	5	3	
Deakin	Daisy D.	m.	PD	6 Dec. 1918	8	2	also 8 Dec., 8:2
Deakin	Henry	o.	PD	1 Oct. 1916	5	5	
Deakin	Henry	o.	PA	9 Oct. 1917	3	6	
Deakin	Margaretha	o.	PA	10 Oct. 1917	3	6	
Deakin	Margaret	o.	PD	1 Oct. 1916	5	5	
Deakin	Margaretha	o.	SRR	24 Aug. 1916	8	2	
Deakin	Mr.	m.	PD	8 July 1917	2	2	
Dean	Grace	d.	PC	24 May 1917	1	6	Cypress Hill; also 25 May, 3:4; 26 May, 6:4
Dean	Grace	d.	PD	25 May 1917	7	5	
Dean	Grace Vivien	d.	PA	25 May 1917	4	4	
Dean	John W.	m.	HT	22 Nov. 1917	5	3	
Dean	Leslie	b.	PD	10 Feb. 1916	8	2	
Dean	Leslie	b.	PA	9 Feb. 1916	1	6	also 8:3
Dean	Oliver	m.	SRR	2 June 1917	8	3	also 6 June, 6:3
Dean	Oliver	m.	HT	7 June 1917	5	4	
Deane	Genevieve	m.	PD	5 Nov. 1916	5	5	
Deane	Genevieve	m.	SRR	6 Nov. 1916	5	4	
Dearborn	Alice	m.	PD	8 Nov. 1917	5	3	
Dearborn	Edith Alice	m.	SRR	7 Nov. 1917	8	1	
Debats	A.	d.	PD	19 Aug. 1917	8	3	
DeBora	A.	b.	PC	2 May 1916	8	4	
DeCarli	Robert	d.	PC	14 Mar. 1917	3	6	
DeCarli	Robert	b.	PA	9 Mar. 1917	5	5	
DeCarli	Robert (son of)	b&d	PA	26 May 1916	4	1	also 27 May, 8:5
DeCarli	Robert D.	b.	PC	10 Mar. 1917	8	4	
Decker	Mary	d.	SRR	20 Mar. 1916	5	1	cremation; also 21 Mar., 7:4
Decker	Mary Jane	d.	PD	19 Mar. 1916	5	1	Oakland; also 21 Mar., 5:6; 22 Mar., 6:3
Decker	Mary Jane	d.	PC	21 Mar. 1916	3	3	
Decker	Vera	m.	PA	5 July 1916	7	4	
Deckert	Vera	m.	PC	6 July 1916	5	1	
Decket	Vera	m.	SRR	5 July 1916	1	4	
DeClercq	Arthur R.	d.	PC	2 May 1918	6	4	
DeClerq	Alfred	d.	PA	1 May 1918	8	3	
DeClerq	Alfred	d.	PD	1 May 1918	8	1	also 2 May, 2:5; 3 May, 8:2
DeClerq	Alfred	d.	SIT	11 May 1918	3	5	
Dedignatti	Ruth	d.	PA	12 Sept. 1917	1	6	

(1) Surname	(2) Given Name	(3)	(4)	(5) Date	(6) Pg	(7) Col	(8) Comments
Deegan	John	d.	PC	1 Sept. 1916	1	5	San Francisco; also 2 Sept., 8:5
Deegan	John	d.	SRR	2 Sept. 1916	6	3	
Deegan	John	d.	PA	29 Aug. 1916	4	4	
Deevey	Dan (son of)	b&d	PA	6 May 1916	3	5	
Deevey	Dan (son of)	b&d	PC	6 May 1916	8	1	
DeFries	Gertrude	m.	PC	1 May 1917	5	3	
DeFries	Gertrude	m.	PD	1 May 1917	8	3	also 2 May, 7:3
DeFries	Gertrude	m.	SRR	30 Apr. 1917	5	3	
DeGoover	Henry	m.	PC	8 Dec. 1918	6	3	
DeGooyer	Henry	m.	ST	6 Dec. 1918	1	5	
DeHay	Jeanette	m.	PD	5 May 1917	2	6	
Dehay	Jeanette	m.	SRR	5 May 1917	3	5	
Dehay	Jeanette	m.	CR	11 May 1917	1	5	
DeHay	Wendell	b.	CR	29 Nov. 1918	8	2	
Dehling	H.	d.	PA	3 Aug. 1917	5	5	
Dehling	Henry	d.	PD	4 Aug. 1917	8	3	
Dei	Felmore	d.	SRR	27 Mar. 1916	5	1	
Dei	Gaetoni	d.	PD	26 Apr. 1917	4	2	Bodega; also 27 Apr., 4:3
Dei	Gaetoni	d.	SRR	26 Apr. 1917	8	6	
Dei	Leonard	o.	SRR	4 Mar. 1916	1	5	
Deis	Felmore	d.	PD	28 Mar. 1916	3	5	Calvary Cemetery, Bodega
Del	Gaetoni	d.	PA	26 Apr. 1917	5	4	
Del	Henry	o.	PC	8 Dec. 1917	3	3	
Del Paggetto	Newton	o.	SIT	14 Mar. 1918	1	5	also 4 May, 1:3
Del Poggetio	E.	b.	PD	19 July 1916	8	2	
Delahy	Andrew	d.	PA	23 Sept. 1916	1	1	
Delahy	Andrew	d.	PC	24 Sept. 1916	1	4	
DeLaMotte	Harry	d.	PC	31 Jan. 1918	3	3	
Delany	Andrew	d.	HT	29 Sept. 1916	2	5	
Delmarty	Noel	d.	PA	25 Oct. 1917	5	4	France
DelMeastro	Al	b.	PA	5 Nov. 1917	8	8	
DeLong	Gertrude	m.	SRR	13 Sept. 1916	8	2	also 18 Sept., 2:4
Delong	Gertrude	m.	PD	17 Sept. 1916	8	3	
DeLong	Gertrude	m.	SRR	7 Aug. 1916	5	1	
DeLong	Gertrude	m.	PC	8 Aug. 1916	4	2	
DelPorto	Fulton	o.	SIT	19 Oct. 1918	2	3	
deMartin	Lillian	d.	PC	4 Jan. 1916	1	5	Catholic Cemetery, Martinez
DeMartini	Emilio	d.	SRR	24 Feb. 1916	5	2	
Demartini	Frank	d.	PA	17 May 1916	4	1	
DeMartini	Frank	d.	PD	17 May 1916	8	1	S. F.
Demartini	Frank	d.	SRR	17 May 1916	4	6	

(1) Surname	(2) Given Name	(3)	(4)	(5) Date	(6) Pg	(7) Col	(8) Comments
Demartini	Frank	d.	PC	18 May 1916	3	3	
DeMartini	Frank	d.	ST	20 May 1916	1	5	
DeMartini	Louis	d.	PA	28 Sept. 1917	4	5	also 1 Oct., 4:3
DeMartini	Louis	d.	PC	29 Sept. 1917	2	2	Calvary Cemetery; also 4:3; 30 Sept., 2:2, 3:6; 2 Oct., 4:3
DeMartini	M., Mrs.	d.	HT	8 Nov. 1916	6	5	
DeMartini	M., Mrs.	d.	SRR	9 Nov. 1916	3	3	
Demenzet	Joseph	d.	ST	28 Oct. 1916	6	5	
Demeo	Joseph	d.	SRR	2 Feb. 1917	5	5	
Demeo	Joseph	d.	PD	3 Feb. 1917	5	2	Calvary Cemetery; also 6 Feb., 3:3
Demmick	O. E.	b.	PD	31 July 1918	6	5	
Demmick	Orville E.	b.	PD	14 Aug. 1916	8	2	
Dempke	Otto	d.	SRR	7 July 1916	8	3	
Dempsey	George	d.	PD	21 Dec. 1918	2	3	
Denahy	Gertrude	m.	PD	26 Aug. 1917	3	5	
DeNeuf	Mignon	m.	PC	26 Mar. 1916	4	4	
DeNeuf	Pauline	m.	PA	25 Mar. 1916	4	3	
Denham	Drury	m.	SRR	13 June 1916	5	1	
Denham	Frank	m.	PC	11 Oct. 1918	5	4	also 13 Oct., 4:4
Denham	Frank	d.	PD	13 Oct. 1918	8	3	France
Denham	Frank	d.	PA	14 Oct. 1918	5	3	France
Denham	Frank P.	m.	PA	12 Oct. 1918	8	5	
Denise	Vivian	m.	HT	5 Dec. 1918	1	2	
Denman	Isabel	d.	PA	14 Sept. 1917	8	5	also 18 Sept., 2:3
Denman	Isabel	d.	PD	15 Sept. 1917	6	5	
Denman	Isabel	p.	PA	19 Sept. 1917	7	4	
Denman	Isabel	p.	PC	20 Sept. 1917	3	4	
Denman	Isabelle	d.	PC	15 Sept. 1917	8	3	
Denner	Alfred	m.	PC	2 Mar. 1918	3	6	
Dennes	William	d.	HT	28 Nov. 1918	7	2	
Denney	Joseph G.	o.	PC	15 Jan. 1916	1	1&2	
Denney	Joseph G.	d.	PC	18 Jan. 1916	8	4	Cypress Hill
Denney	Joseph Gilbert	d.	PA	15 Jan. 1916	5	1&2	also 17 Jan., 4:3
Denning	Earle E.	m.	PC	6 May 1916	2	1	
Dennis	Walter	d.	PA	21 Nov. 1918	2	3	Santa Rosa
Dennis	Walter aka William Whan	d.	PD	21 Nov. 1918	6	2	Stanley's Cemetery; also 8:2; 22 Nov., 1:2
Dennison	Cynthia	d.	SRR	27 Sept. 1916	3	3	Rural Cemetery; also 28 Sept., 8:5
Dennison	Cynthia	m.	PC	28 Sept. 1916	4	6	
Dennison	Cynthia	d.	PD	28 Sept. 1916	5	4	
Dennison	L. D.	m.	SIT	24 Feb. 1916	1	4	also 4 Mar., 3:5
Denny	Joseph G.	d.	PD	16 Jan. 1916	2	2	

(1) Surname	(2) Given Name	(3)	(4)	(5) Date	(6) Pg	(7) Col	(8) Comments
Denny	Joseph Gilbert	d.	HT	20 Jan. 1916	4	2	
Denny	Margaret	d.	PA	27 Mar. 1917	5	2	
Denny	Margaret	d.	PC	28 Mar. 1917	1	5	
Denny	Margaret	d.	PD	28 Mar. 1917	4	2	
Denny	Margaret	d.	SRR	28 Mar. 1917	5	1	
Denton	Hazel	m.	PD	22 May 1918	8	2	also 23 May, 5:4
Denton	Ora W.	m.	PC	28 Dec. 1916	5	5	also 30 Dec., 3:3
DePauli	Maria	m.	PD	3 Apr. 1917	8	2	
DePuncia	Joseph	d.	PC	29 Feb. 1916	4	3	Calvary Cemetery
Derborn	Frank	d.	PD	22 Oct. 1918	6	4	
DeRosa	Lenora	m.	PC	11 June 1916	4	2	also 14 June, 4:2
DeRosa	Manuel	m.	SRR	2 Apr. 1917	5	2	
DeRosa	Manuel	b.	PA	21 Mar. 1918	4	5	
DeRosa	Manuel	m.	PA	3 Apr. 1917	3	7	
DeRosa	Manuel	m.	PC	3 Apr. 1917	3	5	
DeRose	Lenora	m.	PA	10 June 1916	4	2	
DeRose	Lenora	m.	PD	14 June 1916	3	3	
DeRose	Manuel	m.	ST	7 Apr. 1917	3	2	
Derrick	Joseph A.	d.	SRR	14 June 1917	6	4	Oak Mound Cemetery
Derrick	Joseph H.	d.	PD	16 June 1917	6	4	
DeSelles	H. L.	b.	PD	10 Aug. 1918	3	4	
Deskin	Geneva	m.	PD	10 Mar. 1916	2	2	
Detro	John	d.	SRR	10 Jan. 1916	8	6	
Detro	John	d.	PD	11 Jan. 1916	2	4	
Devenceni	Theresa	d.	PC	24 May 1916	1	2	
Devencinsi	Theresa	d.	PA	23 May 1916	1	6	
Devereaux	Richard	d.	PD	5 Mar. 1918	8	2	
Devoia	Manuel	d.	PC	10 Mar. 1918	1	3	
DeVota	Hazel H.	m.	PC	11 July 1918	6	3	
DeVota	Louis	d.	PC	5 Apr. 1918	1	2	
Devoto	David, Jr.	b.	PD	1 Apr. 1917	5	5	
Devoto	David, Jr.	b.	SRR	31 Mar. 1917	2	5	
DeVoto	Hazel	m.	PD	11 July 1918	5	4	
Dewer	Victor R.	m.	PD	2 Nov. 1916	2	2	also 4 Nov., 7:2
Dewey	Beryl Marie	m.	SRR	18 May 1917	1	4	also 21 May, 6:4
Dewey	Beryl Marie	m.	PD	19 May 1917	8	1	
Dewey	Beryl Marie	m.	HT	24 May 1917	5	2	
Dewey	Victor R.	m.	SRR	2 Nov. 1916	3	2	
Dewey	Victor R.	m.	HT	3 Nov. 1916	1	6	
Dianda	D.	p.	PD	3 June 1917	6	3	
Dianda	Domenico	d.	PA	14 May 1917	7	3	
Dianda	Domenico	d.	SRR	14 May 1917	1	2	also 15 May, 8:1
Dibble	Adelle	d.	PD	1 Sept. 1916	5	5	Odd Fellows Cemetery, Sebastopol
Dibble	Dell	d.	ST	2 Sept. 1916	1	2	I.O.O.F. Cemetery

(1) Surname	(2) Given Name	(3)	(4)	(5) Date	(6) Pg	(7) Col	(8) Comments
Dibble	Delle	d.	SRR	31 Aug. 1916	8	5	
Dick	Agnes	m.	ST	1 Jan. 1916	1	1	
Dicke	Carl	o.	HT	22 Aug. 1918	1	2	
Dicke	George	b.	HT	2 Aug. 1917	2	3	
Dicker	Mary Jane	d.	PA	20 Mar. 1916	4	6	
Dickerson	Melvin Rosell	d.	SRR	2 Oct. 1916	7	3	also 8:1
Dickerson	Roe	d.	PD	1 Oct. 1916	8	2	also 3 Oct., 3:3
Dickey	Bessie	m.	PD	21 Nov. 1916	6	4	
Dickey	Bessie E.	m.	SRR	20 Nov. 1916	8	5	
Dickey	George	m.	PC	16 July 1916	1	5	
Dickey	George	m.	PA	18 July 1916	3	4	
Dickey	Phil	d.	HT	1 June 1916	5	3	
Dickman	Charles	o.	PC	19 Nov. 1916	5	5	
Dickman	Charlotta	o.	PC	19 Nov. 1916	5	5	
Dickson	Blair	d.	SRR	1 May 1916	8	3	
Dickson	Blair	d.	SRR	3 May 1916	10	5	
Dickson	Blair W.	d.	PD	3 May 1916	5	3	also 4 May, 6:4
Dickson	Clara Howard	d.	SRR	30 Jan. 1917	4	6	
Dickson	Clara Leslie	d.	PA	30 Jan. 1917	6	4	Sebastopol
Dickson	Frank Morris	m.	PA	18 June 1917	8	5	also 25 June, 2:5
Dickson	Robert	b.	PA	12 Apr. 1918	8	2&5	
Dietze	Ena	m.	PC	7 June 1917	5	2	
Dieu	John	m.	PD	19 Oct. 1917	5	4	
Dilena	Simeon	m.	PA	29 Oct. 1917	4	2	
Dilena	Simon	m.	PC	28 Oct. 1917	8	5	also 30 Oct., 3:4
Dillon	Mary	d.	PA	7 Dec. 1918	4	4	Tomales; also 9 Dec., 4:4
Dillon	Mary	d.	PC	8 Dec. 1918	5	3	also 10 Dec., 4:4
Dillon	Matilda	d.	PA	29 Jan. 1918	7	4	Calvary Cemetery; also 31 Jan., 8:6
Dillon	Matilda	d.	PC	29 Jan. 1918	4	3	Calvary Cemetery; also 5:5; 4 Feb., 5:4
Dimmick	Charity Frances	d.	SRR	17 Jan. 1916	8	1	also 18 Jan., 8:5
Dimmick	Charity Frances Callison	d.	PD	18 Jan. 1916	7	2	
Dimmick	George W.	d.	PD	21 Aug. 1917	5	1	Rural Cemetery; also 22 Aug., 4:2; 23 Aug., 2:4
Dimmick	George W.	d.	SRR	21 Aug. 1917	4	3	also 22 Aug., 8:3
Dimmick	O. E.	b.	SRR	14 Aug. 1916	1	2	
Dinucci	Mary	d.	SRR	13 Dec. 1917	8	5	
Disbrow	Emily	m.	SIT	30 Mar. 1918	1	6	
Disbrow	Emily	m.	PC	4 Apr. 1918	3	3	
Divis	Alfred A.	o.	PA	18 June 1918	3	2	
Divis	Susan	o.	PA	18 June 1918	3	2	
Dixon	Clara	d.	PC	28 Jan. 1917	8	1	Sebastopol

(1) Surname	(2) Given Name	(3)	(4)	(5) Date	(6) Pg	(7) Col	(8) Comments
Dixon	George E.	o.	PD	18 June 1918	5	6	
Dixon	Helen	m.	SRR	27 June 1916	8	2	
Dixon	Helen	m.	SRR	1 July 1916	4	2	
Dixon	Helen Louise	m.	PD	28 June 1916	6	1	
Dixon	Helen Louise	m.	PD	2 July 1916	2	2	
Dixon	Laura	o.	PD	18 June 1918	5	6	
Dixon	Walter C.	m.	SRR	4 May 1917	8	5	also 5 May, 4:2
Dixon	Walter C.	m.	PD	5 May 1917	2	3	
Doane	Emma Lydia	d.	PD	19 Jan. 1918	5	3	Carson City, NV; also 20 Jan., 5:3
Doane	Marian	d.	SRR	22 June 1917	8	3	
Dobbel	Dorothy	m.	SIT	27 July 1918	1	4	
Dobbel	Dorothy	m.	SIT	16 Feb. 1918	1	5	
Dobbel	Dorothy	m.	PD	19 Feb. 1918	5	3	
Dobbel	Dorothy Catherine	m.	PD	21 July 1918	5	3	
Dobbel	Dorothy Catherine	m.	PA	22 July 1918	4	7	
Doda	Elizabeth	d.	PD	1 Oct. 1916	3	2	also 3 Oct., 7:2
Doda	John, Mrs.	d.	PC	1 Oct. 1916	1	3	
Doda	John, Mrs.	d.	PA	30 Sept. 1916	1	5	
Doda	Mary	d.	SRR	30 Sept. 1916	12	1	Rural Cemetery; also 2 Oct., 8:6
Dodds	Jennie	o.	SRR	26 Apr. 1916	8	4	
Dodds	William	o.	SRR	26 Apr. 1916	8	4	
Dodson	Minnie	m.	HT	1 Feb. 1917	8	4	
Dodson	Minnie M.	m.	PC	26 Jan. 1917	5	3	
Dody	John, Mrs.	d.	PD	10 Feb. 1918	8	3	
Doe	Edgar	b.	PA	3 Dec. 1917	5	3	
Doe	Edgar A.	m.	PC	22 Nov. 1917	3	1	
Doelling	Harry	m.	PA	1 Feb. 1918	8	5	also 4 Feb., 4:5
Doelling	Harry	m.	PC	2 Feb. 1918	6	6	also 5 Feb., 4:3
Doelling	Harry	m.	PD	5 Feb. 1918	7	3	
Doggett	Averil	m.	PD	14 Jan. 1917	8	2	
Doggett	Averil	m.	SRR	24 Nov. 1916	3	3	
Doggett	Averill Allison	m.	PD	25 Nov. 1916	7	4	
Doggett	Vina	m.	SRR	15 Jan. 1917	8	1	
Dogliano	George	o.	PD	20 Apr. 1918	5	3	
Dogliano	Joe	o.	PD	20 Apr. 1918	5	3	
Doherty	Edward J.	d.	PC	10 Nov. 1918	1	2	
Dolcini	Arnold	b.	PC	27 Oct. 1918	4	3	
Dolcini	Arnold	b.	PA	28 Nov. 1916	8	3	
Dolcini	Arnold J.	m.	PC	2 Feb. 1916	4	1&2	also 16 Jan., 6:1
Dolcini	Arnold T.	b.	PC	28 Nov. 1916	8	1	
Dolcini	Arnold Tulley	m.	PD	2 Feb. 1916	5	4	
Dolcini	Arthur	m.	SRR	2 Feb. 1916	5	6	
Dolcini	Charles E.	m.	PA	27 Aug. 1918	5	3	

(1) Surname	(2) Given Name	(3)	(4)	(5) Date	(6) Pg	(7) Col	(8) Comments
Dolcini	Charles E.	m.	PC	28 Aug. 1918	6	3	
Dolcini	Dante	d.	PA	11 Oct. 1918	5	4	France; also 12 Oct., 2:4
Dolcini	Lydia Catherine	m.	PA	26 Apr. 1916	4	3	
Dolcinus	Dante	d.	PC	12 Oct. 1918	8	2	France
Dollarhide	Galan M.	d.	PD	13 Feb. 1917	6	1	
Dolsons	Fred	m.	PD	24 Aug. 1916	7	4	
Domenzet	Joseph	d.	SRR	21 Oct. 1916	1	5	cremation; also 23 Oct., 8:5; 24 Oct., 2:2
Domezet	Joseph	d.	PD	22 Oct. 1916	5	4	
Donahue	Annie F.	d.	PA	8 Dec. 1916	7	3	
Donahue	James	d.	SIT	11 Nov. 1916	1	1	
Donahue	James	d.	PD	17 Nov. 1916	8	1	also 18 Nov., 2:3
Donahue	James	d.	SRR	17 Nov. 1916	5	1	also 18 Nov., 5:4
Donahue	James	d.	PC	18 Nov. 1916	1	5	also 19 Nov., 5:6
Donahue	James, Mrs.	d.	SRR	8 Dec. 1916	5	3	
Donahue	James, Mrs.	d.	SIT	9 Dec. 1916	1	5	
Donahue	Joseph	d.	PA	17 Nov. 1916	3	2	
Donaldson	Jeanette	m.	SRR	26 June 1916	8	5	
Donaldson	Jeanette	m.	PC	29 June 1916	6	3	
Donaldson	Jeanette	o.	SRR	1 July 1916	2	2	
Donaldson	Jeanette	o.	SRR	13 Sept. 1916	8	5	
Donaldson	Jeanette	o.	PC	14 Sept. 1916	6	1	
Donaldson	Jennie	o.	PA	13 Sept. 1916	5	4	
Donati	Romilda	m.	PD	25 Feb. 1916	7	2	
Doney	R. C.	b.	PA	16 Oct. 1916	5	4	
Donham	J.	m.	PC	3 Jan. 1918	5	4	
Donley	William	d.	SRR	10 Aug. 1917	3	6	
Donley	William	d.	PC	11 Aug. 1917	4	5	
Donley	William	d.	PD	11 Aug. 1917	6	1	
Donley	William	d.	ST	17 Aug. 1917	1	6	
Donnelly	Ana	o.	PC	2 Feb. 1916	2	2	
Donnelly	Ann	d.	PA	22 July 1918	4	4	Calvary Cemetery; also 24 July, 5:3
Donnelly	Ann	d.	PC	24 July 1918	5	3	Calvary Cemetery; also 23 July, 3:3; 25 July, 4:3
Donnelly	Anna	d.	PD	24 July 1918	2	2	
Donnelly	Ellen	d.	PD	29 Dec. 1916	8	2	
Donnelly	John	d.	PD	15 Mar. 1917	8	6	
Donnelly	John	d.	ST	17 Mar. 1917	1	1	
Donnelly	John J.	d.	PA	1 Feb. 1916	2	3	
Donnelly	John J.	d.	HT	3 Feb. 1917	5	2	
Donnelly	John J.	d.	ST	5 Feb. 1916	8	6	
Donnelly	John James	d.	SRR	3 Feb. 1916	6	4	

(1) Surname	(2) Given Name	(3)	(4)	(5) Date	(6) Pg	(7) Col	(8) Comments
Donnelly	Margaret	d.	ST	29 Nov. 1918	1	6	
Donnelly	Rose	d.	PD	14 Nov. 1918	4	2	
Donnelly	Rose	d.	ST	15 Nov. 1918	1	2	
Donnolly	Dolores	d.	PA	26 Nov. 1918	8	2	
Donnolly	Dolores	d.	PC	27 Nov. 1918	2	3	
Donnolly	Ellen	d.	PA	28 Dec. 1916	5	3	Calvary Cemetery; also 29 Dec., 4:2
Donnolly	Ellen	d.	PC	29 Dec. 1916	4	3	Calvary Cemetery; also 4:6; 30 Dec., 8:2
Donnolly	Margaret	d.	PC	16 Nov. 1918	3	3	
Donogh	Russell	b.	PA	8 Nov. 1918	1	6	also 6:5
Donogh	Russell W.	m.	PC	12 Sept. 1917	4	2	also 13 Sept., 6:3
Donohue	James, Mrs.	d.	PD	8 Dec. 1916	8	1	
Donough	Russell W.	m.	PA	11 Sept. 1917	4	3	also 12 Sept., 3:5
Donovan	C. C.	m.	PD	22 May 1918	8	2	portrait; also 23 May, 5:4
Donston	Mary	m.	PD	17 July 1917	8	3	
Donston	Mary B.	m.	SRR	17 July 1917	5	3	
Donston	Mary B.	m.	PC	18 July 1917	5	2	
Dont	Minnie	m.	PA	18 Jan. 1918	6	2	
Dont	Minnie	m.	PD	19 Jan. 1918	3	4	
Dooley	Elijah	d.	SRR	23 June 1917	7	3	Hopland
Dooley	R. V.	b.	PA	6 Nov. 1917	4	7	also 5:1
Doran	James	d.	HT	18 Oct. 1917	1	3	
Dormetta	Annie	d.	PA	11 Mar. 1916	8	6	Calvary Cemetery; also 13 Mar., 3:6
Dorn	Genevieve Olive	m.	SRR	12 Sept. 1917	4	4	
Dornback	Ella	o.	PD	12 June 1918	3	2	
Dornback	Fred J.	o.	PD	12 June 1918	3	2	
Dornberger	Margaret	m.	SRR	18 Apr. 1917	3	5	
Dornberger	Margaret	m.	PC	4 Aug. 1917	3	2	
Dornberger	Marguerite	m.	PA	3 Aug. 1917	8	5	
Dorset	Fred Edward	m.	PC	16 Dec. 1917	5	3	
Dorsett	Fred	b.	PA	29 Oct. 1917	4	1	also 8:3
Dorsett	Fred Edward	m.	PA	15 Dec. 1916	4	1	also 16 Dec., 4:5
Doss	Amanda M.	d.	PA	9 July 1917	4	3	also 11 July, 6:3
Doss	Amanda M.	d.	PC	10 July 1917	3	4	Two Rock; also 6:4; 11 July, 3:4; 12 July, 5:4
Doss	John M., Mrs.	d.	PD	10 July 1917	3	3	also 12 July, 5:3
Doss	John M., Mrs.	d.	HT	12 July 1917	4	3	
Doss	Mrs.	d.	SRR	9 July 1917	8	4	
Doss	Oliver	o.	PC	4 Dec. 1917	5	4	
Doss	Pearl	m.	PD	11 Oct. 1917	2	6	
Doss	Pearl Elizabeth	m.	PC	10 Aug. 1917	5	4	
Doss	Pearl Elizabeth	m.	SRR	10 Oct. 1917	4	6	

(1) Surname	(2) Given Name	(3)	(4)	(5) Date	(6) Pg	(7) Col	(8) Comments
Doss	Pearl Elizabeth	m.	PD	11 Aug. 1917	6	2	
Doss	Pearl Elizabeth	m.	SRR	11 Aug. 1917	8	5	
Doss	Pearl Elizabeth	m.	PC	11 Oct. 1917	4	3	
Doss	Pearl Elizabeth	m.	PA	9 Oct. 1917	5	3	
Doss	Wilma Eloise	m.	PD	6 July 1918	8	2	
Dostal	Frank	d.	PD	9 Feb. 1918	8	2	
Doty	Abraham H.	d.	PC	10 Feb. 1918	3	2	Two Rock; also 12 Feb., 3:3; 13 Feb., 8:4
Doty	Abraham H.	d.	PA	9 Feb. 1918	4	3	Two Rock; also 11 Feb., 5:3; 12 Feb., 8:4
Doty	Frank	d.	PA	7 Nov. 1918	4	3	Cypress Hill; also 5:5; 8 Nov., 5:4
Doty	Frank	d.	PC	8 Nov. 1918	4	3&4	Cypress Hill
Dougherty	Hazel	m.	SRR	30 Nov. 1917	8	3	
Dougherty	Samuel K.	d.	PA	13 Oct. 1916	1	2	also 3:3; 14 Oct., 3:3; 16 Oct., 4:3; 9 Nov., 4:2
Dougherty	Samuel K.	d.	PD	13 Oct. 1916	8	1	also 14 Oct., 6:3; 15 Oct., 7:5; 17 Oct., 6:3
Dougherty	Samuel K.	d.	SRR	14 Oct. 1916	6	3	also 16 Oct., 8:6; 30 Oct., 6:2
Dougherty	Samuel K.	p.	PC	9 Nov. 1916	3	4	
Dougherty	Samuel K.	d.	PC	13 Oct. 1916	1	6	cremation; also 14 Oct., 1:5, 4:3; 15 Oct., 1:4; 17 Oct., 1:5; 18 Oct., 3:3; 10 Nov., 1:6
Douglas	A. S.	m.	PD	17 Sept. 1918	7	2	
Douglas	Clarence Bruce	m.	PD	4 July 1917	2	2	
Douglas	Hetta Frances	d.	PD	8 Jan. 1918	2	4	also 9 Jan., 6:2; 10 Jan., 3:4
Douglas	June Claire	b.	HT	2 May 1918	8	2	
Douglass	Leon F.	d.	PD	8 May 1918	6	4	
Dove	W. E.	o.	PC	23 Nov. 1917	6	2	
Dow	Eliza V.	d.	PA	3 Jan. 1916	6	4	
Dow	Eliza Veder	d.	HT	6 Jan. 1916	10	5	
Dow	Eliza Veeder	d.	PD	1 Jan. 1916	7	1	Bennett Valley Cemetery; also 4 Jan., 7:3
Dow	Eliza Veeder	d.	SRR	1 Jan. 1916	1	3	also 3 Jan., 8:6
Dow	Eliza Veeder	d.	PC	5 Jan. 1916	3	2	Bennett Valley Cemetery
Dowd	Edward	d.	PA	22 Oct. 1918	5	3	Calvary Cemetery; also 24 Oct., 4:4
Dowd	Edward	d.	PC	22 Oct. 1918	8	5	Calvary Cemetery; also 8:3&4; 25 Oct., 4:4
Dowd	Edward	d.	PD	24 Oct. 1918	2	3	also 25 Oct., 5:2
Dowd	Edward	d.	SIT	26 Oct. 1918	1	1	

(1) Surname	(2) Given Name	(3)	(4)	(5) Date	(6) Pg	(7) Col	(8) Comments
Dowd	Henry L.	o.	SRR	27 Sept. 1917	8	4	
Dowd	Margaret C.	o.	SRR	27 Sept. 1917	8	4	
Downes	E.	d.	PC	28 Mar. 1916	1	2	
Downes	Ernest	d.	PA	28 Mar. 1916	1	3	
Downes	Ernest	d.	PD	28 Mar. 1916	8	1	also 28 Mar., 5:3
Downes	Ernest	d.	SRR	28 Mar. 1916	5	3	cremation; also 29 Mar., 8:4
Downes	Vernon	b.	SRR	16 Oct. 1917	1	2	
Downing	Samuel Uberto	d.	PD	5 June 1918	5	6	also 6 June, 4:2
Downs	Frank	d.	PC	19 Nov. 1918	1	4	also 20 Nov., 5:3
Downs	Frank	d.	PD	19 Nov. 1918	1	4	
Downs	Frank Merrill	d.	PA	19 Nov. 1918	4	5	
Downs	Vernon	b.	SRR	6 Mar. 1916	8	5	
Downs	William	d.	PA	22 Nov. 1917	4	2	also 23 Nov., 8:6
Downs	William	d.	PC	23 Nov. 1917	2	3	Calvary Cemetery; also 5:4; 24 Nov., 4:1
Downs	William	d.	PD	23 Nov. 1917	2	2	
Downs	William	d.	SRR	23 Nov. 1917	7	3	
Doyle	M.	p.	PA	2 Sept. 1916	2	2	will
Doyle	Manville	d.	PA	21 Aug. 1916	4	3	also 23 Aug., 5:5
Doyle	Manville	d.	SRR	21 Aug. 1916	1	4	also 22 Aug., 8:1; 23 Aug., 8:1
Doyle	Manville	d.	PC	22 Aug. 1916	1	4	also 23 Aug., 1:2&3; 24 Aug., 4:5
Doyle	Manville	d.	PD	22 Aug. 1916	8	3	also 23 Aug., 2:1
Doyle	Manville	p.	PC	3 Sept. 1916	1	5	
Dozier	Leon	d.	PD	10 Mar. 1917	1	2	
Drago	Frank	b.	ST	6 July 1917	2	3	
Drago	Margaret	d.	PD	16 May 1918	5	1	
Drago	Margaret T.	d.	PC	17 May 1918	3	5	Sebastopol
Drake	Albert E.	o.	PD	1 May 1918	5	1	
Drake	Annie	o.	SRR	4 Nov. 1916	6	3	
Drake	Arthur	o.	SIT	11 Aug. 1917	1	2	
Drake	Benjamin J.	m.	SRR	19 Apr. 1916	3	4	
Drake	Bernard	o.	SRR	4 Nov. 1916	6	3	
Drake	Carrie	o.	PA	10 Apr. 1918	3	1	
Drake	Edith M.	m.	PD	17 Sept. 1916	6	6	
Drake	Floyd G.	o.	PA	10 Apr. 1918	3	1	
Drake	Josephine	m.	SRR	4 Aug. 1916	6	2	
Drake	L. A.	o.	SIT	2 Feb. 1918	1	7	
Drake	L. A. (Arthur)	o.	SIT	23 Feb. 1918	1	1	also 6 Apr., 1:7
Drake	Mabel Florence	o.	PD	1 May 1918	5	1	
Drand	John	b.	PC	26 Feb. 1918	8	3	
Dray	Emma	d.	PA	3 Feb. 1916	5	3	
Dray	Harry, Mrs.	d.	PA	5 Feb. 1916	8	3	Cypress Hill

(1) Surname	(2) Given Name	(3)	(4)	(5) Date	(6) Pg	(7) Col	(8) Comments
Dray	Harry, Mrs.	d.	PC	6 Feb. 1916	4	3	Cypress Hill
Drees	Adolph	d.	PA	18 Dec. 1917	4	3	Cypress Hill; also 19 De3c., 4:6; 20 Dec., 5:5; 21 Dec., 4:5
Drees	Adolph	d.	PC	19 Dec. 1917	1	3	also 20 Dec., 5:5; 21 Dec., 8:6; 22 Dec., 8:2
Drees	Adolph	d.	PD	19 Dec. 1917	8	3	
Drees	Alvin	o.	PA	12 Dec. 1918	6	1	also 19 Dec., 5:3
Drees	Alvin	o.	PA	23 Nov. 1918	5	5	also 27 Nov., 2:3
Dregenberg	Henry F.	b.	PA	15 Mar. 1918	4	7	
Dresbach	Isabella	d.	PA	21 Aug. 1916	5	4	cremation; also 22 Aug., 5:5
Dresbach	Isabella	d.	PC	22 Aug. 1916	3	3	also 23 Aug., 4:3
Dresbach	Isabelle	d.	PD	22 Aug. 1916	5	3	
Dresel	Otto	o.	SIT	23 Nov. 1918	1	3	
Dressel	Carl	o.	PA	25 Nov. 1918	8	7	
Dresser	August Wellington	d.	SRR	28 Aug. 1916	4	3	also 29 Aug., 8:3
Dresser	Augustus Wellington	d.	PD	27 Aug. 1916	8	4	
Dringenberg	Hattie Florence	d.	PA	29 Mar. 1918	5	5	Two Rock; also 8:5; 1 Apr., 4:7
Dringenburg	Annie	o.	PD	7 Aug. 1918	6	5	adoption
Dringenburg	Christine	o.	PC	6 Aug. 1918	1	3	adoption
Dringenburg	Christine	o.	PD	7 Aug. 1918	6	5	adoption
Dringenburg	Ethlene	o.	PC	6 Aug. 1918	1	3	adoption
Dringenburg	Ethlene	o.	PD	7 Aug. 1918	6	5	adoption
Dringenburg	Fannie	o.	PD	7 Aug. 1918	6	5	adoption
Dringenburg	Florence	o.	PC	6 Aug. 1918	1	3	adoption
Dringenburg	Florence	o.	PD	7 Aug. 1918	6	5	adoption
Dringenburg	Frederick	o.	PC	6 Aug. 1918	1	3	adoption
Dringenburg	Frederick David	o.	PD	7 Aug. 1918	6	5	adoption
Dringenburg	Hattie Florence	d.	PC	30 Mar. 1918	5	4	Two Rock; also 6:1; 31 Mar., 2:3; 1 Apr., 4:1
Dringenburg	Henrietta	o.	PC	6 Aug. 1918	1	3	adoption
Dringenburg	Henrietta	o.	PD	7 Aug. 1918	6	5	adoption
Drinkwater	Austin M.	m.	PD	1 Dec. 1917	2	4	
Drinkwater	Austin M.	m.	ST	30 Nov. 1917	1	3	
Driscoll	Daniel	d.	PA	10 June 1916	4	1	San Francisco; also 12 June, 8:5
Driscoll	Daniel	d.	PC	11 June 1916	3	1	
Driscoll	Lewis P.	m.	PC	20 Sept. 1916	8	5	
Driver	William (dau of)	d.	ST	5 Oct. 1917	8	1	
Drosbach	Frederika	d.	PD	7 Apr. 1918	4	2	I.O.O.F. Cemetery
Dryden	Carla	d.	PD	26 Feb. 1918	4	2	also 5:5; 1 Mar., 2:2
Drysdale	Clarence J.	d.	PC	9 Nov. 1918	2	1	
Drysdale	Florence	m.	PC	13 Sept. 1917	8	6	

(1) Surname	(2) Given Name	(3)	(4)	(5) Date	(6) Pg	(7) Col	(8) Comments
Drysdale	Florence	m.	PD	13 Sept. 1917	5	2	
Drysdale	George Sidney	m.	PD	9 Dec. 1917	6	3	
Du Commun	Lillian	m.	SRR	12 June 1916	1	4	
Dubois	Jessie Leta	m.	PD	3 June 1916	8	2	
DuBois	Leta	m.	SRR	3 June 1916	5	2	
Ducharin	Olive V.	d.	SRR	21 May 1917	8	3	
Ducharm	Olive V.	d.	PD	22 May 1917	5	4	
Ducharn	Olive V.	d.	SRR	23 May 1917	1	4	Rural Cemetery; also 24 May, 5:1
Duchran	William M.	m.	HT	13 June 1918	5	5	
Ducker	Andrew	d.	PA	27 Mar. 1916	8	5	also 28 Mar., 2:6; 29 Mar., 4:5
Ducker	Andrew	d.	SRR	27 Mar. 1916	1	2	
Ducker	Andrew	d.	PC	28 Mar. 1916	1	3	Cypress Hill; also 30 Mar., 5:5
Ducker	Andrew	d.	PD	28 Mar. 1916	5	2	also 29 Mar., 6:1
Duckworth	H. H.	o.	PD	4 Oct. 1916	5	2	adoption
DuCommon	Lillian	m.	PD	11 June 1916	3	2	also 13 June, 6:4
Dudley	Philo F.	b.	SRR	12 Sept. 1916	5	4	
Duerson	Laura/Lucy	d.	PC	19 Mar. 1918	5	6	Cypress Hill; also 6:2; 21 Mar., 4:4
Duerson	Lucia	d.	PA	14 Mar. 1918	3	3	Cypress Hill; also 20 Mar., 4:4
Duerson	Lucie	d.	PD	14 Mar. 1918	6	3	also 19 Mar., 4:2
Duerson	Robert	b.	PD	16 Sept. 1917	3	3	
Duerson	Robert	b.	SRR	17 Sept. 1917	3	4	
Duerson	Robert	b.	PC	18 Sept. 1917	8	2	
Duffy	Sarah M.	m.	PD	18 Nov. 1916	5	5	
Dufranc	Jeanne	d.	SRR	26 May 1917	6	6	
Dufranc	Jeanne	d.	PC	27 May 1917	4	2	
Dufranc	Jeanne	d.	ST	1 June 1917	5	4	
Dufrance	Vital	m.	PD	29 May 1918	6	2	
Duhring	Donald	o.	SIT	22 Dec. 1917	1	5	
Duhring	Frederick	o.	SIT	22 Dec. 1917	1	5	also 29 Dec., 1:6; 26 Jan., 1918, 1:3; 9 Mar., 1918, 1:6; 4 May, 1918, 1:6
Duhring	Frederick	o.	SIT	30 June 1917	3	2	also 18 Aug., 4:4
Duhring	Frederick	o.	PC	4 Apr. 1918	6	3	
Duhring	Frederick	o.	PA	7 Sept. 1917	3	5	
Duhring	Frederick S.	m.	PC	4 Nov. 1916	1	2	
Duhring	Frederick S.	o.	PC	9 Mar. 1918	6	4	
Duhring	Frederick Stearns	m.	PA	16 Feb. 1916	4	3	
Duhring	Frederick Sterns	m.	SRR	18 Feb. 1916	4	6	
Duhring	Frederick, Jr.	m.	SIT	21 Oct. 1916	3	2	also 4 Nov., 1:5
Duie	Jack	m.	SRR	17 Oct. 1917	6	3	

(1) Surname	(2) Given Name	(3)	(4)	(5) Date	(6) Pg	(7) Col	(8) Comments
Duke	Ada	m.	PC	8 Aug. 1917	4	4	
Dukes	Jimmie L.	d.	PC	24 Sept. 1918	1	4	France
Dulac	Emma May	d.	PA	14 Mar. 1916	8	5	Cypress Hill; also 15 Mar., 5:5
Dulac	Emma Mays	d.	PC	14 Mar. 1916	1	5	
Dulac	Ernest	m.	PA	7 Apr. 1917	4	5	
Dulac	Ernest E.	m.	PC	8 Apr. 1917	5	3	
Dulcini	Lydia	m.	PC	27 Apr. 1916	4	3	
Dumas	A.	m.	SIT	12 Oct. 1918	1	3	wife not named
Dun	Arthur	m.	PA	15 May 1917	4	5	
Dun	Arthur	m.	PD	16 May 1917	8	3	
Dun	Arthur	m.	SRR	16 May 1917	2	4	
Dunbar	Charles O., Mrs.	d.	PA	30 Dec. 1918	6	4	
Dunbar	Fanny	d.	PC	31 Dec. 1918	2	3	
Dunbar	Frances	d.	PD	31 Dec. 1918	2	3	Odd Fellows Cemetery; also 4:2
Dunbar	Ora	d.	PD	5 Mar. 1918	3	3	also 4:2
Dunbar	William A.	d.	PD	30 Oct. 1917	6	2	
Dunbar	William A.	d.	PC	31 Oct. 1917	6	3	
Duncan	Edith M.	m.	PC	21 Sept. 1916	2	2	
Duncan	Gertrude	m.	PD	2 Nov. 1918	2	2	
Duncan	Gertrude	m.	PD	20 Oct. 1918	5	2	
Duncan	John	b.	PC	7 June 1917	2	3	
Duncan	Marian B.	m.	SRR	20 Nov. 1917	8	2	
Duncan	R. B.	o.	PC	27 Mar. 1918	8	4	
Dunden	Mary Kelley	d.	PA	7 Jan. 1918	7	3	Calvary Cemetery; also 8 Jan., 4:4, 8:5
Dundon	Mary Kelley	d.	PC	8 Jan. 1918	5	3	also 9 Jan., 8:4
Dundon	Mary Kelley	d.	PD	8 Jan. 1918	5	1	
Dringenburg	Ethel	o.	ST	16 Aug. 1918	1	1	adoption
Dringenburg	Fannie Annie Christine	o.	ST	16 Aug. 1918	1	1	adoption
Dringenburg	Frederick David	o.	ST	16 Aug. 1918	1	1	adoption
Dringenburg	Henrietta Florence	o.	ST	16 Aug. 1918	1	1	adoption
Dunn	George C.	d.	PD	1 June 1918	4	2	also 4 June, 3:3
Dunn	John	d.	PA	31 May 1918	1	3	Calvary Cemetery; also 1 June, 4:3
Dunn	John	d.	PC	1 June 1918	4	4	Calvary Cemetery; also 5:3; 2 June, 8:3
Dunn	Matthew H.	d.	PD	27 Feb. 1918	4	2	also 8:4
Dunne	Theresa	m.	PC	3 May 1916	1	3	
Dunne	Theresa	m.	PC	9 May 1916	6	3	
Dunne	Therese	m.	PA	10 May 1917	4	4	
Dunning	B. F.	b.	PA	18 Feb. 1916	1	3	
Dunning	Emma J.	d.	PA	17 May 1917	4	3	Cypress Hill; also 21 May, 8:5

(1) Surname	(2) Given Name	(3)	(4)	(5) Date	(6) Pg	(7) Col	(8) Comments
Dunning	Emma Jane	d.	PC	18 May 1917	6	1	Liberty Cemetery or Cypress Hill; also 19 May, 4:5; 20 May, 8:3; 22 May, 4:1
Dunton	Fannie	d.	PA	29 July 1918	6	1	Cypress Hill; also 30 July, 5:3
Dunton	Fannie Armstrong	d.	PC	28 July 1918	1	4	Cypress Hill; also 31 July, 4:1
Dupon	Joe	o.	PC	10 Nov. 1918	3	1	
Dupont	Joseph	d.	SRR	3 Feb. 1916	5	3	
Dupont	Joseph	d.	PD	4 Feb. 1916	8	4	also 5 Feb., 2:4
Dupont	Joseph	d.	ST	5 Feb. 1916	1	3	
Dupre	Frank	d.	PA	5 Sept. 1918	6	5	France
Dupre	Frank	d.	PC	6 Sept. 1918	8	6	France
Durand	Victor	d.	PA	24 Oct. 1918	5	4	
Durand	Victor D.	d.	PD	24 Oct. 1918	4	2	Calvary Cemetery; also 6:3; 26 Oct. 3:2
Durando	Felice	d.	PA	20 Nov. 1918	4	7	also 23 Nov., 5:3; 25 Nov., 6:3
Durando	Felice	d.	PC	21 Nov. 1918	6	3	also 26 Nov., 5:4
Durando	Frank	d.	PC	19 Nov. 1918	4	3	
Durbin	Evelyn	d.	PC	23 Dec. 1917	8	3	
Durbrow	Ross	m.	SRR	6 June 1917	3	3	
Duree	Mima Shanks	m.	PC	31 Mar. 1916	5	3	also 4 Apr., 2:1
Durst	David	m.	PD	20 July 1916	8	4	
Durst	David M.	m.	ST	13 May 1916	1	5	also 22 July, 1:2
Durst	David M.	m.	SRR	20 July 1916	4	5	
Durst	David M.	m.	PC	21 July 1916	4	1	
Dutcher	Mary	d.	PD	30 Jan. 1918	8	4	also 2 Feb., 4:2
Dutton	Lucina	d.	PD	20 Aug. 1918	2	1	I.O.O.F. Cemetery; also 4:2; 21 Aug., 5:3
DuVander	Rae	o.	HT	15 Nov. 1917	4	4	
Dye	Joseph	b.	PA	12 Sept. 1918	2	2	
Dye	Joseph	b.	PC	12 Sept. 1918	4	4	
Dyer	Edith	o.	PC	9 Mar. 1917	1	3	died 1889
Dykes	H. H.	o.	PA	26 Oct. 1918	7	3	
Dykes	Harlan	o.	PA	9 Aug. 1918	6	4	
Dykes	Harlan H.	o.	PC	25 May 1917	1	6	
Dykes	Harlan H.	o.	PA	31 May 1918	3	7	
Dykes	Harlan H.	o.	PC	10 Aug. 1918	6	4	
Dykes	Harlan H.	o.	PA	7 Oct. 1918	6	1	

E

(1) Surname	(2) Given Name	(3)	(4)	(5) Date	(6) Pg	(7) Col	(8) Comments
Eades	George H.	d.	PC	28 Nov. 1916	3	3	Calvary Cemetery; also 8:5; 29 Nov., 5:5
Eades	George H.	d.	PD	28 Nov. 1916	8	2	
Eades	George M.	d.	PA	27 Nov. 1916	4	1	also 28 Nov., 8:3
Eagle	William	o.	HT	4 July 1918	5	1	
Eaglin	Elmer	m.	PA	22 Dec. 1916	5	3	
Eaglin	Elmer	m.	PC	23 Dec. 1916	8	4	
Eaglin	Elmer H.	m.	SRR	22 Dec. 1916	3	3	
Eardley	Gladys	m.	SRR	19 June 1917	8	3	
Eardley	Gladys	m.	PD	20 June 1917	2	6	also 21 June, 5:4
Earhart	Philip L.	d.	PC	15 Dec. 1917	8	3	Cypress Hill
Earnest	Helen Pearl	m.	PC	30 Aug. 1916	5	4	
Earnest	Helen Pearl	m.	PD	31 Aug. 1916	6	2	
Easterling	Margaret	m.	SRR	30 Oct. 1916	8	5	
Eastman	Charles A.	d.	PA	28 Dec. 1916	5	1	
Eatheron	Alfred	b.	PC	28 Mar. 1916	5	6	
Eaton	H. W.	m.	PA	30 Mar. 1918	4	1	
Ebbert	Grafton	m.	PD	20 Nov. 1917	3	3	
Eberts	Berwin	m.	PD	20 Feb. 1917	7	2	
Eberts	Berwin	m.	PD	26 Apr. 1917	6	1	
Eby	Carrie	d.	PD	31 Dec. 1918	1	5	
Echell	Mabel	o.	PC	26 Jan. 1918	1	6	
Ecker	Margaret	d.	PA	31 Oct. 1917	4	3	Mt. Olivet, S.F.; also 8:4
Ecker	Margaret	d.	PC	31 Oct. 1917	1	4	Mt. Olivet, S.F.; also 5:6; 1 Nov., 5:6; 2 Nov., 4:3
Eckhart	Nathan	m.	PA	8 Oct. 1918	8	5	
Eckhart	Percy	m.	PD	8 Oct. 1918	2	3	
Eckhart	Percy	m.	PC	9 Oct. 1918	2	2	
Ecklund	Jack	m.	SRR	16 Dec. 1916	3	2	
Eckman	John	d.	PC	5 Apr. 1916	4	2	
Eckman	Madaline Marie	b&d	PA	20 Mar. 1918	6	4	Cypress Hill; also 4:5; 21 Mar., 5:4
Eckman	Madaline Marie	d.	PC	21 Mar. 1918	3	3	Cypress Hill
Eckmann	Nellie Esther	m.	PA	10 Sept. 1918	5	6	
Eckmann	Nellie Esther	m.	PC	11 Sept. 1918	5	3	
Eddington	Fred	b.	PA	2 May 1916	8	5	
Edelman	Harriet	d.	PC	12 Nov. 1918	8	5	cremation; also 13 Nov., 4:4
Edelmann	Harriett	d.	PA	12 Nov. 1918	7	3	cremation
Edgar	James	m.	SRR	26 June 1917	8	6	
Edgeworth	Edward H.	o.	PC	9 Feb. 1918	8	5	also 10 Feb., 1:5
Edgeworth	Edward J.	o.	ST	15 Feb. 1918	1	4	also 8 Mar., 1:5

(1) Surname	(2) Given Name	(3)	(4)	(5) Date	(6) Pg	(7) Col	(8) Comments
Edgeworth	Grace	m.	PD	28 Nov. 1917	6	1	also 5 Dec., 5:3
Edgeworth	Grace	m.	ST	30 Nov. 1917	1	6	also 7 Dec., 1:2
Edington	Fred	b.	PC	2 May 1916	8	4	
Edmester	Grace A.	m.	PD	22 Nov. 1916	6	2	
Edmester	Grace A.	m.	PC	24 Nov. 1916	2	3	
Edmester	Grace A.	m.	ST	25 Nov. 1917	1	1	
Edmunds	August	d.	PD	15 Sept. 1918	5	1	also 17 Sept., 8:2
Edmunds	August	d.	ST	20 Sept. 1918	2	1	
Edmunds	August Richard	d.	PC	15 Sept. 1918	1	5	
Edwards	Bertha A.	o.	PD	31 July 1918	7	2	
Edwards	Charles	d.	PA	4 May 1917	6	5	Rose Cemetery, Santa Rosa; also 5 May, 2:5
Edwards	Charles	d.	SRR	4 May 1917	4	2	
Edwards	Charles	d.	PC	5 May 1917	4	6	Rural Cemetery; also 9 May, 2:2
Edwards	Charles	d.	SRR	7 May 1917	4	3	
Edwards	Charles J.	d.	PD	5 May 1917	4	3	Rural Cemetery; also 8 May, 2:3
Edwards	Eugene	o.	SRR	21 Nov. 1916	4	5	
Edwards	Hazel Margaret	o.	SRR	21 Nov. 1916	4	5	
Edwards	John A.	o.	PD	31 July 1918	7	2	
Edwards	Julia Frances	m.	ST	7 Oct. 1916	8	5	
Edwards	Julia Francis	m.	PC	7 Oct. 1916	5	6	
Edwards	Ralph W.	m.	PD	22 Sept. 1916	6	5	
Edwards	Sarah	d.	PA	10 July 1916	5	4	also 11 July, 5:5; 12 July, 5:3; 13 July, 8:4
Edwards	Sarah A.	d.	SRR	10 July 1916	8	6	Rural Cemetery; also 12 July, 3:5
Edwards	Sarah A.	d.	PC	11 July 1916	4	1	Santa Rosa; also 13 July, 3:2
Edwards	Sarah A.	d.	PD	12 July 1916	8	3	also 13 July, 2:6; 16 July, 6:2
Edwards	Sarah E.	d.	PC	13 Mar. 1917	1	3	Cypress Hill; also 14 Mar., 3:1; 15 Mar., 4:5
Ehlers	Georgina	m.	PA	31 Aug. 1916	5	3	
Ehrier	Louis	d.	PA	31 Dec. 1918	4	5	
Ehrlich	F.	d.	SIT	24 Mar. 1917	1	4	Mountain Cemetery
Ehrlich	F.	d.	PC	25 Mar. 1917	8	1	Sonoma
Ehrlich	Jack	b.	SRR	31 Mar. 1917	6	4	
Ehrlich	Jack	b.	HT	5 Apr. 1917	6	4	
Ehrlich	Jane Henrietta	d.	SRR	16 Nov. 1917	4	4	
Ehrlich	Jane Henrietta	d.	PD	15 Nov. 1917	5	4	Rural Cemetery; also 17 Nov., 2:1
Eickmeyer	Henry	b.	PA	24 May 1918	4	7	
Eisenmayer	Clarence Richard	m.	PD	24 Aug. 1917	3	1	
Ekstrom	Chester Leo	m.	PD	20 June 1917	8	2	

(1) Surname	(2) Given Name	(3)	(4)	(5) Date	(6) Pg	(7) Col	(8) Comments
Ekstrom	Herbert E.	m.	PD	15 May 1918	8	4	
Eldeen/Snider	Verlie	m.	PC	9 June 1918	2	2	also 18 June, 8:2
Elderkin	Edna	m.	PD	22 Sept. 1918	8	3	
Eldred	Norine	m.	SIT	28 July 1917	2	5	
Eldredge	Joseph E.	d.	HT	7 Dec. 1916	7	3	
Eldridge	Joseph B.	d.	SRR	2 Dec. 1916	3	1	
Elfring	John J.	d.	PA	14 Oct. 1918	8	3	
Elfring	John, Jr.	d.	PC	16 Oct. 1918	8	4	Michigan
Eliason	Ruby	m.	PA	2 July 1918	6	4	
Eliason	Ruby F.	m.	PC	28 June 1918	5	4	
Eliason	Ruby F.	m.	PD	30 June 1918	12	3	
Eliggi	Bartolemeo	m.	CR	27 Sept. 1918	1	1	
Elliot	Catherine	d.	PC	16 June 1918	6	1	
Elliot	Dewey	m.	PD	17 Nov. 1917	5	3	
Elliott	Amy	m.	PD	5 May 1917	5	5	
Elliott	Amy	m.	ST	5 May 1917	1	5	
Elliott	Dewey	m.	ST	16 Nov. 1917	1	6	
Elliott	Dewey	m.	PC	17 Nov. 1917	4	5	
Elliott	Dutton	d.	PD	3 Mar. 1918	4	2	also 8:4
Elliott	L. Dewey	m.	SRR	17 Nov. 1917	5	1	
Elliott	Milton	d.	ST	8 Mar. 1918	4	2	Odd Fellows Cem., Santa Rosa
Ellis	Arthur	b.	PA	27 Nov. 1916	4	2	
Ellis	Arthur	m.	PA	31 Jan. 1916	3	3	also 4 Feb., 4:1
Ellis	Arthur C.	b.	PC	28 Nov. 1916	2	3	also 8:1
Ellis	Arthur C.	m.	PC	5 Feb. 1916	5	3	
Ellis	Edward	o.	PD	27 Nov. 1918	8	1	
Ellis	James	m.	PD	3 Apr. 1917	8	2	
Ellis	James	m.	PC	4 Apr. 1917	4	1	
Ellis	James	m.	ST	7 Apr. 1917	3	2	
Ellis	John Dixon	o.	PC	29 May 1918	2	3	
Ellis	John Dixon	o.	PA	18 June 1918	2	1	
Ellis	John Dixon	o.	PC	27 Nov. 1918	8	3	
Ellis	Leander, Mrs.	d.	HT	4 Apr. 1918	5	5	
Ellis	Margaret	o.	PD	27 Nov. 1918	8	1	
Ellis	Margaret Stanley	o.	PC	29 May 1918	2	3	
Ellis	Margaret Sterling	o.	PA	18 June 1918	2	1	
Ellis	Margaret Sterling	o.	PC	27 Nov. 1918	8	3	
Ellis	Nancy Eleanor	d.	PD	30 Mar. 1918	6	5	
Ellis	Russell	d.	PD	24 Oct. 1918	5	2	
Ellison	Ethel	m.	PD	7 Aug. 1918	6	2	
Elmer	William	d.	PC	19 Oct. 1916	5	1	
Elmer	William	d.	SRR	19 Oct. 1916	2	2	also 20 Oct., 3:5
Elmer	William	d.	PA	24 Oct. 1916	8	3	
Elmore	Lois	m.	SRR	15 June 1916	8	3	

(1) Surname	(2) Given Name	(3)	(4)	(5) Date	(6) Pg	(7) Col	(8) Comments
Elmore	Lois	m.	PD	16 June 1916	8	2	
Elmore	Ruby	m.	PC	17 May 1918	1	4	
Elmore	Ruth	m.	PD	17 May 1918	5	4	
Eloza	A.	b.	PC	13 Aug. 1916	5	2	
Elphick	Eugene	m.	SRR	31 July 1917	8	3	
Elphick	Eugene	m.	ST	3 Aug. 1917	1	3	
Elphick	Mary E.	o.	PC	10 Apr. 1918	2	2	
Elphick	May	o.	PA	5 Feb. 1918	5	6	
Elphick	Oscar	o.	PC	13 Apr. 1918	7	6	
Elphick	Oscar F.	o.	PC	10 Apr. 1918	2	2	
Elphick	Oscar F.	o.	PA	5 Feb. 1918	5	6	
Elphick	Ray	b.	PC	4 Sept. 1918	8	5	
Elphick	Roy	b.	PA	31 Aug. 1918	8	4	also 5 Sept., 4:3
Elphick	Sidney	o.	PC	12 Sept. 1918	3	4	
Elphick	Sidney	o.	PC	25 Aug. 1918	3	4	
Elton	Arthur M.	m.	PD	3 Aug. 1918	6	4	
Elwell	Ernest, Mrs.	d.	PC	12 Feb. 1916	1	1	
Elzey	R. H.	b.	SRR	16 Nov. 1916	8	5	
Emeldi	Theodora Marie	m.	PD	8 Sept. 1916	5	4	
Emeldi	Theodora Marie	m.	PD	9 Sept. 1916	3	4	
Emery	Mary	d.	PD	4 Sept. 1918	8	3	
Emmett	Elmer	b.	PA	13 Jan. 1916	8	6	
Endicott	Berry	o.	SRR	23 July 1917	8	1	
Endicott	M. J., Mrs.	d.	PA	25 Mar. 1916	2	3	
Endicott	M. J., Mrs.	d.	PC	25 Mar. 1916	1	6	
Endicott	M. J., Mrs.	d.	PD	25 Mar. 1916	5	3	
Endicott	Mary Jane	d.	SRR	24 Mar. 1916	8	3	also 27 Mar., 2:4
Endicott	Mattie	o.	SRR	23 July 1917	8	1	
Endicott	Mattie	o.	PC	24 July 1917	4	2	
Endicott	Perry	o.	PC	24 July 1917	4	2	
Enemark	Frank R.	m.	PD	18 Nov. 1916	3	2	also 25 Nov., 3:3; 26 Nov., 3:1
Engelke	Lewis	d.	HT	14 Mar. 1918	1	1	
Enger	Martha	m.	PD	13 June 1916	5	4	
Enger	Martha	m.	SRR	13 June 1916	5	1	
England	Arthur	m.	PD	21 Aug. 1917	8	3	
England	Arthur	m.	SRR	21 Aug. 1917	5	3	
England	Elizabeth	d.	PC	1 Sept. 1918	8	4	
England	Elizabeth Hoffman	d.	PD	31 Aug. 1918	4	2	Rural Cemetery; also 8:3
Engler	Charles	b.	PA	31 Jan. 1916	8	6	
Engler	Frank	o.	PC	24 Nov. 1918	1	2	
Engler	Frank	o.	SIT	28 Dec. 1918	1	1	
Engler	Frank C.	o.	SIT	28 Sept. 1918	1	6	
Engler	Matthias	d.	SRR	19 Feb. 1917	8	2	also 20 Feb., 4:3
Engler	Matthias	d.	PA	20 Feb. 1917	3	6	Sonoma

(1) Surname	(2) Given Name	(3)	(4)	(5) Date	(6) Pg	(7) Col	(8) Comments
Engler	Matthias	d.	PD	20 Feb. 1917	7	2	
Enmark	Frank R.	m.	SRR	18 Nov. 1916	8	3	also 25 Nov., 8:4
Enos	Jessie V.	d.	SRR	4 June 1917	10	6	Odd Fellows Cemetery; also 6 June, 5:3
Enos	Jessie V.	d.	PD	5 June 1917	4	3	Odd Fellows Cemetery
Enquist	August	p.	PD	22 Oct. 1918	5	5	
Enquist	August	d.	PD	8 Oct. 1918	4	2	also 9 Oct., 2:5
Enright	John Edwin	m.	PA	6 June 1916	4	7	
Enright	John Edwin	m.	PC	7 June 1916	5	5	also 30 June, 5:2
Enright	John Edwin	m.	PA	29 June 1916	5	2	
Enscoeski	Julius	d.	SRR	7 May 1917	1	3	
Enzenauer	Ethel	m.	PD	3 June 1917	10	3	
Enzenauer	Tiny	o.	HT	18 July 1918	1	2	
Epson	Minnie	m.	PA	7 Jan. 1918	8	5	
Epson	Minnie	m.	PC	8 Jan. 1918	3	5	
Epson	Minnie	m.	PD	8 Jan. 1918	5	5	
Eraldi	Albina	m.	SRR	1 May 1916	1	2	
Eraldi	Albina	m.	PD	2 May 1916	5	2	
Eraldi	Albina	m.	SIT	11 Mar. 1916	1	3	also 29 Apr., 1:6; 6 May, 1:1
Erazmus	Stanley J.	d.	SIT	28 Sept. 1918	4	1	Presidio
Eresa	Luis	m.	PC	17 Apr. 1917	3	3	
Erickson	Andrew G.	d.	SRR	30 Mar. 1916	8	4	
Erickson	Andrew Godfred	d.	PC	1 Apr. 1916	8	3	also 2 Apr., 2:3
Erickson	Andrew Godfred	d.	PA	31 Mar. 1916	10	3	
Erlebach	May	m.	SIT	8 Jan. 1916	4	3	also 17 June, 1:7
Ermentrout	S. J.	d.	PA	15 Nov. 1917	8	2	
Ermentrout	S. J.	d.	SRR	15 Nov. 1917	7	4	
Ermentrout	S. J.	d.	PC	16 Nov. 1917	6	2	
Ermentrout	S. Justina	d.	PD	15 Nov. 1917	5	4	also 17 Nov., 8:2
Ernst	August M.	m.	PD	11 Dec. 1917	5	3	
Ernst	August M.	m.	SRR	11 Dec. 1917	5	4	
Ernst	John L.	d.	PD	16 June 1918	2	3	
Ernston	Martin Alonzo	m.	HT	9 Mar. 1916	1	6	
Errett	Pete	d.	PD	26 Nov. 1918	2	3	also 4:2; 28 Nov., 5:4
Errett	Pete	d.	PC	27 Nov. 1918	6	1	
Errett	Pete	d.	HT	28 Nov. 1918	1	2	
Erwin	Nicholas	d.	PC	4 June 1916	1	5	
Eslick	Daisy Bell	m.	HT	24 Aug. 1916	1	5	
Eslick	Daisy Belle	m.	PD	22 Aug. 1916	2	3	
Espey	Sidney	m.	PC	4 Aug. 1917	8	5	
Esterling	Margaret	m.	SRR	27 June 1916	4	3	
Esterling	Margaret	m.	PD	26 Oct. 1916	2	3	
Estes	George	d.	PC	1 Oct. 1918	5	4	also 5 Oct., 5:4
Estes	George	d.	PD	1 Oct. 1918	5	5	

(1) Surname	(2) Given Name	(3)	(4)	(5) Date	(6) Pg	(7) Col	(8) Comments
Estes	George	d.	ST	11 Oct. 1918	1	1	
Estes	George	d.	PA	30 Sept. 1918	4	4	
Estes	George W., Jr.	d.	SIT	24 June 1916	1	5	Mountain Cemetery
Estes	Madison Eugene	d.	SRR	18 Dec. 1916	5	1	
Estinghausen	William, Mrs.	d.	PD	3 Feb. 1918	8	4	also 6 Feb., 7:1
Ethorne	A.	d.	PA	18 Sept. 1918	8	4	
Eunningham	Hugh	b.	PC	13 May 1916	8	2	
Euphrat	Emanuel F.	m.	PC	26 July 1917	3	5	
Evans	Ada	m.	PD	17 July 1918	5	4	
Evans	Ada	m.	PA	18 July 1918	4	5	
Evans	Alma	m.	PA	23 July 1917	2	3	
Evans	Alma Murial	m.	PC	24 July 1917	3	4	
Evans	Arthur	b.	PA	27 May 1918	5	5	
Evans	Arthur	b.	PC	28 May 1918	6	3	
Evans	Arthur	b.	PA	29 Jan. 1917	8	5	
Evans	Arthur	b.	PC	30 Jan. 1917	8	3	
Evans	Edward	m.	PD	7 Jan. 1916	2	2	
Evans	Edward H.	m.	ST	8 Jan. 1916	1	6	
Evans	Edward R.	m.	SRR	7 Jan. 1916	3	3	
Evans	Elizabeth J.	d.	SRR	30 July 1917	4	2	Ukiah; also 8:6; 1 Aug., 4:4
Evans	Elizabeth J.	d.	PC	31 July 1917	8	4	
Evans	Elizabeth J.	d.	PD	31 July 1917	4	2	Ukiah; also 6:1; 2 Aug., 5:2
Evans	James M.	d.	PD	27 Sept. 1917	4	2	also 28 Sept., 5:2
Evans	James W.	d.	SRR	26 Sept. 1917	2	3	also 27 Sept., 3:4
Evans	John	o.	SRR	24 May 1916	5	2	
Evans	Lillian	m.	SRR	5 Nov. 1917	3	2	
Evans	Lillian	m.	PD	6 Nov. 1917	5	1	
Evans	Margaret	d.	PA	5 Oct. 1916	5	3	
Evans	Ralph	m.	SIT	15 Dec. 1917	1	4	
Evans	Ralph	m.	SRR	30 Nov. 1917	4	2	
Evans	Ralph	m.	PD	7 Dec. 1917	2	3	
Evans	Ralph	m.	SRR	7 Dec. 1917	6	3	
Evans	Roscoe	o.	PA	30 June 1917	4	4	
Evans	Roscoe	o.	PC	1 July 1917	1	4	
Evans	Roscoe	o.	PC	21 Mar. 1917	1	3	
Evans	Roy	o.	PC	17 Apr. 1918	8	4	also 21 Apr., 4:4
Evans	Roy	o.	PC	2 Aug. 1918	6	3	
Evans	Roy	o.	PC	27 Feb. 1918	6	3	
Evans	Roy	o.	PD	6 Dec. 1918	7	3	
Evart	Earl	b.	PC	16 Nov. 1918	5	3	
Evart	Earl	b.	PA	18 Nov. 1918	3	4	
Evart	Robbie	o.	PC	23 Mar. 1916	1	5	portrait
Evart	William, Jr.	b.	PC	2 Sept. 1916	4	2	

(1) Surname	(2) Given Name	(3)	(4)	(5) Date	(6) Pg	(7) Col	(8) Comments
Evarts	Earl	m.	PA	7 May 1918	3	5	
Evarts	Earl	m.	PC	7 May 1918	4	2	
Evarts	Earl	m.	PD	8 May 1918	2	4	
Everett	Armita	m.	PA	15 May 1917	8	7	
Everett	Armita	m.	PC	16 May 1917	8	2	
Ewing	Mary Ann	d.	PA	30 Jan. 1917	4	1	
Ewing	Mary Ann	d.	PC	31 Jan. 1917	3	3	also 2 Feb., 6:4
Ewing	William	d.	PA	15 May 1917	5	3	Cypress Hill; also 17 May. 5:5
Ewing	William	d.	PC	16 May 1917	1	5	Cypress Hill; also 16 May, 8:5; 17 May, 8:5; 18 May, 4:3

F

(1) Surname	(2) Given Name	(3)	(4)	(5) Date	(6) Pg	(7) Col	(8) Comments
Fairbanks	J. F., Mrs.	d.	PD	18 Sept. 1918	8	2	
Fairbanks	Julius F.	d.	PA	16 Sept. 1918	8	2	
Fairbanks	Julius F., Mrs.	d.	PC	18 Sept. 1918	6	3	Sebastopol; also 19 Sept., 2:3
Fairbanks	Loretta	m.	PA	16 Jan. 1918	4	5	
Fairbanks	Loretta	m.	PC	16 Jan. 1918	5	3	also 17 Jan., 4:2
Fairbanks	Robert Gilbert	d.	PC	26 Feb. 1918	3	4	also 4:5; 28 Feb., 4:3
Fairchild	Delia	d.	PA	27 Jan. 1917	2	3	Bloomfield; also 29 Jan., 8:2
Fairchild	Delia M.	d.	PD	27 Jan. 1917	2	4	Bloomfield; also 30 Jan., 5:4
Fairchild	Della	d.	PC	27 Jan. 1917	5	3	also 30 Jan., 2:3, Bloomfield
Fairfield	Delia M.	d.	SRR	27 Jan. 1917	5	4	Bloomfield
Fairman	Mary	d.	ST	1 Jan. 1016	1	3	
Fairman	Mary Elizabeth	d.	SRR	3 Jan. 1916	1	2	
Faithful	Annie L.	d.	PC	12 Jan. 1918	4	5	Mountain Cemetery
Faithful	Annie L.	d.	PD	12 Jan. 1918	6	3	
Fallen	Martin	d.	PD	24 June 1917	4	3	
Fallon	Jack	d.	PD	26 June 1917	8	4	
Fallon	Jack	d.	SRR	26 June 1917	5	1	Vallejo
Fallon	Jack	d.	SIT	30 June 1917	1	5	
Fallon	Martin	d.	SRR	23 June 1917	1	3	also 12:2; 25 June, 8:3
Falmer	Charles F.	m.	PD	29 June 1916	2	5	
Fancher	Frace	m.	PC	11 Jan. 1917	5	3	
Fancher	Grace	m.	PA	10 Jan. 1917	4	2	
Faraone	F.	b.	PA	9 July 1917	2	5	also 8:3
Farley	Mary	d.	PA	29 May 1917	8	5	Valley Ford; also 31 May, 5:2
Farley	Mary	d.	PC	29 May 1917	2	2	Tomales; also 8:3; 30 May, 2:2; 1 June, 5:3
Farley	Mary	d.	PD	1 June 1917	5	1	
Farley	Melvin R.	d.	PA	16 Nov. 1918	4	3	
Farley	Michael	d.	PD	10 Oct. 1917	3	3	
Farley	Michael	d.	SRR	10 Oct. 1917	5	4	Salinas
Farley	William	m.	PC	7 Mar. 1918	8	2	
Farley	William J.	m.	PA	1 Mar. 1918	8	6	
Farmer	Alice	m.	SRR	1 May 1916	8	1	
Farmer	Alice Blanche	m.	PD	2 May 1916	6	1	
Farmer	George	d.	PD	29 June 1918	5	2	Oakland
Farmer	Ralph	m.	PD	27 Dec. 1917	8	4	
Farmer	Ralph	m.	SRR	3 Dec. 1917	8	6	also 27 Dec., 3:5; 29 Dec., 4:2
Farmer	Ralph Arthur	o.	PC	27 July 1918	2	2	
Farmer	Ruth Eleanor	o.	PC	27 July 1918	2	2	

(1) Surname	(2) Given Name	(3)	(4)	(5) Date	(6) Pg	(7) Col	(8) Comments
Farmer	Susanna	d.	PD	7 Aug. 1917	4	2	also 5:3
Farmer	Susanna Savage	d.	SRR	7 Aug. 1917	7	4	also 8 Aug., 4:3; 9 Aug., 4:1
Farmer	Susanna Savage	d.	PC	8 Aug. 1917	8	1	
Farmer	Suzanna S.	o.	SRR	29 June 1917	4	3	
Farnlof	J. Edwin	d.	PD	28 June 1918	4	2	also 8:2; 29 June, 5:4
Faroni	Frank	m.	PC	19 Sept. 1916	5	4	
Faroni	Frank	m.	PC	31 Aug. 1916	4	1	also 13 Sept., 5:3
Faroni	Frank	m.	PA	6 Sept. 1916	5	7	also 11 Sept., 4:6; 18 Sept., 8:5
Farranze	Mr.	d.	ST	19 Apr. 1918	7	5	
Farrell	Angela Helen	m.	PA	27 July 1917	3	5	
Farrell	Angela Helen	m.	PD	27 July 1917	7	1	
Farrell	Gertrude	m.	PC	18 July 1916	2	2	
Farrell	Helen	m.	SRR	27 July 1917	5	5	
Farrell	Helen D.	m.	PC	27 July 1917	3	5	
Farrell	Mary	m.	SIT	27 Apr. 1918	1	7	
Farrell	Mary/Gertrude	m.	PD	27 Apr. 1918	7	5	
Farrell	W. E., Jr.	m.	PA	5 May 1916	6	3	
Farrell	William	d.	SRR	18 Dec. 1916	5	2	also 20 Dec., 5"3
Farrell	William E., Jr.	m.	SRR	4 May 1916	1	2	
Farrell	William E., Jr.	m.	PC	5 May 1916	6	3	
Farrell	William F.	d.	PA	18 Dec. 1916	4	2	portrait; Cypress Hill; also 19 Dec., 5:3, 6:3; 20 Dec., 4:1
Farrell	William F.	d.	PD	19 Dec. 1916	3	1	also 20 Dec., 8:3; 21 Dec., 7:1
Farrell	William Fitzmaurice	d.	PC	19 Dec. 1916	1	3	portrait; Cypress Hill; also 2:2; 20 Dec., 2:4; 21 Dec., 1:3
Farrington	B. F.	d.	PA	27 Feb. 1917	4	3	Cypress Hill; also 1 Mar., 8:4
Farrington	Benjamin Franklin	d.	PC	28 Feb. 1917	1	2	also 2 Mar., 8:4
Farrington	Guy Stevens	m.	PA	12 Mar. 1918	2	2	
Farrington	Nettie	m.	HT	11 Apr. 1918	3	5	
Farwell	Sydney	m.	PD	30 Jan. 1916	7	4	
Faught	Hazel	m.	PD	11 Dec. 1917	5	3	
Faught	Hazel	m.	SRR	11 Dec. 1917	5	4	
Faught	James	d.	PA	13 Jan. 1917	3	4	
Faught	James	d.	PD	14 Jan. 1917	2	2	
Faure	E.	d.	PA	23 Sept. 1918	8	5	Cypress Hill; also 5:5; 26 Sept., 4:5
Faure	Eckhardt	d.	PC	24 Sept. 1918	8	2	Cypress Hill; also 25 Sept., 6:3
Faure	Sophie	d.	PA	10 Nov. 1917	5	4	also 13 Nov., 8:3
Faure	Sophie	d.	PC	11 Nov. 1917	8	3	Cypress Hill; also 14 Nov., 4:4

(1) Surname	(2) Given Name	(3)	(4)	(5) Date	(6) Pg	(7) Col	(8) Comments
Fava	Pietro	d.	PD	16 June 1918	6	2	cremation
Fava	Pietro	d.	ST	22 June 1918	1	5	
Favour	John	m.	SRR	20 Jan. 1916	6	4	
Favour	John	m.	HT	27 Jan. 1916	1	4	
Fay	John	o.	PC	31 Jan. 1917	8	4	
Fay	May	o.	PC	31 Jan. 1917	8	4	
Fay	Patrick	d.	PA	5 Jan. 1917	8	6	also 9 Jan., 6:7
Fay	Patrick	d.	SRR	5 Jan. 1917	8	2	
Fay	Patrick	d.	PC	6 Jan. 1917	8	3	
Fay	Patrick	d.	PD	6 Jan. 1917	8	2	
Fay	Rebecca	d.	PD	21 Apr. 1917	8	5	
Fay	Rebecca	d.	PC	22 Apr. 1917	5	6	
Fay	Rebekah	d.	ST	21 Apr. 1917	1	6	also 28 Apr., 5:3
Faylor	John	d.	PC	5 Feb. 1918	1	2	also 8 Feb., 8:3
Faylor	John Richard	d.	PD	9 May 1918	8	3	
Faylor	John, Jr.	d.	ST	15 Feb. 1918	1	1	
Faylor	Johnnie	d.	PD	5 Dec. 1918	6	6	also 6 Dec., 3:4; 7 Dec., 8:1
Fechtelkotter	Harry	m.	SRR	28 Aug. 1916	3	3	
Fechtelkotter	Harry	m.	PD	29 Aug. 1916	3	3	
Feehan	Gladys	m.	SRR	29 Aug. 1916	7	5	
Fees	William H.	m.	PA	15 Jan. 1917	2	2	
Fees	William H.	m.	PC	16 Jan. 1917	5	5	
Fehrman	Paul	b.	PD	5 Nov. 1916	10	4	
Felciano	Manuel	b.	PD	10 Oct. 1916	3	4	
Feldmeyer	Berdina	m.	PC	3 May 1916	4	4	
Feldmeyer	Birdena E.	m.	SRR	2 May 1916	8	1	also 4 May, 6:2
Feldstein	Herman	b.	PC	1 May 1917	4	4	
Feliz	Mary J.	d.	PA	24 Apr. 1916	2	5	Calvary Cemetery; also 3:3; 26 Apr., 3:4
Feliz	Mary J.	d.	PC	25 Apr. 1916	4	3	Calvary Cemetery; also 26 Apr., 5:1; 27 Apr., 4:2
Feliz	Mary J.	d.	PD	25 Apr. 1916	3	2	also 27 Apr., 5:3
Felle	Louis	d.	PC	3 Mar. 1916	5	5	
Feller	Frank	b.	ST	14 Oct. 1916	2	4	
Feller	Louis	d.	SRR	10 Mar. 1916	4	1	
Feller	Louis	d.	PA	11 Mar. 1916	6	1	Calvary Cemetery, Santa Rosa
Feller	Louis	d.	PA	9 Mar. 1916	2	3	
Fellers	Frank	b.	ST	18 Jan. 1918	8	4	
Felstein	Mr. & Mrs.	b.	PA	4 Jan. 1917	2	4	
Felt	W. W.	b.	HT	4 Oct. 1917	1	1	
Feltes	Charles	o.	PD	26 Feb. 1918	6	1	
Feltes	May	m.	PD	16 Feb. 1917	8	1	
Feltes	May Caroline	m.	SRR	25 Apr. 1917	3	1	
Felton	Clarence	m.	PA	22 May 1916	4	1	

(1) Surname	(2) Given Name	(3)	(4)	(5) Date	(6) Pg	(7) Col	(8) Comments
Felton	Clarence	m.	PC	22 May 1916	5	2	
Felton	Clarence	b.	PA	13 Nov. 1918	5	4	
Fenley	Samuel E.	d.	PA	9 Aug. 1917	2	2	Cypress Hill; also 11 Aug., 8:4
Fenn	Theodore	m.	ST	27 Sept. 1918	1	3	
Fenner	A. L	d.	PD	29 Dec. 1917	2	4	
Fenner	A. L.	d.	SRR	28 Dec. 1917	4	1	
Fenner	Eliza M.	d.	CR	4 May 1917	1	2	
Fenton	Mary	d.	PD	17 Dec. 1918	2	2	Rural Cemetery; also 4:2; 19 Dec., 7:3
Fereira	Manuel Francisco	d.	PC	22 Sept. 1918	5	3	aka Smith; also 6:3
Ferguson	Cecelia	m.	PD	2 May 1916	7	4	
Ferguson	Cecelia	m.	PC	3 May 1916	6	3	
Ferguson	Chester	b.	HT	17 May 1917	5	3	
Ferguson	Martha	d.	PD	3 Nov. 1916	6	3	
Ferguson	Martha	d.	SRR	3 Nov. 1916	5	4	
Ferguson	Mattie	d.	HT	19 Oct. 1916	1	5	
Ferguson	Mattie	d.	PC	19 Oct. 1916	1	5	also 21 Oct., 1:3
Ferguson	Mattie	d.	PD	19 Oct. 1916	8	1	
Ferguson	Mattie	d.	SRR	19 Oct. 1916	4	3	
Ferguson	Mattie M.	d.	SRR	26 June 1916	8	6	also 27 June, 1:5
Ferguson	Mattie Woodward	d.	PD	27 June 1916	3	3	also 28 June, 8:4
Ferguson	Mrs.	d.	PA	19 Oct. 1916	4	5	
Ferguson	N. R.	b.	PA	6 Sept. 1916	4	3	
Ferguson	N. R.	b.	PC	7 Sept. 1916	5	6	
Ferguson	Velma	m.	PC	13 Dec. 1918	4	4	also 17 Dec., 5:5
Ferguson	Velma Crawford	m.	PA	13 Dec. 1918	5	2	also 16 Dec., 5:5
Ferguson	Velma Crawford	m.	PD	13 Dec. 1918	8	3	also 15 Dec., 7:2
Ferguson	W. A.	d.	SRR	7 Nov. 1916	2	3	
Fernandez	Alvina	d.	PC	20 May 1917	5	3	Sebastopol
Ferrari	Eda	m.	PD	4 May 1917	2	2	also 15 May, 2:6
Ferrari	Edith	m.	SRR	14 May 1917	3	5	
Ferreira	Manuel Francisco	d.	PA	21 Sept. 1918	8	5	aka Smith; also 23 Sept., 6:5
Ferria	Mrs. (dau of)	d.	PC	3 Feb. 1918	8	2	
Ferrier	George	m.	PA	27 July 1917	3	5	
Ferroggiaro	Fred A.	m.	PA	2 Aug. 1916	4	3	
Ferroggiaro	Fred A.	m.	PC	4 Aug. 1916	5	2	
Ferroni	Marie	m.	HT	7 Feb. 1918	5	4	
Fessendes	Clarence Silver	d.	PA	14 Aug. 1918	8	1	San Bernardino
Fetch	Harry	m.	SRR	15 July 1916	12	2	
Fetch	Nina	m.	PC	7 May 1918	5	2	
Fetch	Nina	m.	PD	7 May 1918	5	2	
Fetes	Charles E.	m.	PC	29 Feb. 1916	4	4	
Fevrier	George	m.	PD	27 July 1917	7	1	
Fevrier	George	m.	SRR	27 July 1917	5	5	

(1) Surname	(2) Given Name	(3)	(4)	(5) Date	(6) Pg	(7) Col	(8) Comments
Fevrier	George Taylor	m.	PC	27 July 1917	3	5	
Fevrier	Harold	m.	PC	18 July 1916	2	2	
Fick	John F.	d.	PD	7 June 1918	2	5	I.O.O.F. Cemetery; also 8 June, 4:2; 11 June, 8:5
Fick	John F.	d.	PA	8 June 1918	3	6	
Fiel	Ike	d.	PA	13 May 1916	8	3	
Field	C. E.	p.	SRR	5 July 1917	8	2	
Field	Charles Edward	d.	SRR	30 June 1917	6	5	Oak Mound Cemetery
Field	Charles Edward	d.	PC	1 July 1917	6	4	
Field	John T.	d.	SIT	8 June 1918	1	6	
Field	John T.	d.	PD	9 June 1918	3	6	
Field	Walter	o.	SRR	20 Jan. 1916	8	3	
Fields	S.	b.	PC	1 Dec. 1918	5	3	
Figoci	Albert	d.	PC	6 July 1916	1	6	
Filhes	M. L.	o.	PC	15 Oct. 1918	3	3	
Filipini	Anacelto	d.	PA	28 Dec. 1917	4	6	Calvary Cemetery; also 29 Dec., 5:4
Filippini	Amacieto	d.	PC	29 Dec. 1917	4	1	Calvary Cemeetery; also 7:3; 30 Dec., 8:2
Filippini	Emelia	d.	PD	28 Jan. 1917	2	4	also 31 Jan., 2:2
Filippini	Emilia	d.	PA	27 Jan. 1917	4	3	also 29 Jan., 4:5; 30 Jan., 8:3
Filippini	Emilia	d.	PC	27 Jan. 1917	1	4	Calvary Cemetery; also 28 Jan., 3:3, 8:4; 30 Jan., 8:7, 31 Jan., 1:4
Filippini	H.	m.	PC	15 Aug. 1917	8	2	
Filippini	Irene	d.	PC	27 Apr. 1918	2	2	Calvary Cemetery; also 28 Apr., 6:2; 30 Apr., 5:5
Filippini	John	b.	PC	21 Feb. 1917	5	2	
Filippini	Louisa E.	m.	PA	5 Apr. 1916	4	3	also 25 Apr., 5:3; 26 Apr., 5:3
Filippini	Louise	m.	SIT	29 Apr. 1916	5	4	
Filippini	V. C., Mrs.	d.	PD	1 Nov. 1918	2	1	
Filippini	Vegilia	d.	PA	30 Oct. 1918	8	5	Calvary Cemetery; also 31 Oct., 5:4
Filippini	Veglia	d.	PC	31 Oct. 1918	4	2	Calvary Cemetery; also 8:3; 1 Nov., 5:3
Fillipi	Rose	o.	PC	26 Oct. 1916	6	4	
Fillipi	Tony	o.	PC	26 Oct. 1916	6	4	
Fillipini	Louise	m.	PD	27 Apr. 1916	4	2	
Fillippi	Louise E.	m.	PC	6 Apr. 1916	6	1	
Finch	Gordon	m.	SIT	14 Apr. 1917	3	5	
Findley	J. J, Mrs.	d,	HT	7 Dec. 1916	1	2	
Fine	J. W.	d.	PD	24 Feb. 1917	2	5	
Fine	John W.	d.	PC	22 Feb. 1917	1	4	Cypress Hill; also 24 Feb., 1:5, 4:6; 25 Feb., 3:6
Fine	John W.	d.	PA	23 Feb. 1917	6	3	also 26 Feb., 5:4

(1) Surname	(2) Given Name	(3)	(4)	(5) Date	(6) Pg	(7) Col	(8) Comments
Fink	Huldie	d.	PA	16 July 1918	8	5	
Finkelstein	Bessie	m.	PC	29 Apr. 1916	5	2	
Finley	Belle	m.	PD	1 Dec. 1917	6	5	
Finley	Belle	m.	SRR	30 Nov. 1917	5	3	
Finley	Carrie Ann	o.	SRR	17 Feb. 1917	5	6	
Finley	Ernest L.	b.	PD	28 Nov. 1916	8	2	
Finley	Ethel	m.	PA	19 Jan. 1918	3	2	
Finley	Ethel	m.	PD	19 Jan. 1918	8	2	
Finley	Ethel	m.	ST	25 Jan. 1918	3	4	
Finley	Harrison	d.	PD	6 July 1917	7	1	Stanley Cemetery; also 7 July, 4:3
Finley	Harrison	d.	SRR	6 July 1917	5	1	Stanley Cemetery; also 7 July, 8:3; 9 July, 8:1
Finley	Harrison	d.	PC	7 July 1917	3	4	
Finley	Harrison	d.	HT	12 July 1917	4	1	
Finley	Harrison	p.	SRR	12 July 1917	8	4	
Finley	Harry	m.	PA	16 Feb. 1918	4	2	
Finley	Helen Alice	m.	PD	7 July 1918	7	3	also 14 July, 6:1
Finley	Henry	d.	PD	14 Apr. 1917	8	2	
Finley	Henry	d.	SRR	14 Apr. 1917	5	1	
Finley	Henry	d.	ST	14 Apr. 1917	8	4	also 23 Apr., 1:5
Finley	Henry	d.	PC	15 Apr. 1917	4	4	also 2 Apr., 3:3
Finley	Henry	d.	ST	19 Apr. 1918	1	2	Spring Hill Cem.
Finley	Henry	p.	PA	24 Apr. 1918	5	3	
Finley	Henry F.	d.	PD	19 Apr. 1918	4	2	Spring Hill Cemetery; also 6:5
Finley	Henry H.	d.	PA	19 Apr. 1918	7	6	
Finley	Henry H.	d.	PC	20 Apr. 1918	3	1	
Finley	Henry H.	p.	PD	24 Apr. 1918	7	4	
Finley	J. D.	o.	SRR	17 Feb. 1917	5	6	
Finley	James F.	p.	PA	23 Aug. 1917	3	1	
Finley	James F.	p.	PC	24 Aug. 1917	2	3	
Finley	Jefferson	d.	PC	27 Jan. 1918	1	3	
Finley	Jefferson	d.	PD	27 Jan. 1918	5	4	
Finley	Jefferson	d.	PA	28 Jan. 1918	8	3	
Finley	Jefferson	d.	HT	31 June 1918	6	2	
Finley	Jefferson Davis	d.	ST	1 Feb. 1918	4	3	
Finley	Samuel E.	d.	PC	10 Aug. 1917	2	1	Cypress Hill; also 8:3; 12 Aug., 8:4
Finley	Samuel E.	d.	PD	10 Aug. 1917	2	3	
Finley	Samuel E.	d.	SRR	10 Aug. 1917	5	4	
Finley	Winfred	d.	PD	14 Apr. 1917	8	2	
Finley	Winfred	d.	PC	15 Apr. 1917	4	4	also 2 Apr., 3:3
Finley	Winifred	d.	SRR	14 Apr. 1917	5	1	
Finley	Winifred	d.	ST	21 Apr. 1917	1	5	also 14 Apr., 8:4

(1) Surname	(2) Given Name	(3)	(4)	(5) Date	(6) Pg	(7) Col	(8) Comments
Finnie	Ruth Edna	m.	PD	14 June 1917	5	2	
Finsterbusch	Charles Lewis	d.	PA	15 Aug. 1916	8	3	Cypress Hill; also 17 Aug., 5:3
Finsterbusch	Charles Louis	d.	PC	16 Aug. 1916	1	5	Cypress Hill; also 5:3; 18 Aug., 4:1
Finsterbusch	Edith G.	m.	PA	1 May 1918	5	3	also 3 May, 8:3
Finsterbusch	Edith Grace	m.	PC	1 May 1918	5	5	
Fiocchini	Frank	d.	PA	16 May 1917	4	4	Cypress Hill; also 17 May, 4:3; 18 May 5:6. 8:7; 19 May 5:1
Fiori	Henry	d.	PA	23 Nov. 1918	5	3&4	Calvary Cemetery; also 25 Nov., 5:1
Fiori	Henry	d.	PC	24 Nov. 1918	2	2	Calvary Cemetery; also 4:3
Fischer	Anton	d.	PC	10 June 1918	6	6	Sebastopol
Fischer	Elise	d.	PC	17 Dec. 1916	1	3	Sonoma; also 19 Dec., 6:5; 20 Dec., 8:3
Fischer	Ella	m.	PA	22 Jan. 1916	3	4	
Fischer	Ella	m.	SRR	22 Jan. 1916	10	4	
Fischer	Ella	m.	PD	23 Jan. 1916	3	3	
Fischer	Ella	m.	PC	23 Jan. 1916	3	1	
Fischer	Ella	m.	HT	27 Jan. 1916	6	2	
Fischer	Elsie	d.	PA	18 Dec. 1916	4	5	Mountain Cemetery; also 19 Dec., 3:6
Fischer	Elsie	d.	PD	20 Dec. 1916	8	4	
Fischer	Fred	d.	PA	28 Apr. 1917	6	3	
Fischer	Fred	d.	PC	28 Apr. 1917	1	3	
Fischer	G. E., Mrs.	d.	SRR	18 Dec. 1916	4	2	
Fischer	G. F.	d.	PC	4 May 1917	5	2	cremation; also 6:2; 5 May, 6:1; 6 May, 1:4
Fischer	G. F.	d.	PD	4 May 1917	3	4	
Fischer	George F.	d.	PA	3 May 1917	5	4	cremation; also 4 May, 4:7
Fish	Arthur	o.	SIT	9 Feb. 1918	2	5	
Fish	Edward E.	m.	PD	26 Mar. 1918	3	1	
Fishel	John C.	m.	PD	8 Sept. 1916	3	3	
Fisher	Annie	d.	PA	28 Mar. 1916	4	1	Cypress Hill
Fisher	Ella	m.	SIT	29 Jan. 1916	4	4	
Fisher	Eva M.	o.	PD	4 Oct. 1916	5	2	adoption
Fisher	Fred	d.	PA	1 May 1917	2	4	
Fisher	Fred	d.	SRR	28 Apr. 1917	5	2	
Fisher	John	m.	HT	19 July 1917	1	5	
Fisher	John T.	m.	PD	17 July 1917	5	2	
Fisher	Melba	m.	PD	12 May 1917	8	3	
Fisher	Rebecca	d.	SRR	3 Aug. 1917	8	1&5	Rural Cemetery
Fisher	Rebecca	d.	PD	4 Aug. 1917	4	2	also 6:5
Fisher	Willard	d.	SRR	18 Feb. 1916	4	5	also 21 Feb., 3:2
Fisher	Willard	d.	PD	20 Feb. 1916	3	1	also Feb., 6:4

(1) Surname	(2) Given Name	(3)	(4)	(5) Date	(6) Pg	(7) Col	(8) Comments
Fisher	Willard X.	d.	HT	24 Feb. 1916	2	3	
Fisher	Willie R. D.	d.	PD	8 June 1917	5	1	
Fisk	Ann	m.	SRR	28 Dec. 1917	4	1	also 29 Dec., 4:2
Fisk	Ann	m.	PD	29 Dec. 1917	3	1	
Fisk	Frances	d.	ST	15 Nov. 1918	5	3	
Fiske	George J.	b.	PA	20 May 1918	6	2	
Fiske	George J.	b.	PA	8 Mar. 1916	5	4	
Fiske	Ira A.	d.	PA	20 Jan. 1917	2	2	
Fiske	Ira A.	d.	PC	21 Jan. 1917	5	2	also 24 Jan., 4:2
Fitch	Arthur	m.	SRR	21 Sept. 1916	8	6	
Fitch	Arthur	m.	PD	22 Sept. 1916	6	5	
Fitch	Dave	d.	PC	7 Mar. 1917	1	5	Napa; also 9 Mar., 3:6
Fitch	Herminia	d.	PD	2 June 1917	4	3	also 3 June, 2:3
Fitch	Martha M.	d.	HT	3 Mar. 1916	1	5	
Fitch	Martina M.	d.	PA	28 Feb. 1916	3	1	Healdsburg
Fites	Charles E.	m.	PA	23 Feb. 1916	5	4	also 29 Feb., 5:3
Fitts	J. P., Mrs.	d.	PA	20 Aug. 1917	1	5	
Fitts	Mary Jane	d.	SRR	20 Aug. 1917	4	2	
Fitts	Mary Jane	d.	PC	21 Aug. 1917	5	3	
Fitts	Mary Jane	d.	PD	21 Aug. 1917	4	2	also 6:5; 23 Aug., 4:2
Fitzgerald	John	o.	PC	21 Nov. 1918	1	5	
Fitzgerald	Tom	b.	PD	20 July 1917	3	2	
Fitzh	E., Mrs.	d.	SRR	1 June 1917	8	4	
Fitzpatrick	Elmer	d.	SRR	14 May 1917	3	3	Calvary Cemetery, Bodega; also 15 May, 8:1; 16 May, 8:3
Fitzpatrick	Elmer James	d.	PC	15 May 1917	4	3	Bodega; also 5:4; 16 May, 4:3; 17 May, 4:4
Fitzpatrick	Elmer James	d.	PD	15 May 1917	4	3	Bodega
Fitzpatrick	Elmer James	d.	PA	16 May 1917	8	7	Bodega
Fitzpatrick	Lawrence	m.	PD	26 Nov. 1918	1	3	
Fitzpatrick	Lawrence	m.	PA	27 Nov. 1918	8	2	
Fitzpatrick	Lawrence	m.	ST	29 Nov. 1918	1	2	
Fitzpatrick	Thomas	d.	SRR	20 Sept. 1917	4	3	
Flack	Rosie	m.	PC	25 Apr. 1917	8	1	
Flagge	Frederick	d.	PA	7 Jan. 1916	2	5	
Flagge	Frederick	d.	PD	7 Jan. 1916	5	4	
Flagge	Frederick	d.	SRR	7 Jan. 1916	8	5	
Flaherty	Joseph	d.	SRR	8 Feb. 1016	4	2	
Flanagin	C. E.	b.	PA	28 Mar. 1917	1	6	
Fleek	William	d.	PC	6 Sept. 1916	4	3	cremation, ashes to Wisconsin; also 8 Sept., 6:2
Fleek	William H.	d.	PA	5 Sept. 1916	5	4	Janesville, WI; 6 Sept., 1:7; 8 Sept., 4:5
Fleek	William H.	d.	PD	6 Sept. 1916	5	3	

(1) Surname	(2) Given Name	(3)	(4)	(5) Date	(6) Pg	(7) Col	(8) Comments
Flemming	William	m.	PA	31 Dec. 1918	4	2	
Fletcher	Katherine	d.	PC	30 Apr. 1918	6	4	
Flocchini	Frank	d.	PC	22 July 1917	4	4	
Flocchini/Focchini	Frank	d.	PC	18 May 1917	4	3	also 19 May, 8:5
Flockhart	Jack	d.	PD	20 Dec. 1918	8	4	I.O.O.F. Cemetery; also 21 Dec., 4:2; 22 Dec., 2:4
Floochini	Frank	d.	SRR	17 May 1917	8	1	
Floochini	Frank	d.	PD	18 May 1917	5	1	
Florence	Jane	d.	SRR	25 Jan. 1916	8	1	
Florence	Jane	o.	PC	26 Jan. 1916	4	3	
Florence	Jane	d.	PD	26 Jan. 1916	3	1	Guerneville Cemetery
Flores	Jesse (child of)	d.	SRR	30 July 1917	7	3	
Flourney	Alex	m.	PD	3 June 1917	10	3	
Flower	Herbert	o.	SRR	22 Nov. 1916	8	2	
Flower	Louisa	o.	SRR	22 Nov. 1916	8	2	
Focha	Albion	m.	PC	4 May 1918	5	2	
Focha	Ernest F.	d.	SRR	26 Sept. 1917	6	4	
Focha	Ernest F.	d.	PC	28 Sept. 1917	8	2	
Focha	Ernest F.	d.	ST	28 Sept. 1917	1	6	
Focha	Frances Agnes	m.	PC	6 Jan. 1918	5	3	also 17 Jan., 5:3
Focha	Frances Agnes	m.	PA	7 Jan. 1918	4	3	also 16 Jan., 8:5
Fochet	Amelia	m.	SRR	11 Dec. 1916	7	1	
Fochet	Amelia	m.	PC	13 Dec. 1916	5	1	
Fochetti	Abel Wilhelmina	d.	SRR	2 Dec. 1916	5	2	
Fochetti	Abel Wilhelmina	d.	PC	3 Dec. 1916	2	2	
Fochetti	Wilhelmina A.	d.	SIT	2 Dec. 1916	1	7	
Fochettioff	Abel Wilhelmina	d.	PD	2 Dec. 1916	7	1	
Fochs	Frances A.	m.	PD	8 Jan. 1918	5	7	
Focks	Ernest F.	d.	PD	26 Sept. 1917	8	1	
Foerstler	William C.	m.	SRR	30 July 1917	3	4	
Foerstler	William Carl	m.	PD	28 July 1917	7	5	also 31 July, 6:4
Foley	Michael	m.	PD	23 Sept. 1917	6	4	
Foote	Martha A.	d.	SRR	23 Oct. 1917	6	6	
Forbes	Mary	m.	PD	14 Sept. 1916	3	3	
Forbes	Mary	m.	SRR	14 Sept. 1916	8	4	
Ford	George T.	m.	PD	14 Oct. 1917	8	2	
Ford	George T.	m.	PA	15 Oct. 1917	7	5	
Ford	George T.	m.	SRR	15 Oct. 1917	5	3	
Ford	W. A.	m.	SRR	17 Dec. 1917	5	5	also 19 Dec., 8:3
Ford	W. A.	m.	PD	19 Dec. 1917	7	1	also 20 Dec., 6:5
Ford	William Augustus	m.	HT	20 Dec. 1917	1	5	
Fore	Walter	b.	PC	9 June 1917	3	6	
Foreman	Marie	d.	PD	24 Feb. 1917	8	2	
Foresti	Frank	d.	PD	8 Feb. 1917	2	4	Masonic Cemetery, Sebastopol; also 9 Feb., 4:2

(1) Surname	(2) Given Name	(3)	(4)	(5) Date	(6) Pg	(7) Col	(8) Comments
Foresti	Frank A.	d.	SRR	8 Feb. 1917	5	2	Sebastopol
Foresti	Frank V.	d.	PC	10 Feb. 1917	8	5	
Forgerson	Ingeborg	d.	PD	29 Feb. 1916	2	3	Oak Mound Cemetery
Formschlag	August	o.	PD	19 Nov. 1918	6	2	
Formschlag	August	o.	PA	20 Nov. 1918	7	3	
Formschlag	August E.	o.	PC	6 Jan. 1918	5	4	also 22 Mar., 8:5; 23 Mar., 1:2
Formschlag	August E.	o.	PA	7 Jan. 1918	3	4	also 21 Mar., 4:5; 22 Mar., 4:4
Formschlag	Josephine	o.	PC	6 Jan. 1918	5	4	also 22 Mar., 8:5; 23 Mar., 1:2
Formschlag	Josephine M.	o.	PA	7 Jan. 1918	3	4	also 21 Mar., 4:5; 22 Mar., 4:4
Forni	Kate	m.	PD	29 Jan. 1918	2	3	
Forqueras	Antonia	d.	PA	19 Jan. 1918	4	5	Tomales; also 21 Jan., 6:3
Forquerds	Antonia R.	d.	PC	19 Jan. 1918	1	5	Tomales
Forsyth	Henry M., III	b.	PD	18 Apr. 1917	3	4	
Forsyth	Henry M., III	b.	SRR	16 Apr. 1917	5	1	
Forsyth	Jack	b.	PD	27 June 1916	2	4	
Forsyth	Jack, Jr.	d.	PD	29 June 1916	8	2	also 30 June, 8:4
Forsyth	John	d.	HT	10 Feb. 1916	5	2	
Forsyth	John	d.	PD	6 Feb. 1916	8	4	also 8 Feb., 2:4, 5:4
Forsyth	John	d.	SRR	7 Feb. 1916	5	4	also 8 Feb., 8:3
Forsyth	Robert	d.	PA	13 Apr. 1916	4	2	
Forsyth	Robert	d.	SRR	13 Apr. 1916	4	3	Rural Cemetery
Forsyth	Robert	d.	PC	14 Apr. 1916	4	2	
Forsyth	Robert Alexander	d.	PD	13 Apr. 1916	8	4	also 14 Apr., 8:3
Forsythe	Jack	b.	SRR	26 June 1916	7	3	
Forsythe	Jack, Jr.	d.	SRR	29 June 1916	5	4	also 30 June, 8:2
Forsythe	Jack, Jr.	d.	PD	1 July 1916	2	1	
Forsythe	John	d.	ST	12 Feb. 1916	7	4	
Fosdick	Mildrd Ethel	m.	SIT	31 Aug. 1918	1	5	
Foster	Arminda	d.	PA	17 Jan. 1917	2	4	Berkeley
Foster	Arminda	d.	PD	17 Jan. 1917	5	2	Sunset Cemetery, Berkeley
Foster	Arminda	d.	SRR	17 Jan. 1917	5	3	
Foster	Arminda	d.	PC	18 Jan. 1917	3	4	
Foster	Fred Orth	o.	PD	15 Nov. 1918	4	2	name change from Fred Orth
Foster	J. W.	b.	PC	8 Oct. 1916	5	2	
Foster	Jesse Valentine	d.	PA	31 July 1916	1	6	
Foster	Jesse Valentine	d.	PC	1 Aug. 1916	4	1	
Foster	Jesse Valentine	d.	PD	1 Aug. 1916	5	2	
Foster	Lulu E.	d.	PD	6 Apr. 1918	4	2	also 9 Apr., 3:3
Foster	Walter	b.	PA	7 Oct. 1916	5	2	
Foster	William S.	m.	PD	10 Oct. 1917	6	2	
Fowler	Laura T.	d.	PD	13 Oct. 1916	2	2	

(1) Surname	(2) Given Name	(3)	(4)	(5) Date	(6) Pg	(7) Col	(8) Comments
Fox	Delia	m.	PD	7 Mar. 1916	8	1	
Fox	Elizabeth	m.	HT	19 July 1917	1	5	
Fox	Elizabeth Ann	m.	PD	17 July 1917	5	2	
Fox	Henry	d.	HT	29 June 1916	1	2	cremation; also 4 July, 6:5
Fox	Henry	d.	SRR	29 June 1916	8	6	cremation; also 30 June, 2:3
Fox	Henry	d.	PC	30 June 1916	6	4	
Fox	Henry	d.	PD	30 June 1916	7	4	
Fox	Jeremiah "Jerry"	d.	PA	8 Mar. 1916	5	2	Sacramento; also 9 Mar., 6:4
Fox	Mary	d.	PC	4 July 1918	6	4	San Rafael
Fraherty	Joseph	d.	ST	12 Feb. 1916	1	3	
Frail	Emma	d.	ST	16 Nov. 1917	1	2	
Fralich	Free	d.	PA	24 Apr. 1917	8	2	
Fralich	Free	d.	PD	25 Apr. 1917	5	5	
Fralick	Free	d.	SRR	24 Apr. 1917	8	1	
Frampton	Earl	b.	SRR	8 Aug. 1917	6	5	
Frampton	Earl	b.	HT	9 Aug. 1917	1	1	
Francard	Phelomene	d.	SRR	19 May 1917	10	2	
Francard	Philomene	d.	PD	22 May 1917	2	3	
Franceschi	A., Mrs.	d.	PD	18 Sept. 1917	5	2	also 21 Sept., 2:3
Franceschi	Francisco	d.	SRR	17 Sept. 1917	8	3	also 18 Sept., 8:5
Franchesi	Frank, Mrs.	d.	ST	21 Sept. 1917	11	2	Druids Cemetery
Francisco	Ray	o.	PD	17 May 1918	6	1	
Francisco	Ray	o.	PD	10 Aug. 1918	5	1	
Franeschi	A., Mrs.	d.	PC	18 Sept. 1917	1	4	
Franklin	Blandine	m.	PA	20 Oct. 1916	4	3	also 24 Oct., 8:5
Franklin	Blandine	m.	PC	20 Oct. 1916	5	4	
Franklin	Blandine L.	m.	PD	24 Oct. 1916	5	7	
Fraser	Dan	b.	SRR	12 Sept. 1916	5	5	
Fraser	Dan	b.	PD	13 Sept. 1916	6	3	
Frates	Florence A.	m.	PA	15 Feb. 1916	1	1	
Frates	Irene	m.	PC	11 Apr. 1917	6	6	also 12 Apr., 5:2
Frates	Manuel	d.	PA	22 Aug. 1918	5	3	Calvary Cemetery; also 23 Aug., 5:5; 24 Aug., 5:4
Frates	Manuel	d.	PC	22 Aug. 1918	1	2	Calvary Cemetery; also 23 Aug., 5:3; 25 Aug., 8:3
Frates	Mary Glory	d.	PA	19 Jan. 1918	4	4&5	Calvary Cemetery; also 21 Jan., 5:3
Frates	Mary Glory	d.	PC	20 Jan. 1918	6	2&3	
Frati	Frank	d.	PD	1 June 1918	4	2	Calvary Cemetery; also 5:4
Fratini	Casimire	d.	PA	19 Sept. 1917	8	3	Calvary Cemetery; also 21 Sept., 5:5; 22 Sept., 5:6
Fratini	Casimiro	d.	PC	20 Sept. 1917	1	3&5	Calvary Cemetery; also 21 Sept., 8:5; 23 Sept., 8:4
Fraucher	Jessie	m.	PD	16 Aug. 1918	8	4	
Fraucher	Jessie	m.	PC	17 Aug. 1918	6	5	

(1) Surname	(2) Given Name	(3)	(4)	(5) Date	(6) Pg	(7) Col	(8) Comments
Frazier	H. K.	b.	PA	2 July 1918	8	7	
Frazier	Harry K.	m.	PA	14 Mar. 1918	5	4	
Frazier	Harry K.	m.	PC	15 Mar. 1918	4	2	
Frazier	Henry	b.	PC	3 July 1918	5	2	
Frazier	Ruth	d.	PA	26 June 1916	4	3	Ukiah; also 27 June, 7:5
Frazier	Ruth Fern	d.	PD	28 June 1916	2	3	
Frazier	Ruth Fern	d.	PC	27 June 1916	4	3	Ukiah; also 5:4; 28 June, 4:4
Freck	Louis	m.	SIT	30 June 1917	2	4	
Fredericks	Dora M.	m.	PA	29 May 1918	8	5	
Fredericks	Dora M.	m.	PC	30 May 1918	5	4	
Fredericks	Frances	d.	PC	6 July 1916	5	6	Sebastopol
Fredericks	Frances	d.	PD	6 July 1916	1	6	
Fredericks	Franzisca	d.	SRR	5 July 1916	8	6	Sebastopol Odd Fellows
Fredericks	Marty	o.	PC	4 Dec. 1917	5	4	
Fredericks	Mrs.	d.	PA	5 July 1916	1	2	
Fredericks	William	m.	PA	2 Mar. 1917	8	2	
Fredericks	William	m.	PD	2 Mar. 1917	8	2	
Frederickson	Mr. & Mrs.	b.	PC	20 Apr. 1916	8	2	
Freeman	Clara	m.	PD	21 May 1916	10	2	
Freeman	Clara B.	m.	SRR	22 May 1916	5	4	
Freeman	Eliza J.	d.	PA	23 Feb. 1916	5	6	Cypress Hill
Freeman	Emma P.	m.	PC	8 Sept. 1916	8	3	
Freeman	Glen	o.	PA	19 June 1917	1	7	
Freeman	John M.	p.	PC	5 Oct. 1916	5	4	died 1890
Freeman	Lester	d.	PD	30 Aug. 1917	2	3	
Freeman	Lester L.	d.	SRR	27 Aug. 1917	8	3	also 29 Aug., 8:2
Freese	Alice M.	o.	PC	21 Nov. 1917	3	3	
Freese	Charles A.	o.	PC	21 Nov. 1917	3	3	
Freese	Walter	b.	PA	12 Sept. 1917	1	7	also 5:5
Freeze	Elza	m.	PD	23 May 1971	8	2	
Frehan	Gladys L.	m.	PD	3 Sept. 1916	5	3	
Frei	Louis	b.	PA	19 June 1917	5	4&6	
Frei	Louis	b.	PD	20 June 1917	1	6	
Frei	Louis	b.	SRR	20 June 1917	5	2	
Frei	Walter C.	m.	ST	15 Feb. 1918	1	2	
Frei	Walter T.	m.	PC	10 Feb. 1918	1	4	
Freitas	Andre T.	d.	PC	26 May 1917	6	3	
Freize	Willard Elbert	d.	PD	4 Feb. 1916	9	2	
Frelich	Fred	d.	HT	26 Apr. 1917	1	4	
Frellson	Hans	d.	PA	17 Sept. 1918	5	4	
French	Vida Rachael	m.	PC	21 Apr. 1917	2	3	
French	Vida Rachael	m.	SRR	19 Apr. 1917	5	2	
French	Vida Rachel	m.	ST	21 Apr. 1917	8	5	
Frese	Elza	m.	SRR	22 May 1917	10	3	
Frese	Lloyd	b.	SRR	8 Nov. 1917	6	6	

(1) Surname	(2) Given Name	(3)	(4)	(5) Date	(6) Pg	(7) Col	(8) Comments
Fresher	Elmer J.	d.	PA	5 Sept. 1918	2	5	
Fresher	Elmer L.	d.	PD	5 Sept. 1918	3	1	France; portrait; also 6 Sept., 1:6
Freshour	Christopher Columbus	d.	SRR	8 May 1917	6	4	
Freshour	Christopher Columbus	d.	HT	10 May 1917	5	2	Oak Mound Cemetery
Frieze	Willard E.	d.	SRR	3 Feb. 1916	8	2	also 4 Feb., 3:2
Friis	Christine	m.	PD	17 Oct. 1917	6	5	
Friis	Elene	m.	PD	10 Oct. 1917	2	1	
Friis	Elene	m.	SRR	10 Oct. 1917	5	1	
Friis	Elene	m.	PA	9 Oct. 1917	5	4	also 16 Oct., 4:5
Frisch	F. W.	b.	HT	30 Mar. 1916	1	5	
Frisk	Charles E.	d.	PD	5 Sept. 1917	7	3	
Fritsch	John	d.	PD	12 Oct. 1917	8	4	
Fritsch	John Raymond	d.	PA	11 Oct. 1917	5	1	Cypress Hill; also 12 Oct., 4:1
Fritsch	John Raymond	d.	PC	12 Oct. 1917	4	5	also 13 Oct., 5:4
Fritsch	John Raymond	d.	SRR	12 Oct. 1917	3	6	
Fritsch	Mecham	m.	PA	4 June 1918	4	4	also 8 June, 4:5; 10 June, 5:4
Fritsch	Walter M.	m.	PD	9 June 1918	7	1	
Fritsch	Walter Mecham	m.	PC	10 June 1918	1	1	
Fritsch	Walter Mecham	m.	PC	7 Apr. 1918	5	4	
Fritsch	Walter Mecham	m.	PD	7 Apr. 1918	5	1	
Frittz	Fillmore	b.	SRR	20 Sept. 1917	8	4	
Fritz	Filmore	m.	SRR	26 Aug. 1916	4	2	
Frohlking	William	d.	PA	5 Jan. 1916	4	5	cremation; also 5:3; 7 Jan., 7:3
Frohlking	William	d.	PC	6 Jan. 1916	5	2	cremation; also 6:4
Frost	Walter	d.	PC	14 Apr. 1918	4	3	
Frugoli	Joe	o.	PD	2 July 1918	8	1	
Frus	Elaine Christine	m.	PC	16 Oct. 1917	1	5	also 17 Oct., 5:3
Fry	Frances	m.	PD	9 Dec. 1917	6	3	
Fry	Peter	b.	SRR	24 July 1916	5	3	
Fucha	Ewald A.	m.	SRR	16 Oct. 1916	8	4	
Fuetterer	C.	d.	SRR	4 Dec. 1916	5	1	
Fuettrer	C.	d.	PD	3 Dec. 1916	6	4	
Fullagar	Caroline	d.	SRR	29 June 1917	8	2&6	Stanley's Cemetery
Fullegar	Caroline	d.	PA	30 June 1917	7	3	
Fuller	Frank	o.	PA	23 May 1917	5	4	
Fuller	Frank	o.	PC	24 May 1917	1	4	
Fuller	Harry	o.	ST	27 Dec. 1918	1	3	
Fuller	John Isaac	d.	PC	1 Apr. 1918	5	2	Cypress Hill; also 2 Apr., 4:3
Fuller	John Isaac	d.	PA	2 Apr. 1918	4	1	Cypress Hill; also 4 Apr., 4:2

(1) Surname	(2) Given Name	(3)	(4)	(5) Date	(6) Pg	(7) Col	(8) Comments
Fuller	Percy	b.	PC	8 Aug. 1916	5	2	
Fulton	James	d.	PA	26 Mar. 1917	5	7	
Fulton	James	d.	SRR	26 Mar. 1917	8	5	
Fulton	James N.	d.	PD	27 Mar. 1917	1	4	
Fulwider	Earl N.	m.	PD	3 June 1916	5	3	
Fulwider	Earl H.	m.	PA	2 June 1916	2	4	
Fulwider	Earl N.	m.	SRR	31 May 1916	8	1	also 3 June, 4:1
Funke	Emilie	d.	PD	20 May 1917	1	3	
Funke-Wagner	Emeline	d.	SRR	21 May 1917	8	3	Alameda
Funte	Emily Wagner	d.	PA	19 May 1917	5	3	
Furber	Elbridge G.	d.	PD	29 Feb. 1916	5	1	also 1 Mar., 6:1
Furber	Eldridge	d.	HT	3 Mar. 1916	1	3	
Furber	Eldridge G.	d.	SRR	29 Feb. 1916	5	1	also 1 Mar., 9:3
Furgerson	Jugeborg	d.	HT	3 Mar. 1916	1	5	
Furlong	Charles E.	m.	PC	6 Jan. 1918	5	3	also 17 Jan., 5:3
Furlong	Charles E.	o.	PA	7 Jan. 1918	4	3	also 16 Jan., 8:5
Furlong	Charles E.	m.	PD	8 Jan. 1918	5	7	
Furlong	E. J.	d.	PA	29 Feb. 1916	5	2	
Furlong	Kathryn	m.	PC	16 Feb. 1917	8	2	
Furlong	Kathryn	m.	SRR	16 Feb. 1917	6	5	
Furlong	Kathryn A.	m.	PC	21 Jan. 1917	5	4	
Furlong	Kathryn A.	m.	PA	22 Jan. 1917	5	3	also 15 Feb., 4:5
Furlong	Patrick	d.	PA	13 Mar. 1916	5	3	also 14 Mar., 4:5; 16 Mar., 5:2
Furlong	Patrick	d.	ST	18 Mar. 1916	1	3	
Furlong	Patrick A.	d.	SRR	13 Mar. 1916	8	3	
Furlong	Patrick A.	d.	PC	16 Mar. 1916	5	4	Catholic Cemetery
Furlong	Patrick A.	d.	PD	16 Mar. 1916	6	3	Sebastopol Cemetery
Furlong	Robert A.	d.	PC	14 Mar. 1916	1	4	Catholic Cemetery
Furlong	Sarah	m.	PC	27 Sept. 1916	4	3	
Furlong	Sarah	m.	ST	30 Sept. 1916	8	4	
Furlong	Thomas	m.	PD	29 Mar. 1918	8	2	
Furlong	Thomas	m.	PC	30 Mar. 1918	6	5	
Furlong	Thomas	m.	ST	5 Apr. 1918	1	6	
Fyfe	Ed S.	d.	ST	23 Aug. 1918	1	5	
Fyfe	Edward F.	d.	PD	23 Aug. 1918	3	4	

G

(1) Surname	(2) Given Name	(3)	(4)	(5) Date	(6) Pg	(7) Col	(8) Comments
Gablin	Clifford	d.	PC	29 Apr. 1916	1	7	
Gablin	Cliftord	d.	SRR	28 Apr. 1916	1	4	
Gablin	Clifton	d.	PA	28 Apr. 1916	5	4	
Gabriele	John S.	m.	PC	29 May 1917	4	1	also 1 May, 5:4
Gabrielle	John E.	m.	PA	30 Apr. 1917	5	1	
Gaff	Walter Harold	m.	SRR	15 Sept. 1917	4	2	
Gaffney	Andrew	d.	PA	13 Nov. 1917	2	6	
Gaffney	Andrew	d.	ST	16 Nov. 1917	2	5	
Gaffney	Andrew	d.	PD	2 Nov. 1917	5	4	legal ruling; also 13 Nov., 3:1
Gaffney	Andrew	d.	PC	4 Nov. 1917	2	2	also 14 Nov., 3:5
Gaffney	Miles	d.	PA	24 Aug. 1916	5	4	Bodega; also 25 Aug., 5:3; 26 Aug., 6:3
Gaffney	Miles	d.	SRR	24 Aug. 1916	1	2	also 25 Aug., 4:1; 26 Aug., 5:2
Gaffney	Miles	d.	PC	25 Aug. 1916	1	6	also 26 Aug., 6:4; 27 Aug., 4:1
Gaffney	Miles	d.	PD	26 Aug. 1916	5	1	also 27 Aug., 1:6
Gaffney	Miles	d.	ST	26 Aug. 1916	1	5	Bodega
Gaffney	Miles	d.	PD	8 Dec. 1916	2	1	also 9 Dec., 2:7
Gaffney	William	m.	SRR	21 May 1917	1	5	
Gaffney	William	m.	PD	22 May 1917	7	3	
Gaffney	William	m.	PA	23 May 1917	2	6	
Gaffney	William	m.	PC	23 May 1917	4	2	
Gaffney	William	m.	ST	25 May 1917	2	3	
Gage	Charles G.	d.	PC	5 Sept. 1917	8	5	Novato; also 6 Sept., 8:1; 7 Sept., 4:1
Gaige	A. E.	d.	PC	12 Mar. 1918	3	2	
Gaige	A. E.	d.	PA	9 Mar. 1918	2	3	
Gaige	Albert E.	d.	PD	10 Mar. 1918	4	3	
Gaige	Albert R.	d.	SIT	14 Mar. 1918	1	7	Mountain Cemetery
Gaines	Clark H.	m.	SIT	21 Dec. 1918	2	3	
Gaines	Paul	m.	PA	20 June 1918	4	4	
Galard	Nicholas	d.	PD	24 Jan. 1918	2	3	Calvary Cemetery; also 4:2; 29 Jan., 2:1
Galdden	Geneva	m.	SRR	13 Jan. 1916	8	4	
Gale	Bert	o.	SIT	29 Sept. 1917	1	1	
Gale	Earl R.	o.	PC	1 Dec. 1917	1	5	
Gale	Eliza	d.	PA	11 Apr. 1916	4	3	Cypress Hill; also 5:2; 13 Apr., 4:4
Gale	Eliza	d.	PD	13 Apr. 1916	7	1	
Gale	Eliza A.	d.	PC	11 Apr. 1916	1	6	also 12 Apr., 3:3; 14 Apr., 5:1

(1) Surname	(2) Given Name	(3)	(4)	(5) Date	(6) Pg	(7) Col	(8) Comments
Gale	Eliza E.	d.	SRR	11 Apr. 1916	3	4	
Gale	Elsie	m.	PD	28 Oct. 1916	2	3	
Gale	Georg Lavinia	d.	SIT	30 Nov. 1918	1	1	Santa Rosa
Gale	Georgia Lavinia	d.	PD	26 Nov. 1918	1	6	also 28 Nov., 3:1
Gale	Georgia Lavinia	d.	PC	27 Nov. 1918	3	4	
Gale	John M.	m.	PA	29 June 1918	4	7	
Gale	Marie T.	m.	PA	18 Oct. 1916	5	4	also 19 Oct., 6:9
Gale	Mary	m.	PC	7 May 1918	2	3	
Gale	Riley	d.	PA	19 Sept. 1916	4	3	cremation; also 20 Sept., 5:5
Gale	Riley	d.	SRR	19 Sept. 1916	1	4	also 20 Sept., 8:1, 8:5
Gale	Riley	d.	PC	20 Sept. 1916	2	1	cremation; also 22 Sept., 2:2
Gale	Riley	d.	PD	20 Sept. 1916	2	2	Oakland; also 21 Sept., 6:2
Gale	Thorn P.	m.	PD	16 Dec. 1917	3	3	
Gale	Thorn P.	m.	SRR	20 Aug. 1917	3	4	
Gale	Thorn P.	m.	PC	21 Aug. 1917	6	1	
Gale	Thornbrough	m.	SRR	15 Dec. 1917	6	1	
Gale	Wallace B.	m.	PA	25 May 1916	4	4	
Gale	Wallace P.	m.	PD	26 May 1916	6	2	
Gale	Wallace R.	m.	PC	26 May 1916	8	5	
Gale	Marie F.	m.	PC	19 Oct. 1916	3	3	
Galehouse	Ira W.	o.	PA	17 Aug. 1918	2	3	
Galehouse	Ira W.	o.	PC	18 Aug. 1918	4	3	
Galesworthy	Jane	d.	SRR	8 Mar. 1917	4	4	Sebastopol
Gallagher	Charles H.	m.	ST	6 May 1916	1	3	
Gallagher	Charles Hugh	m.	PC	4 May 1916	8	2	
Gallagher	John P.	o.	PA	21 Aug. 1918	6	4	
Gallagher	Lorellia	m.	SRR	20 Oct. 1916	5	1	
Gallagher	Loretta	m.	SRR	1 Dec. 1916	7	3	
Gallagher	Loretta	m.	PA	19 Oct. 1916	5	4	
Gallagher	Loretta	m.	PC	19 Oct. 1916	8	3	
Gallagher	Loretta	m.	PC	2 Dec. 1916	5	4	
Gallagher	Loretta	m.	PD	20 Oct. 1916	1	4	
Gallagher	Loretta	m.	SRR	22 Nov. 1916	2	1	
Gallagher	Loretta	m.	PA	29 Nov. 1916	4	3	
Gallagher	Loretta	m.	PD	30 Nov. 1916	8	4	
Gallagher	Mrs.	d.	PA	14 Nov. 1918	1	5	
Gallagher	Mrs.	d.	PD	14 Nov. 1918	6	3	
Gallard	Nick	d.	SIT	26 Jan. 1918	4	5	
Gallaway	Crystal	m.	HT	12 Oct. 1916	1	1	
Gallaway	Crystal	m.	SRR	6 Oct. 1916	4	3	also 10 Oct., 3:1; 18 Oct., 3:6
Gallaway	Crystal	m.	PC	7 Oct. 1916	5	3	also 11 Oct., 1:4; 13 Oct., 3:6
Gallaway	Crystal	m.	PD	7 Oct. 1916	2	4	
Gallaway	Elizabeth	m.	HT	11 July 1918	1	1	

(1) Surname	(2) Given Name	(3)	(4)	(5) Date	(6) Pg	(7) Col	(8) Comments
Gallaway	Elizabeth	m.	PD	12 July 1918	2	3	
Galli	Norma	d.	PD	27 Dec. 1918	3	1	Calvary Cemetery; also 4:2
Galli/Calli	Ester Josephine	d.	PD	11 Aug. 1918	4	2	also 8:2
Gallion	Henry B.	d.	HT	5 July 1917	4	3	
Gallion	Henry B.	d.	SRR	6 July 1917	6	6	
Galloway	Elizabeth	m.	PC	12 July 1918	3	1	
Galvin	Mary E.	d.	PD	18 Jan. 1918	3	1	
Gambini	Peter A. R.	m.	SRR	8 Feb. 1917	8	4	
Gambini	Peter A. R.	m.	PD	9 Feb. 1917	5	1	
Gamboni	Adele	d.	PA	16 Apr. 1917	5	4	Calvary Cemetery; also 17 Apr., 5:4
Gamboni	Adele	d.	PC	18 Apr. 1917	4	3	Calvary Cemetery
Gamboni	Arnold	m.	PA	1 Oct. 1918	5	3	
Gamboni	Battista	p.	PA	30 Sept. 1918	6	4	
Gambonini	Arnold	m.	PC	2 Oct. 1918	8	3	
Gambonini	Baptista	d.	PA	19 Sept. 1918	4	3	Calvary Cemetery; also 7:5; 21 Sept., 5:3
Gambonini	Baptista	d.	PC	19 Sept. 1918	1	3	also 22 Sept., 4:4
Gambonini	Catherine	d.	PC	27 May 1917	1	6	Calvary Cemetery; also 29 May, 3:3; 30 May, 5:4
Gambonini	Catherine	d.	PA	28 May 1917	8	3&7	Calvary Cemetery; also 29 May, 4:5
Gambonini	Ermenia	m.	PC	2 Nov. 1917	6	5	
Gambonini	Ermenia	m.	PA	31 Oct. 1917	5	2	
Gammage	Jules C.	o.	PC	3 Oct. 1917	5	5	
Gammage	Lottie F.	o.	PC	3 Oct. 1917	5	5	
Ganagni	James	b.	PC	22 Feb. 1917	5	2	
Gangloff	Teresa	d.	PC	17 Nov. 1917	3	2	
Gangloff	Theresa	d.	ST	16 Nov. 1917	1	5	
Gannon	Elizabeth K.	d.	PD	30 Jan. 1917	8	2	
Garaventa	Gormola	d.	PD	10 Feb. 1916	1	1	
Garaventa	James	d.	SRR	10 Feb. 1916	5	2	also 11 Feb., 5:2
Garaventa	Jimmie	d.	ST	12 Feb. 1916	8	4	
Garcer	Joseph	m.	PC	25 Apr. 1917	8	1	
Garcia	Firmin	m.	PD	8 Sept. 1916	5	4	
Garcia	Firmin	m.	PD	9 Sept. 1916	3	4	
Garcia	Michael	b.	PC	28 Apr. 1916	8	6	
Gard	Amelia	o.	SRR	18 Aug. 1916	8	1	
Gard	Amelia	o.	SRR	27 Nov. 1916	8	5	
Gard	Amelia	o.	PD	28 Nov. 1916	2	5	
Gard	Amelia Lawrence	m.	PD	5 Sept. 1918	6	2	
Gard	Arley	o.	SRR	18 Aug. 1916	8	1	
Gard	Arley	o.	SRR	27 Nov. 1916	8	5	
Gard	Arley	o.	PD	28 Nov. 1916	2	5	
Gard	James	b.	PA	19 Feb. 1918	8	2	

(1) Surname	(2) Given Name	(3)	(4)	(5) Date	(6) Pg	(7) Col	(8) Comments
Gard	James	b.	PC	20 Feb. 1918	8	3	
Gard	James F.	m.	PA	5 May 1917	2	6	
Gardiner	Alice	o.	PA	21 Dec. 1918	3	6	also 23 Dec., 2:2
Gardiner	C. V.	o.	SRR	27 Jan. 1916	5	1	
Gardiner	Clarence Leroy	m.	SRR	13 July 1916	1	5	
Gardiner	Clarence LeRoy	m.	PC	14 July 1916	3	4	
Gardiner	Clayson V.	o.	PD	29 Dec. 1917	3	4	
Gardiner	Louise	o.	SRR	27 Jan. 1916	5	1	
Gardiner	Louise A.	o.	PD	29 Dec. 1917	3	4	
Gardiner	W. B.	m.	PC	30 Nov. 1918	5	3	
Gardiner	Waldron B.	m.	PA	29 Nov. 1918	4	4	
Gardiner	Waldron R.	o.	PA	21 Dec. 1918	3	6	also 23 Dec., 2:2
Gardner	George W.	d.	PD	22 Nov. 1916	5	2	
Gardner	George W.	d.	SRR	22 Nov. 1916	3	3	Alexandria, MN
Gardner	George W.	d.	ST	25 Nov. 1917	1	2	
Gardner	Louise A.	o.	PA	27 Jan. 1916	3	6	
Gardner	O. V.	o.	PA	27 Jan. 1916	3	6	
Garloff	Ben	o.	ST	6 Oct. 1918	1	2	
Garloff	Herman	o.	ST	14 June 1918	5	3	
Garloff	Herman J.	m.	PA	14 Nov. 1917	4	3	
Garloff	Herman J.	m.	PC	15 Nov. 1917	3	1	
Garloff	Mamie	m.	ST	26 Aug. 1916	5	2	
Garloff	Mamie	m.	PC	27 Aug. 1916	6	2	
Garloff	William	b.	ST	21 Apr. 1917	7	2	
Garner	Addie	d.	SRR	27 May 1916	10	6	
Garner	Addie	d.	PD	28 May 1916	2	3	
Garner	Robert	m.	PD	7 Aug. 1918	6	2	
Garofalo	Bernice	d.	PA	25 Jan. 1916	3	6	
Garrett	Ida	m.	PD	1 June 1917	8	1	
Garrigan	Florence	d.	PA	31 Aug. 1917	1	5	
Garrison	Florence	d.	PC	1 Sept. 1917	1	4	also 6 Sept., 3:4
Garrison	Florence	d.	PD	1 Sept. 1917	8	4	Rural Cemetery; also 2 Sept., 4:3; 5 Sept., 5:3
Garrison	Florence	d.	SRR	31 Aug. 1917	1	4	also 1 Sept., 1:2; 4 Sept., 5:4
Garsoll	Lena Frances	m.	PD	11 Oct. 1917	7	2	
Gartaroli	Harry	m.	SRR	1 May 1916	1	2	
Garvin	Nora S.	m.	PD	14 Sept. 1916	3	5	
Garzelli	Clemente	b.	PA	2 July 1918	5	6	
Garzoli	Lena Frances	m.	PC	30 Sept. 1917	5	4	also 11 Oct., 5:4
Garzolli	Lena Francis	m.	PA	9 Oct. 1917	5	6	
Gaspari	Jennie	d.	SRR	7 May 1917	1	4	Calvary Cemetery; also 9 May, 2:3
Gaspari	Jennie	d.	PD	8 May 1917	4	3	Calvary Cemetery; also 5:7; 9 May, 4:3; 11 May, 8:4
Gasper	Harry	d.	PC	8 Dec. 1916	8	3	

(1) Surname	(2) Given Name	(3)	(4)	(5) Date	(6) Pg	(7) Col	(8) Comments
Gasper	Henry	d.	PA	7 Dec. 1916	4	5	
Gasper	Joseph	d.	PA	12 June 1916	4	4&5	Cypress Hill; also 14 June, 5:4
Gasper	Joseph I.	d.	PC	13 June 1916	3	1	Calvary Cemetery; also 5:3, 8:4; 15 June, 3:4; 16 June, 3:3
Gaston	G. Russell	b.	PA	3 July 1918	8	3	
Gaston	Russell	m.	PC	1 Sept. 1917	5	2	
Gaston	Russell	m.	PA	28 Sept. 1917	4	3	also 1 Oct., 5:4
Gaston	Russell	m.	PC	28 Sept. 1917	3	4	also 30 Sept., 6:6; 2 Oct., 6:3
Gates	Benjamin Franklin	d.	PA	15 Nov. 1918	5	3	Cypress Hill
Gates	Benjamin Franklin	d.	PC	16 Nov. 1918	2	2	
Gates	H. H.	d.	ST	7 Apr. 1917	1	5	
Gates	Henry H.	d.	SRR	31 Mar. 1917	5	6	
Gates	Henry Harrison	d.	PA	30 Mar. 1917	4	5	
Gates	Henry Harrison	d.	PC	31 Mar. 1917	4	1	
Gates	Henry Harrison	d.	PD	31 Mar. 1917	8	1	
Gates	W. A.	d.	PD	19 Mar. 1918	5	2	
Gatson	Russell	m.	PA	1 Sept. 1917	2	4	
Gautier	Leopold	m.	PD	9 Sept. 1917	7	4	
Gaydou	Charles H.	d.	SRR	3 Dec. 1917	7	3	
Gazelli	Clementi	b.	PC	3 July 1918	5	2	
Geanini	Henry (child of)	d.	PC	6 Sept. 1916	7	3	Olema
Gease	Julius	m.	PA	10 July 1918	4	6	
Gedes	F. B.	d.	PD	20 Apr. 1918	5	2	
Gee	Yong	d.	SRR	21 Aug. 1916	1	6	
Geegus	Louis	d.	PD	28 July 1917	8	3	
Geggus	Louis	d.	SRR	28 July 1917	5	3	
Geggus	Louis	d.	CR	3 Aug. 1917	1	1	
Geiger	Elizabeth J.	d.	PD	18 June 1918	7	3	I.O.O.F. Cemetery; also 19 June, 4:2
Geiger	Otto	m.	PD	5 Sept. 1918	6	2	
Geldermann	William	o.	SIT	11 Aug. 1917	1	2	
Gells	Elsie May	m.	PC	13 Sept. 1916	5	4	
Gemetti	Antone	d.	PD	1 Nov. 1918	2	2	also 2 Nov., 6:5
Gemetti	Antone	d.	PC	31 Oct. 1918	4	4	
Genazzi	Fred	m.	PC	17 Oct. 1917	4	2	
Genazzi	Fred	m.	PD	18 Oct. 1917	3	3	
Genazzi	H. H., Mrs.	d.	ST	17 May 1918	5	4	
Genezzi	Fred	m.	PA	16 Oct. 1917	8	3	
Genther	Ray	m.	PD	8 Oct. 1916	3	1	
George	Earmon A.	o.	PD	7 Aug. 1918	6	5	adoption
George	H. A.	o.	PA	10 Aug. 1918	3	6	portrait
George	H. A.	o.	ST	16 Aug. 1918	5	3	portrait
George	H. A.	o.	PA	17 Aug. 1918	4	6	portrait; also 24 Aug., 7:5

(1) Surname	(2) Given Name	(3)	(4)	(5) Date	(6) Pg	(7) Col	(8) Comments
George	Harmon A.	o.	PC	6 Aug. 1918	1	3	adoption
George	Henry A.	o.	ST	16 Aug. 1918	1	1	adoption
George	John	d.	ST	22 Nov. 1918	2	2	
Gerden/Gerdes	Frederick Bernard	d.	PA	18 Apr. 1918	5	7	Muscatine, Iowa; also 19 Apr., 8:4
Gerdes	Frederick Bernhard	d.	PC	19 Apr. 1918	4	3	Muscatine, Iowa; also 8:4; 21 Apr., 2:2
Gerear	Josef	m.	PA	23 Apr. 1917	5	4	
Gericke	Agnes	m.	PA	23 Apr. 1917	5	3	
Gericke	Agnes	m.	PC	24 Apr. 1917	5	1	
Gericke	Agnes	m.	SRR	24 Apr. 1917	5	2	
Gericke	Agnes	m.	SIT	28 Apr. 1917	1	3	
Germanino	Mary	d.	SRR	29 Aug. 1917	4	3	Calvary Cemetery; also 30 Aug., 8:1
Germanino	Mary	d.	PD	30 Aug. 1917	8	5	
Gerson	Abraham	b.	PA	24 Mar. 1917	4	3	
Gerson	Abraham	b.	PC	25 Mar. 1917	5	5	
Gertridge	Carl	b.	PD	9 Oct. 1918	5	3	
Gertsen	Carl Stanley	o.	PC	22 Mar. 1916	1	6	portrait
Gesse	Julius	m.	PC	11 July 1918	8	2	
Geurkink	William Bernard	d.	PC	11 Nov. 1917	1	2	Cypress Hill; also 13 Nov., 8:3
Ghisletta	A.	b.	PA	14 Sept. 1917	4	4	
Ghisletti	A.	b.	PA	28 Feb. 1916	5	5	
Giacometti	Louis	m.	PA	10 Feb. 1916	4	1	
Giacometti	Louis	b.	PA	3 Aug. 1916	8	4	
Giacomini	Olive	m.	PA	5 May 1916	6	3	
Giacomini	Olive M.	m.	SRR	4 May 1916	1	2	
Giacomini	Olive M.	m.	PC	5 May 1916	6	3	
Giacomini	P.	b.	PC	21 Sept. 1916	5	4	
Giando	Frank, Jr.	d.	SRR	3 Oct. 1917	1	3	
Gibbons	Vernon	b.	PA	8 May 1917	8	3	
Gibbs	Frank	d.	PA	15 Jan. 1918	5	3	Benicia; also 16 Jan., 2:1
Gibbs	Frank	d.	PC	16 Jan. 1918	1	5	
Gibbs	Giles	d.	PA	19 Nov. 1918	8	1	
Gibbs	Giles	d.	PC	19 Nov. 1918	3	5	Cypress Hill; also 21 Nov., 3:2
Gibbs	Giles	d.	PA	20 Nov. 1918	5	6	
Gibbs	Walter	d.	PD	3 Mar. 1916	3	3	Masonic Cemetery, Sebastopol
Gibbs	Walter	d.	SRR	3 Mar. 1916	4	3	
Gibbs	Walter	d.	ST	4 Mar. 1916	8	3	
Giberson	C. M.	p.	PC	14 Jan. 1917	1	4	
Giberson	Charles	d.	SRR	11 Jan. 1917	6	3	
Giberson	Charles McChesney	d.	PA	10 Jan. 1917	5	4	also 12 Jan., 8:5
Giberson	Charles McChesney	d.	PC	10 Jan. 1917	8	2	Two Rock; also 11 Jan., 4:4

(1) Surname	(2) Given Name	(3)	(4)	(5) Date	(6) Pg	(7) Col	(8) Comments
Giberson	Charles McChesney	d.	PD	11 Jan. 1917	1	4	
Giberson	Meribah Jane	d.	PA	24 July 1916	5	2	Two Rock
Giberson	Meribah Jane	d.	PC	25 July 1916	1	3	Two Rock; also 3:4; 26 July, 3:4, 4:4; 27 July, 8:2
Gibsdon	Clyde	m.	PD	23 Nov. 1916	2	3	
Gibson	Claudius	d.	PA	11 Apr. 1916	5	2&3	Cypress Hill; also 12 Apr., 5:1
Gibson	Claudius Somers	d.	PC	11 Apr. 1916	1	5	Cypress Hill; also 4:1; 13 Apr., 6:6
Gibson	Clyde	b.	PA	15 Nov. 1917	5	2	
Gibson	Clyde	m.	PC	6 Oct. 1916	8	3	
Gibson	Clyde C.	m.	PA	21 Nov. 1916	4	3	
Gibson	Clyde C.	m.	PC	22 Nov. 1916	1	4	
Gibson	Clyde C.	m.	SRR	22 Nov. 1916	7	4	
Gibson	Forrest	o.	PD	24 Aug. 1918	6	5	
Gibson	George	d.	SRR	14 July 1917	8	6	I.O.O.F. Cemetery; also 16 July, 1:4
Gibson	Kate	m.	PD	21 June 1916	2	2	
Gibson	L. B., Mrs.	d.	PD	27 Sept. 1918	3	3	
Gibson	Lenora	m.	HT	14 June 1917	6	3	
Gibson	Leona	m.	PA	20 June 1918	8	3	
Gibson	Leona	m.	PC	20 June 1918	1	4	also 21 June, 4:3
Gibson	Lucena B.	d.	PA	24 Sept. 1918	4	6	Cypress Hill; also 5:5; 26 Sept., 5:3
Gibson	Otis	b&d	PC	9 Apr. 1918	4	2	Calvary Cemetery
Giffen	George W.	d.	PD	25 Nov. 1916	6	3	
Gilandi	America	o.	PC	6 Dec. 1917	3	4	also 14 Dec., 1:6
Gilardi	Allan T.	d.	PC	25 Sept. 1918	3	4	also 8:4; 27 Sept., 3:2
Gilardi	Allen	d.	SIT	28 Sept. 1918	3	5	
Gilardi	Allen Thomas	d.	PA	24 Sept. 1918	4	3	Calvary Cemetery; also 5:5; 25 Sept., 2:6
Gilardi	Allen Thomas	d.	PD	26 Sept. 1918	3	3	also 27 Sept., 2:5
Gilardi	Americo	o.	PC	28 July 1917	8	2	
Gilardi	Ames	b.	PC	18 Apr. 1917	4	4	
Gilardi	Andrew	b.	PA	22 Nov. 1917	1	3	also 7:7
Gilardi	Andy	b.	PC	22 Nov. 1917	3	2	
Gilardi	Catherine Marie	m.	PC	8 July 1917	1	5	also 11 July, 5:2; 12 July, 5:2
Gilardi	Catherine Marie	m.	SRR	10 July 1917	6	4	also 11 July, 4:1
Gilardi	Catherine Marie	m.	PA	11 July 1917	3	4	
Gilardi	Edith Agatha	m.	PA	17 May 1916	6	4	also 24 May, 4:4
Gilardi	Edith Agatha	m.	PC	17 May 1916	4	3	also 25 May, 1:3
Gilardi	Frank	o.	PC	27 July 1918	6	3	
Gilardi	Frank F.	o.	PA	25 July 1918	4	7	
Gilardi	Frank J.	o.	SRR	14 May 1917	10	1	
Gilardi	Frank J.	o.	PC	15 May 1917	8	4	
Gilardi	Irene	o.	PA	25 July 1918	4	7	

(1) Surname	(2) Given Name	(3)	(4)	(5) Date	(6) Pg	(7) Col	(8) Comments
Gilardi	Irene	o.	PC	27 July 1918	6	3	
Gilardi	Katherine	m.	PD	11 July 1917	8	2	also 12 July, 6:5
Gilardi	Margery	d.	SIT	28 Sept. 1918	3	5	
Gilardi	Marjory	d.	PC	25 Sept. 1918	3	4	also 8:4; 27 Sept., 3:2
Gilardi	Marjory Louise	d.	PA	24 Sept. 1918	4	3	Calvary Cemetery; also 5:5; 25 Sept., 2:6
Gilardi	Marjory Louise	d.	PD	26 Sept. 1918	3	3	also 27 Sept., 2:5
Gilardy	Albert Joseph	b.	ST	16 Aug. 1918	6	1	born 19 Feb. 1914
Gilbert	Arthur	m.	PD	19 Apr. 1918	8	4	
Gilbert	Arthur	m.	PC	20 Apr. 1918	2	2	
Gilbert	W. S.	d.	PD	24 Nov. 1918	7	4	
Gilbert	William	d.	PD	27 June 1916	8	2	
Gilbert	William	d.	SIT	1 July 1916	1	7	
Gilbert	William J.	d.	PC	27 June 1916	1	2	
Gilbertson	M. L., Mrs.	d.	PD	27 July 1916	8	5	Two Rock Churchyard
Gildred	Alfred	o.	PD	16 Nov. 1917	6	2	
Gildred	Gertrude	o.	PD	16 Nov. 1917	6	2	
Giles	Elizabeth	m.	PA	29 Nov. 1916	8	4	
Giles	Elizabeth	m.	PC	30 Nov. 1916	1	5	
Giles	Elsie	m.	PA	12 Sept. 1916	4	3	
Giles	Elsie	m.	PD	13 Sept. 1916	1	6	
Giles	Elsie	m.	SRR	13 Sept. 1916	5	2	
Gilkey	Howard	m.	SRR	6 June 1916	8	3	
Gillam	Sam	d.	PA	11 July 1917	5	3	
Gillespie	Benjamin	d.	HT	14 Dec. 1916	1	4	
Gillespie	Benjamin	d.	SRR	14 Dec. 1916	3	3	Olive Hill Cemetery
Gillespie	Benjamin	d.	PC	15 Dec. 1916	1	6	
Gillespie	Benjamin	d.	PD	16 Dec. 1916	6	2	
Gillespie	Ruth	m.	PD	30 May 1917	6	4	
Gillett	Charles	m.	PD	14 Sept. 1916	3	3	
Gillett	Charles, Mrs.	d.	SRR	14 Jan. 1916	5	1	also 17 Jan., 4:3
Gillette	Charles, Mrs.	d.	PD	14 Jan. 1916	5	3	also 15 Jan., 6:4; 16 Jan., 1:2
Gillettt	Charles	m.	SRR	14 Sept. 1916	8	4	
Gilliam	Samuel Jackson	d.	PC	12 July 1917	3	5	Rural Cemetery; also 14 July, 8:4
Gilliam	Samuel Jackson	d.	PD	12 July 1917	2	4	also 4:3; 14 July 3:2
Gilliam	Samuel Jackson	d.	SRR	13 July 1917	8	3	
Gilman	Barbara	m.	PD	22 June 1918	5	4	
Gilman	Becky	d.	PA	10 Jan. 1917	3	3	
Gilman	Fred W., Mrs.	d.	PD	11 Jan. 1917	2	1	I.O.O.F. Cemetery; also 13 Jan., 6:5
Gilman	Gladys	m.	PC	15 Aug. 1917	8	1	
Gilman	Gladys A.	m.	SRR	14 Aug. 1917	8	4	also 15 Aug., 8:3; 16 Aug., 5:3
Gilman	Helen	d.	PC	18 Dec. 1917	7	5	

(1) Surname	(2) Given Name	(3)	(4)	(5) Date	(6) Pg	(7) Col	(8) Comments
Gilman	Rebecca Curtis	d.	SRR	10 Jan. 1917	1	3	also 12 Jan., 2:3
Gilman	Rebecca Curtis	d.	PC	11 Jan. 1917	1	6	
Gilman	William	m.	PD	6 Oct. 1917	2	1	
Gilmer	Harvey, Mrs.	d.	PA	29 Nov. 1916	5	1	Sebastopol
Gilmer	Vera	d.	PC	29 Nov. 1916	3	4	Sebastopol; also 30 Nov., 8:1
Gilmer	Vera	d.	SRR	29 Nov. 1916	4	1	Sebastopol Masonic Cemetery
Gilmer	Vera	d.	PD	30 Nov. 1916	6	2	
Gilmore	Annie	o.	PD	12 July 1918	3	3	
Gilmore	Annie D.	d.	PA	1 Apr. 1918	3	5	Cypress Hill
Gilmore	Annie Delaney	d.	PC	30 Mar. 1918	1	3	Cypress Hill; also 2 Apr., 2:2
Gilmore	Annie Delaney	d.	PD	30 Mar. 1918	3	2	Petaluma; also 4:2; 2 Apr., 7:3
Gilmore	Minerva Ruth	m.	SRR	9 Nov. 1916	8	5	
Gilmore	Mrs.	d.	ST	5 Apr. 1918	1	2	
Gilmore	W. B.	o.	CR	8 June 1917	1	2	
Gilmore	W. S.	o.	PD	12 July 1918	3	3	
Gingery	Joseph	d.	PC	1 Jan. 1918	3	5	Sebastopol; also 3 Jan., 5:6
Gingery	Joseph	d.	PD	1 Jan. 1918	4	2	also 6:2; 3 Jan., 2:2
Gingery	Joseph	d.	SIT	5 Jan. 1918	3	4	
Ginini	Tillo	d.	PC	4 Feb. 1918	3	6	
Giovannia	Tony (son of)	d.	ST	8 Nov. 1918	5	6	Occidental
Giovannini	A. (son of)	d.	PD	3 Nov. 1918	1	2	also 8 Nov., 2:2
Girolo	A.	b.	PA	7 June 1917	8	3	
Givanovich	Captain	d.	PC	7 Mar. 1918	8	5	on ship sunk by German submarine
Givins	T.	b.	PC	23 Oct. 1918	8	2	
Giwaltney	Benjamin	b.	SRR	2 Nov. 1916	10	3	
Gladden	Fred W.	b.	HT	30 Oct. 1918	1	2	
Glando	Frank	d.	PD	4 Oct. 1917	5	2	
Glando	Frank, Jr.	d.	PC	4 Oct. 1917	1	1	
Glando	John, Jr.	d.	PA	4 Oct. 1917	8	4	Oakland
Glatfelder	Clement	d.	SRR	15 Dec. 1917	12	1	
Glatfelder	Vinicia Anna	d.	PD	14 Dec. 1917	4	2	Odd Fellows Cemetery; also 6:2
Glazier	Harry	b.	PA	9 Jan. 1917	8	4	
Glazier	Hazel	d.	PA	8 July 1918	5	7	Santa Rosa
Glazier	Hazel	d.	PC	9 July 1918	3	4	Santa Rosa
Glazier	Walter	b.	PA	26 Feb. 1916	4	4	
Gleason	Harry	m.	PD	17 Nov. 1917	2	4	
Gleason	Lee Harry	m.	PA	19 Nov. 1917	6	5	
Gleason	Leo Harry	m.	SRR	17 Nov. 1917	6	3	also 30 Nov., 4:1
Gleason	Leo Harry	m.	PC	18 Nov. 1917	3	3	
Gleason	Mac	m.	PD	29 Mar. 1918	8	2	
Gleason	Mae	m.	PC	30 Mar. 1918	6	5	

(1) Surname	(2) Given Name	(3)	(4)	(5) Date	(6) Pg	(7) Col	(8) Comments
Gleason	May	m.	ST	5 Apr. 1918	1	6	
Gleeson	Elizabeth Eileen	m.	PA	27 Apr. 1916	5	4	
Gleiser	J. Harry	b.	PD	3 Sept. 1916	7	2	
Glenn	William	d.	PA	31 May 1917	5	4	also 1 June, 7:4; 2 June, 3:3
Glenn	William	d.	PC	1 June 1917	5	3	also 2 June, 8:2; 3 June, 1:5
Glenn	William	d.	PC	13 Nov. 1917	3	3	
Glenn	William	d.	PD	13 Nov. 1917	7	2	also 14 Nov., 5:2
Glenson	Leo	m.	PC	1 Dec. 1917	2	1	
Glines	Mabel	m.	PD	7 Jan. 1917	7	1	
Gobbi	Henry D.	m.	HT	12 Oct. 1916	1	6	
Gobbi	Maggie	o.	PC	5 Feb. 1918	1	3	
Goddard	Evelyn	m.	PD	12 Apr. 1916	2	4	
Goddard	Evelyn	m.	SRR	12 Apr. 1916	7	5	
Goddard	Hazel	m.	HT	25 Oct. 1917	1	5	
Goddard	Hazel	m.	PD	27 Oct. 1917	7	3	
Goddard	Jesse	b.	HT	21 Feb. 1918	7	2	
Godding	Blaine C.	m.	SRR	13 Jan. 1916	8	4	
Godozi	Mary	d.	PD	29 June 1918	8	3	
Goess	George	d.	PA	11 June 1917	6	3	
Goess	George	d.	SRR	11 June 1917	3	2	
Goess	George	d.	PD	13 June 1917	7	2	also 14 June, 3:3
Goess	George	d.	SIT	16 June 1917	2	1	
Goetzen	Ann	d.	PA	11 Sept. 1918	4	1	Cypress Hill
Goetzen	Ann	d.	PC	11 Sept. 1918	8	5	Cypress Hill; also 12 Sept., 4:4
Goldberg	Lillian	m.	HT	14 Nov. 1918	8	4	
Goldberg	Lillian	m.	PD	11 Nov. 1918	8	3	
Goldman	Leopold	o.	PA	20 Feb. 1917	8	6	
Goldsworthy	Jane	d.	PD	9 Mar. 1917	8	3	
Goldworthy	Jane	d.	PC	10 Mar. 1917	1	6	
Gonela	child	d.	HT	4 Oct. 1917	1	5	
Gonella	Carmine, Mrs.	d.	PD	7 Dec. 1917	3	4	also 9 Dec., 8;4
Gonella	J. (son of)	d.	PD	16 Mar. 1918	5	5	
Gonella	Louis	d.	SRR	10 Nov. 1916	2	1	Druids Cemetery
Gonnella	Amerigo	d.	SRR	19 June 1917	8	1&5	Bodega Calvery Cemetery
Gonnella	Amerigo	d.	PD	20 June 1917	4	3	Bodega; also 8:5
Gonnella	Amerigo	d.	PC	21 June 1917	5	4	also 22 June, 8:4
Gonnella	C. Mrs.	d.	ST	14 Dec. 1917	6	3	Bodega
Gonnella	Carmine	d.	SRR	6 Dec. 1917	8	2	
Gonnella	Carmine	d.	PC	7 Dec. 1917	4	4	Calvary Cemetery, Bodega; also 11 Dec., 2:2
Gonnella	L.	d.	PC	11 Nov. 1916	2	3	Druid's Cemetery
Gonnella	Louis	d.	PD	10 Nov. 1916	8	6	
Gonnella	Louis	d.	ST	11 Nov. 1916	3	2	Druid's Cemetery
Gonsalves	George	m.	PA	3 July 1917	8	5	

(1) Surname	(2) Given Name	(3)	(4)	(5) Date	(6) Pg	(7) Col	(8) Comments
Gonsalves	George E.	m.	PC	4 July 1917	4	3	
Gonsalves	George S.	m.	SRR	3 July 1917	8	1	
Gonsalves	Mr. & Mrs.	b.	PA	19 Apr. 1918	4	5	
Gonsalves	Mrs.	d.	PA	15 Feb. 1916	5	4	Calvary Cemetery; also 16 Feb., 8:6; 17 Feb., 10:6
Goodbrake	Jack James	m.	PA	20 Mar. 1916	4	5	
Goodbrake	James	m.	PC	21 Mar. 1916	8	5	
Goodman	Harvey M.	m.	PD	9 Dec. 1916	2	3	
Goodman	Nellie	d.	SRR	17 Dec. 1917	8	2	
Goodman	Nellie	d.	PA	18 Dec. 1917	11	5	
Goodman	Nellie Arnold	d.	PC	18 Dec. 1917	3	2	
Goodman	Nellie Arnold	d.	PD	18 Dec. 1917	5	1	also 20 Dec., 2:5
Goodman	Nellie Arnold	d.	HT	20 Dec. 1917	7	3	
Goodman	Samuel	m.	PA	26 Mar. 1917	4	3	
Goodman	Samuel	m.	PC	27 Mar. 1917	5	1	
Goodwin	Aaron	d.	PC	26 Jan. 1917	5	5	
Goodwin	Georgianna F.	m.	PC	15 Dec. 1917	8	3	also 16 Dec., 5:3
Goodwin	Georginna Catherine	m.	PA	15 Dec. 1917	4	3	
Goodwin	Gladys	d.	PA	28 Dec. 1918	4	1	Calvary Cemetery; also 5:2; 30 Dec., 5:1
Goodwin	Harry	d.	PD	31 Mar. 1918	3	3	also 3 Apr., 8:1
Goodwin	Henrietta Gladys	d.	PC	28 Dec. 1918	8	3	also 29 Dec., 5:3; 31 Dec., 8:3
Goodwin	J.	o.	PA	10 Apr. 1918	4	2	
Goodwin	Linwood	o.	PC	1 Dec. 1918	4	4	
Goodwin	Pearl	m.	PA	23 June 1917	5	3	
Goodwin	Pearl	m.	PC	24 June 1917	4	4	
Goodwin	Pearl	m.	PD	24 June 1917	2	2	
Goodwin	William Julius	d.	HT	8 Aug. 1918	1	5	
Goodyear	Lloyd	m.	PD	13 Nov. 1917	6	1	
Goodyear	Lloyd	m.	PD	25 Dec. 1917	8	3	also 27 Dec., 6:3
Goodyear	Lloyd	m.	SRR	26 Dec. 1917	5	4	
Goodyear	Lloyd	m.	HT	3 Jan. 1918	8	4	
Goodyear	Lloyd S.	m.	PC	14 Nov. 1917	3	4	
Goodyear	Lloyd S.	m.	PC	27 Dec. 1917	1	3	also 29 Dec., 8:2
Gordan	Frank	o.	PA	19 Jan. 1918	5	2	adoption
Gordenker	Martha	m.	SRR	22 Jan. 1916	2	3	
Gordenker	Martha	m.	SRR	5 Sept. 1916	6	2	
Gordenker	Martha	m.	PD	6 Sept. 1916	7	2	
Gordon	Nancy A.	d.	PD	31 Dec. 1918	4	2	Rural Cemetery
Gore	Chester A.	m.	SRR	22 Sept. 1916	6	5	also 25 Sept., 8:5
Gorgerson	Mary	o.	PD	26 Jan. 1918	5	5	
Gorgerson	William	o.	PD	26 Jan. 1918	5	5	
Gorman	Mary I.	m.	PD	30 Dec. 1917	7	2	
Gorman	Stanley	d.	PA	12 Apr. 1918	5	2	France

(1) Surname	(2) Given Name	(3)	(4)	(5) Date	(6) Pg	(7) Col	(8) Comments
Gorman	Stanley	d.	PC	13 Apr. 1918	3	4	France in British Army
Gorman	Stanley	d.	PD	13 Apr. 1918	2	4	British Army
Gorski	Charles	d.	PD	12 July 1917	5	3	
Gosch	Earnest	d.	PD	23 Dec. 1917	8	1	
Gossage	Josephine	m.	PD	27 Oct. 1917	8	3	
Gossage	Josephine	m.	PC	28 Oct. 1917	4	3	
Gottenberg	Emmett	m.	SIT	28 Dec. 1918	1	5	
Gotvig	Samuel	o.	PD	24 Oct. 1918	3	4	
Goudy	Harry A.	m.	ST	17 May 1918	1	1	
Goudy	Henry A.	m.	PD	14 May 1918	7	3	
Goudy	Henry A.	m.	PA	17 May 1918	3	2	
Goudy	Henry A.	m.	PC	17 May 1918	1	3	
Gould	Anna	d.	PD	21 Aug. 1917	8	5	also 22 Aug., 2:4
Gould	Anna	d.	SRR	21 Aug. 1917	4	5	
Gould	Luetta	m.	PC	17 Mar. 1917	4	6	
Gould	Mary Ann	d.	PC	22 Aug. 1917	3	6	Santa Rosa
Gould	Nathaniel	d.	PA	25 Jan. 1916	4	5	also 8:5; 26 Jan., 8:5
Gould	Nathaniel	d.	PC	25 Jan. 1916	1	1&4	Cypress Hill; also 26 Jan., 2:3; 27 Jan., 4:2
Gould	Nathaniel	d.	SRR	25 Jan. 1916	5	4	also 27 Jan., 5:1
Gould	Nathaniel	d.	HT	27 Jan. 1916	1	3	
Gould	Nathaniel	d.	PD	27 Jan. 1916	5	4	
Gow	Ah	d.	PA	23 Aug. 1918	3	4	
Gow	Ah	d.	PD	23 Aug. 1918	8	5	
Gow	Ah	d.	PC	24 Aug. 1918	8	3	
Gow	George	b.	PA	24 Apr. 1918	4	4	also 25 Apr., 4:2
Gow	George	b.	PC	25 Apr. 1918	4	4	
Gowans	Andrew, Jr.	b.	PC	18 Feb. 1917	4	3	
Grabner	Fred, Mrs.	d.	HT	20 Apr. 1916	6	5	Oak Mound Cemetery
Grabner	Katherine	d.	SRR	18 Apr. 1916	3	3	
Graeff	John U.	d.	PA	1 Feb. 1917	4	3	Sebastopol; also 5:4; 2 Feb., 3:4
Graeff	John U.	d.	PC	2 Feb. 1917	8	5	
Graeff	John W.	d.	PD	2 Feb. 1917	8	3	Odd Fellows, Sebastopol; also 3 Feb., 8:3
Graeff	John W.	d.	SRR	2 Feb. 1917	6	1	
Graff	Lillebelle	m.	PC	22 May 1916	5	2	
Graff	Lilliebell	m.	PA	22 May 1916	4	1	
Graff	Mike	d.	HT	14 Feb. 1918	1	4	
Graff	Walter E.	m.	PA	15 Sept. 1917	4	1	
Graham	A. D., Mrs.	d.	PD	21 June 1916	6	1	
Graham	A. D., Mrs.	d.	SIT	24 June 1916	1	7	
Graham	Eleanor	d.	PC	19 June 1918	3	3	Cypress Hill; also 4:3; 20 June, 4:4; 21 June, 5:1
Graham	Eleanor	d.	PD	20 June 1918	2	3	also 21 June, 6:7

(1) Surname	(2) Given Name	(3)	(4)	(5) Date	(6) Pg	(7) Col	(8) Comments
Graham	Hazeldean	m.	PD	22 May 1918	5	2	
Graham	Joe	o.	PC	29 May 1917	3	5	
Graham	Joseph E.	d.	PA	13 Mar. 1918	4	4	
Graham	Joseph E.	d.	PC	14 Mar. 1918	1	2	
Graham	Joseph M.	d.	PA	15 Aug. 1916	4	5	Suisun
Graham	Joseph M.	d.	PC	15 Aug. 1916	1	3	
Graham	Mary A.	o.	PC	16 Jan. 1916	6	2	
Graham	Mrs.	d.	PC	21 June 1916	1	4	
Graham	Richard	d.	PA	5 Sept. 1916	4	1	cremation
Graham	Richard	d.	PC	6 Sept. 1916	1	6	
Graham	Robert	m.	PC	22 Feb. 1918	6	5	
Graham	Robert	m.	ST	22 Feb. 1918	8	5	
Graham	T. J., Mrs.	d.	PA	18 June 1918	4	4	
Graham	T. J., Mrs.	p.	PA	24 June 1918	6	4	will
Graham	T. J., Mrs.	p.	PC	25 June 1918	5	3	
Graham	Tony, Mrs.	d.	PA	20 June 1916	8	3	
Graham	Will	b.	SRR	13 July 1916	1	2	
Graham	William Howard	d.	PD	27 Dec. 1918	4	2	Guerneville; also 28 Dec., 3:4
Graig	Belle	m.	PD	27 Sept. 1916	6	1	
Granice	Grace I.	m.	SIT	3 Nov. 1917	1	5	
Granice	H. H.	p.	PD	22 July 1917	3	4	
Granice	H. H.	p.	SIT	1 Apr. 1916	1	7	also 25 Nov., 4:7
Granice	H. H.	p.	SIT	3 Mar. 1917	1	4	also 24 Mar., 1:3; 21 July, 1:1
Grant	Antone	d.	PA	10 May 1917	5	3	Calvary Cemetery; also 11 May, 2:3
Grant	Antone	d.	PC	11 May 1917	5	5	also 12 May, 4:6
Grant	Charles	o.	CR	8 June 1917	1	5	also 6 July, 1:1; 27 July, 1:1
Grant	Charles	o.	SRR	27 July 1917	8	3	
Grant	Charles	o.	CR	13 Apr. 1917	1	2	
Grant	Joseph	b.	PA	22 Sept. 1916	4	4	
Grant	Joseph	b.	PC	23 Sept. 1916	5	3	
Grant	Manuel	d.	PA	9 Jan. 1917	4	5	Calvary Cemetery; also 11 Jan., 2:4
Grant	Manuel	d.	PC	9 Jan. 1917	1	6	Calvary Cemetery; also 8:1; 10 Jan., 2:2; 12 Jan., 8:3
Grant	Ralph	m.	SRR	2 Jan. 1917	3	3	
Grant	Ralph	m.	PD	30 Dec. 1916	6	2	
Grant	Ralph Delano	m.	SRR	30 Dec. 1916	6	3	
Grant	Ralph Delano	m.	HT	4 Jan. 1917	1	3	
Grant	Charles	o.	PD	7 July 1917	6	1	
Grass	Elizabeth	d.	ST	2 Sept. 1916	3	3	
Grass	Elizabeth	d.	PA	28 Aug. 1916	4	4	also 30 Aug., 3:5
Grass	Elizabeth	d.	PC	29 Aug. 1916	1	4	also 30 Aug., 5:2; 31 Aug., 1:5; Mt. Olivet

(1) Surname	(2) Given Name	(3)	(4)	(5) Date	(6) Pg	(7) Col	(8) Comments
Grass	Elizabeth	d.	SRR	31 Aug. 1916	6	3	
Grass	Mike	d.	PC	12 Feb. 1918	1	1	
Grass	Peter	d.	PA	13 Apr. 1916	4	4	Mt. Olivet, S.F.; also 14 Apr., 2:2, 5:5; 15 Apr., 4:6
Grass	Peter	d.	PC	14 Apr. 1916	3	3	also 15 Apr., 5:2; 16 Apr., 2:2
Grass	Peter	d.	PD	14 Apr. 1916	8	1	
Grass	Peter	d.	SRR	17 Apr. 1916	5	3	
Grass	Peter	p.	PA	18 Apr. 1916	5	1	
Grass	Peter	d.	ST	22 Apr. 1916	6	3	
Grass	Elizabeth	d.	PD	27 Aug. 1916	1	4	also 30 Aug., 8:1
Graumlich	Caroline	d.	PC	7 Jan. 1917	1	3	
Graves	Alexander S.	o.	SRR	19 Dec. 1916	4	4	
Graves	Alexander S.	o.	PA	20 Dec. 1916	1	5	
Graves	E. C.	b.	PD	3 Dec. 1918	6	4	
Graves	Edwin C.	m.	PC	1 Oct. 1916	8	5	
Graves	Edwin C.	m.	SRR	30 Sept. 1916	1	5	
Graves	Elwin	m.	PD	1 Oct. 1916	7	5	
Graves	John W.	d.	PD	18 Mar. 1917	6	2	also 20 Mar., 1:6
Graves	Rose	o.	SRR	19 Dec. 1916	4	4	
Graves	Rose	o.	PA	20 Dec. 1916	1	5	
Graves	Wesley	d.	SRR	17 Mar. 1917	6	3	
Graves	Zennie B.	m.	PA	22 Sept. 1916	8	4	
Graves	Zennie B.	m.	PC	23 Sept. 1916	3	3	
Gravitt	Marguerite	m.	PC	11 June 1918	3	3	
Gray	Donald	o.	PD	22 June 1918	5	5	
Gray	Donald	o.	PD	19 Dec. 1918	5	3	
Gray	Floyd M.	d.	SRR	27 Mar. 1916	5	3	also 28 Mar., 3:1
Gray	Floyd M.	d.	PD	28 Mar. 1916	5	2	also 29 Mar., 2:2
Gray	Hugh	d.	PA	15 Jan. 1918	5	3	Cypress Hill; also 16 Jan., 6:4, 8:3; 17 Jan., 5:6
Gray	Hugh	d.	PC	16 Jan. 1918	1	3	Cypress Hill; also 17 Jan., 5:6; 18 Jan., 4:4
Gray	James	d.	SRR	3 Aug. 1916	5	1	Rural Cemetery
Gray	James	d.	PC	5 Sept. 1918	3	5	
Gray	James Washington	d.	PD	4 Sept. 1918	5	1	Rural Cemetery
Gray	James Wilson	d.	PC	4 Aug. 1916	4	3	
Gray	Martin, Jr.	b.	PD	3 July 1918	3	4	
Gray	Mary	d.	PA	21 Aug. 1918	7	4	
Gray	Mary	d.	HT	22 Aug. 1918	1	1	also 29 Aug., 5:5
Gray	Mary	d.	PC	22 Aug. 1918	8	2	
Gray	Mary	d.	PD	22 Aug. 1918	2	4	
Gray	Samuel	d.	PA	26 Feb. 1917	4	5	Cypress Hill; also 28 Feb., 4:5
Gray	Samuel	d.	PC	27 Feb. 1917	1	2	also 28 Feb., 8:1; 1 Mar., 3:3

(1) Surname	(2) Given Name	(3)	(4)	(5) Date	(6) Pg	(7) Col	(8) Comments
Gray	Samuel	d.	PD	27 Feb. 1917	5	3	Petaluma
Gray	Susannah	d.	PC	6 Mar. 1917	4	1	also 7 Mar., 8:4
Gray	Susannah Edwards	d.	PA	5 Mar. 1917	2	3	also 6 Mar., 4:3
Gray	Will	b.	HT	28 Nov. 1918	7	4	
Gray	William	o.	SRR	23 July 1917	1	5	also 24 July, 1:4; 25 July, 4:1
Grayson	Anna W.	d.	PD	2 Feb. 1918	2	1	
Graziani	Celia	o.	PD	6 Apr. 1917	2	4	
Graziani	Emil	o.	SIT	17 Feb. 1917	2	3	
Graziani	Emil	o.	PD	6 Apr. 1917	2	4	
Grear	Earl C.	m.	PD	16 Dec. 1917	6	3	
Greeley	Benjamin	o.	PD	20 Nov. 1917	6	3	
Greeley	Marian	o.	PD	20 Nov. 1917	6	3	
Green	Anna	d.	PA	29 May 1917	8	5	Calvary Cemetery; also 31 May, 5:5
Green	Anna	d.	PC	30 May 1917	3	1	also 6:4
Green	Anna	d.	PD	1 June 1917	6	3	
Green	Anna	d.	ST	1 June 1917	2	3	
Green	Annie	d.	SRR	28 May 1917	4	3	
Green	Arthur Reginald	d.	PA	30 Mar. 1916	4	4	Auburn
Green	Arthur Reginald	d.	PC	30 Mar. 1916	1	4	Auburn; also 31 Mar., 8:5
Green	David	d.	PC	17 Sept. 1918	3	4	cremation; also 19 Sept., 3:3
Green	David J.	d.	PA	16 Sept. 1918	8	5	cremation; also 18 Sept., 8:3
Green	Elsie	m.	SRR	25 May 1917	6	4	
Green	Elsie	m.	HT	31 May 1917	5	4	
Green	Elsie M.	m.	HT	28 Dec. 1916	1	3	
Green	Elsie M.	m.	SRR	28 Dec. 1916	3	2	
Green	Elsie M.	m.	PD	29 Dec. 1916	6	5	
Green	Frank, Mrs.	d.	SRR	9 Dec. 1916	5	3	
Green	Ida E.	o.	SRR	7 Feb. 1916	8	2	
Green	Ira	m.	PD	9 Jan. 1917	3	1	
Green	Ira G.	m.	SRR	8 Jan. 1917	3	5	
Green	L. D.	m.	HT	3 Feb. 1917	5	2	
Green	Lincoln D.	m.	SRR	29 Jan. 1916	10	3	
Green	Lincoln D.	m.	PD	30 Jan. 1916	5	4	
Green	Olive Victoria	d.	PA	11 Dec. 1916	5	3	Santa Rosa; also 12 Dec., 4:2
Green	Olive Victoria	d.	PC	12 Dec. 1916	5	5	Woodland, Yolo County; also 13 Dec., 5:3
Green	Olive Victoria	d.	PD	12 Dec. 1916	5	6	
Green	Owen	o.	SRR	7 Feb. 1916	8	2	
Green	Perry W.	b.	SRR	29 Sept. 1917	8	6	
Green	R. F.	b.	CR	1 June 1917	4	2	
Green	Richard	d.	PD	14 Aug. 1916	1	6	Oakland
Green	Richard	d.	SRR	14 Aug. 1916	8	5	cremation
Green	Stella	m.	PD	18 Nov. 1916	5	1	
Green	Stella	m.	CR	6 Sept. 1918	1	4	

(1) Surname	(2) Given Name	(3)	(4)	(5) Date	(6) Pg	(7) Col	(8) Comments
Green	W. C.	o.	PD	31 Dec. 1918	5	1	
Green	Wallace	d.	SRR	25 Aug. 1917	7	6	
Green	Wallace	d.	PC	27 Aug. 1917	5	2	
Green	Walter	b.	SRR	15 Nov. 1916	5	3	
Green	Willett	d.	PA	29 Sept. 1917	5	6	
Green	Willitt	d.	PC	2 Oct. 1917	8	3	Sayville, New York; also 9 Oct., 8:5
Greene	E. E.	o.	PD	8 Feb. 1916	6	1	
Greening	Sadie	m.	PD	25 May 1918	5	6	
Greening	William	d.	PA	10 Apr. 1917	5	5	
Greening	William	d.	PC	10 Apr. 1917	3	5	also 4:2; 11 Apr., 8:3
Greening	William	d.	ST	14 Apr. 1917	3	2	
Greenstein	Mary	m.	SRR	11 Apr. 1917	1	5	
Greenstein	Mary	m.	PC	12 Apr. 1917	8	3	
Greenstein	Mary	m.	PA	13 Apr. 1917	5	5	
Greenway	Mary	o.	PD	1 Jan. 1918	3	3	also 17 Jan., 7:5
Greenway	William C.	o.	PD	1 Jan. 1918	3	3	also 17 Jan., 7:5
Gregg	Nelson	d.	PA	24 Apr. 1916	8	3	cremation; also 25 Apr., 6:4; 26 Apr., 3:2
Gregg	Nelson	d.	PC	25 Apr. 1916	5	5	cremation; also 26 Apr., 5:2; 27 Apr., 8:3
Gregg	Nelson G.	d.	PD	26 Apr. 1916	3	2	cremation; also 27 Apr., 7:1
Gregg	Nelson G.	d.	ST	29 Apr. 1916	5	4	
Gregg	Nelson George	d.	SRR	24 Apr. 1916	4	2	also 25 Apr., 8:2; 26 Apr., 8:5
Gregory	A. H., Mrs.	d.	SRR	21 June 1916	4	1	San Luis Obispo; also 22 June, 5:2
Gregory	A. H., Mrs.	d.	ST	24 June 1916	1	3	San Luis Obispo
Gregory	Albert J.	m.	PC	20 Mar. 1916	6	1	
Gregory	Amelia H.	d,	PC	21 June 1916	1	7	also 23 June, 1:4
Gregory	Amelia Hartwell	d.	PD	21 June 1916	6	3	San Luis Obispo; also 22 June, 3:5; 23 June, 6:4
Gregory	Arthur J.	m.	PC	19 Mar. 1916	6	1	
Gregory	May M.	m.	SRR	26 July 1916	5	3	
Gregory	May M.	m.	PD	27 July 1916	8	2	
Gregory	Morio	d.	PC	3 Nov. 1918	5	2	
Gregory	Thomas, Mrs.	m.	PA	26 July 1916	4	3	
Gregson	Marjorie Esther	m.	SRR	13 July 1916	1	5	
Gregson	Marjorie Esther	m.	PC	14 July 1916	3	4	
Gregson	R.	m.	PA	1 Aug. 1917	3	4	
Gregson	Richard	m.	SRR	31 July 1917	7	3	
Gregson	Richard	m.	PC	1 Aug. 1917	3	4	
Gregson	Richard	m.	PD	1 Aug. 1917	2	2	
Gregson	Richard	m.	ST	17 Aug. 1917	1	3	
Greson	Elsa	m.	SRR	18 Jan. 1917	5	1	
Gressot	Evelyn D.	o.	CR	20 Dec. 1918	1	3	

(1) Surname	(2) Given Name	(3)	(4)	(5) Date	(6) Pg	(7) Col	(8) Comments
Gruenhagan	Henry	b.	SRR	1 Dec. 1916	7	3	
Gruenhagen	Eli	d.	PD	22 Feb. 1918	5	4	
Grueninald	Victor	d.	PC	11 Jan. 1917	1	2	
Guaspari	Peter	d.	SRR	8 Feb. 1917	8	1	
Guaspari	Peter	d.	PD	9 Feb. 1917	4	2	also 5:3; 13 Feb., 2:5
Guasteri	Peter	d.	SRR	12 Feb. 1917	8	8	
Guay	John	d.	PC	23 Apr. 1916	6	3	
Guder	M.	b.	PA	12 Oct. 1916	1	4	
Guenther	W. Earl	m.	PA	5 Oct. 1916	1	5	
Guenza	Siro	d.	SRR	1 Oct. 1917	3	3	Calvary Cemetery; also 8:5
Guenza	Siro	d.	PD	30 Sept. 1917	8	2	also 2 Oct., 2:1; 3 Oct., 2:3
Guerkink	B. W.	d.	PA	11 Nov. 1917	4	5	Cypress Hill
Guerkink	D. W.	d.	PD	14 Nov. 1917	8	1	
Guernsey	Hazel	d.	PC	22 May 1918	8	2	also 26 May, 2:2
Guerrera	Alfrede	d.	HT	25 Jan. 1917	8	4	Oak Mound Cemetery
Guevari	Maria Teresa	m.	ST	28 Sept. 1917	1	3	
Guggia	Josephine	m.	PA	29 Oct. 1917	4	2	
Guggia	Mary	m.	PC	28 Oct. 1917	8	5	also 30 Oct., 3:4
Gughelmetti	Leland	o.	PD	7 Sept. 1917	6	3	
Gughelmetti	Marino	m.	HT	20 June 1918	5	2	
Guglielmenti	Alfred J.	m.	PD	11 July 1917	8	2	also 12 July, 6:5
Guglielmetti	Alfred	b.	PA	4 June 1918	4	5	
Guglielmetti	Alfred J.	m.	PC	8 July 1917	1	5	also 11 July, 5:2; 12 July, 5:2
Guglielmetti	Alfred J.	m.	SRR	10 July 1917	6	4	also 11 July, 4:1
Guglielmetti	Alfred J.	m.	PA	11 July 1917	3	4	
Guglielmetti	Leland	m.	PD	14 July 1918	6	5	wife not named
Guglielmetti	Leland J.	m.	PD	14 June 1918	8	4	
Guglielmetti	Marino	m.	PD	18 June 1918	7	1	
Gugliemetti	Louis	b.	PC	4 Aug. 1916	8	5	
Gugliemetti	Nole	b.	PD	10 Aug. 1916	2	5	
Guidotti	Jeanette	m.	SRR	27 Nov. 1916	5	4	
Guilford	Mrs.	d.	PD	2 May 1916	8	3	
Guilfoyle	Mary	d.	SIT	6 May 1916	3	3	
Guilfoyle	Mrs.	d.	SRR	2 May 1916	7	2	St. Vincent's Cemetery
Guilfoyle	Patrick, Mrs.	d.	PA	2 May 1916	8	6	
Guinnae	David A.	o.	SRR	11 Nov. 1916	6	2	
Guinnae	Melciana	o.	SRR	11 Nov. 1916	6		
Guintero	Nick	d.	PD	5 Nov. 1916	10	4	also 7 Nov., 8:3
Gularte	George S.	m.	PA	24 Dec. 1917	5	3	
Gulberson	Agnes L.	o.	PD	13 Nov. 1917	5	4	
Gulberson	Agnes Loretta	o.	PA	23 Oct. 1917	4	2	
Gulberson	Wallace	o.	PD	13 Nov. 1917	5	4	
Gulberson	Wallace	o.	PA	23 Oct. 1917	4	2	
Gullard	Murial	m.	PD	30 Aug. 1917	8	3	
Gullard	Muriel	m.	SRR	29 Aug. 1917	6	2	

(1) Surname	(2) Given Name	(3)	(4)	(5) Date	(6) Pg	(7) Col	(8) Comments
Gully	Charles	o.	HT	6 Dec. 1917	1	3	
Gunther	Emma	m.	PC	4 Aug. 1917	8	5	
Guomas	Ernest	m.	PA	2 Aug. 1918	3	5	
Guptill	Ruby M.	m.	SRR	2 May 1917	8	5	
Gustafason	Gustasf	m.	SIT	25 May 1918	1	3	
Gustafsen	Esther R. E.	m.	SRR	23 Nov. 1916	8	4	
Gustafson	Esther E.	m.	PD	30 July 1918	7	3	
Gustafson	Esther M.	m.	HT	1 Aug. 1918	2	3	
Gutermute	Sherman	b.	PD	25 Apr. 1917	8	4	
Gutermute	Sherwin	b.	PA	8 June 1918	5	2	also 8:3
Gutermute	Sherwin	b.	PC	22 Apr. 1917	5	1	
Gutermute	Sherwin	b.	PA	23 Apr. 1917	5	3	
Gutermute	Sherwin	b.	SRR	24 Apr. 1917	6	2	
Gutermute	Sherwin	m.	PA	28 Sept. 1916	7	4	
Gutermute	Sherwin	m.	PC	28 Sept. 1916	5	4	
Guthrie	C. M.	b.	PA	27 Oct. 1916	8	6	
Guthrie	Charles M.	b.	PC	27 Oct. 1916	5	6	
Gwin	Ancil E.	o.	SRR	25 July 1917	2	3	also 27 Aug., 4:1; 4 Sept., 8:5
Gwin	Ancil W.	o.	PD	25 July 1917	3	2	
Gwin	Myrtle	o.	PD	25 July 1917	3	2	
Gwin	Myrtle	o.	SRR	25 July 1917	2	3	also 27 Aug., 4:1; 4 Sept., 8:5
Gwinn	Pearl	m.	SRR	13 Mar. 1917	2	4	
Gwinn	Walter	m.	SRR	3 Apr. 1916	4	4	

H

(1) Surname	(2) Given Name	(3)	(4)	(5) Date	(6) Pg	(7) Col	(8) Comments
Haase	William	d&o	PA	24 June 1916	5	3	also 27 June, 1:4; 28 June, 1:4, 5:1
Haase	William	d.	PC	24 June 1916	1	1	also 27 June, 6:3; 28 June, 1:2
Hackett	Miranda Barnes	d.	PA	20 Jan. 1917	3	4	Ukiah
Hackett	Sally Robinson	d.	SIT	10 Nov. 1917	1	5	Mountain Cemetery
Hackett	Sarah E. V.	d.	PC	10 Nov. 1917	6	4	Sonoma
Hackman	J. C.	b.	PA	2 Apr. 1917	4	5	
Hackman	J. C. (dau of)	d.	PC	4 Apr. 1917	3	5	
Haddick	Joseph N.	d.	SRR	5 Jan. 1916	6	5	
Haddick	Mary	d.	PD	1 Oct. 1916	1	5	also 3 Oct., 8:3
Haddock	Mary	d.	SRR	2 Oct. 1916	4	2	
Hadermann	Johanna	m.	PA	26 June 1917	2	3	
Hadermann	Johanna	m.	PC	27 June 1917	8	4	
Hadermann	Johanna	m.	PA	27 Aug. 1917	1	4	also 2:4
Hadermann	Johanna	m.	PC	28 Aug. 1917	4	5	
Hadermann	Johanna	m.	PD	28 Aug. 1917	8	3	
Hadlock	Leonard	b.	PA	16 Oct. 1916	1	6	
Hadrich	Charles F. Hugo, Jr.	m.	PD	25 Nov. 1916	7	4	
Hadrich	Hugo	m.	PD	14 Jan. 1917	8	2	
Hadrich	Hugo	m.	SRR	15 Jan. 1917	8	1	
Hadrich	Hugo, Jr.	m.	SRR	24 Nov. 1916	3	3	
Haechl	Elene Bond	m.	PD	30 Jan. 1916	7	4	also 8:7
Haehl	Walter	m.	SRR	3 Feb. 1917	3	5	
Hagedohm	Dorothy Augustine	d.	PA	30 July 1918	8	3	Cypress Hill; also 31 July, 5:5; 1 Aug., 5:5
Hagedohm	Dorothy Augustine	d.	PC	31 July 1918	3	4	Cypress Hill; also 4:3; 1 Aug., 4:3; 2 Aug., 4:3
Hagedorn	Dorothy	d.	PD	31 July 1918	8	2	also 2 Aug., 3:5
Hagens	George W.	d.	SRR	24 Oct. 1916	5	4	
Hagens	George W.	d.	PD	26 Oct. 1916	8	5	
Hagland	Charles E.	d.	PC	18 May 1916	4	3	Cypress Hill; also 19 May, 4:3
Hahman	Henrietta	d.	PD	16 Apr. 1918	2	3	portrait; also 5:2; 17 Apr., 4:2; 18 Apr., 2:3
Hahman	Henrietta	d.	SIT	20 Apr. 1918	5	1	
Hahman	Henrietta A.	p.	PD	26 Apr. 1918	2	3	will
Hahmann	Henrietta	d.	PA	16 Apr. 1918	6	4	
Hahmann	Henrietta Ann	d.	PC	16 Apr. 1918	6	4	
Hahn	Bertha	m.	PC	12 June 1917	8	4	
Hahn	Bertha A.	m.	PA	3 May 1917	5	2	
Hahn	Bertha A.	m.	PC	3 May 1917	6	3	

(1) Surname	(2) Given Name	(3)	(4)	(5) Date	(6) Pg	(7) Col	(8) Comments
Hahn	Fred	m.	SRR	26 June 1916	8	5	
Hahn	Fred	m.	PC	29 June 1916	6	3	
Hahn	Fred G.	o.	SRR	13 Sept. 1916	8	5	
Hahn	Fred G.	o.	PC	14 Sept. 1916	6	1	
Hahn	Fred H.	o.	SRR	1 July 1916	2	2	
Hahn	Fred J.	o.	PA	13 Sept. 1916	5	4	
Haigh	W. H.	d.	PA	26 Dec. 1918	8	5	
Haigh	W. Rainey	d.	HT	19 Dec. 1918	4	3	
Haines	Serena	d.	PD	30 Dec. 1916	8	1	
Hair	Edith	m.	PD	20 June 1917	3	2	
Hair	Edith	m.	SRR	20 June 1917	3	5	
Hair	Edith	m.	ST	22 June 1917	7	6	
Hair	Ruth	m.	ST	13 May 1916	1	5	also 22 July, 1:2
Hair	Ruth	m.	PD	20 July 1916	8	4	
Hair	Ruth	m.	SRR	20 July 1916	4	5	
Hair	Ruth Marie	m.	PC	21 July 1916	4	1	
Halberg	Elizabeth	m.	SIT	7 Sept. 1918	1	7	
Halberg	Oscar A.	m.	PA	12 Jan. 1917	6	4	
Haley	Ray	m.	PC	4 July 1918	5	4	
Haley	Robert	b.	PA	17 July 1916	1	1	
Haley	Robert	b.	PA	13 July 1918	1	7	
Haley	Roy	m.	HT	4 July 1918	1	3	
Haley	William A.	m.	PD	2 July 1918	2	3	
Haley	William Edward	d.	HT	10 Jan. 1918	1	4	Oak Mound Cemetery
Hall	Alma E.	m.	PA	15 Sept. 1917	4	1	
Hall	Alma Elizabeth	m.	SRR	15 Sept. 1917	4	2	
Hall	Amy	d.	PD	25 Aug. 1917	7	4	
Hall	Arthur L.	b.	PA	18 July 1918	4	2	also 8:7
Hall	Beatrice	m.	SRR	15 June 1917	8	6	
Hall	Beth Campbell	o.	SRR	6 Aug. 1917	1	4	
Hall	Beth Campbell	o.	PA	6 Aug. 1917	5	6	
Hall	Carrie E.	m.	PD	12 Sept. 1916	6	4	
Hall	Clara	o.	PD	9 Feb. 1918	6	4	
Hall	Denia	d.	SIT	2 June 1917	1	6	
Hall	Edward	b.	PD	2 Dec. 1917	3	2	
Hall	Edward	b.	SRR	3 Dec. 1917	6	3	
Hall	Eugene F.	o.	PD	9 Feb. 1918	6	4	
Hall	H. E.	b.	PA	15 Jan. 1916	4	6	also 8:5
Hall	Harley	m.	SRR	29 Aug. 1916	7	5	
Hall	Harley	b.	PD	5 Apr. 1917	3	3	
Hall	Harley A.	m.	PD	3 Sept. 1916	5	3	
Hall	Harry S.	b.	PA	13 Mar. 1916	5	7	also 8:7
Hall	Howard	m.	PC	11 Aug. 1917	5	3	
Hall	James Robert	d.	PA	23 Feb. 1916	4	1	
Hall	John	d.	SRR	12 Mar. 1917	8	5	also 13 Mar., 8:2&3

(1) Surname	(2) Given Name	(3)	(4)	(5) Date	(6) Pg	(7) Col	(8) Comments
Hall	John	d.	PD	13 Mar. 1917	4	3	also 8:5
Hall	Lynwood	m.	PA	21 June 1918	8	3	also 24 June, 8:3
Hall	Lynwood	m.	PD	22 June 1918	3	5	
Hall	M. D.	o.	PA	6 Aug. 1917	5	6	
Hall	M. D.	o.	SRR	6 Aug. 1917	1	4	
Hall	Maitland G.	d.	SRR	17 Oct. 1916	8	1	also 18 Oct., 6:4; 19 Oct., 8:1
Hall	Maitland, Jr.	d.	PA	17 Oct. 1916	5	5	
Hall	Maitland, Jr.	d.	PD	18 Oct. 1916	6	3	also 19 Oct., 8:4; 20 Oct., 6:4
Hall	Mildred	m.	SRR	24 June 1916	12	6	
Hall	Nell	m.	SRR	7 Sept. 1917	8	4	also 13 Sept., 5:3
Hall	Nell	m.	PD	8 Sept. 1917	8	3	also 13 Sept., 8:2
Hall	Nellie	m.	PC	24 Apr. 1917	5	2	also 25 Apr., 5:3
Hall	Nellie M.	m.	PA	24 Apr. 1917	5	3	
Hall	Olive Fay	o.	PD	20 Feb. 1917	3	4	
Hall	Oliver	o.	SRR	15 Jan. 1916	10	1	also 17 Feb., 8:6
Hall	Oliver	o.	PD	20 Feb. 1917	3	4	
Hall	Oliver F.	o.	PA	17 Jan. 1916	3	5	also 1 Feb., 6:3; 17 Feb., 4:4; 18 Feb., 1:6
Hall	Oliver P.	o.	PD	18 Feb. 1916	7	3	
Hall	Olivia	m.	PA	13 Aug. 1917	8	3	
Hall	Olivia	m.	SRR	13 Aug. 1917	8	5	
Hall	Olivia	o.	SRR	15 Jan. 1916	10	1	also 17 Feb., 8:6
Hall	Olivia	o.	PA	17 Jan. 1916	3	5	also 1 Feb., 6:3; 17 Feb., 4:4; 18 Feb., 1:6
Hall	Olivia Fay	o.	PD	18 Feb. 1916	7	3	
Hall	Robert	d.	SRR	12 June 1916	5	4	
Hall	Robert	d.	HT	15 June 1916	3	3	
Hall	Robert	d.	SIT	17 June 1916	1	1	
Hall	Robert	p.	SIT	17 Feb. 1917	1	4	
Hall	Robert James	d.	PC	24 Feb. 1916	5	5	Mountain View Cemetery
Hall	Roxania	d.	HT	31 Jan. 1918	1	5	
Hall	Stephanie	m.	PD	1 Mar. 1918	8	3	
Hall	Thirza	d.	PD	1 June 1917	8	2	
Hall	Thirza	d.	PC	2 June 1917	8	5	
Hall	Thirza D.	d.	SRR	1 June 1917	3	4	
Hall	Thomas	d.	PD	10 Dec. 1918	8	3	Rural Cemetery; also 11 Dec., 6:2
Hall	Thomas	d.	PD	26 Feb. 1918	8	1	
Hall	Thomas	d.	PD	30 Nov. 1918	4	6	Canada of wounds received in France
Hall	W. P.	o.	PC	4 Jan. 1916	6	3	
Hall	Walter	d.	PD	27 Nov. 1918	8	3	
Hall	Walter C.	d.	PA	26 Nov. 1918	4	3	Bloomfield; also 5:7; 27 Nov., 4:2; 28 Nov., 5:5
Hall	Walter C.	d.	PC	27 Nov. 1918	1	4	also 5:3; 28 Nov., 5:3; 30 Nov., 8:4

(1) Surname	(2) Given Name	(3)	(4)	(5) Date	(6) Pg	(7) Col	(8) Comments
Hall	Walter C.	d.	ST	29 Nov. 1918	7	2	
Hall	Weston	m.	PD	10 Dec. 1918	5	1	
Hall	William C.	m.	PD	10 Nov. 1917	7	2	
Hall	William Clyde	m.	PC	10 Nov. 1917	3	5	
Hall	William Clyde	m.	SRR	9 Nov. 1917	8	2	
Hall	William P.	o.	PC	5 Jan. 1916	1	4	
Hallberg	Oscar	m.	HT	17 Jan. 1918	3	1	
Hallberg	Oscar	m.	ST	18 Jan. 1918	1	3	
Hallberg	Oscar A.	m.	PD	12 Jan. 1918	3	1	also 13 Jan., 3:4
Hallberg	Oscar A.	m.	PC	13 Jan. 1918	1	6	
Hallengren	Lind and baby	d.	HT	14 June 1917	5	3	
Halley	Alice Siever	o.	PD	22 Oct. 1918	3	3	
Halley	Frank	o.	PD	22 Oct. 1918	3	3	
Halley	Wanda	m.	PA	8 June 1916	6	2	
Halley	Wanda	m.	PC	8 June 1916	1	5	
Halley	Wanda	m.	SRR	8 June 1916	5	2	
Halton	James	d.	SRR	27 Nov. 1916	6	2	
Halverson	Clara M. R.	o.	PC	30 Dec. 1916	3	4	
Halverson	Harold C.	o.	PC	30 Dec. 1916	3	4	
Ham	J. T.	d.	PC	7 Apr. 1918	1	4	
Ham	J. T.	d.	PA	8 Apr. 1918	3	1	
Ham	James Taylor	d.	PD	7 Apr. 1918	8	2	also 10 Apr., 7:5; 13 Apr., 6:3
Hamilton	Eugene	o.	PA	18 Mar. 1916	6	4	
Hamilton	Harry E.	m.	SRR	14 Jan. 1916	4	4	
Hamilton	L.	d.	PD	27 Oct. 1918	6	1	
Hamilton	L., Mrs.	d.	HT	30 Oct. 1918	1	5	
Hamilton	Mrs.	d.	SIT	3 Mar. 1918	1	3	
Hamilton	Nellie	o.	PA	18 Mar. 1916	6	4	
Hamilton	Will	d.	PA	6 Mar. 1918	8	3	
Hamilton	William N.	d.	PC	6 Mar. 1918	1	5	
Hamilton	Pearl	m.	PD	22 Sept. 1916	6	5	
Hamlin	Oliver, Jr.	m.	PC	26 Mar. 1916	4	4	
Hamlin	R. E.	b.	SRR	2 Aug. 1916	5	4	
Hamm	Joe	o.	PC	18 Dec. 1918	3	2	
Hamm	Louise	m.	PA	1 Sept. 1917	3	5	
Hamm	Louise	m.	PA	25 Aug. 1917	5	3	also 31 Aug., 4:4
Hamm	Louise Marie	m.	PC	27 Aug. 1917	3	4	also 31 Aug., 3:2; 2 Sept., 5:5
Hammargren	Virginia	d.	PA	7 May 1917	4	5	Cypress Hill
Hammargren	Virginia	d.	PC	8 May 1917	8	4	Cypress Hill
Hammerman	Elsie C.	m.	PC	23 Jan. 1917	7	4	
Hammerman	Elsie M. C.	m.	PA	22 Jan. 1917	2	2	
Hammerman	Henry	d.	PA	20 Nov. 1918	5	5	Mt. Olivet; also 21 Nov., 2:5; 23 Nov., 2:5
Hammermann	George	b.	PA	28 Dec. 1916	8	6	

(1) Surname	(2) Given Name	(3)	(4)	(5) Date	(6) Pg	(7) Col	(8) Comments
Hammermann	Henry	d.	PC	21 Nov. 1918	6	3	San Francisco; also 22 Nov., 6:5
Hammett	John	d.	PD	29 Oct. 1918	6	5	Vallejo
Hammett	John Bassett	d.	PC	30 Oct. 1918	2	1	Vallejo
Hammond	Leslie	o.	PD	11 Jan. 1918	2	1	
Hamner	Joseph	d.	PD	9 June 1918	3	7	also 15 June, 5:1
Hampton	Gerald P.	m.	PC	1 July 1917	8	3	
Hampton	Gerald R.	m.	PA	29 June 1917	8	1	
Hampton	Nellie	o.	PC	25 Mar. 1916	5	6	
Hampton	Nellie A.	o.	SRR	25 Mar. 1916	6	5	
Hance	Louise K.	m.	PD	22 Sept. 1916	6	5	
Hancock	John	d.	SRR	21 July 1916	5	5	
Hancock	Morris	m.	PD	8 Mar. 1918	8	4	
Hancock	Morris W.	m.	PD	3 May 1918	4	1	also 22 May, 5:5
Hane	J.	d.	SRR	7 Jan. 1916	1	3	also 10 Jan., 4:4
Hane	J.	d.	PD	9 Jan. 1916	5	1	
Hanee	Louise K.	m.	SRR	21 Sept. 1916	8	6	
Hanks	Mary Ann	o.	SRR	18 July 1917	8	6	
Hanks	Mary Ann	o.	ST	20 July 1917	3	4	
Hanks	Paul	o.	PA	9 Nov. 1918	1	2	
Hanks	William Wallace	o.	SRR	18 July 1917	8	6	
Hanks	William Wallace	o.	ST	20 July 1917	3	4	
Hanley	A. Siever	o.	PD	12 Oct. 1917	3	4	
Hanley	Alice S.	o.	SRR	10 Oct. 1917	4	6	
Hanley	Alice Siever	o.	SRR	28 Aug. 1917	4	1	
Hanley	Alice Sievers	o.	PD	29 Aug. 1917	6	3	
Hanley	Frank	o.	SRR	10 Oct. 1917	4	6	
Hanley	Frank	o.	PD	12 Oct. 1917	3	4	
Hanley	Frank	o.	SRR	28 Aug. 1917	4	1	
Hanley	Frank	o.	PD	29 Aug. 1917	6	3	
Hanlin	Charles	d.	PA	24 June 1918	4	6	Calvary Cemetery; also 8:1; 25 June, 5:4
Hanlin	Charles	d.	PC	25 June 1918	8	3	also 26 June, 3:4
Hanlin	Charles	d.	PD	26 June 1918	3	2	
Hanlon	Alice Agnes	m.	PA	24 May 1917	2	3	also 11 June, 6:5
Hanlon	Alice Agnes	m.	PC	3 June 1917	8	2	also 6 June, 8:2
Hanlon	John F.	d.	PD	3 July 1917	3	1	
Hanna	Jessica	o.	PA	6 Apr. 1916	3	3	
Hanna	Peter N.	o.	PA	6 Apr. 1916	3	3	
Hans	Jacob	d.	PD	13 Oct. 1918	4	2	
Hansen	Alma	m.	PA	24 Dec. 1917	5	2	
Hansen	Alma	m.	PC	28 Dec. 1917	4	5	
Hansen	Alma	m.	PA	5 Mar. 1918	4	5	also 6 Mar., 4:5
Hansen	Alma Theresa	m.	PC	6 Mar. 1918	4	5	also 7 Mar., 5:3
Hansen	Carl	b.	PA	22 May 1916	1	3	

(1) Surname	(2) Given Name	(3)	(4)	(5) Date	(6) Pg	(7) Col	(8) Comments
Hansen	Carl	b.	PC	22 May 1916	5	2	
Hansen	Ed	b.	HT	15 Nov. 1917	3	4	
Hansen	Elmira	m.	PD	18 Nov. 1917	3	4	
Hansen	Elmira	m.	SRR	2 Oct. 1917	2	3	
Hansen	Elmira	m.	PC	21 Nov. 1917	6	2	
Hansen	Elmira	m.	SIT	29 Sept. 1917	1	6	
Hansen	Evnar	m.	PD	27 Aug. 1918	3	1	
Hansen	Frank H. (son of)	d.	PC	8 Mar. 1917	5	6	Cypress Hill; also 9 Mar., 3:6
Hansen	Frank H. (son of)	d.	PA	7 Mar. 1917	8	3	
Hansen	Frieda	m.	PC	7 Mar. 1917	5	3	
Hansen	Frieda Elsie	m.	PA	16 Mar. 1917	8	3	
Hansen	Ingeborg Marie	m.	SRR	20 Sept. 1916	8	1	
Hansen	Ingeborg Marie	m.	PC	21 Sept. 1916	5	4	
Hansen	Ingelory Marie	m.	PA	20 Sept. 1916	8	1	
Hansen	Joe	o.	PC	28 Nov. 1917	1	3	
Hansen	Margaret	d.	SRR	19 Nov. 1917	8	1	also 20 Nov., 8:2; 21 Nov., 8:3
Hansen	Margaret	d.	PD	20 Nov. 1917	5	3	also 22 Nov. 8:1
Hansen	Marie	d.	PC	12 Nov. 1916	1	5	Cypress Hill; also 14 Nov., 2:2; 15 Nov., 8:1
Hansen	Marie Elizabeth	d.	PA	13 Nov. 1916	7	5	Cypress Hill; also 14 Nov., 5:5
Hansen	Olaf	p.	SRR	6 July 1917	8	3	
Hansen	Ole	d.	PC	26 June 1917	8	2	
Hansen	Ole/Olaf	d.	SRR	25 June 1917	5	5	Rural Cemetery; also 26 June, 6:3
Hansen	S. C.	d.	PD	23 Nov. 1918	1	3	France
Hansen	Sam C.	o.	PA	16 Nov. 1918	5	2	
Hansen	Sam C.	o.	PC	5 Nov. 1918	5	5	
Hansen	Soren (Sam)	d.	PA	23 Nov. 1918	3	4	France
Hansen	Soren (Sam)	d.	PC	23 Nov. 1918	1	3	France
Hansen	Tony	o.	PC	28 Nov. 1917	1	3	
Hanson	Anna	d.	PC	12 Dec. 1918	1	2	Cypress Hill; also 15 Dec., 5:4; 17 Dec., 5:4
Hanson	Anna L.	d.	PA	12 Dec. 1918	8	5	Cypress Hill; also 13 Dec., 8:4,&7; 16 Dec., 5:3
Hanson	Carl	b.	PA	17 Aug. 1918	4	4	
Hanson	Carl	b.	PC	18 Aug. 1918	5	3	
Hanson	Edna	m.	HT	24 May 1917	1	4	
Hanson	Elmire	m.	SRR	19 Nov. 1917	6	1	
Hanson	Frank	b.	PC	7 Mar. 1917	5	6	
Haraszthy	Caroline	o.	SRR	23 Feb. 1017	1	4	adoption
Haraszthy	Maury	o.	SIT	3 Mar. 1917	2	5	adoption
Harazthy	Juanita	m.	PC	28 Oct. 1916	5	3	
Harbine	Alice	d.	PD	13 Mar. 1917	4	3	Occidental; also 8:3
Harbine	Alice	d.	SRR	13 Mar. 1917	5	4	also 20 Mar., 4:2

(1) Surname	(2) Given Name	(3)	(4)	(5) Date	(6) Pg	(7) Col	(8) Comments
Harbine	Alice	d.	PC	14 Mar. 1917	1	3	
Harbine	Florence	m.	ST	12 Feb. 1916	1	2	
Harbine	Jennie Alice	d.	ST	17 Mar. 1917	1	2	also 6:2
Hardin	Clarence	m.	PA	22 May 1917	5	2	also 23 May, 8:3
Hardin	Clarence	m.	SRR	25 May 1917	3	5	
Hardin	Clarence E.	m.	SRR	22 May 1917	4	1	
Hardin	Clarence E.	m.	PC	23 May 1917	8	2	also 24 May, 1:3
Hardin	Harold	m.	SRR	10 Oct. 1917	5	1	
Hardin	Harold	m.	PD	10 Oct. 1917	2	1	
Hardin	Harold	m.	PA	9 Oct. 1917	5	4	also 16 Oct., 4:5
Hardin	Harold J.	m.	PD	17 Oct. 1917	6	5	
Hardin	Harold Jefferson	m.	PC	16 Oct. 1917	1	5	also 17 Oct., 5:3
Hardin	Ida Gross	m.	PC	16 Mar. 1916	5	2	
Hardin	Jeffie	m.	PC	15 Feb. 1918	5	3	
Hardin	Louis	o.	PA	16 Nov. 1918	8	6	
Hardin	Louis	o.	PC	20 Nov. 1918	3	6	
Hardin	Mary	d.	SRR	10 May 1917	10	2	
Hardin	Mary	d.	PD	11 May 1917	4	3	also 5:2; 12 May, 4:3
Hardin	Mary M. McMinn	d.	PC	11 May 1917	4	3	Cypress Hill; also 6:1; 13 May, 5:3
Hardin	Mary Melvina	d.	PA	10 May 1917	4	4	Cypress Hill; also 12 May, 5:4
Hardin	Milton J.	m.	PA	24 July 1917	2	2	
Hardin	Milton J.	m.	PC	25 July 1917	4	4	
Hardin	Rolla	b.	PA	11 Aug. 1916	4	5	
Harding	Edward F.	m.	PD	25 Apr. 1916	1	4	
Harding	Milo	b.	SRR	29 May 1916	8	4	
Harding	Milo	b.	PD	30 May 1916	8	3	
Hardman	Walter	o.	PD	27 Apr. 1917	5	6	
Hardt	George	d.	SRR	22 July 1916	5	2	
Hardt	George H.	d.	PA	21 July 1916	4	3	also 21 July, 6:4; 24 July, 3:5
Hardt	George H.	d.	PC	22 July 1916	1	5	San Francisco; also 25 July, 2:2, 4:1
Harford	Lyman	b.	PA	28 Mar. 1916	2	3	
Harlan	Ellis	o.	HT	3 Jan. 1918	1	5	
Harlan	J.	d.	PD	30 June 1916	8	1	Riverside Cemetery
Harlan	J.	d.	SRR	30 June 1916	5	3	Cloverdale
Harlan	J. M.	d.	PC	11 July 1916	3	5	
Harlan	J. M.	d.	PA	11 July 1916	2	4	
Harlan	John T.	d.	CR	20 Mar. 1917	1	2	Santa Cruz
Harlan	John T.	d.	PD	20 Mar. 1917	5	3	Santa Cruz
Harlan	John T.	d.	SRR	20 Mar. 1917	2	3	
Harlan	John T.	d.	ST	24 Mar. 1917	3	3	
Harlan	Vaughan	o.	HT	27 Dec. 1917	1	1	
Harlan	Vaughan	o.	HT	29 Nov. 1917	7	1	

(1) Surname	(2) Given Name	(3)	(4)	(5) Date	(6) Pg	(7) Col	(8) Comments
Harlan	Vaughan	o.	PD	9 Aug. 1918	7	1	
Harlan	Vaughan H.	o.	HT	8 Aug. 1918	1	4	
Harlan	Vaughn	o.	PD	11 May 1918	7	1	
Harlin	Joseph	d.	PD	1 July 1916	7	1	
Harmon	Elizabeth	d.	SRR	6 Nov. 1917	8	1	also 7 Nov., 8:2
Harmon	Elizabeth	d.	PD	8 Nov. 1917	4	2	Rural Cemetery; also 9 Nov., 6:4
Harmon	Roy	m.	PA	31 Jan. 1916	4	5	also 1 Feb., 3:6
Harmon	Russell	o.	PC	26 Sept. 1918	3	3	
Harmon	Sarah J.	d.	HT	29 Nov. 1917	3	3	
Harms	Clarence	o.	PC	1 Dec. 1918	4	4	
Harms	Clarence	o.	PC	25 Sept. 1918	4	3	
Harms	Fred	b.	PC	14 Sept. 1916	8	3	
Harms	Fred	b.	PA	7 Dec. 1917	4	7	
Harper	Fred	d.	PA	29 Oct. 1918	3	3	also 1 Nov., 6:3
Harper	Grace	d.	PD	5 Jan. 1918	6	1	
Harper	Margaret	d.	SIT	19 Jan. 1918	1	6	
Harper	Margaret	d.	PC	20 Jan. 1918	5	6	
Harriett	Ida Hazel	m.	SRR	1 June 1917	3	4	
Harrington	J. M.	m.	PA	2 July 1918	6	4	
Harrington	Jere M.	m.	PC	28 June 1918	5	4	
Harrington	Jerem	m.	PD	30 June 1918	12	3	
Harrington	Jesse	o.	PC	10 Feb. 1918	3	4	
Harrington	Sidney	d.	ST	12 Aug. 1916	1	3	
Harrington	Sidney	d.	PD	9 Aug. 1916	5	4	
Harrington	Sydney	d.	PC	6 Aug. 1916	2	1&2	also 8 Aug., 5:5
Harrington	Sydney	d.	SRR	7 Aug. 1916	4	2	
Harrington	W.	o.	PA	2 Apr. 1918	3	4	
Harris	Arthur L.	m.	PD	10 Nov. 1917	8	1	also 14 Nov., 5:1
Harris	Arthur L.	d.	SRR	10 Nov. 1917	8	3	
Harris	Arthur L.	d.	PC	11 Nov. 1917	1	4	
Harris	Catherine A.	d.	PA	5 Feb. 1917	5	3	also 7 Feb., 8:5
Harris	Catherine A.	d.	PC	6 Feb. 1917	4	2&5	Cypress Hill; also 8 Feb., 3:2&3
Harris	Catherine A.	d.	PD	6 Feb. 1917	8	5	
Harris	Catherine A.	d.	SRR	6 Feb. 1917	5	3	
Harris	Claude	m.	PD	3 Feb. 1916	3	3	
Harris	Earl L.	m.	PD	25 May 1916	3	4	
Harris	Elizabeth	d.	SRR	22 Apr. 1916	10	6	
Harris	Frank	m.	PA	1 May 1918	5	3	also 3 May, 8:3
Harris	Frank	m.	PC	1 May 1918	5	5	
Harris	Fred	o.	HT	15 Apr. 1918	2	4	
Harris	Fred	o.	HT	29 Aug. 1918	5	4	also 3 Oct., 3:3; 30 Oct., 1:4
Harris	Hall	m.	SRR	2 Feb. 1916	10	6	
Harris	Janette	m.	PD	8 July 1917	2	2	

(1) Surname	(2) Given Name	(3)	(4)	(5) Date	(6) Pg	(7) Col	(8) Comments
Harris	Jeanette	m.	SIT	7 July 1917	1	5	
Harris	Joseph	d.	SRR	11 Dec. 1916	4	3	also 13Dec., 6:4
Harris	Joseph	o.	PC	26 Jan. 1916	1	3	
Harris	Joseph W.	d.	PC	12 Dec. 1916	1	5	also 14 Dec., 8:4
Harris	Joseph W.	d.	PD	12 Dec. 1916	6	1	
Harris	Mary	m.	PD	16 June 1917	6	3	
Harris	Mary B.	m.	PD	10 May 1917	5	1	
Harris	Mary B.	m.	SRR	10 May 1917	3	3	also 11 May, 1:2
Harris	N. B., Miss	m.	PC	11 July 1917	7	4	
Harris	Phebe Fulkerson	d.	PD	2 Nov. 1917	2	4	Fulkerson Cemetery; also 4:2; 4 Nov., 2:2
Harris	Phoebe Fulkerson	d.	SRR	1 Nov. 1917	1	3	also 3 Nov., 1:6
Harris	Phoebe Fulkerson	d.	PC	2 Nov. 1917	8	4	
Harrow	Albert C.	o.	SRR	6 Nov. 1917	4	3	
Harrow	Lucy A.	o.	SRR	6 Nov. 1917	4	3	
Harsen	John H.	d.	HT	3 Feb. 1917	5	2	
Harsen	John S.	d.	SRR	31 Jan. 1916	5	4	
Harsen	John S.	d.	ST	5 Feb. 1916	3	6	
Hart	Edward H.	d.	SRR	26 Sept. 1917	8	2	portrait
Hart	Edward H.	d.	PA	27 Sept. 1917	2	3	portrait; also 29 Sept., 5:7
Hart	Edward H.	d.	PD	27 Sept. 1917	8	3	portrait
Hart	Edward H.	d.	ST	28 Sept. 1917	1	5	
Hart	Emmet	d.	SRR	16 Dec. 1916	10	4	also 18 Dec., 6:1
Hart	Emmet	d.	PC	17 Dec. 1916	1	4	
Hart	Emmet	d.	PA	19 Dec. 1916	2	2	
Hart	Emmet	d.	PD	19 Dec. 1916	5	5	
Hart	Emmet	p.	PC	22 Dec. 1916	6	1	
Hart	Ernest	p.	SRR	20 Dec. 1916	6	4	
Hart	Euphemia	m.	HT	23 Nov. 1916	6	4	
Hart	J. A.	b.	SRR	27 Feb. 1917	8	1	
Hart	Jesse	m.	SRR	7 July 1916	8	2	
Hart	Jesse B.	m.	PD	17 Oct. 1916	5	1	
Hart	Jesse Bruner	m.	SRR	16 Oct. 1916	8	1	
Hart	Lou	m.	PD	9 Dec. 1916	2	3	
Hart	Louise	m.	PD	26 Apr. 1917	8	3	
Hart	Louise	m.	SRR	26 Apr. 1917	5	4	also 1 May, 6:1
Hart	Louise M.	m.	PC	27 Apr. 1917	8	3	
Hart	Ruth	m.	PA	18 Dec. 1917	18	3	
Hart	Ruth	m.	PD	19 Dec. 1917	6	1	
Hart	Ruth N.	m.	PC	18 Dec. 1917	1	2	
Hart	Ruth N.	m.	SRR	19 Dec. 1917	5	1	
Harter	Harold	m.	CR	3 Aug. 1917	1	2	
Harter	Nellie	d.	PD	16 June 1917	2	1	
Harter	Nellie Eva	d.	CR	8 June 1917	1	3	cremation
Hartman	Frank	o.	PD	13 Sept. 1918	2	3	

(1) Surname	(2) Given Name	(3)	(4)	(5) Date	(6) Pg	(7) Col	(8) Comments
Hartman	Lizzie	d.	PA	16 Mar. 1917	5	2	
Hartman	Lizzie	d.	PD	17 Mar. 1917	3	4	
Hartman	Lizzie	d.	SRR	17 Mar. 1917	5	3	
Hartman	Lizzie	d.	ST	24 Mar. 1917	3	2	
Hartman	Mrs.	d.	SIT	17 Mar. 1917	1	1	
Hartman	Nina	d.	PC	18 Jan. 1918	5	3	
Hartsock	Fred E.	m.	PD	7 Dec. 1917	5	6	
Hartsock	Freedom E.	m.	SRR	6 Dec. 1917	8	1	
Harvey	Charles	m.	SIT	20 Oct. 1917	1	7	
Harvey	Charles L.	m.	PD	19 Oct. 1917	7	4	
Harvey	Euphane	d.	HT	17 Feb. 1916	1	3	
Harvey	Euphemia	d.	SRR	15 Feb. 1916	2	3	
Harvey	Helen	m.	PC	29 Mar. 1917	5	2	
Harvey	Lester, Mrs.	d.	PC	31 Oct. 1916	6	4	Cypress Hill
Harvey	M.	b.	SRR	7 Feb. 1916	5	2	
Harvey	Naomi	d.	PA	28 Oct. 1916	8	7	Cypress Hill; also 30 Oct., 4:5
Harvey	Naomi	d.	PC	28 Oct. 1916	1	5	
Haselswerdt	Cora	m.	SRR	8 Apr. 1916	1	5	
Haselswerdt	Cora	m.	PC	9 Apr. 1916	1	3	
Haskell	Florence	d.	PD	23 Dec. 1916	5	5	
Haskell	Mary	d.	PA	26 Apr. 1916	5	4	also 28 Apr., 5:5
Haskell	Mary	d.	PC	27 Apr. 1916	1	6	cremation; also 5:1; 29 Apr., 5:5
Haskell	Mary	d.	PD	27 Apr. 1916	8	3	
Haslett	James Robert	d.	PA	5 July 1916	3	4	also 7 July, 3:5
Haslett	James Robert	d.	PC	6 July 1916	4	2	also 8 July, 8:5
Hasse	William	d.	SRR	22 June 1916	5	3	also 24 June, 7:3; 28 June, 1:1; 29 June, 4:1; 30 June, 8:3
Hassel	Esther	m.	PD	8 May 1917	8	3	
Hasseltine	Stella	m.	PD	10 Apr. 1917	8	4	
Hassey	E. Q. (dau of)	b&d	PA	24 Mar. 1917	4	5	
Hastings	Ruby	m.	PD	7 Dec. 1918	2	5	also 8 Dec., 8:2
Hastings	W. W.	m.	SRR	19 Sept. 1916	3	4	also 20 Sept., 8:6
Hastings	Walton	m.	SRR	26 Aug. 1916	4	2	
Hatch	Sylvia	m.	SIT	21 Dec. 1918	2	3	
Hathaway	Frank	d.	PC	8 July 1917	8	5	
Hathaway	Frank	d.	PD	8 July 1917	5	3	
Hatton	Carl	d.	PC	10 Jan. 1918	1	5	also 12 Jan., 4:6; 20 Jan., 5:5; 23 Jan., 1:6
Hatton	Earl	d.	PC	5 June 1918	1	4	Bloomfield
Hatton	Earl	d.	PD	5 June 1918	6	3	Cypress Hill
Hatton	Earl	d.	ST	25 Jan. 1918	2	1	
Hatton	Earl F.	d.	PA	9 Jan. 1918	5	1	Cypress Hill; also 14 Jan., 7:4; 21 Jan., 4:1; 22 Jan., 5:3
Hatton	James	d.	PC	28 Nov. 1916	1	4	

(1) Surname	(2) Given Name	(3)	(4)	(5) Date	(6) Pg	(7) Col	(8) Comments
Hatton	James	d.	PD	28 Nov. 1916	3	4	
Hauck	Edith	o.	SRR	13 Aug. 1917	5	5	
Hauck	Edith	o.	PA	14 Aug. 1917	7	4	
Hauck	John	m.	SRR	30 June 1917	10	3	also 5 July, 3:5
Hauck	John Edgar	m.	PD	1 July 1917	3	2	also 4 July, 5:2
Hauck	William	o.	SRR	13 Aug. 1917	5	5	
Hauck	William	o.	PA	14 Aug. 1917	7	4	
Haufe	Albert	o.	SRR	15 Feb. 1916	3	2	
Haufe	Nettie E.	o.	SRR	15 Feb. 1916	3	2	
Haultman	A. J.	b.	PA	7 May 1918	4	2	also 9 May, 6:4
Haupt	Louis	m.	PD	13 Feb. 1917	2	5	
Haupt	Louis	m.	PC	14 Feb. 1917	2	3	
Haven	Maude Agler	d.	SIT	30 Mar. 1918	1	1	
Havens	C. I.	d.	PA	28 Apr. 1916	4	3	
Havens	Charles I.	d.	SRR	28 Apr. 1916	1	4	
Havens	Charles I.	d.	PC	29 Apr. 1916	5	6	
Havens	Charles I.	d.	PD	29 Apr. 1916	5	2	San Francisco
Hawes	William H.	m.	ST	5 Oct. 1917	8	2	
Hawkins	Ethel	d.	PA	14 Oct. 1918	1	4	Cypress Hill; also 17 Oct., 4:4; 18 Oct., 5:3, 8:4; 19 Oct., 4:2; 16 Nov., 3:5; 18 Nov., 4:5
Hawkins	Ethel Merritt	d.	PC	16 Oct. 1918	8	3	also 18 Oct., 1:2; 19 Oct., 5:3; 20 Oct., 8:2
Hawkins	G. W.	o.	PA	23 Oct. 1918	8	3	also 26 Oct., 1:5
Hawkins	G. W.	o.	PD	23 Oct. 1918	6	2	
Hawkins	G. W.	o.	PC	24 Oct. 1918	2	2	
Hawkins	George	o.	PC	10 Dec. 1918	1	5	
Hawkins	Helen	o.	PD	10 Dec. 1918	8	1	
Hawkins	Helen	o.	PA	23 Oct. 1918	8	3	also 26 Oct., 1:5
Hawkins	Helen A.	o.	PC	24 Oct. 1918	2	2	
Hawkins	Mildred	m.	SIT	25 May 1918	1	3	
Hawley	Gail	m.	PD	21 Aug. 1917	8	3	
Hawley	Gail	m.	SRR	21 Aug. 1917	5	3	
Hawley	Gladys	m.	PD	19 June 1917	2	1	
Hawley	Gladys Fayo	m.	SRR	18 June 1917	8	5	
Hayden	Joe	d.	PD	15 Dec. 1916	8	3	aka Joseph T. Miles
Hayes	Jean	m.	PC	12 June 1918	5	1	
Hayes	William	m.	PC	21 Nov. 1918	4	3	
Hayes	William E.	b.	PC	1 May 1917	4	4	
Hayes	William E.	b.	PA	3 May 1917	7	3	
Hayne	Ellen	m.	PC	21 Sept. 1916	1	5	also 22 Sept., 3:3; 14 Sept., 4:4; Cypress Hills
Hayne	Ellen C.	d.	PA	21 Sept. 1916	5	4	also 22 Sept., 4:4
Hayne	Laura	m.	ST	27 Sept. 1918	1	3	

(1) Surname	(2) Given Name	(3)	(4)	(5) Date	(6) Pg	(7) Col	(8) Comments
Hayne	Rose Neva	o.	SRR	25 Mar. 1916	6	6	
Hays	G. W.	d.	SIT	10 June 1916	1	1	
Hays	George	d.	PA	6 June 1916	1	6	Cypress Hill; also 7 June, 5:5
Hays	George	d.	PC	6 June 1916	1	4	also 8 June, 8:3
Hays	William Collins	m.	PA	4 Dec. 1917	7	4	
Hayward	Jack	o.	SRR	25 Mar. 1916	6	6	
Hazard	Elizabeth Rachel	d.	HT	2 May 1918	4	4	
Hazelton	Ruth M.	m.	PD	5 Sept. 1918	6	5	
Hazelwood	Jean	m.	PD	26 Aug. 1917	3	5	
Hazen	Frank	o.	HT	22 Nov. 1917	1	3	
Hazen	Frank	o.	SRR	22 Nov. 1917	3	3	
Hazen	Myra	o.	HT	22 Nov. 1917	1	3	
Hazen	Myra F.	o.	SRR	22 Nov. 1917	3	3	
Hazlett	Herman	m.	PA	2 Nov. 1917	5	1	also 3 Nov., 8:3; 5 Nov., 4:3
Hazlett	Herman J.	m.	PC	3 Nov. 1917	4	3	also 4 Nov., 8:4; 6 Nov., 3:4
Hazlett	Stellamae	d.	SRR	26 June 1917	8	1	
Hazlett	Stellamae	d.	PD	27 June 1917	7	2	
Hazz	L.	o.	PD	25 June 1918	5	1	also 26 June, 8:3
Heald	C. E.	m.	SRR	20 June 1917	3	5	
Heald	C. E.	m.	ST	22 June 1917	7	6	
Heald	C. F.	m.	PD	20 June 1917	3	2	
Healey	Claire M.	m.	PA	9 Dec. 1918	6	1	
Healey	Claire Marie	m.	PC	8 Dec. 1918	1	2	
Healey	Earl	o.	PA	31 July 1918	3	4	
Healey	Eugene	b.	PD	24 Oct. 1916	2	3	
Hearn	William J.	d.	PC	11 May 1916	1	6	Cypress Hill; also 12 May, 5:3; 13 May, 8:1
Hearn	William J.	d.	SRR	12 May 1916	5	3	
Hearn	William J.	d.	PD	13 May 1916	3	4	
Hearn	William J.	d.	PA	10 May 1917	5	5	Calvary Cemetery; also 11 May, 8:3; 12 May, 5:5
Hearns	Charles	m.	PC	3 July 1918	4	3	
Hearns	Charles H.	m.	PA	3 July 1918	4	6	
Heaton	Charles	m.	PD	14 Dec. 1916	3	2	
Heaton	Charles C.	m.	SRR	13 Dec. 1916	3	1	
Heber	Mr. & Mrs.	b.	SIT	28 Dec. 1918	3	5	
Heberling	Leonard	d.	SRR	21 Apr. 1917	10	6	Odd Fellows Cemetery; 23 Apr., 8:3; 24 Apr., 4:4
Heberling	Leonard I.	d.	ST	21 Apr. 1917	1	2	also 28 Apr., 8:5
Hedges	George	d.	PA	30 Jan. 1917	8	5	
Hedrich	Eliza Ann	d.	PD	2 July 1918	8	4	
Hedrick	Clyde Warton	m.	PD	4 Aug. 1917	7	1	
Hefrichter	Jane	d.	PA	27 Jan. 1916	5	4	Cypress Hill; also 29 Jan., 5:3
Hefrichter	Jane	d.	SRR	27 Jan. 1916	5	3	
Hefty	Lydia	d.	PD	1 Sept. 1917	2	3	cremation

(1) Surname	(2) Given Name	(3)	(4)	(5) Date	(6) Pg	(7) Col	(8) Comments
Hefty	Lydia	d.	SRR	31 Aug. 1917	8	2	cremation
Hehir	Lyman	m.	SRR	29 Aug. 1916	8	1	
Hehir	Lyman	m.	PD	30 Aug. 1916	3	4	
Hein	Tillie A.	m.	SRR	7 Mar. 1917	8	1	
Heinsen	George	o.	PC	11 Sept. 1918	3	4	
Heinsen	George	o.	PC	15 Sept. 1917	3	3	
Heiser	J. W.	d.	SIT	21 Dec. 1918	2	5	
Heitz	Emma	m.	HT	23 May 1918	3	5	
Heitz	Henry	d.	PD	30 Apr. 1916	1	4	also 1 May,1:1
Helberg	Elizabeth	m.	PD	8 Sept. 1918	3	4	
Helberg	Minnie Clara	d.	SRR	20 May 1916	9	3	
Helberg	Valerie	m.	SIT	24 Aug. 1918	1	1	
Helberg	Valerie	m.	PC	27 Aug. 1918	5	2	
Helberg	William (child of)	d.	SIT	20 May 1916	3	1	
Helberg	William, Jr.	m.	SIT	18 May 1918	1	5	
Helgas	Victor	m.	PA	9 June 1916	4	1	also 24 June, 8:5; 26 June, 5:6; 29 June, 6:5
Helgas	Victor	m.	PC	10 June 1916	8	3	also 25 June, 5:5; 27 June, 3:1
Helgas	Victor	m.	SRR	12 June 1916	1	6	
Helin	Charles E.	m.	PD	16 Sept. 1917	3	3	
Hellberg	Valerie	m.	PD	25 Aug. 1918	7	4	
Hellengren	Lind, Mrs. & Child	d.	PD	7 June 1917	8	1	also 8 June, 5:2; 8:2; 9 June, 8:4
Heller	Wilhelmina	d.	PA	17 Nov. 1917	5	6	
Heller	Wilhelmina	d.	PD	17 Nov. 1917	8	1	also 18 Nov., 4:2
Heller	Wilhelmina	d.	SRR	17 Nov. 1917	5	2	also 19 Nov., 8:2
Helm	Frances	o.	PC	3 Jan. 1918	8	4	
Helm	Pete J.	d.	PD	22 Sept. 1916	1	4	
Helm	Peter J.	d.	PC	23 Sept. 1916	6	1	Cloverdale
Helman	Louis W.	m.	PD	18 Nov. 1916	5	5	
Helmes	R.	b.	PC	1 Dec. 1918	5	3	
Hemenover	Adah	o.	SRR	9 June 1917	5	4	
Hemenover	Adah	o.	SRR	13 July 1917	3	3	
Hemenover	Adah	o.	PD	14 July 1917	2	5	
Hemenover	Dudley	o.	SRR	9 June 1917	5	4	
Hemenover	Dudley	o.	PD	14 July 1917	2	5	
Hemenover	Dudley	o.	PD	9 June 1918	5	3	also 19 June, 5:1
Hemenover	Dudley	o.	PD	13 Aug. 1918	2	3	
Hemenover	Dudley	o.	PD	28 Sept. 1918	8	1	
Hemenover	Dudley A.	o.	SRR	13 July 1917	3	3	
Hemmingsen	Knut	b.	PC	4 Apr. 1918	5	1	
Henderlong	Martha V.	m.	PD	27 Aug. 1918	3	1	
Henderson	George	b.	SRR	24 Sept. 1917	6	4	
Henderson	John	d.	SRR	12 Jan. 1917	2	3	also 15 Jan., 5:2

(1) Surname	(2) Given Name	(3)	(4)	(5) Date	(6) Pg	(7) Col	(8) Comments
Hendricks	Estella	m.	HT	22 June 1916	2	3	
Hendricks	Stella	m.	PD	23 June 1916	3	5	
Hendry	Howard W.	m.	PD	12 June 1917	8	1	
Hendry	Howard W.	m.	SRR	12 June 1917	8	3	
Hendy	S. J.	m.	PD	20 Nov. 1917	1	2	
Henessy	Dan	d.	PC	7 Aug. 1918	1	4	
Henley	M. J.	b.	PC	13 Mar. 1917	4	4	
Henley	Mary	d.	PA	6 Nov. 1917	4	1	Calvary Cemetery; also 7 Nov., 8:5; 8 Nov., 4:6
Henley	Mary Cecilia	d.	PC	7 Nov. 1917	4	3	also 8 Nov., 3:5; 9 Nov., 8:1
Henley	Mike	b.	PA	12 Mar. 1917	6	3	
Hennessey	Don	d.	PD	7 Aug. 1918	2	4	also 8 Aug., 8:5
Hennessy	Dan	d.	PA	6 Aug. 1918	5	1	also 4:2
Henning	Ellie E.	o.	PA	8 July 1918	4	6	
Henning	Thomas Theodore	o.	PA	8 July 1918	4	6	
Henricksen	Anna	o.	PD	21 June 1918	6	6	
Henricksen	Charles	o.	PD	21 June 1918	6	6	
Hensen	Elmira	m.	PC	30 Sept. 1917	8	3	
Henshaw	Danford	d.	PA	1 Feb. 1916	4	1	Cypress Hill; also 2 Feb., 5:6, 8:3; 3 Feb., 5:4
Henshaw	Danford	d.	PD	2 Feb. 1916	8	1	
Henshaw	Danford Alfonso	o.	PC	2 Feb. 1916	8	2	
Henshaw	Danforth	d.	PC	4 Feb. 1916	4	3	Cypress Hill
Herberger	Carl	d.	PA	20 May 1918	5	4	Cypress Hill; also 21 May, 8:5
Herberger	Carl	d.	PC	21 May 1918	4	1&4	Liberty Cemetery; also 22 May, 5:4
Herberger	Carl	d.	PD	22 May 1918	3	4	
Herbert	Gladys	m.	ST	10 Aug. 1917	3	3	
Herbert	Gladys	m.	SRR	26 Mar. 1917	5	3	
Herbert	Gladys	m.	PA	7 Aug. 1917	8	2	
Herbert	Gladys	m.	SRR	7 Aug. 1917	8	4	also 8 Aug., 6:4
Herbert	Gladys	m.	PC	8 Aug. 1917	1	5	
Herbert	Mason	d.	PC	31 July 1917	1	3	
Herbert	Mason	d.	SRR	31 July 1917	8	4	
Herbert	Miss	m.	HT	5 July 1917	3	3	
Herbert	W. F.	m.	PA	7 Jan. 1918	2	6	
Herbert	William	m.	PD	6 Jan. 1918	5	4	
Herbert	William F.	m.	PC	8 Jan. 1918	6	4	
Herbert	William H.	d.	PC	7 Nov. 1916	5	3	
Herbert	William M.	d.	PA	7 Nov. 1916	5	4	Presidio
Hererling	Leonard	d.	PD	24 Apr. 1917	4	3	Odd Fellows Cemetery; also 25 Apr., 8:3
Herfurth	Cornelia	m.	HT	14 June 1917	6	3	
Herman	Frank J.	m.	ST	24 June 1916	1	2	

(1) Surname	(2) Given Name	(3)	(4)	(5) Date	(6) Pg	(7) Col	(8) Comments
Herman	Ray	m.	PC	1 Feb. 1916	4	2	
Hermansen	Herman	o.	PA	15 June 1917	5	5	
Hermanson	H. A.	o.	PA	4 Jan. 1918	6	4	
Herold	Charles	m.	PA	21 Mar. 1917	8	4	
Herold	Charles	m.	PC	21 Mar. 1917	5	3	
Heron	James	d.	PD	26 Mar. 1916	5	3	Rural Cemetery; also 29 Mar., 6:4
Heron	James	d.	SRR	27 Mar. 1916	5	5	also 28 Mar., 8:4
Heron	John	d.	SRR	30 Oct. 1916	4	4	
Heron	John	d.	PD	31 Oct. 1916	8	3	
Herrick	Albert	m.	SRR	27 June 1916	8	2	
Herrick	Albert	m.	SRR	1 July 1916	4	2	
Herrick	Albert B.	m.	PD	2 July 1916	2	2	
Herrick	Albert B., Jr.	m.	PD	28 June 1916	6	1	
Herrick	Clyde Warton	m.	SRR	4 Aug. 1917	2	3	
Herrick	Emerson	m.	PC	28 Apr. 1918	5	3	
Herrick	Emerson Brown	m.	SRR	29 Dec. 1917	4	1	
Herrick	Emerson Brown	m.	PC	30 Dec. 1917	5	4	
Herrington	Claude	o.	PD	4 July 1916	7	5	divorced; married 5 days
Herrington	Martha	o.	PD	4 July 1916	7	5	divorced; married 5 days
Hershberger	Ruby	m.	SRR	30 July 1917	3	4	
Hertz	Emma	m.	PD	24 May 1918	3	1	
Heryford	Roy	m.	PC	30 Aug. 1916	5	4	
Heryford	Roy	m.	PD	31 Aug. 1916	6	2	
Herzog	Frank	d.	PD	17 Nov. 1916	5	2	
Herzog	Frank	d.	SRR	17 Nov. 1916	8	3	also 20 Nov., 8:4
Hesler	Edward Francis	m.	PD	1 June 1917	8	4	
Hess	John	o.	PD	23 July 1918	2	3	
Hess	Sophie	d.	PA	25 May 1918	1	5	aka Sophie Wright
Hess	Sophie	d.	PC	26 May 1918	2	3	Cypress Hill; also 28 May, 2:1; 29 May, 5:4
Hess	Sophie	p.	PC	29 May 1918	1	3	will; also 11 June, 2:2
Hess	Sophie	p.	PD	30 May 1918	5	2	aka Sophia Wright
Hess	Sophie	p.	PD	11 June 1918	8	4	
Hess	Sophie	p.	PA	11 Dec. 1918	5	4	also 13 Dec., 5:4
Hess	Sophie	p.	PD	11 Dec. 1918	3	3	also 12 Dec., 3:1; 13 Dec., 2:4
Hess	Walter	b.	SRR	22 Nov. 1917	5	2	
Hesse	Charles F.	d.	SIT	15 Apr. 1916	1	1	
Hesse	Charles F.	d.	PA	8 Apr. 1916	1	3	also 7 Apr., 4:1; 10 Apr., 1:3
Hesse	Charles F.	m.	SRR	8 Apr. 1916	5	4	
Hesse	Charles F.	d.	PC	9 Apr. 1916	8	1	
Hesse	Rachael	m.	PA	8 Apr. 1916	4	1	
Hesse	Rachael	m.	PD	9 Apr. 1916	8	3	
Hesse	Rachel	m.	SRR	8 Apr. 1916	1	2	

(1) Surname	(2) Given Name	(3)	(4)	(5) Date	(6) Pg	(7) Col	(8) Comments
Hesse/Haase	William	d.	PD	22 June 1916	5	1	S.F.; also 23 June, 1:5; 24 June, 5:1; 28 June, 8:1; 29 June, 5:2
Hessel	Esther	m.	SRR	8 May 1917	7	4	
Hessel	Frances	m.	SRR	6 June 1916	8	3	
Hesseline	Stella	m.	PC	7 Apr. 1917	6	5	
Hesseltine	Stella	m.	SRR	5 Apr. 1917	8	2	also 7 Apr., 3:4
Hessler	Edward Francis	m.	SRR	1 June 1917	3	1	
Hessler	Everett Francis	m.	SRR	21 May 1917	8	3	
Hesslet	Edward Francis	m.	PD	22 May 1917	2	4	
Heugett	Mrs.	d.	SIT	27 Apr. 1918	1	5	Valley Cemetery
Heugitt	Bert	o.	SIT	27 Oct. 1917	1	5	
Heugitt	John	d.	SIT	12 Oct. 1918	1	3	
Heugitt	John	d.	PC	13 Oct. 1918	5	4	
Hevel	W. T.	m.	PD	10 Apr. 1917	8	4	
Hewett	Ernest	d.	PA	12 Apr. 1916	7	5	
Hewgett	John, Mrs.	d.	PD	26 Apr. 1918	6	2	
Hewitt	Archie R.	o.	ST	12 Oct. 1917	3	2	
Hewitt	Archie R.	o.	HT	18 Oct. 1917	2	2	
Hewitt	Bert	o.	PC	30 Oct. 1917	6	3	
Hewitt	Ernest Ellsworth	m.	SRR	10 Apr. 1916	1	4	
Hewitt	Ernest Ellsworth	d.	PC	11 Apr. 1916	4	2	
Hiatt	Charles	m.	SRR	2 Dec. 1916	3	2	
Hiatt	Charles	m.	PD	3 Dec. 1916	8	3	
Hiatt	Charles	m.	HT	7 Dec. 1916	7	4	
Hiatt	Earl	d.	PA	22 Oct. 1918	5	7	
Hiatt	Elizabeth	d.	CR	6 July 1917	1	2	
Hiatt	Jane	d.	PD	7 July 1917	5	4	
Hickman	Wade	d.	PD	3 Nov. 1918	8	3	
Hickman	Wade H.	d.	PC	3 Nov. 1918	5	3	
Hicks	Henrietta C.	m.	PD	17 Sept. 1916	7	2	
Hicks	May	m.	PD	17 Oct. 1917	8	3	
Higby	Bianca	d.	PD	19 Feb. 1918	5	5	
Higgins	J. W.	o.	PD	30 Sept. 1916	2	1	
Higgins	John	d.	PC	26 Oct. 1916	1	6	
Higgins	Mabel	o.	PD	30 Sept. 1916	2	1	
Higgins	Walter Henry	d.	SRR	9 Apr. 1917	3	4	
High	Minnie B.	m.	PD	14 Aug. 1918	6	5	
Highmanick	John Hammond	m.	PC	25 June 1916	5	5	also 27 June, 3:1
Hihn	E. D.	m.	PC	15 Feb. 1918	5	3	
Hildebrand	Gus	m.	HT	18 Jan. 1917	8	4	
Hildebrandt	Laura	d.	SRR	25 Apr. 1917	6	6	
Hildebrant	Laura	d.	PD	26 Apr. 1917	5	2	
Hilderbrand	Gus	m.	SRR	17 Jan. 1917	3	1	
Hilgerloh	Helen	m.	PD	2 Nov. 1916	2	2	also 4 Nov., 7:2

(1) Surname	(2) Given Name	(3)	(4)	(5) Date	(6) Pg	(7) Col	(8) Comments
Hilgerloh	Helen	m.	SRR	2 Nov. 1916	3	2	
Hilgerloh	Helen	m.	HT	3 Nov. 1916	1	6	
Hiliendahl	Eva	d.	PD	19 Oct. 1918	6	1	Tuolumne County
Hill	Bena E.	o.	PC	8 Dec. 1918	3	4	
Hill	Benia	o.	PD	31 Dec. 1918	8	3	
Hill	Dolph B.	b.	PA	18 June 1917	5	4	also 8:6
Hill	Dolph Brice	m.	PC	16 May 1916	5	1	also 7 June, 5:4
Hill	Dolph Brice	m.	PD	8 June 1916	2	1	
Hill	Dolph Brice	b.	PC	19 June 1917	2	2	also 6:3
Hill	Dolph P.	m.	PA	16 May 1916	7	5	also 7 Jun, 5:3
Hill	Gill P.	o.	PC	8 Dec. 1918	3	4	
Hill	Harry Elwood	m.	PC	21 Apr. 1917	5	3	
Hill	Herbert	o.	PC	24 Aug. 1918	1	3	
Hill	Humphrey	d.	SIT	19 Aug. 1916	1	2	
Hill	Josephine	d.	ST	11 Jan. 1918	1	4	
Hill	Josephine F.	d.	PA	9 Jan. 1918	5	3	Cypress Hill; also 10 Jan., 5:3; 11 Jan., 7:5
Hill	Josephine P.	d.	PD	10 Jan. 1918	8	3	
Hill	Josephine P.	d.	PC	9 Jan. 1918	1	2	also 4:3; 10 Jan., 4:5; 11 Jan., 4:3
Hill	Josie	p.	PA	16 Jan. 1918	6	5	
Hill	Mary B.	d.	PA	23 Apr. 1917	4	5	Liberty Cemetery; also 24 Apr., 8:6; 25 Apr., 8:2
Hill	Mary B.	d.	PC	24 Apr. 1917	2	3	Liberty Cemetery; also 5:4; 26 Apr., 8:4
Hill	Samuel	d.	PD	20 May 1916	8	5	
Hill	Samuel	d.	SRR	20 May 1916	7	2	
Hill	William E.	o.	PD	31 Dec. 1918	8	3	
Hillbrandt	Laura	d.	HT	26 Apr. 1917	1	3	
Hillerdahl	Edward	m.	PD	1 Jan. 1918	5	3	
Hilles	Family	o.	PD	18 Nov. 1917	5	1	Canadian Army
Hillis	E.	o.	PC	23 Nov. 1917	2	1	
Hillis	Noble	o.	ST	23 Nov. 1917	1	5	
Hillis	R.	o.	PC	15 Nov. 1917	1	2	
Hillis	Raymond	o.	ST	23 Nov. 1917	1	5	
Hillis	Roy	d.	ST	23 Nov. 1917	1	5	Ypres, France
Hills	Percy	m.	PD	27 Oct. 1917	7	3	
Hills	Percy J.	m.	HT	25 Oct. 1917	1	5	
Himle	Alma	d.	PD	8 Sept. 1918	7	3	Rural Academy; also 11 Sept., 4:2
Hink	Claus J.	m.	PA	4 Mar. 1916	5	7	
Hinkley	Eleanor	d.	SRR	6 Nov. 1916	1	6	also 7 Nov., 4:1
Hinshaw	Harold	m.	PC	27 Nov. 1918	4	3	
Hinshaw	Sabry	p.	PA	21 Aug. 1916	1	4	
Hinshaw	Wilma	m.	PA	8 Oct. 1918	8	5	

(1) Surname	(2) Given Name	(3)	(4)	(5) Date	(6) Pg	(7) Col	(8) Comments
Hinshaw	Wilma	m.	PC	9 Oct. 1918	2	2	
Hinslaw	Wilma	m.	PD	8 Oct. 1918	2	3	
Hirst	Samuel	d.	PD	22 Nov. 1917	6	1	
Hiser	John	d.	HT	12 Dec. 1918	17	4	
Hiser	William	d.	PD	20 Dec. 1918	8	3	
Hiser	William J.	d.	PA	20 Dec. 1918	8	4	
Hitchcock	John	d.	PA	27 Nov. 1917	2	4	
Hitchcock	John	d.	PD	27 Nov. 1917	8	3	Odd Fellows Cemetery; also 29 Nov., 4:2; 1 Dec., 3:4
Hitchcock	John	d.	SRR	27 Nov. 1917	5	3	I.O.O.F. Cemetry; also 8:3; 30 Nov., 8:3
Hitchcock	John	d.	HT	29 Nov. 1917	1	3	
Hitchcock	John, Jr.	o.	PD	18 July 1918	5	2	
Hixon	John	b.	HT	26 Oct. 1916	6	4	
Hoadley	Mervyn J.	d.	PD	5 Apr. 1918	6	5	also 16 Apr., 5:1
Hoadley	Myrvam	d.	PC	6 Apr. 1918	3	4	
Hoag	David E.	d.	SRR	11 Sept. 1916	8	5	
Hoag	David E.	d.	PA	7 Sept. 1916	5	1	also 8 Sept., 8:5
Hoag	David E.	d.	PC	8 Sept. 1916	1	4	Bloomfield; also 9 Sept., 8:5
Hoag	David Elmer	d.	PD	12 Sept. 1916	3	1	
Hoch	Fred W.	d.	PD	4 Aug. 1918	8	1	France
Hocker	George	o.	PC	8 Mar. 1918	8	3	
Hocker	George A.	o.	SRR	6 Mar. 1916	5	2	
Hockin	Anabel	m.	PD	18 Oct. 1917	8	1	
Hockin	Gertrude	m.	PD	7 July 1918	7	3	
Hocking	Alfred	m.	PD	14 Aug. 1918	6	5	
Hodge	Levi	d.	PD	17 Feb. 1916	5	2	Illinois
Hodge	Levi	d.	SRR	17 Feb. 1916	5	5	Sycamore, IL; also 26 Feb., 4:1
Hodges	Vivien C.	m.	ST	24 Mar. 1917	1	2	
Hodgson	Gladys	m.	PA	10 Nov. 1917	8	4	
Hodgson	Gladys	m.	SRR	10 Nov. 1917	5	1	portrait
Hodgson	Gladys	m.	PD	11 Nov. 1917	10	1	
Hodgson	Gladys	m.	PD	13 Jan. 1918	7	1	also 19 Jan., 2:4; 20 Jan., 7:1
Hodgson	Gladys	m.	PA	19 Jan. 1918	6	2	
Hodgson	Irene	m.	PA	6 Apr. 1918	3	4	
Hodgson	Irene Mae	m.	PD	7 Apr. 1918	5	1	
Hodgson	Madge	m.	PA	4 June 1918	4	4	also 8 June, 4:5; 10 June, 5:4
Hodgson	Mae	m.	PC	10 June 1918	1	1	
Hodgson	Mae Irene	m.	PC	7 Apr. 1918	5	4	
Hodgson	May	m.	PD	9 June 1918	7	1	portrait
Hoe	Martin	d.	SRR	8 Oct. 1917	8	5	also 4 Oct., 8:3
Hoe	Martin	d.	PD	9 Oct. 1917	5	3	also 10 Oct., 6:4
Hoeh	Flora	m.	SRR	12 June 1916	1	5	
Hoeh	Fred	o.	PD	7 May 1918	2	4	

(1) Surname	(2) Given Name	(3)	(4)	(5) Date	(6) Pg	(7) Col	(8) Comments
Hoeh	Fred	d.	PD	28 Sept. 1918	8	1	
Hoeh	Fred W.	d.	PC	4 Aug. 1918	1	3	France
Hoff	Walter	m.	PD	7 June 1918	5	2	
Hoffa	Joseph	m.	PD	16 Jan. 1916	10	2	
Hoffer	Fred, Sr.	d.	PA	2 Dec. 1918	5	2	Cypress Hill; also 8:4; 3 Dec., 2:8, 4:8
Hoffer	Frederick, Sr.	d.	PC	3 Dec. 1918	4	3	Cypress Hill; also 4 Dec., 5:3
Hoffer	Gertrude	m.	PD	20 Nov. 1917	3	3	
Hoffer	Virgil	m.	HT	11 Jan. 1917	6	3	
Hoffer	Virgil	m.	PD	3 Jan. 1917	8	3	
Hoffer	Virgil	m.	SRR	3 Jan. 1917	5	2	
Hoffer	Virgil	m.	PC	4 Jan. 1917	5	6	
Hofrichter	Jane	d.	PC	30 Jan. 1916	4	4	Cypress Hill
Hogan	Howard H.	d.	PA	20 Aug. 1917	3	3	
Hogan	Stella Mae	m.	PC	16 Mar. 1918	6	4	
Hogan	Stella May	m.	PA	15 Mar. 1918	4	3	
Hogan	William Marr	d.	PD	6 Apr. 1918	6	1	
Hoirup	Sine C.	m.	PC	4 Oct. 1916	1	4	
Holcomb	Albert S.	b.	SRR	25 Jan. 1916	6	3	
Holl	Emil	d.	SRR	3 Mar. 1916	8	4	
Holl	W. Terrill	m.	PA	21 July 1916	8	3	
Holland	Alva Burton	d.	SRR	21 July 1917	6	3	
Holland	Alva Burton	d.	PD	22 July 1917	3	3	
Holland	Eva	m.	PD	1 Jan. 1918	5	3	
Hollaway	Patrick E.	o.	PD	5 Oct. 1918	8	1	also 10 Oct., 4:2; 11 Oct., 2:2
Holle	Henry	b.	PA	11 Oct. 1916	8	7	
Hollegreen	Stanford Healon	d.	PA	6 June 1917	1	1	also 11 June, 7:2
Hollengreen	Mary	d.	PA	6 June 1917	1	1	
Hollengreen	Mary	d	SRR	6 June 1917	1	2	also 8 June, 6:4; 9 June, 5:1; 11 June, 6:4
Hollengreen	Mary & child	d.	PC	7 June 1917	1	3	
Hollengreen	Mary (child of)	d.	ST	8 June 1917	1	6	
Hollengreen	Stanford Heaton	d	SRR	6 June 1917	1	2	also 8 June, 6:4; 9 June, 5:1; 11 June, 6:4
Hollingsworth	Dale	m.	SRR	31 May 1916	5	3	
Hollingsworth	Gale	m.	PA	1 June 1916	8	3	
Hollingworth	Dale	m.	PC	1 June 1916	5	2	
Holm	J. M.	o.	PC	11 Jan. 1918	5	3	
Holmer	Jep	d.	PD	29 Nov. 1917	4	2	also 1 Dec., 2:4
Holmes	Adolph	o.	PC	28 Nov. 1917	1	2	
Holmes	Alta May	o.	PC	16 Apr. 1916	4	3	portrait
Holmes	Jennie	d.	PD	2 Apr. 1918	3	5	Evergreen Cemetery
Holmes	Jennie	d.	HT	9 Apr. 1918	8	4	Evergreen Cemetery
Holmes	Kate	m.	PC	13 Dec. 1916	3	4	
Holmes	Katie	m.	PA	14 Dec. 1916	8	5	

(1) Surname	(2) Given Name	(3)	(4)	(5) Date	(6) Pg	(7) Col	(8) Comments
Holmes	Lester S.	m.	PC	5 June 1917	4	2	
Holmes	Nathan	o.	PC	5 Nov. 1918	1	5	
Holmes	Nathan C.	o.	PA	5 Nov. 1918	5	5	
Holmstead	Cora Ella	m.	ST	5 Oct. 1917	8	2	
Holrup	Eine C.	m.	PA	2 Oct. 1916	5	5	also 4 Oct., 8:5
Holst	Hazel	o.	SRR	26 Sept. 1916	3	5	
Holst	Hazel	o.	PD	7 Nov. 1916	5	2	
Holst	Hazel	o.	SRR	7 Nov. 1916	5	1	
Holst	James	o.	SRR	26 Sept. 1916	3	5	
Holst	James	o.	PD	7 Nov. 1916	5	2	
Holst	James	o.	SRR	7 Nov. 1916	5	1	
Holst	Mollie	m.	PD	15 Oct. 1918	3	6	
Holt	Homer E.	m.	PD	21 Nov. 1916	5	1	
Holt	W. Terrill	m.	SIT	3 June 1916	1	1	also 8 July, 1:7; 22 July, 1:6
Holt	W. Terrill	m.	PC	12 July 1916	5	2	
Holt	W. W.	m.	PC	3 June 1916	4	6	
Holt	William Terril	m.	SRR	21 July 1916	5	4	
Holt	William Terrill	m.	SRR	3 June 1916	7	6	
Holt	William Therrill	m.	PD	16 July 1916	6	2	
Homer	George	m.	CR	20 Apr. 1917	1	5	
Hong	Hom	d.	PA	12 Mar. 1917	4	4	also 13 Mar., 8:3; 15 Mar., 1:3, 5:5
Hong	Hom	d.	SRR	12 Mar. 1917	1	6	also 13 Mar., 8:1; 16 Mar., 5:2
Hong	Hom	d.	PC	13 Mar. 1917	8	3	also 16 Mar., 1:3; 24 Mar., 1:3; 27 Mar., 4:3
Hong	Hom	d.	ST	17 Mar. 1917	1	6	
Honigan	Polly	m.	PD	14 June 1918	8	4	
Hood	Alzina	m.	PD	5 Feb. 1918	8	4	
Hood	James Galloway	d.	PD	25 Dec. 1918	4	2	Rural Cemetry; also 8:2; 27 Dec., 6:2
Hooper	George W., Jr.	d.	SIT	2 Nov. 1918	1	5	
Hooper	J. Austin	d.	PA	13 June 1917	5	3	Greenville, MS; also 14 June, 2:4
Hooper	J. Austin	d.	SRR	14 June 1917	8	4	
Hoover	J. M.	d.	HT	14 Dec. 1916	1	3	
Hopcroft	Gunda Coralie	d.	PA	15 Feb. 1916	5	3	also 16 Feb., 6:4
Hope	Bert	o.	PD	4 Nov. 1917	2	1	
Hope	Herbert	o.	HT	11 May 1916	1	3	
Hope	Herbert	o.	PD	6 July 1917	6	2	
Hopecroft	Gunda Corelie	d.	PC	15 Feb. 1916	4	2	Cypress Hill
Hopf	C. Luis	d.	PC	1 Aug. 1916	3	3	
Horgan	Eugene	d.	PD	18 Jan. 1916	5	3	Bodega Cemetery; also 20 Jan., 8:1
Horgan	Eugene	d.	SRR	19 Jan. 1916	7	3	Bodega
Horling	Wilhelmina	d.	PA	1 May 1917	8	3	Cypress Hill

(1) Surname	(2) Given Name	(3)	(4)	(5) Date	(6) Pg	(7) Col	(8) Comments
Horling	Wilhelmina	d.	PC	1 May 1917	3	4	Cypress Hill; also 2 May, 5:5
Horling	Wilhelmina	d.	PA	30 Apr. 1917	2	5	
Horn	J. W.	d.	PD	24 Jan. 1918	1	2	
Horn	J. W., Mrs.	d.	SRR	4 Aug. 1916	6	1	
Horn	John W.	d.	PA	24 Jan. 1918	3	4	portrait; Lorraine, Ohio; also 25 Jan., 4:5, 8:3; 26 Jan., 5:1; 28 Jan., 6:4; 2 Feb., 5:5
Horn	John W.	p.	PA	28 Jan. 1918	3	1	will
Horn	John William	d.	PC	24 Jan. 1918	1	3	Cypress Hill, Loraine, Ohio; also 25 Jan., 3:2; 26 Jan., 1:5; 27 Jan., 8:3; 29 Jan., 6:2; 2 Feb., 8:2; 5 Feb., 5:3
Horn	John William	p.	PC	29 Jan. 1918	5	3	
Horn	Mrs.	d.	PD	4 Aug. 1916	7	3	Healdsburg
Horn	Mrs.	d.	PC	5 Aug. 1916	3	3	San Francisco
Horn	Ruby	m.	SRR	3 Apr. 1916	2	2	
Hornbuckle	Thomas Edward	d.	PA	6 June 1917	6	3	Santa Rosa; also 8 June, 8:1
Hornbuckle	Thomas J.	d.	PD	7 June 1917	3	4	also 8 June, 8:5
Hornbuckle	Thomas Jefferson	d.	SRR	7 June 1917	8	2	
Hornsby	Eliza	d.	PC	30 Oct. 1917	6	4	
Horr	Frank	d.	PA	5 Sept. 1916	3	3	
Horr	Frank	d.	PC	6 Sept. 1916	2	2	
Horr	Frank	d.	PD	6 Sept. 1916	7	3	
Hosmer	Winslow	d.	PD	8 Mar. 1917	7	3	cremation; also 9 Mar., 7:4
Hosmer	Winslow Simon	d.	SRR	6 Mar. 1916	8	6	cremation; also 7 Mar., 8:2; 8 Mar., 8:4
Hoster	Willard S.	m.	PD	28 Dec. 1918	3	1	
Hotchkiss	Anna	m.	PD	25 June 1918	6	2	
Hotchkiss	Anna	m.	HT	27 June 1918	5	1	
Houck	Fred	b.	PA	19 Feb. 1917	8	1	
Houck	Mary L.	m.	PC	5 June 1917	4	2	
Hough	Grace	m.	PA	28 Mar. 1916	5	2	
House	Elizabeth	d.	PA	28 Oct. 1916	5	7	
House	W. A.	m.	PD	12 May 1917	8	3	
Houseman	Emeline	d.	PC	18 Apr. 1918	3	2&4	Cypress Hill; also 20 Apr., 4:3
Houseman	Emmaline	d.	PA	17 Apr. 1918	5	4	Cypress Hill; also 19 Apr., 5:4
Houts	May	d.	SRR	17 Mar. 1916	8	1	also 18 Mar., 8:4; 20 Mar., 8:3
Houts	May McConnell	d.	PA	17 Mar. 1916	4	4	Santa Rosa; also 18 Mar., 2:6
Houts	May McCouell	d.	HT	23 Mar. 1916	1	2	
Houts	McConnell, Mrs.	d.	PC	21 Mar. 1916	2	1	
Howard	Ada May	m.	HT	3 Jan. 1918	1	5	
Howard	Edward S.	m.	PA	21 June 1918	8	3	also 24 June, 8:3
Howard	Edward S.	m.	PD	22 June 1918	3	5	

(1) Surname	(2) Given Name	(3)	(4)	(5) Date	(6) Pg	(7) Col	(8) Comments
Howard	Eleanor	m.	PD	18 Jan. 1918	8	4	also 29 Jan., 5:1
Howard	Fred	m.	ST	1 July 1916	7	4	
Howard	Fred W.	m.	SRR	28 June 1916	8	5	
Howard	Fred W.	m.	PD	29 June 1916	5	1	
Howard	Fred W.	m.	PD	2 July 1916	2	2	
Howard	Henry	m.	SRR	3 Mar. 1916	6	2	
Howard	Henry Ward	m.	PD	3 Mar. 1917	5	2	
Howard	James	m.	SRR	26 July 1917	6	6	wife not named
Howard	James F.	d.	PA	25 Mar. 1918	6	1	
Howard	James F.	d.	PC	26 Mar. 1918	5	4	Cypress Hill; also 6:2; 27 Mar., 4:4
Howard	James G.	m.	HT	26 July 1917	8	3	wife not named
Howard	Mary E.	m.	PD	5 June 1918	6	4	
Howard	Ward D.	d.	PC	10 Nov. 1918	5	3	
Howard	Ward D.	d.	ST	8 Nov. 1918	1	3	
Howe	Edward "Ned"	d.	PC	19 Jan. 1917	8	3	
Howe	Stanley	o.	PD	22 Dec. 1917	2	·1	
Howell	Raymond Myron	d.	PC	9 Nov. 1918	8	2	Calvary Cemetery, Santa Rosa
Howell	Raymond Myron	d.	PD	9 Nov. 1918	4	2	also 6:2
Howie	Margaret A. C.	p.	PD	11 July 1917	5	4	
Howie	Mrs.	d.	SRR	3 July 1917	8	4	Bloomfield
Howie	Mrs.	d.	PC	4 July 1917	1	1	Bloomfield
Hoyle	Clarence Wallace	d.	PA	23 Apr. 1918	2	2	
Hoyle	Clarence Wallace	d.	PD	23 Apr. 1918	8	4	
Hoyle	G. W.	m.	PC	25 Nov. 1916	5	3	
Hoyle	George	m.	SIT	30 Nov. 1918	1	4	
Hoyle	George W.	m.	PA	22 Nov. 1918	4	5	
Hoyle	George W.	m.	PC	23 Nov. 1918	8	2	also 24 Nov., 4:4
Hoyle	George W.	m.	PD	23 Nov. 1918	5	1	also 24 Nov., 6:4, 10:2
Hoyle	George W.	m.	CR	29 Nov. 1918	1	3	
Hoyle	James H.	m.	PD	24 Feb. 1918	5	5	wife not named
Hoyle	Maggie Irene	d.	PA	28 Feb. 1917	6	4	
Hoyle	Maggie Irene	d.	PC	28 Feb. 1917	1	5	also 2 Mar. 1:4
Hoyle	Maggie Irene	d.	PD	28 Feb. 1917	8	3	I.O.O.F. Cemetery; also 2 Mar., 5:4
Hoyle	Maggie Irene	d.	SRR	28 Feb. 1917	5	1	I.O.O.F. Cemetery; also 8:3; 1 Mar., 10:6
Hoyle	Maggie Irene	d.	CR	3 Mar. 1917	1	3	
Hoyt	Henry, Mrs.	d.	SRR	24 Apr. 1916	5	1	
Hozz	Louis	o.	PA	24 June 1918	5	4	
Huckabay	Fern	m.	PD	2 Dec. 1917	6	3	also 18 Dec., 8:3
Huckabay	Maude	m.	PD	5 May 1917	2	3	
Huckabay	Maude Sarah	m.	SRR	4 May 1917	8	5	also 5 May, 4:2
Huckaby	Fern	m.	SRR	3 Dec. 1917	2	4	also 17 Dec., 2:3

(1) Surname	(2) Given Name	(3)	(4)	(5) Date	(6) Pg	(7) Col	(8) Comments
Huddard	Alfred	m.	PC	6 July 1916	5	1	
Huddart	Alfred	m.	PA	5 July 1916	7	4	
Huddart	Alfred	m.	SRR	5 July 1916	1	4	
Huddleston	Laura	m.	SRR	28 Sept. 1916	5	4	
Huddleston	Lena	m.	PD	28 Sept. 1916	6	4	
Hudson	Clarence R.	m.	HT	14 June 1917	6	3	
Huff	Binn/Bion H.	d.	PC	24 May 1918	4	3	also 26 May, 5:3; 28 May, 5:3
Huff	Bion	d.	PA	23 May 1918	5	3	Cypress Hill; also 27 May, 2:6
Huff	Bion	d.	PD	25 May 1918	5	4	Petaluma
Huffman	Frances	m.	PC	15 June 1917	5	2	also 19 June, 8:4
Huffman	Frances	m.	PA	18 June 1917	4	4	
Huffman	Frances	m.	PD	20 June 1917	3	1	
Huffman	Francis	m.	HT	21 June 1917	7	4	
Huffman	Mary	m.	PD	17 Sept. 1916	6	7	
Huffman	May	d.	HT	16 Aug. 1917	8	2	
Huffman	May	d.	SRR	17 Aug. 1917	6	6	
Huffman/ Hoffman	Frances	m.	SRR	21 June 1917	6	6	
Huffner	Ed L.	m.	PD	17 Sept. 1916	6	7	
Hug	Warnie	o.	SRR	23 Feb. 1916	1	4	
Hughes	Arthur	m.	SRR	1 Mar. 1916	10	4	
Hughes	Arthur	m.	PD	2 Mar. 1916	2	2	
Hughes	Arthur	m.	PC	3 Mar. 1916	6	6	
Hughes	Cecil E.	m.	HT	28 Dec. 1916	1	3	
Hughes	Cecil E.	m.	PD	29 Dec. 1916	6	5	
Hughes	Everett	m.	SRR	24 Aug. 1917	6	4	
Hughes	Everett Cecil	m.	SRR	28 Dec. 1916	3	2	
Hughes	Georgia	m.	ST	7 Apr. 1917	3	2	
Hughes	Georgie	m.	HT	12 Apr. 1917	6	3	
Hughes	Sarah	d.	PD	16 Dec. 1917	8	3	Quincy, IL; also 18 Dec., 4:2
Hughes	Sarah	d.	SRR	17 Dec. 1917	3	3	Quincy, Illinois; also 8:3; 18 Dec., 6:3
Hughes	Stanley	d.	PD	23 Oct. 1918	8	1	Vallejo
Hughes	Viiola	m.	HT	15 June 1916	2	4	
Hughmanick	John Hammond	m.	PA	24 June 1916	8	5	also 26 June, 5:6; 29 June, 6:5
Hulbert	Harry E.	m.	SRR	13 Feb. 1917	2	2	
Hulbert	Harry E.	m.	CR	17 Feb. 1917	1	4	
Hulbert	Lawrence	b.	CR	29 Nov. 1918	8	2	
Hulbert	Olive M.	m.	PC	29 Mar. 1918	3	4	
Hull	Albert Bennett	d.	PC	22 May 1917	4	4	cremation; also 23 May, 4:1; 24 May, 1:5
Hull	Joseph Albert Bennett	d.	PA	21 May 1917	5	4	cremation; also 8:1; 23 May, 2:1
Hull	Silas W.	m.	PD	24 Aug. 1916	3	1	

(1) Surname	(2) Given Name	(3)	(4)	(5) Date	(6) Pg	(7) Col	(8) Comments
Hull	Silas W.	m.	SRR	24 Aug. 1916	6	5	
Hull	Silas William	m.	ST	26 Aug. 1916	1	2	
Hull	William E.	d.	ST	24 May 1918	8	4	
Hullen	Peter H.	m.	PD	22 Sept. 1918	8	3	
Hultman	A. G.	b.	PC	8 May 1918	4	3	
Humphries	Sarah H.	d.	ST	8 June 1917	1	3	
Hunger	Elmer G.	m.	PD	11 Nov. 1917	8	3	
Hunt	Alice	d.	ST	16 Nov. 1917	1	3	Odd Fellows Cem.
Hunt	Alice	d.	PA	17 Nov. 1917	6	1	Sebastopol
Hunt	Alice Maude	d.	PD	14 Nov. 1917	2	1	also 4:2; 16 Nov., 4:2
Hunt	Alice Maude	d.	SRR	14 Nov. 1917	8	4	Masonic Cemetery, Sebastopol; also 6 Nov., 8:5
Hunt	Alice Maude Wadsworth	d.	PC	14 Nov. 1917	1	5	Sebastopol
Hunt	C. A.	b.	PA	16 Oct. 1917	8	4&5	
Hunt	Clyde	m.	PC	18 June 1916	5	4	also 27 June, 4:1
Hunt	Clyde	b.	SRR	15 June 1917	6	4	
Hunt	Clyde	b.	PD	16 June 1917	2	2	
Hunt	Clyde	b.	PC	17 June 1917	2	3	
Hunt	Clyde	b.	PA	18 June 1917	1	6	also 8:6
Hunt	Clyde	m.	PA	18 Apr. 1916	5	2	
Hunt	Clyde E.	m.	PA	26 June 1916	7	4	
Hunt	Clyde E.	m.	SRR	26 June 1916	8	5	
Hunt	Clyde E.	m.	PD	2 July 1916	2	2	
Hunt	Clyde E.	m.	SRR	17 Apr. 1916	8	3	
Hunt	Clyde E.	m.	PC	18 Apr. 1916	4	4	
Hunt	Clyde Everett	m.	PD	27 June 1916	3	3	
Hunt	Elizabeth	m.	PA	20 June 1918	4	4	
Hunt	Frances	m.	PA	20 June 1918	4	4	
Hunt	G. W.	m.	ST	11 Mar. 1916	1	5	
Hunt	George	m.	SRR	2 Feb. 1916	7	3	also 6 Mar., 1:2; 13 Mar., 8:3
Hunt	George W.	m.	PA	3 Feb. 1916	3	6	
Hunt	Grover	o.	ST	8 Mar. 1918	1	3	
Hunt	M. G.	d.	PA	27 Dec. 1916	4	5	
Hunt	M. G.	b.	PC	28 Dec. 1916	4	1	
Hunt	Oscar	m.	PD	29 Sept. 1916	2	1	
Hunt	Walter	m.	ST	18 Ma.r 1916	7	3	
Hunter	Eugene	o.	SRR	8 May 1916	4	4	
Hunter	Eugene	o.	PA	10 Aug. 1916	2	2	
Hunter	Eugene	o.	PD	8 Aug. 1916	3	4	
Hunter	Grover	b.	PA	10 May 1917	4	3&5	
Hunter	Henry	d.	PD	4 Nov. 1916	1	3	
Hunter	Henry A.	d.	PA	3 Nov. 1916	8	3	
Hunter	Henry A.	d.	SRR	3 Nov. 1916	9	3	Shiloh Cemetery; also 4 Nov., 7:1

(1) Surname	(2) Given Name	(3)	(4)	(5) Date	(6) Pg	(7) Col	(8) Comments
Hunter	Henry A.	d.	PC	4 Nov. 1916	1	3	
Hunter	Johnathan	d.	PC	8 Apr. 1916	2	3	
Hunter	Jonathan	d.	PA	3 Apr. 1916	6	3	
Hunter	Jonathan	d.	PD	4 Apr. 1916	3	1	
Hunter	Jonathan	d.	SIT	8 Apr. 1916	1	7	Mountain Cemetery
Hunter	Leslie	o.	SRR	8 May 1916	4	4	
Hunter	Leslie	o.	PA	10 Aug. 1916	2	2	
Hunter	Leslie	o.	PD	8 Aug. 1916	3	4	
Hunter	Leslie M.	m.	SRR	5 Oct. 1917	5	3	
Huntington	Alta Renshaw	d.	PD	28 Oct. 1917	8	3	also 30 Oct., 4:2; 6:2; Nov., 3:5
Huntington	Alta Renshaw	d.	SRR	29 Oct. 1917	5	4	also 10:3; 30 Oct., 8:1; 31 Oct., 4:1
Huntington	Arthur Erva	m.	PD	27 July 1918	6	1	
Huntington	Eva	m.	SRR	1 Dec. 1916	8	5	
Huntington	Eva	m.	PD	28 Nov. 1916	7	3	also 30 Nov., 8:3; 2 Dec., 6:4
Huntington	Eva	m.	PC	29 Nov. 1916	5	1	
Huntington	Eva	m.	ST	9 Dec. 1916	1	2	
Huntley	Garfield	d.	PD	27 Oct. 1918	4	2	Sebastopol; also 5:3
Huntley	Garfield	d.	PC	29 Oct. 1918	2	3	Sebastopol
Huntley	Jasper	d.	PD	12 Apr. 1918	6	5	
Huntley	Jasper	d.	PC	7 Apr. 1918	4	2	Bloomfield; also 9 Apr., 5:5; 10 Apr., 8:4
Huntley	Jasper	d.	PA	8 Apr. 1918	8	5	Bloomfield; also 9 Apr., 8:5
Huntley	Richard Howard	d.	PD	16 Apr. 1916	1	2	
Huntley	Vincent	d.	PA	27 Dec. 1918	4	5&7	Cypress Hill; also 28 Dec., 4:4
Huntley	Vincent	d.	PC	28 Dec. 1918	4	4	also 29 Dec., 6:2
Huntley	Vincent	d.	PD	28 Dec. 1918	5	3	
Hurd	John	d.	SRR	27 Mar. 1916	8	2	also 29 Mar., 8:3
Hurd	John	d.	PD	28 Mar. 1916	8	4	also 30 Mar., 5:3
Hurlbutt	Willard A.	m.	PD	5 Sept. 1918	6	5	
Hurley	child	d.	PA	10 June 1916	4	5	
Hurner	Edward	d.	PA	14 Dec. 1918	4	4	Cypress Hill; also 16 Dec., 4:5
Hurshburger	Ruby	m.	PD	28 July 1917	7	5	also 31 July, 6:4
Hurskey	Everett	b.	SRR	7 Mar. 1917	8	4	
Hurst	Ruth C.	m.	PD	3 Jan. 1918	4	2	
Hurst	Ruth Charlotte	m.	PC	3 Jan. 1918	7	5	
Hushower	Marie	o.	SRR	22 Nov. 1917	3	3	
Huskey	Evart	o.	SRR	6 Jan. 1916	10	5	
Huskey	Everett	b.	PD	8 Mar. 1917	8	2	
Husler	Alwyn	o.	PA	30 Nov. 1918	5	3	
Husler	Dorothy E.	m.	PC	2 May 1916	1	2	
Husler	Dorothy E.	m.	PA	29 Apr. 1916	5	1	also 1 May, 5:4

(1) Surname	(2) Given Name	(3)	(4)	(5) Date	(6) Pg	(7) Col	(8) Comments
Husler	Elwyn	o.	PC	10 Nov. 1918	3	3	
Hussey	E. O. (dau of)	d.	PC	25 Mar. 1917	5	4	Calvary Cemetery
Hutchinson	Edward A.	m.	PA	5 Apr. 1916	6	1	
Hutchinson	Ellen	d.	PC	29 Jan. 1918	8	3	also 4 Feb., 4:3
Hutchinson	Ellen	d.	PD	29 Jan. 1918	8	2	
Hutchinson	Ethel Frances	m.	PD	18 June 1916	3	1	
Hutchinson	Lester	m.	PD	17 Oct. 1917	8	3	
Hutchison	Ellen	d.	PA	28 Jan. 1918	8	5	Cypress Hill; also 29 Jan., 4:4; 31 Jan., 4:2
Hutton	Earl F.	d.	PA	5 June 1918	4	5	Bloomfield
Hyatt	Robert	o.	PC	12 Nov. 1918	3	2	
Hyde	George	m.	PC	1 Sept. 1917	5	5	
Hyde	George	m.	PD	31 Aug. 1917	8	2	
Hyde	George	m.	SRR	31 Aug. 1917	4	4	

I & J

(1) Surname	(2) Given Name	(3)	(4)	(5) Date	(6) Pg	(7) Col	(8) Comments
Iddings	Mr. & Mrs.	b.	PA	18 Dec. 1916	4	6	
Ielhorini	Thomas Gerald	o.	PC	31 Mar. 1916	1	3	portrait
Iles	Alonzo Thomas	d.	PD	16 Oct. 1918	5	4	also 17 Oct., 3:3
Iles	Alozo Thomas	d.	PA	17 Oct. 1918	8	5	
Iles	Tom	d.	PC	16 Oct. 1918	1	3	
Imhlmann	Alba	m.	SRR	7 Jan. 1916	5	2	
Ingalls	Ruth	d.	PD	22 Oct. 1918	5	5	
Ingalls	Ruth	d.	HT	24 Oct. 1918	1	3	
Ingerson	Grace	m.	PA	22 Jan. 1916	4	3	
Ingerson	Grace	m.	PC	27 Feb. 1916	3	4	
Ingerson	Grace	m.	PA	28 Feb. 1916	3	4	
Ingerson	Grace M.	m.	PC	29 Feb. 1916	3	1	
Ingham	Ernest	o.	SRR	13 Jan. 1917	2	3	British Army
Ingham	Ernest	o.	PD	5 Oct. 1917	6	2	
Inglet	Bessie	m.	SRR	21 Nov. 1916	3	3	
Inglet	Bessie	m.	PA	22 Nov. 1916	4	2	
Inglet	Bessie	m.	PC	22 Nov. 1916	1	2	
Inglet	Bessie	m.	PD	22 Nov. 1916	3	2	
Ingram	James Luther	d.	ST	10 Mar. 1917	1	2	I.O.O.F. Cemetery
Ingram	James Luther	d.	SRR	8 Mar. 1917	8	3	Sebastopol
Ingram	James Luther	d.	PD	9 Mar. 1917	3	3	
Inwood	William	d.	PA	28 Feb. 1916	1	7	Guerneville; also 2 Mar., 2:5
Inwood	William	d.	SRR	28 Feb. 1916	8	3	
Inwood	William	d.	PD	29 Feb. 1916	3	5	also 1 Mar., 6:3
Ioap	Selina	m.	PA	2 Feb. 1918	6	2	also 4 Feb., 5:4
Irving	Thomas F.	d.	PC	15 Feb. 1916	3	1	Olema Cemetery
Irwin	Joseph W.	d.	PD	13 Nov. 1918	5	1	
Irwin	Joseph W.	d.	PC	14 Nov. 1918	3	2	
Irwin	Sam M.	o.	ST	16 Aug. 1918	3	2	
Irwin	Settyra	d.	SRR	24 May 1916	6	6	
Irwin	Settyra	d.	PC	25 May 1916	1	4	
Irwin	Setyra	d.	PD	25 May 1916	2	4	Odd Fellows Cemetery, Sebastopol
Irwin	Setyra	d.	ST	27 May 1916	1	4	
Irwin	Thomas	m.	PA	3 Aug. 1918	3	4	
Isaacs	Sarah	p.	SRR	23 Aug. 1916	8	3	
Isaacs	Sarah A.	d.	SRR	15 Aug. 1916	6	3	
Isaacs	Sarah A.	d.	PC	16 Aug. 1916	1	2	
Isaacs	Sarah A.	d.	PD	16 Aug. 1916	6	2	
Isaacs	Sarah A.	d.	HT	17 Aug. 1916	1	4	
Isaia	Mary	d.	PD	1 Mar. 1916	8	3	

(1) Surname	(2) Given Name	(3)	(4)	(5) Date	(6) Pg	(7) Col	(8) Comments
Isaia	Mary	d.	SRR	1 Mar. 1916	6	4	
Ivans	Mary	d.	PD	6 Apr. 1918	4	2	also 6:4; 14 Apr., 7:5
Iversen	Martin	b.	PA	8 Dec. 1916	8	6	
Iverson	Caroline	m.	PC	17 Mar. 1917	5	5	
Iverson	Louis	m.	PA	25 Apr. 1916	6	3	
Iverson	Louis	m.	SRR	26 Apr. 1916	8	1	
Ives	Daisy	m.	SRR	26 Dec. 1916	8	5	
Ives	Daisy	m.	PC	27 Dec. 1916	4	1	
Ives	Daisy	m.	PD	27 Dec. 1916	5	5	
Ives	E. H.	m.	SRR	8 May 1916	5	1	
Ives	Paula A.	m.	PD	11 Jan. 1916	5	3	
Ives	Pauline	m.	SRR	10 Jan. 1916	1	2	
Ives	R. H.	m.	SIT	6 May 1916	4	5	
Iwamoto	Equisoku	o.	PD	3 Apr. 1918	5	2	
Iwamoto	Tsuji Okunara	o.	PD	3 Apr. 1918	5	2	
Iwaoka	K.	b.	PD	12 May 1918	8	3	
Jack	Harry	p.	SRR	12 Jan. 1916	8	2	
Jack	Harry	o.	PC	18 Apr. 1918	1	2	
Jack	Harry A.	d.	ST	8 Jan. 1916	1	6	
Jackman	J. C. (dau of)	d.	PA	3 Apr. 1917	8	2	San Rafael
Jackober	C.	b.	SIT	21 Oct. 1916	4	2	
Jacks	Harry	d.	PC	9 Jan. 1916	6	3	
Jacks	Harry A.	d.	SRR	5 Jan. 1916	4	5	also 6 Jan., 4:1; 7 Jan., 4:4, 6:5; Sebastopol
Jacks	Harry A.	o.	PC	6 Jan. 1916	3	2	
Jacks	Harry, Jr.	d.	PA	5 Jan. 1916	3	1	
Jacks	Henry	d.	PD	5 Jan. 1916	1	2	also 6 Jan., 6:3; 8 Jan., 8:2
Jackson	Carl W.	m.	PA	15 Feb. 1916	1	1	
Jackson	Carlisle P.	m.	PD	26 Apr. 1918	6	5	
Jackson	Clementina	d.	PA	4 Feb. 1916	2	3	
Jackson	Clementine	d.	PC	4 Feb. 1916	4	3	
Jackson	Grace A.	m.	PA	1 Nov. 1917	4	5	
Jackson	Grace A.	m.	PC	2 Nov. 1917	8	5	
Jackson	John B.	b&d	PA	18 Nov. 1918	4	3&7	
Jackson	John B. (dau of)	b&d	PC	19 Nov. 1918	5	4	
Jackson	Lizzie	d.	PC	13 Apr. 1917	3	4	
Jackson	William	m.	PC	21 Jan. 1917	5	5	
Jackson	William	m.	PA	22 Jan. 1917	2	5	also 12 Feb., 6:1
Jackson	William G.	m.	PC	6 Feb. 1917	4	6	also 11 Feb., 5:3; 13 Feb., 5:4
Jacobi	Bell	m.	PC	26 Apr. 1916	5	4	
Jacobs	Cameron	b.	PD	3 Jan. 1918	5	4	
Jacobs	Carl	b.	PC	12 Nov. 1916	4	5	
Jacobs	Carl	b.	PA	13 Apr. 1916	5	5	

(1) Surname	(2) Given Name	(3)	(4)	(5) Date	(6) Pg	(7) Col	(8) Comments
Jacobs	Carl	b.	PC	14 Apr. 1916	8	2	
Jacobs	Carl	b.	PA	14 Nov. 1916	8	5	
Jacobs	George H.	d.	PD	2 Jan. 1916	11	1	
Jacobs	George W.	d.	HT	30 Oct. 1918	1	4	
Jacobs	J., Mrs.	d.	PC	19 July 1916	4	1	
Jacobs	Lorita	m.	PD	25 Oct. 1917	3	4	
Jacobs	Matthew	d.	PA	16 Aug. 1916	7	3	
Jacobs	Matthew	d.	PC	16 Aug. 1916	1	4	
Jacobs	Murray	d.	PD	2 Feb. 1918	8	3	
Jacobs	Thomas R.	d.	PD	25 Dec. 1917	8	1	
Jacobs	Thomas R.	d.	PA	26 Dec. 1917	2	3	also 4:3; 27 Dec., 5:6
Jacobs	Thomas R.	d.	SRR	26 Dec. 1917	8	1	also 27 Dec., 3:4
Jacobsen	Albert	m.	PA	26 Nov. 1917	4	7	
Jacobsen	Albert H.	m.	PC	27 Nov. 1917	3	3	
Jacobsen	Albert Henry	m.	PC	15 Dec. 1917	5	4	
Jacobsen	Harry	b.	PA	19 Sept. 1917	4	7	also 5:4
Jacobsen	Harry M.	m.	PC	11 Nov. 1916	5	3	
Jacobsen	J. E.	d.	PD	31 July 1917	8	3	also 2 Aug., 8:2
Jacobsen	J. H.	d.	SRR	23 May 1917	6	3	also 24 May, 6:5
Jacobsen	J. H.	d.	PD	23 May 1971	8	4	also 26 May, 6:5
Jacobsen	Jacob	m.	PD	7 May 1916	7	2	
Jacobsen	Jacob C.	m.	PA	6 May 1916	5	1	
Jacobsen	Jacob C.	m.	SRR	8 May 1916	5	2	
Jacobsen	Jacob Emil	d.	PA	30 July 1917	5	4	Cypress Hill; also 1 Aug., 8:5
Jacobsen	Jacob Emil	d.	PC	31 July 1917	5	3	also 1 Aug, 3:6; 2 Aug., 8:3
Jacobsen	Nels	d.	PA	7 Feb. 1917	7	2	Cypress Hill; also 8 Feb., 2:3; 10 Feb., 2:2, 8:5
Jacobsen	Nels	d.	PC	7 Feb. 1917	1	2	Cypress Hill; also 8 Feb., 8:6; 9 Feb., 2:1; 10 Feb., 4:5; 11 Feb., 6:6
Jacobsen	Nels L.	m.	PA	2 Oct. 1916	5	5	also 4 Oct., 8:5
Jacobsen	Niels L.	m.	PC	4 Oct. 1916	1	4	
Jacobsen	Victor Leroy	d.	PA	20 Nov. 1918	5	4	Cypress Hill; also 21 Nov., 5:2
Jacobsen	Victor LeRoy	d.	PC	21 Nov. 1918	5	3	Cypress Hill; also 22 Nov., 5:4
Jacobson	J. H.	d.	HT	31 May 1917	16	3	
Jacobson	Peter	d.	PD	27 Oct. 1918	6	3	
Jaggers	Homer	m.	SRR	16 Aug. 1917	6	6	
James	Georga	m.	PD	9 May 1916	7	7	
James	Jesse	b.	PA	16 June 1916	5	7	also 8:4
James	Lester Ray	b.	PD	14 Dec. 1918	7	4	

(1) Surname	(2) Given Name	(3)	(4)	(5) Date	(6) Pg	(7) Col	(8) Comments
Jamesen	Arthur Roy	m.	PC	8 Sept. 1917	5	3	also 15 Sept., 5:2; 16 Sept., 1:5
Jameson	Arthur Roy	m.	PA	7 Sept. 1917	5	4	also 15 Sept., 3:3
Jameson	Arthur Roy	m.	SRR	8 Sept. 1917	8	5	
Jameson	Arthur Roy	m.	PD	9 Sept. 1917	2	1	also 16 Sept., 3:3
Jamison	Dan J.	b.	PA	26 May 1916	4	1	also 27 May, 8:5
Jamison	Dan J.	b.	PC	26 May 1916	8	2	
Jamison	E. E.	d.	PA	29 Oct. 1918	3	4	
Jamison	Earle E.	d.	PD	29 Oct. 1918	3	1	Clarence, MO; also 30 Oct., 3:3
Jamison	Mabel	m.	PC	21 July 1916	4	2	
Janda	Mary	d.	HT	17 Feb. 1916	1	3	
Janda	Mary Jane	d.	ST	12 Feb. 1916	8	3	
Jappan	Otto Christian	d.	PC	8 June 1917	8	4	also 10 June, 4:2
Jappen	Otto	d.	PA	8 June 1917	1	4	Mt. Olivet, S.F.; also 9 June, 4:3
Jaque	Frank M.	o.	PD	11 Apr. 1917	8	2	
Jason	Fred	m.	PA	4 Jan. 1918	5	4	
Jason	Fred	m.	PC	5 Jan. 1918	5	6	also 9 Jan., 5:4
Jason	John	d.	PC	20 Sept. 1916	1	5	
Jason	Rollin	o.	PA	19 Jan. 1918	5	2	adoption
Jasperson	Henrietta	m.	PD	23 Sept. 1917	6	4	
Jeffries	Sylverine	m.	PD	18 June 1918	7	1	
Jeffries	Sylvertine	m.	HT	20 June 1918	5	2	
Jenkins	C. P.	m.	PD	6 Jan. 1918	8	1	
Jenkins	Clifford P.	m.	PD	25 June 1918	6	5	
Jenkins	Clifford P.	m.	PD	4 July 1918	3	6	
Jenkins	Emma	m.	PC	3 Mar. 1917	6	5	
Jenkins	Gilbert C.	m.	SRR	24 Feb. 1916	5	4	
Jenkins	Hulda	m.	SRR	11 Aug. 1917	3	2	
Jenkins	Hulda	m.	PD	12 Aug. 1917	1	2	
Jennings	Margaret	m.	PC	18 Jan. 1916	6	2	
Jennings	Marguerite	m.	PA	17 Jan. 1916	5	5	
Jenny	Adam	d.	PA	5 July 1916	3	3	
Jensen	Anna	m.	SRR	17 Aug. 1916	6	1	
Jensen	Annie	m.	PC	17 Aug. 1916	5	3	
Jensen	Arthur	m.	PD	27 July 1917	8	3	also 31 July, 7:1
Jensen	Arthur H.	m.	SRR	27 July 1917	5	3	also 30 July, 8:3
Jensen	Behtra H.	o.	PC	14 Nov. 1916	8	3	
Jensen	Bertha	o.	PD	10 Oct. 1916	7	4	
Jensen	Bertha	o.	PC	7 Nov. 1916	5	4	
Jensen	Bertha	o.	PD	7 Nov. 1916	6	4	
Jensen	Bertha H.	o.	PC	10 Oct. 1916	8	5	
Jensen	Bertha H.	o.	SRR	7 Nov. 1916	5	1	
Jensen	Bertha H.	o.	PA	9 Oct. 1916	5	1	also 13 Nov., 1:3

(1) Surname	(2) Given Name	(3)	(4)	(5) Date	(6) Pg	(7) Col	(8) Comments
Jensen	Bertha H.	o.	SRR	9 Oct. 1916	3	6	
Jensen	Carl B.	m.	PA	10 Apr. 1917	2	3	
Jensen	Edna	m.	SIT	25 May 1918	2	7	
Jensen	Elvia Guldager	d.	PC	30 July 1916	5	4	Tomales; also 1 Aug., 6:3
Jensen	Erick, Mrs.	d.	PA	28 Apr. 1916	8	5	Cypress Hill
Jensen	Erick, Mrs.	d.	PC	28 Apr. 1916	5	5	also 2 May, 6:3
Jensen	Fred (son of)	d.	PD	27 Oct. 1918	4	2	
Jensen	H. J.	o.	PC	7 Nov. 1916	5	4	
Jensen	H. J.	o.	PD	7 Nov. 1916	6	4	
Jensen	H. P.	o.	PC	10 Oct. 1916	8	5	
Jensen	H. P.	o.	PD	10 Oct. 1916	7	4	
Jensen	H. P.	o.	PC	14 Nov. 1916	8	3	
Jensen	H. P.	o.	SRR	7 Nov. 1916	5	1	
Jensen	H. P.	o.	PA	9 Oct. 1916	5	1	also 13 Nov., 1:3
Jensen	H. P.	o.	SRR	9 Oct. 1916	3	6	
Jensen	Hans P.	m.	PA	16 Jan. 1918	4	5	
Jensen	Hans P.	m.	PC	16 Jan. 1918	5	3	also 17 Jan., 4:2
Jensen	Harold	d.	PA	19 Aug. 1918	1	4	also 5:5
Jensen	Harold	d.	PC	20 Aug. 1918	1	3	
Jensen	Harold	d.	HT	22 Aug. 1918	1	5	
Jensen	Hilmer	o.	PD	30 Nov. 1918	2	3	
Jensen	Hilmer W.	o.	ST	29 Nov. 1918	8	4	
Jensen	J. B.	o.	PD	15 June 1918	8	4	
Jensen	Joseph	o.	PC	2 Aug. 1917	1	5	
Jensen	Martin	o.	PC	19 Nov. 1918	3	1	
Jensen	Martin Henry	d.	PA	12 Dec. 1918	4	3	Cypress Hill; also 13 Dec., 5:3
Jensen	Martin Henry	d.	PC	13 Dec. 1918	8	3	also 14 Dec., 5:6
Jensen	Minnie	m.	PC	24 Nov. 1916	4	1	
Jensen	Minnie	m.	SRR	24 Nov. 1916	10	5	
Jensen	Minnie	m.	PA	25 Nov. 1916	3	4	
Jensen	Minnie E.	m.	PC	3 Jan. 1918	5	4	
Jensen	Minnie E.	m.	PA	4 Jan. 1918	8	3	
Jensen	Minnie E.	m.	PD	5 Jan. 1918	2	5	
Jensen	Peter	m.	PA	20 Sept. 1916	8	1	
Jensen	Peter	m.	SRR	20 Sept. 1916	8	1	
Jensen	Peter	m.	PC	21 Sept. 1916	5	4	
Jensen	Victor	b.	PA	13 Dec. 1918	3	1	
Jensen	Victor	b.	PA	24 Apr. 1916	2	6	also 8:4
Jensen	Victor	b.	PC	25 Apr. 1916	8	4	
Jertosio	Joe	d.	SRR	19 Apr. 1916	8	6	
Jertosio	Joe	d.	PC	20 Apr. 1916	8	3	
Jertosio	Joseph	d.	PD	20 Apr. 1916	5	3	
Jesse	J. W.	m.	PD	1 Mar. 1916	8	2	

(1) Surname	(2) Given Name	(3)	(4)	(5) Date	(6) Pg	(7) Col	(8) Comments
Jesse	J. W.	m.	PA	2 Mar. 1916	3	1	
Jesse	J. W.	m.	ST	4 Mar. 1916	1	1	
Jesse	L. W.	m.	SRR	1 Mar. 1916	4	4	
Jessen	Grace	o.	PC	14 Apr. 1916	1	2	portrait
Jessen	Paul C.	d.	PA	25 Oct. 1916	4	6	
Jessen	Paul Christian	d.	PC	26 Oct. 1916	1	5	Cypress Hill; also 8:2; 27 Oct., 8:2; 28 Oct., 8:3
Jessup	Henry H.	d.	PC	2 Mar. 1917	5	4	Holy Cross, S.F.
Jewett	Daryl	d.	PD	4 Dec. 1918	7	7	France; also 8 Dec., 6:1
Jewett	Daryl	d.	PC	5 Dec. 1918	6	4	France
Jewett	Earl	o.	PA	16 Nov. 1918	8	1	
Jewett	Earl	o.	PC	16 Nov. 1918	8	2	also 17 Nov., 3:4
Jewett	Earl	o.	PC	18 Sept. 1918	5	4	
Jinks	Martin	b.	HT	11 Oct. 1917	5	3	
Joap	Selina	m.	PC	3 Feb. 1918	8	3	
Jobe	Fred, Mrs.	d.	ST	25 Mar. 1916	1	5	I.O.O.F. Cemetery
Jobe	T. F.	m.	PD	4 Jan. 1918	8	4	
Johns	A. W.	b.	PA	6 Sept. 1918	5	2	
Johns	Watson	m.	PD	8 May 1917	5	3	
Johns	Watson	m.	SRR	8 May 1917	2	3	
Johns	Watson	m.	PD	27 June 1917	5	3	
Johns	Watson	m.	HT	28 June 1917	1	3	
Johns	Watson	b.	PD	1 Oct. 1918	2	5	
Johns	Watson Lee	m.	SRR	26 June 1917	8	4	
Johns	Watson Lee	m.	PC	27 June 1917	8	2	
Johnson	Albert	m.	SRR	2 June 1916	6	1	
Johnson	Albert	d.	PD	25 June 1918	3	2	
Johnson	Alice M.	m.	ST	13 Dec. 1918	9	4	
Johnson	Anna M.	d.	PD	21 Mar. 1917	1	5	
Johnson	Anna Maria	d.	ST	24 Mar. 1917	3	2	
Johnson	Anna Marie	d.	PA	20 Mar. 1917	6	3	Cypress Hill; also 23 Mar., 8:7
Johnson	Anna Marta	d.	SRR	21 Mar. 1917	5	4	
Johnson	Anna Martha	d.	PC	21 Mar. 1917	1	2	Cypress Hill; also 4:2; 24 Mar., 5:6, 8:4
Johnson	Beatrice	d.	PA	8 June 1918	7	5	
Johnson	Benjamin	d.	PD	18 Oct. 1917	2	4	
Johnson	Charles	d.	SRR	29 May 1916	5	2	
Johnson	Charles D.	d.	PD	30 May 1916	3	4	also 1 June, 5:4
Johnson	Charles Elmer	d.	PC	19 Dec. 1917	4	4	Bloomfield; also 21 Dec., 6:4
Johnson	Charles L.	d.	PD	12 July 1918	3	5	
Johnson	Charles L.	d.	PC	13 July 1918	3	3	
Johnson	Clyde D.	d.	PC	16 Nov. 1916	8	6	

(1) Surname	(2) Given Name	(3)	(4)	(5) Date	(6) Pg	(7) Col	(8) Comments
Johnson	Edna Louise	m.	SRR	19 Dec. 1916	4	5	
Johnson	Edward	m.	PC	21 July 1916	4	2	
Johnson	Edwin	m.	SIT	29 Apr. 1916	1	1	
Johnson	Evelyn	m.	SRR	6 Dec. 1917	8	6	
Johnson	Evelyn	m.	PD	7 Dec. 1917	6	4	
Johnson	Evelyn Marie	m.	PD	22 Feb. 1916	6	5	
Johnson	Evelyn Marjorie	m.	PA	18 Feb. 1916	1	1	
Johnson	Fay	b.	PA	12 Sept. 1917	5	5	
Johnson	Felitha	o.	PD	26 July 1916	2	3	
Johnson	Frank B.	b.	PA	23 May 1916	1	3	
Johnson	George	d.	ST	16 Dec. 1916	1	3	
Johnson	George W.	d.	HT	14 Dec. 1916	1	2	Oak Mound Cemetery; also 23 Dec., 1"2
Johnson	George W.	d.	SRR	14 Dec. 1916	3	1	
Johnson	George W.	d.	PD	15 Dec. 1916	7	1	
Johnson	George W.	d.	PC	17 Dec. 1916	5	2	
Johnson	Gertrude	d.	PD	25 Apr. 1917	2	4	
Johnson	Gertrude Alma Ingeborg	d.	PC	22 Apr. 1917	4	3	Cypress Hill; also 24 Apr., 2:2; 25 Apr., 8:4
Johnson	Gertrude Alma Ingeborg	d.	SRR	25 Apr. 1917	5	4	
Johnson	Gertrude Alma Ingeborg	d.	PA	23 Apr. 1917	2	4	Cypress Hill; also 24 Apr., 4:5
Johnson	Gus Charles	m.	PA	2 Sept. 1918	5	6	
Johnson	Gus Charles	m.	PC	4 Sept. 1918	4	2	
Johnson	H. H.	o.	PD	26 July 1916	2	3	
Johnson	Hayward	m.	PC	5 Sept. 1917	4	2	
Johnson	Haywood	m.	PD	6 Sept. 1917	7	5	
Johnson	Haywood	m.	SIT	8 Sept. 1917	4	7	
Johnson	Helen C.	m.	PD	10 Sept. 1918	6	1	
Johnson	Helen Clover	m.	PD	17 Sept. 1918	8	3	
Johnson	Homer	b.	ST	1 July 1916	6	3	
Johnson	Inez A.	m.	PA	3 July 1917	8	5	
Johnson	Inez A.	m.	SRR	3 July 1917	8	1	
Johnson	Inez A.	m.	PC	4 July 1917	4	3	
Johnson	Jeanette	o.	PD	10 Oct. 1916	6	3	
Johnson	Jeanette	o.	SRR	7 Nov. 1917	1	3	
Johnson	Jeanette B.	o.	SRR	9 Oct. 1916	8	1	
Johnson	Jeannette	m.	PD	10 Feb. 1918	7	1	
Johnson	John P.	m.	PD	9 Apr. 1918	2	2	
Johnson	Karl V.	m.	PA	19 Mar. 1918	6	6	
Johnson	Leonard	o.	SRR	5 Jan. 1916	8	2	
Johnson	Leonard M.	o.	SRR	8 Jan. 1917	5	3	
Johnson	Leonard M.	o.	PA	9 Jan. 1917	3	3	
Johnson	Leonard M.	o.	PC	9 Jan. 1917	1	5	
Johnson	Lillian	m.	ST	14 Oct. 1916	1	5	

(1) Surname	(2) Given Name	(3)	(4)	(5) Date	(6) Pg	(7) Col	(8) Comments
Johnson	Lolita	m.	PD	4 July 1918	3	6	
Johnson	Lolita	m.	PD	6 Jan. 1918	8	1	
Johnson	Mabel	m.	HT	11 Jan. 1917	6	3	
Johnson	Mabel	m.	PD	3 Jan. 1917	8	3	
Johnson	Mabel	m.	SRR	3 Jan. 1917	5	2	
Johnson	Mabel	m.	PC	4 Jan. 1917	5	6	
Johnson	Margaret C.	o.	PC	8 May 1918	2	2	
Johnson	Martin	b.	PA	25 Feb. 1918	4	1&4	
Johnson	Mary Alice	d.	SIT	20 Jan. 1917	1	3	
Johnson	Mary E.	d.	PA	17 Feb. 1917	4	5	
Johnson	Mr.	m.	PC	2 Apr. 1916	5	3	
Johnson	N. Albert	m.	SRR	9 June 1916	2	3	
Johnson	Nannie	m.	PC	16 Mar. 1918	8	5	also 22 Mar., 8:2
Johnson	Nannie	m.	PC	18 Apr. 1916	5	5	also 2 May, 3:1
Johnson	Neva	o.	SRR	5 Jan. 1916	8	2	
Johnson	Neva F.	o.	SRR	8 Jan. 1917	5	3	aka Neva Needham
Johnson	Neva F.	o.	PC	9 Jan. 1917	1	5	
Johnson	Nora S.	o.	PA	9 Jan. 1917	3	3	
Johnson	Nota M.	m.	PD	8 Feb. 1918	7	1	
Johnson	Peter, Mrs.	d.	PA	12 Nov. 1918	4	1	
Johnson	Peter, Mrs.	d.	PC	13 Nov. 1918	6	1	
Johnson	Richard	d.	PD	11 Jan. 1918	5	4	also 12 Jan., 4:2
Johnson	Roscoe	m.	SRR	13 June 1916	7	2	
Johnson	Roscoe	b.	PD	11 Apr. 1917	8	2	
Johnson	Roy	d.	PD	24 Dec. 1918	8	3	France
Johnson	Roy	d.	PD	8 Dec. 1918	6	3	
Johnson	Ruby	m.	SRR	19 Apr. 1916	3	4	
Johnson	Ruth	m.	PA	31 Dec. 1917	4	2	
Johnson	Ruth Nannie	m.	PA	18 Apr. 1916	2	4	also 29 Apr., 7:5; 1 May, 5:3
Johnson	Sydney C.	m.	PC	1 Oct. 1918	2	1	
Johnson	Velmer	m.	PD	24 Aug. 1916	3	1	
Johnson	Velmer Vernida	m.	SRR	24 Aug. 1916	6	5	
Johnson	Vernita	m.	ST	26 Aug. 1916	1	2	
Johnson	Violet	o.	PC	8 May 1918	2	2	
Johnson	W. L.	m.	PD	28 Oct. 1916	2	3	
Johnson	Wesley	b.	PA	15 Sept. 1917	5	2	
Johnson	William	o.	PD	10 Oct. 1916	6	3	
Johnson	William	b.	PD	11 Dec. 1917	3	3	
Johnson	William	d.	SRR	8 Dec. 1916	8	6	
Johnson	William	d.	PD	9 Dec. 1916	2	2	
Johnson	William B.	o.	SRR	7 Nov. 1917	1	3	
Johnston	Frank	b.	PC	24 May 1916	8	2	
Johnston	Frank	b.	PA	13 Feb. 1918	5	7	
Johnston	James W.	d.	PD	4 Oct. 1917	4	2	also 5:4

(1) Surname	(2) Given Name	(3)	(4)	(5) Date	(6) Pg	(7) Col	(8) Comments
Johnston	James Westley	d.	SRR	3 Oct. 1917	6	4	also 4 Oct., 8:2; 5 Oct., 4:1
Johnston	Lolita	m.	PD	25 June 1918	6	5	
Johnston	Maude	m.	SRR	16 July 1917	3	4	also 18 July, 8:3
Johnston	Maude	m.	PD	17 July 1917	8	2	also 19 July, 2:5
Johnston	Robert	d.	SRR	25 Nov. 1916	5	2	also 27 Nov., 8:5
Johnston	Robert L.	d.	PD	25 Nov. 1916	2	1	also 26 Nov., 10:3; 28 Nov., 3:1
Johnston	W. J. (child of)	d.	PD	19 Dec. 1917	8	2	
Johnston	William	b.	SRR	10 Dec. 1917	8	3	
Johnston	William	b.	PC	12 Dec. 1917	6	1	
Johonson	William B.	o.	SRR	9 Oct. 1916	8	1	
Joiner	William D., Jr.	m.	PA	26 Dec. 1917	5	3	
Jolly	Mabel Clare	m.	SRR	28 June 1917	8	6	
Jonas	Alice M.	m.	PD	1 Mar. 1916	8	2	
Jonas	Alice M.	m.	SRR	1 Mar. 1916	4	4	
Jones	Alfred B.	m.	PD	20 July 1916	2	3	
Jones	Alfred Benonia	m.	HT	20 July 1916	1	1	
Jones	Alice M.	m.	PA	2 Mar. 1916	3	1	
Jones	Alice M.	m.	ST	4 Mar. 1916	1	1	
Jones	Alvie	m.	PD	22 June 1918	5	4	
Jones	Anna	o.	SRR	23 Sept. 1916	3	3	
Jones	Annie	o.	SRR	24 Sept. 1917	8	1	
Jones	Annie	d.	PD	9 Apr. 1918	5	4	Rural Cemetery; also 12 Apr., 8:3; 16 Apr., 4:2; 17 Apr., 2:2
Jones	Benoni	m.	SRR	3 July 1916	3	6	
Jones	Carroll	d.	PD	23 Dec. 1917	8	1	Bloomfield; also 25 Dec., 4:2; 27 Dec., 5:1
Jones	Carroll	d.	PA	24 Dec. 1917	4	3	Bloomfield; also 27 Dec., 3:5
Jones	Cecil	m.	PD	24 Oct. 1916	5	2	
Jones	Cethie	m.	SRR	21 Oct. 1916	7	4	
Jones	Cethil	m.	HT	20 Oct. 1916	1	5	
Jones	Charles E.	d.	SRR	15 Dec. 1916	10	4	
Jones	Clora May	o.	PC	8 Apr. 1916	1	3	portrait
Jones	Earl P.	o.	SRR	24 Sept. 1917	8	1	
Jones	Earle P.	o.	SRR	23 Sept. 1916	3	3	
Jones	Genevieve	d.	PD	19 Apr. 1918	3	2	
Jones	Guy P.	m.	SRR	21 Aug. 1916	5	1	
Jones	Helen	m.	PD	1 Sept. 1916	3	3	
Jones	Helen	m.	SRR	25 Aug. 1916	6	1	also 31 Aug., 6:1
Jones	Helen	m.	HT	31 Aug. 1916	1	6	
Jones	Irvin	b.	PA	11 Mar. 1918	8	5	
Jones	James Lloyd	m.	PD	26 Apr. 1917	8	3	also 1 May, 5:1
Jones	John	m.	PC	4 Apr. 1918	8	4	

(1) Surname	(2) Given Name	(3)	(4)	(5) Date	(6) Pg	(7) Col	(8) Comments
Jones	John	m.	PD	5 Apr. 1918	3	3	
Jones	John Oscar	d.	PD	28 Nov. 1916	8	2	
Jones	John Oscar	d.	SRR	28 Nov. 1916	5	3	Oakland; also 29 Nov., 4:3
Jones	Mabel	m.	PD	23 Nov. 1916	2	3	
Jones	Mabel	m.	SIT	28 Dec. 1918	1	5	
Jones	Mabel	m.	PC	6 Oct. 1916	8	3	
Jones	Mary	d.	SRR	19 Oct. 1917	4	3	
Jones	Mary Jane	d.	PA	18 Oct. 1917	4	3	Cypress Hill; also 19 Oct., 5:3; 20 Oct., 4:4
Jones	Mary Jane	d.	PC	19 Oct. 1917	2	2	Cypress Hill; also 3:4; 20 Oct., 2:2; 21 Oct., 5:3
Jones	Mary Jane	d.	PD	20 Oct. 1917	3	3	
Jones	Mr. & Mrs.	b.	ST	7 Apr. 1917	2	3	
Jones	Olive	o.	HT	4 July 1918	1	3	
Jones	Olive	o.	HT	26 Sept. 1918	1	4	also 17 Oct., 3:1; 30 Oct., 6:3
Jones	Orby	d.	PC	13 Oct. 1918	5	4	
Jones	Orson A.	d.	PD	16 Jan. 1918	4	2	McPeak's Cemetery
Jones	Orvia L.	d.	ST	18 Oct. 1918	1	1	France
Jones	Orvie L.	d.	PA	19 Oct. 1918	8	5	France
Jones	Oscar	d.	PC	15 Jan. 1918	1	2	
Jones	Patrick Carroll	d.	PC	23 Dec. 1917	1	5	also 27 Dec., 1:5
Jones	Patrick Carroll	d.	SRR	26 Dec. 1917	8	5	Bloomfield
Jones	Phillip Mills, Dr. & Mrs.	d.	PC	30 Nov. 1916	6	4	
Jones	Rebecca	d.	PA	25 May 1917	4	3	Cypress Hill; also 6:1; 26 May, 1:3
Jones	Rebecca	d.	PC	25 May 1917	1	2	also 26 May, 3:4; 27 May, 4:3
Jones	Rebecca	d.	PD	26 May 1917	3	4	
Jones	Rebecca	d.	SRR	26 May 1917	7	4	
Jones	Sallie	m.	SRR	22 Sept. 1916	6	5	also 25 Sept., 8:5
Jones	Seth	m.	PA	19 Mar. 1918	4	3	
Jones	Seth W.	m.	PA	5 Mar. 1918	4	1	
Jones	Seth W.	m.	PC	6 Mar. 1918	8	4	also 19 Mar., 8:3
Jones	T. K.	o.	PC	3 Jan. 1918	5	5	
Jones	William	o.	PC	15 Feb. 1917	1	5	
Joppini	Evelina	d.	SRR	21 May 1917	6	3	
Joppini	Evelina	d.	PD	22 May 1917	3	3	Calvary Cemetery; also 4:3; 23 May, 6:4
Jordan	Georgiana	d.	SRR	6 Jan. 1916	10	3	cremation; also 7 Jan., 3:3; 8 Jan., 3:4
Jordan	Georgiana W.	d.	PD	6 Jan. 1916	8	3	Oakland
Jordan	Jesse J.	b.	PD	30 Oct. 1918	5	3	
Jorgensen	Ann M.	m.	PC	8 May 1918	5	4	

(1) Surname	(2) Given Name	(3)	(4)	(5) Date	(6) Pg	(7) Col	(8) Comments
Jorgensen	Evelyn	m.	PA	16 Feb. 1918	8	3	
Jorgensen	Evelyn	m.	PC	16 Feb. 1918	4	2	also 17 Feb., 8:3
Jorgensen	Evelyn	m.	PD	19 Feb. 1918	7	1	
Jorgensen	Florence	m.	PC	7 May 1918	4	2	
Jorgensen	Florence	m.	PD	8 May 1918	2	4	
Jorgensen	Otilio	m.	PD	19 Oct. 1916	6	4	also 4 Nov., 1:5
Jorgensen	Otillo	m.	PA	18 Oct. 1916	5	2	also 4 Nov., 4:4
Jorgensen	Otillo	m.	PC	18 Oct. 1916	1	5	also 3 Nov., 6:5; 4 Nov., 4:6
Jorgensen	Robert	m.	SRR	18 Jan. 1917	5	1	
Joseph	Ethel	o.	PA	11 July 1916	4	3	also 26 July, 4:2
Joseph	Ethel	o.	PC	27 July 1916	6	4	
Joseph	Ethel	o.	PD	27 July 1916	7	5	
Joseph	Ethel I.	o.	PC	2 Aug. 1917	8	3	
Joseph	Ethel L.	o.	SRR	11 July 1916	1	5	also 26 July, 8:6
Joseph	Ethel L.	o.	SRR	1 Aug. 1917	4	3	
Joseph	J. W.	o.	PA	11 July 1916	4	3	also 26 July, 4:2
Joseph	J. W.	o.	SRR	11 July 1916	1	5	also 26 July, 8:6
Joseph	J. W.	o.	PC	27 July 1916	6	4	
Joseph	J. W.	o.	PD	27 July 1916	7	5	
Joseph	J. W.	o.	SRR	1 Aug. 1917	4	3	
Joseph	J. W.	o.	PC	2 Aug. 1917	8	3	
Josephs	Ethel L.	o.	PA	1 Aug. 1917	5	6	
Josephs	J. W.	o.	PA	1 Aug. 1917	5	6	
Joslin	Jason W.	d.	PD	19 Sept. 1918	4	2	Presidio
Joy	W. H.	d.	PD	18 Oct. 1916	2	5	also 8 Nov., 6:4
Jud	Pauline	d.	PD	3 May 1918	2	3	Rural Cemetery; also 4:2; 7 May, 5:2
Juilliard	Charles	d.	PD	22 Dec. 1917	4	2	also 8:1; 25 Dec., 3:4
Juilliard	Charles F.	d.	PA	22 Dec. 1917	2	6	
Julliard	C. D.	d.	SRR	19 Dec. 1917	5	2	also 20 Dec., 4:5; 22 Dec., 5:3; 24 Dec., 4:5
Jump	Terry	m.	PD	5 Nov. 1916	5	5	
Jump	Terry	m.	SRR	6 Nov. 1916	5	4	
Jurd	Landis	m.	HT	11 July 1918	2	2	
Jurd	Landis	o.	HT	7 Mar. 1918	1	4	also 25 Apr., 3:1
Jurd	Landis A.	o.	HT	15 Apr. 1916	1	3	
Jurgens	Cora Isabelle	d.	PD	3 Feb. 1917	3	3	
Jurgensen	Florence	m.	PA	7 May 1918	3	5	
Jurgensen	Harmina	m.	PC	18 Jan. 1918	5	3	
Jurgensen	Harry	m.	PA	15 Jan. 1918	5	5	
Jurgensen	Harry	m.	PC	16 Jan. 1918	8	4	
Jurgensen	Harry	m.	PD	16 Jan. 1918	6	1	
Jurgensen	Herminia	m.	PA	19 Jan. 1918	4	5	also 21 Jan., 4:4

K

(1) Surname	(2) Given Name	(3)	(4)	(5) Date	(6) Pg	(7) Col	(8) Comments
Kaelin	Edwin	b.	SRR	29 Oct. 1917	8	6	
Kafantario	George	b.	SRR	28 Feb. 1917	8	4	
Kai	Kichimatsu	d.	SRR	12 Aug. 1916	4	5	cremation
Kaiser	Joseph, Mrs.	o.	PA	17 Jan. 1918	4	3	
Kaiser	Will H., Jr.	m.	PA	2 Sept. 1916	4	3	
Kaiser	William	m.	PD	2 Sept. 1916	1	6	
Kaiser	William S.	m.	PC	2 Sept. 1916	1	2	also 3 Sept., 8:2
Kane	Thomas	m.	PC	8 Sept. 1917	8	4	wife not named
Kane	Thomas P.	m.	PD	12 Sept. 1917	3	1	
Kanode	John O.	m.	PD	5 Sept. 1917	7	4	
Karmmuller/ Kornmuller	Wilhelm	m.	PA	20 July 1916	4	4	also 21 July, 3:6
Kaski	Matt	d.	SIT	21 July 1917	1	4	
Katen	Frank	d.	PA	31 May 1917	5	5	
Katen	Frank, Jr.	o.	PC	5 Aug. 1917	1	1	also 7 Aug., 8:4
Katen	Josephine	d.	PA	6 July 1917	4	2	
Katen	Josephine	d.	PC	7 July 1917	1	5	Calvary Cemetery
Katen	Mary	d.	PA	16 July 1917	8	1	Calvary Cemetery
Katen	Mary	d.	PC	17 July 1917	6	4	Calvary Cemetery
Katen	Mary	d.	SRR	17 July 1917	8	5	
Katen	Rita R.	m.	PC	30 Mar. 1917	4	5	also 8 Apr., 3:3
Katen	Will	b.	PA	17 Dec. 1917	4	2	
Katen	William L.	m.	PA	1 Mar. 1917	8	2	
Katen	William L.	m.	PC	2 Mar. 1917	5	1	
Katen	William L.	m.	PD	2 Mar. 1917	8	3	
Katen	William L.	m.	SRR	2 Mar. 1917	3	2	
Katten	Frank	o.	SRR	6 Aug. 1917	4	1	
Kayada	C.	d.	SRR	25 Apr. 1917	5	5	
Kaye	Charles I.	d.	PD	19 July 1916	8	2	Santa Cruz
Kaye	E.	d.	SRR	17 July 1916	5	2	
Kearney	James	o.	SIT	9 Mar. 1918	1	6	
Keating	Thomas	m.	PC	7 July 1916	7	5	
Keating	Tom	d.	PD	30 Oct. 1918	8	4	
Keaveny	Frank	d.	PC	25 Oct. 1917	4	4	Calvary Cemetery
Keavney	Frank	d.	PA	24 Oct. 1917	8	5	also 25 Oct.,5:6; Calvary Cemetery
Keavney	Frank	d.	PD	25 Oct. 1917	8	2	Calvary Cemetery, Petaluma
Kee	George	b.	PD	13 Feb. 1917	2	2	
Kee	Nellie	m.	PC	10 Feb. 1917	1	6	
Kee	Nellie	m.	PA	13 Feb. 1917	6	4	
Keech	Clara Mae	d.	PC	20 Nov. 1918	8	4	England

(1) Surname	(2) Given Name	(3)	(4)	(5) Date	(6) Pg	(7) Col	(8) Comments
Keegan	Dolo	o.	PA	8 Feb. 1917	5	4	
Keegan	Dolo	o.	SRR	8 Feb. 1917	1	2	
Keegan	Dolo	o.	PC	9 Feb. 1917	3	6	
Keegan	Elizabeth	d.	PC	10 Aug. 1917	8	3	
Keegan	Elizabeth	d.	PD	10 Aug. 1917	3	4	Calvary Cemetery; also 4:2; 11 Aug., 3:3; 14 Aug., 5:4
Keegan	Elizabeth	d.	SRR	9 Aug. 1917	8	1	Calvary Cemetery; also 10 Aug., 8:3; 13 Aug., 5:4
Keegan	Harry	b.	PA	3 May 1918	2	4	also 4:3
Keegan	Harry	m.	PC	17 Aug. 1916	5	3	
Keegan	Harry	m.	SRR	17 Aug. 1916	6	1	
Keegan	Harry	b.	PA	28 Nov. 1916	8	3	
Keegan	Harry	b.	PD	28 Nov. 1916	5	3	
Keegan	Harry	b.	PC	29 Nov. 1916	3	6	
Keegan	James	m.	PC	13 Sept. 1917	8	6	
Keegan	James	m.	PD	13 Sept. 1917	5	2	
Keegan	William	o.	PA	8 Feb. 1917	5	4	
Keegan	William	o.	SRR	8 Feb. 1917	1	2	
Keegan	William	o.	PC	9 Feb. 1917	3	6	
Keel	William	m.	PA	21 Oct. 1916	8	4	
Keeler	William	m.	HT	13 Jan. 1916	8	5	
Keeler	William	m.	SRR	13 Jan. 1916	8	3	
Keeley	Celia Elizabeth	d.	PD	26 May 1916	8	3	also 30 May, 3:3
Keeley	Elizabeth	d.	SRR	29 May 1916	1	5	
Keenan	Mary	d.	PC	12 Mar. 1918	4	4	Holy Cross, S.F.; also 13 Mar., 3:2
Keene	Lillian I.	m.	PA	29 June 1917	8	1	
Keene	Paul A.	m.	HT	11 July 1918	1	1	
Keene	Paul A.	m.	PC	12 July 1918	3	1	
Keene	Paul A.	m.	PD	12 July 1918	2	3	
Kehoe	Edward F.	b.	PA	15 June 1916	8	3	
Keig	William C.	b.	PA	1 Mar. 1916	6	2	also 8:4
Keiser	Amanda	o.	PD	19 June 1918	3	1	also 20 June, 3:1
Keiser	Joseph, Mrs.	o.	PD	17 Jan. 1918	1	7	
Keiser	Michael	d.	PA	19 Jan. 1918	5	4	Calvary Cemetery; also 22 Jan., 4:2; 23 Jan., 4:5
Keiser	Michael, Sr.	d.	PC	23 Jan. 1918	3	5	also 24 Jan., 6:2
Keiser	Minerod	d.	PD	23 July 1916	8	4	Calvary Cemetery; also 27 July, 8:5
Keiser	Minerod	d.	SRR	24 July 1916	5	1	Calvary Cemetery; also 26 July, 8:4
Keiser	Minerod	d.	PA	24 July 1916	2	4	Calvary Cemetery

(1) Surname	(2) Given Name	(3)	(4)	(5) Date	(6) Pg	(7) Col	(8) Comments
Keiser	Minerod	d.	PC	25 July 1916	4	4	also 27 July, 4:4
Keiser	Mrs.	d.	PC	4 Apr. 1916	1	5	
Keller	E. A.	o.	PA	20 Apr. 1916	2	5	
Keller	Joseph	m.	PA	7 Jan. 1918	8	5	
Keller	Joseph	m.	PC	8 Jan. 1918	3	5	
Keller	Joseph	m.	PD	8 Jan. 1918	5	5	
Keller	Susan M.	o.	PA	20 Apr. 1916	2	5	
Keller	Vernon	o.	PD	14 Mar. 1918	7	1	
Keller	Vernon	o.	ST	16 Aug. 1918	1	5	
Keller	Vernon E.	o.	PC	11 Aug. 1918	6	3	
Kelley	Evelyn	m.	PC	25 Sept. 1917	1	5	
Kelley	Howard	b.	ST	25 Nov. 1917	3	4	
Kelley	Irving	m.	PC	16 Oct. 1917	5	3	
Kelley	J. W., Mrs.	d.	PD	30 June 1916	5	4	
Kelley	J. W., Mrs.	d.	PC	1 July 1916	3	3	
Kelley	James W.	d.	ST	24 Aug. 1917	1	2	
Kelley	James W.	p.	ST	31 Aug. 1917	5	4	
Kelley	James William	d.	PC	25 Aug. 1917	8	4	
Kelley	Mary E.	m.	PA	25 Sept. 1917	4	6	
Kellgren	Hugo	m.	PD	7 July 1918	7	3	
Kelly	J. W., Mrs.	d.	SRR	30 June 1916	5	3	
Kelly	J. W., Mrs.	d.	PD	2 July 1916	6	3	Odd Fellows Cemetery
Kelly	J. W., Mrs.	d.	SRR	3 July 1916	5	2	
Kelly	James W.	p.	SRR	29 Aug. 1917	4	5	
Kelly	James William	d.	PD	24 Aug. 1917	4	2	Odd Fellows Cemetery; also 8:2
Kelly	James William	d.	SRR	24 Aug. 1917	4	3	
Kelly	John H.	o.	PC	29 July 1917	1	4	
Kelly	Lillian	m.	PD	20 Oct. 1918	5	3	
Kelly	Lillian M.	m.	ST	25 Oct. 1918	1	2	
Kelly	Mary Agnes	d.	ST	1 July 1916	1	4	
Kemp	Thomas	d.	PC	18 Dec. 1918	6	3	
Kendall	Thelma	m.	PC	25 Dec. 1917	3	2	
Kendall	Thelma	m.	PA	27 Dec. 1917	4	3	
Kendall	Thelma	m.	PD	27 Dec. 1917	2	2	
Kennedy	Edward H.	b.	SRR	15 June 1917	2	3	
Kennedy	Elbert	o.	PC	3 May 1918	4	3	
Kennedy	Elbert	m.	PC	25 Sept. 1917	1	6	
Kennedy	Herbert/Elbert	o.	PC	8 Feb. 1918	1	4	also 15 Feb., 1:3; 27 Feb., 3:5; 6 Mar., 3:3
Kennedy	Lawrence	d.	PA	2 Nov. 1918	4	1	
Kennedy	Lawrence	d.	PC	5 Nov. 1918	8	2	Sebastopol
Kennedy	Lawrence	d.	ST	8 Nov. 1918	1	2	
Kennedy	W. A.	d.	ST	22 Dec. 1916	1	6	

(1) Surname	(2) Given Name	(3)	(4)	(5) Date	(6) Pg	(7) Col	(8) Comments
Kennedy	Warren	d.	SRR	18 Dec. 1916	5	3	
Kennel	Josephine	m.	PD	7 Dec. 1917	2	3	
Kennel	Josephine	m.	SRR	7 Dec. 1917	6	3	
Kennell	Josie	m.	SIT	15 Dec. 1917	1	4	
Kennell	Josie	m.	SRR	30 Nov. 1917	4	2	
Kent	Edwin, Jr.	m.	PD	23 June 1917	2	2	
Keppie	Ann D.	d.	PD	22 Feb. 1916	5	4	
Keppie	Anna O.	d.	PA	18 Feb. 1916	3	4	also 14 Feb., 5:3
Kerbey	Samuel	b.	PC	20 May 1916	5	4	
Kerbey	Sarah Ann	d.	PA	23 Apr. 1917	4	3	
Kerbey	Sarah Ann	d.	PC	24 Apr. 1917	8	3	Cypress Hill; also 25 Apr., 4:4
Kerbey	Sarah Ann	d.	PD	25 Apr. 1917	7	1	
Kerfoot	Leland	m.	PD	29 Dec. 1917	2	1	
Kerfoot	Leland B.	m.	PC	29 Dec. 1917	5	2	
Kernan	Arthur Thomas	m.	PD	27 June 1916	7	5	
Kerner	Henry	m.	PD	11 June 1916	3	2	
Kerner	Henry	m.	SRR	12 June 1916	1	4	
Kerner	Lillian F.	m.	PC	1 July 1917	8	3	
Kerr	Arthur	m.	PC	22 Feb. 1918	2	2	
Kerrey	S. A.	b.	PA	19 May 1916	1	7	also 3:4
Kerrigan	George	d.	PC	11 Jan. 1916	5	2	Cypress Hill
Kerrigan	Walter	d.	SRR	20 Dec. 1916	2	3	
Kerrison	A. C.	d.	PD	12 June 1917	5	3	
Kerrison	Alfred George	d.	PA	2 June 1917	4	1	Cypress Hill; also 6 June, 5:3; 11 June, 8:3
Kerrison	Alfred George	d.	PC	3 June 1917	1	3	also 5 June, 1:4; 6 June, 1:4; 8 June, 8:4; 12 June, 4:5
Kerrison	George	d.	PA	3 Jan. 1916	1	3	Cypress Hill; also 4 Jan., 6:4; 10 Jan., 4:5
Kerrison	George	d.	PC	4 Jan. 1916	1	4	
Kerrison	George	d.	PD	4 Jan. 1916	5	3	Cypress Hill Cemetery, Petaluma
Kerrison	George	d.	SRR	4 Jan. 1916	5	1	
Kerrison	Walter	d.	PA	26 Dec. 1916	7	5	
Kerrison	Walter A.	d.	PC	3 Jan. 1917	4	5	
Kerrison	Walter Alfred	d.	PC	20 Dec. 1916	5	3	also 24 Dec., 1:7; 27 Dec., 8:7
Kerrison	Walter W.	d.	PD	20 Dec. 1916	8	2	also 23 Dec., 2:3
Kersten	Fred John	d.	SRR	7 July 1916	6	5	
Kessel	Leland	m.	PA	30 Oct. 1917	4	3	
Ketchum	O. C.	b.	PD	16 Feb. 1916	5	2	
Ketchum	O. C.	b.	SRR	16 Feb. 1916	6	4	
Ketels	Gus	b.	PC	21 Feb. 1917	5	2	

(1) Surname	(2) Given Name	(3)	(4)	(5) Date	(6) Pg	(7) Col	(8) Comments
Key	Helen Mortimer	d.	PD	10 Nov. 1918	5	3	
Keyes	Lillian	d.	SIT	23 June 1917	1	3	
Keyser	L. E., Mrs.	d.	PC	5 Apr. 1916	4	3	cremation, ashes buried Cypress Hill; also 7 Apr., 3:3
Keyser	Lucie E.	d.	PA	4 Apr. 1916	5	1	cremation; also 8:7
Kidd	Edward	o.	PA	6 July 1916	4	5	
Kidd	Edward	o.	PA	13 July 1917	5	5	
Kidd	Edward	o.	PD	13 July 1917	2	2	
Kidd	Maud	o.	PA	6 July 1916	4	5	
Kidd	Maude	o.	PA	13 July 1917	5	5	
Kidd	Maude	o.	PD	13 July 1917	2	2	
Kiesbuye	Jack/Jacob	d.	PC	1 Apr. 1917	1	4	Cypress Hill; also 3 Apr., 5:5; 4 Apr., 1:3; 5 Apr., 5:1
Kiesbuye	Jacob	d.	PA	31 Mar. 1917	4	3	Cypress Hill; also 3 Apr., 6:3; 4 Apr., 8:1
Kiesbuye	Jacob	d.	SRR	5 Apr. 1917	9	1	
Kieser	N. L.	m.	PC	26 Apr. 1916	5	4	
Kihara	David	m.	SRR	19 Apr. 1917	5	2	
Kihara	David S.	m.	PC	21 Apr. 1917	2	3	
Kihara	David S.	m.	ST	21 Apr. 1917	8	5	
Kill	Edward	o.	PC	14 July 1917	3	2	
Kill	Maude	o.	PC	14 July 1917	3	2	
Kimberly	Martha	m.	SRR	8 June 1917	6	4	
Kimes	Edward T.	m.	SRR	17 Oct. 1917	8	1	
Kimes	Edward T.	m.	PD	18 Oct. 1917	7	2	
Kimes	Esther	d.	PD	23 Mar. 1917	5	4	also 25 Mar., 4:3
Kimes	Esther	d.	SRR	23 Mar. 1917	8	3	
Kimes	Esther	d.	ST	24 Mar. 1917	1	5	
Kincaid	Ruth	o.	SIT	21 Oct. 1916	1	2	also 4 Nov., 1:5
Kincaid	Ruth	m.	PC	4 Nov. 1916	1	2	
Kindle	Marion Frances	d.	PD	5 Nov. 1916	6	5	
Kindler	Robert Mervin	d.	PD	4 Sept. 1918	4	2	Rural Cemetery; also 5 Sept., 6:4; 6 Sept., 6:4
King	Ana L.	d.	ST	2 Nov. 1917	1	3	
King	Catherine Frances	m.	SRR	21 May 1917	8	3	
King	Catherine Frances	m.	PD	22 May 1917	2	4	
King	Catherine Frances	m.	PD	1 June 1917	8	4	
King	Catherine Frances	m.	SRR	1 June 1917	3	1	
King	Clara	m.	PD	26 May 1918	7	6	
King	Clara	m.	PA	28 May 1918	6	3	
King	Clara Laverne	m.	PC	28 May 1918	3	4	
King	Fred	d.	PD	12 May 1918	4	2	Shiloh Cemetery; also 6:4; 14 May, 6:5

(1) Surname	(2) Given Name	(3)	(4)	(5) Date	(6) Pg	(7) Col	(8) Comments
King	John E., Jr.	m.	PA	17 July 1918	6	6	
King	Joseph	b.	SRR	26 Jan. 1916	8	6	
King	Nellie Gertrude	m.	SRR	22 Nov. 1917	6	6	
Kingman	I. Wayland	d.	PD	26 Sept. 1917	4	2	also 28 Sept., 7:1
Kingman	Wyland	d.	SRR	26 Sept. 1917	4	5	also 28 Sept., 6:4
Kingsbury	E. L.	d.	SRR	16 Apr. 1917	1	2	
Kingsbury	Elonzo I.	d.	PD	14 Apr. 1917	4	3	also 5:2
Kingwell	F. B.	m.	PD	19 Jan. 1918	3	4	
Kingwell	Francis B.	m.	PA	18 Jan. 1918	6	2	
Kinkead	Ruth	m.	PA	16 Feb. 1916	4	3	
Kinkead	Ruth	m.	SRR	18 Feb. 1916	4	6	
Kinkle	Marion Francis	d.	SRR	4 Nov. 1916	6	5	Calvary Cemetery
Kinne	Ethel	m.	SIT	24 Feb. 1916	1	4	also 4 Mar., 3:5
Kinne	Eudora May	m.	PD	12 May 1918	7	5	also 16 May, 6:4
Kinne	Eudora May	m.	PA	13 May 1918	8	5	also 15 May, 5:7; 17 May, 3:1
Kinne	Eudora May	m.	PC	16 May 1918	5	2	
Kinne	Walter	m.	PD	15 Jan. 1918	3	2	
Kinsella	J. A.	o.	PD	2 Aug. 1916	6	1	
Kinsella	Mabel Irene	o.	PD	2 Aug. 1916	6	1	
Kinsey	Effie A.	m.	SRR	29 Dec. 1916	6	3	
Kirkham	Fred	m.	PA	4 May 1917	7	4	
Kirkland	Blanche Hannah	m.	PC	11 Mar. 1916	5	4	
Kirkland	Harry B.	o.	PD	22 June 1917	3	1	
Kirkland	Harry B.	o.	SRR	22 June 1917	5	3	
Kirkland	Harry B.	o.	PC	23 June 1917	3	5	
Kirkland	Lulu	o.	PD	22 June 1917	3	1	
Kirkland	Lulu	o.	SRR	22 June 1917	5	3	
Kirkland	Lulu	o.	PC	23 June 1917	3	5	
Kirkland	Mabel Irene	d.	PC	20 Sept. 1918	1	2	Bloomfield; also 21 Sept., 3:2; 24 Sept., 4:3
Kirkland	Mable Irene	d.	PA	20 Sept. 1918	5	5	
Kisbeau	John	d.	PD	1 Apr. 1917	5	2	
Kisbue	Jack	d.	SRR	31 Mar. 1917	1	2	
Kiser	Charles	d.	PC	13 Feb. 1917	3	6	Napa
Kiser	J., Mrs.	o.	PC	17 Jan. 1918	1	3	also 18 Jan., 4:3
Kiser	Lillian	m.	PA	30 Sept. 1916	5	1	
Kiser	Teresa	d.	SIT	21 Apr. 1917	3	2	
Kiser	Theodore	o.	SIT	30 Mar. 1918	1	7	
Kiser	William J.	d.	PC	21 Dec. 1918	1	5	
Klein	Charles	d.	PA	7 Feb. 1916	5	4	
Klemgard	J. G.	m.	PD	20 June 1917	2	6	also 21 June, 5:4
Klemgard	James G.	m.	SRR	19 June 1917	8	3	
Klick/Klink	Harry	d.	PD	25 Mar. 1917	4	3	also 27 Mar., 1:2

(1) Surname	(2) Given Name	(3)	(4)	(5) Date	(6) Pg	(7) Col	(8) Comments
Klink	Harry W.	d.	PC	25 Mar. 1917	4	2	
Klink	Henry W.	d.	SRR	24 Mar. 1917	8	6	Guerneville; also 26 Mar., 8:3
Klusing	Dorothy	m.	HT	10 Feb. 1916	1	2	
Knapp	John	d.	PC	15 Feb. 1918	4	5	
Knecht	Marie	m.	SRR	23 Apr. 1917	8	4	
Knecht	Marie	m.	PD	24 Apr. 1917	2	3	
Knell	Fred	d.	PC	13 Dec. 1916	1	2	
Knight	Bernice E.	m.	PD	3 Apr. 1917	8	2	
Knight	Bernice E.	m.	PC	4 Apr. 1917	4	1	
Knight	Bernice E.	m.	ST	7 Apr. 1917	3	2	
Knight	Clara I.	m.	PA	10 Sept. 1917	5	4	also 11 Sept., 2:3
Knight	Clara L.	m.	PC	11 Sept. 1917	5	3	also 12 Sept., 3:4
Knolle	Frank	b.	SIT	6 July 1918	4	4	
Knolle	Frank	m.	PD	7 Apr. 1916	7	2	
Knolle	Frank	m.	SRR	7 Apr. 1916	8	6	
Knolle	Frank	m.	PC	8 Apr. 1916	2	2	
Knolls	Frank	m.	SIT	1 Apr. 1916	2	5	
Knoop	Catherine	m.	SRR	11 Aug. 1917	2	3	
Knott	Ethel	m.	PC	15 Sept. 1918	5	3	
Knott	Ethel I.	m.	ST	20 Sept. 1918	5	1	
Knott	Ethel L.	m.	PD	15 Sept. 1918	4	2	
Knott	Ethel Lillian	m.	SIT	14 Sept. 1918	2	4	
Knounberg	Charles H.	m.	PC	10 June 1918	1	4	
Knowell	Emily	d.	SRR	10 Jan. 1916	8	2	Calvary Cemetery; also 12 Jan., 1:4
Knowles	Belva	o.	SRR	18 Jan. 1917	3	5	
Knowles	Belva	o.	PD	19 Jan. 1917	5	2	
Knowles	W. H., Jr.	o.	SRR	18 Jan. 1917	3	5	
Knowles	W. H., Jr.	o.	PD	19 Jan. 1917	5	2	
Knowles	William H.	d.	PA	15 Apr. 1918	5	4	Canfield Cemetery; also 18 Apr., 4:1
Knowles	William H.	d.	PC	16 Apr. 1918	5	3&6	Canfield Cemetery; also 17 Apr., 4:4; 19 Apr., 6:3
Knowles	William H.	d.	PD	16 Apr. 1918	5	3	also 20 Apr., 5:2
Knowlton	C. D.	b.	PA	8 June 1917	5	2	
Knowlton	Cyrus	m.	PC	25 Jan. 1916	3	1	also 6 Jan. 4:1
Knowlton	Cyrus	m.	PD	26 Jan. 1916	3	2	
Knowlton	Cyrus D.	m.	PA	6 Jan. 1916	5	2	also 22 Jan., 7:4; 24 Jan., 5:4
Knowlton	Cyrus D.	m.	SRR	7 Jan. 1916	5	2	
Knownburg	Charles Henry	d.	PD	9 June 1918	5	2	
Knox	Jeremiah	d.	PA	24 Jan. 1917	8	4&5	Fulton; also 25 Jan., 7:2
Knox	Jeremiah, Mrs.	d.	PD	25 Jan. 1917	2	5	

(1) Surname	(2) Given Name	(3)	(4)	(5) Date	(6) Pg	(7) Col	(8) Comments
Knox	Jeremiah, Mrs.	d.	PC	24 Jan. 1917	4	1	Fulton; also 8:2; 25 Jan., 4:6; 26 Jan., 4:1
Knudsen	C.	b.	PA	30 Aug. 1917	5	7	
Knudsen	Peder C.	m.	PC	28 Feb. 1917	3	4	
Knudson	Arthur J.	m.	PD	14 May 1918	3	5	
Koch	Walter	d.	PC	20 Nov. 1918	4	4	21 Nov., 3:4
Koch	Walter	d.	PD	20 Nov. 1918	4	7	
Kochman	Gertrude	m.	HT	14 Nov. 1918	3	3	
Kochman	Gertrude	m.	PD	15 Nov. 1918	3	3	
Kockler	Charles E.	m.	PD	13 Apr. 1917	4	2	
Kockores	John	d.	SRR	21 May 1917	6	3	
Koeboon	J.	d.	SIT	15 Dec. 1917	1	4	
Koehler	Annie	d.	PD	7 Feb. 1917	6	5	
Koehler	Annie	d.	PC	8 Feb. 1917	1	5	
Koeing	Lizzie	d.	CR	27 Sept. 1918	4	1	Healdsburg
Koenig	Anton	d.	SIT	15 Dec. 1917	1	6	also 22 Dec., 4:4
Koenig	Anton	d.	PD	16 Dec. 1917	6	4	
Koenig	Elizabeth	d.	SIT	21 Sept. 1918	1	4	Healdsburg; also 28 Sept., 1:6
Koenig	Elizabeth Agnes	d.	PD	21 Sept. 1918	8	3	Oak Mound Cemetery; also 24 Sept., 7:2
Koenig	Elizabeth Agnes	d.	PC	22 Sept. 1918	8	2	
Koenig	Frank, Mrs.	d.	PA	21 Sept. 1918	5	7	Sonoma
Koenig	John	m.	PA	24 Jan. 1917	8	6	
Koenig	John	m.	PC	25 Jan. 1917	2	2	
Koford	Ed	o.	PD	17 Dec. 1918	3	3	
Koford	Peter	d.	PD	30 Jan. 1918	5	4	also 2 Feb., 4:2; 3 Feb., 2:7
Kohl	Helen Flora	m.	SRR	31 May 1917	4	1	
Kohler	Annie	d.	SRR	8 Feb. 1917	3	4	
Kohler	E.	b.	PC	16 Apr. 1918	5	6	
Kohler	Ernest	b.	HT	21 Sept. 1916	4	2	
Kolkmeer	Freda Clara	m.	PC	1 June 1917	5	4	
Kolkmeyer	Freda	m.	PA	1 June 1917	6	5	
Kolkmeyer	Freda	m.	PC	5 Aug. 1917	5	1	also 7 Aug., 3:4 & 6
Kolkmeyer	Frieda	m.	PA	4 Aug. 1917	3	4	also 6 Aug., 4:3
Konnamon/Kin namon	Mary	m.	PD	20 Nov. 1917	1	2	
Kopf	Anna	d.	PA	15 Jan. 1916	2	3	Santa Rosa; also 17 Jan., 2:6
Kopf	Anna	d.	HT	20 Jan. 1916	4	2	
Kopf	C. Louis	d.	PD	1 Aug. 1916	2	3	Oakland cremation; also 3 Aug., 3:1
Kopf	C. Louis	p.	SRR	29 Aug. 1916	5	4	
Kopf	C. Louis	p.	PC	30 Aug. 1916	4	2	also 2 Sept., 2:2

(1) Surname	(2) Given Name	(3)	(4)	(5) Date	(6) Pg	(7) Col	(8) Comments
Kopf	C. Louis	p.	PC	5 Oct. 1916	2	2	
Kopf	Catherine	d.	SRR	14 Jan. 1916	8	4	also 15 Jan., 10:3; 17 Jan., 4:2
Kopf	Catherine	o.	PC	15 Jan. 1916	8	3	
Kopf	Katherine	d.	PD	15 Jan. 1916	5	4	also 16 Jan., 1:2; 18 Jan., 5:2
Kopf	Louis	d.	SRR	31 July 1916	1	3	
Kopf	Louis	d.	PA	1 Aug. 1916	3	1	cremation; also 3 Aug., 6:5
Kopf	Roy V.	m.	PA	29 May 1918	8	5	
Kopf	Roy V.	m.	PC	30 May 1918	5	4	
Koplake	Amelia	m.	PA	5 May 1917	2	6	
Korbel	L. V.	b.	PA	22 July 1916	4	2	
Korbel	L. V.	b.	PC	23 July 1916	8	3	
Korbel	L. V.	b.	PA	13 Nov. 1918	4	4	also 5:4
Korbel	L. V.	b.	PC	13 Nov. 1918	4	1	
Korbel	Leo	b.	PD	23 July 1916	6	4	
Koski	Matt	d.	PA	14 July 1917	2	3	
Koski	Matt	d.	PD	14 July 1917	8	3	also 17 July, 4:2
Koski	Matt	d.	SRR	14 July 1917	5	3	
Koski	Matt	d.	PC	15 July 1917	3	4	also 17 July, 8:5
Koss	Marie	m.	PC	11 Dec. 1917	7	4	
Koss	Marie	m.	PD	12 Dec. 1917	3	2	
Kothgassner	Wilhelmina	d.	SRR	28 Dec. 1916	8	3	Rural Cemetery
Kovary	Morris	d.	PA	1 Oct. 1917	8	4	
Kovary	Morris	d.	SRR	1 Oct. 1917	8	6	
Kovary	Morris	d.	PC	2 Oct. 1917	1	2	
Kovary	Morris	d.	PD	2 Oct. 1917	6	2	
Kowell	Emily	d.	PD	11 Jan. 1916	2	4	
Kramer	Albert F.	m.	PA	5 Mar. 1917	6	6	
Kramer	Albert F.	m.	PC	6 Mar. 1917	1	5	
Kreh	Carl H.	d.	PA	29 Oct. 1918	1	4	
Kreh	Chistiana	d.	PC	19 Oct. 1916	5	3	Cypress Hill; also 21 Oct., 6:5; 24 Oct., 3:5; 25 Oct., 4:4
Kreh	Christina	d.	PA	18 Oct. 1916	5	5	Cypress Hill; also 21 Oct., 8:7
Kreh	Edward	d.	PD	14 June 1918	2	5	France
Kreh	Edward C.	d.	PC	24 Aug. 1918	1	3	France
Kreh	Edward Carl	d.	PC	12 May 1918	1	1	France; also 21 May, 5:4; 22 May, 2:2; 13 June, 1:3; 16 June, 2:1
Kreh	Edward Carl	d.	PD	12 May 1918	6	3	France

(1) Surname	(2) Given Name	(3)	(4)	(5) Date	(6) Pg	(7) Col	(8) Comments
Kreh	Edward Karl	d.	PA	18 May 1918	1	3	France; also 8:4; 20 May, 4:6; 24 June, 3:6
Kreh	William	m.	PA	2 Sept. 1918	5	5	
Kreh	William	m.	PC	4 Sept. 1918	3	3	
Kreider	B. B.	m.	PA	14 July 1917	5	3	
Kreider	B. R.	m.	PC	15 July 1917	4	3	
Kricke	Amelia	m.	SRR	23 July 1917	4	5	
Krieder	Carl	m.	PD	16 Aug. 1916	2	3	
Krieke	Amelia Anna	m.	PD	24 July 1917	6	1	
Kroft	Dorothea	m.	PA	25 Aug. 1917	8	5	
Kroft	Dorothea	m.	PC	27 Aug. 1917	5	5	
Kroft	Dorothy	m.	PD	26 Aug. 1917	8	4	
Kruger	Hattie	o.	PA	24 Sept. 1917	4	4	
Kruger	Hattie F.	o.	PC	13 Aug. 1918	5	2	
Kruger	Hattie F.	o.	SRR	24 Sept. 1917	8	3	
Kruger	Louis J.	o.	PC	13 Aug. 1918	5	2	
Kruger	Louis J.	o.	PA	24 Sept. 1917	4	4	
Kruger	Louis J.	o.	SRR	24 Sept. 1917	8	3	
Krugh	Claude	o.	SRR	11 Feb. 1916	5	1	
Krugh	Claude	o.	PA	12 Feb. 1916	3	5	
Krugh	Claude	o.	PD	12 Feb. 1916	3	2	
Krugh	Daisy	o.	PD	12 Feb. 1916	3	2	
Krugh	Daisy D.	o.	SRR	11 Feb. 1916	5	1	
Krugh	Daisy D.	o.	PA	12 Feb. 1916	3	5	
Kruse	C. C.	b.	PD	18 Apr. 1917	6	5	
Kruse	Freda	d.	PC	11 June 1918	1	3	
Kruse	Stanley	d.	PD	10 Jan. 1917	8	3	
Kruse	Stanley	d.	SRR	9 Jan. 1917	5	2	
Kruse	Viola	m.	SRR	10 Jan. 1917	4	5	also 12 Jan., 2:2
Kruse	Viola	m.	PD	11 Jan. 1917	1	7	also 13 Jan., 6:3
Kruse	Viola	m.	HT	18 Jan. 1917	6	4	
Kruse	Viola	m.	SRR	23 Nov. 1916	5	1	
Krusick	Eva E.	m.	PD	25 Feb. 1916	7	2	
Krutmeyer	Clarence	d.	PA	10 July 1917	5	3	also 11 July, 5:4; 12 July, 6:3
Kuck	Henry	d.	PA	4 May 1918	1	3	Cypress Hill; also 6 May, 5:5
Kuck	Henry	d.	PC	4 May 1918	4	2	Cypress Hill; also 7 May, 4:4
Kuenster	Urania	b.	SRR	5 Apr. 1916	5	1	
Kuhlberg	E. C., Mis	m.	PC	12 Sept. 1917	4	2	also 13 Sept., 6:3
Kuhnle	Irene Genevieve	m.	PD	11 Oct. 1917	3	3	also 25 Oct., 8:3
Kuhnle	Irene Genevieve	m.	PC	10 Oct. 1917	1	5	also 25 Oct., 6:3
Kuhnle	Irene Genevieve	m.	PA	9 Oct. 1917	5	1	also 24 Oct., 4:4

(1) Surname	(2) Given Name	(3)	(4)	(5) Date	(6) Pg	(7) Col	(8) Comments
Kulberg	Al	m.	PC	1 Oct. 1916	1	6	
Kulberg	Al	m.	PA	2 Oct. 1916	6	5	
Kulberg	Engre C.	m.	PA	11 Sept. 1917	4	3	also 12 Sept., 3:5
Kunde	Kurt G.	m.	SIT	9 Feb. 1918	1	5	
Kundsen	Jennie T.	m.	SIT	24 Mar. 1916	1	7	
Kurlander	Frank	m.	PD	22 June 1918	5	4	
Kurlander	Hulda May	b.	PD	4 Oct. 1918	3	4	
Kurnmuller	Wilheim	m.	PD	21 July 1916	1	5	
Kurtmeyer	Clarence	d.	PD	11 July 1917	8	1	
Kurtmeyer	Clarence	d.	SRR	11 July 1917	5	1	
Kurtmeyer	Clarence	d.	ST	13 July 1917	3	2	
Kutschmar	Paul	m.	SRR	12 June 1916	1	2	
Kuykendall	Helen	m.	PD	26 Aug. 1916	8	1	
Kuykendall	Helen	m.	SRR	3 Aug. 1916	3	3	portrait; also 26 Aug., 4:1
Kuykendall	Helen	m.	PA	4 Aug. 1916	2	7	also 28 Aug., 8:2
Kuykendall	Helen	m.	PC	4 Aug. 1916	3	4	also 20 Aug., 5:4; 27 Aug., 5:4
Kuypers	Stanley	o.	PD	22 Dec. 1917	5	3	
Kuypers	Stanley	o.	SRR	22 Dec. 1917	5	4	
Kyle	John	o.	PC	27 Feb. 1918	5	4	
Kyle	John P.	o.	PC	27 Aug. 1917	4	6	
Kynoch	Emma Alvilla	d.	PC	24 Dec. 1916	1	4	

L

(1) Surname	(2) Given Name	(3)	(4)	(5) Date	(6) Pg	(7) Col	(8) Comments
Labourdette	Laurence	m.	PC	4 Jan. 1916	2	2	
Labourdette	Lawrence, Miss	m.	PA	3 Jan. 1916	4	5	
Lacey	Albert	m.	ST	8 Nov. 1918	1	2	
Lackey	A.	d.	PA	24 Jan. 1917	5	4	also 25 Jan., 5:5; 26 Jan., 8:6
Lackey	Alexander	d.	PC	26 Jan. 1917	8	1	Cypress Hill; also 27 Jan., 8:2;
Lackey	Sarah	d.	PA	18 May 1918	7	4	Cypress Hill; also 8:5; 20 May, 3:6, 7:5
Lackey	Sarah	d.	PC	19 May 1918	4	3	Cypress Hill; also 21 May, 5:4
Lacque	Alexander	d.	PC	25 Jan. 1917	8	2	also 26 Jan., 3:3
Ladara	Anna L.	m.	PC	10 Mar. 1917	5	2	
LaFevre	Ocelta B.	m.	HT	13 Jan. 1916	3	6	
Lafranchi	Alfonso	m.	PD	11 Oct. 1917	7	2	
Lafranchi	Alfonso	m.	PC	30 Sept. 1917	5	4	also 11 Oct., 5:4
Lafranchi	Alfonso	m.	PA	9 Oct. 1917	5	6	
Lafranchi	Anita	m.	PA	1 Oct. 1918	5	3	
Lafranchi	Anita Elvira	m.	PC	2 Oct. 1918	8	3	
LaFranchi	Jimmie	d.	PC	19 Oct. 1918	1	5	
Lagomarsino	Albert	b.	PD	31 Jan. 1917	8	2	
Lagomarsino	Albert	b.	SRR	31 Jan. 1917	2	3	
Lagomarsino	Rosa	d.	SRR	5 Feb. 1917	5	3	
Lagomarsino	Rosa	d.	PC	6 Feb. 1917	5	3	
Lagomarsino	Rose	d.	PD	6 Feb. 1917	8	1	
Lahue	Edward	m.	PA	15 Mar. 1916	1	4	also 16 Mar., 10:6
Lahue	Edward	m.	PC	16 Mar. 1916	5	2	
LaHue	Edward	m.	ST	18 Mar. 1916	1	2	
Laird	Amarinta Arabell	m.	PD	21 Aug. 1917	8	3	
Lakesman	Frances	d.	PD	9 May 1916	5	1	
Lamar	A. E.	b.	SRR	2 Nov. 1916	4	2	
Lamar	Ruth	d.	PD	5 Nov. 1916	9	7	
Lamb	Edward Thomas	b.	SRR	19 Oct. 1916	7	4	
Lambert	Inez	d.	PD	21 Dec. 1918	7	1	
Lambert	Inez	d.	CR	27 Dec. 1918	4	2	
Lambert	Julia	m.	PD	8 Mar. 1918	8	4	
Lambert	Rae	m.	PD	3 May 1918	4	1	also 22 May, 5:5
Lammon	Clarence W.	m.	PD	26 July 1916	2	3	
Lamont	Jessie	d.	PD	12 Feb. 1918	8	3	
Lamont	Jessie Loranger	d.	PA	11 Feb. 1918	8	5	
Lampson	A.	d.	SRR	12 Mar. 1917	6	5	Olive Hill Cemetery; also 15 Mar., 6:4

(1) Surname	(2) Given Name	(3)	(4)	(5) Date	(6) Pg	(7) Col	(8) Comments
Lampson	Abbie	d.	SRR	13 Mar. 1916	2	2	
Lampson	August	d.	PD	13 Mar. 1917	5	1	
Lampson	August	d.	HT	15 Mar. 1917	1	5	
Lampson	Augustus	d.	PC	14 Mar. 1917	4	3	Geyserville
Lampson	Everett David	m.	PD	13 Dec. 1918	3	3	
Lampson	Everett David	m.	HT	7 Nov. 1916	5	3	
Lampson	Warren	m.	PD	27 Oct. 1917	7	5	
Lance	Ora L.	m.	PC	28 Dec. 1917	6	5	
Lance	Osa L.	m.	PD	27 Dec. 1917	6	1	
Landborough	James Arthur	d.	SIT	21 Dec. 1918	3	5	
Lander	Walter	d.	PD	15 Aug. 1916	8	1	
Lander	Walter	d.	PC	25 Aug. 1916	1	4	also 26 Aug., 1:5
Lander	Walter	d.	SRR	25 Aug. 1916	5	2	
Lander	Walter	d.	PA	26 Aug. 1916	4	6	Coalinga
Landrum	Martha	o.	PD	20 June 1918	2	2	
Landrum	William Y.	o.	PD	20 June 1918	2	2	
Landsborough	James A.	d.	PD	15 Dec. 1918	10	1	
Lane	George B.	o.	PD	27 July 1918	6	3	
Lane	Lettie A.	m.	PD	7 June 1916	5	3	also 8 June, 7:5
Lane	Lottie	m.	SRR	7 June 1916	8	2	
Lane	Lottie E.	o.	PD	27 July 1918	6	3	
Lane	Vera	m.	PD	2 Dec. 1917	10	4	
Lane	Vera	m.	HT	29 Nov. 1917	2	3	
Laneur	Louis	d.	PA	14 June 1917	2	5	also 11 June, 1:6 (original story)
Lang	N. F.	b.	PA	10 May 1917	4	5	
Lang	N. F.	b.	PC	11 May 1917	8	5	
Langdon	Charles	m.	HT	3 Jan. 1918	1	5	
Langdon	Ima B.	d.	PC	10 May 1917	2	2	I.O.O.F. Cemetry, Sebastopol; also 12 May, 6:3
Lange	Nels Frederick	m.	PC	18 June 1916	4	3	also 27 June, 5:3
Lange	Nils F.	m.	PA	26 June 1916	5	4	also 27 June, 5:3
Langer	Elmer S.	m.	PC	4 Feb. 1917	6	2	
Languer	Louis	d.	PD	12 June 1917	5	1	
Languer	Louis	d.	SRR	20 June 1917	4	2	
Lanka	Albert	b.	PA	4 Sept. 1917	5	5	
Lanker	Albert	b.	PA	12 May 1916	5	5	
Lanker	Albert	b.	PC	13 May 1916	8	2	
Lanker	Albert, Jr.	d.	PC	21 May 1916	4	1	Cypress Hill
Lanker	Mary	d.	PA	25 Nov. 1916	5	3	
Lanker	Mary	d.	PC	26 Nov. 1916	4	2	also 28 Nov., 4:2
Lanzi	F.	b.	PA	13 Apr. 1916	5	5	
Lanzi	F.	b.	PC	14 Apr. 1916	8	2	
Laplant	Oliver	d.	SRR	7 Apr. 1916	4	5	

(1) Surname	(2) Given Name	(3)	(4)	(5) Date	(6) Pg	(7) Col	(8) Comments
Laplante	Oliver Snavi	d.	PC	7 Apr. 1916	4	1	Bloomfield; also 8 Apr., 1:2
Lapoint	Fred	d.	PA	15 Oct. 1917	5	5	
LaPort	Guy	d.	PD	9 Feb. 1917	2	1	
Large	R.	b.	PA	23 May 1916	5	3	
Large	Reginald	b.	PC	24 May 1916	8	2	
Large	Reginald	b.	PC	15 May 1918	4	3	
Larimer	Robert	m.	PD	14 May 1918	8	2	also 16 May, 6:5
Larimer	Robert	m.	PD	9 Apr. 1918	7	1	
Larramore	Mr.	d.	SIT	22 June 1918	4	4	
Larsen	Chris	m.	PA	16 Mar. 1917	8	3	
Larsen	Stella M.	m.	CR	8 Nov. 1918	4	3	
Larsen	Tillie	o.	PC	9 Apr. 1918	8	4	
Laseroni	Isabel	m.	PD	15 Feb. 1917	8	3	
Lasker	Albert, Jr.	d.	PA	20 May 1916	5	7	
Lass	Henry F.	p.	SRR	24 Oct. 1917	8	3	will
Lassen	Chris	m.	PC	7 Mar. 1917	5	3	
Lassley	Leila	m.	PC	21 Aug. 1917	6	1	
Lassley	Leili	m.	SRR	20 Aug. 1917	3	4	
Latell	Elsie E.	m.	PA	26 June 1916	5	4	also 27 June, 5:3
Latell	Elsie Elizabeth	m.	PC	18 June 1916	4	3	also 27 June, 5:3
Laton	Harry	d.	PA	25 Aug. 1916	5	4	
Laton	John W.	d.	HT	8 Aug. 1918	6	4	
LaTorres	Robert	m.	SIT	14 Apr. 1917	3	2	
LaTorres	Robert	m.	PD	7 Apr. 1917	6	5	
Latson	Charles	d.	PC	10 Nov. 1918	5	4	Cypress Hill; also 13 Nov., 3:3; 14 Nov., 4:3
Latson	Charles	d.	PA	9 Nov. 1918	4	2	Cypress Hill; also 12 Nov., 5:7; 13 Nov., 5:5
Lau	Julia	d.	PA	20 Aug. 1917	2	3	Santa Rosa; also 4:4; 22 Aug., 5:3
Lau	Julia	d.	SRR	20 Aug. 1917	3	6	also 22 Aug., 8:5
Lau	Julia	d.	PC	21 Aug. 1917	2	2	Santa Rosa; also 3:3; 23 Aug., 5:5
Lau	Julia	d.	PD	21 Aug. 1917	4	2	also 23 Aug., 2:5
Laufenberg	George	m.	PA	18 Dec. 1916	5	3	also 20 Dec., 5:3
Laufenberg	George	m.	PC	19 Dec. 1916	8	2	also 21 Dec., 1:6
Laufenburg	George	m.	PD	21 Dec. 1916	8	2	
Lauggero	Luigi	o.	PD	26 May 1917	5	6	
Laughlin	Gail Everil	m.	PD	16 Sept. 1917	7	4	
Laughlin	Gail Evert	m.	SRR	17 Sept. 1917	5	1	
Laumann	John	m.	PD	30 Nov. 1916	5	6	
Laumann	John, Jr.	m.	SRR	29 Nov. 1916	8	6	
Laundmann	Martha	o.	PD	12 Apr. 1918	6	1	
Laundmann	William	o.	PD	12 Apr. 1918	6	1	

(1) Surname	(2) Given Name	(3)	(4)	(5) Date	(6) Pg	(7) Col	(8) Comments
Laurent	Ernest	b.	SRR	5 Sept. 1917	4	3	
Laurent	Julia	d.	SRR	8 Feb. 1917	4	1	
Laurent	Julia	d.	PD	9 Feb. 1917	4	2	
Laurenzi	Peter (dau of)	d.	PC	3 Feb. 1918	8	2	
Laveroni	Olive	m.	PC	1 Oct. 1916	1	6	
Law	Lily	d.	SRR	26 Dec. 1916	8	6	Oakland
Law	Lily	d.	PD	27 Dec. 1916	5	3	
Law	Mrs.	m.	PA	26 May 1917	8	1	
Law	Mrs.	m.	PC	27 May 1917	8	5	
Lawler	Helen Marie	d.	SIT	10 Nov. 1917	1	4	
Lawler	Helen Marie	d.	PA	11 Nov. 1917	5	4	also 14 Nov., 5:1; 15 Nov., 4:4; 16 Nov., 5:5
Lawler	Helen Marie	d.	PD	13 Nov. 1917	5	3	
Lawler	Helen Marie	d.	SRR	13 Nov. 1917	5	1	
Lawler	Helene Marie	d.	PC	13 Nov. 1917	3	4	also 14 Nov., 8:2; 15 Nov., 2:2; 17 Nov., 5:3
Lawlor	Isabel	d.	PA	28 Jan. 1918	7	4	
Lawlor	John G., Mrs.	d.	PD	29 Jan. 1918	2	4	
Lawrence	Clara	m.	PD	5 Sept. 1918	6	2	
Lawrence	George E.	m.	SRR	15 June 1916	8	3	
Lawrence	George E.	m.	PD	16 June 1916	8	2	
Lawrence	Jennie	m.	PD	19 Oct. 1917	5	4	
Lawrence	Jessie	m.	SRR	17 Oct. 1917	6	3	
Lawrence	Margaret	m.	PD	13 Sept. 1917	5	3	
Lawrence	Margaret	m.	SRR	13 Sept. 1917	5	4	
Lawrence	Margaret	m.	SRR	29 Sept. 1917	4	4	
Lawrence	Vera A.	m.	PA	14 Nov. 1917	4	2	
Lawrence	Vera Arcissa	m.	PD	15 Nov. 1917	6	5	
Lawrence	Vera A.	m.	SRR	14 Nov. 1917	6	6	
Lawri	Francs Anna	m.	PD	20 June 1917	8	2	
Lawson	Daniel	d.	PD	17 May 1918	4	2	cremation; also 8:2
Lawson	George E.	o.	PD	27 Aug. 1916	1	6	
Lawson	George E.	o.	SRR	28 Aug. 1916	5	5	
Lawson	Ivan G.	m.	PA	11 Feb. 1916	5	3	
Lawson	Jesse H.	b.	PC	27 July 1916	8	5	
Lawson	Martha	d.	SRR	10 July 1916	5	4	I.O.O.F. Cemetery; also 8:5; 11 July, 8:3; 12 July, 3:5
Lawson	Martha H.	d.	PA	10 July 1916	5	2	
Lawson	Martha H.	d.	PC	11 July 1916	4	7	
Lawson	Martha H.	d.	PD	11 July 1916	2	2	also 12 July, 8:3; 13 July, 8:3
Lawson	Mary	d.	PD	1 Mar. 1918	2	4	also 4:2
Lawson	Mary	d.	PD	2 Mar. 1918	4	2	also 5 Mar., 6:4
Lawson	Mary	o.	SRR	28 Aug. 1916	5	5	

(1) Surname	(2) Given Name	(3)	(4)	(5) Date	(6) Pg	(7) Col	(8) Comments
Lawson	Mary	m.	SRR	28 Nov. 1916	6	4	
Lawson	Mary L.	o.	PD	27 Aug. 1916	1	6	
Layne	Jessie	m.	PD	5 Jan. 1918	3	5	
Lazarini	Adele	o.	SRR	4 Mar. 1916	1	5	
Lazzaroni	Adele	o.	PD	20 Nov. 1917	6	3	
Lazzaroni	G.	o.	PD	20 Nov. 1917	6	3	
Lea	Alonzo F.	d.	PC	27 Oct. 1916	1	5	Big Valley, Lake County; also 29 Oct., 8:1
Lea	Alonzo F.	d.	PD	27 Oct. 1916	8	1	
Lea	Alonzo F.	d.	SRR	27 Oct. 1916	5	1	Geyserville
Lea	Christina	m.	CR	6 July 1917	1	1	
Lea	Elizabeth	d.	PD	23 Oct. 1917	7	2	
Lea	Elizabeth	d.	SRR	4 Sept. 1917	5	1	also 5 Sept., 8:6
Lea	Elizabeth	d.	PC	5 Sept. 1917	1	5	
Lea	Elizabeth	d.	ST	7 Sept. 1916	5	2	
Lea	Elizabeth Trower	d.	PD	5 Sept. 1917	5	3	
Lea	Frederick	d.	PD	11 Sept. 1918	4	2	also 5:1, 8:2; 12 Sept., 4:2; 13 Sept., 6:3
Lea	Frederick	d.	PA	6 Sept. 1918	8	2&3	also 12 Sept., 5:5
Lea	Frederick	d.	PC	6 Sept. 1918	1	4	also 12 Sept., 8:3
Lea	Orlando	d.	PA	26 Dec. 1916	4	5	
Lea	Orlando	d.	SRR	26 Dec. 1916	4	1	Kelseyville; also 27 Dec., 8:4
Lea	Orlando	d.	PD	27 Dec. 1916	2	3	also 28 Dec., 2:2
Leach	A. D.	d.	PD	15 Nov. 1916	3	4	
Leach	A. D.	d.	SRR	16 Nov. 1916	8	66	
Leach	Henry W.	m.	HT	13 June 1918	3	4	
Leach	Henry W.	m.	PD	14 June 1918	2	3	
Leach	John	d.	PA	11 May 1918	2	2	Cypress Hill; also 14 May, 4:3
Leach	John	d.	PC	11 May 1918	1	3	Cypress Hill; also 15 May, 4:5
Leach	John W.	b.	PA	3 May 1917	5	3	
Leahy	Jeremiah	d.	PD	9 Aug. 1916	6	1	
Leahy	Lillian	m.	PA	20 June 1916	1	7	also 21 June, 5:1; 26 June, 5:4
Leahy	Lillian	m.	PC	21 June 1916	8	3	also 27 June, 5:2
Leake	Ralph Wesley	b.	SRR	3 July 1916	10	4	
Leavy	P. F.	d.	PA	16 July 1918	4	3	also 18 July, 3:7; 19 July, 8:3
Leavy	Patrick F.	d.	PC	16 July 1918	1	2	
Leavy	Patrick F.	d.	PD	17 July 1918	6	5	
Leazinsky	Dora	d.	PA	13 Feb. 1917	4	3	also 15 Feb., 5:4
LeBaron	Clyde	b.	PD	24 Mar. 1918	3	5	
LeBaron	Clyde	b.	PA	25 Mar. 1918	3	4	

(1) Surname	(2) Given Name	(3)	(4)	(5) Date	(6) Pg	(7) Col	(8) Comments
LeBaron	Clyde Leslie	d.	PD	23 Nov. 1916	2	1	San Francisco; also 24 Nov., 6:5
LeBaron	Clyde Lester	d.	SRR	22 Nov. 1916	1	3	also 23 Nov., 5:3
LeBaron	Clyde, Jr.	d.	PA	22 Nov. 1916	1	3	also 24 Nov., 2:5
LeBaron	Clyde, Jr.	d.	PC	23 Nov. 1916	1	1	also 24 Nov., 1:3; 25 Nov., 8:5
LeBaron	H. M.	b.	PA	26 May 1917	5	4	
LeBaron	Harrison	b.	PC	27 June 1916	8	1	
LeBaron	Harrison, Jr.	b.	PC	27 May 1917	4	4	
LeBaron	Robert Palmer	d.	PA	22 Nov. 1916	1	3	also 24 Nov., 2:5
LeBaron	Robert Palmer	d.	SRR	22 Nov. 1916	1	3	also 23 Nov., 5:3
LeBaron	Robert Palmer	d.	PC	23 Nov. 1916	1	1	also 24 Nov., 1:3; 25 Nov., 8:5
LeBaron	Robert Palmer	d.	PD	23 Nov. 1916	2	1	San Francisco; also 24 Nov., 6:5
LeBrun	Eddie	o.	ST	13 Dec. 1918	1	2	
LeBrun	M. A.	m.	PC	15 Sept. 1918	5	3	
LeBrun	M. A.	m.	PD	15 Sept. 1918	4	2	
LeBrun	M. A.	m.	ST	20 Sept. 1918	5	1	
LeBrun	Michael A.	m.	SIT	14 Sept. 1918	2	4	
Ledford	William	m.	CR	8 Nov. 1918	4	3	
Ledger	Alexander C.	d.	SRR	13 Nov. 1917	8	2	Riverside Cemetery
Ledger	Alexander C.	d.	PD	14 Nov. 1917	2	2	
Lee	Galen	b.	PD	10 Jan. 1918	8	2	
Lee	Galen E.	m.	SRR	18 Sept. 1916	2	2	
Lee	George C.	b.	PD	5 Sept. 1918	5	4	
Lee	Mary	m.	SRR	3 Dec. 1917	8	4	
Lee	Rachel	m.	PD	22 June 1918	3	4	also 25 June, 7:5
Lee	W. H.	o.	SRR	10 Oct. 1916	1	4	
Lee	Walter S.	m.	SRR	25 July 1917	3	1	
Leese	Arthur R.	d.	PC	26 Oct. 1918	5	4	
Leete	John	m.	SRR	28 May 1917	3	3	
LeFevre	Ocella	m.	SRR	10 Jan. 1916	8	5	
Leffingwell	Margaret A.	d.	PC	17 Apr. 1917	3	5	Cypress Hill; also 5:5; 18 Apr., 3:6; 19 Apr., 5:3
Leffingwell	Margaret A.	d.	PA	18 Apr. 1917	4	6	Cypress Hill
Leggett	Alta	m.	PD	7 June 1918	3	5	
Leggett	Chester	m.	SRR	11 Aug. 1917	2	3	
Leggett	Donna Z.	m.	PD	9 Dec. 1917	6	1	also 11 Dec., 6:5
Leggett	Henry	d.	PA	19 May 1917	5	3	
Leggett	Henry B.	d.	PC	20 May 1917	1	3	
Leggett	Henry B.	d.	PD	20 May 1917	8	1	also 22 May, 5:5
Leggett	Henry B.	d.	SRR	21 May 1917	8	3	
Leggett	Julienne	m.	SRR	1 Oct. 1917	4	3	
Leggett	Julienne	m.	PD	2 Oct. 1917	2	3	

(1) Surname	(2) Given Name	(3)	(4)	(5) Date	(6) Pg	(7) Col	(8) Comments
Leggett	Nellie	m.	SRR	29 July 1916	10	4	
Leggett	Nellie	m.	SRR	27 Sept. 1916	5	3	
Leggett	Nellie	m.	PC	28 Sept. 1916	3	4	
Leggett	Raford Wesley	m.	SRR	20 July 1916	8	2	
Leggett	Rayford	m.	SRR	15 Aug. 1916	8	5	
Leggett	Rayford	m.	PD	16 Aug. 1916	6	4	
Leggett	Thomas, Jr.	m.	SRR	11 Aug. 1917	3	2	
Lehman	M. D.	d.	PA	28 Feb. 1918	5	3	Salem Cemetery
Lehman	Max David	d.	PC	25 Feb. 1918	8	4	Salem Cemetery; also 1 Mar., 4:4
Lehrke	Albert W.	d.	SRR	3 May 1917	8	3	
Lehrke	Albert W.	d.	PD	4 May 1917	2	2	
Leibert	Celestine	m.	PC	20 July 1916	5	4	
Leighton	J. W.	d.	PA	1 Aug. 1918	4	4	also 2 Aug., 3:4
Leighton	J. W.	d.	PD	2 Aug. 1918	8	3	
Leighton	W.	d.	PC	3 Aug. 1918	2	2	
Leisen	Mamie	d.	PA	26 June 1918	1	3	also 27 June, 3:2
Leisen	Mamie	d.	PD	26 June 1918	1	6	Rural Cemeetery; also 27 June, 8:2; 28 June, 4:2, 5:4; 29 June, 3:5
Leiser	George	m.	SIT	16 Sept. 1916	1	4	also 23 Sept., 1:1
Leiser	George	m.	PD	19 Sept. 1916	2	2	
Leiser	George	m.	SRR	9 Sept. 1916	7	4	also 10:4; 19 Sept., 8:6
Leithmann	Louis	m.	SRR	16 July 1917	6	3	
Lencioni	Amastasia	d.	HT	20 Apr. 1916	6	2	
Lencioni	Fred, Mrs.	d.	PD	4 Sept. 1918	8	3	
Lencioni	Nathan	d.	PC	7 Feb. 1917	4	5	
Lencioni	Nathan	d.	HT	8 Feb. 1917	6	3	
Lencioni	Susie	d.	HT	5 Sept. 1918	5	5	
Lencioni	Theresa	m.	PC	29 May 1917	4	1	
Lencioni	Theresa	m.	SRR	28 Apr. 1917	10	3	also 30 Apr., 4:2
Lencioni	Theresa	m.	PD	29 Apr. 1917	5	3	
Lenhardt	Dick	o.	PA	22 Jan. 1918	2	5	
Lenhart	Lee	b.	PD	11 Apr. 1917	8	2	
Lent	Ethel Marie	m.	PA	21 Jan. 1916	5	3	
Lent	Ethel Marie	m.	PC	22 Jan. 1916	6	3	
Lentz	W. E.	b.	PD	11 May 1918	6	5	
Lentz	Walter	m.	PD	26 May 1917	5	5	
Lentz	Walter	m.	SRR	26 May 1917	6	1	
Lentz	Walter	m.	PD	3 June 1917	5	1	
Lenzi	Arturo	m.	SRR	3 Aug. 1916	6	1	
Leonard	Mary J.	d.	PA	24 Sept. 1917	5	6	
Leonard	Mary J.	d.	PD	25 Sept. 1917	6	5	also 26 Sept., 6:3
Leonard	Mary Jane	d.	SRR	24 Sept. 1917	1	2	also 25 Sept., 4:2
Leonardini	John	d.	PD	13 Nov. 1917	1	5	

(1) Surname	(2) Given Name	(3)	(4)	(5) Date	(6) Pg	(7) Col	(8) Comments
Leonardini	Maria	o.	SRR	5 Jan. 1916	10	5	
Leonardini	Marie	o.	SRR	8 Feb. 1016	5	6	
Leonardini	Paolo	o.	SRR	5 Jan. 1916	10	5	
Leonardini	Paolo	o.	SRR	8 Feb. 1016	5	6	
Lepori	Anton	d.	PD	4 June 1916	5	2	also 6 June, 6:3
Lepori	Anton	d.	PA	5 June 1916	4	2	
Lepori	Antoni	d.	SRR	3 June 1916	10	3	also 5 June, 1:3
Leppo	Frank	m.	PC	7 May 1918	5	2	
Leppo	Frank	m.	PD	7 May 1918	5	2	
Lerda	Delphine	m.	PC	4 Aug. 1916	5	2	
Lerer	Gertrude	m.	PA	26 Mar. 1917	4	3	
Lerer	Gertrude	m.	PC	27 Mar. 1917	5	1	
Leroux	Paul	d.	CR	18 Oct. 1918	4	2	
Leroux	Paul	d.	PD	23 Oct. 1918	5	2	
Leroux	Paul J.	d.	PC	23 Oct. 1918	4	3	
Lescioni	Domenico	d.	HT	24 Jan. 1918	1	1	
Leslie	Charles W.	m.	PD	25 June 1918	6	2	
Leslie	Charles W.	m.	HT	27 June 1918	5	1	
Less	Bud	o.	HT	10 Oct. 1918	8	2	
Leszinsky	Dora	d.	PC	14 Feb. 1917	4	4	cremation; also 5:4; 15 Feb., 4:4; 16 Feb., 4:4, 1:3
Leszinsky	Dora	d.	SRR	15 Feb. 1917	1	2	
Letcher	Katherine	d.	PA	24 Apr. 1918	5	7	
Letold	Alice	m.	SRR	19 Sept. 1916	3	4	also 20 Sept., 8:6
Letold	Alice M.	m.	SRR	26 Aug. 1916	4	2	
Lette	John	m.	PD	27 May 1917	8	1	
Leucioni	Domenico	d.	PC	25 Jan. 1918	3	4	
Leverau	Hattie La Dow	m.	PD	1 Jan. 1918	3	4	
Leveroni	Oliva	m.	PA	2 Oct. 1916	6	5	
Leveroni	Victor	m.	PD	18 Nov. 1917	3	4	
Leveroni	Victor	m.	SRR	19 Nov. 1917	6	1	
Leveroni	Victor	m.	SRR	2 Oct. 1917	2	3	
Leveroni	Victor	m.	PC	21 Nov. 1917	6	2	
Leveroni	Victor	m.	SIT	29 Sept. 1917	1	6	
Leveroni	Victor	m.	PC	30 Sept. 1917	8	3	
Leveroni	Victor	b.	SIT	31 Aug. 1918	3	5	
Levrenzini	Edward	b.	HT	26 July 1917	8	1	
Levy	B. M.	b.	SRR	17 Jan. 1916	1	5	
Levy	Bernard	b.	SRR	12 Sept. 1917	7	4	
Levy	Mark	d.	SRR	6 Apr. 1917	6	5	
Levy	R. M.	b.	PD	18 Jan. 1916	3	5	
Levy	Robert	d.	SRR	26 July 1917	8	3	
Lewis	Alonzo	d.	SRR	26 Dec. 1916	4	2	
Lewis	Alonzo	d.	PD	27 Dec. 1916	3	5	

(1) Surname	(2) Given Name	(3)	(4)	(5) Date	(6) Pg	(7) Col	(8) Comments
Lewis	C. M.	m.	HT	1 Feb. 1917	8	4	
Lewis	C. M.	b.	HT	7 Feb. 1918	1	2	
Lewis	Calvin McM.	m.	PC	26 Jan. 1917	5	3	
Lewis	Etha Lillian	m.	SRR	5 Nov. 1917	8	1	
Lewis	Etha Lillian	m.	PD	6 Nov. 1917	2	3	
Lewis	Etha Lillian	m.	PC	7 Nov. 1917	2	2	
Lewis	Florence	d.	CR	1 June 1917	1	2	
Lewis	Harry	m.	PA	10 June 1916	4	2	
Lewis	Harry	m.	PC	11 June 1916	4	2	also 14 June, 4:2
Lewis	Harry	m.	PD	14 June 1916	3	3	
Lewis	Harry D.	m.	ST	17 June 1916	1	2	
Lewis	J. Hall	m.	PA	8 Oct. 1917	4	5	also 9 Oct., 4:6
Lewis	Joe	d.	SIT	9 Feb. 1918	4	7	Mountain Cemetery
Lewis	John	d.	PC	10 Feb. 1918	4	3	Mountain Cemetery
Lewis	John	d.	PD	10 Feb. 1918	8	4	
Lewis	Julia	m.	PA	2 Oct. 1916	4	3	
Lewis	Julia	m.	PC	2 Oct. 1916	8	4	
Lewis	Julia	m.	SRR	2 Oct. 1916	8	3	
Lewis	Manuel	o.	PC	18 Apr. 1916	1	4	portrait
Lewis	Marie	o.	PC	18 Apr. 1916	1	4	portrait
Lewis	Marshall	m.	SRR	21 Dec. 1917	7	2	
Lewis	William	b.	PA	23 July 1917	5	3	
Lewis	William	m.	PA	17 Oct. 1916	2	4	
Lewis	William	m.	PC	19 Oct. 1916	3	2	
Leymance	B. J.	o.	PD	5 Dec. 1918	3	4	
Libarle	Hans John	m.	PA	3 Jan. 1916	4	5	
Libby	George	d.	SRR	27 Jan. 1917	3	1	
Libby	George H.	d.	ST	2 Feb. 1917	1	1	
Libby	George H.	d.	PC	28 Jan. 1917	1	1	
Libby	George H.	d.	PD	28 Jan. 1917	3	3	
Libby	George H.	d.	PA	29 Jan. 1917	3	3	
Libby	Grace	m.	ST	8 Nov. 1918	1	2	
Lichau	Henry	d.	PA	31 Dec. 1917	5	1	also 8:5
Lichau	Henry P.	d.	PD	1 Jan. 1918	3	5	
Lichau	Henry P.	d.	PA	2 Jan. 1918	4	4	
Lichau	Henry Philip	d.	PC	1 Jan. 1918	6	1&2	also 3 Jan., 4:4
Liebert	Esther	o.	PC	27 May 1916	3	3	adoption
Liebert	Mabel	o.	PC	27 May 1916	3	3	adoption
Liebert	Nanette	o.	PC	27 May 1916	3	3	adoption
Liethman	James	m.	PD	17 July 1917	3	3	
Liggett	Thomas, Jr.	m.	PD	12 Aug. 1917	1	2	
Lightfoot	Eliza	d.	CR	6 Apr. 1917	1	4	Riverside Cemetery
Lightner	John S.	d.	PA	7 Jan. 1918	8	3	
Lightner	S.	d.	PC	8 Jan. 1918	4	1	
Lilly	C. P.	m.	PD	9 Dec. 1916	2	5	

(1) Surname	(2) Given Name	(3)	(4)	(5) Date	(6) Pg	(7) Col	(8) Comments
Lind	C. W., Mrs.	d.	PA	5 Aug. 1916	1	3	
Lind	Dollie	d.	PD	4 Aug. 1916	8	3	also 8 Aug., 3:4
Lind	Dolly	d.	SRR	4 Aug. 1916	8	6	also 5 Aug., 10:6; 7 Aug., 3:3
Lind	Dolly	d.	PC	5 Aug. 1916	1	6	Rural Cemetery; also 6 Aug., 3:5
Lindemann	M., Miss	d.	PA	3 July 1918	6	2	
Lindemenn	George	b.	SRR	21 Aug. 1917	3	2	
Lindemenn	George	b.	PD	22 Aug. 1917	6	2	
Lindemenn	Sidney	m.	SRR	13 Nov. 1916	7	3	
Lindermann	Mercedes	d.	PD	4 July 1918	3	4	Shiloh Cemeetery; also 6 July, 4:2; 7 July, 5:3
Lindermann	William	d.	PA	2 Aug. 1918	1	4	
Lindermann	William	d.	PD	3 Aug. 1918	6	2	
Lindholm	Charles E.	b.	PA	27 Apr. 1918	8	2	
Lindholm	Ruth	d.	PD	19 Nov. 1918	5	1	England
Lindholm	Viola	d.	PD	19 Nov. 1918	5	1	England
Lindholm	Violet	d.	PD	15 Oct. 1918	5	3	France
Lindley	Leo Lee	m.	PD	27 May 1917	6	1	
Lindley	Leo Lee	m.	SRR	28 May 1917	3	4	
Lindley	Melba	m.	SIT	14 Apr. 1917	3	5	
Lindley	P.	o.	PC	14 Nov. 1918	4	3	
Lindsay	Hattie	d.	HT	12 Dec. 1918	1	2	
Lindsey	Alpheus C.	m.	PD	18 Aug. 1918	10	2	
Lindsley	Alfred	m.	PD	14 Sept. 1916	3	5	
Lindsley	Alfred	m.	SRR	14 Sept. 1916	7	4	
Lindsley	William	d.	PD	3 Oct. 1917	4	2	Rural Cemetery; also 8:3; 6 Oct., 2:6
Lindsley/Lindsay	William	d.	SRR	3 Oct. 1917	4	5	Rural Cemetery; also 5 Oct., 8:3
Linebaugh	Edna	d.	PD	4 Jan. 1916	8	1	
Linebaugh	Edna	d.	SRR	4 Jan. 1916	4	1	also 5 Jan., 8:1
Linebaugh	Edna Marion	d.	ST	8 Jan. 1916	1	2	
Linebaugh	George	m.	PA	11 Jan. 1917	8	4	
Linebaugh	George	m.	PC	11 Jan. 1918	4	5	
Linebaugh	George	m.	PD	11 Jan. 1918	2	4	
Lingenfelser	Eusebia	m.	SIT	14 Apr. 1917	3	2	
Lingenfelser	Eusebia	m.	PD	7 Apr. 1917	6	5	
Linscot	Hazel	m.	PA	11 Feb. 1916	5	3	
Linsley	Raymond	b.	PD	19 Oct. 1916	8	4	
Linsley	Winfield Scott	d.	PD	11 Nov. 1918	8	4	also 13 Nov., 6:4; 14 Nov., 5:2, 6:3
Lippi	Dean Orlando	m.	SRR	14 May 1917	6	3	
Lippi	Dean Orlando	m.	PD	15 May 1917	5	4	
Lippitt	Frank	d.	PD	16 Aug. 1917	5	1	also 17 Aug., 2:1

(1) Surname	(2) Given Name	(3)	(4)	(5) Date	(6) Pg	(7) Col	(8) Comments
Lippitt	Frank K.	d.	PA	14 Aug. 1917	5	6	Cypress Hill; also 15 Aug., 4:5; 16 Aug., 3:3
Lippitt	Frank K.	d.	SRR	15 Aug. 1917	8	1	also 17 Aug., 4:5
Lippitt	Frank K.	d.	PC	16 Aug. 1917	1	6	also 17 Aug., 5:3
Lippitt	Frank K.	p.	PA	20 Aug. 1917	6	3	
Lippitt	Frank K.	p.	PC	21 Aug. 1917	8	3	
Lissen/Nissen	Ella Marie	m.	PA	6 July 1916	2	6	also 4:4
Litcher	Katherine	d.	PC	30 Apr. 1918	3	3	Cypress Hill; also 2 May, 5:3
Lithwin	August	m.	SRR	1 Sept. 1917	6	3	
Lithwin	August	m.	PD	2 Sept. 1917	6	2	
Little	James F.	d.	PC	3 Jan. 1917	2	1	also 4 Jan., 6:2
Little	James J.	d.	PD	4 Jan. 1917	5	2	
Little	James P.	d.	PA	2 Jan. 1917	3	3	Calvary Cemetery; also 3 Jan., 4:1
Little	James P.	d.	PC	31 Dec. 1916	4	3	
Littleton	Julia	m.	HT	17 Jan. 1918	8	4	
Littleton	Virginia	d.	SRR	1 Jan. 1916	3	4	Rural Cemetery
Litzuis	Henrietta	d.	SIT	12 Feb. 1916	1	3	
Livernash	Alberta	m.	PC	1 Sept. 1917	5	5	
Livernash	Alberta	m.	PD	31 Aug. 1917	8	2	
Livernash	Alberta	m.	SRR	31 Aug. 1917	4	4	
Livernash	Magaret	m.	PD	2 Dec. 1916	2	1	also 15 Dec., 6:4
Livernash	Margaret	m.	PA	12 Dec. 1916	5	5	
Livernash	Margaret	m.	SRR	2 Dec. 1916	7	4	
Livernash	Margaret	m.	PC	3 Dec. 1916	3	1	also 12 Dec., 8:5; 14 Dec., 4:3
Livernash	Marjorie	m.	SIT	2 Dec. 1916	1	3	also 16 Dec., 1:3
Livingston	E. S., Mrs.	d.	CR	27 July 1917	1	2	
Livingston	Ermine	d.	PD	27 July 1917	7	5	Cloverdale
Lobb	William	d.	PA	17 Mar. 1916	4	6	
Lobb	William	d.	SRR	17 Mar. 1916	4	3	
Locan	Ruby Hall	m.	PA	26 Aug. 1916	6	1	
Locan	Ruby Hall	m.	PD	26 Aug. 1916	6	3	
Locan	Ruby Hall	m.	PC	29 Aug. 1916	4	6	
Locatelli	Mr.	d.	PD	21 June 1916	7	3	Shiloh Cemetery
Lock	Ernest	m.	PD	19 June 1917	8	2	
Lock	Ernest	m.	SRR	19 June 1917	3	6	
Lock	Ernest	m.	PC	20 June 1917	5	1	
Lock	Ernest	m.	PA	22 Aug. 1917	1	5	
Lock	Joe	o.	SIT	24 Mar. 1917	1	5	
Locke	Beryl	m.	PD	7 June 1916	5	3	also 8 June, 8:4
Locke	Beryl	m.	SRR	7 June 1916	8	1	
Locke	Ernest	m.	PA	19 June 1917	3	3	

(1) Surname	(2) Given Name	(3)	(4)	(5) Date	(6) Pg	(7) Col	(8) Comments
Locke	Ernest	m.	SRR	15 Aug. 1917	4	4	also 22 Aug., 5:2; 23 Aug., 4:4
Locke	Ernest	m.	PC	16 Aug. 1917	5	3	also 23 Aug., 5:4
Locke	Gladys	d.	SRR	19 June 1916	5	3	also 20 June, 8:5
Locke	Gladys	d.	PD	20 June 1916	2	5	also 21 June, 2:3
Lockett	Bizonia	d.	PD	26 Oct. 1918	5	3	
Lockett	Lizonia	d.	PC	27 Oct. 1918	8	2	
Lockhart	Ethel	m.	PD	23 Dec. 1916	5	4	
Lockhart	Robert	d.	PD	10 Mar. 1917	1	4	also 11 Mar., 4:3; 13 Mar., 5:4
Lockhart	Robert	d.	SRR	10 Mar. 1917	5	1	also 12 Mar., 8:2
Lockwood	Hattie E.	m.	SRR	5 Jan. 1916	4	6	
Loftus	Billy	d.	PD	1 May 1918	2	5	also 2 May, 2:4
Loftus	William	d.	PC	1 May 1918	1	2	also 2 May, 5:3; 3 May, 2:3
Loftus	William	d.	ST	3 May 1918	2	3	
Loftus	William	d.	SIT	4 May 1918	4	5	
Loftus	William	d.	PA	30 Apr. 1918	5	5	Calvary Cemetery; also 1 May, 4:5; 2 May, 4:4, 5:3
Logan	Robert S.	d.	SRR	14 Feb. 1917	3	1	Oak Mound Cemetery
Logan	Robert S.	d.	PA	15 Feb. 1917	6	3	
Logan	Robert S.	d.	PD	15 Feb. 1917	2	3	
Logan	Robert S.	d.	HT	8 Feb. 1917	1	2	
Lombard	Marcel	d.	PA	29 Oct. 1918	5	1	France
Lombard	Marcel	d.	PC	30 Oct. 1918	1	6	France
Lombardi	Felice	d.	PC	10 Nov. 1918	5	3	
Lombardi	Felice	d.	PD	10 Nov. 1918	4	2	also 5:4; 13 Nov., 6:2
Lombardi	Lucia	d.	PD	21 June 1918	4	2	Calvary Cemetery; also 8:5; 25 June, 3:3
Lombari	Joseph	m.	PD	13 Jan. 1918	6	6	also 18 Jan., 5:5
Lombari	Lucia	d.	PC	22 June 1918	2	3	
Lomont	Jesse Leranger	d.	PC	12 Feb. 1918	8	4	cremation; also 15 Feb., 6:4
Lomont	Sybilla	m.	SRR	21 Aug. 1916	5	1	
London	Jack	p.	SRR	29 June 1917	5	1	
London	Jack	p.	SRR	1 Dec. 1916	1	3	also 2 Dec., 1:5, 10:6; 3 Dec., 3:4; 11 Dec., 5:1; 18 Dec., 8:3
London	Jack	p.	SIT	16 Feb. 1918	3	4	
London	Jack	p.	PC	2 Dec. 1916	8	3	also 19 Dec., 1:5
London	Jack	p.	PD	2 Dec. 1916	3	1	will; also 3 Dec., 1:3; 19 Dec., 2:1
London	Jack	d.	PA	23 Nov. 1916	2	2	his ranch; also 24 Nov., 5:3; 25 Nov., 6:3; 28 Nov., 3:4

(1) Surname	(2) Given Name	(3)	(4)	(5) Date	(6) Pg	(7) Col	(8) Comments
London	Jack	d.	PC	23 Nov. 1916	1	5	also 24 Nov., 1:6
London	Jack	d.	PD	23 Nov. 1916	1	1	also 24 Nov., 1:4, 8:1; 25 Nov., 8:1; 28 Nov., 5:1
London	Jack	d.	SRR	23 Nov. 1916	1	5	cremation; also 24 Nov., 10:4; 27 Nov., 6:2
London	Jack	d.	SIT	25 Nov. 1916	1	1	also 2 Dec., 1:1
London	Jack	p.	PA	29 Nov. 1916	4	4	also 19 Dec., 3:3
London	Jack	p.	SIT	9 Dec. 1916	1	1	
Lonergan	Daniel	d.	PC	27 Feb. 1917	3	3	
Lonergan	Daniel C.	d.	PA	26 Feb. 1917	5	4	also 28 Feb., 4:5
Lonergan	Daniel C.	d.	PD	27 Feb. 1917	5	4	
Lonergan	Daniel C.	d.	SRR	27 Feb. 1917	7	3	Petaluma
Long	Edd G.	d.	PD	26 May 1917	8	1	
Long	Edd G.	d.	SRR	26 May 1917	5	3	I.O.O.F. Cemetery; also 10:6; 28 May, 8:3
Long	Edd G.	d.	HT	31 May 1917	1	4	
Long	Edward	d.	PA	29 May 1917	2	5	
Long	Harry	o.	HT	14 Mar. 1918	1	5	
Long	Henry	m.	HT	17 Jan. 1918	8	4	
Long	John T.	b.	SRR	29 Sept. 1917	8	6	
Long	Joseph	d.	PA	1 July 1916	4	6	Cypress Hill; also 5:4; 3 July, 3:1
Long	Joseph	d.	PC	2 July 1916	5	5	Calvary Cemetery; also 4 July, 4:3
Long	Joseph	d.	SRR	3 July 1916	6	4	
Long	Mae	d.	PC	6 Nov. 1918	3	4	
Long	Mae Piezzi	d.	PD	2 Nov. 1918	3	1	I.O.O.F. Cemetery; also 4:2; 5 Nov., 2:5
Long	Mae Piezzi	d.	PD	29 Oct. 1918	8	2	
Long	Mae Piezzi	d.	PA	30 Oct. 1918	6	5	also 5 Nov., 4:6
Long	Sarah	d.	SRR	28 Sept. 1916	8	1&6	29 Sept., 5:4, 8:8
Long	Sarah Lucy Francona	d.	PD	29 Sept. 1916	5	3	also 30 Sept., 2:4
Long	W. I.	d.	PD	1 Oct. 1916	5	1	
Long/DeLong	Gertrude	m.	PC	19 Sept. 1916	8	4	
Longsine	Addie	m.	PD	4 Jan. 1918	3	5	
Longuine	Addie	m.	SRR	28 Dec. 1917	8	5	
Lonkey	Lloyd	m.	PD	18 Aug. 1916	3	5	
Loomis	John W.	m.	PC	20 May 1916	6	2	
Loosemore	Emma	d.	PD	1 Nov. 1916	5	4	
Lopez	Dorothy	m.	SRR	23 Oct. 1917	4	4	
Lopez	Joseph	d.	PD	11 Nov. 1918	4	5	
Lopus	J.	o.	PA	30 Sept. 1918	5	3	
Lopus	John	o.	PC	1 Oct. 1918	8	3	also 1 Nov., 2:2
Lopus	John	o.	PD	1 Oct. 1918	3	5	

(1) Surname	(2) Given Name	(3)	(4)	(5) Date	(6) Pg	(7) Col	(8) Comments
Lopus	John	o.	PA	31 Oct. 1918	4	1	
Lopus	Joseph	o.	PA	16 Nov. 1918	4	4	
Lopus	Joseph	b.	PA	20 Nov. 1916	1	6	
Lopus	Minnie	o.	PC	1 Oct. 1918	8	3	also 1 Nov., 2:2
Lopus	Minnie	o.	PD	1 Oct. 1918	3	5	
Lopus	Minnie	o.	PA	30 Sept. 1918	5	3	
Lopus	Minnie Dunker	o.	PA	31 Oct. 1918	4	1	
Lords	Delphine	m.	PA	2 Aug. 1916	4	3	
Lorenz	Mr. & Mrs.	b.	PA	24 Jan. 1917	8	5	
Lorenzen	Catherine	d.	PA	7 May 1917	5	5	Liberty Cemetery; also 8:5; 9 May, 5:4
Lorenzen	Catherine Christine	d.	PC	8 May 1917	5	3	also 10 May, 5:3
Lorenzen	Catherine Christine	d.	SRR	8 May 1917	6	4	
Lorenzen	Philip	b.	PC	15 Nov. 1918	4	3	
Lorenzen	Phillip	b.	PA	24 Feb. 1916	5	7	
Lorenzine	Ida	m.	SRR	23 Oct. 1917	4	4	
Lorenzini	Edward	b.	SRR	26 July 1917	6	4	
Lorenzini	Ida	m.	HT	25 Oct. 1917	7	4	
Lorenzini	Ida	m.	PC	26 Oct. 1917	5	4	
Lorenzini	Ida	m.	PD	26 Oct. 1917	5	2	
Loughery	Harold K., Mrs.	d.	PD	1 Nov. 1918	3	3	
Loughery	Marguerite	d.	PD	30 Oct. 1918	8	2	Holy Cross Cemetery, SF; also 31 Oct., 3:2
Loughery	Marguerite	d.	PA	31 Oct. 1918	6	3	
Loughrey	Marguerite Frances	d.	PC	31 Oct. 1918	6	4	
Lounibos	John	d.	PA	19 Sept. 1917	8	5	Sonoma; also 22 Sept., 8:3
Lounibos	John	d.	PC	21 Sept. 1917	1	3	also 25 Sept., 6:4
Lounibos	John	d.	PD	21 Sept. 1917	8	4	
Lounibos	John	d.	SRR	21 Sept. 1917	7	3	
Lounibos	John	d.	SIT	22 Sept. 1917	1	7	
Lourdeaux	Aline	m.	SRR	11 May 1916	8	4	
Loustalot	Lee	d.	PA	19 Nov. 1918	3	3	Oakland; also 4:4; 22 Nov., 2:4
Loustalot	Lee	d.	PD	19 Nov. 1918	5	3	also 20 Nov., 5:5
Lovejoy	Frances M.	m.	PA	30 Mar. 1918	4	1	
Lovejoy	Frank E.	d.	PA	22 May 1917	4	5	Cypress Hill; also 23 May, 4:3
Lovejoy	Frank E.	d.	PC	23 May 1917	1	4	Cypress Hill; also 24 May, 1:2
Lovejoy	Frank E.	d.	SRR	23 May 1917	6	4	
Lovejoy	Frank E.	d.	PD	23 May 1917	8	2	
Loveland	Emmett A.	o.	PD	23 Nov. 1917	3	2	also 18 Dec., 3:2
Loveland	Ernest A.	o.	SRR	17 Dec. 1917	8	3	
Loveland	Mary E.	o.	SRR	17 Dec. 1917	8	3	
Loveland	Mary E.	o.	PD	23 Nov. 1917	3	2	also 18 Dec., 3:2

(1) Surname	(2) Given Name	(3)	(4)	(5) Date	(6) Pg	(7) Col	(8) Comments
Lowell	Frank	m.	SIT	28 Sept. 1918	3	1	
Lowell	Hattie J.	d.	SIT	8 Jan. 1916	1	3	Cypress Lawn, S.F.
Lowery	Florence E.	m.	PD	28 Dec. 1916	8	3	
Lowery	Florence E.	m.	SRR	28 Dec. 1916	7	4	
Lownes	J. C.	b.	HT	25 July 1918	1	3	
Lowrey	Helen	m.	PD	3 Aug. 1918	6	4	
Lowry	Gladys	d.	SRR	29 Jan. 1917	2	3	
Lowry	Gladys	d.	PD	30 Jan. 1917	6	2	
Lubbock	Harry	o.	PD	23 Apr. 1918	5	3	
Lucas	Edna	m.	PD	8 June 1917	3	3	
Lucas	Edna	m.	SRR	8 June 1917	6	2	
Lucas	Edna	m.	SRR	25 Apr. 1917	8	1	
Lucas	Edna	m.	PD	26 Apr. 1917	2	3	
Lucas	Emanuel	d.	PD	3 Jan. 1918	6	4	also 4 Jan., 4:2; 5 Jan., 6:4
Lucas	Lavina	m.	SRR	20 July 1916	8	2	
Lucas	Lavina	m.	SRR	15 Aug. 1916	8	5	
Lucas	Leta A.	m.	SRR	25 Apr. 1916	8	5	
Lucchetti	A.	d.	SRR	23 May 1916	4	2	Cloverdale
Lucchetti	Antone	d.	PA	22 May 1916	1	6	
Luce	Elmer	m.	PD	21 Nov. 1916	6	4	
Luce	Elmer E.	m.	SRR	20 Nov. 1916	8	5	
Lucifer	William	b.	SRR	17 May 1917	4	5	
Ludeman	John Herman	m.	PA	21 Jan. 1916	5	3	
Ludeman	John Herman	m.	PC	22 Jan. 1916	6	3	
Luff	Eva	d.	SRR	17 Jan. 1916	8	2	
Luff	Eva	o.	PC	18 Jan. 1916	6	1	
Luff	Eva	d.	PC	19 Jan. 1916	3	2	Cypress Hill
Luff	Eva	d.	PD	19 Jan. 1916	2	4	Petaluma
Luff	Eva C.	d.	PA	17 Jan. 1916	4	1&4	Cypress Hill; also 18 Jan., 5:4
Luglas	Hetta Frances	d.	PC	8 Jan. 1918	1	2	
Lukas	Lavina	m.	PD	16 Aug. 1916	6	4	also 22 Aug., 6:4
Lukens	Charles B.	o.	PC	3 Feb. 1918	5	5	
Lukens	Charles R.	o.	PA	1 Feb. 1918	6	2	
Lukens	Charles R.	o.	PC	7 Nov. 1918	4	4	
Lukens	Nellie	o.	PA	1 Feb. 1918	6	2	
Lukens	Nellie M.	o.	PC	3 Feb. 1918	5	5	
Lukens	Nellie M.	o.	PC	7 Nov. 1918	4	4	
Luker	Vera	o.	SRR	21 June 1916	1	2	also 4:1
Luker	Vesta	m.	PD	22 June 1916	7	3	
Lukins/Lukens	Charles R.	o.	PA	6 Nov. 1918	5	7	also 9 Nov., 8:7
Lukins/Lukens	Nellie	o.	PA	6 Nov. 1918	5	7	also 9 Nov., 8:7

(1) Surname	(2) Given Name	(3)	(4)	(5) Date	(6) Pg	(7) Col	(8) Comments
Lumsden	Charles	d.	PA	29 Oct. 1918	1	3	Cypress Hill; also 30 Oct., 4:2, 5:3; 1 Nov., 4:2; 2 Nov., 3:4
Lumsden	Charles	d.	PC	30 Oct. 1918	4	3	Cypress Hill; also 31 Oct., 2:3; 5 Nov., 4:4
Lumsden	Louise Ducker	m.	PA	19 July 1917	4	2	
Lumsden	Robert M.	m.	PC	4 Jan. 1918	4	5	
Lund	Annie	m.	PA	29 Sept. 1918	5	3	
Lundgren	Mr. & Mrs.	b.	PA	28 Dec. 1916	8	6	
Lundholm	Charles E.	b.	PC	28 Apr. 1918	6	5	
Lundholm	Ruth	d.	PA	1 Nov. 1918	1	2	also 5:3; 2 Nov., 2:3; 18 Nov., 4:5
Lundholm	Ruth	o.	PC	20 Mar. 1918	4	3	also 9 Apr., 8:4
Lundholm	Ruth V.	d.	PC	2 Nov. 1918	1	3	Morn Hill, Winchester, England; also 5:3; 6 Nov., 6:2; 16 Nov., 5:2; 19 Nov., 8:3; 27 Nov., 6:4
Lundholm	Viola	d.	PA	14 Oct. 1918	5	4	England; also 21 Oct., 5:4; 1 Nov., 1:2
Lundholm	Viola	d.	PC	15 Oct. 1918	1	4	South Sea, England; also 16 Oct., 8:4; 17 Oct., 8:4; 22 Oct., 4:4
Lundholm	Viola	d.	PD	17 Oct. 1918	8	1	England; also 22 Oct., 2:2
Lundholm	Viola	d.	PC	2 Nov. 1918	1	3	Morn Hill, Winchester, England; also 19 Nov., 8:3; 27 Nov., 6:4
Lundholm	Viola	o.	PC	9 Apr. 1918	8	4	
Lunger	Elmer	m.	SRR	3 Feb. 1917	10	2	
Lutgens	Harry M.	b.	PC	16 June 1918	8	4	
Luttrell	Frank M.	d.	PD	3 Dec. 1916	2	3	
Luttrell	H. L., Mrs.	d.	PD	24 Nov. 1918	8	3	Mountain Cemetery
Luttrell	Nettie Law	d.	SIT	23 Nov. 1918	1	5	
Lyle	George	m.	SRR	23 June 1917	12	3	
Lyman	Ann	d.	SRR	21 June 1917	5	1	
Lyman	Ann	d.	ST	22 June 1917	1	4	Odd Fellows Cem.
Lyman	Annie	d.	PA	21 June 1917	2	3	
Lyman	Annie	d.	PD	21 June 1917	2	6	also 23 June, 6:5
Lyman	Annie	d.	PC	22 June 1917	7	3	
Lyman	Bessie	d.	PC	30 Sept. 1916	3	4	Sebastopol; also 1 Oct., 4:6
Lyman	Bessie	d.	ST	30 Sept. 1916	1	4	also 7 Oct., 3:4
Lyman	Gene	b.	PA	25 Apr. 1918	4	2	
Lyman	James H.	o.	ST	30 Aug. 1918	1	5	
Lyman	James H.	o.	PD	31 Aug. 1918	7	3	
Lyman	James H.	o.	SRR	5 Dec. 1917	8	4	

(1) Surname	(2) Given Name	(3)	(4)	(5) Date	(6) Pg	(7) Col	(8) Comments
Lyman	Jean	b.	PC	25 Apr. 1918	4	4	
Lyman	Oma E.	o.	ST	30 Aug. 1918	1	5	
Lyman	Oma E.	o.	PD	31 Aug. 1918	7	3	
Lyman	Oma T.	o.	SRR	5 Dec. 1917	8	4	
Lyman	W. J., Mrs.	d.	PA	29 Sept. 1916	4	5	Sebastopol; also 2 Oct., 4:1
Lyman	W. J., Mrs.	d.	PD	30 Sept. 1916	8	3	
Lyman	W. J., Mrs.	d.	SRR	30 Sept. 1916	11	3	
Lyman	William J.	m.	SRR	27 June 1917	8	2	also 2 July, 6:2
Lyman	William J.	m.	ST	29 June 1917	1	2	
Lynch	Bertha W.	o.	PC	22 Aug. 1918	8	4	
Lynch	Catherine	d.	PA	17 June 1918	4	4	Calvary Cemetery; also 20 June, 8:5
Lynch	Catherine	d.	PC	18 June 1918	3	3	Calvary Cemetery; also 19 June, 5:4; 21 June, 4:1
Lynch	Catherine	d.	PD	19 June 1918	6	5	
Lynch	Elizabeth	d.	PA	10 Jan. 1916	5	5	Cypress Hill; also 11 Jan., 1:5
Lynch	Elizabeth	d.	PC	11 Jan. 1916	1	3	
Lynch	Elizabeth	d.	SRR	11 Jan. 1916	8	6	
Lynch	Elizabeth	d.	PC	12 Jan. 1916	4	3	Cypress Hill
Lynch	Elizabeth	d.	PD	12 Jan. 1916	6	4	
Lynch	Johanna	d.	PA	7 Dec. 1918	5	3	Calvary Cemetery; also 8:3; 9 Dec., 4:2
Lynch	Johanna	d.	PC	8 Dec. 1918	1	5	Calvary Cemetery; also 4:4; 10 Dec., 4:4
Lynch	Joseph H.	d.	SRR	21 Aug. 1916	8	3	
Lynch	Joseph H.	d.	PD	22 Aug. 1916	7	4	
Lynch	Marian	d.	PC	9 May 1918	3	4	
Lynch	Patrick Joseph	d.	PA	12 Aug. 1918	5	2	Calvary Cemetery; also 13 Aug., 5:7
Lynch	Patrick Joseph	d.	PC	13 Aug. 1918	4	3	also 18 Aug., 5:4
Lynch	Patrick Joseph	d.	PD	14 Aug. 1918	3	4	
Lynch	William Allan	o.	PC	22 Aug. 1918	8	4	
Lynn	Cenora M.	d.	PD	12 Oct. 1918	6	2	I.O.O.F. Cemetery; also 13 Oct., 4:2
Lynness	L., Mrs.	m.	SIT	28 Sept. 1918	3	1	
Lyons	Adelaide	d.	PD	20 June 1917	2	4	
Lyons	Adelene	d.	ST	22 June 1917	8	4	
Lyons	Virgil	m.	SRR	30 Nov. 1917	8	3	

M

(1) Surname	(2) Given Name	(3)	(4)	(5) Date	(6) Pg	(7) Col	(8) Comments
McAllister	Fred Shelby	m.	PD	28 Dec. 1916	8	3	
Maas	Charles F.	d.	PD	28 Jan. 1917	2	6	
Maas	Claus Frederich	d.	SRR	27 Jan. 1917	10	1	also 29 Jan., 5:2
Maas	Claus Frederick	d.	PC	27 Jan. 1917	5	3	also 8:4; 30 Jan., 4:2
Maass	Claus F.	d.	PA	26 Jan. 1917	5	4	Cypress Hill; also 29 Jan., 3:5
Macdonald	Helen Gertrude	m.	PC	14 Nov. 1917	6	3	also 15 Nov., 6:4
Macdonald	John Richard	m.	PC	8 July 1916	3	3	
Macfarlane	Dorothy	m.	PD	15 July 1917	2	4	
MacGregor	Milton	o.	SRR	8 Nov. 1917	8	6	
Mache	Americo F.	m.	SRR	16 May 1917	5	3	
Mache	Americo Franquille	m	PD	16 May 1917	3	4	
Mache	Americo Tranquilli	m.	PC	12 May 1917	5	5	
Mache	Angelo	d.	PD	17 Feb. 1917	8	2	also 18 Feb., 1:5; 20 Feb., 5:1
Mache	Angelo	d.	ST	17 Feb. 1917	5	3	also 24 Feb., 1:6
Mache	Angelo	d.	PC	18 Feb. 1917	4	4	Sebastopol; also 21 Feb., 3:2
Mache	Angelo	d.	PA	19 Feb. 1917	8	3	
Mache	John	d.	PC	15 Oct. 1916	1	3	Sebastopol; also 18 Oct., 1:6
Mache	John	d.	PD	15 Oct. 1916	5	1	also 19 Oct., 6:5
Mache	John	d.	SRR	16 Oct. 1916	5	5	Calvary Cemetery; also 17 Oct., 3:5
Mache	John	d.	ST	21 Oct. 1916	1	6	Masonic Cemetery
Mache	Stephen	m.	PC	5 Sept. 1918	5	4	
Mache	Stephen A.	m.	PA	4 Sept. 1918	8	2	
Macherini	F. E. "Toots"	m.	PD	9 Nov. 1917	5	3	
Machlan	Albert E.	d.	PC	20 Jan. 1918	8	2	
Mack	W. E.	b.	SRR	5 Jan. 1916	10	1	
Mackenzie	Elizabeth Graham	m.	PA	19 June 1917	4	5	also 21 June, 7:3; 29 June, 8:5; 5 July, 3:5
Mackenzie	Elizabeth Graham	m.	PC	20 June 1917	6	4	also 28 June, 8:2
Mackenzie	Elizabeth Graham	m.	PD	20 June 1917	2	3	
Mackenzie	Elizabeth Graham	m.	PC	4 July 1917	5	4	
Mackenzie	Miss	m.	SRR	30 June 1917	5	4	
MacKinnon	John	d.	PA	22 May 1917	5	1	
Mackinnon	John	d.	PD	22 May 1917	8	1	also 23 May, 1:3; 4:3; 26 May, 8:2
MacKinnon	John	d.	SRR	22 May 1917	5	3	I.O.O.F. Cemetery; also 25 May, 8:3
MacLane	Harold Austin	o.	PC	15 July 1916	3	3	

(1) Surname	(2) Given Name	(3)	(4)	(5) Date	(6) Pg	(7) Col	(8) Comments
MacQuiddy	Lynn	o.	SIT	16 June 1917	1	3	also 11 Aug., 1:1
MacQuiddy	Lynn	m.	SIT	25 May 1918	2	7	
Madalina	F.	b.	PA	23 Mar. 1916	4	2	
Maddalens/ Maddalina	Joseph	d.	PC	12 Jan. 1918	4	3	also 15 Jan., 6:5
Maddalina	Joseph	d.	PA	11 Jan. 1917	5	3	Calvary Cemetery; also 12 Jan., 8:3; 14 Jan., 8:3
Maddams	S. B.	b.	PA	25 Nov. 1918	7	5	
Madden	Esther	m.	PD	20 June 1917	8	2	
Maddock	Fred W.	o.	PA	6 July 1918	6	3	
Maddocks	Dorothy	m.	ST	22 Apr. 1916	1	2	
Maddocks	Dorothy Oliva	m.	PC	19 Apr. 1916	5	3	
Maddocks	Winthrop	d.	ST	30 Nov. 1917	1	2	
Maddocks	Winthrop	d.	PD	4 Dec. 1917	7	2	
Maddocks	Winthrop	d.	SRR	4 Dec. 1917	5	1	
Maddocks	Winthrop	d.	PC	5 Dec. 1917	8	3	
Maddox	Fred	o.	PA	22 Aug. 1918	3	3	
Maddox	Serena	m.	SRR	23 June 1917	5	1	
Maddux	Lee	b.	PD	24 Nov. 1917	2	3	
Maddux	Lee	b.	PD	8 Mar. 1916	8	2	
Maddux	Mark	d.	PD	14 May 1918	2	4	Fulkerson Cemetery; also 4:2; 15 May, 6:5
Maddux	Mark W.	d.	PC	14 May 1918	5	4	
Maddux	Mr. & Mrs.	b.	SRR	7 Mar. 1916	2	3	
Mader	Constance Marie	m.	PD	22 June 1918	6	1	also 23 June, 7:1
Madison	Clifton	d.	PD	24 Nov. 1918	6	3	France
Madison	Clifton	d.	HT	28 Nov. 1918	8	1	France
Madison	Clinton R.	d.	PA	25 Nov. 1918	3	3	France
Madison	Clinton R.	d.	SIT	30 Nov. 1918	1	3	
Madison	Clinton Rice	d.	PC	24 Nov. 1918	1	3	France
Madison	Hans	d.	PD	31 Dec. 1918	4	2	also 7:3
Madsen	John	d.	PA	9 Dec. 1918	3	3	France
Maffei	Annabile	b.	SIT	3 Nov. 1917	3	3	
Maffei	Annibale	o.	SIT	11 Aug. 1917	1	2	
Maffei	Annibale (son of)	d.	SIT	6 Oct. 1917	1	5	
Maffei	Oliva	o.	SIT	15 Dec. 1917	1	5	
Maffei	Olivio	o.	SIT	30 June 1917	3	2	
Maffia	John	d.	ST	5 Apr. 1918	1	5	
Maffia	M.	b.	PA	8 Mar. 1918	5	2&3	
Maffini	Earnest	d.	PD	11 Nov. 1918	4	5	also 12 Nov., 4:2
Magatelli	D.	m.	SRR	10 Jan. 1916	8	4	
Magatelli	Domencia	d.	PC	29 Dec. 1917	5	5	
Magatelli	Domenica	o&d	PD	28 Dec. 1917	8	1	also 29 Dec., 3:3, 4:2
Magatelli	Domenica	d.	SRR	28 Dec. 1917	8	3	Calvary Cemetery; also 31 Dec., 3:5

(1) Surname	(2) Given Name	(3)	(4)	(5) Date	(6) Pg	(7) Col	(8) Comments
Magatelli	Domenico	d.	PD	19 Apr. 1918	5	4	Calvary Cemetery; also 20 Apr., 4:2, 6:4; 23 Apr., 6:3
Magatelli	Domenico	o&d	PD	28 Dec. 1917	8	1	also 29 Dec., 3:3; 4:2; 30 Dec., 7:2
Magatelli	Dominico	d.	PA	18 Apr. 1918	4	4	also 19 Apr., 7:3
Magatelli	Dominico	o.	PC	28 Dec. 1917	1	3	
Magatilli	D.	m.	PD	11 Jan. 1916	3	1	
Magee	John Flemm	m.	PC	17 Aug. 1917	8	5	
Magetti	Robert	o.	PC	10 Dec. 1918	1	4	
Maggatelli	Domencio	o.	PC	19 Apr. 1918	6	5	
Maggenti	Antonio	m.	SRR	23 Oct. 1917	4	4	
Maggenti	Antonio	m.	HT	25 Oct. 1917	7	4	
Maggenti	Antonio	m.	PC	26 Oct. 1917	5	4	
Maggenti	Antonio	m.	PD	26 Oct. 1917	5	2	
Maggetti	Joseph	d.	PA	2 May 1918	5	4	Calvary Cemetery; also 3 May, 4:5; 4 May, 4:3
Maggetti	Joseph	d.	PC	2 May 1918	6	5	Calvary Cemetery; also 3 May, 5:1; 4 May, 8:2
Maggetti	Josephina	d.	PC	28 June 1917	1	6	also 29 June, 6:3; 30 June, 6:3
Maggetti	Josephine	d.	PA	28 June 1917	4	1	Calvary Cemetery; also 5:7
Maggetti	Josephine	d.	PC	1 July 1917	1	3	
Maggetti	Robert	o.	PA	9 Dec. 1918	8	1	
Magnetelli	D., Mrs.	d.	PA	29 Dec. 1917	6	5	
Magowan	Agnes	d.	PA	20 May 1916	4	1	Cypress Hill; also 22 May, 5:3
Magowan	Agnes	d.	PD	21 May 1916	3	3	Cypress Hill Cemetery, Petaluma; also 23 May, 3:4
Magowan	Agnes	d.	SRR	22 May 1916	4	1	
Magowan	Agnes S.	d.	PC	21 May 1916	5	2&6	Cypress Hill; also 22 May, 4:3
Magowan	Samuel James	d.	PA	7 Jan. 1918	4	4	Cypress Hill; also 8 Jan., 5:4
Magowan	Samuel James, Jr.	d.	PC	8 Jan. 1918	3	1&3	also 9 Jan., 3:1
Magowan	Samuel James, Jr.	d.	PD	8 Jan. 1918	5	3	
Maher	Bridget	d.	PD	7 Nov. 1916	6	3	
Maher	Margaret	d.	SRR	6 Nov. 1916	9	6	also 10:6; 8 Nov., 2:4
Mahler	Charles	o.	PC	1 Mar. 1918	6	4	
Mahler	Charles	m.	PC	25 Sept. 1917	1	5	
Mahler	Charles E.	m.	PA	25 Sept. 1917	4	6	
Mahler	Henry J.	m.	PC	21 June 1916	8	3	also 27 June, 5:2
Mahler	Henry, Jr.	m.	PA	20 June 1916	1	7	also 21 June, 5:1; 26 June, 5:4

(1) Surname	(2) Given Name	(3)	(4)	(5) Date	(6) Pg	(7) Col	(8) Comments
Mahoney	J. M.	b.	PA	16 Feb. 1918	5	1	
Mahoney	J. M.	b.	PC	17 Feb. 1918	5	6	
Mahoney	Mary E.	d.	PC	22 May 1916	2	1	Sonoma
Mahoney	Redmond H.	m.	PD	11 July 1918	5	4	
Maile	Robert	b.	PD	8 Mar. 1917	8	2	
Maile	Robert	b.	SRR	8 Mar. 1917	5	4	
Makee	Alva N. Charlotte	m.	PD	22 June 1918	5	4	
Makee	George	m.	SRR	23 June 1917	12	3	also 25 June, 6:1; 3 July, 6:4
Makee	Mr.	m.	PC	24 June 1917	5	4	
Makee	Mr.	m.	ST	29 June 1917	6	5	
Maker	Ernest	d.	PA	5 Nov. 1918	5	6	
Makham	Andrew	d.	PA	2 Mar. 1918	8	1	also 6 Mar., 4:4
Malacarne	May	m.	PD	28 Dec. 1918	8	3	
Malacarne	May H.	m.	SIT	28 Dec. 1918	1	3	
Malacreadi	M., Mrs.	d.	PD	22 June 1918	7	1	Druid's Cemetery
Malacreadi	M., Mrs.	d.	PC	23 June 1918	8	3	Druid's Cemetery
Malacreda	Marcello	d.	ST	10 Feb. 1917	8	4	
Malacreda	Marcello	d.	PD	8 Feb. 1917	2	2	Druid's Cemetery; also 9 Feb., 4:2
Malacreda	Marcello	d.	SRR	8 Feb. 1917	2	3	
Malacreda	Marcello	d.	PC	9 Feb. 1917	3	5	
Malacredi	Margharita	d.	ST	22 June 1918	1	2	
Malandra	Ferdinand	o.	PC	10 Aug. 1917	3	5	
Maldonaldo	Mercedes Angulo	d.	SIT	2 Feb. 1918	1	6	
Mallory	Elaine	d.	PD	4 Mar. 1916	8	4	
Mallory	Elaine	d.	SRR	4 Mar. 1916	5	3	also 6 Mar., 8:2
Mallory	Margaret F.	m.	PD	8 Sept. 1916	3	3	
Mallory	Wes	o.	PD	15 May 1918	3	4	
Mallory	West	o.	PD	4 July 1918	6	1	also 8 Aug., 7:1
Malm	Irene	m.	PD	19 Apr. 1917	2	3	
Malm	Irene	m.	SRR	19 Apr. 1917	3	1	
Malmgren	Margareta C.	d.	PA	6 May 1918	4	6	Akron, Iowa; also 13 May, 4:4; 24 May, 8:3
Malmgren	Margreta Christina	d.	PC	7 May 1918	6	3	also 14 May, 3:1
Malone	Martin	d.	PD	18 Jan. 1916	5	3	Annapolis Cemetery
Malone	Martin A.	d.	SRR	18 Jan. 1916	2	3	
Malone	Susan	d.	PA	3 Dec. 1918	8	3	
Malone	Susan	d.	PC	3 Dec. 1918	1	2	
Malone	Susan	d.	PD	5 Dec. 1918	6	7	
Maloney	Mary E.	d.	SIT	27 May 1916	1	3	
Maloney	Redmond J.	m.	PC	11 July 1918	6	3	
Maloof	Fifie	m.	PD	28 Dec. 1918	3	1	
Maloof	Helen	d.	SRR	5 Nov. 1917	8	6	
Maloof	Helen	d.	PD	6 Nov. 1917	5	3	also 7 Nov., 2:3

(1) Surname	(2) Given Name	(3)	(4)	(5) Date	(6) Pg	(7) Col	(8) Comments
Maloof	Helen Jabor	d.	PC	6 Nov. 1917	3	4	
Malpiede	John, Sr.	d.	HT	15 Aug. 1918	8	3	
Malsetti	Henry	m.	PC	16 Aug. 1917	6	2	
Mambretti	Alex	o.	PD	16 Nov. 1917	6	2	also 2 Dec., 5:7
Mambretti	Alexander	o.	SRR	27 Dec. 1917	8	4	
Mambretti	Leana Fresti	o.	PD	16 Nov. 1917	6	2	also 2 Dec., 5:7
Mambretti	Lena Foresti	o.	SRR	27 Dec. 1917	8	4	
Manakins	Bert	m.	PA	31 Dec. 1917	4	2	
Mancini	Pietro	d.	PD	19 Nov. 1918	4	2	also 5:4; 21 Nov., 3:4
Mane	Ann	o.	PC	1 Apr. 1916	5	5	
Mane	Anna	o.	SRR	30 June 1916	1	5	
Mane	Anna	o.	PC	1 July 1916	6	3	also 4 Aug., 3:5
Mane	James	o.	SRR	30 June 1916	1	5	
Mane	James	o.	PA	1 July 1916	3	5	
Mane	James	o.	PC	1 July 1916	6	3	also 4 Aug., 3:5
Mane	James	o.	PC	1 Apr. 1916	5	5	
Mane	Paul	m.	PC	14 Aug. 1917	5	1	
Maney	Josephine	m.	PA	16 May 1916	7	5	also 7 June, 5:3
Maney	Josephine	m.	PD	8 June 1916	2	1	also 11 June, 7:4
Maney	Josephine Mason	m.	PC	16 May 1916	5	1	also 7 June, 5:4
Mangan	Matthew	m.	PC	24 Feb. 1917	1	5	
Mangiatini	Marcisso	m.	PD	18 Nov. 1917	10	3	
Manina	Julius	m.	PD	19 Jan. 1918	8	2	
Mann	Florence	m.	PD	29 Jan. 1918	5	3	
Mann	Joseph	m.	SRR	23 Nov. 1916	5	1	
Mann	Joseph	m.	SRR	10 Jan. 1917	4	5	
Mann	Joseph	m.	PD	11 Jan. 1917	1	7	also 13 Jan., 6:3
Mann	Joseph	m.	HT	18 Jan. 1917	6	4	
Manney	Edward T.	d.	PA	18 Nov. 1918	5	3	
Manning	James Joseph	d.	PA	20 Jan. 1916	4	1	Cypress Hill; also 21 Jan., 10:6; 22 Jan., 6:3
Manning	James Joseph	o.	PC	21 Jan. 1916	1	6	
Manning	James Joseph	d.	SRR	21 Jan. 1916	8	4	
Manning	John Joseph	d.	PD	21 Jan. 1916	5	1	
Mannuck	Mike	m.	PC	28 Oct. 1916	5	3	
Mano	Paul	m.	PA	14 Aug. 1917	5	2	
Mansfield	Eliza/Elizabeth	d.	PD	13 Apr. 1918	2	2	Forestville; also 4:3; 14 Apr., 4:2
Manton	Edward George	d.	PD	14 Sept. 1916	8	5	San Francisco
Mantua	Julius	m.	PA	19 Jan. 1918	3	2	
Mantua	Julius	m.	ST	25 Jan. 1918	3	4	
Manuel	H. C.	d.	PC	16 Apr. 1918	2	2	
Manuel	Harvey	d.	PD	6 Apr. 1918	8	3	
Manuel	Hiram C.	d.	SIT	13 Apr. 1918	1	7	
Maracci	Albert	d.	PA	8 Oct. 1917	5	3	

(1) Surname	(2) Given Name	(3)	(4)	(5) Date	(6) Pg	(7) Col	(8) Comments
Maracci	Alfred	d.	SRR	8 Oct. 1917	1	5	
Maracci	Alfred	d.	PC	9 Oct. 1917	1	6	
Marall	Frank	d.	PA	24 Jan. 1916	6	4	
Marall	Frank S.	d.	PC	25 Jan. 1916	6	4	also 27 Jan., 8:4
Marango	George Frederick	m.	PC	5 June 1918	5	3	
Marango	Verlie	m.	PA	5 June 1918	8	5	aka Verlie Snider/Snyder; also 17 June, 5:4
Marchant	Martha J.	d.	PD	15 Aug. 1916	1	4	also 26 Aug., 8:1
Marchant	Martha J.	d.	SRR	25 Aug. 1916	4	2	also 26 Aug., 5:4
Marchant	Martha Jane	d.	PC	2 Sept. 1916	6	3	Santa Rosa
Marcher	Hazel	d.	PD	2 Oct. 1918	5	3	
Marchi	Oliva	d.	PD	8 June 1918	8	4	
Marchi	Oliva	d.	PC	10 June 1918	6	5	
Marcucci	Fortunato	d.	PA	18 Apr. 1918	8	3	Calvary Cemetery; also 20 Apr., 5:2
Marcucci	Fortunato	d.	PC	19 Apr. 1918	3	3&4	Calvary Cemetery; also 20 Apr., 3:4; 21 Apr., 8:2
Marcucci	Peter	d.	SIT	10 Feb. 1917	1	7	also 4:2
Marcucci	Peter	d.	HT	8 Feb. 1917	5	3	
Marcucci	Peter	d.	PD	8 Feb. 1917	6	2	
Marcucci	Peter	d.	PA	7 Feb. 1917	6	5	
Marcus	Frank G.	m.	SRR	3 Aug. 1916	2	6	also 7 Aug., 7:3
Marcus	Henry G.	m.	SRR	3 Aug. 1916	2	6	also 7 Aug., 7:3; 8 Aug., 6:1; 9 Aug., 2:3
Marcus	Martha	m.	PA	20 Mar. 1916	5	3	
Marcus	Martha	d.	PC	21 Mar. 1916	5	3	
Marcy	Zeph	o.	SIT	11 Aug. 1917	1	1	
Marcy	Zeph	o.	SIT	29 Sept. 1917	1	1	
Mari	Battista	o.	SRR	11 Jan. 1916	8	1	
Marin	Harold Jesse	d.	PC	23 July 1918	6	2	France
Marion	Angelo	m.	PC	7 Apr. 1917	5	3	also 8 Apr., 5:3
Marion	Angelo N.	m.	PD	8 Apr. 1917	7	3	
Marion	Nellie	d.	PC	26 Jan. 1916	4	3	Calvary Cemetery
Marion	Nellie E.	d.	PC	25 Jan. 1916	8	3	Calvary Cemetery
Marion	Nellie Ellen	d.	PA	24 Jan. 1916	4	3	Calvary Cemetery; also 25 Jan., 8:3
Marion	Vernal	m.	PA	12 July 1916	5	1	
Marion	Vernal K.	m.	PC	13 July 1916	4	2	
Marjarolf	A., Mrs.	d.	PD	6 Jan. 1917	3	2	
Markham	Andrew	d.	PC	2 Mar. 1918	4	5	also 6 Mar., 8:2
Markham	Sanford	m.	SRR	15 June 1917	8	6	
Markley	W. A.	d.	PA	28 Oct. 1916	1	3	
Marnell	Thomas J.	d.	PD	14 Feb. 1918	1	3	Santa Cruz
Maroni	George	m.	PC	29 May 1917	4	1	

(1) Surname	(2) Given Name	(3)	(4)	(5) Date	(6) Pg	(7) Col	(8) Comments
Maroni	George	m.	SRR	28 Apr. 1917	10	3	also 30 Apr., 4:2
Maroni	George	m.	PD	29 Apr. 1917	5	3	
Marquart	George	m.	PD	28 Oct. 1917	8	2	
Marquart	George S.	m.	PC	30 Oct. 1917	3	4	
Marriott	W. Joseph Stacey	m.	ST	7 Sept. 1916	8	4	
Marriott	W. Joseph Stacey	m.	PA	8 Sept. 1917	4	5	
Marrithews	Robert	b.	PD	7 May 1918	2	3	
Mars	Charles W.	b.	SRR	28 May 1917	5	3	
Marsden	Virginia	m.	HT	16 Aug. 1917	4	4	
Marsden	Virginia	m.	PD	22 Aug. 1917	8	5	
Marshall	Annie	m.	PA	8 June 1918	3	5	
Marshall	Antone	b.	PA	15 Sept. 1917	5	2	
Marshall	Aretus	d.	SRR	13 Oct. 1917	10	4&5	also 15 Oct., 3:6
Marshall	Aretus	b.	SRR	8 Aug. 1916	7	4	
Marshall	Elsie J.	m.	PD	2 Mar. 1918	2	3	
Marshall	Frank	m.	PD	17 Feb. 1918	8	2	
Marshall	Frank A.	m.	PD	23 Nov. 1917	5	4	
Marshall	Frank H.	m.	SRR	23 Nov. 1917	6	5	
Marshall	Frank H.	m.	PC	24 Nov. 1917	5	2	
Marshall	Hattie	d.	PC	13 Feb. 1918	1	2	Graton; also 19 Feb., 8:4
Marshall	Hattie	d.	PD	14 Feb. 1918	4	3	also 20 Feb., 7:1
Marshall	Hattie	d.	ST	22 Feb. 1918	1	1	
Marshall	Ida	d.	PD	1 Jan. 1918	8	3	
Marshall	Ida F.	o.	PA	21 Aug. 1918	3	3	portrait
Marshall	James	d.	PA	25 Jan. 1916	7	3	Calvary Cemetery; also 8:1; 26 Jan., 7:4; 27 Jan., 8:5
Marshall	James	p.	PA	29 Jan. 1916	4	3	
Marshall	James George	o.	PC	26 Jan. 1916	3	1	
Marshall	James George	d.	PC	28 Jan. 1916	4	3	Cypress Hill
Marshall	M. J., Mrs.	d.	SRR	19 Dec. 1916	3	4	Green Valley Cemetery; also 21 Dec., 9:3
Marshall	M. J., Mrs.	d.	PC	20 Dec. 1916	1	5	Methodist Cemetery, Green Valley
Marshall	M. J., Mrs.	d.	PD	20 Dec. 1916	2	3	also 23 Dec., 2:3
Marshall	M. P., Mrs.	d.	PA	20 Dec. 1916	3	1	
Marshall	Sarah J.	m.	PC	22 Feb. 1916	5	4	
Marshall	Tony	m.	PD	29 Sept. 1918	7	3	
Marshall	W. W., Mrs.	d.	PC	7 Aug. 1917	5	5	Willows; also 9 Aug., 3:2
Marslof	Charles J.	m.	PC	1 Oct. 1916	8	2	also 2 Oct., 2:1
Martin	Anna	m.	PD	1 May 1918	2	3	
Martin	Charles	m.	PA	16 Feb. 1918	8	3	
Martin	Charles	m.	PD	19 Feb. 1918	7	1	
Martin	Charles L.	m.	PC	16 Feb. 1918	4	2	also 17 Feb., 8:3

(1) Surname	(2) Given Name	(3)	(4)	(5) Date	(6) Pg	(7) Col	(8) Comments
Martin	Chester Miller	m.	PC	18 Apr. 1917	3	3	
Martin	Dexter M.	d.	PA	5 Feb. 1916	5	3	also 7 Feb., 8:3
Martin	Edward Franklin	m.	PA	26 July 1916	4	3	
Martin	Edward Franklin	m.	SRR	26 July 1916	5	3	
Martin	Edward Franklin	m.	PD	27 July 1916	8	2	
Martin	Effie	m.	SRR	13 Feb. 1917	2	2	
Martin	Effie	m.	CR	17 Feb. 1917	1	4	
Martin	Elizabeth	m.	PA	21 July 1917	4	3	
Martin	Elizabeth	m.	PC	21 July 1917	5	2	
Martin	Elizabeth	m.	ST	3 Aug. 1917	3	3	
Martin	Elizabeth Graham	m.	PD	22 July 1917	7	4	
Martin	Francis W.	m.	PA	24 Apr. 1918	4	5	
Martin	Francis W.	m.	PC	28 Apr. 1918	6	2	also 30 Apr., 5:4
Martin	Harold Jesse	d.	PD	24 July 1918	8	2	France
Martin	Joseph	d.	PA	11 Jan. 1916	8	3	
Martin	Joseph	d.	PD	12 Jan. 1916	8	3	
Martin	Josephine	m.	PD	10 Oct. 1916	2	4	
Martin	Josephine	m.	PC	11 Oct. 1916	6	1	
Martin	Josephine	m.	PA	3 Oct. 1916	5	2	
Martin	Josephine	m.	SRR	3 Oct. 1916	8	3	
Martin	Josephine	m.	ST	7 Oct. 1916	1	2	also 14 Oct., 1:2
Martin	Lois J.	m.	PD	23 Nov. 1918	1	5	
Martin	Marie	m.	PD	1 Sept. 1916	2	2	
Martin	Marie	m.	SRR	1 Sept. 1916	3	5	
Martin	Marion Brown	d.	PC	15 Dec. 1917	8	2	
Martin	Mary Ann	d.	PC	3 Sept. 1916	5	2	
Martin	Maude E.	m.	PC	18 Apr. 1917	3	3	
Martin	Olive	d.	PD	30 Jan. 1918	3	4	
Martin	Olive	d.	PA	31 Jan. 1918	4	3	
Martin	Paul	b.	PA	13 Feb. 1918	5	7	
Martin	Sarah	m.	PC	7 Apr. 1917	5	3	also 8 Apr., 5:3
Martin	Sarah M.	m.	PD	8 Apr. 1917	7	3	
Martinelli	Guiseppe	d.	PC	20 July 1918	8	2	
Martinelli	Guiseppe	d.	PD	20 July 1918	4	2	Sebastopol; also 23 July, 6:5
Martinelli	Guiseppe	d.	ST	26 July 1918	3	2	
Martinelli	Guiseppe	d.	PD	1 Aug. 1918	2	3	
Martinelli	Irene	d.	PA	28 Aug. 1917	1	4	Olema; also 29 Aug., 3:6
Martinelli	Irene	d.	PD	29 Aug. 1917	8	4	
Martinelli	Robert	b.	PA	4 May 1916	4	5	
Martinelli	Robert	b.	PA	29 July 1918	5	6	
Martinelli	Robert A.	b.	PA	7 May 1917	8	6	
Martinez	Leia	d.	SRR	10 Jan. 1916	8	5	
Martini	Albert	o.	ST	20 Sept. 1918	3	2	

(1) Surname	(2) Given Name	(3)	(4)	(5) Date	(6) Pg	(7) Col	(8) Comments
Martini	Emilio	d.	HT	24 Feb. 1916	1	5	
Martini	Louis	d.	PA	15 June 1918	5	6	
Martini	Louis	d.	PC	16 June 1918	3	4	Calvary Cemetery; also 18 June, 5:4
Martinoni	Matilda	d.	SIT	7 Sept. 1918	1	5	also 14 Sept., 2:3
Marucci	Peter	d.	ST	17 Feb. 1917	3	2	
Marx	Margaret Houston	d.	SRR	12 Sept. 1917	8	5	Oakland
Marzarolf	A., Mrs.	d.	SRR	5 Jan. 1917	8	5	
Marzolf	Antoinette	d.	PA	5 Jan. 1917	5	1	Cypress Hill
Marzolf	Antonette	d.	PC	6 Jan. 1917	5	3	Cypress Hill; also 9 Jan., 1:4
Marzolf	Charles	m.	PA	15 Sept. 1916	4	4	also 30 Sept., 5:4; 2 Oct., 5:3
Marzolf	Charles J.	m.	PC	26 Aug. 1916	5	4	
Marzolf	Fred	m.	PC	16 Feb. 1917	8	2	
Marzolf	Fred	m.	SRR	16 Feb. 1917	6	5	
Marzolf	Frederick G.	m.	PC	21 Jan. 1917	5	4	
Marzolf	Frederick G.	m.	PA	22 Jan. 1917	5	3	also 15 Feb., 4:5
Mascarini	Erminia	m.	SRR	22 Nov. 1916	5	2	
Mascenti	A.	b.	PA	21 Sept. 1918	1	5	
Mascherini	F. E., Jr.	m.	HT	8 Nov. 1917	1	1	
Mascherini	Faust E., Jr.	m.	SRR	13 Nov. 1917	7	5	
Maschiorini	Henry T.	m.	SIT	5 Jan. 1918	3	3	
Masciaroni	Erminia	m.	PA	21 Nov. 1916	5	3	also 22 Nov., 8:6
Masciaroni	Florence	m.	PA	11 Oct. 1916	4	4	
Masciorini	Erminia	m.	PC	29 Oct. 1916	5	2	also 22 Nov., 4:2
Masciorini	Florence	m.	PC	8 Oct. 1916	4	2	also 11 Oct., 1:2; 12 Oct., 1:5
Masciorini	Florence	m.	SRR	9 Oct. 1916	4	5	
Masciorini	Henry T.	m.	PC	25 Dec. 1917	1	3	also 28 Dec., 4:6; 29 Dec., 5:6
Masciorini	Henry T.	m.	PA	26 Dec. 1917	7	4	
Mascoroni	Erminia	m.	PD	22 Nov. 1916	3	2	
Masdonair	Helen Gertrude	m.	PC	10 Nov. 1917	1	2	
Mason	Elizabeth	o.	PD	19 Apr. 1916	7	1	
Mason	Frank	o.	SRR	18 Apr. 1916	6	3	
Mason	Frank	o.	PD	19 Apr. 1916	7	1	
Mason	Garret C.	d.	HT	17 Jan. 1918	3	1	
Mason	Garrett C.	d.	PA	12 Jan. 1917	5	3	Cypress Hill; also 14 Jan., 5:4, 8:6; 16 Jan., 5:4, 8:3&5; 17 Jan., 5:4
Mason	Garrett C.	d.	PC	13 Jan. 1918	1	3	Cypress Hill; also 15 Jan., 2:1; 17 Jan., 1:6; 18 Jan., 8:5
Mason	Garrett C.	d.	PD	13 Jan. 1918	5	4	
Mason	Katie	d.	PC	28 Dec. 1916	1	5	also 29 Dec., 8:1

(1) Surname	(2) Given Name	(3)	(4)	(5) Date	(6) Pg	(7) Col	(8) Comments
Mason	Lizzie	o.	SRR	18 Apr. 1916	6	3	
Mason	Lucy	b.	SRR	27 July 1916	1	3	
Mason	William, Mrs.	d.	ST	24 May 1918	4	4	
Mason	William, Mrs.	d.	PD	30 May 1918	5	1	
Massanti	A.	m.	SRR	26 Oct. 1916	5	1	
Massie	J. W.	d.	PA	22 July 1916	3	4	
Massie	James A.	d.	PC	22 July 1916	1	2	
Masters	Gertrude McPherson	d.	SRR	7 Nov. 1916	8	1	also 9 Nov. 5:2
Masters	Gertrude McPherson	d.	PD	8 Nov. 1916	2	5	Beeson Cemetery; also 9 Nov., 7:4; 10 Nov., 5:3
Masters	Larry	m.	PD	29 Aug. 1918	2	4	
Masters	Leslie	m.	SRR	25 Sept. 1916	3	6	
Mastin	D. M.	d.	PC	8 Feb. 1916	5	4	Cypress Hill
Mastin	Dexter M.	d.	PC	6 Feb. 1916	1	3	
Mastrup	James	d.	PC	7 Jan. 1917	8	4	also 9 Jan., 3:4
Mastrup	James	d.	PA	8 Jan. 1917	1	4	
Mastrup	James	d.	PD	9 Jan. 1917	7	2	
Matazoni	Joseph	b.	SRR	29 Sept. 1917	8	6	
Maters	L. H.	o.	ST	30 Nov. 1917	5	4	
Mathers	Wes	o.	PD	12 Sept. 1918	2	3	
Mathers	Wesley	o.	ST	13 Sept. 1918	1	2	
Mathews	Harry	d.	PC	1 Sept. 1916	8	1	
Mathews	John	d.	PC	8 Oct. 1916	4	1	Cypress Hill; also 10 Oct., 4:2
Mathews	Maryetta	d.	HT	5 Oct. 1916	4	1	
Mathews	Mildred	m.	PA	1 Nov. 1917	5	2	
Mathewson	Frances	d.	SIT	8 July 1916	1	7	
Mathewson	Harley P., Mrs.	d.	PD	13 July 1916	6	4	
Mathewson	Harley P., Mrs.	d.	SRR	13 July 1916	5	3	
Mathias	A. B.	b.	PA	27 June 1916	5	4	
Matieu	Jose	b.	PD	1 Feb. 1916	8	3	
Matson	Arthur	b.	PC	6 June 1917	8	4	
Matsuma	S.	b.	PA	31 Dec. 1917	4	5	
Mattazoni	Amiel	m.	PD	2 Apr. 1918	3	3	
Mattei	V. C.	b.	PA	22 July 1918	3	6	also 8:1
Mattei	V. C.	b.	PD	24 July 1918	7	2	
Matthew	Hettie Belle	m.	SRR	3 Aug. 1916	2	6	also 7 Aug., 7:3; 8 Aug., 6:1; 9 Aug., 2:3
Matthew	W. S.	b.	PD	28 May 1918	3	4	
Matthew	Winfield Scott	b.	PD	3 Sept. 1916	7	2	
Matthew	Winfield Scott, Jr.	b.	PD	27 Aug. 1916	1	6	
Matthews	Harry	d.	PA	30 Aug. 1916	7	4	
Matthews	Harry	d.	PD	31 Aug. 1916	8	3	10 yrs

(1) Surname	(2) Given Name	(3)	(4)	(5) Date	(6) Pg	(7) Col	(8) Comments
Matthews	James	b.	PD	1 Jan. 1916	6	4	
Matthews	John	m.	PD	25 May 1918	5	6	
Matthews	John W.	d.	PA	9 Oct. 1916	8	5	Cypress Hill
Matthews	Maryella	d.	PD	1 Oct. 1916	7	3	also 6 Oct., 6:3
Matthews	Maryette	d.	SRR	2 Oct. 1916	6	1	Shiloh Cemetery
Matthews	Mildred	m.	PC	1 Nov. 1917	3	4	also 25 Nov., 5:3
Matthews	Mildred May	m.	PA	26 Nov. 1917	5	5	
Matthews	Sarah	d.	PA	21 July 1917	8	4	Cypress Hill
Matthews	Sarah H.	d.	PC	22 July 1917	5	3	Cypress Hill
Matthews	Wesley	o.	PC	6 Dec. 1918	1	3	
Matthias	John Brown	b.	PC	14 Nov. 1916	4	5	
Mattos	N. P.	b.	PA	22 Sept. 1916	4	4	
Mattri	Antone	b.	PC	21 Feb. 1917	5	2	
Matzen	Arthur	b.	PA	8 Mar. 1916	5	4	
Matzen	Peter	m.	PC	8 Sept. 1916	8	3	
Matzen	Theodore	b.	PA	7 Apr. 1916	5	5	
Maury	Nellie	m.	SRR	24 Jan. 1916	1	2	
Maxenti	Amencio (son of)	b&d	PC	8 Aug. 1917	5	4	also 9 Aug., 4:1
Maxwell	J. H.	d.	SRR	7 Nov. 1916	3	3	
May	Anna F.	d.	PA	1 May 1916	2	7	
May	Charles	d.	PA	19 May 1916	2	2	
May	Charles	d.	PC	20 May 1916	1	5	San Francisco; also 21 May, 5:1
May	Charles	d.	PD	20 May 1916	8	1	
May	Emily	m.	SRR	6 May 1916	10	5	
May	Emily	m.	PD	7 May 1916	3	1	
Mayer	Emily	m.	SRR	23 Nov. 1917	5	1	
Mayes	Ethel Piezzi	d.	PC	2 Nov. 1918	1	2	also 6 Nov., 3:4
Mayes	Ethel Piezzi	d.	PD	2 Nov. 1918	3	1	I.O.O.F. Cemetery; also 4:2; 5 Nov., 2:5
Mayes	Ethel Piezzi	d.	PA	5 Nov. 1918	4	6	
Mayfield	G. W.	o.	PA	2 Mar. 1916	7	4	
Mayfield	George W.	o.	SRR	28 Apr. 1916	5	2	
Mayfield	George W.	o.	PC	30 Apr. 1916	2	2	
Mayfield	Lucy A.	o.	PA	2 Mar. 1916	7	4	
Mayfield	Lucy A.	o.	SRR	28 Apr. 1916	5	2	
Mayfield	Lucy A.	o.	PC	30 Apr. 1916	2	2	
Mayfield	Milton	d.	SRR	30 July 1917	8	3	
Mayfield	Mr.	d.	PD	31 July 1917	4	2	Rural Cemetery
Mayfield	Mr. & Mrs.	o.	SRR	1 Mar. 1916	10	3	
Maynor	Nellie	d.	PD	20 July 1918	7	1	Sebastopol
Mays	Anna	d.	SRR	19 Oct. 1917	8	2	also 20 Oct., 10:2; 22 Oct., 4:4
Mays	Joseph B.	o.	SRR	5 Sept. 1917	4	4	
Mays	Katheryn	o.	SRR	5 Sept. 1917	4	4	

(1) Surname	(2) Given Name	(3)	(4)	(5) Date	(6) Pg	(7) Col	(8) Comments
McCaubrey	George T.	d.	HT	27 Jan. 1916	5	2	
McCaughey	James, Mrs.	d.	PA	11 Dec. 1917	7	4	Sebastopol
McCaughey	James, Mrs.	d.	PD	11 Dec. 1917	8	3	Sebastopol; also 13 Dec., 4:2; 14 Dec., 6:4
McCaughey	James, Mrs.	d.	SRR	11 Dec. 1917	5	3	Sebastopol
McCaughey	James, Mrs.	d.	PC	12 Dec. 1917	5	4	Sebastopol
McCaughey	Nancy	d.	ST	14 Dec. 1917	1	5	also 21 Dec., 7:2
McCaw	Wallace	d.	PA	12 Dec. 1917	6	7	Oakland
McClain	Lavina	m.	PA	27 Nov. 1918	8	2	
McClary	Bell	m.	ST	8 Jan. 1916	1	6	
McClary	Belle	m.	PD	7 Jan. 1916	2	2	
McClary	Belle	m.	SRR	7 Jan. 1916	3	3	
McClear	J. M., Mrs.	d.	PD	14 Dec. 1918	6	2	Riverside Cemetery
McClear	M. J., Mrs.	d.	CR	13 Dec. 1918	1	5	Riverside Cemetery
McClish	Harold R.	m.	PD	1 Dec. 1917	2	1	also 2 Dec., 5:5
McClish	Harold R.	m.	SRR	1 Dec. 1917	3	2	
McClish	Harold Ralph	m.	HT	6 Dec. 1917	1	4	
McClure	Mary	d.	PC	7 Jan. 1917	5	1	also 10 Jan., 4:1
McConnell	Fred	b.	SRR	25 July 1916	5	1	
McConnell	Fred	b.	HT	27 July 1916	4	5	
McConnell	Fred W.	b.	HT	6 June 1918	8	4	
McConnell	Fred W.	b.	PD	7 June 1918	3	5	
McConnell	Pearl	m.	SRR	6 Apr. 1916	2	4	
McCoon	Horace C.	d.	HT	13 July 1916	5	5	
McCord	Jane	d.	SRR	13 Feb. 1917	8	5	I.O.O.F. Cemetery; also 15 Feb., 8:1
McCord	Jane	d.	PD	14 Feb. 1917	3	4	also 4:2
McCord	Julius C.	o.	SRR	31 May 1916	5	3	
McCord	Julius C.	o.	HT	1 June 1916	4	3	
McCord	Julius C.	o.	SRR	21 Aug. 1916	8	5	
McCord	Julius E.	o.	PD	22 Aug. 1916	7	5	
McCord	Mary	o.	PD	22 Aug. 1916	7	5	
McCord	Mary	m.	HT	27 Sept. 1917	4	3	
McCord	Mary E.	o.	SRR	31 May 1916	5	3	
McCord	Mary E.	o.	HT	1 June 1916	4	3	
McCord	Mary E.	o.	SRR	21 Aug. 1916	8	5	
McCormack	Percival	m.	PA	19 Dec. 1917	4	3	
McCormack	Percival	m.	PD	20 Dec. 1917	5	3	
McCormack	W. A.	d.	PC	22 Feb. 1918	5	4	
McCormick	Percival	m.	PC	20 Dec. 1917	5	3	
McCoubrey	George E.	d.	PC	25 Jan. 1916	6	2	Cypress Hill
McCoubrey	George Frederick	d.	PA	21 Jan. 1916	5	5	Cypress Hill; also 24 Jan., 7:4
McCoubrey	George T.	o.	PC	21 Jan. 1916	1	5	
McCoubrey	George T.	d.	SRR	21 Jan. 1916	8	3	

(1) Surname	(2) Given Name	(3)	(4)	(5) Date	(6) Pg	(7) Col	(8) Comments
McCoubrey	George T.	d.	PD	22 Jan. 1916	6	4	
McCoy	Olive L.	m.	PD	24 Aug. 1916	7	4	
McCray	Eva	d.	PD	14 Feb. 1917	8	3	
McCray	Eva	d.	SRR	14 Feb. 1917	5	5	
McCray	Warren	d.	PD	5 Dec. 1918	8	3	
McCready	Thomas	m.	PA	3 Oct. 1918	4	3	
McCready	Thomas	m.	PD	3 Oct. 1918	3	1	
McCready	Thomas	m.	ST	6 Oct. 1918	1	4	
McCuistion	Thomas H.	d.	PD	14 Nov. 1918	3	1	Canadian Army
McCuistion	Viola	d.	PD	21 Mar. 1917	4	3	also 6:5
McCuistion	Viola	d.	SRR	21 Mar. 1917	5	4	I.O.O.F. Cemetery; also 23 Mar., 8:6
McCulloch	Dora	m.	SRR	21 Aug. 1916	8	5	
McCullough	Charles	m.	PA	2 Jan. 1918	3	5	
McCullough	Charles	m.	PC	3 Jan. 1918	3	3	also 4 Jan., 8:4
McCullough	James	d.	PA	19 May 1917	5	4	also 21 May, 3:6
McCullough	John	d.	PC	25 Apr. 1917	6	1	
McCullum	George	d.	PD	10 Dec. 1916	5	1	
McCutheon	Elizabeth	m.	PA	2 Sept. 1918	5	6	
McCuthin	Elizabeth	m.	PC	4 Sept. 1918	4	2	
McCutochi	Peter	d.	PC	7 Feb. 1917	1	4	
McDaniel	Olive	m.	PD	11 Apr. 1917	8	3	also 15 Apr., 6:1
McDaniel	Olive	m.	SRR	12 Apr. 1917	8	6	
McDaniels	Alma	m.	PD	13 Dec. 1917	5	3	
McDaniels	Anna	m.	PC	15 Dec. 1917	2	1	
McDermott	A., Mrs.	o.	SRR	7 Jan. 1916	5	1	
McDermott	D. W.	d.	PD	19 Dec. 1918	7	1	
McDermott	D. W.	o.	PD	25 Jan. 1916	3	2	
McDermott	David	d.	HT	12 Dec. 1918	16	3	
McDermott	David W.	o.	HT	13 Jan. 1916	6	5	also 27 Jan., 3:5
McDermott	David W.	o.	PD	2 Oct. 1917	8	4	
McDermott	David W.	o.	HT	4 Oct. 1917	1	5	
McDermott	David W.	o.	SRR	7 Jan. 1916	5	1	
McDermott	Flora	m.	SRR	2 Oct. 1917	4	5	
McDermott	Flora	o.	PD	25 Jan. 1916	3	2	
McDermott	Flora	o.	HT	4 Oct. 1917	1	5	
McDermott	Flora	m.	HT	4 Oct. 1917	1	5	
McDermott	Flora A.	o.	HT	13 Jan. 1916	6	5	also 27 Jan., 3:5
McDermott	Flora A.	o.	PD	2 Oct. 1917	8	4	
McDermott	Flora A.	m.	PD	2 Oct. 1917	8	4	also 3 Oct., 2:5
McDermott	John	d.	PC	16 Nov. 1918	5	3	
McDermott	Mary	m.	ST	11 Jan. 1918	1	5	
McDermott	Will	o.	PA	16 Sept. 1918	4	1	
McDermott	Will	o.	PC	17 Sept. 1918	8	4	
McDermott	Will	o.	PA	3 Dec. 1918	4	5	

(1) Surname	(2) Given Name	(3)	(4)	(5) Date	(6) Pg	(7) Col	(8) Comments
McDonald	Bessie	o.	PC	5 Dec. 1917	4	2	
McDonald	Cora	m.	PD	17 July 1917	2	3	
McDonald	Cora	m.	SRR	17 July 1917	3	4	
McDonald	Helen	d.	PC	12 Feb. 1918	4	3	also 19 Feb., 5:3
McDonald	Helen Gertrude	m.	PA	10 Nov. 1917	7	7	also 13 Nov., 5:5; 14 Nov., 5:3
McDonald	James P.	m.	PD	12 Mar. 1918	4	2	
McDonald	James P.	m.	PD	7 Sept. 1916	1	6	
McDonald	John Glenn	m.	PC	24 Sept. 1916	5	2	
McDonald	John Richard	m.	PA	6 July 1916	2	6	also 4:4
McDonald	Joy	m.	ST	8 Mar. 1918	1	5	
McDonald	Joy Bernice	m.	PC	12 Mar. 1918	6	3	
McDonald	Joy Bernice	m.	PD	12 Mar. 1918	3	5	
McDonald	Mak L.	d.	PC	9 Mar. 1917	5	4	
McDonald	Marie	d.	ST	3 May 1918	1	3	San Francisco
McDonald	Marie	d.	PC	30 Apr. 1918	3	5	
McDonald	Marie A.	d.	PD	28 Apr. 1918	4	2	San Francisco; also 8:2; 30 Apr., 5:4
McDonald	Mark	d.	SIT	17 Mar. 1917	4	1	
McDonald	Mark	d.	SRR	8 Mar. 1917	1	3	also 10 Mar., 8:1
McDonald	Mark L.	d.	HT	15 Mar. 1917	3	4	
McDonald	Mark L.	d.	CR	17 Mar. 1917	1	4	
McDonald	Mark L.	d.	PA	8 Mar. 1917	5	3	
McDonald	Mark L.	d.	PD	9 Mar. 1917	8	1	portrait; also 10 Mar., 4:3
McDonald	Marshall B.	m.	SRR	1 Nov. 1917	4	1	
McDonald	Marshall B.	m.	PD	2 Nov. 1917	2	3	
McDonald	Marshall B.	m.	ST	2 Nov. 1917	4	3	
McDonald	Marshall Bell	m.	PC	28 Oct. 1917	8	5	also 2 Nov., 1:2
McDonald	Olive Lenora	m.	PC	22 Mar. 1917	5	6	
McDonald	Ralphine North	d.	PA	26 June 1918	2	5	
McDonald	Ralphine North	d.	PC	26 June 1918	3	3	
McDonald	Ralphine North	d.	PD	26 June 1918	3	3	also 28 June, 8:1
McDonald	Sarah Hattie	d.	PD	21 Jan. 1917	6	4	also 23 Jan., 2:6
McDonald	W. A.	o.	PC	5 Dec. 1917	4	2	
McDonald	Wallace	o.	PC	4 Dec. 1917	5	4	
McDonough	Marie	m.	HT	13 June 1918	3	4	
McDonough	Marie	m.	PD	14 June 1918	2	3	
McDowell	William	b.	PA	29 Jan. 1917	8	5	
McDowell	William	b.	PC	30 Jan. 1917	8	3	
McFadden	Edna	d.	PA	26 Oct. 1918	4	5	Reno, Nevada; also 30 Oct., 5:3
McFadden	Edna	d.	PC	27 Oct. 1918	8	3	
McFadden	Marie	d.	PC	14 Dec. 1918	8	4	also 15 Dec., 5:4; 17 Dec., 4:4; 31 Dec., 5:3

(1) Surname	(2) Given Name	(3)	(4)	(5) Date	(6) Pg	(7) Col	(8) Comments
McFadden	Marie	d.	PD	15 Dec. 1918	8	4	
McFadden	Marie/Sandi	d.	PA	14 Dec. 1918	5	4	Cypress Hill; also 16 Dec., 4:1; 27 Dec., 8:4; 30 Dec., 3:6
McFadden	Watson	m.	PA	1 Nov. 1917	4	5	
McFadden	Watson	m.	PC	2 Nov. 1917	8	5	
McFarlane	Dorothy	m.	SRR	16 July 1917	5	1	
McFarlane	H. M.	m.	HT	10 Feb. 1916	1	1	
McGahan	Mildred	m.	PD	3 Mar. 1917	8	3	
McGan	Miltie	d.	HT	8 Nov. 1917	8	4	
McGann	Mary A.	d.	PD	7 Nov. 1917	3	4	Rural Cemetery; also 8 Nov. 4:2
McGann	Metta	d.	SRR	7 Nov. 1917	8	2&3	Rural Cemetery; also 9 Nov., 3:4
McGarcy	Russell	m.	PC	8 Apr. 1917	5	4	
McGarey	Russell	m.	PD	8 Apr. 1917	8	3	
McGee	John	d.	PD	9 Aug. 1918	2	4	
McGeein	Roland	o.	PD	18 Oct. 1917	6	5	
McGeorge	LeRoy	m.	PD	10 Apr. 1917	8	4	
McGeorge	Roy	m.	SRR	5 Apr. 1917	8	2	also 7 Apr., 3:4
McGeorge	Roy	m.	PC	7 Apr. 1917	6	5	
McGill	Frank	o.	SIT	29 Sept. 1917	3	2	
McGimpsey	Catherine	d.	PC	9 Apr. 1918	5	4	Sonoma
McGimpsey	J. M.	b.	PA	30 Sept. 1916	8	3&4	
McGimpsey	Katherine	d.	PD	10 Apr. 1918	6	3	
McGimsey	Catherine Morris	d.	SIT	13 Apr. 1918	1	3	
McGimsey	J. M., Mrs.	d.	PA	6 Apr. 1918	4	3	Sonoma; also 8 Apr., 2:4
McGimsey	Milton	b.	SIT	30 Sept. 1916	4	6	
McGovern	Anna Loretta	m.	PA	18 June 1917	8	5	also 25 June, 2:5
McGovern	Clara Josephine	m.	PC	8 Apr. 1917	5	4	
McGovern	Clara Josephine	m.	PD	8 Apr. 1917	8	3	
McGovern	Clara Josephine	m.	SRR	9 Apr. 1917	4	6	
McGovern	Josephine	m.	PA	5 Apr. 1917	5	5	
McGowan	Daisy Fedora	m.	PD	28 May 1916	3	1	
McGraham	Mildred	m.	CR	3 Mar. 1917	1	2	
McGrath	Charles	b.	SRR	21 Aug. 1916	2	2	
McGrath	John	d.	PA	18 Jan. 1917	8	5	also 20 Jan., 4:7
McGrath	John	d.	PC	19 Jan. 1917	8	4	also 20 Jan., 5:2; 21 Jan., 5:5
McGrath	Joseph E.	d.	PA	21 Feb. 1916	4	7	
McGray	Warren	d.	PC	7 Dec. 1918	6	2	
McGrew	Hazel	m.	PD	19 Apr. 1918	8	4	
McGrew	Hazel	m.	PC	20 Apr. 1918	2	2	
McGuire	Jacob	o.	PD	4 Aug. 1916	6	1	
McGuire	Jacob	o.	SRR	7 Aug. 1917	1	3	

(1) Surname	(2) Given Name	(3)	(4)	(5) Date	(6) Pg	(7) Col	(8) Comments
McGuire	Mary E.	m.	PC	1 Sept. 1917	4	4	also 2 Sept., 5:4
McGuire	Mary E.	m.	PD	1 Sept. 1917	8	5	also 2 Sept., 8:4
McGuire	Mary E.	m.	SRR	1 Sept. 1917	8	6	
McGuire	Mary E.	o.	PD	4 Aug. 1916	6	1	
McGuire	Mary E.	o.	SRR	7 Aug. 1917	1	3	
McGuire	Mary Elizabeth	m.	PA	1 Sept. 1917	5	3	
McHarvey	Alice	o.	SRR	4 May 1916	1	3	
McHarvey	C. F.	o.	SRR	4 May 1916	1	3	
McHarvey	Friend	o.	SIT	4 Mar. 1916	1	3	
McHugh	George	m.	PD	10 Oct. 1916	2	4	
McHugh	George	m.	PC	11 Oct. 1916	6	1	
McHugh	George	m.	PA	3 Oct. 1916	5	2	
McHugh	George	m.	SRR	3 Oct. 1916	8	3	
McHugh	George	m.	ST	7 Oct. 1916	1	2	also 14 Oct., 1:2
McIntosh	Andrew	b.	PC	6 Sept. 1918	8	2	
McIntyre	Mary	o.	SRR	10 May 1917	4	6	
McIntyre	Mary M.	o.	SRR	16 July 1917	8	2	
McIntyre	R. H.	o.	SRR	10 May 1917	4	6	
McIntyre	Ray H.	o.	SRR	16 July 1917	8	2	
McIntyre	Robert	m.	PC	3 Jan. 1918	7	5	
McIntyre	William R.	m.	PD	3 Jan. 1918	4	2	
McIsaacs	Margaret	d.	PD	25 Oct. 1918	4	2	also 27 Oct., 1:2
McIsaacs	Margaret	d.	PC	26 Oct. 1918	8	3	
McKay	Millie	m.	PA	15 Jan. 1917	2	2	
McKay	Millie	m.	PC	16 Jan. 1917	5	5	
McKee	Harry B.	m.	SRR	17 May 1917	8	6	
McKenna	Alice	d.	SRR	29 May 1916	7	2	
McKenna	Peter, Mrs.	d.	PC	1 Apr. 1916	8	4	
McKenna	Peter, Mrs.	d.	PD	1 Apr. 1916	2	3	
McKenna	Peter, Mrs.	d.	SRR	31 Mar. 1916	3	1	
McKenzie	James	d.	PA	21 June 1917	7	4	
McKenzie	James	d.	PD	21 June 1917	1	4	
McKeon	Eugene J.	d.	PD	22 May 1918	3	1	
McKeon	Harriet Ehrlich	d.	SIT	25 May 1918	1	5	Mountain Cemetery
McKerman	Florence Devlin	d.	SRR	17 Nov. 1917	5	5	
McKernan	Florence Devlin	d.	PD	17 Nov. 1917	8	4	also 20 Nov., 6:5
McKillop	H.	b.	PA	9 Jan. 1917	8	4	
McKinley	Duncan	o.	PA	8 Nov. 1918	4	2	
McKinney	Dudley T.	o.	PD	20 Dec. 1918	2	1	
McKinnon	Alexander	m.	PD	3 Sept. 1916	5	3	
McKinnon	Hugh	m.	PA	11 Apr. 1917	6	3	also 27 Apr., 5:3
McKinnon	Hugh R.	m.	PC	13 Apr. 1917	5	3	also 27 Apr., 5:3
McKinnon	John	d.	PC	22 May 1917	1	3	I.O.O.F. Cemetery, Santa Rosa; also 23 May, 1:2&3

(1) Surname	(2) Given Name	(3)	(4)	(5) Date	(6) Pg	(7) Col	(8) Comments
McKinnon	Leslie	o.	SIT	7 Sept. 1918	3	4	
McKnight	John	d.	SRR	26 Dec. 1917	8	5	
McKoon	Horace	d.	PD	9 July 1916	1	2	also 11 July, 7:4; 12 July, 8:2
McKoon	Horace	d.	SRR	10 July 1916	5	5	
McLachlan	Albert E.	d.	PD	20 Jan. 1918	8	4	
McLain	Agatha	m.	PC	1 Dec. 1917	2	1	
McLain	Lavina	m.	PD	26 Nov. 1918	1	3	
McLane	Anita	m.	SRR	19 May 1916	5	1	
McLane	Harold	o.	SRR	14 July 1916	5	1	
McLane	Harold A.	o.	SRR	21 Feb. 1917	1	6	
McLane	Harold Austin	o.	PC	9 May 1917	4	6	
McLane	Harold Austin	o.	PD	10 May 1917	5	5	
McLane	Margaret	o.	SRR	14 July 1916	5	1	
McLane	Margaret	o.	PC	15 July 1916	3	3	
McLane	Marguerite	o.	PD	10 May 1917	5	5	
McLane	Marguerite Mae	o.	PC	9 May 1917	4	6	
McLane	Marguerite Mae	o.	SRR	21 Feb. 1917	1	6	
McLaren	Elizabeth	d.	PA	1 May 1916	4	6	also 2 May, 4:4
McLaughlin	Catherine	d.	PA	4 Jan. 1918	8	5	Calvary Cemetery; also 5 Jan., 4:1
McLaughlin	Catherine	d.	PC	4 Jan. 1918	5	3	Calvary Cemetery; also 5 Jan., 3:6; 6 Jan., 6:3
McLaughlin	Frank	d.	PC	30 Mar. 1918	1	4	
McLaughlin	Franklin	d.	PA	30 Mar. 1918	3	3	
McLaughlin	Joseph	d.	PC	1 Jan. 1918	2	3	
McLaughlin	Joseph	d.	PA	28 Dec. 1917	4	4	Calvary Cemetery; also 31 Dec., 8:7
McLaughlin	Joseph	d.	PC	29 Dec. 1917	5	4	
McLean	Agatha	m.	PD	17 Nov. 1917	2	4	
McLean	Agatha	m.	SRR	17 Nov. 1917	6	3	also 30 Nov., 4:1
McLean	Agatha	m.	PC	18 Nov. 1917	3	3	
McLean	Agatha	m.	PA	19 Nov. 1917	6	5	
McLearan	Elizabeth	d.	PC	30 Apr. 1916	5	5	Cypress Hill; also 2 May, 5:3, 6:2; 3 May, 1:1
McLees	James	d.	PC	11 Feb. 1917	5	5	Calvary Cemetery
McLenahan	Isabella	d.	PD	9 May 1917	3	2	Rural Cemetery; also 4:3
McLenahan	Isabella	d.	SRR	9 May 1917	10	3	
McLenehan	William, Mrs.	d.	SIT	12 May 1917	1	7	
McLeod	Ella	m.	SRR	6 July 1916	8	2	also 8 July, 4:1
McLeod	Ella	m.	PC	7 July 1916	4	4	
McLure	Robert D.	m.	PC	28 Dec. 1916	6	1	
McMath	E. M.	b.	SRR	29 Oct. 1917	3	4	
McMeans	May	m.	PD	10 June 1916	5	5	also 11 June, 7:1

(1) Surname	(2) Given Name	(3)	(4)	(5) Date	(6) Pg	(7) Col	(8) Comments
McMeans	May Alice	m.	SRR	10 June 1916	2	1	also 12 June, 6:6; 17 June, 4:1
McMenamin	John (son of)	b&d	ST	23 Sept. 1916	10	3	I.O.O.F. Cemetery
McMichaels	Absalom B.	d.	HT	21 Mar. 1918	8	5	
McMillan	Henry	d.	PD	20 Mar. 1917	5	1	
McMillan	Henry	d.	SRR	20 Mar. 1917	2	5	
McMillan	Lena Alice	m.	SRR	6 May 1916	10	5	
McMillan	Lena Alice	m.	PD	7 May 1916	3	1	
McMinn	Frederic	o.	PD	21 Sept. 1918	6	1	portrait
McMinn	J. Frederic	o.	PD	27 Oct. 1918	3	1	
McMullen	Ed	m.	PD	25 May 1918	6	3	
McMullen	Emma	o.	PD	13 Aug. 1918	5	3	
McMullen	Smith	o.	PD	13 Aug. 1918	5	3	
McMullin	Russell	m.	PA	5 Apr. 1917	5	5	
McMullin	Russell McGarcy	m.	SRR	9 Apr. 1917	4	6	
McNab	James	d.	PA	14 Mar. 1916	4	4	also 16 Mar., 4:4
McNab	James	p.	PA	24 Mar. 1916	8	5	
McNab/McNabb	Evelyn	d.	PA	5 June 1918	8	3	also 7 June, 3:6
McNabb	Evelyn	d.	PC	6 June 1918	3	3	also 7 June, 8:4
McNally	Ray G.	b.	PA	8 Sept. 1918	5	4	also 7:4
McNally	Ray G.	b.	PC	8 Sept. 1918	5	4	
McNally	Raymond	m.	PA	16 Sept. 1916	3	4	
McNally	Raymond	m.	PC	17 Sept. 1916	5	2	
McNally	Raymond	m.	SRR	18 Sept. 1916	2	1	
McNally	Raymond	m.	SRR	21 Nov. 1916	1	4	also 23 Nov., 2:3
McNally	Raymond	m.	PA	22 Nov. 1916	5	3	
McNally	Raymond	m.	PC	23 Nov. 1916	5	3	
McNamara	T. B.	d.	PC	21 Oct. 1916	1	6	Green Valley Cemetery
McNamara	Thomas B.	d.	SRR	17 Oct. 1916	5	1	Green Valley Cemetery; also 18 Oct., 8:3; 19 Oct., 5:6
McNamara	Tom	d.	PA	17 Oct. 1916	5	5	Green Valley; also 18 Oct., 8:5; 19 Oct., 4:2
McNamara	Tom M.	d.	PD	18 Oct. 1916	2	3	portrait; Green Valley Cemetery; also 19 Oct., 8:5; 20 Oct., 1:5
McNeal	Gene Lenora	d.	SRR	11 Oct. 1917	5	2	also 12 Oct., 7:3
McNear	Amanda	d.	SRR	16 Apr. 1917	3	4	
McNear	Amanda	d.	PC	18 Apr. 1917	3	3	
McNear	E. Denman	o.	PA	29 Aug. 1918	7	5	
McNear	E. Denman	o.	PA	7 Feb. 1918	1	5	paper filed after 6 Apr. 1918
McNear	E. Denman	o.	PC	8 Feb. 1918	1	3	also 9 Feb., 1:6; 12 Feb., 1:4; 17 Feb., 6:4; 17 Mar., 1:3; 31 Mar., 6:3

(1) Surname	(2) Given Name	(3)	(4)	(5) Date	(6) Pg	(7) Col	(8) Comments
McNear	Einnim	m.	PA	20 Apr. 1917	4	3	
McNear	Ezekiel Denman	o.	PC	27 Nov. 1917	1	3	
McNear	George	o.	PC	30 Apr. 1916	5	1	portrait
McNear	George B., Jr.	m.	SRR	30 June 1917	5	4	
McNear	George P. Jr.	o.	PA	14 May 1917	8	3	
McNear	George P., Jr.	o.	PC	15 May 1917	5	3	
McNear	George P., Jr.	m.	PC	20 June 1917	6	4	also 28 June, 8:2
McNear	George P., Jr.	m.	PC	4 July 1917	5	4	
McNear	George Plummer, Jr.	m.	PA	19 June 1917	4	5	also 21 June, 7:3; 29 June, 8:5; 5 July, 3:5
McNear	George W.	o.	PC	4 Jan. 1916	4	2	
McNear	George, Jr.	m.	PD	20 June 1917	2	3	
McNear	J. A.	p.	PA	1 July 1918	6	1	
McNear	John	d.	PD	20 June 1918	8	1	also 22 June, 2:3
McNear	John A.	o.	PC	16 May 1917	3	3	
McNear	John A.	d.	PA	19 June 1918	4	2	Cypress Hill; also 20 June, 5:6; 21 June, 4:3
McNear	John A.	d.	ST	22 June 1918	6	1	
McNear	John A.	p.	PC	2 July 1918	3	4	will
McNear	John A.	p.	PD	2 July 1918	8	4	
McNear	John A.	o.	PC	24 Dec. 1916	5	4	
McNear	John, Sr.	d.	PC	20 June 1918	1	2	Cypress Hill; also 8:4; 21 June, 4:2&3, 8:2; 22 June, 1:4
McNee	Royal J. H.	o.	PD	24 Sept. 1918	2	5	Canadian Army
McNeil	Gene Lenora	d.	PD	9 Oct. 1917	8	4	
McNeil	Irvin A.	d.	PD	16 May 1916	2	3	Shiloh Cemetery; also 19 May, 6:5
McNeil	James	b.	PA	23 May 1917	4	5	
McNeill	Irvin A.	d.	SRR	15 May 1916	5	3	Shiloh Cemetery
McPeak	Donald E.	m.	SRR	5 Nov. 1917	3	2	
McPeak	Donald E.	m.	PD	6 Nov. 1917	5	1	
McPhearson	Mr. & Mrs.	b.	PC	24 July 1917	8	4	
McPherson	Early	d.	HT	3 Nov. 1916	1	1	
McPherson	Early	d.	PD	31 Oct. 1916	3	3	
McPherson	Gertrude	m.	SRR	25 Sept. 1916	3	6	
McPherson	Gertrude	d.	PC	9 Nov. 1916	2	1	
McPherson	Harold	b.	HT	14 Sept. 1916	1	4	
McPherson	Mr. & Mrs.	b.	PA	23 July 1917	5	3	
McPherson-Masters	Gertrude	d.	HT	8 Nov. 1916	1	3	
McReclus	Alfred	d.	SRR	15 Sept. 1917	6	6	
McReynolds	B. L.	b&d	PA	10 Jan. 1916	1	3	also 8:3
McSween	Jane	d.	PC	3 June 1917	5	7	Cypress Hill
McTear	R. R.	b.	SRR	27 Feb. 1917	1	2	
McWilliams	George F.	d.	HT	17 Oct. 1918	8	3	

(1) Surname	(2) Given Name	(3)	(4)	(5) Date	(6) Pg	(7) Col	(8) Comments
McWilliams	James C.	m.	PD	18 Oct. 1917	2	4	
Meacham	Charles	o.	PD	13 Feb. 1917	5	1	
Meacham	Mary	m.	PD	31 Aug. 1918	2	5	
Mead	Albert Miller	m.	PD	12 Aug. 1916	8	4	
Mead	Lee	d.	PA	4 Dec. 1917	5	6	
Mead	Lee	d.	PC	4 Dec. 1917	1	5	
Mead	Lee	d.	PD	5 Dec. 1917	5	3	
Mead	Lee	d.	SRR	5 Dec. 1917	5	2	
Meadows	John	b.	PA	16 Sept. 1916	5	4	
Meadows	John	d.	PC	17 Sept. 1916	4	4	
Meadows	John	b.	PD	17 Sept. 1916	8	4	
Meadows	John	b.	SRR	18 Sept. 1916	7	3	
Meadows	Thomas	d.	PA	8 Nov. 1918	4	3	
Meadows	Thomas	d.	PC	8 Nov. 1918	8	4	Presidio; also 9 Nov., 1:4
Meads	Willis	m.	PD	18 Jan. 1918	8	4	also 29 Jan., 5:1
Means	Alma	m.	SRR	16 Dec. 1916	3	2	
Means	Emelda Josephine	d.	ST	20 Sept. 1918	7	2	
Mecham	Frank A.	d.	PD	3 June 1916	8	1	also 6 June, 7:1
Mecham	Franklyn A.	d.	PA	2 June 1916	4	4	Liberty Cemetery; also 3 June, 8:3; 5 June, 1:4
Mecham	Franklyn A.	d.	PC	3 June 1916	1	3&4	Liberty Cemetery; also 6 June, 6:2
Mechan	Walter	m.	PA	6 Apr. 1918	3	4	
Medley	James	m.	PA	18 Dec. 1917	11	4	
Medrano	J. T.	b.	PD	29 Feb. 1916	2	4	
Meeham	Frank A.	p.	PA	13 June 1916	8	3	
Meeham	Franklyn A.	d.	SRR	2 June 1916	1	4	also 5 June, 1:4
Meeker	Amzi Pennington	d.	PD	24 Dec. 1918	6	1	
Meeker	M. C.	p.	SRR	14 Jan. 1916	5	3	
Meeker	M. C.	p.	ST	15 Jan. 1916	1	1	
Meeker	Maurine	m.	SRR	10 July 1916	8	5	also 11 July, 2:3
Meeker	Maurine	m.	PC	11 July 1916	5	1	
Meeker	Maurine	m.	PD	11 July 1916	3	4	
Meeker	Melvin C.	m.	PC	7 Oct. 1916	5	6	
Meeker	Melvin C.	m.	ST	7 Oct. 1916	8	5	
Meeker	Merton	o.	PD	8 Oct. 1918	3	1	
Meeker	Roy T.	m.	PD	8 May 1917	8	3	
Meeker	Roy T.	m.	SRR	8 May 1917	7	4	
Meeks	J. C.	m.	PC	22 Feb. 1918	3	3	wife not named
Meeks	J. C. (Case)	o.	PA	11 June 1917	8	5	
Mefia	(son)	d.	PC	7 Apr. 1918	2	3	
Mehrtens	Ana Meese	d.	SRR	29 Jan. 1916	1	2	also 31 Jan., 8:2
Mehrtens	Anna M.	d.	PD	30 Jan. 1916	5	2	Odd Fellows Cemetery
Meier	Gus	b.	SRR	1 May 1917	1	1	

(1) Surname	(2) Given Name	(3)	(4)	(5) Date	(6) Pg	(7) Col	(8) Comments
Meineri	Elizabeth A.	d.	SRR	4 Aug. 1916	6	2	
Meinert	Elizabeth	d.	PD	4 Aug. 1916	3	2	
Meisner	Frank	m.	SRR	25 May 1917	6	5	
Meisser	Margaret May	b.	HT	15 Aug. 1918	5	3	
Meitszch	Margaret	d.	PD	6 Nov. 1917	5	1	Calvary Cemetery; also 7 Nov., 4:2; 6:4; 8 Nov., 7:1
Meitzsch	Charles E.	d.	SRR	6 Dec. 1917	8	4	
Meitzsch	Charles E.	d.	PD	7 Dec. 1917	7	1	
Meitzsch	Margaret A.	d.	SRR	5 Nov. 1917	6	5	also 7 Nov., 8:4
Melehan	James	b.	PC	26 May 1916	8	2	
Melehan	Mattie	d.	PA	9 Jan. 1917	2	3	San Jose; also 13 Jan., 3:5
Melesi	Guiseppe	d.	SRR	17 June 1916	1	3	
Melesi	Mr.	d.	PD	21 June 1916	7	3	Shiloh Cemetery
Meller	Lillian Rose	m.	PC	24 Feb. 1917	1	5	
Mello	Maria C.	m.	PA	22 May 1917	8	3	
Melo	Mary	m.	PC	19 May 1917	4	6	
Melovidoff	Frank C.	o.	PC	17 Aug. 1918	3	4	
Memini	Peter	d.	SRR	22 Jan. 1916	6	4	Fulton
Memini	Peter	d.	PD	23 Jan. 1916	1	4	
Menne	Henry	d.	PD	27 July 1917	8	1	Calvary Cemetery; also 29 July, 4:2; 31 July, 8:1
Menne	Henry	d.	SRR	27 July 1917	5	1	also 28 July, 5:3
Menne	Henry	d.	PC	28 July 1917	4	4	
Merchant	I. S.	d.	PA	18 Feb. 1916	6	5	
Merchant	T. S.	d.	PD	20 Feb. 1916	8	1	
Merchant	T. S.	d.	HT	24 Feb. 1916	1	1	also 8:3
Merchant	Thomas S.	o.	PC	18 Feb. 1916	?	3	
Merchant	Thomas S.	d.	SRR	17 Feb. 1916	8	2	also 21 Feb., 10:4
Merken	Matilda	m.	PC	19 Apr. 1918	5	3	
Merlo	John	b.	SRR	28 Dec. 1916	4	4	
Merrihew	Robert	m.	PD	19 June 1917	1	5	
Merrill	Maud	d.	SRR	15 Mar. 1917	6	5	Olive Hill Cemetery
Merrill	Robert G.	d.	HT	18 July 1918	3	2	
Merriott	Joseph S.	m.	PD	9 Sept. 1917	2	3	
Merriott	Joseph Stacey	m.	PC	8 Sept. 1917	1	3	
Merrithew	Robert	m.	SRR	19 June 1917	3	4	
Merritt	Emma J.	d.	CR	20 Apr. 1917	1	4	
Merritt	Esther Hardin	d.	PA	3 June 1916	4	5	Cypress Hill; also 5 June, 4:5&7; 6 June, 8:5
Merritt	Esther Jimella	d.	PC	4 June 1916	8	3	
Merritt	George, Mrs.	d.	PC	6 June 1916	6	3	Cypress Hill; also 7 June, 6:3
Merritt	J. F.	o.	PD	23 Oct. 1918	6	2	

(1) Surname	(2) Given Name	(3)	(4)	(5) Date	(6) Pg	(7) Col	(8) Comments
Merritt	J. F.	o.	PC	24 Oct. 1918	2	2	
Merritt	J. T.	o.	PA	23 Oct. 1918	8	3	also 26 Oct., 1:5
Merritt	John	d.	PA	14 June 1916	4	3	Liberty Cemetery; also 16 June, 5:1
Merritt	John	d.	PD	15 June 1916	5	2	Liberty Churchyard, Petaluma; also 16 June, 2:3
Merritt	John	d.	SRR	15 June 1916	4	6	
Merritt	John	o.	PC	10 Dec. 1918	1	5	
Merritt	John	d.	PA	16 Sept. 1916	4	3	also 18 Sept., 4:3
Merritt	John	d.	PC	16 Sept. 1916	1	4	Calvary Cemetery; also 6:2
Merritt	John	d.	PD	17 Sept. 1916	2	2	
Merritt	John	d.	PC	19 Sept. 1916	6	3	
Merritt	John	p.	PC	20 Sept. 1916	7	3	
Merritt	John	p.	PA	21 Sept. 1916	3	5	
Merritt	John, Sr.	d.	PC	14 June 1916	1	6	Liberty Cemetery; also 16 June, 5:1; 17 June, 4:3, 8:3
Merritt	John, Sr.	d.	ST	17 June 1916	3	4	
Merryfield	Clara	m.	PD	5 May 1917	5	3	
Merz	Bertha	d.	PC	1 May 1918	5	4	Calvary Cemetery; also 2 May, 3:4; 3 May, 6:7
Merz	Bertha Miranda	d.	PA	24 Apr. 1918	4	2	Calvary Cemetery; also 1 May, 2:4; 2 May, 5:6
Messenger	Amy Caroline	d.	PD	9 Oct. 1917	8	3	also 10 Oct., 4:2
Messenger	Amy Caroline	d.	SRR	9 Oct. 1917	3	2	also 10 Oct., 5:3
Methu	Jose	b.	SRR	1 Feb. 1916	2	3	
Metzger	Eli	d.	PD	20 Dec. 1918	5	4	
Metzger	Eli	d.	PC	21 Dec. 1918	2	2	
Meuh	Robert Herbert	m.	SRR	3 June 1916	4	1	also 7 June, 8:1
Meuh	Robert Herbert	m.	PD	7 June 1916	5	3	
Meuting	Anna	m.	SRR	7 May 1917	5	5	
Meuting	Charlotte Rose	m.	PC	11 Apr. 1917	1	3	
Meuting	William	m.	ST	14 Sept. 1917	2	3	
Meuting	William	m.	SRR	8 Sept. 1917	1	4	also 11 Sept., 10:2
Meuting	William F.	m.	PA	12 Sept. 1917	4	3	
Meuting	William F.	d.	PD	19 Dec. 1916	2	1	also 21 Dec., 5:5
Meuting	William P.	m.	PD	6 Sept. 1917	6	3	also 12 Sept., 2:4
Meyer	Al (dau of)	b&d	PA	28 Jan. 1916	8	6	
Meyer	Anna	m.	PD	9 July 1916	3	4	
Meyer	Anthony	b.	PC	20 Sept. 1918	5	4	
Meyer	Anthony R.	m.	PC	24 Apr. 1917	5	2	also 25 Apr., 5:3
Meyer	E.	d.	PA	16 Oct. 1916	5	5	
Meyer	E.	d.	SRR	16 Oct. 1916	1	5	
Meyer	E.	d.	PC	17 Oct. 1916	1	4	also 18 Oct., 3:4

(1) Surname	(2) Given Name	(3)	(4)	(5) Date	(6) Pg	(7) Col	(8) Comments
Meyer	Elizabeth G.	m.	SRR	2 Oct. 1916	5	2	
Meyer	Francesca	d.	PA	18 Jan. 1917	5	4	Calvary Cemetery; also 19 Jan., 5:3; 20 Jan., 3:3
Meyer	Franciska	d.	PC	18 Jan. 1917	8	3	also 20 Jan., 5:2; 21 Jan., 4:4
Meyer	Jerome	d.	SIT	21 Oct. 1916	1	2	
Meyer	Knut	d.	PC	11 July 1917	1	6	
Meyer	Louis	m.	HT	14 Nov. 1918	3	3	
Meyer	Louis	m.	PD	15 Nov. 1918	3	3	
Meyer	William J., Mrs.	d.	SRR	18 Nov. 1916	5	3	Alameda
Meyer	Wilma Hayden	d.	PC	29 Aug. 1917	4	6	
Meyer	Wilma Hayden	d.	PC	29 Aug. 1917	8	4	also 30 Aug., 5:6
Meyerholtz	Alma	m.	PC	21 Nov. 1916	4	2	
Meyers	Carleen	m.	PA	16 Sept. 1916	3	4	
Meyers	Carleen	m.	PC	17 Sept. 1916	5	2	
Meyers	Carleen	m.	SRR	18 Sept. 1916	2	1	
Meyers	Carleen	m.	PA	22 Nov. 1916	5	3	
Meyers	Carleen	m.	PC	23 Nov. 1916	5	3	
Meyers	Carline	m.	SRR	21 Nov. 1916	1	4	also 23 Nov., 2:3
Meyers	Helen Margaret	d.	PC	31 Dec. 1916	3	3	also 3:6
Meyers	Helena M.	d.	PA	30 Dec. 1916	4	1	
Meyers	Helene	d.	PC	3 Jan. 1917	2	1	Cypress Hill
Meyers	Helene M.	d.	PD	30 Dec. 1916	3	1	
Meyers	Joseph	d.	PA	22 Jan. 1916	7	3	
Meyers	Joseph	d.	HT	27 Jan. 1916	5	2	
Meyers	Larene E.	m.	PC	5 Feb. 1916	5	3	
Meyers	Leonard	o.	PC	13 Feb. 1918	3	4	
Meyers	Lorene	m.	PA	31 Jan. 1916	3	3	also 4 Feb., 4:1
Meyers	Margaret	d.	PA	2 Jan. 1917	8	5	
Meyers	W. A.	b.	PC	20 Apr. 1916	8	2	
Meyers	Wilma	d.	SRR	29 Aug. 1917	2	4	
Mezzera	Paul P.	m.	PA	29 Aug. 1917	2	1	
Mezzeri	Paul	m.	PC	29 Aug. 1917	5	5	also 30 Aug., 5:2
Michael	Mr. & Mrs.	b.	PC	27 June 1916	8	1	
Michaels	Mr. & Mrs.	b.	PA	26 June 1916	5	1	
Michelletti	Stefano	m.	PD	10 Dec. 1916	8	2	
Michelletti	Stefano	m.	SRR	11 Dec. 1916	8	4	
Mickelsen	M.	b.	PC	25 Nov. 1916	5	3	
Mickelsen	Peter	d.	PA	20 Nov. 1918	4	4	
Mickelsen	Peter	m.	PC	20 Nov. 1918	5	4	
Mickle	Archibald E.	d.	SRR	24 Dec. 1917	3	3	
Middagh	Elizabeth	m.	PA	4 Dec. 1916	4	2	
Middagh	Elizabeth	o.	PD	5 Dec. 1916	5	4	
Middagh	Elizabeth Mae	m.	PC	5 Dec. 1916	8	2	
Middagh	John R.	o.	PC	5 Dec. 1916	8	2	

(1) Surname	(2) Given Name	(3)	(4)	(5) Date	(6) Pg	(7) Col	(8) Comments
Middagh	John R.	o.	PD	5 Dec. 1916	5	4	
Mierneri	Elizabeth A.	d.	ST	5 Aug. 1916	2	4	
Miesner	Frank	m.	PD	26 May 1917	6	2	
Mighell	Jack	m.	PC	5 Jan. 1916	3	1	
Miglian	John	m.	PC	19 Apr. 1918	5	3	
Mihovilovich	Victoria	d.	PD	19 Nov. 1918	4	2	also 5:3; 20 Nov., 7:4
Mikkelsen	M.	b.	PA	7 Mar. 1918	4	3	
Milani	Antoinette	m.	SRR	3 Aug. 1916	6	1	
Milen	Clent E.	m.	PC	4 Aug. 1917	3	2	
Miles	J. P.	d.	PC	19 Dec. 1916	8	6	aka Joe Hayden
Miles	Joseph T.	d.	PD	15 Dec. 1916	8	3	aka Joe Hayden
Miles	Joseph T.	d.	SRR	15 Dec. 1916	5	2	aks Joe Hayden
Miles	Lily C.	m.	PD	30 Aug. 1917	8	3	
Milesi	Guiseppe	d.	PA	17 June 1916	2	4	also 19 June, 4:5
Milesi	Guiseppi	d.	PC	18 June 1916	6	5	also 20 June, 8:3
Mill	Percy Albert	m.	PC	23 May 1918	4	4	
Miller	Ada	o.	SRR	20 Apr. 1916	8	4	
Miller	Ada L.	o.	PA	20 Apr. 1916	4	3	
Miller	Ada L.	o.	SRR	30 Apr. 1917	8	2	
Miller	Al	d.	SIT	1 Sept. 1917	3	2	
Miller	Bertha	m.	PA	28 Sept. 1916	7	4	
Miller	Bertha	m.	PC	28 Sept. 1916	5	4	
Miller	Beulah	m.	PD	27 Dec. 1917	6	1	
Miller	Beulah	m.	PC	28 Dec. 1917	6	5	
Miller	C. Z.	b.	SRR	9 Nov. 1917	4	4	
Miller	Charles	b.	PD	13 Jan. 1917	5	1	
Miller	Charles	b.	SRR	13 Jan. 1917	5	2	also 18 Jan., 8:1; 19 Jan., 5:2
Miller	Charles	b.	PC	14 Jan. 1917	3	6	
Miller	Charles	b.	PA	15 Jan. 1917	4	3	
Miller	Charles P.	o.	PD	29 Dec. 1916	5	3	
Miller	Charles P.	o.	SRR	29 Dec. 1916	3	4	
Miller	Charles Raymond	d.	SRR	19 Nov. 1917	5	3	
Miller	Clinton	o.	PC	1 Dec. 1918	4	4	
Miller	Clinton	o.	PC	17 Apr. 1918	4	3	
Miller	Earl	d.	PA	2 Jan. 1917	7	4	
Miller	Earl	d.	SRR	2 Jan. 1917	1	3	
Miller	Earl	d.	PC	3 Jan. 1917	1	6	also 14 Jan., 1:5
Miller	Earl	d.	PD	3 Jan. 1917	6	3	also 19 Jan., 2:1; 24 Jan., 5:2
Miller	Earl	d.	HT	4 Jan. 1917	1	1	
Miller	Edna	m.	PC	21 Mar. 1916	8	5	
Miller	Edna J.	m.	PA	20 Mar. 1916	4	5	
Miller	Elsie (son of)	b.	SIT	16 Sept. 1916	1	7	Holy Cross, S.F.
Miller	Estel	m.	PD	30 May 1917	5	2	

(1) Surname	(2) Given Name	(3)	(4)	(5) Date	(6) Pg	(7) Col	(8) Comments
Miller	Fana	m.	SRR	23 Aug. 1917	8	4	
Miller	Fawn	m.	PD	24 Aug. 1917	2	3	
Miller	Fay A.	o.	PA	19 May 1917	7	4	
Miller	Fred R.	o.	SRR	30 Apr. 1917	8	2	
Miller	Frederick	o.	PA	20 Apr. 1916	4	3	
Miller	Frederick	o.	SRR	20 Apr. 1916	8	4	
Miller	George	d.	SRR	23 Apr. 1917	1	2	
Miller	George	d.	PD	24 Apr. 1917	8	4	
Miller	George W.	d.	PD	30 Aug. 1918	3	5	
Miller	George William	d.	HT	29 Aug. 1918	1	3	Oak Mound Cemetery
Miller	Harold	o.	HT	30 Oct. 1918	6	2	
Miller	Henry	d.	PD	12 Oct. 1918	4	2	Healdsburg; also 8:3
Miller	Isaac	o.	SRR	27 July 1916	3	5	
Miller	Isaac	o.	PC	28 July 1916	8	3	
Miller	Isaac	o.	PD	28 July 1916	6	3	
Miller	Isaac	o.	PA	14 Mar. 1916	4	6	
Miller	Isaac	o.	SRR	14 Mar. 1916	1	3	
Miller	J. H.	b.	PC	7 Apr. 1918	2	1	
Miller	J. J.	d.	PA	5 Feb. 1917	6	7	
Miller	Joe	b.	SRR	29 Aug. 1916	6	1	
Miller	Joe	b.	PD	3 Sept. 1916	7	2	
Miller	Joe	b.	PC	31 Aug. 1916	8	1	
Miller	John	d.	PD	9 Jan. 1918	2	5	
Miller	John J.	d.	SRR	5 Feb. 1917	3	1	also 5:2
Miller	John J.	d.	PC	6 Feb. 1917	8	4	
Miller	John J.	d.	PD	6 Feb. 1917	5	7	
Miller	Kattie	o.	PA	14 Mar. 1916	4	6	
Miller	Kittie	o.	PD	28 July 1916	6	3	
Miller	Kittie	o.	SRR	14 Mar. 1916	1	3	
Miller	Kitty I.	o.	PC	28 July 1916	8	3	
Miller	Kitty L.	o.	SRR	27 July 1916	3	5	
Miller	L. G.	o.	PD	21 June 1918	5	1	
Miller	Lucy	d.	PD	1 Feb. 1916	8	4	Shiloh Cemetery
Miller	Lucy	d.	HT	3 Feb. 1917	5	2	Shiloh Cemetery
Miller	Lucy	d.	SRR	31 Jan. 1916	8	3	
Miller	Mamie Nellie	m.	SRR	7 July 1917	8	4	
Miller	Martha E.	m.	PA	19 Sept. 1917	5	7	
Miller	Martha E.	m.	SRR	20 Sept. 1917	4	3	
Miller	Mary	m.	ST	8 Jan. 1916	7	4	
Miller	Rachael Debbie	m.	PA	8 Sept. 1917	4	5	
Miller	Rachael Dobbie	m.	PC	8 Sept. 1917	1	3	
Miller	Rachel D.	m.	PD	9 Sept. 1917	2	3	
Miller	Rachel Dobbie	m.	ST	7 Sept. 1916	8	4	
Miller	Rebecca	o.	PD	29 Dec. 1916	5	3	
Miller	Rebecca	o.	SRR	29 Dec. 1916	3	4	

(1) Surname	(2) Given Name	(3)	(4)	(5) Date	(6) Pg	(7) Col	(8) Comments
Miller	Thomas Richards	d.	PD	22 Sept. 1916	1	5	Holy Cross Cemetery, San Francisco; 1 yr.
Miller	Velana	m.	SRR	21 Feb. 1916	1	6	
Miller	Velma	m.	PD	22 Feb. 1916	2	2	
Miller	William	d.	PA	16 Mar. 1913	4	3	
Miller	William Anderson	d.	SRR	20 Dec. 1916	2	4	
Miller	William L.	d.	PD	19 Dec. 1916	2	3	
Miller	William Lynn	d.	PA	18 Dec. 1916	5	5	
Miller	William Lynn	d.	SRR	18 Dec. 1916	5	4	
Miller	Willian Lynn	d.	PC	19 Dec. 1916	4	4	
Miller	Willis	o.	CR	13 Apr. 1917	1	2	
Millerick	Dave	b.	PC	11 Feb. 1917	4	2	
Millerick	J. A.	d.	PD	23 Jan. 1917	8	4	
Millerick	Jack/John	d.	PC	27 Sept. 1917	1	1	also 28 Sept., 6:5; 30 Sept., 3:6
Millerick	James	d.	SRR	23 Jan. 1917	2	1	
Millerick	James	d.	SIT	27 Jan. 1917	1	7	
Millerick	James A.	d.	PA	22 Jan. 1917	2	5	also 24 Jan., 4:7
Millerick	James A.	d.	PC	23 Jan. 1917	3	6	Calvary Cemetery; also 8:3; 24 Jan., 3:6; 25 Jan., 2:3
Millerick	John	d.	PA	27 Sept. 1917	5	6	Calvary Cemetery; also 8:5; 23 Sept., 5:1; 29 Sept., 8:3
Mills	Allan	b.	PD	24 Jan. 1917	8	5	
Mills	Elaine	m.	ST	6 Dec. 1918	1	5	
Mills	Elaine	m.	PC	8 Dec. 1918	6	3	
Mills	George W.	d.	PD	28 Apr. 1918	2	5	
Mills	Helen T.	d.	PC	19 Feb. 1918	3	3	Cypress Hill; also 4:2; 20 Feb., 3:3, 5:6; 21 Feb., 4:4
Mills	Helen Todd	d.	PA	18 Feb. 1918	5	1	Cypress Hill; also 20 Feb., 4:3
Mills	Kate	o.	SRR	12 Nov. 1917	8	1	
Mills	Kate	o.	HT	15 Nov. 1917	2	3	
Mills	Lilly C.	m.	SRR	29 Aug. 1917	2	4	
Mills	Pauline	o.	SRR	28 Nov. 1916	10	3	also 29 Nov., 8:5
Mills	Pauline	o.	PC	29 Nov. 1916	8	1	also 2 Dec., 2:2
Mills	Pauline	o.	PD	29 Nov. 1916	7	1	also 30 Nov., 3:3
Mills	Percy	m.	PD	23 May 1918	5	2	
Mills	Percy Albert	m.	PA	22 May 1918	4	5	also 1 June, 4:5
Mills	Percy M.	o.	PA	14 Aug. 1917	2	3	
Mills	Ray	m.	PA	8 Feb. 1916	6	5	also 12 Feb., 2:3
Mills	Robert	o.	SRR	28 Nov. 1916	10	3	also 29 Nov., 8:5
Mills	Robert	o.	PC	29 Nov. 1916	8	1	also 2 Dec., 2:2
Mills	Robert	o.	PD	29 Nov. 1916	7	1	also 30 Nov., 3:3

(1) Surname	(2) Given Name	(3)	(4)	(5) Date	(6) Pg	(7) Col	(8) Comments
Mills	Roy Hudson	m.	PD	12 Feb. 1916	2	4	
Mills	William C.	o.	SRR	12 Nov. 1917	8	1	
Mills	William C.	o.	HT	15 Nov. 1917	2	3	
Milne	C. E.	m.	SRR	18 Apr. 1917	3	5	
Milne	Clent E.	m.	PA	3 Aug. 1917	8	5	
Minck	Marguerite	m.	PA	19 Mar. 1918	4	3	
Minck	Marguerite	m.	PA	5 Mar. 1918	4	1	
Minck	William, Jr.	d.	PC	7 Nov. 1918	1	4	France
Miner	Clement A.	m.	SRR	10 Jan. 1917	2	2	
Miner	Clement L.	m.	PA	9 Jan. 1917	5	1	
Ming	C., Mrs.	d.	PD	10 Feb. 1916	1	5	Mountain Home Cemetery, Oakland
Ming	C., Mrs.	d.	SRR	10 Feb. 1916	5	3	Oakland
Minick	Marguerite	m.	PC	6 Mar. 1918	8	4	also 19 Mar., 8:3
Minor	Peter	b.	PD	20 Mar. 1917	8	2	
Minott	Anna	d.	ST	21 Oct. 1916	1	3	
Minott	Anna H.	d.	PD	18 Oct. 1916	2	2	
Minott	Anna Hopkins	d.	SRR	17 Oct. 1916	6	5	Sebastopol
Miser	Ross	b.	HT	23 May 1918	8	4	
Mitchel	Frank	m.	SRR	2 Aug. 1917	6	3	
Mitchell	Adela Jane	d.	SRR	13 Oct. 1917	10	3	also 15 Oct., 8:3
Mitchell	Adele Jane	d.	PD	14 Oct. 1917	7	4	also 16 Oct., 3:4
Mitchell	E., Mrs.	m.	PD	18 Oct. 1917	2	4	
Mitchell	Ellsworth	m.	SRR	10 June 1916	11	2	also 17 June, 4:1
Mitchell	Ernest	o.	HT	8 Nov. 1917	3	5	
Mitchell	Frank	o.	HT	2 May 1918	7	3	
Mitchell	Frank	m.	HT	2 Aug. 1917	1	3	
Mitchell	Hannah	d.	PD	29 Mar. 1918	8	2	
Mitchell	Irma	m.	SRR	17 Jan. 1917	3	1	
Mitchell	Irma	m.	HT	18 Jan. 1917	8	4	
Mitchell	Jacob	d.	CR	13 Sept. 1918	1	3	also 20 Sept., 1:1
Mitchell	Robert G.	d.	PC	16 July 1918	2	1	
Mitchell	Ross F.	m.	PC	11 June 1918	3	3	
Mitchell	Victor	d.	PA	5 May 1916	2	6	
Mize	Albert	d.	PD	11 Apr. 1918	3	2	also 14 Apr., 6:1
Mize	Albert	d.	PC	12 Apr. 1918	5	3	
Mock	Jane Thornton	d.	PD	3 Aug. 1917	8	1	also 4 Aug., 4:2; 5 Aug., 5:1; 7 Aug., 2:3
Mock	Jane Thornton	d.	SRR	3 Aug. 1917	5	3	also 8:1; 6 Aug., 8:2
Mock	Jane Thorston	d.	PA	3 Aug. 1917	6	5	
Mock	Sarah Jane	d.	PC	3 Aug. 1917	8	3	
Modini	James	m.	SIT	2 Dec. 1916	1	3	also 16 Dec., 1:3
Modini	James L.	m.	PA	12 Dec. 1916	5	5	
Modini	James L.	m.	PD	2 Dec. 1916	2	1	also 15 Dec., 6:4
Modini	James L.	m.	SRR	2 Dec. 1916	7	4	

(1) Surname	(2) Given Name	(3)	(4)	(5) Date	(6) Pg	(7) Col	(8) Comments
Modini	James L.	m.	PC	3 Dec. 1916	3	1	also 12 Dec., 8:5; 14 Dec., 4:3
Moehring	Laria M.	m.	SRR	14 Jan. 1916	4	4	
Moffatt	Margaret	m.	PA	24 Apr. 1918	3	4	
Mohl	Emiel	d.	PA	6 Nov. 1916	1	4	cremation; also 7 Nov., 3:3, 8:3; 8 Nov., 8:1
Mohl	Emiel	d.	PC	7 Nov. 1916	8	3	cremation; also 8 Nov., 8:4; 9 Nov., 3:3
Molfsen	Albert Christian	m.	PD	7 Jan. 1917	7	1	
Molinaro	Mr. & Mrs.	b.	PA	13 Apr. 1917	5	5	
Molinaro	Mr. & Mrs.	b.	PC	14 Apr. 1917	8	5	
Moll	Emil	d.	PA	3 Mar. 1916	4	3	
Moll	Emil	d.	PD	3 Mar. 1916	2	1	also 4 Mar., 7:1
Moll	Emil	o.	PC	4 Mar. 1916	3	1	
Moll	Emile	d.	ST	4 Mar. 1916	1	2	
Moll	Florine	m.	PA	30 July 1917	4	3	
Moll	Florine	m.	PC	31 July 1917	3	3	
Moll	Florine	m.	PD	31 July 1917	5	1	
Moller	Alfred	m.	PA	22 Mar. 1918	5	4	
Moller	Alfred	m.	PC	24 Mar. 1918	3	4	
Moller	Gyde	m.	PC	28 Feb. 1917	3	4	
Moller	Richard	d.	SRR	28 Nov. 1916	5	2	
Moller	William Richard	d.	PA	27 Nov. 1916	5	4	also 28 Nov., 4:4, 8:1; 29 Nov., 8:3
Moller	William Richard	d.	PC	28 Nov. 1916	4	3	also 6:2; 29 Nov., 8:5; 30 Nov., 6:2
Moller	William Richard	d.	PD	28 Nov. 1916	1	2	
Molseed	Robert T.	o.	PA	8 Nov. 1918	5	1	
Molseed	Robert T.	o.	PC	8 Nov. 1918	5	1	
Moltsen	Albert Christian	m.	PD	8 Feb. 1917	2	4	
Moltzen	A. C.	m.	PA	6 Jan. 1917	5	4	also 6 Feb., 8:4; 7 Feb., 4:3
Moltzen	Albert C.	m.	SRR	6 Feb. 1917	8	1	
Moltzen	Albert Christian	m.	PC	24 Nov. 1916	6	5	
Moltzen	Christian	m.	PA	23 Nov. 1916	5	3	
Moltzen	Christian	m.	PD	24 Nov. 1916	5	2	
Moltzen	Christian	m.	SRR	24 Nov. 1916	3	2	
Moltzen	Christian	m.	PC	6 Jan. 1917	8	2	also 7 Feb., 5:2; 8 Feb., 4:1
Momboisse	Victoria	d.	PD	17 July 1917	6	4	
Momboisse	Victorine	d.	PA	16 July 1917	4	5	Calvary Cemetery; also 5:3; 17 July, 4:3
Mombroisse	Victorine	d.	PC	15 July 1917	8	2	also 18 July, 4:3
Monell	Anna T.	o.	PD	26 Apr. 1918	3	3	
Monell	James E.	o.	PD	26 Apr. 1918	3	3	
Monett	C. D.	b.	PA	26 Mar. 1918	8	2	

(1) Surname	(2) Given Name	(3)	(4)	(5) Date	(6) Pg	(7) Col	(8) Comments
Moni	Frank	d.	PC	12 Feb. 1918	4	4	Calvary Cemetery
Moni	Frank	d.	PA	6 Feb. 1918	4	5	also 11 Feb., 2:4
Moni	Frank	d.	PC	6 Feb. 1918	4	2	
Monroe	Calvin	m.	PC	12 Dec. 1916	6	4	
Monroe	Calvin	m.	SIT	9 Dec. 1916	1	3	
Monroe	George Lee	d.	SIT	13 Oct. 1917	1	7	
Montafi	Daria	d.	SRR	1 Oct. 1917	2	3	
Montafi	Daria	d.	SRR	29 Sept. 1917	10	2	
Montafi	Darla	d.	PC	30 Sept. 1917	1	4	
Montafi	Doris	d.	PD	30 Sept. 1917	2	2	also 5 Oct., 7:3
Montessoro	Catherine	o.	PC	1 Apr. 1916	1	3	portrait
Montford	Charles	d.	SRR	15 Jan. 1916	10	5	I.O.O.F. Cemetery
Montgomery	Claudius	d.	PD	10 Dec. 1918	1	5	
Montgomery	Hugh C.	m.	PD	15 May 1917	6	3	
Montgomery	Margaret	d.	PA	5 July 1916	4	2	also 6 July, 6:2
Montgomery	Margaret	d.	PC	6 July 1916	5	3	also 6:2; 7 July, 3:3
Montgomery	Margaret	d.	SRR	6 July 1916	8	3	
Montgomery	Raleigh Claude	m.	SRR	14 May 1917	10	3	
Montgomery	W. W.	b.	PA	16 June 1917	5	2	also 8:2
Montgomery	William	d.	SRR	25 Aug. 1916	5	1	
Montijo	Daniel	m.	SRR	14 July 1917	8	2	
Montiyo	Daniel	m.	PC	17 July 1917	2	1	
Moodey	Rose	m.	SRR	7 July 1916	8	2	
Moodey	Rose	m.	PD	17 Oct. 1916	5	1	
Moodey	W. A.	d.	PA	15 Feb. 1917	5	4	Bloomfield; also 17 Feb., 2:5
Moodey	W. A.	d.	SRR	15 Feb. 1917	8	3	also 16 Feb., 4:5; 17 Feb., 5:6; 19 Feb., 8:1
Moody	Frank I.	o.	SRR	22 June 1917	5	4	
Moody	Frank L.	o.	PD	22 June 1917	8	4	
Moody	Howard	m.	SRR	21 Nov. 1916	3	3	
Moody	Howard	m.	PA	22 Nov. 1916	4	2	
Moody	Howard	m.	PC	22 Nov. 1916	1	2	
Moody	Howard	m.	PD	22 Nov. 1916	3	2	
Moody	Logan	m.	PD	22 Aug. 1916	2	3	
Moody	Logan	m.	HT	24 Aug. 1916	1	5	
Moody	Logan	b.	HT	30 Aug. 1917	2	5	
Moody	Mary	d.	SRR	6 Sept. 1916	6	3	also 7 Sept., 6:3
Moody	Rosa K.	o.	PD	22 June 1917	8	4	
Moody	Rosa K.	o.	SRR	22 June 1917	5	4	
Moody	Rose Carlyle	m.	SRR	16 Oct. 1916	8	1	
Moody	William A.	d.	PC	18 Feb. 1917	4	6	Bloomfield; also 21 Feb., 6:4
Moody	William Alexander	d.	PD	16 Feb. 1917	4	2	Bloomfield; also 6:4; 17 Feb., 5:4; 20 Feb., 6:4

(1) Surname	(2) Given Name	(3)	(4)	(5) Date	(6) Pg	(7) Col	(8) Comments
Mooers	Maude E.	o.	SRR	16 Feb. 1917	4	3	
Mooers	Maude E.	o.	PD	9 Dec. 1916	5	5	
Mooers	Wiliam H.	o.	PD	9 Dec. 1916	5	5	
Mooers	William H.	o.	SRR	16 Feb. 1917	4	3	
Moore	Archie S.	d.	PD	13 Mar. 1917	8	2	
Moore	Archie S.	d.	SRR	13 Mar. 1917	6	2	
Moore	C. S.	d.	SRR	21 Aug. 1916	6	2	
Moore	Dewey	m.	ST	27 Sept. 1918	1	2	
Moore	Florence	m.	PA	10 Dec. 1918	3	4	
Moore	Florence	m.	PC	8 Dec. 1918	4	2	
Moore	Francis	b&d	SRR	7 Oct. 1916	5	5	
Moore	Frederick R.	o.	PD	16 Aug. 1918	5	1	
Moore	Helen	m.	PC	24 Apr. 1918	5	2	
Moore	James	d.	PA	15 June 1918	8	5	
Moore	James	d.	PC	15 June 1918	1	4	
Moore	James	d.	PA	17 June 1918	4	6	Calvary Cemetery
Moore	James E.	d.	PC	16 June 1918	6	1	Calvary Cemetery; also 18 June, 8:4
Moore	James, Mrs.	d.	PC	20 Oct. 1918	5	4	Tomales; also 22 Oct., 3:4
Moore	John	d.	PD	21 Oct. 1916	8	2	also 22 Oct., 7:2
Moore	John	d.	ST	21 Oct. 1916	5	3	
Moore	Leola	m.	PC	29 Mar. 1918	5	4	
Moore	Lola/Leola	m.	PD	28 Mar. 1918	8	3	also 29 Mar., 5:5
Moore	Marion	m.	SRR	30 June 1916	8	5	
Moore	N. P.	b.	SRR	14 May 1917	1	2	
Moore	Neil	m.	PD	2 May 1916	7	4	
Moore	Neil	m.	PC	3 May 1916	6	3	
Moore	O. S.	d.	PA	19 Aug. 1916	4	3	Cypress Hill; also 5:4; 21 Aug., 4:1
Moore	O. S.	d.	PC	20 Aug. 1916	8	4	Cypress Hill; also 22 Aug., 3:4
Moore	Rebecca	d.	SRR	13 May 1916	1	5	
Moore	Rebecca	d.	PC	14 May 1916	4	5	
Moore	Rebecca	d.	PD	14 May 1916	6	1	also 16 May, 6:3
Moore	Robert	d.	ST	8 Jan. 1916	1	2	
Moore	W. S.	d.	SRR	6 Apr. 1917	4	3	
Moore	W. S.	d.	PD	7 Apr. 1917	5	4	Lakeport
Moorhead	Thomas	d.	PD	3 Jan. 1917	3	2	
Moraes	M.	d.	PC	16 Apr. 1918	5	4	Calvary Cemetery; also 17 Apr., 4:3; 19 Apr., 8:4
Moraes	Manuel	d.	PA	16 Apr. 1918	4	3	Calvary Cemetery; also 18 Apr., 4:5
Moraes	Maria A. Silva	d.	PC	17 Feb. 1917	5	3	also 21 Feb., 3:4

(1) Surname	(2) Given Name	(3)	(4)	(5) Date	(6) Pg	(7) Col	(8) Comments
Moraes	Marie A. Silva	d.	PA	16 Feb. 1917	5	5	Calvary Cemetery; also 20 Feb., 8:3
Moran	Sydney	b.	PD	16 June 1916	8	5	
Moran	Sydney D.	b.	SRR	16 June 1916	5	3	
Moreland	W. W., Mrs.	d.	PD	27 Dec. 1918	8	2	
Morelli	Alvino	d.	PC	4 June 1918	5	4	
Morelli-Filippini	Irene	d.	PA	27 Apr. 1918	4	1	Calvary Cemetery; also 29 Apr., 4:1
Moretti	Battista	d.	PA	8 Jan. 1917	6	4	Calvary Cemetery; also 10 Jan., 4:3
Moretti	Battista	d.	PC	9 Jan. 1917	1	4	also 3:6
Moretti	C.	m.	PA	17 Mar. 1917	5	2	also 23 Mar., 5:3
Moretti	C.	m.	PC	18 Mar. 1917	8	5	also 24 Mar., 1:5
Moretti	Camille	o.	SRR	13 June 1917	1	2	
Moretti	Camille	o.	PD	7 Aug. 1917	5	5	
Moretti	Camille	o.	SRR	7 Aug. 1917	3	5	
Moretti	Camillo	o.	PA	29 June 1918	4	7	
Moretti	Linda	o.	SRR	13 June 1917	1	2	
Moretti	Linda	o.	PA	29 June 1918	4	7	
Moretti	Linda	m.	PA	29 June 1918	4	7	
Moretti	Linda	m.	PA	25 Aug. 1917	4	4	also 29 Aug., 2:5
Moretti	Linda	o.	PD	7 Aug. 1917	5	5	
Moretti	Linda	o.	SRR	7 Aug. 1917	3	5	
Moretti	Linda M.	m.	PC	27 Aug. 1917	5	4	
Moretti	R.	o.	PC	20 Nov. 1917	6	4	
Morey	Clyde L.	d.	PC	28 Dec. 1918	6	4	France
Morgan	Howard	d.	PC	1 Mar. 1918	6	3	
Morgan	Maudy Frances	m.	HT	30 Mar. 1916	2	3	
Morgensen	Magnus	o.	PC	29 Dec. 1918	4	2	
Mori	B.	m.	SIT	27 Oct. 1917	1	5	also 17 Nov., 1:7
Morifawa	R.	o.	PD	12 May 1918	6	1	also 14 May, 8:1
Morita	Yoshiko	d.	PD	3 Mar. 1916	3	3	I.O.O.F. Cemetery, Sebastopol
Morita	Yoshiko	d.	SRR	3 Mar. 1916	4	3	
Morley	Mr.	m.	PC	7 May 1918	2	3	
Morris	Effie L.	d.	PA	21 May 1917	5	4	Cypress Hill; also 8:3, 23 May, 5:2; 24 May, 5:4
Morris	Effie L.	d.	PC	22 May 1917	2	1	also 25 May, 8:4
Morris	Jack	b.	ST	20 July 1917	2	3	
Morris	Jack	o.	CR	20 Mar. 1917	1	3	
Morris	Jack	b.	PA	4 Dec. 1917	4	2	
Morris	Jack	b.	PC	5 Dec. 1917	5	5	
Morris	John	b.	PD	18 Aug. 1918	2	2	
Morris	Marie	m.	PC	24 Sept. 1916	5	2	

(1) Surname	(2) Given Name	(3)	(4)	(5) Date	(6) Pg	(7) Col	(8) Comments
Morris	Melvin	d.	SRR	7 Nov. 1917	8	2	Fulton Cemetery; also 10 Nov., 7:6
Morris	Melvin	d.	PC	8 Nov. 1917	1	5	
Morris	Melvin	d.	PD	8 Nov. 1917	4	2	also 8:3
Morris	Russell	b.	PA	15 Sept. 1916	8	6	
Morris	Selma	m.	PC	27 Nov. 1918	4	3	
Morris	T. D.	d.	PD	19 Oct. 1916	3	3	
Morris	T. D.	d.	SRR	19 Oct. 1916	4	4	
Morris	Thomas D.	d.	PA	18 Oct. 1916	6	3	also 19 Oct. 2:7; Mountain View, Oakland
Morris	Thomas David	d.	PC	18 Oct. 1916	1	3	Oakland; also 20 Sept., 1:6
Morris	William	m.	PA	20 Oct. 1916	4	3	also 24 Oct., 8:5
Morris	William	m.	PC	20 Oct. 1916	5	4	
Morris	William H.	m.	PD	24 Oct. 1916	5	7	
Morrison	Alva	m.	PA	8 Apr. 1916	4	1	
Morrison	Alva	m.	SRR	8 Apr. 1916	1	2	
Morrison	Alva	m.	PD	9 Apr. 1916	8	3	
Morrison	Alvah	o.	SRR	3 Dec. 1917	8	2	also 12 Dec., 4:4
Morrison	Alvah H.	d.	PD	24 Dec. 1918	5	4	I.O.O.F. Cemetery; also 25 Dec., 4:2; 27 Dec., 6:1
Morrison	B. G.	b.	HT	14 Nov. 1916	1	3	
Morrison	Burk Guy	m.	PD	15 Jan. 1916	5	3	
Morrison	Estelle	d.	PD	21 Feb. 1917	4	2	also 8:3; 22 Feb., 4:2
Morrison	Estelle	d.	SRR	21 Feb. 1917	4	3	also 5:3; 23 Feb., 4:3
Morrison	Leslie	m.	SRR	1 June 1917	3	4	
Morrison	Lester	m.	PD	1 June 1917	8	1	
Morrison	Rachel E.	o.	SRR	3 Dec. 1917	8	2	also 12 Dec., 4:4
Morrow	J. A.	d.	PD	2 Aug. 1917	8	4	
Morrow	James	d.	PC	12 Mar. 1918	3	3	
Morrow	Mary	d.	PD	14 Mar. 1918	2	5	also 4:2
Morrow	Mary Susan	d.	PC	14 Mar. 1918	4	4	also 16 Mar., 6:4
Morrow	Mary Susan	p.	PD	24 Aug. 1918	2	3	
Mortensen	Emma	d.	PA	31 May 1916	4	1	cremation; also 1 June, 4:5
Mortensen	Emma	d.	PC	1 June 1916	3	2	San Francisco
Mortenson	Nelson, Mrs.	d.	SRR	1 June 1916	6	2	
Mortimer	J. K.	d.	SRR	12 July 1916	3	5	Rural Cemetery; also 5:3
Mortimer	John K.	d.	PD	12 July 1916	6	2	
Morton	Alexander	d.	PD	30 May 1916	7	4	
Morton	F. L., Mrs.	d.	PA	5 Nov. 1917	6	1	Sacramento
Morton	James Edward	d.	PD	14 Feb. 1918	4	3	Rural Cemetery; also 8:1; 15 Feb., 4:2

(1) Surname	(2) Given Name	(3)	(4)	(5) Date	(6) Pg	(7) Col	(8) Comments
Morton	Permilla L.	d.	PC	6 Nov. 1917	8	5	Sacramento; also 7 Nov., 6:3
Morton	Robert A.	d.	ST	3 June 1916	1	3	
Morton	Robert Alexander	d.	SRR	29 May 1916	8	6	
Morton	Robert Alexander	d.	PC	30 May 1916	5	3	
Moscowite	Isadore	d.	PC	22 Dec. 1918	8	2	France
Moscowitz	P. W.	o.	SIT	17 Aug. 1918	6	7	also 23 Nov., 1:2
Moscowitz	P. W.	o.	PC	17 Sept. 1918	2	2	
Moskowite	Isadore	d.	PA	24 Dec. 1918	6	2	France
Moskowite	Isadore W.	d.	PD	22 Dec. 1918	2	3	France
Moskowitz	Isadore W.	d.	SIT	21 Dec. 1918	2	3	portrait; France
Mossi	Anne	m.	PD	3 July 1918	3	2	
Mossi	Annie	m.	PA	3 July 1918	4	3	
Mossisey	Margaret	d.	SRR	6 Aug. 1917	1	4	aka Sister Mary Catherine; also 7 Aug., 2:1
Mossisey	Margaret	d.	PC	7 Aug. 1917	8	2	aka Sister Mary Catherine
Mothern	Pressley	b.	SRR	17 Mar. 1917	6	5	
Mothorn	Clem	d.	PA	14 Sept. 1917	2	4	
Mothorn	Emily C.	d.	PD	26 Jan. 1918	2	3	
Mothorn	Emily Elizabeth	d.	HT	31 Jan. 1918	1	2	
Mothorn	F. C. "Clem"	d.	PD	14 Sept. 1918	5	2	
Mothorn	Herma	m.	HT	20 July 1916	1	1	
Mothorn	Herman	m.	SRR	3 July 1916	3	6	
Mothorn	Irma	m.	PD	20 July 1916	2	3	
Mothorn	Pressley	b.	HT	22 Mar. 1917	7	4	
Motti	Rosa	d.	ST	5 May 1917	1	2	
Motti	Rosaline Damonte	d.	ST	5 May 1917	1	2	
Mouyer	Louis	m.	SRR	11 May 1916	8	4	
Mowry	W. A.	d.	ST	2 Nov. 1917	4	3	Pleasant Hill; also 7:3
Mowry	W. A.	d.	SRR	30 Oct. 1917	8	3	
Mowry	W. A.	d.	PC	31 Oct. 1917	8	4	
Mowry	W. A.	d.	PD	31 Oct. 1917	4	2	also 6:1
Moy	Fung	d.	SRR	19 Nov. 1917	8	2	
Mozzolini	Angelo	d.	PC	16 Jan. 1917	5	6	Calvary Cemetery
Much	Herbert N.	m.	PC	8 June 1916	6	3	
Mudget	Charles Austin	m.	PA	13 June 1918	4	3	also 22 June, 5:7; 24 June, 4:1
Mudget	Charles Austin	m.	PC	14 June 1918	5	2	also 25 June, 5:4
Muegler	Albert	m.	SRR	15 July 1916	5	1	
Muegler	Helen	m.	SRR	15 July 1916	5	1	
Mueller	C. H.	o.	PA	20 July 1917	4	3	
Mueting	William F.	d.	PC	19 Dec. 1916	8	3	
Mugler	Albert Muller	m.	PD	18 July 1916	3	2	

(1) Surname	(2) Given Name	(3)	(4)	(5) Date	(6) Pg	(7) Col	(8) Comments
Mugler	Helen Frances	m.	PD	18 July 1916	3	2	
Mulford	Ola Ward	d.	SRR	25 Nov. 1916	9	5	Riverside Cemetery
Mulhall	James	m.	PC	11 Dec. 1917	7	4	
Mulhall	James	m.	PD	12 Dec. 1917	3	2	
Mulkey	Bertine	m.	PD	14 Sept. 1918	8	3	
Mullane	Myrtle	d.	PA	5 July 1916	8	3	
Mullen	(child)	d.	PC	22 Nov. 1917	1	3	
Mullen	J. J.	b.	PD	27 Mar. 1917	2	3	
Mullen	Nora	m.	SIT	15 Dec. 1917	2	3	
Mullen	Nora	m.	PC	18 Dec. 1917	3	3	
Mullen	Norma E.	m.	SRR	11 Dec. 1917	7	3	
Muller	Christine	d.	HT	5 Apr. 1917	1	3	
Muller	Mrs.	d.	SRR	19 Dec. 1916	4	4	
Muller	Mrs.	d.	PC	3 Apr. 1917	8	2	cremation
Muller	W. A.	d.	PD	19 Dec. 1916	5	4	
Mulligan	G. Julius	m.	PD	16 Feb. 1917	8	1	
Mulligan	George Julian	m.	SRR	25 Apr. 1917	3	1	
Mulloy	Mary	d.	SRR	1 Oct. 1917	4	4	
Mumma	Maude	m.	PD	4 Aug. 1917	7	1	
Mumma	Mela Maude	m.	SRR	4 Aug. 1917	2	3	
Munday	Julia Scudder	d.	PA	16 Feb. 1916	5	4	Cypress Hill; also 8:6
Munday	Julia Scudder	d.	PC	17 Feb. 1916	3	1	Cypress Hill; also 19 Feb., 4:2
Munday	Thomas, Mrs.	d.	SRR	16 Feb. 1916	6	4	
Mundurf	Edgar	m.	PD	30 May 1917	5	2	
Munfrey	Edmund	d.	PC	20 Nov. 1917	2	3	
Munfrey	Edward	d.	SIT	24 Nov. 1917	1	4	
Munk	Fred L.	m.	PC	16 Jan. 1917	1	5	
Munro	Rosa	m.	PA	27 Dec. 1917	5	3	
Murdoch	Merton	m.	PD	1 Dec. 1918	10	2	
Murdock	Mary	d.	PA	26 Sept. 1916	4	3	
Murdock	Mary	d.	PC	26 Sept. 1916	1	5	
Murdock	Mary	d.	PD	26 Sept. 1916	1	2	also 27 Sept., 6:3; 28 Sept., 2:1
Murdock	Mary	d.	SRR	26 Sept. 1916	5	1	also 27 Sept., 8:4
Murdock	Mary	p.	SRR	6 Nov. 1916	10	3	
Mureslin	Marta	m.	PD	13 Apr. 1917	4	2	
Murofushi	Mr.	o.	SRR	7 Feb. 1916	1	3	
Murofusi	Masaye	d.	PD	7 Jan. 1917	10	2	
Murphy	Alice	d.	PD	30 May 1918	8	3	Druid's Cemetery; also 5 June, 7:4
Murphy	Estella	o.	PD	10 Oct. 1916	6	4	
Murphy	Estelle	o.	PC	12 Apr. 1916	1	3	
Murphy	Estelle	o.	SRR	21 Feb. 1916	10	5	also 11 Apr., 1:2
Murphy	Estelle C.	o.	PA	26 Apr. 1917	5	3	

(1) Surname	(2) Given Name	(3)	(4)	(5) Date	(6) Pg	(7) Col	(8) Comments
Murphy	Estelle C.	o.	SRR	26 Apr. 1917	1	2	
Murphy	Estelle C.	o.	PC	27 Apr. 1917	5	3	
Murphy	Francis Donald	m.	PD	6 July 1918	8	2	
Murphy	George B.	b.	PA	23 Aug. 1916	3	3	also 8:3
Murphy	George B.	b.	PC	24 Aug. 1916	5	2	
Murphy	Harry	b.	PA	5 Sept. 1916	1	2&3	
Murphy	J.	d.	SRR	28 June 1916	8	4	
Murphy	J.	m.	PA	29 June 1916	2	2	
Murphy	J.	d.	PC	29 June 1916	8	4	
Murphy	John C.	d.	PC	10 Feb. 1917	4	3	
Murphy	John C.	d.	CR	17 Feb. 1917	1	4	
Murphy	John C.	d.	PD	9 Feb. 1917	3	1	also 10 Feb., 4:2; 13 Feb., 2:3
Murphy	John C.	d.	SRR	9 Feb. 1917	5	1	Rural Cemetery; also 12 Feb., 8:2
Murphy	Joseph	d.	PD	29 June 1916	8	1	also 30 June, 7:1
Murphy	Louise	d.	PA	4 Aug. 1917	5	6	Cypress Hill; also 7 Aug., 5:6
Murphy	Louise A.	d.	PC	5 Aug. 1917	4	5	Cypress Hill; also 5:3; 8 Aug., 5:3
Murphy	Mary Constance	o.	PC	26 Mar. 1916	1	4	portrait
Murphy	P. H.	d.	PA	18 Aug. 1916	4	3	also 19 Aug., 4:1; 21 Aug., 4:1
Murphy	P. J.	d.	PD	23 Jan. 1917	1	3	
Murphy	P. J. "Prince"	d.	SRR	23 Jan. 1917	5	2	
Murphy	Patrick H.	d.	PC	19 Aug. 1916	1	5&6	Cypress Hill; also 22 Aug., 4:3
Murphy	Peter	o.	PC	30 Oct. 1917	8	3	
Murphy	Peter L.	o.	PC	6 June 1916	1	2	also 13 June, 2:1
Murphy	Peter L.	o.	PD	10 Oct. 1916	6	4	
Murphy	Peter L.	o.	PC	12 Apr. 1916	1	3	
Murphy	Peter L.	o.	PA	21 Feb. 1916	5	3	also 10 Apr., 1:7; 11 Apr., 4:4
Murphy	Peter L.	o.	SRR	21 Feb. 1916	10	5	also 11 Apr., 1:2
Murphy	Peter L.	o.	PA	26 Apr. 1917	5	3	
Murphy	Peter L.	o.	SRR	26 Apr. 1917	1	2	
Murphy	Peter L.	o.	PC	27 Apr. 1917	5	3	
Murphy	Peter L.	o.	SRR	29 Oct. 1917	10	5	
Murphy	Ray	o.	PC	2 Aug. 1917	3	3	
Murphy	Richard W.	d.	PD	16 May 1916	3	1	Riverside Cemetery, Cloverdale
Murphy	Richard W.	d.	SRR	16 May 1916	3	3	
Murphy	Robert	m.	PA	19 Jan. 1918	4	5	also 21 Jan., 4:4
Murphy	Robert	o.	PC	2 Aug. 1917	3	3	
Murphy	Robert W.	m.	PC	18 Jan. 1918	5	3	

(1) Surname	(2) Given Name	(3)	(4)	(5) Date	(6) Pg	(7) Col	(8) Comments
Murphy	Stella	o.	PA	21 Feb. 1916	5	3	also 10 Apr., 1:7; 11 Apr., 4:4
Murphy	Stella McGrew	o.	PC	6 June 1916	1	2	also 13 June, 2:1
Murphy	William A.	d.	PA	7 July 1916	4	5	Calvary Cemetery; also 8 July, 8:4; 10 July, 5:1
Murphy	William A.	d.	PC	7 July 1916	1	5	Calvary Cemetery; also 8 July, 5:2, 8:3; 9 July, 5:2; 11 July, 2:1
Murphy	William A.	d.	SRR	7 July 1916	6	3	
Murphy	William A.	d.	PD	8 July 1916	5	1	
Murray	Annie	m.	PD	3 Aug. 1918	2	3	
Murray	Billy	o.	PA	16 May 1917	4	6	
Murray	Burd M.	m.	PD	6 Dec. 1918	1	6	also 3:1
Murray	Catherine Elizabeth	d.	PD	1 Oct. 1918	4	2	Sebastopol; also 8:2
Murray	George William	m.	PD	22 Feb. 1916	6	5	
Murray	George Willis	m.	PA	18 Feb. 1916	1	1	
Murray	Hilda	m.	PA	5 Oct. 1916	1	5	
Murray	Hilda Mae	m.	PD	8 Oct. 1916	3	1	
Murray	J. C.	m.	SRR	4 Aug. 1916	6	2	
Murray	Kate	d.	PC	1 Oct. 1918	8	3	Sebastopol
Murray	Kate	d.	PD	29 Sept. 1918	8	1	
Murray	Kate	d.	ST	6 Oct. 1918	1	6	
Murray	Perry, Mrs.	d.	PD	24 Feb. 1918	3	5	
Murthin	Minnie	m.	PD	16 Dec. 1917	3	3	
Murthin	Minnie	m.	SRR	20 Aug. 1917	3	4	
Murthin	Minnie	m.	PC	21 Aug. 1917	6	1	
Murthin	Minnie E.	m.	SRR	15 Dec. 1917	6	1	
Musselman	George	d.	PD	1 Apr. 1917	1	2	
Musselman	George	d.	SRR	2 Apr. 1917	2	4	Sebastopol
Musselman	George	d.	PC	3 Apr. 1917	4	1	Sebastopol
Musselman	Jesse	d.	PD	1 Jan. 1918	2	7	
Musselman	Jesse	d.	SRR	27 Dec. 1917	8	3	Pleasant Hill Cemetery; also 31 Dec., 6:2
Musselman	Jesse	d.	PD	28 Dec. 1917	3	4	Pleasant Hill Cemetery; also 4:2
Musselman	Jesse	d.	PC	29 Dec. 1917	7	3	
Musselman	Robert	o.	HT	16 May 1918	7	2	
Musseln	Jesse	d.	HT	3 Jan. 1918	6	4	
Musting	William F.	d.	SRR	18 Dec. 1916	8	6	
Mutha	Frank, Jr.	b.	PD	23 Apr. 1918	8	4	
Myer	A. R.	b.	PA	19 Sept. 1918	6	2	also 8:7
Myer	Anthony R.	m.	PA	24 Apr. 1917	5	3	
Myers	Joe	d.	SRR	21 Jan. 1916	8	4	
Myers	Joe	d.	PD	22 Jan. 1916	6	3	
Myers	Lawrence	d.	PA	5 Nov. 1918	5	6	
Myers	Leland	o.	PA	21 Mar. 1918	6	5	

(1) Surname	(2) Given Name	(3)	(4)	(5) Date	(6) Pg	(7) Col	(8) Comments
Myers	Leland	o.	PA	25 Oct. 1918	4	3	
Myers	Leland	o.	PC	29 Oct. 1918	5	4	
Myers	Leland H.	o.	PA	4 Dec. 1918	5	3	
Mynatt	Carl	o.	PC	5 Oct. 1918	8	2	

N

(1) Surname	(2) Given Name	(3)	(4)	(5) Date	(6) Pg	(7) Col	(8) Comments
Nader	Charles	m.	SRR	7 Sept. 1917	8	4	also 13 Sept., 5:3
Nader	Charles	m.	PD	8 Sept. 1917	8	3	also 13 Sept., 8:2
Nagel	Arthur	d.	PC	2 Dec. 1916	8	4	
Nagle	Arthur	d.	SRR	1 Dec. 1916	8	1	also 2 Dec., 10:6; 4 Dec., 5:1
Nagle	Arthur	d.	PD	2 Dec. 1916	3	3	also 3 Dec., 6:4
Nagle	Helen	m.	PD	12 Feb. 1916	2	4	
Nagle	Helen	m.	PA	8 Feb. 1916	6	5	also 12 Feb., 2:3
Nagle	John	d.	PC	19 July 1918	1	3	
Nagle	John	d.	PD	20 July 1918	6	3	
Nance	Margaret	d.	PD	29 Dec. 1916	3	3	
Narcizo	Mary	m.	PA	12 Sept. 1916	4	4	also 14 Sept., 5:4
Narcizo	Mary	m.	PC	13 Sept. 1916	4	4	also 15 Sept., 7:3
Nash	Martha	d.	SRR	22 Nov. 1916	1	3	Franklyn, Idaho; also 23 Nov., 5:3; 24 Nov., 5:3
Nash	Martha	d.	PD	23 Nov. 1916	2	1	Franklin, Idaho; also 24 Nov., 3:1
Nash	Martha A.	d.	PA	22 Nov. 1916	1	3	also 23 Nov., 8:4
Nash	Martha A.	d.	PC	23 Nov. 1916	1	1	Franklin, Idaho; also 24 Nov., 1:3; 25 Nov., 5:3
Nauert	Fannie	d.	PA	5 Dec. 1918	4	1	cremation; also 6 Dec.,5:4; 9 Dec.. 8:2; 10 Dec.. 6:2; 11 Dec., 8:3
Nauert	Fannie	d.	PC	5 Dec. 1918	1	2	also 11 Dec., 4:3; 12 Dec., 5:4
Nauert	Fannie Light	d.	PD	6 Dec. 1918	3	2	
Nauert	Frank	o.	PC	1 June 1917	5	6	
Nauert	Frank	o.	PC	27 Sept. 1917	8	4	
Nauert	Fredda	m.	PA	7 Aug. 1918	4	3	
Nauert	Fredda	m.	PC	8 Aug. 1918	3	4	
Nauert	Fredda	m.	PD	8 Aug. 1918	2	3	
Naughton	Mary	d.	PA	16 Oct. 1917	6	5	Calvary Cemetery; also 17 Oct., 4:1
Naughton	Mary	d.	SRR	16 Oct. 1917	8	2	
Naughton	Mary	d.	PC	18 Oct. 1917	8	3	
Nauman	Lawrence	m.	PC	18 Nov. 1917	6	4	
Naumann	Lawrence	m.	ST	16 Nov. 1917	1	1	
Naumann	Lawrence	m.	PD	17 Nov. 1917	4	2	
Naumann	Ludwig	d.	PD	21 Sept. 1918	5	5	
Navani	Baptista	d.	PD	27 Feb. 1917	4	2	Calvary Cemetery; also 5:3
Navani	R.	d.	SRR	26 Feb. 1917	8	2	
Neal	Alamatia	m.	PC	20 Dec. 1918	8	3	

(1) Surname	(2) Given Name	(3)	(4)	(5) Date	(6) Pg	(7) Col	(8) Comments
Neal	Almatia	o.	PA	27 July 1917	5	4	
Neal	Almatia	o.	PD	28 July 1917	4	2	
Neal	Calmatia	o.	PC	28 July 1917	8	5	
Neal	Leslie F.	o.	PA	27 July 1917	5	4	
Neal	Leslie F.	o.	PC	28 July 1917	8	5	
Neal	Lester F.	o.	PD	28 July 1917	4	2	
Near	Chris	d.	PA	26 Dec. 1916	4	5	
Near	Chris	d.	PD	27 Dec. 1916	3	1	also 28 Dec., 3:1
Near	Christopher	d.	SRR	26 Dec. 1916	8	6	also 27 Dec., 8:2
Near	Christopher D.	p.	SRR	16 Jan. 1917	1	5	
Near	Christopher David	d.	PC	27 Dec. 1916	3	3	
Negrini	Joseph	d.	PD	31 Oct. 1916	2	2	
Neidrusthane	Harry	d.	SRR	15 Dec. 1916	10	4	
Neilsen	Anna	m.	PD	7 May 1916	7	2	
Neilson	Hannah	m.	PA	6 May 1916	5	1	
Nell	Susanna	m.	PA	18 Dec. 1917	11	4	
Nelligan	Joseph	b.	SRR	25 Apr. 1916	8	5	
Nelligan	Joseph	b.	SRR	7 Nov. 1917	8	1	
Nelson	Alfred	o.	PC	4 Dec. 1918	3	4	
Nelson	Andrew Thomas	m.	HT	29 Nov. 1917	2	3	
Nelson	Charles	b.	PA	23 May 1917	4	5	
Nelson	Clyde	o.	PC	18 Apr. 1918	3	4	
Nelson	Emery	m.	PD	8 July 1917	5	4	
Nelson	Emma C.	m.	PC	28 Dec. 1916	5	5	also 30 Dec., 3:3
Nelson	Harold	m.	PD	1 May 1917	5	1	
Nelson	Harold	m.	SRR	1 May 1917	3	2	
Nelson	Harry E.	d.	PC	30 Aug. 1918	3	2	
Nelson	Harvey E.	m.	PC	15 May 1917	3	3	also 16 May, 5:3
Nelson	Harvey E.	m.	PA	16 May 1917	4	3	
Nelson	John	b.	PA	3 July 1918	8	3	
Nelson	John	b.	PA	13 Oct. 1916	4	6	
Nelson	John T.	o.	PA	31 May 1917	5	4	
Nelson	Margaret J.	d.	SRR	1 Apr. 1916	5	3	Ashland, OR; also 3 Apr., 7:6
Nelson	Margaret J.	d.	PD	2 Apr. 1016	4	2	Ashland, OR
Nelson	Margery Leymance	d.	HT	13 Jan. 1916	1	6	Oak Mound Cemetery
Nelson	Mary	m.	PD	8 July 1917	5	4	
Nelson	Mary	d.	SRR	19 Sept. 1916	6	3	Oak Mound Cemetery
Nelson	Mary	d.	PD	20 Sept. 1916	2	2	Oak Mound Cemetery
Nelson	Mary	d.	HT	21 Sept. 1916	1	2	
Nelson	Rose G.	o.	PA	31 May 1917	5	4	
Nelson	Samuel	m.	PD	7 Mar. 1916	8	1	
Nelson	William	m.	PC	16 Mar. 1918	8	5	also 22 Mar., 8:2
Nelson	Thomas	m.	PD	2 Dec. 1917	10	4	
Nesbit	Andrew Jackson	d.	PA	2 Apr. 1918	6	4	

(1) Surname	(2) Given Name	(3)	(4)	(5) Date	(6) Pg	(7) Col	(8) Comments
Nesbit	Eva	m.	PC	11 Oct. 1918	5	4	also 13 Oct., 4:4
Nesbit	Rudolph William Whan	d.	PD	21 Nov. 1918	8	1	France
Nesbitt	Andrew Jackson	d.	PD	31 Mar. 1918	4	2	also 7:2; 2 Apr., 7:3
Nesbitt	Eva Elizabeth	m.	PA	12 Oct. 1918	8	5	
Nesbitt	James Robert	d.	PA	8 July 1918	5	5	Cypress Hill; also 8:6
Nesbitt	James Robert	d.	PC	9 July 1918	2	1	Cypress Hill; also 6:3; 10 July, 5:4
Nesbitt	Randolf	d.	PA	19 Nov. 1918	5	4	France
Nesbitt	Randolph	d.	PC	20 Nov. 1918	1	3	France
Nesbitt	Will J.	d.	PA	6 Dec. 1917	4	3	also 7 Dec., 6:3; 11 Dec., 13:4
Nesbitt	Will J., Jr.	d.	PD	13 Dec. 1917	7	2	
Nesbitt	Will, Jr.	d.	SRR	8 Dec. 1917	6	3	Cypress Hill; also 11 Dec., 8:3; 13 Dec., 2:3
Nesbitt	William J., Jr.	d.	PC	7 Dec. 1917	4	3	Cypress Hill; also 8 Dec., 1:5; 11 Dec., 4:3, 5:6; 12 Dec., 5:1; 13 Dec., 8:3; 16 Dec., 7:5
Neview	Hilda M.	d.	PA	27 Feb. 1917	8	5	Cypress Hill; also 1 Mar., 8:6
Neview	Hilda M.	d.	PC	28 Feb. 1917	4	5	Cypress Hill; also 8:5; 1 Mar., 8:4; 2 Mar., 4:3
Neview	Hilda M.	d.	SRR	28 Feb. 1917	6	3	
Newbert	Clara M.	o.	HT	4 Oct. 1917	7	2	
Newbert	William P.	o.	HT	4 Oct. 1917	7	2	
Newcomb	Irene	m.	PD	23 Mar. 1918	8	3	
Newcomb	Irene	m.	ST	29 Mar. 1918	1	1	
Newcomb	Irene	m.	PC	31 Mar. 1918	2	2	
Newell	Esther Alice	d.	PD	30 June 1918	7	3	
Newell	Paul C.	m.	PD	10 Sept. 1918	6	1	
Newell	Paul C.	m.	PD	17 Sept. 1918	8	3	
Newland	Harry D.	m.	PD	6 Oct. 1917	2	1	
Newman	Frank	d.	SRR	24 Aug. 1916	5	2	cremation; also 25 Aug., 8:4; 29 Aug., 5:3
Newman	Frank C.	d.	PD	24 Aug. 1916	8	4	also 25 Aug., 8:3
Newman	Frank C.	d.	PC	25 Aug. 1916	6	4	cremation; also 30 Aug., 2:2
Newman	Ludwig	d.	PA	20 Sept. 1918	4	5	
Newman	Ludwig	d.	PC	21 Sept. 1918	1	3	
Newman	M. C.	d.	PD	10 Nov. 1916	6	5	
Newman	Walden Charles	d.	PA	9 Nov. 1916	8	5	Cypress Hill; also 10 Nov., 4:5
Newman	Walden Charles	d.	PC	9 Nov. 1916	1	4	also 10 Nov., 8:2; 11 Nov., 4:1
Nicholas	Leland	b.	SIT	8 Jan. 1916	1	4	
Nichols	Margaret	m.	PA	15 Feb. 1917	5	7	also 20 Feb., 5:2

(1) Surname	(2) Given Name	(3)	(4)	(5) Date	(6) Pg	(7) Col	(8) Comments
Nichols	Margaret	m.	PD	16 Feb. 1917	6	4	also 21 Feb., 6:2
Nichols	Sarah Margaret	m.	PC	21 Feb. 1917	1	4	
Nichols	Vernon	o.	HT	20 Dec. 1917	4	1	
Nichols	Vernon	o.	PD	24 Nov. 1918	5	3	
Nichols	Vernon	o.	HT	3 Oct. 1918	7	1	
Nichols	William E.	d.	PD	19 July 1918	8	1	Oakland; also 23 July, 2:2
Nicholson	Andrew G.	d.	PC	10 Apr. 1918	8	3	
Nickerson	E. D.	d.	HT	17 Jan. 1918	1	5	
Nickerson	Z. D.	d.	PD	18 Jan. 1918	3	1	
Nicolisen	Carl	b.	PC	1 Dec. 1917	5	3	
Nicolisen	Carl	b.	PA	30 Nov. 1917	4	6	
Nielsen	Carl	m.	ST	8 Mar. 1918	1	5	
Nielsen	Carl W.	m.	PC	12 Mar. 1918	6	3	
Nielsen	Louis	d.	PA	14 Aug. 1918	4	5	Two Rock; also 5:5; 16 Aug., 4:5
Nielsen	Louis	d.	PC	14 Aug. 1918	8	3	Two Rock; also 15 Aug., 5:3; 17 Aug., 4:3
Nielsen	N. P.	b.	PA	18 Sept. 1918	8	2	
Nielson	Alma O.	o.	PA	18 Feb. 1918	5	2	
Nielson	Andrea Sophie	d.	PD	6 Aug. 1918	4	2	also 5:4; 8 Aug., 2:1
Nielson	Anna	m.	SRR	8 May 1916	5	2	
Nielson	Carl W.	m.	PD	12 Mar. 1918	3	5	
Nielson	Lauritz	o.	PA	18 Feb. 1918	5	2	
Nielson	Louis	d.	PD	15 Aug. 1918	8	4	
Nieman	Rolina	m.	PC	1 Dec. 1917	5	1	also 25 Dec., 6:3
Nieman	Rolina	m.	PA	30 Nov. 1917	8	3	also 24 Dec., 8:3
Niestrath	Maybelle	m.	PD	25 Aug. 1918	2	5	
Nisson	Carl W.	m.	PD	17 July 1918	5	4	
Nisson	Carl W.	m.	PA	18 July 1918	4	5	
Nisson	Christian	m.	PA	20 Dec. 1918	8	3	
Nisson	Christian	m.	PC	20 Dec. 1918	8	3	
Nisson	Christine	m.	PA	20 Nov. 1918	4	4	
Nisson	Christine E.	m.	PC	20 Nov. 1918	5	4	21 Nov., 3:4
Nisson	Claudina J.	d.	PA	10 Dec. 1917	5	4	Two Rock; also 11 Dec., 12:4
Nisson	Claudinia	d.	SRR	10 Dec. 1917	6	4	
Nisson	Claudinia	d.	PC	9 Dec. 1917	1	5	Two Rock; also 4:5; 12 Dec., 8:3
Nisson	E. P., Mrs.	d.	PD	12 Dec. 1917	3	2	
Nisson	Ella Marie	m.	PC	8 July 1916	3	3	
Nisson	Viggo	b.	PA	25 Oct. 1916	4	5	
Nisson	Viggo	b.	PC	26 Oct. 1916	5	6	
Noack	Frederick	m.	ST	15 Apr. 1916	1	2	also 22 Apr., 1:1
Noack	Maxwell	m.	SRR	10 Apr. 1916	1	4	also 8 May, 6:2

(1) Surname	(2) Given Name	(3)	(4)	(5) Date	(6) Pg	(7) Col	(8) Comments
Noack	Maxwell F.	m.	PD	18 Apr. 1916	3	1	
Noack	Maxwell Frederick	m.	PC	11 Apr. 1916	4	3	
Noble	Madge	m.	PD	17 Sept. 1918	7	2	
Noble	Percy	o.	PA	16 Sept. 1918	4	2	
Noble	Percy	d.	PC	17 Sept. 1918	1	5	
Noble	Percy	d.	PD	17 Sept. 1918	2	5	
Noble	Ralph Weyman	m.	SRR	21 Aug. 1916	8	5	
Nobles	Harry A.	m.	PC	22 Feb. 1916	5	4	
Noc	William Joseph	m.	SRR	5 Oct. 1917	5	3	
Nofler	Harrison	d.	SRR	7 July 1916	8	5	
Nofler	Harrison	d.	PD	8 July 1916	8	3	
Nonella	Stephen	d.	SIT	19 Oct. 1918	1	1	
Nonella	Sylvester	d.	PA	17 Oct. 1918	5	2	
Nonella	Sylvester	d.	PC	17 Oct. 1918	1	2	Sonoma
Nonella	Sylvester	d.	PD	18 Oct. 1918	5	4	also 20 Oct., 3;3
Nonella	William	b.	PC	10 Oct. 1916	5	6	
Nonella	William	b.	PD	10 Oct. 1916	6	5	
Nonella	William	b.	PA	9 Oct. 1916	1	2	
Noonan	Ella	m.	PA	15 May 1917	5	6	
Noonan	Ella	m.	SRR	15 May 1917	8	3	
Noonan	Ella	m.	PD	16 May 1917	8	3	
Noonan	Paul	b.	PC	4 July 1918	8	3	
Norbury	Cecil John	m.	PD	18 June 1916	3	1	
Norden	Augusta	m.	PA	3 Aug. 1918	3	4	
Noriel	Joseph	b.	PA	4 Sept. 1917	5	5	also 5 Sept., 6:6
Noriel	Will	o.	PC	6 Dec. 1917	1	3	
Noriel	Zenas	m.	PA	3 Apr. 1916	4	1	
Noriel	Zenos	m.	SRR	5 Apr. 1916	3	4	
Norrbom	Mrs.	d.	PD	25 Oct. 1916	2	3	
Norrbom	Peter	m.	SIT	8 Jan. 1916	4	3	also 17 June, 1:7
Norrbom	Sarah	d.	SIT	28 Oct. 1916	1	3	Mountain Cemetery
Norrbom	Sarah T.	d.	PC	28 Oct. 1916	3	1	
Norris	E. R.	b.	PD	20 Jan. 1916	2	2	
Norris	Irene	m.	SRR	31 May 1917	3	3	
Norris	Irene	m.	PD	1 June 1917	6	4	
Northern	Frank T.	d.	PA	15 Nov. 1918	5	1&6	Cypress Hill; also 18 Nov., 5:1
Northern	Frank Thomas	d.	PC	15 Nov. 1918	8	2	Cypress Hill; also 16 Nov., 3:2; 17 Nov., 2:3; 19 Nov., 3:2
Northrup	Charles	d.	PD	30 Nov. 1918	5	2	
Northrup	Charles F.	d.	PA	27 Nov. 1918	4	4	also 29 Nov., 5:4
Northrup	Charles Frederich	d.	PC	28 Nov. 1918	5	3	also 8:4
Norton	Irene	o.	PD	17 July 1917	6	3	
Norton	Raymond	o.	PD	17 July 1917	6	3	

(1) Surname	(2) Given Name	(3)	(4)	(5) Date	(6) Pg	(7) Col	(8) Comments
Norwood	Captain	d.	SIT	7 Apr. 1917	1	2	
Norwood	H. H.	d.	SRR	9 Apr. 1917	6	1	also 11 Apr., 8:2
Nothern	Frank Thomas	d.	PD	16 Nov. 1918	8	4	
Notrica	Albert	m.	SRR	4 May 1917	2	4	
Notries	Albert	m.	PD	4 May 1917	1	2	
Noumensen	Katinka	m.	SIT	26 Jan. 1918	1	2	
Nowell	Adelia	d.	PD	9 Feb. 1918	4	3	also 7:4; 12 Feb., 6:2
Nowlin	Ernest C.	o.	PD	30 July 1918	6	3	
Nowlin	Mary L.	o.	PD	30 July 1918	6	3	
Nutting	Myrtle	m.	PA	19 May 1916	8	7	
Nutting	Myrtle	m.	PC	19 May 1916	5	3	
Nyedegger	Frederick G.	m.	PD	15 Nov. 1917	4	2	
Nygren	G. E.	d.	SRR	4 Jan. 1916	10	2	Bennett Valley

O

(1) Surname	(2) Given Name	(3)	(4)	(5) Date	(6) Pg	(7) Col	(8) Comments
Oakley	Maynard	b.	PA	9 May 1916	5	2&7	
Oakley	Maynard	b.	PC	10 May 1916	8	2	
Oates	James W.	d.	HT	3 Feb. 1917	5	1	cremation
Oates	James Wyatt	d.	SRR	17 Jan. 1916	3	4	
O'Banion	Hannah	d.	PA	3 Dec. 1917	5	5	Cypress Hill; also 5 Dec., 5:5
O'Banion	Hannah Pauline	d.	PC	4 Dec. 1917	6	3	also 6 Dec., 5:4
O'Bannion	Roy	m.	PC	27 Sept. 1918	4	3	
Obear	Charles	m.	HT	23 May 1918	3	5	
Obear	Eva	m.	PD	15 Dec. 1916	6	1	
O'Bear	Charles	m.	PD	24 May 1918	3	1	
O'Bear	Charles	o.	ST	7 Apr. 1917	3	2	
Ober	Bessie I.	m.	PD	27 Sept. 1916	6	1	
Obert	J. M.	m.	PA	8 Oct. 1918	6	5	
O'Brien	J. T.	o.	PC	19 July 1917	1	4	
O'Brien	Pam	m.	PD	4 June 1918	2	1	also 7 June, 8:5; 8 June, 5:7
O'Brien	V. W.	d.	PC	15 Nov. 1916	8	3	Stotesbury, MO; also 16 Nov., 8:4
O'Brien	Vernie W.	d.	PA	14 Nov. 1916	8	6	Stotesburg, MO
O'Brien	Vernon	o.	PD	13 July 1918	2	3	
O'Brien/O'Bryan	Arthur Leander	d.	PD	12 May 1917	2	2	also 13 May, 4:3
O'Bryan	Arthur L.	d.	SRR	11 May 1917	1	6	
O'Callaghan	Mary	m.	PD	9 May 1916	7	7	
O'Connel	John	d.	ST	27 Dec. 1918	8	4	
O'Connell	John	d.	PC	28 Dec. 1918	8	4	
O'Connor	Robert	o.	PC	17 Sept. 1918	1	2	
O'Connor	Thomas	o.	PD	26 June 1918	5	1	
Odgers	Clara	d.	ST	22 June 1917	1	3	Gilliams Cemetery
Odgers	John W., Mrs.	d.	PD	20 June 1917	2	4	
Odgers	John W., Mrs.	d.	PC	21 June 1917	5	6	
O'Donovan	Bartholomew	o.	PD	20 Jan. 1918	1	2	
O'Donovan	Bartholomew	d.	PC	26 Jan. 1918	8	5	
O'Donovan	Bartholomew	d.	PD	26 Jan. 1918	4	3	Calvary Cemetery; also 5:1
Oeacha	Chris	d.	PA	25 June 1917	3	4	Napa
Oehlmann	Otto	b.	PD	1 Aug. 1917	3	5	
Oeltjen	George	b.	PC	11 Jan. 1917	5	1	
Oeltjen	George	m.	PC	18 Jan. 1916	6	2	
Oeltjen	George H.	m.	PA	17 Jan. 1916	5	5	
Oeltjen	Matilda L.	m.	PC	8 Sept. 1918	5	3	also 10 Sept., 4:1
Oeltjen	Tillie	m.	PA	9 Sept. 1918	4	5	also 8 Sept., 8:5

(1) Surname	(2) Given Name	(3)	(4)	(5) Date	(6) Pg	(7) Col	(8) Comments
Ofdenkamp	Kathryn Isabel	m.	PA	4 May 1917	7	4	
Offut	Lewis Walker	o.	PC	21 Apr. 1918	1	4	
Offut	Louis	o.	PC	16 Dec. 1917	1	2	
Offutt	Charles G.	m.	PD	26 Aug. 1917	8	4	
Offutt	Charles G.	m.	PC	27 Aug. 1917	5	5	
Offutt	Charles, Jr.	m.	PA	25 Aug. 1917	8	5	
Offutt	Ella	m.	PA	15 Sept. 1916	4	4	also 30 Sept., 5:4; 2 Oct., 5:3
Offutt	Ella Mae	m.	PC	26 Aug. 1916	5	4	
Offutt	Ella May	m.	PC	1 Oct. 1916	8	2	also 2 Oct., 2:1
Offutt	Lewis	d.	PC	7 May 1918	3	4	
Offutt	Lewis	o.	PC	24 May 1918	1	3	
Offutt	Mildred	m.	PA	17 Aug. 1918	4	5	
Offutt	Mildred	m.	PC	18 Aug. 1918	5	2	
Offutt	Will	b.	PA	10 June 1918	5	3	
Offutt	William	b.	PC	4 May 1916	8	5	
Ogan	Lester	d.	PC	11 Apr. 1918	3	4	I.O.O.F. Cemetery
Ogan	Lester	d.	PD	10 Apr. 1918	7	1	
Ogan	Lester	d.	PA	12 Apr. 1918	8	1	
Ogan	Lester	d.	ST	5 Apr. 1918	1	4	I.O.O.F. Cem.
Ogburn	Edith	m.	PD	1 Oct. 1916	7	5	
Ogburn	Edith	m.	SRR	30 Sept. 1916	1	5	
Ogburn	Edith L.	m.	PC	1 Oct. 1916	8	5	
Ogle	Frances	m.	PD	27 Oct. 1917	7	5	
Ogle	Fred	m.	SRR	26 Feb. 1916	10	3	
Ogle	Fred C.	m.	PA	26 Feb. 1916	5	4	
Ogle	Fred Cecil	m.	PC	26 Feb. 1916	2	3	
Ogle	Grover	o.	PC	28 July 1918	3	3	
O'Hallaran	Tim	d.	PD	21 July 1918	2	4	
O'Halloran	Timothy	d.	PA	20 July 1918	4	1	also 22 July, 5:2
O'Halloran	Timothy	d.	SIT	27 July 1918	1	3	also 3 Aug., 1:5
O'Hannan	Timothy	d.	PC	21 July 1918	8	2	
Ohlson	N. E.	d.	PD	10 Feb. 1917	2	2	
Olberg	Harry, Jr.	m.	PC	22 May 1916	3	2	
Oldberg	Harry	m.	PA	22 May 1916	1	4	also 23 May, 7:4
Oldberg	Harry J.	m.	PD	23 May 1916	3	4	
Oldberg	Harry J., Jr.	m.	PA	30 Mar. 1916	6	3	
O'Leary	Dollie	m.	SRR	7 July 1917	8	2	
O'Leary	Dollie	m.	PD	8 July 1917	2	4	
O'Leary	John	m.	SIT	29 Apr. 1916	5	4	
O'Leary	John F.	d.	PC	25 Apr. 1916	3	2	Holy Cross, S.F.; also 4:2; 26 Apr., 4:4
O'Leary	John P.	d.	PA	24 Apr. 1916	8	4	Holy Cross, S.F.; also 25 Apr., 7:3

(1) Surname	(2) Given Name	(3)	(4)	(5) Date	(6) Pg	(7) Col	(8) Comments
O'Leary	Ruby	d.	SRR	2 May 1917	3	5	Guerneville; also 3 May, 8:4
O'Leary	Ruby May	d.	PD	2 May 1917	4	3	Guerneville; also 8:3; 4 May, 3:5
Oleson	Elsie A.	m.	PC	12 May 1916	6	1	
Olin	Cyrus	m.	SIT	15 Sept. 1917	1	5	
Olin	Edith	d.	PC	19 Oct. 1918	4	6	
Olin	Edith	d.	PD	19 Oct. 1918	8	3	Rural Cemetery; also 24 Oct., 4:2; 26 Oct., 6:4
Olin	Silas W.	m.	PC	11 Sept. 1917	4	4	
Olin	Silas W.	m.	SRR	8 Sept. 1917	8	5	
Oliver	Joseph	m.	SRR	16 June 1917	10	5	
Oliver	Joseph	m.	PC	17 June 1917	5	1	
Olmstead	Helen	m.	PC	12 July 1917	3	3	
Olmstead	Helen Matlack	m.	PA	15 May 1917	4	6	also 25 June, 2:6; 12 July, 4:4
Olmstead	Stephen Horatio	d.	PC	27 Dec. 1916	4	3	Cypress Hill; also 24 Dec., 4:1
Olmsted	Helen	m.	PD	16 May 1917	4	2	
Olmsted	Helen	m.	SRR	25 June 1917	1	4	
Olmsted	Helen	m.	PD	12 July 1917	2	5	
Olmsted	Helen	m.	SRR	12 July 1917	5	2	
Olmsted	Helen M.	m.	SRR	15 May 1917	3	4	
Olmsted	Helen Matlack	m.	PC	16 May 1917	5	3	
Olmsted	Stephen H.	d.	PD	24 Dec. 1916	4	2	
Olney	Adelia M.	d.	PD	19 May 1918	4	2	Odd Fellows Cemetery; also 5:2; 22 May, 5:1
Olney	Harry	d.	GT	1 Jan. 1916	1	2	
Olsen	Adolph	m.	PA	18 Oct. 1916	5	2	also 4 Nov., 4:4
Olsen	Adolph	m.	PC	18 Oct. 1916	1	5	also 3 Nov., 6:5; 4 Nov., 4:6
Olsen	Adolph	m.	PD	19 Oct. 1916	6	4	also 4 Nov., 1:5
Olson	Adolph	b.	PA	10 Aug. 1917	5	4&5	
Olson	Minnick	m.	PC	17 Sept. 1916	6	2	
Olson	Minnick	m.	PA	18 Sept. 1916	4	6	also 19 Sept., 4:5; 20 Sept., 7:5
Olson	Minnick	m.	PC	20 Sept. 1916	4	1	
Olson	Minnick	b.	PA	5 Oct. 1917	4	5	
Olson	Otto	m.	PD	3 Aug. 1917	2	1	
Olson	Otto	m.	SRR	3 Aug. 1917	3	2	
Olson	Segrid	d.	PA	2 May 1916	5	1&7	Cypress Hill
Olson	Sigured/Sigfred	d.	PC	2 May 1916	1	2	Cypress Hill; also 4 May, 5:4
Olson	Thora	m.	PA	31 Dec. 1918	4	2	
Oltmann	L. W.	m.	HT	11 Apr. 1918	3	5	
Oluffs	Pauline	m.	PA	16 Dec. 1918	5	4	

(1) Surname	(2) Given Name	(3)	(4)	(5) Date	(6) Pg	(7) Col	(8) Comments
Olufs	Pauline	m.	PC	4 Dec. 1918	8	4	
O'Neill	Jennie	d.	PA	10 Mar. 1917	5	1	also 13 Mar., 5:3
O'Neill	Jennie	d.	PC	11 Mar. 1917	4	1	also 13 Mar., 4:1; 14 Mar., 8:3
O'Neill	Jennie A.	d.	PC	14 Aug. 1917	5	2	moved from Cypress Hill to Calvary Cemetery
O'Neill	Will T.	b.	PC	24 June 1916	8	1	
Ordahl	George	b.	SRR	28 Aug. 1916	8	4	
Ordahl	George	b.	PD	29 Aug. 1916	6	3	
Ornbaum	Alma May	m.	PD	6 Oct. 1917	2	1	
Ornbaum	Annabelle	o.	PD	9 Aug. 1917	3	4	
Ornbaum	Breck	o.	PD	9 Aug. 1917	3	4	
Ornbaum	Daisy	m.	PD	6 Oct. 1917	2	1	
Ornbaun	Ananbelle	o.	SRR	9 Aug. 1917	3	4	also 27 Aug., 4:1; 5 Sept., 2:3
Ornbaun	Breck	o.	SRR	9 Aug. 1917	3	4	also 27 Aug., 4:1; 5 Sept., 2:3
Orr	J. S.	d.	SRR	13 Nov. 1916	8	4	
Orr	James Sherman	d.	PD	14 Nov. 1916	8	4	
Orr	James Sherman	d.	PC	21 Nov. 1916	3	2	Duncan's Mills
Orsolini	Paul	d.	PD	12 Dec. 1916	2	3	
Orsolini	Paul	d.	SRR	8 Dec. 1916	8	2	also 11 Dec., 1:4
Orth	Fred	o.	PD	15 Nov. 1918	4	2	name change to Fred Orth Foster
Osborn	Alexander	d.	ST	15 June 1917	1	2	
Osborn	Alexander	d.	PC	17 June 1917	3	2	
Osborn	Minot	m.	SRR	18 May 1917	6	5	
Osborn	Minto F.	o.	SRR	27 Aug. 1917	8	6	
Osborn	William H.	o.	SRR	27 Aug. 1917	8	6	
Osborne	Will	b.	HT	30 Mar. 1916	2	3	
Oscha	Chris	d.	PD	26 June 1917	8	1	
Oscha	Chris	d.	SRR	26 June 1917	5	3	
Oscha	Chris	d.	PC	28 June 1917	7	5	
Osecha	Chris	d.	SIT	30 June 1917	4	4	
Oster	Henry	m.	PD	6 Feb. 1917	2	2	
Oster	Ottmar	d.	PD	17 Nov. 1918	1	4	France
Oster	Otto H.	d.	PC	16 Nov. 1918	1	3	France
Oster	Ottomar H.	d.	PA	16 Nov. 1918	5	4	France
Oster	Walter	m.	PC	3 Feb. 1917	4	1	also 17 Feb., 4:5; 20 Feb., 5:3
Oster	Walter	m.	SRR	5 Feb. 1917	5	1	also 20 Feb., 7:3
Oster	Walter Henry	m.	PA	19 Feb. 1917	3	4	
Ostersen	Walter	b.	PA	28 Feb. 1918	6	4	
Ostrander	Frances	m.	SRR	27 June 1917	8	2	also 2 July, 6:2
Ostrander	Frances	m.	ST	29 June 1917	1	2	
Ostrander	Wilbur C.	m.	SRR	27 June 1917	8	2	

(1) Surname	(2) Given Name	(3)	(4)	(5) Date	(6) Pg	(7) Col	(8) Comments
Ott	George	b.	PC	6 Mar. 1917	4	1	
Ott	George H.	b.	PA	6 Mar. 1917	7	4	
Ott	Gerald Herbert	d.	PA	7 Mar. 1917	5	3	also 8 Mar., 6:5
Ott	Gerald Herbert	d.	PC	8 Mar. 1917	1	5	also 9 Mar., 8:5
Ottavionio	Mario	d.	PC	3 Nov. 1918	1	4	Calvary Cemetery; also 8 Nov., 4:3; 10 Nov., 4:2
Otterbeck	Evelyn	m.	SRR	14 July 1917	8	2	
Otterbeck	Evelyn	m.	PC	17 July 1917	2	1	
Ottman	Joseph	m.	PC	21 Nov. 1916	4	2	
Ottoboni	Lina	m.	PD	2 Apr. 1918	3	3	
Ottonella	Vittrio	o.	SIT	11 Aug. 1917	1	1	
Ottoviano	Mario	d.	PA	9 Nov. 1918	5	4	
Overington	Charles H.	o.	PD	27 Apr. 1918	8	3	also 28 Apr., 3:2
Overmeyer	Leanore	d.	PD	13 Sept. 1917	3	4	
Overstreet	Mollie	m.	PD	10 Oct. 1917	6	2	
Overton	Grace	m.	PA	7 Apr. 1917	4	5	
Overton	Grace V.	m.	PC	8 Apr. 1917	5	3	
Overton	Gwendolyn	m.	PD	8 Dec. 1917	8	3	also 9 Dec., 7:1
Overton	Gwendolyn	m.	SRR	8 Dec. 1917	4	2	
Overton	Gwendolyn	m.	PC	9 Dec. 1917	6	3	
Overton	John H.	d.	PA	2 Dec. 1918	5	3	Cypress Hill; also 8:4; 3 Dec., 4:4
Overton	John H.	d.	PC	3 Dec. 1918	5	3&4	also 5 Dec., 6:3
Overton	John H.	d.	PD	3 Dec. 1918	6	3	
Overton	Laurene	m.	PA	10 Dec. 1917	2	2	
Overton	Laurene	m.	PD	2 Dec. 1917	7	1	also 9 Dec., 7:1
Overton	Laurine	m.	SRR	8 Dec. 1917	4	1	
Overton	Laurine	m.	PC	9 Dec. 1917	5	4	
Overton	M. E., Mrs.	d.	PD	11 Oct. 1916	8	4	
Overton	M. E., Mrs.	d.	SRR	11 Oct. 1916	5	3	Mountain View, Oakland
Overton	M. W., Mrs.	d.	PA	10 Oct. 1916	3	4	Mountain View, Oakland
Overton	Mitchell R.	m.	PD	18 Nov. 1916	5	1	
Owen	B. J.	b.	SRR	13 Mar. 1916	3	2	triplets
Owens	Charles	d.	SRR	1 Dec. 1916	8	4	
Owens	Charles Anderson	d.	PD	2 Dec. 1916	8	1	
Owens	Lizzie	d.	ST	1 Jan. 1916	7	5	
Oxley	James D.	o.	SRR	29 Oct. 1917	1	4	
Oxley	James D.	o.	PD	30 Oct. 1917	2	3	
Oxley	Marie	o.	PD	30 Oct. 1917	2	3	
Oxley	Marie J.	o.	SRR	29 Oct. 1917	1	4	

P & Q

(1) Surname	(2) Given Name	(3)	(4)	(5) Date	(6) Pg	(7) Col	(8) Comments
Pacheco	Gill	d.	PA	15 Nov. 1918	3	6	Tomales; also 5:1; 16 Nov., 4:4
Pacheco	Gill	d.	PC	15 Nov. 1918	8	3	Tomales; also 16 Nov., 3:5; 17 Nov., 5:3
Pacilli	Raphael	d.	PD	16 Nov. 1918	3	4	
Packscher	Samuel D.	m.	PD	23 May 1918	7	3	also 25 May, 2:5; 22 June, 3:5
Packwood	Esther	d.	HT	19 Dec. 1918	4	1	
Packwood	Esther	d.	PD	27 Dec. 1918	6	1	also 31 Dec., 7:1
Packwood	Esther	d.	PC	28 Dec. 1918	2	2	
Packwood	Stella	d.	PD	28 Dec. 1918	8	1	also 31 Dec., 3:2
Packwood	Stella	d.	PC	29 Dec. 1918	1	4	
Padilli	Antone	b.	PA	31 Mar. 1916	6	6	
Page	Albert	b.	SRR	18 Sept. 1917	4	4	
Page	Albert E.	b.	PD	19 Sept. 1917	3	4	
Page	Anna	d.	PD	10 July 1918	6	1	
Page	Emma W.	d.	HT	17 May 1917	1	2	
Page	Emma W.	d.	ST	18 May 1917	3	3	
Paine	Edwin	d.	PC	23 Nov. 1917	2	3	
Paine	Edwin	d.	SIT	24 Nov. 1917	3	1	
Paisley	Helen Marie	m.	SRR	3 Jan. 1917	8	5	
Paisley	Helen Marie	m.	PC	4 Jan. 1917	5	4	
Paisley	Helen Marie	m.	PD	4 Jan. 1917	3	2	
Pallady	Helen	m.	PD	20 Nov. 1917	2	3	
Pallady	Helen	m.	HT	22 Nov. 1917	5	3	
Pallady	Ruth	m.	PD	16 Sept. 1917	3	3	
Pallo	Victoria	m.	PC	22 Nov. 1917	3	1	
Palmer	Charles Edward	o.	PC	8 Feb. 1918	8	2	
Palmer	Elsia	d.	PD	10 May 1918	8	2	
Palmer	George W.	m.	PD	20 Oct. 1918	5	3	
Palmer	George W.	m.	ST	25 Oct. 1918	1	2	
Palmer	Lucy	d.	PC	29 Dec. 1916	1	6	
Palmer	Mary	d.	PC	14 Apr. 1916	1	4	also 15 Apr., 1:5
Palmer	Mary E.	d.	PA	14 Apr. 1916	8	3&5	
Palmer	Mary Emily	d.	PD	14 Apr. 1916	8	1	
Palmer	Mary Emily	d.	SRR	14 Apr. 1916	5	3	Alameda
Palmerlee	Edith	m.	SRR	24 Apr. 1916	8	2	
Paltini	Ernest	m.	PD	28 July 1917	3	2	
Palucci	Louis	b.	PA	4 Jan. 1917	2	4	
Palucci	Louis	b.	PC	5 Jan. 1917	5	5	
Pancrazi	Josephine	m.	PD	21 Nov. 1916	6	5	
Pancrazi	Julius	m.	PD	30 May 1918	2	3	

(1) Surname	(2) Given Name	(3)	(4)	(5) Date	(6) Pg	(7) Col	(8) Comments
Pancrazi	Julius	m.	SIT	8 June 1918	1	7	
Panerazi	Josephine Florence	m.	SIT	25 Nov. 1916	1	3	
Panosh	Joseph W.	o.	PD	9 Feb. 1918	6	4	
Panosh	Mac B.	o.	PD	9 Feb. 1918	6	4	
Paolini	Mary	m.	PD	13 Jan. 1918	6	6	also 18 Jan., 5:5
Papera	Dide	m.	PD	14 May 1918	7	3	also 15 May, 7:3
Pardee	George W.	d.	PD	15 Oct. 1918	5	4	
Pardee	Lusitta	m.	PD	15 May 1918	8	4	
Pare	Theles	d.	SRR	28 Nov. 1917	8	4	Sebastopol
Pare	Thels	d.	PD	29 Nov. 1917	8	4	
Pare	Thies	d.	PC	29 Nov. 1917	4	4	
Pare	Thles	d.	PA	28 Nov. 1917	5	5	
Parent	Arthur	m.	PD	4 Jan. 1918	6	2	
Parent	Arthur W.	m.	PA	3 Jan. 1918	8	3	
Parent	Arthur W.	m.	PC	4 Jan. 1918	3	5	
Pareria	George	m.	PA	30 Apr. 1917	4	5	
Pareto	George	m.	SRR	23 Oct. 1917	4	4	
Pariera	George	m.	PC	26 Apr. 1917	1	1	also 1 May, 3:5
Paris	Walter	b.	PC	15 Mar. 1918	6	3	
Park	E. E.	d.	SRR	19 June 1916	5	1	San Francisco; also 20 June, 8:4
Park	Everett E.	d.	PC	20 June 1916	6	2	
Park	J. A.	d.	PD	8 May 1917	6	2	Petaluma
Park	John C.	d.	PA	1 May 1917	7	4	Cypress Hill; also 7 May, 4:4
Park	John C.	d.	PC	2 May 1917	4	3	Cypress Hill; also 4 May, 8:1; 8 May, 4:1
Park	John C.	d.	SRR	7 May 1917	6	4	
Park	Roy	d.	PA	22 Oct. 1918	5	5	San Mateo Co.; also 23 Oct., 2:2
Park	Roy	d.	PC	23 Oct. 1918	8	4	Cypress Hill; also 24 Oct., 5:4
Parker	Bessie	m.	PD	13 Feb. 1917	2	5	
Parker	Bessie	m.	PC	14 Feb. 1917	2	3	
Parker	H. E., Mrs.	d.	PD	18 Dec. 1917	8	4	
Parker	Henry	d.	PA	22 Jan. 1917	6	3	Cypress Hill; also 23 Jan., 2:2
Parker	Henry	d.	PC	23 Jan. 1917	5	5	also 24 Jan., 3:3
Parker	J. T.	m.	PA	17 Aug. 1917	4	2	
Parker	John T.	m.	PC	17 Aug. 1917	1	3	
Parker	Josephine	d.	PD	2 July 1918	3	2	also 3 July, 8:2
Parker	Mr.	o.	SRR	29 Jan. 1916	10	4	
Parker	Raymond	b.	PC	22 May 1918	5	4	
Parker	Stanley S.	m.	PC	16 July 1918	6	2	
Parkerson	George	d.	HT	15 Aug. 1918	1	1	
Parkinson	George	d.	PD	14 Aug. 1918	8	2	

(1) Surname	(2) Given Name	(3)	(4)	(5) Date	(6) Pg	(7) Col	(8) Comments
Parkinson	George	m.	PC	14 Sept. 1916	6	4	
Parkinson	George A.	m.	PA	12 Sept. 1916	5	3	
Parkinson	George A.	b.	PA	14 Feb. 1918	4	5	
Parks	Albert	m.	SRR	22 July 1916	5	1	also 24 July, 8:1; 27 July, 5:3
Parks	Albert	m.	SIT	29 July 1916	3	5	
Parks	D.	m.	PC	18 Aug. 1918	5	2	
Parks	D. D.	m.	PA	17 Aug. 1918	4	5	
Parks	George	d.	PD	3 Mar. 1917	8	5	Willows, Glenn County
Parks	Marjorie	o.	PD	7 Dec. 1917	8	1	
Parks	Thomas I.	o.	PD	7 Dec. 1917	8	1	
Parmarlee	Edith A.	m.	PD	25 Apr. 1916	2	2	
Paroli	Dominica	m.	PD	11 Jan. 1916	3	1	
Parolia	Dominica	m.	SRR	10 Jan. 1916	8	4	
Parr	Barbara	m.	PD	10 Apr. 1917	8	4	
Parrish	Janet	m.	PD	24 Sept. 1916	1	6	
Partrick	Jasper	d.	SRR	25 Apr. 1917	5	2	
Partridge	Frank	m.	PC	12 June 1918	5	1	
Pasquet	August	d.	PC	10 June 1917	1	5	also 12 June, 6:2
Pasquet	August	d.	PD	10 June 1917	2	1	also 12 June, 3:1
Pasquet	Emil	d.	PD	10 June 1917	2	1	also 12 June, 3:1
Pasquet	Emile	d.	PC	10 June 1917	1	5	also 12 June, 6:2
Pasquet	Esther	d.	PD	10 June 1917	2	1	also 12 June, 3:1
Pasquet	Ethel	d.	PC	10 June 1917	1	5	also 12 June, 6:2
Pasquet	Jacques	d.	PC	10 June 1917	1	5	also 12 June, 6:2
Pasquet	Joseph	d.	PD	10 June 1917	2	1	also 12 June, 3:1
Pasquet	Joseph	p.	SRR	13 June 1917	1	3	
Pasquet	Joseph & 3 children	d.	PA	9 June 1917	1	2	also 11 June, 7:5
Pasquet	Joseph & 3 children	d.	SRR	9 June 1917	1	3	Esther, Ceasar & Emil; also 11 June, 3:2, 5:1
Passarino	Margy	m.	PD	2 Mar. 1917	8	2	
Passarino	Peter	o.	HT	20 Dec. 1917	1	2	
Pastagnasso	Harry	m.	SRR	29 Apr. 1916	8	5	
Patchett	John	b.	PD	17 July 1918	6	4	
Patrick	Corydon	m.	PD	25 Dec. 1917	8	1	also 27 Dec., 2:5
Patrick	Corydon A.	m.	SRR	26 Dec. 1917	5	5	
Patrick	M. L., Mrs.	d.	PD	17 July 1917	2	2	
Patrick	Moriah L.	d.	SRR	16 July 1917	5	6	
Patten	Dick	d.	PC	3 June 1917	4	6	
Patten	Feliz Leon	d.	SRR	30 Aug. 1916	2	3	
Patten	Leo	d.	PD	31 Aug. 1916	8	5	
Patten	R. R.	d.	PA	5 June 1917	1	4	
Patten	Richard R.	d.	HT	7 June 1917	1	3	
Patterson	Charles L.	d.	SIT	5 Jan. 1918	1	5	
Patterson	Elizabeth	d.	HT	19 Dec. 1918	8	3	

(1) Surname	(2) Given Name	(3)	(4)	(5) Date	(6) Pg	(7) Col	(8) Comments
Patterson	Elizabeth	d.	PC	28 Dec. 1918	6	2	
Patterson	Geneva	m.	HT	3 Feb. 1917	5	2	
Patterson	Geneva E.	m.	SRR	29 Jan. 1916	10	3	
Patterson	Geneva E.	m.	PD	30 Jan. 1916	5	4	
Patterson	Mary Belle	m.	ST	16 Nov. 1917	1	6	
Patterson	Mary Belle	m.	PC	17 Nov. 1917	4	5	
Patterson	Mary Belle	m.	PD	17 Nov. 1917	5	3	
Patterson	Mary Belle	m.	SRR	17 Nov. 1917	5	1	
Patterson	Nellie	m.	SRR	1 Mar. 1916	10	4	
Patterson	Nellie	m.	PD	2 Mar. 1916	2	2	
Patterson	Nellie	m.	PC	3 Mar. 1916	6	6	
Patterson	S. G.	o.	PA	15 July 1918	7	4	
Patteson	Charles F.	d.	PC	1 Jan. 1918	1	3	also 4 Jan., 5:6
Patteson	Charles J. "Ned"	d.	PD	1 Jan. 1918	8	1	also 4 Jan., 5:3
Patteson	Charles L. "Ned"	d.	PA	3 Jan. 1918	4	7	Healdsburg
Patteson	Charles Leroy "Ned"	d.	HT	3 Jan. 1918	1	1	also 10 Jan., 5:3
Patteson	Don C.	m.	SRR	31 July 1916	8	1	
Patteson	Don C.	m.	PC	2 Aug. 1916	5	2	
Patteson	Don C.	m.	HT	3 Aug. 1916	3	2	
Patteson	Elizabeth	d.	PD	27 Dec. 1918	5	1	
Patteson	Jack	o.	HT	7 June 1917	2	5	
Patteson	Jack	o.	HT	18 Oct. 1917	1	2	
Patteson	Jack	o.	PC	29 Aug. 1917	6	3	
Patteson	Martha Washington	b.	PD	24 Feb. 1918	5	1	
Patteson	Ned	o.	SRR	31 Dec. 1917	4	3	
Patteson	Ralph	m.	SRR	19 May 1916	5	1	
Patteson	Wayne	m.	HT	1 Feb. 1917	6	4	
Patteson	Wayne	m.	SRR	27 Jan. 1917	3	5	
Patteson	Wayne	m.	PC	28 Jan. 1917	6	2	
Patteson	Wayne "Curley"	m.	PD	27 Jan. 1917	1	3	
Pattison	Don C.	m.	PA	1 Aug. 1916	3	1	
Pattison	Don C.	o.	PA	24 Apr. 1916	3	5	
Pattison	Gussie	o.	PA	24 Apr. 1916	3	5	
Patton	Edna	m.	PC	21 Nov. 1916	1	4	
Patton	Florence E.	m.	PD	12 Oct. 1917	6	3	
Patton	Robert R.	d.	SRR	4 June 1917	10	3	
Patton	Robert R.	d.	PD	5 June 1917	7	2	
Patton	Robert R.	d.	PC	6 June 1917	3	3	
Pauchon	Charlotte	m.	SRR	25 Apr. 1916	8	5	
Paul	Frederick K.	m.	PA	10 July 1917	5	6	
Paula	George	m.	PC	13 Dec. 1916	3	4	
Paula	George	m.	PA	14 Dec. 1916	8	5	
Paula	Lena	m.	PA	3 Dec. 1917	4	3	
Paula	Manuel, Jr.	b.	PA	14 Oct. 1918	5	4	
Paula	Wilhelmina	m.	PC	27 Nov. 1917	5	3	also 4 Dec., 5:2

(1) Surname	(2) Given Name	(3)	(4)	(5) Date	(6) Pg	(7) Col	(8) Comments
Paula	Wilhelmina	m.	ST	30 Nov. 1917	1	5	
Pauli	Caroline	d.	SIT	1 Apr. 1916	1	3	
Pauli	Caroline	d.	PD	28 Mar. 1916	3	3	Sonoma Cemetery
Pauli	Caroline	d.	SRR	29 Mar. 1916	3	5	
Pauli	Harold	b.	SIT	25 May 1918	4	3	
Pauli	Harold	b.	PC	13 Jan. 1917	5	1	
Pauli	Robert	d.	SIT	15 Apr. 1916	3	2	
Paulson	Alma L.	o.	SRR	9 Mar. 1916	5	3	
Paulucci	Frank	d.	PA	6 Dec. 1917	5	3	Calvary Cemetery; also 7 Dec., 5:4; 10 Dec., 5:3
Paulucci	Frank	d.	PC	6 Dec. 1917	1	6	also 7 Dec., 3:5; 11 Dec., 2:1
Payn	Willie	m.	HT	13 Jan. 1916	8	5	
Payne	Willie	m.	SRR	13 Jan. 1916	8	3	
Payner	Walter C.	m.	PD	5 Sept. 1918	2	3	also 5 Sept., 2:5
Paysen	Pauline	d.	PC	2 Mar. 1917	3	5	also 3 Mar., 6:1; 4 Mar., 3:1; 6 Mar., 5:4
Paysen	Pauline	d.	ST	3 Mar. 1917	5	2	
Paysen	Pauline Christine	d.	PA	1 Mar. 1917	4	5	Cypress Hill; also 5:2; 5 Mar., 5:2
Pearce	Clara	d.	PC	26 Nov. 1918	8	3	
Pearman	Emma	d.	PD	16 Jan. 1916	9	4	
Pearson	Dorris	o.	PC	9 Nov. 1917	2	2	
Pearson	James Russell	d.	PD	12 Dec. 1916	2	2	
Pearson	James Russell	d.	ST	16 Dec. 1916	1	1	Gilliam Cemetery
Pease	Raymond	d.	HT	31 May 1917	3	2	Sacramento
Pease	Raymond H.	d.	SRR	26 May 1917	6	3	Sacramento
Peck	Raymond W.	m.	PA	19 July 1917	4	2	
Peckham	Frank	d.	PD	13 Apr. 1918	7	3	
Peckham	George D.	m.	PD	30 Aug. 1918	2	3	
Peckham	George D.	m.	CR	6 Sept. 1918	1	4	
Pedersen	Arthur	m.	PA	19 Jan. 1918	5	3	
Pedersen	Arthur A.	m.	PC	20 Jan. 1918	5	3	
Pedersen	Hans N.P.	d.	PA	27 Jan. 1916	4	3&4	also 29 Jan., 4:2
Pedersen	Ivar	o.	PC	27 Nov. 1917	1	5	
Pedersen	Ivar	o.	PC	8 Feb. 1918	1	4	also 12 Feb., 8:3
Pedersen	Jay Frederick	m.	PD	5 May 1918	3	1	
Pedersen	Marcus	b.	PA	19 Nov. 1917	5	7	
Pederson	Ivar	o.	PC	18 Apr. 1918	1	2	
Pederson	M. C.	b.	PC	14 Nov. 1917	3	6	
Pedigo	Olney	o.	SIT	29 June 1918	1	7	portrait
Pedigo	Olney G.	m.	PC	1 May 1917	5	3	
Pedigo	Olney G.	m.	PD	1 May 1917	8	3	also 2 May, 7:3
Pedigo	Olney G.	m.	SRR	30 Apr. 1917	5	3	
Pedigo	W. M.	m.	PD	24 Aug. 1917	2	3	
Pedranti	Constantine	d.	PA	27 Aug. 1918	3	3	France

(1) Surname	(2) Given Name	(3)	(4)	(5) Date	(6) Pg	(7) Col	(8) Comments
Pedranti	Constantino	d.	PC	27 Aug. 1918	1	3	France
Pedroni	Charles	m.	SRR	7 May 1917	5	5	
Pedroni	Emelio	d.	PA	10 Mar. 1917	5	6	also 12 Mar., 6:5
Pedroni	Emilio	d.	PC	11 Mar. 1917	4	3&6	Calvary Cemetery; also 14 Mar., 3:5
Pedroni	Mr. & Mrs.	b.	PD	3 May 1918	6	2	
Pedrotti	Angie A.	m.	SRR	10 Jan. 1917	2	2	
Pedrotti	Angie A.	m.	PA	9 Jan. 1917	5	1	
Pedrotti	Ernestine	m.	PA	19 June 1918	8	3	also 26 June, 8:5
Pedrotti	Ernestine	m.	PD	20 June 1918	8	3	
Pedrotti	Ernestine	m.	PC	21 June 1918	3	4	
Pedrotti	Ind	m.	PC	3 June 1916	6	2	
Pedrotti	P.	m.	PC	20 July 1916	5	4	
Pedrotti	Pearl D.	o.	PD	20 June 1916	5	4	
Pedrotti	Perle D.	o.	SRR	3 June 1916	3	3	also 19 June, 5:5
Pedrotti	Sayia D.	o.	PD	20 June 1916	5	4	
Pedrotti	Sylvia	o.	SRR	3 June 1916	3	3	also 19 June, 5:5
Peek	Ella	d.	PA	25 Nov. 1918	5	2	
Peerman	Leonara Shudy	d.	SRR	10 Mar. 1916	8	5	
Peery	Thomas	d.	PA	9 June 1916	3	3	
Peery	Thomas	d.	SRR	9 June 1916	5	2	I.O.O.F. Cemetery; also 10 June, 11:4
Peery	Thomas E.	d.	HT	15 June 1916	3	3	
Peery	Thomas Evans	d.	PD	9 June 1916	3	4	Odd Fellows Cemetery; also 13 June, 3:2
Peery	Viola	m.	PD	25 July 1917	3	2	
Peery	Viola	m.	PC	15 Sept. 1917	6	4	also 19 Oct., 4:1
Peery	Viola Mildred	m.	PA	24 July 1917	2	5	also 28 July, 2:5
Peery	Viola Mildred	m.	PC	25 July 1917	3	4	
Pelequin	Theophiele	d.	PA	22 Apr. 1918	5	3	
Pelier	Adelia	m.	PC	20 Sept. 1916	4	6	
Pellacio	Enio	o.	PA	8 Sept. 1918	6	1	
Pellascio	Alfred	d.	PA	18 Oct. 1918	8	3	Calvary Cemetery; also 19 Oct., 2:2, 4:6, 3:3; 21 Oct., 5:6
Pellascio	Alfred	d.	PC	19 Oct. 1918	8	3	also 20 Oct., 6:3; 22 Oct., 8:4
Pellascio	Alfred	d.	PD	20 Oct. 1918	2	2	
Pellascio	Enio	o.	PC	8 Sept. 1918	6	2	
Peller	Adelia	m.	SRR	21 Sept. 1916	5	1	
Pellini	Bessie	d.	PD	15 Jan. 1918	3	3	also 16 Jan., 4:2
Peloquin	Theophiele	d.	PC	22 Apr. 1918	3	4	
Peloquin	Uldrick	b.	PC	1 Aug. 1916	8	4	
Pember	Esther	m.	HT	7 June 1917	5	4	
Pember	Ethel	m.	SRR	2 June 1917	8	3	also 6 June, 6:3
Pence	J. C.	d.	SRR	19 Oct. 1917	4	2	

(1) Surname	(2) Given Name	(3)	(4)	(5) Date	(6) Pg	(7) Col	(8) Comments
Pence	Jacob	d.	PD	19 Oct. 1917	3	5	also 20 Oct., 4:2
Pendergast	John L.	m.	PD	24 Aug. 1916	7	4	
Pendleton	Charles	b.	PA	27 Mar. 1916	8	3	
Pendleton	Hubert W.	d.	PC	11 Jan. 1916	4	1	Calvary Cemetery
Pendleton	Hubert Warren	d.	PA	8 Jan. 1916	4	6	also 10 Jan., 7:5
Pendleton	Hubert Warren	o.	PC	9 Jan. 1916	1	3	
Pendleton	John	d.	SRR	20 Nov. 1917	5	3	
Penn	Ila Irene	m.	PD	26 May 1916	6	2	
Penn	Irene	m.	PA	25 May 1916	4	4	
Penn	Irene	m.	PC	26 May 1916	8	5	
Penrotti	L.	b.	HT	17 Oct. 1918	4	2	
Penry	Sam	o.	HT	23 May 1918	5	2	
Peolquin	Ulderick	b.	PA	1 Aug. 1916	5	7	
Peoples	Curtis	b.	PC	6 Sept. 1918	8	2	
Peoples	Curtiss	b.	PA	4 Sept. 1918	8	4	
Peoples	Gladys	m.	PD	21 July 1917	3	3	
Peoples	Gladys F.	m.	ST	3 Aug. 1917	2	3	
Peoples	Gladys Lucile	m.	PC	21 July 1917	5	1	also 22 July, 5:1
Peoples	Gladys Lucille	m.	PA	20 July 1917	8	4	
Peoples	John W.	m.	SRR	15 Mar. 1917	2	3	
Peoples	John W.	m.	PD	16 Mar. 1917	5	4	
Peoples	John Worth	m.	PA	15 Mar. 1917	4	4	
Peoples	John Worth	m.	PC	16 Mar. 1917	4	5	
Peoples	John Worth	b.	PA	29 Mar. 1918	4	3	
Peoples	Joseph	d.	PD	8 July 1916	8	3	Calvary Cemetery
Peoples	Joseph	d.	SRR	8 July 1916	5	2	also 10 July, 3:4, 8:4
Peoples	Josephine Irene	m.	PA	19 Feb. 1917	3	4	
Peoples	Josephine Irene	m.	PC	3 Feb. 1917	4	1	also 17 Feb., 4:5; 20 Feb., 5:3
Peoples	Josephine Irene	m.	SRR	5 Feb. 1917	5	1	also 20 Feb., 7:3
Peoples	Josephine Irene	m.	PD	6 Feb. 1917	2	2	
Peoples	S. Z.	o.	PC	14 Feb. 1918	1	3	also 21 Feb., 1:3
Peoples	S. Z.	o.	PC	31 Mar. 1918	3	3	
Peoples	Stuart Z.	o.	PA	14 Feb. 1918	2	4	also 18 Mar., 8:3
Peracca	Anton (children of)	d.	PD	14 Feb. 1917	8	3	
Peracca	Catherine	d.	PA	13 Feb. 1917	1	4	Cypress Hill; also 14 Feb., 1:4; 15 Feb., 5:4
Peracca	Catherine	d.	PC	14 Feb. 1917	1	5	also 15 Feb., 1:4
Peracca	Catherine	d.	ST	17 Feb. 1917	3	2	
Peracca	Stephen	d.	PC	14 Feb. 1917	1	5	also 15 Feb., 1:4
Peracca	Stephen	d.	ST	17 Feb. 1917	3	2	
Peracca	Stephen	d.	PA	13 Feb. 1917	1	4	Cypress Hill; also 14 Feb., 1:4; 15 Feb., 5:4
Peracca	Victor	d.	PC	14 Feb. 1917	1	5	also 15 Feb., 1:4
Perazzo	David	d.	CR	4 Oct. 1918	1	4	
Perazzo	Pete	o.	SIT	30 Mar. 1918	2	6	

(1) Surname	(2) Given Name	(3)	(4)	(5) Date	(6) Pg	(7) Col	(8) Comments
Percival	Mr.	m.	ST	8 Jan. 1916	7	4	
Percival	Richard E.	d.	PA	22 Nov. 1917	4	3	Providence, R.I.
Percival	Richard H.	d.	PC	23 Nov. 1917	3	4	Providence, R.I.
Percival	Richard R.	d.	PD	23 Nov. 1917	2	4	
Percy	Donald	m.	PD	25 Jan. 1917	8	5	
Percy	Donald	b.	SRR	29 Aug. 1917	6	2	
Percy	Donald	b.	PD	30 Aug. 1917	7	1	
Peri	Esinolila	d.	PD	9 Mar. 1917	6	5	also 10 Mar., 2:5, 4:3
Peri	Espinolia/Essilina	d.	SRR	9 Mar. 1917	5	3	also 10 Mar., 1:3; 12 Mar., 8:2
Perigo	William	m.	SRR	23 Aug. 1917	8	4	
Peristein	Harry	m.	PC	21 Mar. 1916	5	3	
Perkins	Alice Lennon	m.	PC	21 Apr. 1917	5	3	
Perkins	John Henry	d.	SRR	12 Feb. 1917	8	5	also 13 Feb., 8:4; 15 Feb., 8:1
Perkins	John Henry	d.	PD	13 Feb. 1917	6	2	also 14 Feb., 4:2; 16 Feb., 7:4
Perkinson	Susan E.	o.	PD	29 May 1918	8	2	
Perle	Arthur	o.	SIT	14 Dec. 1918	3	7	
Perley	Marie	d.	SRR	12 Feb. 1917	5	4	Rural Cemetery
Perley	Marie Edwards	d.	PD	11 Feb. 1917	1	3	Rural Cemetery; also 4:2; 13 Feb., 3:5
Perlstein	Harry	m.	PA	20 Mar. 1916	5	3	
Perolini	Joseph	m.	PA	8 Sept. 1918	8	3	
Perrett	Andrew	m.	SRR	1 Sept. 1916	3	5	
Perrett	Andrew Guy	m.	PD	1 Sept. 1916	2	2	
Perri	Adeline	m.	PA	10 Feb. 1916	4	1	
Perrier	E. C.	b.	PA	28 Jan. 1916	5	1	
Perring	Leo	d.	PA	10 Sept. 1917	6	2	
Perring	Leo	d.	PC	11 Sept. 1917	1	5	also 12 Sept., 8:5
Perring	Leo	d.	SRR	11 Sept. 1917	5	3	
Perring	Leo	d.	PD	12 Sept. 1917	3	2	
Perrish	Janet	m.	SRR	25 Sept. 1916	5	2	
Perry	Arthur	d.	PA	28 Dec. 1918	8	3	
Perry	Frank	b.	PA	11 Oct. 1917	5	3&7	
Perry	Gertrude	o.	PA	10 Oct. 1917	3	6	
Perry	Gertrude H.	o.	SRR	4 June 1917	1	2	
Perry	Gertrude H.	o.	SRR	9 Oct. 1917	5	3	
Perry	John	o.	PA	10 Oct. 1917	3	6	
Perry	John A.	o.	SRR	4 June 1917	1	2	
Perry	John A.	o.	SRR	9 Oct. 1917	5	3	
Perry	John W.	d.	PA	27 July 1918	7	5	
Perry	John W.	d.	PD	28 July 1918	5	4	
Perry	Joseph W.	d.	PA	18 Nov. 1918	5	2	also 19 Nov., 8:5
Perry	Joseph W.	d.	PC	19 Nov. 1918	3	2&5	Calvary Cemetery; also 20 Nov., 5:4

(1) Surname	(2) Given Name	(3)	(4)	(5) Date	(6) Pg	(7) Col	(8) Comments
Perry	Mary	d.	PA	3 Jan. 1918	4	5	Calvary Cemetery; also 5 Jan., 4:3
Perry	Mary	d.	PC	3 Jan. 1918	1	5	Calvary Cemetery; also 3:2; 4 Jan., 6:2; 6 Jan., 4:5
Perry	Mary	d.	PC	30 Jan. 1918	8	2	Calvary Cemetery; also 31 Jan., 6:4; 2 Feb., 4:1
Perry	Mary Smith	d.	PA	29 Jan. 1918	4	5	Calvary Cemetery; also 1 Feb., 5:5
Perry	Rachael Ann	d.	PD	11 Jan. 1918	4	2	Fulkerson Cemetery
Perry	Rachel Ann	d.	PC	11 Jan. 1918	6	4	Santa Rosa
Perry	Rose	m.	PC	12 Dec. 1916	3	4	
Perry	Rose	m.	PA	19 Feb. 1917	5	4	
Perry	Rose	m.	PC	20 Feb. 1917	4	4	
Perry	Rosie	m.	PA	11 Dec. 1916	5	5	
Perry	Wes	o.	SIT	11 Aug. 1917	1	2	
Persons	Diadamia	d.	PC	23 Jan. 1917	5	4	
Persons	Diadamia	d.	PD	23 Jan. 1917	8	2	
Persons	Diadamin	d.	PA	22 Jan. 1917	5	4	Sissons
Pesenti	Frank	d.	PD	1 Oct. 1916	5	2	
Pesenti	Frank	d.	SRR	3 Oct. 1916	7	4	Calvary Cemetery
Pete	James	d.	ST	15 June 1917	1	2	
Peter	Edward	o.	PC	22 Apr. 1918	4	4	
Peter	Edward	o.	PA	23 Apr. 1918	4	3	
Peter	Edward	o.	PD	23 Apr. 1918	3	5	
Peter	Josephine	o.	PC	22 Apr. 1918	4	4	
Peter	Josephine	o.	PA	23 Apr. 1918	4	3	
Peter	Josephine	o.	PD	23 Apr. 1918	3	5	
Peters	Clive	d.	PC	4 May 1918	3	4	
Peters	Ebe M.	m.	PC	15 Aug. 1917	8	2	
Peters	Edward	o.	SRR	3 Mar. 1916	8	2	also 21 Mar., 8:2
Peters	Eleanor	d.	PA	11 Nov. 1916	5	3	Cypress Hill
Peters	Eleanor	d.	PC	12 Nov. 1916	4	1	Cypress Hill; also 7:6; 14 Nov., 8:2
Peters	Eleanor	m.	PA	15 Oct. 1917	4	3	
Peters	Eleanor	m.	PC	16 Oct. 1917	3	4	
Peters	Helen	m.	PD	29 Dec. 1917	2	1	
Peters	Helen E.	m.	PA	28 Dec. 1917	3	3	
Peters	Helen E.	m.	PC	29 Dec. 1917	5	2	
Peters	J. L.	m.	PA	28 Dec. 1917	3	3	
Peters	John	m.	PC	29 Oct. 1918	4	4	
Peters	John H.	m.	PA	28 Oct. 1918	3	3	
Peters	John H.	m.	PA	30 Sept. 1918	4	5	
Peters	Josephine	o.	SRR	3 Mar. 1916	8	2	also 21 Mar., 8:2
Peters	Julia M.	m.	PC	15 May 1917	3	3	also 16 May, 5:3
Peters	Julia M.	m.	PA	16 May 1917	4	3	

(1) Surname	(2) Given Name	(3)	(4)	(5) Date	(6) Pg	(7) Col	(8) Comments
Peters	Rudolph	o.	PC	28 Aug. 1918	6	1	
Peters	William	d.	PD	21 July 1917	8	2&3	
Peters	William C.	d.	PA	20 July 1917	5	6	also 21 July, 2:3
Peters	William C.	d.	SRR	20 July 1917	1	4	also 21 July, 10:6; 23 July, 6:6
Peters	William C.	d.	PC	21 July 1917	5	6	also 22 July, 5:3
Petersen	Alma	m.	PC	3 Oct. 1917	3	5	
Petersen	Andrew	d.	PC	5 May 1916	4	2	cremation
Petersen	Charles	d.	PC	27 July 1916	4	4	cremation; also 1 Aug., 4:2; 3 Aug., 4:2
Petersen	Charles C.	m.	PC	30 Nov. 1916	1	5	
Petersen	Genevieve	o.	PC	6 Apr. 1916	1	5	portrait
Petersen	Geoge	m.	PC	27 June 1917	8	4	
Petersen	George	m.	PA	26 June 1917	2	3	
Petersen	George	m.	PC	28 Aug. 1917	4	5	
Petersen	H. P.	b.	PC	4 Sept. 1918	8	5	
Petersen	Hana Nells	d.	PC	28 Jan. 1916	5	6	Cypress Hill; also 30 Jan., 4:2
Petersen	Hansine S.	m.	PC	1 Nov. 1917	8	3	
Petersen	Hansine S.	m.	SRR	1 Nov. 1917	1	2	
Petersen	Hansine S.	m.	PA	31 Oct. 1917	8	5	
Petersen	Harry	b.	PC	2 May 1918	6	6	
Petersen	Hattie	m.	PC	25 Dec. 1917	1	3	also 28 Dec., 4:6; 29 Dec., 5:6
Petersen	Hattie	m.	PA	26 Dec. 1917	7	4	
Petersen	Hattie	m.	SIT	5 Jan. 1918	3	3	
Petersen	Henry, Mrs.	d.	PC	25 July 1916	4	3	
Petersen	Ivar	o.	PA	6 Dec. 1918	2	3	
Petersen	Louis	m.	PC	26 Apr. 1916	8	3	
Petersen	Martin E.	o.	PA	23 Apr. 1918	4	3	
Petersen	Minnie	o.	PA	23 Apr. 1918	4	3	
Petersen	N.	b.	PC	13 May 1916	8	2	
Petersen	Wilhelmina	d.	PA	28 Mar. 1917	5	4	
Petersen	Wilhelmina	d.	PC	29 Mar. 1917	4	3	Cypress Hill; also 30 Mar., 5:4; 1 Apr., 4:2
Peterson	A.	b.	SRR	27 June 1916	8	1	
Peterson	A. L.	b.	ST	14 Oct. 1916	8	4	
Peterson	Alga Johanna	d.	PC	25 Jan. 1916	5	2	Cypress Hill; also 28 Jan., 4:3
Peterson	Andrew	d.	PA	4 May 1916	1	3	cremation; also 6 May, 3:3
Peterson	Anna	m.	PC	2 Mar. 1918	3	6	
Peterson	C.	b.	PC	30 Jan. 1917	8	3	
Peterson	C. C.	b.	PA	12 Jan. 1917	4	3	
Peterson	C. E.	b.	PA	13 Mar. 1916	8	7	
Peterson	Carl	d.	HT	22 Aug. 1918	1	4	

(1) Surname	(2) Given Name	(3)	(4)	(5) Date	(6) Pg	(7) Col	(8) Comments
Peterson	Carl	d.	PD	23 Aug. 1918	4	2	
Peterson	Catherine Price	d.	PA	9 Dec. 1918	5	6	Cypress Hill; also 10 Dec., 8:5; 11 Dec., 5:1
Peterson	Charles	d.	PA	28 July 1916	5	4	
Peterson	Charles C.	m.	PA	29 Nov. 1916	8	4	
Peterson	Christian	d.	SRR	3 May 1916	10	4	
Peterson	Christian	b.	PA	29 Jan. 1917	8	5	
Peterson	Constable	b.	SIT	29 Apr. 1916	3	6	
Peterson	Edward	o.	PD	23 Apr. 1918	3	5	
Peterson	Elizabeth Cordelia	m.	PD	26 Apr. 1917	8	3	also 1 May, 5:1
Peterson	George	m.	PA	27 Aug. 1917	1	4	also 2:4
Peterson	George	m.	PD	28 Aug. 1917	8	3	
Peterson	George	b.	PA	4 Jan. 1917	5	4	
Peterson	Hansine	m.	PD	2 Nov. 1917	6	5	
Peterson	Harold	m.	PA	11 Oct. 1916	4	4	
Peterson	Harold	m.	PC	8 Oct. 1916	4	2	also 11 Oct., 1:2; 12 Oct., 1:5
Peterson	Harold	m.	SRR	9 Oct. 1916	4	5	
Peterson	Hattie	m.	PA	28 Dec. 1917	4	3	
Peterson	Hedvig A.	m.	PA	26 Feb. 1916	5	4	
Peterson	Henrietta	m.	PC	26 Feb. 1916	2	3	
Peterson	Henrietta	m.	SRR	26 Feb. 1916	10	3	
Peterson	Henry	m.	SRR	13 Aug. 1917	8	5	
Peterson	Howard W.	m.	PD	2 June 1916	7	3	
Peterson	Howard Wright	m.	SRR	1 June 1916	1	2	
Peterson	J. O., Mrs.	d.	PA	24 Jan. 1916	4	5	
Peterson	J. R.	m.	PD	30 June 1918	9	1	
Peterson	Jens Christian	d.	ST	6 May 1916	1	6	Oakland
Peterson	Johanna	d.	ST	10 Aug. 1917	1	5	
Peterson	Johanna	d.	PC	12 Aug. 1917	3	2	
Peterson	Julius R.	m.	PA	1 July 1918	5	3	
Peterson	Katheryn A.	d.	PD	10 Dec. 1918	3	4	Petaluma; also 8:3; 11 Dec., 2:3; 12 Dec., 3:2
Peterson	Kathryn Price	d.	PC	10 Dec. 1918	4	3	Cypress Hill; also 11 Dec., 3:4; 12 Dec., 5:3
Peterson	Lucendia	d.	ST	24 Feb. 1917	3	4	
Peterson	Ludencia	d.	PD	16 Feb. 1917	4	2	Sebastopol; also 8:5
Peterson	Ludencia	d.	SRR	16 Feb. 1917	4	5	also 5:5
Peterson	Ludencia	p.	ST	24 Mar. 1917	6	4	
Peterson	Malcolm	m.	PD	12 Oct. 1916	5	1	
Peterson	Malcolm	m.	PA	7 Oct. 1916	5	2	also 11 Oct., 4:4
Peterson	Malcolm	m.	PC	8 Oct. 1916	4	2	also 12 Oct., 1:5
Peterson	Malcolm	m.	SRR	9 Oct. 1916	4	5	also 12 Oct., 5:4
Peterson	Martin E.	o.	PC	22 Apr. 1918	4	4	also 14 May, 5:4
Peterson	Minnie	o.	PC	22 Apr. 1918	4	4	also 14 May, 5:4
Peterson	Minnie E.	o.	PD	23 Apr. 1918	3	5	

(1) Surname	(2) Given Name	(3)	(4)	(5) Date	(6) Pg	(7) Col	(8) Comments
Peterson	Mr. & Mrs.	b.	SIT	28 Dec. 1918	3	5	
Peterson	N.	b.	PA	12 May 1916	5	5	
Peterson	Olga	d.	PA	25 Jan. 1916	5	4	Cypress Hill; also 8:5; 27 Jan., 2:4
Peterson	Olga	d.	PC	26 Jan. 1916	2	2	Cypress Hill
Peterson	P. A.	d.	HT	10 Feb. 1916	5	1	
Peterson	P. A.	d.	PD	3 Feb. 1916	8	2	also 8 Feb., 3:3
Peterson	P. A.	d.	SRR	3 Feb. 1916	6	3	Masonic Cemetery, Sebastopol; also 7 Feb., 5:2
Peterson	P. August	d.	ST	5 Feb. 1916	1	6	
Peterson	Ruby	m	PD	27 July 1917	8	3	also 31 July, 7:1
Peterson	Ruby	m.	SRR	27 July 1917	5	3	also 30 July, 8:3
Peterson	Rudolph	b.	PC	3 Dec. 1918	1	6	
Peterson	Rudolph	b.	PD	3 Dec. 1918	1	3	
Peterson	Rudolph J.	m.	PC	30 June 1918	1	3	
Peterson	Rudolph J.	b.	PA	4 Dec. 1918	2	6&7	
Peterson	Samuel J.	d.	PA	2 May 1916	5	6	also 3 May, 6:5
Peterson	Samuel J.	d.	PD	3 May 1916	2	5	
Peterson	Valma	m.	SRR	29 Aug. 1916	8	1	
Peterson	Velma	m.	PD	30 Aug. 1916	3	4	
Peterson	William	m.	PD	7 July 1917	5	3	
Peterson	William	m.	SRR	7 July 1917	6	5	
Peterson	William	m.	PA	13 Aug. 1917	8	3	
Peterson	Willie	m.	PC	6 July 1917	5	1	
Peterson	Willie	m.	SIT	7 July 1917	1	3	
Peterson	Wilson	b.	SRR	16 Sept. 1916	7	4	
Petes	Joe	b.	ST	11 Nov. 1916	3	4	
Petray	Donald	o.	HT	7 Nov. 1916	8	5	
Petray	Gladys Valentine	m.	PD	11 Aug. 1917	2	3	
Petray	Gladys Valentine	m.	SRR	11 Aug. 1917	6	1	
Petray	Gladys Valentine	m.	PC	12 Aug. 1917	1	4	
Petray	James A.	o.	PA	24 Aug. 1918	4	1	portrait
Petray	William J.	d.	SRR	8 Sept. 1917	6	6	Oak Mound Cemetery
Pettis	Elida T.	o.	PD	7 Feb. 1917	8	3	
Pettis	William F.	m.	PD	23 Apr. 1918	6	4	
Pettis	William F.	o.	SRR	6 Feb. 1917	4	3	
Pettis	William F.	o.	PD	7 Feb. 1917	8	3	
Pettis	Zilda T.	o.	SRR	6 Feb. 1917	4	3	
Pettits	William F.	m.	PC	22 Apr. 1918	1	6	
Pettles	I. N., Mrs.	d.	HT	31 Aug. 1916	1	3	Oak Mound Cemetery
Peugh	Christina	d.	SRR	10 Oct. 1917	8	5	also 11 Oct., 8:2
Peugh	Christina A.	d.	PD	11 Oct. 1917	3	4	also 12 Oct., 7:2
Peugh	Christina A.	d.	PC	12 Oct. 1917	6	3	Rural Cemetery
Peyser	Hattie	d.	PA	6 Apr. 1917	8	4	

(1) Surname	(2) Given Name	(3)	(4)	(5) Date	(6) Pg	(7) Col	(8) Comments
Pfaff	Henry	d.	PC	2 Oct. 1916	1	5	Loraine, Ohio; also 4 Oct., 5:4
Pfaff	Henry	d.	PA	3 Oct. 1916	1	6	
Pfaff	Frank	m.	PD	10 Sept. 1916	3	2	
Pfefferie	Edna	d.	PC	5 Jan. 1916	6	2	
Pfeifer	F. C.	m.	SRR	29 Aug. 1917	2	4	
Pfeifer	F. C.	m.	PD	30 Aug. 1917	8	3	
Pfeifer	Ruth	m.	PD	1 May 1917	5	1	
Pfeifer	Ruth	m.	SRR	1 May 1917	3	2	
Pfohl	Frank	m.	PC	21 Nov. 1916	1	4	
Phair	Carter	m.	ST	1 Mar. 1918	3	2	
Phair	Carter N.	m.	PC	27 Feb. 1918	2	3	
Phair	Lucy	m.	PC	11 Nov. 1916	5	3	
Phares	French	m.	SRR	28 June 1917	8	6	
Phares	J. S.	b.	PD	24 May 1918	5	4	
Pharish	Walter	b.	PA	18 Mar. 1916	8	6	
Pharish	Walter	b.	PC	20 Mar. 1916	8	5	
Phariss	Alice	m.	PC	30 Nov. 1918	5	3	
Pharris	Alice	m.	PA	29 Nov. 1918	4	4	
Pharris	Cecil	m.	PA	26 June 1917	2	5	
Pharris	Cecil	m.	ST	29 June 1917	8	1	
Pharris	Cecil O.	m.	PD	17 June 1917	2	6	also 27 June, 6:3
Pharris	Cecil O.	m.	SRR	18 June 1917	2	3	also 27 June, 8:5
Pharris	Cecil O.	m.	PC	19 June 1917	5	3	26 June, 5:3
Phelps	Purvis M.	m.	PD	8 June 1917	2	1	
Phelps	Purvis Mabel	m.	CR	8 June 1917	1	3	
Philbrick	Jean	m.	PC	1 Feb. 1916	4	2	
Philbrick	Jean	m.	PA	31 Jan. 1916	4	5	also 1 Feb., 3:6
Philips	W. W., Mrs.	d.	PD	17 Mar. 1916	6	1	also 19 Mar., 2:4, 3:5
Phillips	A. L.	o.	PD	6 Mar. 1917	8	3	adoption
Phillips	A. L.	o.	PC	7 Mar. 1917	3	4	adoption
Phillips	Bennett	d.	PC	11 May 1916	6	2	
Phillips	Catherine	d.	SRR	11 July 1917	8	2	also 12 July, 8:6
Phillips	Catherine	d.	PD	12 July 1917	7	4	Odd Fellows Cemetery; also 13 July, 8:3
Phillips	Daphne	o.	PC	10 Apr. 1917	8	3	
Phillips	Dick	d.	PD	17 May 1918	8	1	also 18 May, 7:3
Phillips	Ed	m.	PD	5 June 1918	3	1	
Phillips	F. H.	o.	PA	22 Aug. 1918	3	3	
Phillips	Gertrude	m.	SRR	8 Nov. 1917	3	1	
Phillips	Gertrude E.	m.	SIT	10 Nov. 1917	1	7	
Phillips	Gertrude E.	m.	HT	8 Nov. 1917	3	1	
Phillips	Harold	m.	HT	14 Nov. 1918	8	2	also 5 Dec., 1:2
Phillips	Harold F.	m.	PD	30 Nov. 1918	7	2	
Phillips	Henry	o.	PC	21 Aug. 1917	1	1	

(1) Surname	(2) Given Name	(3)	(4)	(5) Date	(6) Pg	(7) Col	(8) Comments
Phillips	J.	d.	PC	26 Feb. 1918	6	2&4	also 27 Feb., 3:3; 28 Feb., 4:1
Phillips	J., Mr. & Mrs.	o.	PC	17 Mar. 1916	3	1	
Phillips	Jack	d.	ST	1 Mar. 1918	8	5	
Phillips	Jacob "Jack"	p.	PC	1 Mar. 1918	5	5	
Phillips	Jacob "Jack"	d.	PA	25 Feb. 1918	4	2	
Phillips	John	o.	PC	14 Sept. 1918	4	1	
Phillips	John	d.	PD	26 Feb. 1918	8	4	
Phillips	John Pressley	m.	PD	26 Oct. 1918	5	1	
Phillips	John Pressley	m.	PA	28 Oct. 1918	6	3	
Phillips	Lucy	o.	PA	25 Sept. 1917	5	3	
Phillips	Lucy Anita	o.	SRR	17 May 1917	5	3	
Phillips	Lucy Anita	o.	PD	18 May 1917	6	3	
Phillips	Philip E.	o.	PD	20 Dec. 1918	3	2	
Phillips	S. E.	m.	HT	13 June 1918	4	4	
Phillips	Teresa	o.	PD	8 Sept. 1918	8	1	
Phillips	Vernie I.	m.	SRR	2 May 1917	8	5	
Phillips	Vernie L.	m.	PD	2 May 1917	6	5	
Phillips	W. B.	o.	PA	25 Sept. 1917	5	3	
Phillips	W. W., Mrs.	d.	SRR	17 Mar. 1916	8	4	
Phillips	William B.	o.	PD	18 May 1917	6	3	
Phillips	William J.	o.	PD	8 Sept. 1918	8	1	
Phillips	William R.	o.	SRR	17 May 1917	5	3	
Phillyss	Duvall	m.	HT	11 Oct. 1917	1	5	
Phillyss	Vernie I.	m.	HT	3 May 1917	4	5	
Philpott	Jefferson P.	m.	PD	6 Dec. 1918	8	2	also 8 Dec., 8:2
Philpott	Thomas H.	o.	PD	1 May 1918	6	2	
Pianti	Oliver Sauve de la	d.	PA	6 Apr. 1916	2	3	Bloomfield
Piazza	Albert	d.	PD	28 Nov. 1917	8	2	
Piazza	Albert	d.	SRR	28 Nov. 1917	6	6	
Picetti	Jack	b.	SIT	11 Nov. 1916	1	7	
Picetti	Jack	b.	PC	19 Nov. 1916	4	5	
Picinnini	Frank	b.	PD	28 May 1918	6	7	
Pickerill	Dayle Elwood	d.	ST	24 Mar. 1917	1	5	
Pickering	Ivy	m.	ST	6 Dec. 1918	2	3	
Pickle	Herbert	m.	SRR	6 Mar. 1916	8	1	
Pickle	Herbert	m.	PD	7 Mar. 1917	5	3	
Pickrell	J. T.	b.	SRR	26 Feb. 1916	10	2	
Pieper	Richard H.	m.	PA	30 Nov. 1917	8	3	also 24 Dec., 8:3
Pieper	Richard H.	m.	PC	1 Dec. 1917	5	1	also 25 Dec., 6:3
Pieratt	Ellender Wanda	d.	PC	30 May 1917	2	2	
Pieratt	James	d.	PD	15 Sept. 1917	8	2	Sonoma
Pieratt	James S.	d.	SRR	15 Sept. 1917	6	4	Sonoma
Pieratt	Jim	d.	SIT	22 Sept. 1917	3	4	

(1) Surname	(2) Given Name	(3)	(4)	(5) Date	(6) Pg	(7) Col	(8) Comments
Pierce	Arthur A.	d.	PD	24 Aug. 1918	8	1	Gilliam Cemetery; also 28 Aug., 6:5; 31 Aug., 4:2
Pierce	Arthur A.	d.	PC	25 Aug. 1918	3	2	
Pierce	Arthur A.	d.	ST	6 Sept. 1918	8	2	
Pierce	Clara	d.	PA	25 Nov. 1918	5	4	also 26 Nov., 8:6
Pierce	Clara	d.	PD	26 Nov. 1918	5	4	Bloomfield; also 27 Nov., 3:2
Pierce	Clara M.	d.	ST	29 Nov. 1918	1	4	
Pierce	E. I.	b.	PA	23 July 1918	5	6&7	
Pierce	E. M.	m.	PC	7 Sept. 1918	8	5	
Pierce	Edna L.	m.	PA	25 Sept. 1917	4	5	
Pierce	Edna L.	m.	SRR	25 Sept. 1917	4	4	also 26 Sept., 4:3
Pierce	Edna L.	m.	PC	27 Sept. 1917	5	5	
Pierce	Edna Langley	m.	PD	26 Sept. 1917	5	3	also 27 Sept., 3:4
Pierce	J. G.	d.	PA	27 Nov. 1916	4	2	Sebastopol
Pierce	J. K.	o.	PC	24 Feb. 1917	8	2	also 27 Feb., 2:1
Pierce	E. M.	m.	PD	8 Sept. 1918	3	3	
Piereni	Rebecca J.	d.	PC	11 June 1916	8	5	Odd Fellows Cemetery, Sebastopol
Pierini	Fred V.	m.	ST	14 Oct. 1916	1	5	
Pierini	Rebecca	d.	SRR	12 June 1916	3	6	Sebastopol
Pierini	Rebecca	d.	ST	17 June 1916	4	1	
Pierson	Marian	m.	PD	27 May 1917	6	1	
Pierson	James Russell	d.	SRR	12 Dec. 1916	7	5	
Pierson	Marion	m.	SRR	28 May 1917	3	4	
Pierson	T. C., Mrs.	d.	PD	14 Apr. 1918	4	2	also 8:1; 17 Apr., 2:1
Pierson	T. C., Mrs.	d.	PC	17 Apr. 1918	4	4	
Pilkington	Thomas J.	d.	PA	22 Dec. 1917	6	5	also 24 Dec., 5:7
Pilkington	Thomas J.	d.	PC	22 Dec. 1917	1	3	
Pilkington	Thomas J.	d.	PD	23 Dec. 1917	7	3	
Pilkington	Thomas J.	d.	SRR	24 Dec. 1917	10	2	
Pillar	Lillie	o.	SRR	16 July 1917	8	2	
Pillar	Lillie	o.	PD	17 July 1917	6	3	
Pillar	Thomas	o.	SRR	16 July 1917	8	2	
Piller	Thomas	o.	PD	17 July 1917	6	3	
Pillow	Anna	d.	PD	12 Dec. 1916	1	3	extra edition
Pillow	Anna	d.	SRR	12 Dec. 1916	4	2	County Armagh, Ireland; also 13 Dec., 6:6
Pillow	Anna	d.	ST	16 Dec. 1916	1	5	Ireland
Pina	Louis	d.	PD	27 Dec. 1918	4	2	Hopland; also 6:4
Pinchers	Marie	m.	PD	20 Sept. 1917	5	2	
Pinches	Marie	m.	SRR	19 Sept. 1917	5	1	
Pinches	Marie	m.	PD	27 Nov. 1917	7	1	
Pinches	Marie Genevieve	m.	SRR	26 Nov. 1917	8	1	
Pinches	William S.	d.	PD	14 Nov. 1916	2	3	
Pinches	William Samuel	d.	SRR	13 Nov. 1916	1	2	also 3:2; 14 Nov., 6:2

(1) Surname	(2) Given Name	(3)	(4)	(5) Date	(6) Pg	(7) Col	(8) Comments
Pine	William H.	m.	PD	22 July 1916	8	4	
Ping	Ah	d.	SRR	15 Jan. 1917	8	3	
Pinschower	Marion	d.	SRR	27 Aug. 1917	3	4	
Pinschower	Marion	d.	PD	28 Aug. 1917	6	2	
Pippin	Thomas C., Mrs.	d.	PD	14 Jan. 1917	1	6	
Pippin	Thomas C., Mrs.	d.	PA	15 Jan. 1917	6	5	
Pippin	Thomas C., Mrs.	d.	SRR	15 Jan. 1917	5	5	
Pippin	Thomas G., Mrs.	d.	PC	16 Jan. 1917	1	6	Guerneville
Pisani	Isabel	d.	PA	27 Aug. 1917	3	3	Italian Cemetery, S. F.; also 28 Aug., 6:5
Pisani	Isabel	d.	PC	28 Aug. 1917	3	4	Italian Cemetery, S.F.; also 4:6; 29 Aug., 4:3
Pitkin	Cora	m.	PC	11 Aug. 1917	5	3	
Pitt	D. W.	b.	PA	4 June 1918	4	5	
Pitt	D. W.	b.	PC	7 Mar. 1917	5	6	
Pitt	Daniel W.	m.	PA	6 June 1916	5	6	
Pitt	Daniel W.	m.	PC	6 June 1916	5	1	
Pitt	Leland	m.	PA	2 Jan. 1917	8	1	
Pitt	Leland	m.	PC	3 Jan. 1917	3	3	
Pitt	Leland	m.	PC	31 Dec. 1916	4	2	
Pitts	James	d.	PA	3 Dec. 1918	3	5	Oakland; also 4 Dec., 2:2
Pitts	James	d.	PC	3 Dec. 1918	8	3	Oakland; also 4 Dec., 8:2
Placentini	Celide	o.	PA	10 Oct. 1917	3	6	
Placentini	Pietro	o.	PA	10 Oct. 1917	3	6	
Plaff	Henry	d.	PD	4 Oct. 1916	4	2	Lorain, Ohio
Plaff	Henry	d.	SRR	4 Oct. 1916	7	4	Lorain, Ohio
Plank	Reta	d.	PD	10 Mar. 1917	4	3	Gilliam Cemetery
Plank	Retta	d.	ST	10 Mar. 1917	5	4	Gilliam Cemetery
Plark	John C.	d.	PD	2 May 1917	7	3	
Plum	Mr. & Mrs.	b.	SRR	11 Aug. 1916	4	3	
Plum	William	m.	PD	17 July 1917	2	3	
Plum	William	m.	SRR	17 July 1917	3	4	
Plummer	Henry	b.	PC	11 Aug. 1918	8	2	
Plummer	Henry E.	b.	PC	16 Apr. 1916	8	4	
Plummer	R. A.	b.	PA	19 Apr. 1916	4	3	
Plunket	Albert Wylie	b.	PD	6 Oct. 1916	3	5	
Poat	Mary A.	d.	SRR	20 Apr. 1916	8	4	also 21 Apr., 8:5; 22 Apr., 1:3
Poe	Ina Alma	m.	ST	2 Feb. 1917	3	5	
Poehlmann	Max	o.	PA	18 Oct. 1918	5	3	also 23 Oct., 4:3; 24 Oct., 4:3
Poehlmann	Max	o.	PC	19 Oct. 1918	4	3	also 24 Oct., 1:2; 25 Oct., 8:3
Pohley	Margaret	m.	PD	22 Sept. 1916	5	1	
Pohley	Margaret	m.	SRR	22 Sept. 1916	2	4	
Pohley	Margaret	m.	PC	23 Sept. 1916	6	3	

(1) Surname	(2) Given Name	(3)	(4)	(5) Date	(6) Pg	(7) Col	(8) Comments
Pohley	Mary	d.	PA	22 Sept. 1916	5	7	
Pohlman	Ed	b.	SRR	20 Dec. 1916	2	2	
Polantri	Richard B.	m.	PA	4 Aug. 1916	2	4	
Polastri	Richard	m.	SRR	3 Aug. 1916	8	5	
Polastri	Richard B.	m.	PD	2 Aug. 1916	5	6	
Polgetto	E. Del	b.	SRR	18 July 1916	5	1	
Poliquin	Teko	d.	PD	23 Apr. 1918	8	2	
Polland	Alice Margaret	m.	PA	12 Mar. 1918	2	2	
Pom	Candin Albert	d.	ST	29 Apr. 1916	12	5	
Pometta	Dominic	d.	PA	9 Nov. 1917	4	4	also 10 Nov., 6:4; 12 Nov., 8:3
Pometta	Domonic	d.	PC	10 Nov. 1917	1	3	Calvary Cemetery; also 4:4; 13 Nov., 4:4
Pomi	Candin Albert	d.	PD	1 May 1916	1	6	also 3 May, 4:2
Pomi	Candin Albert	d.	SRR	2 May 1916	2	5	Petaluma Catholic Cemetery
Pomi	Candin Albert	d.	PA	29 Apr. 1916	4	5	
Pomi	Candin Albert	d.	PC	29 Apr. 1916	1	4	Calvary Cemetery; also 8:3; 5 May, 5:2
Pomi	Mr. & son	d.	PC	20 May 1916	1	3	moved from Santa Rosa Cemetery to Calvary Cemetery
Ponca	Amelia	d.	ST	10 Mar. 1917	8	4	Bodega
Poncetta	Gullia	m.	PD	19 Sept. 1916	8	3	
Poncetta	Rocca	m.	PD	26 Nov. 1916	4	2	
Poncetta	Rocco	d.	PD	2 Nov. 1918	7	5	
Poncetta	Rocco	m.	SRR	25 Nov. 1916	4	4	
Poncetta	Rocco	d.	PA	30 Oct. 1918	4	4	
Poncetta	Rocco	d.	PD	30 Oct. 1918	8	2	also 31 Oct., 4:2
Poncia	Fazzio	d.	PA	19 Oct. 1917	5	2	
Poncia	John	d.	PA	21 Dec. 1916	4	3	Tomales; also 22 Dec., 4:4; 23 Dec., 5:1
Poncia	John	d.	PC	22 Dec. 1916	8	6	Tomales; also 23 Dec., 4:7; 24 Dec., 8:3
Poncia	Joseph	d.	PA	25 Feb. 1916	4	2	Calvary Cemetery; also 28 Feb., 4:3
Poncia	Maddalena	m.	PA	10 July 1918	4	6	
Poncia	Magdalena	m.	PC	11 July 1918	8	2	
Poncia	Peter (dau of)	d.	PA	10 Mar. 1917	3	6	
Poncis	Joseph	d.	PD	25 Feb. 1916	8	3	
Pond	Archie B.	m.	PC	11 Apr. 1917	1	3	
Pond	Melvin	d.	PA	18 Mar. 1918	5	4	
Pond	Melvin	d.	PC	19 Mar. 1918	4	2	
Pongnacca	Tony	d.	PC	3 Jan. 1917	1	5	
Poniletti	Andrew	o.	SRR	16 Aug. 1917	6	1	
Poniletti	Romilda	o.	SRR	16 Aug. 1917	6	1	

(1) Surname	(2) Given Name	(3)	(4)	(5) Date	(6) Pg	(7) Col	(8) Comments
Pontaletto	Andrea	m.	PD	25 Feb. 1916	7	2	
Ponti	Peter	d.	SRR	23 Aug. 1916	7	4	
Pontiletti	Andrew	o.	SRR	18 Oct. 1917	5	5	
Pontiletti	Romilda	o.	SRR	18 Oct. 1917	5	5	
Ponzo	Filippi	d.	SRR	17 Jan. 1917	3	4	Oak Mound Cemetery
Ponzo	Peter	m.	PD	20 June 1916	5	3	
Ponzo	Peter	m.	HT	22 June 1916	2	3	
Pool	Chester	b.	PD	5 Apr. 1918	7	2	
Pool	Chester H.	m.	PD	15 Feb. 1916	8	3	
Pool	Chester R.	m.	SRR	15 Feb. 1916	5	2	
Pool	Ebba	m.	PC	16 Jan. 1916	1	5	
Pool	Elba	m.	PD	16 Jan. 1916	10	2	
Pool	George E.	o.	PD	21 Dec. 1918	4	2	I.O.O.F. Cemetery; also 8:1; 24 Dec., 5:2
Poole	Elba	m.	SRR	15 Jan. 1916	4	4	
Poole	Elba	m.	HT	20 Jan. 1916	4	1	
Poole	Fedora	d.	PD	15 Nov. 1916	2	3	also 18 Nov., 2:2
Poole	Seodoria	d.	PC	16 Nov. 1916	4	5	I.O.O.F. Cemetery
Poole	Seodoris	d.	SRR	15 Nov. 1916	8	5	I.O.O.F. Cemetery; also 17 Nov., 10:6
Pooler	Harry	d.	SIT	3 Mar. 1917	1	6	Mountain Cemetery
Pope	William	d.	SRR	23 July 1917	5	5	
Pope	William D.	d.	PD	22 July 1917	4	2	Odd Fellows Cemetery; also 8:2
Popp	Frederich William	m.	PD	1 May 1918	5	4	
Poppe	Raymond	m.	HT	27 July 1916	1	4	also 17 Aug., 1:5
Poppe	Raymond	m.	SIT	29 July 1916	1	1	also 19 Aug., 1:5
Poppe	Raymond	m.	PD	12 Aug. 1916	2	4	
Poppe	Raymond	m.	SRR	14 Aug. 1916	5	5	
Poppe	Raymond	m.	PA	17 Aug. 1916	4	2	
Poppe	Rymond	m.	PC	13 Aug. 1916	1	5	
Popper	Rudolph	m.	SRR	14 Feb. 1917	8	1	also 17 Feb., 6:3
Popper	Rudolph	m.	PC	15 Feb. 1917	8	6	
Popper	Rudolph	m.	PD	15 Feb. 1917	5	4	
Poppini	Joseph, Mrs.	d.	PA	22 May 1917	3	6	
Porter	Albert G.	o.	SRR	1 June 1917	1	5	
Porter	Elizabeth Dabney	d.	PD	23 Aug. 1918	8	2	also 27 Aug., 4:2; 29 Aug., 6:4
Porter	Fred C.	o.	PA	4 Oct. 1916	5	6	
Porter	Frederick	o.	PC	14 Feb. 1917	6	3	
Porter	Frederick C.	o.	PC	14 Mar. 1917	8	4	
Porter	Frederick C.	o.	PC	5 Oct. 1916	5	4	
Porter	Missouri Ann	d.	HT	15 Aug. 1918	5	3	
Porter	Nell W.	o.	SRR	1 June 1917	1	5	
Porter	Nellie	o.	PD	15 Jan. 1918	3	1	
Porter	Peter	o.	PD	15 Jan. 1918	3	1	

(1) Surname	(2) Given Name	(3)	(4)	(5) Date	(6) Pg	(7) Col	(8) Comments
Porter	Rose	m.	PA	15 May 1917	4	5	
Porter	Rose	m.	PD	16 May 1917	8	3	
Porter	Rose	m.	SRR	16 May 1917	2	4	
Porter	Rosette	o.	PC	14 Feb. 1917	6	3	
Porter	Rosette C.	o.	PC	14 Mar. 1917	8	4	
Porter	Rosette Cantel	o.	PC	5 Oct. 1916	5	4	
Porter	Rosette Cartel	o.	PA	4 Oct. 1916	5	6	
Porter	S. L.	o.	PC	29 Jan. 1918	3	4	
Portolan	Anselmo	d.	CR	15 Nov. 1918	8	1	
Portolo	Anselmo	d.	PA	13 Nov. 1918	4	2	Cloverdale
Post	Lucius R.	m.	SRR	3 May 1917	3	1	
Post	Mary A.	d.	PD	21 Apr. 1916	8	4	I.O.O.F. Cemetery; also 23 Apr., 3:3
Potter	Charles R.	m.	PD	1 Mar. 1918	8	3	
Potter	Charles R.	m.	PC	27 Feb. 1918	2	3	also 1 Mar., 5:2
Potter	Charles R.	m.	SIT	3 Mar. 1918	4	2	
Potter	Elizabeth	d.	SIT	15 Sept. 1917	1	7	cremation
Potter	Elizabeth Ann	d.	PC	14 Sept. 1917	1	4	
Potter	Elmer	b.	PA	27 Apr. 1916	3	3	
Potter	Elmer	b.	PC	28 Apr. 1916	8	6	
Potter	Elmer Milne	d.	PA	10 July 1916	4	5	
Potter	Elmer Milne	d.	PC	11 July 1916	8	4	also 12 July, 5:5
Potter	Ethel	d.	PA	8 Dec. 1917	6	3	
Potter	Ethel	d.	PC	8 Dec. 1917	1	2	
Potter	Ethel Sarah	d.	SIT	15 Dec. 1917	1	3	
Potter	Glen	m.	PA	3 Aug. 1917	8	3	
Potter	Glen	m.	PC	4 Aug. 1917	4	3	
Potter	Hugh	m.	PC	2 July 1916	4	2	
Potter	J. H.	o.	SRR	14 Sept. 1916	1	3	
Potter	James	d.	PD	24 Nov. 1918	6	4	
Potter	James	d.	HT	28 Nov. 1918	8	1	
Potter	James A.	d.	PA	23 Nov. 1918	5	3&4	Cypress Hill; also 25 Nov., 8:5
Potter	James A.	d.	PC	24 Nov. 1918	6	6	Cypress Hill; also 8:4; 26 Nov., 3:2
Potter	Mary	m.	SRR	9 June 1916	8	4	
Potter	Stephen D.	d.	PD	11 May 1916	2	3	Kelseyville
Potter	Stephen D.	d.	SRR	11 May 1916	5	3	
Potter	Hugh	m.	PA	1 July 1916	1	4	also 3 July, 5:3
Potwine	William	d.	PA	30 Aug. 1917	4	5	
Potwine	William E.	d.	SRR	29 Aug. 1917	4	1	also 8:3
Potwine	William Edward	d.	PD	30 Aug. 1917	8	1	also 31 Aug., 6:5; 2 Sept., 6:1; 12 Sept., 7:1; 16 Sept., 6:1
Potwine	William Edward	d.	ST	31 Aug. 1917	4	2	
Poulin	Louis	d.	PC	24 July 1917	4	6	

(1) Surname	(2) Given Name	(3)	(4)	(5) Date	(6) Pg	(7) Col	(8) Comments
Poulin	Louis	d.	PD	24 July 1917	8	4	
Poulin	Louis	d.	SRR	24 July 1917	6	5	Stanley Cemetery; also 8:5
Powell	Raymond Myron	d.	PA	9 Nov. 1918	3	3	
Power	John	d.	ST	2 Nov. 1917	1	6	
Powers	John W.	d.	PD	6 Nov. 1917	8	1	
Powers	John W.	d.	PC	7 Nov. 1917	8	1	
Powers	Maurice	m.	PA	20 June 1918	4	4	
Powers	Zelma	m.	PD	14 May 1918	3	5	
Pozzi	America	o.	PA	3 Dec. 1918	2	6	
Pozzi	America	o.	PC	3 Dec. 1918	1	3	
Pozzi	Archie	m.	PD	28 Mar. 1918	8	3	also 29 Mar., 5:5
Pozzi	Archie R.	m.	PC	29 Mar. 1918	5	4	
Pozzi	Linda	m.	PA	4 June 1918	4	1	
Pozzi	Linda	m.	PA	21 Mar. 1917	8	4	
Pozzi	Linda	m.	PC	21 Mar. 1917	5	3	
Pozzi	Linda M.	m.	PC	4 June 1918	5	3	
Pozzi	Luggi	o.	PC	26 Oct. 1916	8	3	
Pozzi	Luigi	o.	SRR	25 Oct. 1916	8	2	
Pozzi	Luigi	o.	PC	9 Jan. 1918	2	2	
Pozzi	Luigi Carlo	d.	SRR	18 June 1917	6	3	
Pozzi	Luigi Carlo	d.	PC	19 June 1917	3	4	
Pozzi	Luigi Carlo	d.	ST	22 June 1917	4	2	also 6:5
Pozzi	Lydia	o.	SRR	25 Oct. 1916	8	2	
Pozzi	Lydia	o.	PC	26 Oct. 1916	8	3	
Pozzi	Lydia	o.	PC	9 Jan. 1918	2	2	
Pozzi	Lydia	m.	PC	9 Jan. 1918	2	2	
Pozzi	Rosalia	m.	PC	19 Sept. 1917	4	1	
Pranj	Frederick	m.	PC	4 Dec. 1918	5	3	
Prato	Frank	d.	PC	10 Sept. 1916	1	3	
Prato	Frank	d.	PD	10 Sept. 1916	3	2	
Prato	Frank	d.	SRR	9 Sept. 1916	1	5	also 11 Sept., 5:5
Pratt	Earl	m.	SRR	16 July 1917	3	4	also 18 July, 8:3
Pratt	Earl	m.	PD	17 July 1917	8	2	also 19 July, 2:5
Pratt	Earl	b.	PC	8 Nov. 1918	5	1	
Pratt	Earl	b.	PA	9 Nov. 1918	6	4	
Pratt	Eugenia	m.	PC	28 Dec. 1916	6	1	
Pratt	Frank E.	d.	PD	30 Mar. 1918	8	3	
Presley	Alden	d.	PA	23 June 1917	6	3	
Pressley	Gertrude	o.	PD	20 Nov. 1917	6	3	
Pressley	Gertrude	o.	SRR	9 Oct. 1917	4	2	
Pressley	Gertrude	o.	PD	10 Oct. 1917	1	3	
Pressley	Hugh A.	o.	PD	10 Oct. 1917	1	3	
Pressley	Hugh A.	o.	PD	20 Nov. 1917	6	3	
Pressley	Hugh A.	o.	SRR	9 Oct. 1917	4	2	

(1) Surname	(2) Given Name	(3)	(4)	(5) Date	(6) Pg	(7) Col	(8) Comments
Preston	Charles F.	d.	HT	11 Oct. 1917	2	3	
Preston	Charlotte	d.	SRR	11 Dec. 1917	8	1	Petaluma; also 12 Dec., 8:2; 13 Dec., 3:4
Preston	Charlotte	d.	PA	12 Dec. 1917	6	3	Cypress Hill; also 13 Dec., 5:6
Preston	Charlotte	d.	PC	12 Dec. 1917	1	4	Cypress Hill; also 13 Dec., 4:5; 14 Dec., 4:4
Preston	Charlotte	d.	PD	12 Dec. 1917	5	5	Petaluma; also 13 Dec., 4:2; 14 Dec., 5:3
Preston	Elden	d.	ST	15 Jan. 1916	1	2	
Preston	Josie	m.	PD	8 Oct. 1918	7	2	
Preston	Mabel	m.	HT	22 Nov. 1917	5	3	
Price	Carrie	m.	PD	1 June 1917	6	5	
Price	Carrie Francis	m.	SRR	31 May 1917	1	6	
Price	Dorothy B.	m.	SRR	31 July 1917	8	3	
Price	Dorothy P.	m.	ST	3 Aug. 1917	1	3	
Price	Estella	m.	SRR	26 June 1916	8	5	
Price	Estella	m.	PD	27 June 1916	3	3	
Price	Estella May	m.	SRR	17 Apr. 1916	8	3	
Price	Estella May	m.	PC	18 Apr. 1916	4	4	
Price	Estelle	m.	PC	18 June 1916	5	4	also 27 June, 4:1
Price	Ethel M.	o.	PA	12 Mar. 1918	8	4	
Price	George	d.	PC	28 Nov. 1918	2	2	
Price	George W.	m.	PD	19 Oct. 1916	6	1	
Price	James B.	o.	PA	12 Mar. 1918	8	4	
Price	Katheryn	m.	PD	30 June 1918	9	1	
Price	Katheryn	m.	PA	1 July 1918	5	3	
Price	Kathryn A.	m.	PC	30 June 1918	1	3	
Price	Laura	m.	PD	26 Mar. 1918	3	1	
Price	Leroy	m.	HT	10 Jan. 1918	4	3	
Price	Leroy	d.	HT	15 Apr. 1918	5	5	
Price	Leroy	d.	PA	15 Apr. 1918	4	4	
Price	Leroy	d.	PD	16 Apr. 1918	6	2	
Price	Miss	m.	PA	18 Apr. 1916	5	2	
Price	Roy	d.	PC	16 Apr. 1918	6	4	
Price	Stella	m.	PA	26 June 1916	7	4	
Price	Stella	m.	PD	2 July 1916	2	2	
Price	Will	m.	PD	1 Jan. 1918	3	3	
Price	Will	m.	PA	29 Dec. 1917	4	2	also 31 Dec., 7:5
Price	Will	b.	PA	5 Nov. 1918	5	5	
Price	William	m.	PC	1 Jan. 1918	5	3	
Price	William B.	m.	PC	30 Dec. 1917	4	4	
Price	Zellah Luck	m.	SRR	3 May 1917	3	1	
Prince	Earl Raymond	m.	SRR	7 Mar. 1917	8	1	
Pritchett	Eliza	d.	HT	30 Mar. 1916	8	5	Geyserville

(1) Surname	(2) Given Name	(3)	(4)	(5) Date	(6) Pg	(7) Col	(8) Comments
Pritchett	Elizabeth	d.	PD	28 Mar. 1916	5	5	Olive Hill Cemetery, Geyserville
Pritchett	Elizabeth	d.	SRR	29 Mar. 1916	3	5	Olive Hill Cemetery
Proctor	Charles	m.	SRR	26 Jan. 1916	5	3	also 4 Mar., 5:1
Proctor	Charles I.	m.	HT	27 Jan. 1916	1	6	also 4 Mar., 2:3
Proctor	George A.	b.	SRR	21 Aug. 1916	5	4	
Proctor	Sarah	d.	SRR	18 Sept. 1916	6	4	
Proctor	Sarah J.	d.	PD	19 Sept. 1916	8	3	Oak Mound Cemetery
Proctor	Sarah J.	d.	HT	21 Sept. 1916	1	2	
Proctor	Walter	b.	PD	29 Aug. 1916	8	1	
Proctor	Walter L.	b.	SRR	28 Aug. 1916	8	2	
Pronini	Isadore	m.	PA	19 June 1918	8	3	also 26 June, 8:5
Pronini	Isadore	m.	PC	21 June 1918	3	4	also 27 June, 5:3
Prononi	Isadore	m.	PD	20 June 1918	8	3	
Prout	Florence	m.	CR	11 May 1917	1	5	
Prout	Stephen	m.	PD	2 Nov. 1916	8	1	
Prout	W. J.	d.	CR	20 Sept. 1918	1	4	Riverside Cemetery
Provines	Louis B.	m.	SRR	8 June 1917	6	4	
Prows	Fred	b.	HT	15 Mar. 1917	3	4	
Prowse	H.	m.	PC	9 Aug. 1917	1	5	
Prowse	H.	d.	PC	9 Aug. 1917	1	5	
Prowse	H. S.	m.	SIT	11 Aug. 1917	1	3	
Prowse	H. S.	d.	SIT	11 Aug. 1917	1	3	
Prowse	H. S.	m.	PD	9 Aug. 1917	8	3	
Prowse	S. E.	m.	SRR	9 Aug. 1917	5	1	
Prowse	S. E.	d.	SRR	9 Aug. 1917	5	1	
Prunty	Elizabeth Ruth	m.	PD	15 Feb. 1916	8	3	
Prunty	Elizabeth Ruth	m.	SRR	15 Feb. 1916	5	2	
Puget	Henry	b.	PA	2 Apr. 1917	3	5	also 4:5
Puja	John	b.	PA	18 July 1917	4	6	
Pursell	Georgia	m.	SRR	4 Jan. 1917	1	3	
Pursell	Georgia	m.	PC	5 Jan. 1917	5	2	
Pursell	John	d.	PA	27 Feb. 1917	8	3	
Pursell	John	d.	PD	27 Feb. 1917	8	3	portrait; also 2 Mar., 4:2
Pursell	John	d.	SRR	27 Feb. 1917	5	1	also 23 Feb., 8:3; 2 Mar., 10:3
Pursell	John	d.	PC	3 Mar. 1917	5	3	
Purvine	Lena	m.	PD	20 Dec. 1917	5	3	
Purvine	Lena A.	m.	PA	19 Dec. 1917	4	3	
Purvine	Lena Aletha	m.	PC	20 Dec. 1917	5	3	
Putzker	Ralph Waldo	m.	PD	27 May 1917	5	4	
Puzzi	Henry	o.	PC	17 Oct. 1918	3	4	
Quackenbusch	C. Edward	m.	PC	18 Oct. 1918	5	3	
Quartaroli	Frank	m.	SRR	26 Sept. 1917	5	3	
Quartaroli	Harry	m.	SIT	11 Mar. 1916	1	3	also 29 Apr., 1:6; 6 May, 1:1

(1) Surname	(2) Given Name	(3)	(4)	(5) Date	(6) Pg	(7) Col	(8) Comments
Quartaroli	Peter	d.	SIT	9 Nov. 1918	1	2	
Quartermass	Emma	m.	SRR	16 Aug. 1917	6	6	
Quartoroli	Harry	m.	PD	2 May 1916	5	2	
Queen	Mary S.	m.	SRR	23 June 1917	12	3	
Queener	Doris	m.	SRR	22 July 1916	5	1	also 24 July, 8:1; 27 July, 5:3
Queener/Volmeer	Doris	m.	SIT	29 July 1916	3	5	
Quentin	William	d.	PC	6 Nov. 1918	1	4	
Quigley	Fred	o.	PD	17 July 1917	2	2	
Quigley	Frederick	d.	SRR	13 Nov. 1916	1	2	
Quigley	Frederick	d.	PD	14 Nov. 1916	2	3	
Quigley	Margaret	o.	PD	17 July 1917	2	2	
Quincy	Fred	o.	PD	4 July 1916	7	5	
Quincy	Marguerite	o	PD	4 July 1916	7	5	
Quinlan	Lydia	d.	PA	18 Jan. 1918	4	2	
Quinlan	Lydia	d.	PC	19 Jan. 1918	4	1	cremation
Quinlan	Lydia	d.	PD	19 Jan. 1918	8	4	
Quinlin	Mrs.	d.	PA	4 Mar. 1918	4	4	Cypress Hill
Quinn	Frank	d.	SRR	5 Sept. 1917	4	3	San Francisco
Quinn	James	d.	SRR	19 June 1917	8	3	Calvary Cemetery; also 20 June, 8:2; 22 June, 8:6
Quinn	James	d.	PD	20 June 1917	8	2	Calvary Cemetery; also 22 June, 4:3; 23 June; 2:2
Quinn	James	d.	PC	21 June 1917	5	4	
Quintero	Annie	m.	PD	10 Oct. 1916	3	1	
Quintero	Annie	m.	SRR	9 Oct. 1916	8	2	
Quintero	Nick	d.	SRR	4 Nov. 1916	12	4	

R

(1) Surname	(2) Given Name	(3)	(4)	(5) Date	(6) Pg	(7) Col	(8) Comments
Rabben	William	b.	PA	27 Mar. 1917	5	4	
Rabben	William	b.	PC	28 Mar. 1917	5	6	
Rachetti	Pacifico	d.	PC	6 May 1916	2	2	
Rafael	M. E., Mrs.	d.	PD	11 Apr. 1918	3	3	
Raffellio	Palo, Mrs.	d.	HT	30 Mar. 1916	3	3	
Rafferty	Nellie	m.	PD	9 June 1918	2	5	
Ragain	Edith Belle	d.	PD	12 Nov. 1916	7	4	also 14 Nov., 5:4; 16 Nov., 8:3
Ragain	Edith Belle	d.	SRR	13 Nov. 1916	5	4	Rural Cemetery; also 14 Nov., 6:3; 15 Nov., 8:2
Ragain	Edith Belle	d.	PC	14 Nov. 1916	3	3	
Ragin	Domenico	m.	PC	20 Sept. 1918	4	3	
Ragle	Margaret I.	p.	PD	6 Feb. 1918	2	3	
Ragle	Margaret J.	d.	PD	2 Feb. 1918	3	1	Masonic Cemetery; also 4:2
Ragle	Margaret Jane	d.	ST	1 Feb. 1918	1	2	also 8 Feb., 7:4
Ragle	Margaret Jane	p.	ST	8 Feb. 1918	7	3	
Raines	Elliott M.	d.	SRR	5 Mar. 1917	7	3	also 6 Mar., 4:1
Rains	Elliott	d.	PD	6 Mar. 1917	2	3	Odd Fellows Cemetery; also 4:2
Ramaticci	Lily	m.	PC	9 July 1918	1	3	
Ramaticci	Romeo	b.	PA	11 June 1917	8	7	
Ramatici	Lily	m.	PA	9 July 1918	5	7	
Ramatici	Lily	m.	PD	9 July 1918	8	4	
Ramatici	Linda	m.	PA	17 Mar. 1917	5	2	also 23 Mar., 5:3
Ramatici	Linda	m.	PC	18 Mar. 1917	8	5	also 24 Mar., 1:5
Rambo	Esther Irene	m.	SRR	18 July 1917	4	3	also 4 Aug., 8:4; 6 Aug., 8:3
Rambo	Esther Irene	m.	PD	19 July 1917	3	1	also 7 Aug., 3:3
Rambo	Esther Irene	m.	ST	20 July 1917	4	2	also 10 Aug., 7:3
Rambo	Esther Irene	m.	SIT	11 Aug. 1917	1	4	
Rambo	Esther Rene	m.	PC	12 Aug. 1917	2	3	
Rambo	Milton G.	m.	PD	23 June 1918	6	1	
Ramos	Antone	m.	PA	1 Nov. 1916	7	4	
Ramos	Josephine	d.	PA	24 July 1916	4	1	Calvary Cemetery; also 8:1; 26 July, 4:1
Ramos	Josephine	d.	PC	25 July 1916	4	2	also 6:3; 27 July, 4:3
Ramos	Lena	m.	PC	26 Apr. 1917	1	1	also 1 May, 3:5
Ramos	Lena	m.	PA	30 Apr. 1917	4	5	
Ramos	Rosaline	m.	PD	5 June 1917	3	3	
Ramos	Rosaline	m.	PC	6 June 1917	3	5	
Ramos	Rosaline	m.	ST	8 June 1917	1	2	

(1) Surname	(2) Given Name	(3)	(4)	(5) Date	(6) Pg	(7) Col	(8) Comments
Ramos	Tony	m.	PC	31 Oct. 1916	6	5	also 26 Nov., 4:3
Rand	Charles	d.	SIT	10 Aug. 1918	1	5	
Randall	Grace	o.	PA	23 June 1916	8	7	
Randall	Grace I.	o.	SRR	7 June 1916	8	5	
Randall	Grace I.	o.	PC	8 June 1916	8	4	
Randall	Helen	m.	PD	9 Jan. 1917	3	1	
Randall	Helen Mar	m.	SRR	8 Jan. 1917	3	5	
Randall	Horace	o.	SRR	7 June 1916	8	5	
Randall	Horace	o.	PC	8 June 1916	8	4	
Randall	Horace C.	o.	PA	23 June 1916	8	7	
Randolph	Annie	m.	SIT	10 June 1916	1	2	
Randt	Charles	d.	PC	7 Aug. 1918	1	3	
Randt	Charles	d.	PD	7 Aug. 1918	8	5	
Randt	Charles	d.	PA	8 Aug. 1918	3	6	San Francisco
Raney	William Garnett	b.	SRR	4 Dec. 1917	1	3	
Ranker	Mildred	m.	PD	24 May 1918	2	4	
Ranker	Mildred	m.	SIT	25 May 1918	1	4	
Rankin	Julius C.	d.	PD	17 Oct. 1918	3	3	
Rankin	Kate	d.	PD	7 Jan. 1917	6	4	
Rankin	Kate Alice	d.	PA	6 Jan. 1917	3	4	Cypress Hill; also 8 Jan., 2:2
Rankin	Kate Alice	d.	PC	6 Jan. 1917	1	3	Cypress Hill; also 8:1; 9 Jan., 8:2
Rankin	Kate Alice	d.	SRR	8 Jan. 1917	5	2	
Rankin	L. Elmer	d.	SRR	13 Sept. 1917	1	4	
Rankin	L. Elmer	d.	PC	14 Sept. 1917	1	1	Cypress Hill; also 3:5; 15 Sept., 3:6; 16 Sept., 4:1
Rankin	L. Elmer	d.	ST	21 Sept. 1917	6	3	
Rankin	L. Elmer "Ed"	d.	PD	14 Sept. 1918	5	1	
Rankin	Lowry Elmer	d.	PA	13 Sept. 1917	1	3	Cypress Hill; also 15 Sept., 4:7
Raschetti	Pacifico	d.	PA	2 May 1916	5	5	
Rasmussen	Arthur L.	m.	PA	17 May 1916	4	6	also 25 May, 5:5
Rasmussen	Arthur Lawrence	m.	PC	17 May 1916	8	5	also 25 May, 1:4
Rasmussen	Arthur Lawrence	m.	PA	19 Apr. 1916	3	4	
Rasmussen	Arthur Lawrence	m.	PC	19 Apr. 1916	3	3	
Rasmussen	E.	d.	PA	21 Sept. 1918	4	4	
Rasmussen	N. P.	b.	PA	24 Feb. 1916	5	7	
Rasmussen	Peter	m.	PA	11 Sept. 1916	4	5	
Rasmussen	Peter	m.	PC	12 Sept. 1916	5	2	
Rasmussen	Rasmus	m.	PA	18 Oct. 1916	5	2	also 4 Nov., 4:4
Rasmussen	Rasmus	m.	PC	18 Oct. 1916	1	5	also 3 Nov., 6:5; 4 Nov., 4:6
Rasmussen	Rasmus	m.	PD	19 Oct. 1916	6	4	also 4 Nov., 1:5
Raszat	Adolf	m.	SRR	21 Sept. 1916	6	6	

(1) Surname	(2) Given Name	(3)	(4)	(5) Date	(6) Pg	(7) Col	(8) Comments
Raszat	Adolf	m.	SRR	24 Nov. 1916	10	3	
Rathbone	Albert	b.	PD	6 Dec. 1916	4	2	
Rathbone	Albert	b.	SRR	6 Dec. 1916	4	2	
Rathbone	Leland	m.	PD	8 Apr. 1917	6	1	
Rathbone	Lillie Jeanette	m.	PD	31 Jan. 1917	3	2	
Rathbone	Lillie Jeanette	m.	SRR	31 Jan. 1917	7	4	
Rauch	Tom	o.	PD	4 May 1918	7	4	
Rauch	Tom	o.	PD	9 Feb. 1918	6	1	
Raulet	Annyta	o.	PD	14 May 1918	5	2	
Raulet	Annyta	o.	PD	30 July 1918	6	3	
Raulet	Charles	o.	PD	14 May 1918	5	2	
Raulet	Charles	o.	PD	30 July 1918	6	3	
Raup	William	d.	PD	9 Dec. 1916	8	3	
Rawlings	Pearl	m.	PD	11 Aug. 1918	9	5	
Rawlins	Pearl	m.	PD	5 Sept. 1918	8	3	
Rawlinson	Amy	m.	SRR	11 Jan. 1916	3	3	
Rawls	Robert	d.	PC	18 Jan. 1918	3	3	
Rawls	Robert A.	d.	HT	17 Jan. 1918	1	1	
Rawls	Robert A.	d.	PD	20 Jan. 1918	2	4	
Rawson	Matilda D.	d.	PD	28 Apr. 1918	2	2	
Raymond	C. F.	o.	HT	30 Aug. 1917	1	1	
Raymond	Charles F.	o.	PD	26 Aug. 1917	3	4	
Raymond	Charles F.	o.	PD	29 Aug. 1917	6	4	
Raymond	Charles F.	o.	PC	30 Aug. 1917	3	3	
Rayner	Walter	m.	PA	5 Sept. 1918	3	3	
Reading	George A.	o.	SRR	19 Jan. 1917	5	3	adoption
Reams	Ellsworth	d.	PC	30 Nov. 1918	6	4	France
Reams	Mannie E.	m.	SRR	7 Sept. 1916	1	3	also 9 Sept., 10:1; 11 Sept., 8:6
Reams	Mannie Ellsworth	m.	PD	12 Sept. 1916	8	3	
Reams	Mannie Ellsworth	d.	PD	28 Nov. 1918	6	1	France
Reams	Mannie Elsworth	m.	PA	8 Sept. 1916	5	3	
Reams	Mannie Elworth	m.	PC	8 Sept. 1916	8	3	
Reavis	Clair	m.	PD	7 Dec. 1918	2	5	also 8 Dec., 8:2
Reavis	Clair W.	o.	PD	21 Sept. 1917	3	4	
Reavis	Clarence	o.	PD	20 Nov. 1917	6	3	also 27 Nov., 5:4
Reavis	Frances L.	o.	PD	20 Nov. 1917	6	3	also 27 Nov., 5:4
Reavis	Francis L.	o.	PD	21 Sept. 1917	3	4	
Redden	Sadie	d.	SRR	2 Aug. 1917	8	4	Rural Cemetery; also 3 Aug., 8:1
Redden	Sadie	d.	PD	3 Aug. 1917	7	2	Rural Cemetery; also 4 Aug., 4:2
Redford	Russell	d.	PA	24 Jan. 1918	5	1	France
Redmond	Frank	d.	PD	12 Aug. 1916	5	3	
Redmond	Frank	d.	PA	14 Aug. 1916	4	5	

(1) Surname	(2) Given Name	(3)	(4)	(5) Date	(6) Pg	(7) Col	(8) Comments
Redmond	Frank M.	d.	SRR	12 Aug. 1916	1	4	
Redmond	Frank M.	d.	PC	13 Aug. 1916	1	1	
Redmond	Levi	d.	SRR	21 Mar. 1917	8	2	
Redmond	Levi	d.	PD	22 Mar. 1917	8	4	
Redner	Charles	m.	PD	22 June 1918	6	1	also 23 June, 7:1
Reed	Isaac B.	o.	PA	1 May 1917	5	3	
Reed	James	d.	PA	2 June 1917	5	1	Calvary Cemetery; also 4 June, 8:2
Reed	James	d.	PD	3 June 1917	9	1	
Reed	James	d.	PC	5 June 1917	8	2	Calvary Cemetery
Reed	Joe	b.	PD	20 Sept. 1916	2	3	
Reed	Quincy	m.	PA	1 May 1917	5	3	also 2 May, 2:5
Reed	Quincy	m.	SRR	1 May 1917	8	2	
Reed	Quincy	m.	PC	2 May 1917	4	3	
Reed	Quincy	m.	PD	2 May 1917	8	5	
Reedy	B. C., Mrs.	d.	SIT	7 Dec. 1918	2	7	
Reese	B. S.	d.	PD	7 Sept. 1917	5	1	
Reese	George	m.	SRR	11 Jan. 1916	3	3	
Reese	S. B.	d.	HT	6 Sept. 1917	1	4	
Regan	E. D.	b.	PC	5 Dec. 1917	5	5	
Regan	Ed D.	b.	PA	3 Dec. 1917	5	3	
Regin	Domenico	m.	PA	19 Sept. 1918	3	5	
Regoni	Antone	o.	SRR	13 Nov. 1916	8	5	
Regoni	Antonio	o.	SRR	24 Dec. 1917	10	3	
Regoni	Celestine	o.	SRR	13 Nov. 1916	8	5	
Regoni	Celestine	o.	SRR	24 Dec. 1917	10	3	
Regoni	Celestino	o.	PD	14 Nov. 1916	2	2	
Regucci	Filippo	b.	PC	1 Dec. 1917	5	5	
Reibli	Christine	o.	PD	6 Nov. 1917	6	3	
Reichart	Hans	d.	PA	24 June 1918	1	4	
Reichart	Hans	d.	PD	25 June 1918	5	3	
Reichert	Hans	d.	PC	25 June 1918	1	2	
Reichert	Hans	d.	HT	27 June 1918	1	2	
Reid	Daniel	d.	PA	2 July 1918	5	3	Cypress Hill; also 3 July, 4:4, 7:2; 5 July, 1:3
Reid	Daniel	d.	PC	3 July 1918	1	4	Cypress Hill; also 8:2; 6 July, 5:4
Reid	Daniel	d.	PD	6 July 1918	2	3	
Reid	J. W.	o.	PA	23 Apr. 1918	4	3	
Reid	Joseph B.	d.	PD	3 Dec. 1918	3	5	Rural Cemetery; also 4:2; 5 Dec., 3:3
Reid	Maude M.	o.	PA	23 Apr. 1918	4	3	
Reilly	Richard	d.	PA	9 Oct. 1918	8	5	
Reilly	Richard	d.	PC	9 Oct. 1918	4	2	Oakland; also 10 Oct., 8:4

(1) Surname	(2) Given Name	(3)	(4)	(5) Date	(6) Pg	(7) Col	(8) Comments
Reiman	Walter	d.	PC	19 Oct. 1918	4	6	
Reiman	Walter	d.	PD	19 Oct. 1918	8	3	Shiloh Cemetery; also 22 Oct., 3:1
Reimers	Anita A.	m.	PA	4 Mar. 1916	5	7	
Reimers	William	d.	SRR	26 Dec. 1916	8	1	
Reimers	William	d.	HT	28 Dec. 1916	8	5	
Reis	Oscar	m.	PA	19 May 1916	8	7	also 22 May, 5:1
Reis	Oscar	m.	PC	20 May 1916	4	4	also 22 May, 4:1
Reise	Charles	m.	PD	27 Oct. 1917	8	3	
Reise	Charles	m.	PC	28 Oct. 1917	4	3	
Reise	Charles G.	m.	SRR	1 Dec. 1917	3	4	
Reise	Charles G.	m.	PD	2 Dec. 1917	8	2	
Remmel	Charles	o.	HT	3 Jan. 1918	1	5	
Rencurel	Augustine	m.	PA	29 Jan. 1916	8	7	
Reniff	Mary	d.	PA	5 Aug. 1918	8	2&5	Cypress Hill
Reniff	Mary	d.	PC	6 Aug. 1918	3	1&2	Cypress Hill; also 7 Aug., 2:2; 8 Aug., 4:3
Reniff	Mary	d.	PD	6 Aug. 1918	4	2	Cypress Hill; also 5:2; 8 Aug., 2:4
Renolds	Laura	m.	PD	1 July 1917	2	1	also 1 Aug., 8:5; 3 Aug., 2:3; 4 Aug., 8:2
Renworth	Nora T.	m.	PD	23 Oct. 1917	7	4	
Renz	Millie Alvin	d.	PC	11 July 1916	5	7	Calvary Cemetery; also 12 July, 8:5
Renz	Millie Alvina	d.	PA	10 July 1916	5	6	Calvary Cemetery; also 11 July, 5:3
Rescendes	William	d.	PD	20 July 1918	6	1	France
Resendes	Tony	m.	PC	10 Dec. 1918	3	4	
Resendes	Tony	m.	PA	3 Dec. 1918	5	1	also 9 Dec., 2:2
Resendes	William	d.	ST	26 July 1918	1	5	France
Resendes	William J.	d.	PA	20 July 1918	7	4	France
Resendes	William J.	d.	PC	20 July 1918	1	4	France
Respini	America	m.	PC	27 Sept. 1916	4	3	
Respini	America	m.	ST	30 Sept. 1916	8	4	
Respini	Henry	b.	PC	18 Apr. 1916	8	1	
Respini	Robert	m.	PC	27 Apr. 1916	4	3	
Respini	Robert M.	m.	PA	26 Apr. 1916	4	3	
Respini	Silvio	m.	PD	26 Aug. 1917	3	5	
Rester	Lillian	m.	PD	8 July 1917	5	4	
Revalli/Rivillie	George	d.	PD	7 Aug. 1918	5	1	also 9 Aug., 7:2
Revellie	George	d.	PA	6 Aug. 1918	4	4	
Revie	Archie	o.	SIT	20 Oct. 1917	1	5	
Revie	Arvilla C.	m.	PA	5 May 1917	3	3	
Revie	Arvilla C.	m.	PC	5 May 1917	3	3	
Revie	Arvilla C.	m.	SIT	12 May 1917	2	5	
Revie	Charles	o.	SIT	11 Aug. 1917	1	1	

(1) Surname	(2) Given Name	(3)	(4)	(5) Date	(6) Pg	(7) Col	(8) Comments
Revie	Charles	o.	SIT	20 Oct. 1917	1	5	
Revie	Ernest	d.	PC	20 Feb. 1918	7	4	
Revie	Ernest	d.	SIT	23 Feb. 1918	1	5	
Reynolds	Anita	m.	PD	28 Oct. 1917	8	2	
Reynolds	Anita	m.	PC	30 Oct. 1917	3	4	
Reynolds	Edwin	d.	PA	3 Jan. 1918	7	4	
Reynolds	Edwin	d.	PC	3 Jan. 1918	2	2	
Reynolds	Emma	m.	PD	4 Feb. 1916	8	3	
Reynolds	Harold	m.	PC	17 May 1918	1	4	
Reynolds	Harold V.	m.	PD	17 May 1918	5	4	
Reynolds	Louis E.	d.	PC	7 June 1916	4	3	
Reynolds	Sarah	d.	PD	15 June 1917	2	5	
Reynolds	Sarah	d.	ST	15 June 1917	4	3	Gilliam Cemetery
Rhoades	Annie Nelson	d.	PD	27 July 1917	3	1	also 31 July, 3:2
Rhoads	Annie Nelson	d.	SRR	26 July 1917	8	3	also 28 July, 2:1, 10:6; 30 July, 8:5
Rhoads	Annie Nelson	d.	PC	27 July 1917	8	2	Santa Rosa
Rhoads	Samuel	o.	SRR	26 Mar. 1917	3	1	
Rhodes	Henry	d.	PD	26 July 1916	7	1	
Rhodes	Henry	d.	SRR	26 July 1916	3	5	
Rhodes	James E.	m.	PD	16 June 1917	6	3	
Riboni	Amelia	o.	SRR	2 Aug. 1917	4	1	
Riboni	Emma R.	o.	PD	3 Aug. 1917	2	2	
Riboni	John	o.	SRR	2 Aug. 1917	4	1	
Riboni	John	o.	PD	3 Aug. 1917	2	2	
Rice	Arthur F.	b.	ST	7 Sept. 1916	8	3	
Rice	Bryan	o.	PA	20 Feb. 1918	4	5	
Rice	Ethel	o.	PA	20 Feb. 1918	4	5	
Rice	Ethel	o.	PC	31 Oct. 1918	3	3	
Rice	Ethel M.	o.	PA	27 July 1918	8	2	
Rice	Ethel M.	o.	PC	27 July 1918	3	3	
Rice	Ethel M.	o.	PA	1 Nov. 1918	4	5	
Rice	Ethel M.	o.	PC	12 Mar. 1918	3	3	
Rice	Ethel M.	o.	PD	2 Dec. 1917	5	7	
Rice	Ethel M.	o.	PD	2 Nov. 1918	3	1	
Rice	Ethel M.	o.	PD	20 Feb. 1918	2	3	also 21 Feb., 8:4
Rice	Ethel M.	o.	PC	20 Nov. 1917	4	5	
Rice	Ethel M.	o.	PC	28 Oct. 1917	1	5	
Rice	Helen M.	m.	PA	2 Nov. 1918	8	2	
Rice	Helen M.	m.	PC	3 Nov. 1918	5	3	
Rice	James	o.	PD	20 Feb. 1918	2	3	also 21 Feb., 8:4
Rice	James B.	o.	PA	27 July 1918	8	2	
Rice	James B.	o.	PC	12 Mar. 1918	3	3	
Rice	James B.	o.	PD	2 Nov. 1918	3	1	
Rice	James B.	o.	PC	20 Nov. 1917	4	5	

(1) Surname	(2) Given Name	(3)	(4)	(5) Date	(6) Pg	(7) Col	(8) Comments
Rice	James B.	o.	PC	28 Oct. 1917	1	5	
Rice	James B.	o.	PC	31 Oct. 1918	3	3	
Rice	James Bryan	o.	PA	1 Nov. 1918	4	5	
Rice	James R.	o.	PD	2 Dec. 1917	5	7	
Rich	Edwin	o.	PD	20 Mar. 1918	2	1	
Rich	Mr.	m.	SRR	24 Apr. 1917	6	4	
Rich	Mr.	m.	PD	25 Apr. 1917	2	5	
Richard	James L.	d.	SRR	11 Nov. 1916	8	6	
Richard	W. N.	b.	SRR	14 Nov. 1916	7	6	
Richards	(dau. of)	b&d	PD	23 Nov. 1917	2	2	
Richards	Albert	d.	PA	16 Aug. 1916	3	5	
Richards	Albert	d.	PC	16 Aug. 1916	1	5	
Richards	Albert	d.	PD	16 Aug. 1916	8	1	
Richards	Albert	d.	SRR	16 Aug. 1916	5	1	also 17 Aug., 7:3
Richards	Edwin (child of)	d.	SRR	2 Jan. 1917	3	5	
Richards	Ernet L.	o.	PD	27 Aug. 1918	2	3	
Richards	George	d.	PD	5 Feb. 1918	3	3	Calvary Cemetery; also 6 Feb., 8:3
Richards	Theodor	d.	PD	12 Feb. 1918	8	3	Holy Cross, S.F.; also 13 Feb., 4:2; 15 Feb., 3:3
Richards	Theodor	d.	SIT	16 Feb. 1918	1	3	
Richards	Theodore	d.	PC	12 Feb. 1918	4	4	Holy Cross, S.F.; also 13 Feb., 4:6; 14 Feb., 4:6; 16 Feb., 6:3
Richards	Theodore F.	d.	PA	12 Feb. 1918	8	3	
Richards	Thomas Joseph	o.	SIT	28 Sept. 1918	3	4	
Richards	Vernon	b.	HT	21 Mar. 1918	2	2	
Richardson	C. C.	b.	PA	24 July 1918	6	4	
Richardson	Ed B.	o.	SRR	5 Sept. 1917	7	3	
Richardson	F. H. R.	m.	PC	5 Nov. 1918	5	3	
Richardson	Lewis	m.	PD	29 June 1916	8	4	
Richardson	Lewis	m.	SRR	29 June 1916	5	3	
Richardson	Lewis Everett	m.	PD	13 Aug. 1918	3	3	
Richardson	Lydia	d.	SRR	12 Dec. 1916	4	1	
Richardson	Lydia Esther	d.	PD	12 Dec. 1916	5	3	
Richardson	Mabel	m.	PC	1 Apr. 1918	4	3	
Richardson	Mabel	m.	PA	16 Mar. 1918	4	4	also 1 Apr., 5:5
Richardson	Mabel	m.	PC	17 Mar. 1918	5	4	
Richardson	Mary E.	d.	PA	20 May 1918	3	2	Cypress Hill; also 4:5; 21 May, 4:5
Richardson	Mary E.	d.	PC	21 May 1918	4	3	Cypress Hill; also 22 May, 4:2
Richardson	Sarah Myrtle	o.	SRR	5 Sept. 1917	7	3	
Richardson	W. H.	d.	SRR	5 Feb. 1917	5	4	

(1) Surname	(2) Given Name	(3)	(4)	(5) Date	(6) Pg	(7) Col	(8) Comments
Richardson	William	b.	PA	23 Oct. 1916	5	7	
Richardson	William H.	d.	PA	18 May 1917	4	3	
Richardson	William H.	d.	PA	16 Jan. 1917	1	4	also 23 Jan., 1:3; 24 Jan., 2:2; 3 Feb., 5:6
Richardson	William H.	d.	PC	17 Jan. 1917	4	4	also 18 Jan., 4:2; 4 Feb., 1:6
Richert	Constant	d.	PC	1 Jan. 1918	4	1	
Richinca	Peter	d.	PA	10 Dec. 1917	8	5	also 11 Dec., 12:1
Richini	Peter	d.	PD	11 Dec. 1917	7	1	
Richter	Fred	d.	PA	27 Dec. 1916	5	3	
Rickman	D. H., Mrs.	d.	PA	2 Nov. 1916	3	4	
Rickman	D. H., Mrs.	d.	PC	31 Oct. 1916	3	4	
Rickman	D. H., Mrs.	d.	SRR	31 Oct. 1916	5	4	also 2 Nov., 10:6
Rickman	Elizabeth	d.	PD	31 Oct. 1916	3	1	also 1 Nov., 2:2
Rickman	Mary Elizabeth	d.	HT	3 Nov. 1916	1	1	
Ridgeway	Lawrence	d.	PC	7 Aug. 1918	2	1	
Ridley	Elsie V.	o.	PD	15 Jan. 1918	3	1	
Ridley	Ernest	o.	PD	29 June 1918	6	3	
Ridley	Ernest	o.	PD	15 Jan. 1918	3	1	
Riebli	Arnold B.	o.	PC	6 Nov. 1917	5	1	
Riebli	Christina A.	o.	PC	6 Nov. 1917	5	1	
Riegelhuths	J., Mrs.	d.	SIT	21 Apr. 1917	1	5	
Riemers	William	d.	PD	27 Dec. 1916	1	4	
Ries	Oscar	m.	PC	29 Apr. 1916	5	2	
Riester	Arrington L.	d.	PD	4 Sept. 1918	5	4	
Riewerts	Arnold	o.	PC	4 Dec. 1917	5	4	
Righetti	Leno	m.	PD	1 June 1918	3	1	also 4 June, 3:5
Rignell	Gus	d.	SRR	23 Aug. 1916	8	4	
Rignell/Bignell	Gus	d.	PA	23 Aug. 1916	5	2	also 24 Aug., 6:1
Rigoni	Antonio	o.	SRR	8 Jan. 1917	4	4	
Rigoni	Celestine	o.	SRR	8 Jan. 1917	4	4	
Riley	Michael C.	d.	PA	10 Apr. 1916	4	1	Calvary Cemetery; also 8:6; 12 Apr., 1:3
Riley	Michael C.	m.	PC	9 Apr. 1916	1	3	Calvary Cemetery; also 11 Apr., 4:1; 13 Apr., 8:4
Riley	Robert J.	b.	PA	12 Oct. 1916	1	4	
Rinaldi	Vincenzo	d.	SRR	26 Apr. 1916	5	5	Cloverdale; also 28 Apr., 8:2
Rinehart	Sadie	m.	PD	2 Mar. 1917	8	2	
Rinehart	Sadie F.	m.	PA	2 Mar. 1917	8	2	
Ringgressy	C. F.	o.	PC	15 Dec. 1918	3	1	
Rinkle	Lorenz	m.	PD	16 Aug. 1918	8	4	
Rinkle	Lorenz	m.	PC	17 Aug. 1918	6	5	
Rinola	Tomasini	m.	CR	24 June 1917	1	3	
Rinziessy	A. P.	o.	PC	8 Feb. 1918	8	4	also 17 Feb., 4:4

(1) Surname	(2) Given Name	(3)	(4)	(5) Date	(6) Pg	(7) Col	(8) Comments
Riscioni	George	d.	PA	10 Jan. 1917	7	2	Calvary Cemetery; also 11 Jan., 5:4
Riscioni	George	d.	PC	8 Jan. 1918	1	2	Calvary Cemetery; also 9 Jan., 1:6, 4:1; 10 Jan., 8:1; 12 Jan., 1:5
Ristau	Mable	m.	PC	1 Oct. 1918	2	1	
Roach	Lena	m.	PC	11 July 1918	6	5	
Robbins	David	d.	SRR	25 July 1916	8	1	also 26 July, 8:5
Robbins	David M.	d.	PD	26 July 1916	3	4	
Robbins	Florence	d.	PD	21 Feb. 1918	7	2	
Robbins	James Franklin	d.	HT	10 Jan. 1918	1	2	Oak Mound Cemetery
Robbins	James Franklin	d.	PD	5 Jan. 1918	7	1	
Roberts	Albert Charles	m.	PD	30 May 1918	8	2	
Roberts	Annie Lyle	d.	PC	21 Apr. 1918	5	3	Cypress Hill; also 22 Apr., 6:3
Roberts	Annie Lyle	d.	PA	22 Apr. 1918	2	4	Cypress Hill
Roberts	Annie Lyle	d.	PD	23 Apr. 1918	6	2	
Roberts	Arthur C.	d.	HT	31 Jan. 1918	4	4	Geyserville
Roberts	Charles O.	m.	SRR	20 Mar. 1917	1	3	
Roberts	Edward	m.	SRR	8 Nov. 1916	8	5	also 9 Nov., 2:1
Roberts	Ernest G.	b.	PA	30 Nov. 1917	4	6	
Roberts	Fletcher	b.	PA	1 May 1916	6	6	also 8:4
Roberts	Fletcher	b.	PC	27 Nov. 1917	8	5	
Roberts	Frank	d.	PA	17 Aug. 1917	5	4	Cypress Hill; also 20 Aug., 1:4
Roberts	Frank	d.	PC	17 Aug. 1917	6	3	Cypress Hill; also 8:3; 19 Aug., 6:3; 21 Aug., 8:1
Roberts	Frank	d.	SRR	17 Aug. 1917	8	3	Cypress Hill; also 18 Aug., 8:3; 20 Aug., 5:3
Roberts	Frank	p.	PA	23 Aug. 1917	4	3	
Roberts	Frank, Mrs.	d.	SRR	10 Feb. 1917	4	2	
Roberts	Franklin	d.	PD	18 Aug. 1917	4	2	Cypress Hill Cemetery; also 6:1
Roberts	Harriet	d.	PC	8 May 1918	1	4	Cypress Hill; also 8 May, 8:4; 10 May, 4:4; 11 May, 4:2
Roberts	Harriet	d.	PD	9 May 1918	3	5	
Roberts	Harriett	d.	PA	7 May 1918	5	4	Cypress Hill; also 10 May, 5:7
Roberts	Hugh	d.	PA	24 Jan. 1917	5	3	also 29 Jan., 5:2
Roberts	Hugh J.	d.	PC	25 Jan. 1917	1	5	also 26 Jan., 5:5; 27 Jan., 5:1; 28 Jan., 3:6, 5:1; 30 Jan., 3:4
Roberts	Logan	m.	SRR	28 Nov. 1916	6	4	
Roberts	Mary	d.	PC	10 Feb. 1916	5	5	Cypress Hill

(1) Surname	(2) Given Name	(3)	(4)	(5) Date	(6) Pg	(7) Col	(8) Comments
Roberts	Mary	d.	SRR	5 Feb. 1916	10	6	Petaluma; also 7 Feb., 4:1; 9 Feb., 8:3
Roberts	Mary	d.	PA	6 Feb. 1917	4	5	Cypress Hill; also 8 Feb., 2:3; 10 Feb., 4:3
Roberts	Mary	d.	SRR	6 Feb. 1917	4	1	
Roberts	Mary	d.	PA	7 Feb. 1916	4	3	also 9 Feb., 3:5
Roberts	Mary	d.	PD	7 Feb. 1917	6	4	also 11 Feb., 8:2
Roberts	Mary	d.	PC	8 Feb. 1916	4	1	
Roberts	Mary	d.	PD	8 Feb. 1916	5	1	Petaluma Cemetery; also 10 Feb., 2:3
Roberts	Mary Elizabeth	d.	PC	7 Feb. 1917	5	3	Cypress Hill; also 8 Feb., 6:1; 10 Feb., 5:6; 11 Feb., 5:4
Roberts	Mary J.	p.	PA	24 June 1916	3	3	
Roberts	Mary J.	p.	PA	23 Aug. 1917	4	3	
Roberts	Mary Jane	d.	PC	16 Feb. 1916	5	5	Cypress Hill
Roberts	Sadie	m.	PC	21 Feb. 1917	1	1	
Roberts	Sadie V.	m.	SRR	20 Feb. 1917	1	2	
Roberts	Susan	d.	SRR	22 May 1916	8	3	Rural Cemetery; also 24 May, 8:5
Roberts	Susan B.	d.	PD	23 May 1916	7	2	also 25 May, 3:4
Roberts	W. T.	m.	PC	1 Sept. 1917	4	4	also 2 Sept., 5:4
Roberts	Will	m.	SRR	1 Sept. 1917	8	6	
Roberts	William T.	m.	PD	1 Sept. 1917	8	5	also 2 Sept., 8:4
Roberts	William Thomas	m.	PA	1 Sept. 1917	5	3	
Roberts	Edwin A.	m.	PD	9 Nov. 1916	6	4	
Robertson	Evan Clinton	m.	PA	2 Jan. 1918	5	3	
Robertson	Evan Clinton	m.	PC	3 Jan. 1918	1	4	
Robertson	Isaac Nathan	d.	SRR	31 Dec. 1917	8	3	
Robertson	John	p.	PC	1 Nov. 1917	3	4	
Robertson	John W.	d.	PD	29 Sept. 1916	1	6	Masonic Cemetery, Sebastopol
Robertson	John W.	d.	SRR	29 Sept. 1916	5	6	Sebastopol
Robertson	John W.	d.	PA	30 Sept. 1916	6	4	Sebastopol
Robertson	John W.	d.	PC	30 Sept. 1916	6	1	
Robertson	John W.	d.	ST	30 Sept. 1916	1	6	Masonic Cemetery
Robertson	Josie	d.	PD	19 July 1916	8	3	San Francisco
Robertson	Sidney H.	d.	PC	18 Aug. 1918	8	2&5	Bloomfield; also 20 Aug., 6:3
Robertson/Robinson	Sidney H.	d.	PD	18 Aug. 1918	7	4	also 20 Aug., 2:4
Robinson	Benjamin	d.	SRR	17 Oct. 1917	8	4	also 22 Oct., 4:4
Robinson	Benjamin M.	d.	PC	18 Oct. 1917	1	5	
Robinson	Bob	o.	PA	24 Aug. 1918	4	3	
Robinson	Charlotte Anne	b.	ST	5 Oct. 1917	8	4	
Robinson	Dorothea Lincoln	d.	ST	26 Aug. 1916	1	2	

(1) Surname	(2) Given Name	(3)	(4)	(5) Date	(6) Pg	(7) Col	(8) Comments
Robinson	Dorothy Lincoln	d.	PD	22 Aug. 1916	6	2	Gilliam Cemetery; 6 yrs; typhoid
Robinson	Dorothy Lincoln	d.	PC	24 Aug. 1916	1	6	Gillman Cemetery
Robinson	Emma	m.	PA	3 July 1918	4	6	
Robinson	Eugene	m.	SRR	23 June 1917	5	1	
Robinson	Eugene	o.	PD	3 Nov. 1918	8	1	
Robinson	Eugene	o.	PC	6 Nov. 1918	2	2	
Robinson	J. W.	m.	PC	11 Mar. 1917	5	5	wife not named
Robinson	John Ormsby	d.	PD	7 Sept. 1918	4	2	cremation, also 5:3
Robinson	John Ormsby	d.	PC	8 Sept. 1918	4	5	
Robinson	John Ormsby	d.	PA	9 Sept. 1918	8	5	
Robinson	Lucile	m.	PA	8 June 1916	6	2	
Robinson	Lucille	m.	SRR	8 June 1916	5	2	
Robinson	Lucy	m.	PC	8 June 1916	1	5	
Robinson	M., Mrs.	m.	PC	3 July 1918	4	3	
Robinson	Montgomery	d.	SRR	18 Mar. 1916	10	6	also 21 Mar., 8:6, 22 Mar., 10:3
Robinson	Montgomery	d.	PD	22 Mar. 1916	8	3	
Robinson	Rhoda	m.	PD	30 Jan. 1916	8	7	
Robinson	Sidney H.	d.	PA	17 Aug. 1918	4	6	Bloomfield; also 19 Aug., 5:1
Robinson	Walter "Bobby"	o.	PC	25 Aug. 1918	1	4	
Robinson	William Dexter	d.	PA	17 July 1916	4	3	cremation
Robinson	William Dexter	d.	PC	18 July 1916	3	1	
Robinson	William H.	d.	PA	31 Oct. 1916	2	4	cremation; also 1 Nov., 8:5; 3 Nov., 6:4
Robinson	William H.	d.	PC	31 Oct. 1916	1	2	cremation; also 3 Nov., 4:2; 4 Nov., 1:5
Robuson	George	d.	PA	30 Nov. 1917	4	4	
Rochat	Fuller	o.	SIT	8 June 1918	1	1	
Roche	A. J.	p.	PD	28 Dec. 1916	3	4	
Rochester	Eva	d.	PD	17 Mar. 1916	2	1	
Rock	Marie	m.	SRR	3 Apr. 1916	4	4	
Rockhold	H. W.	m.	PA	5 May 1917	3	3	
Rockhold	H. W.	m.	SIT	12 May 1917	2	5	
Rockhold	Harry W.	m.	PC	5 May 1917	3	3	
Rodehaver	Lillion	m.	PC	10 Apr. 1917	5	2	
Rodehaver	Ray H.	m.	PA	26 May 1917	8	1	
Rodehaver	Ray H.	m.	PC	27 May 1917	8	5	
Roderick	Frank S.	b.	PA	14 Nov. 1917	4	4	also 5:2
Roderick	Joseph	d.	PA	22 May 1917	5	3	Calvary Cemetery; also 23 May, 5:2; 25 May, 4:5
Roderick	Joseph	d.	PC	23 May 1917	4	3	Calvary Cemetery; also 8:3; 24 May, 3:3; 25 May, 3:1; 26 May, 7:4

(1) Surname	(2) Given Name	(3)	(4)	(5) Date	(6) Pg	(7) Col	(8) Comments
Rodgers	Anna Belle	m.	PA	23 Nov. 1916	5	3	
Rodgers	Anna Belle	m.	SRR	24 Nov. 1916	3	2	
Rodgers	Anna Belle	m.	SRR	6 Feb. 1917	8	1	also 8 Feb., 5:3
Rodgers	Anna Belle	m.	PA	6 Jan. 1917	5	4	also 6 Feb., 8:4; 7 Feb., 4:3
Rodgers	Anna Belle	m.	PD	7 Jan. 1917	7	1	
Rodgers	Anna Belle "Patsy"	m.	PC	6 Jan. 1917	8	2	also 7 Feb., 5:2; 8 Feb., 4:1
Rodgers	Anna Belle "Patsy"	m.	PD	8 Feb. 1917	2	4	
Rodgers	Anna Belle "Patsy"	m.	PD	24 Nov. 1916	5	2	
Rodgers	Annabelle	m.	PC	24 Nov. 1916	6	5	
Rodgers	Charles	b.	PA	13 June 1916	4	3	
Rodgers	Irene	o.	PA	1 May 1917	3	2	
Rodgers	Irene	o.	SRR	18 Sept. 1916	8	2	
Rodgers	Irene	o.	PA	19 Sept. 1916	3	1	
Rodgers	Irene	o.	SRR	30 Apr. 1917	8	2	
Rodgers	Isaac	o.	SRR	18 Sept. 1916	8	2	
Rodgers	Isaac B.	o.	SRR	30 Apr. 1917	8	2	
Rodgers	Manuel Perry	d.	PA	19 May 1916	5	4	Calvary Cemetery; also 22 May, 5:1
Rodgers	Manuel Perry	d.	PC	19 May 1916	1	2	Calvary Cemetery; also 20 May, 1:1, 5:5; 22 May, 4:4
Rodgers	Robert Collins	b.	PD	3 Jan. 1917	6	5	
Rodgers	William	m.	PD	18 June 1916	5	2	
Rodgers	William	m.	PA	12 Sept. 1916	4	4	also 14 Sept., 5:4
Rodgers	William	d.	SRR	19 Dec. 1916	5	1	
Rodgers	William A.	m.	PC	13 Sept. 1916	4	4	also 15 Sept., 7:3
Rodgers	William T.	b.	SRR	3 Jan. 1917	7	4	
Rodriquez	Mary	m.	PA	22 Nov. 1916	6	4	
Roemer	Robert G.	m.	CR	8 June 1917	1	3	
Roemer	Robert G.	m.	PD	8 June 1917	2	1	
Rogain	Bessie	m.	PD	27 May 1917	8	1	
Rogers	Elizabeth	m.	PA	27 Aug. 1918	5	3	
Rogers	Elizabeth	m.	PC	28 Aug. 1918	6	3	
Rogers	Frank	m.	PA	5 Sept. 1917	6	4	
Rogers	Frank	m.	PC	6 Sept. 1917	5	2	
Rogers	Frank P.	m.	PC	24 Aug. 1917	5	5	
Rogers	Frank P.	m.	PD	24 Aug. 1917	3	1	
Rogers	Franklin	o.	PD	20 Dec. 1917	3	3	
Rogers	Franklin N.	o.	SRR	5 Sept. 1917	4	4	
Rogers	Franklin N.	o.	SRR	7 Dec. 1917	8	2	also 19 Dec., 4:1
Rogers	George	o.	PC	31 Oct. 1916	8	1	
Rogers	Irene	o.	PC	31 Oct. 1916	8	1	
Rogers	Isaac	o.	PA	19 Sept. 1916	3	1	

(1) Surname	(2) Given Name	(3)	(4)	(5) Date	(6) Pg	(7) Col	(8) Comments
Rogers	Lucy	o.	PD	20 Dec. 1917	3	3	
Rogers	Lucy B.	o.	SRR	5 Sept. 1917	4	4	
Rogers	Lucy R.	o.	SRR	7 Dec. 1917	8	2	also 19 Dec., 4:1
Rogers	Otillie Catherine	m.	PC	19 Sept. 1916	5	4	
Rogers	Ottile Catherine	m.	PC	31 Aug. 1916	4	1	also 13 Sept., 5:3
Rogers	Ottilie	m.	PA	6 Sept. 1916	5	7	also 11 Sept., 4:6; 18 Sept., 8:5
Rogers	Samuel W.	d.	PD	23 Nov. 1918	1	6	
Rogers	Stewart	m.	SRR	26 Dec. 1916	8	5	
Rogers	Stewart	m.	PC	27 Dec. 1916	4	1	
Rogers	Stuart	m.	PD	27 Dec. 1916	5	5	
Rogers	William	d.	PD	19 Dec. 1916	7	3	also 21 Dec., 3:4
Rogers	William	d.	PA	20 Dec. 1916	6	6	
Rogers	William	d.	PC	20 Dec. 1916	4	4	I.O.O.F. Cemetery, Sebastopol
Rogers	William	d.	ST	22 Dec. 1916	1	4	
Rogers	William T.	d.	SRR	8 May 1917	6	5	
Rogers	William T.	d.	HT	10 May 1917	3	2	Oak Mound Cemetery
Rohde	Johanna	m.	PC	18 May 1918	3	4	
Rohde	Johanna	m.	PC	22 Apr. 1918	5	2	
Rohrer	Edward	d.	SRR	10 May 1917	10	5	also 11 May, 4:1
Rohrer	Edward	d.	PA	11 May 1917	5	4	Santa Rosa
Rohrer	Edward	d.	PD	11 May 1917	8	4	also 12 May, 4:3; 7:2
Rohrer	Edward	d.	PC	12 May 1917	6	3	
Rohrer	William H.	m.	PA	14 Nov. 1917	4	2	
Rohrer	William H.	m.	SRR	14 Nov. 1917	6	6	
Rohrer	William H.	m	PD	15 Nov. 1917	6	5	
Roix	R. J.	m.	SRR	17 May 1917	2	3	
Roix	Raymond J.	m.	PD	17 May 1917	2	2	also 5:6
Rollins	Fred	b.	PA	1 Nov. 1916	1	4	
Roloff	George F.	d.	PD	23 May 1971	8	2	
Roloff	George J.	m.	SRR	22 May 1917	10	3	
Romaine	William G., Jr.	m.	PD	26 Aug. 1916	8	1	
Romaine	William, Jr.	m.	SRR	3 Aug. 1916	3	3	also 26 Aug., 4:1
Romaine	William, Jr.	m.	PA	4 Aug. 1916	2	7	also 28 Aug., 8:2
Romaine	William, Jr.	m.	PC	4 Aug. 1916	3	4	also 20 Aug., 5:4; 27 Aug., 5:4
Roman	Albertine	m.	PD	14 Sept. 1916	3	5	also 5:1
Roman	Albertine C.	m.	SRR	14 Sept. 1916	7	4	
Romanoff	Anton	m.	SRR	22 Jan. 1916	2	3	
Romanov	Anton	m.	SRR	5 Sept. 1916	6	2	
Romanov	Anton	m.	PD	6 Sept. 1916	7	2	
Romson	Mr.	m.	SIT	3 Nov. 1917	1	5	
Romwall	Charles	d.	PC	11 Jan. 1918	1	3	also 13 Jan., 8:3; 15 Jan., 3:3

(1) Surname	(2) Given Name	(3)	(4)	(5) Date	(6) Pg	(7) Col	(8) Comments
Romwall	Charles	d.	ST	18 Jan. 1918	4	1	
Romwall	Charles	d.	PD	11 Jan. 1918	5	3	also 12 Jan., 4:2, 8:2
Romwall	Charles J.	d.	PA	11 Jan. 1917	4	4	Cypress Hill; also 12 Jan., 4:6; 14 Jan., 4:4
Ronco	John	m.	PD	29 Oct. 1918	7	2	
Ronquie	Phillipine	d.	SIT	15 Apr. 1916	3	3	
Ronselli	Eivetia	m.	PC	20 Mar. 1916	6	1	
Ronsheimer	Howard	m.	PD	2 Nov. 1918	2	2	
Ronsheimer	Howard	m.	PD	20 Oct. 1918	5	2	
Roof	L. E.	b.	SRR	18 July 1917	8	3	
Root	Jennie	d.	SRR	13 May 1916	1	3	
Root	Jennie	d.	PC	14 May 1916	3	2	
Root	Jennie C.	d.	PA	15 May 1916	4	1	
Roper	Charles	d.	HT	14 June 1917	4	2	
Rorrison	Arthur	d.	PA	5 Aug. 1918	5	5	Cypress Hill; also 6:2
Rorrison	Arthur	d.	PC	6 Aug. 1918	8	2	Cypress Hill; also 7 Aug., 8:3; 8 Aug., 5:2
Rorrison	Arthur	d.	PD	7 Aug. 1918	6	4	
Rosa	Harriet	o.	SRR	12 Dec. 1916	8	2	
Rosa	Harriet	o.	PC	13 Dec. 1916	3	6	
Rosa	W. D.	o.	PC	13 Dec. 1916	3	6	
Rosa	William D.	o.	SRR	12 Dec. 1916	8	2	
Rosasco	Charles	m.	HT	7 Feb. 1918	5	4	
Roschetti	Pacificio	d.	SRR	5 May 1916	5	2	
Roschetti	Pacillco	d.	PD	3 May 1916	8	2	
Rose	Edward	d.	ST	20 May 1916	4	3	Odd Fellows Cemetery
Rose	Emma B.	o.	PA	4 Oct. 1916	4	4	
Rose	Emma Buskey	o.	SRR	4 Oct. 1916	8	5	
Rose	Emma Buskey	o.	PC	5 Oct. 1916	1	5	
Rose	Frank Curtis	d.	PD	1 Sept. 1916	3	2	
Rose	Frank Curtis	d.	SRR	31 Aug. 1916	8	4	
Rose	Guy	b.	PD	14 Sept. 1916	3	5	
Rose	J. W.	d.	PD	29 Aug. 1918	6	3	
Rose	J. W.	d.	PC	30 Aug. 1918	6	1	
Rose	J. W.	d.	HT	5 Sept. 1918	1	1	
Rose	Jerry	b.	PA	10 May 1917	4	5	
Rose	Jerry	b.	PC	11 May 1917	8	5	
Rose	John	m.	PC	27 Nov. 1917	5	3	also 4 Dec., 5:2
Rose	John	m.	PA	3 Dec. 1917	4	3	
Rose	John	m.	ST	30 Nov. 1917	1	5	
Rose	John Wesley	d.	PD	11 Sept. 1918	5	5	
Rose	John Wesley	m.	PD	21 Aug. 1917	8	3	
Rose	Lee	o.	PD	12 Oct. 1917	5	2	adoption
Rose	Lerora	m.	ST	17 June 1916	1	2	
Rose	Manuel	m.	SRR	11 Dec. 1916	7	1	

(1) Surname	(2) Given Name	(3)	(4)	(5) Date	(6) Pg	(7) Col	(8) Comments
Rose	Manuel	m.	PC	13 Dec. 1916	5	1	
Rose	W. A.	d.	PA	16 Mar. 1917	3	2	
Rose	William A.	d.	PC	16 Mar. 1917	8	2	
Rose	William Perry	o.	PA	4 Oct. 1916	4	4	
Rose	William Perry	o.	SRR	4 Oct. 1916	8	5	
Rose	William Perry	o.	PC	5 Oct. 1916	1	5	
Roselli	A.	d.	PA	22 Jan. 1918	5	5	
Roselli	Elvezio	o.	PA	13 Sept. 1918	2	3	
Roselli	Elvezio	o.	PD	14 Sept. 1918	4	2	
Roselli	Elvis	o.	PA	30 Oct. 1918	3	4	
Roselli	Sylvester	d.	PA	20 Jan. 1917	4	5	Calvary Cemetery; also 22 Jan., 6:4
Roselli	Sylvester	d.	PC	23 Jan. 1917	8	5	Calvary Cemetery
Roselli	Sylvester	d.	SRR	23 Jan. 1917	2	5	
Rosen	Lennie	m.	SRR	4 Oct. 1916	8	4	
Rosen	Lenny	m.	PA	4 Oct. 1916	5	3	
Rosen	Lenny	m.	PC	5 Oct. 1916	3	3	
Rosenbach	Blanche	m.	SRR	2 July 1917	6	5	
Rosenbach	Blanche	m.	HT	5 July 1917	4	2	
Rosenberg	Harold	m.	HT	14 Nov. 1918	8	4	
Rosenberg	Harold B.	m.	PD	11 Nov. 1918	8	3	
Rosenberg	M.	b.	SRR	2 May 1917	6	6	
Rosenberg	M. M.	b.	HT	3 May 1917	3	4	
Rosenberg	M. M.	b.	PD	4 May 1917	6	3	
Ross	Carl	o.	PC	21 Mar. 1917	1	3	
Ross	Eddie	o.	ST	26 July 1918	8	4	
Ross	George	m.	PA	24 May 1917	2	3	also 4 June, 6:5
Ross	George John	m.	PC	3 June 1917	8	2	also 6 June, 8:2
Ross	Harriet	o.	PA	12 Dec. 1916	4	4	
Ross	Harriet	o.	PD	12 Dec. 1916	5	4	
Ross	Jean Pithlado	m.	SRR	1 Jan. 1916	6	1	
Ross	Karl	d.	PA	10 Dec. 1918	6	3	France
Ross	Karl	d.	PD	11 Dec. 1918	3	4	France
Ross	Kemp	o.	PD	21 Apr. 1918	7	1	
Ross	Kemp	o.	PD	4 Dec. 1918	2	3	
Ross	Leonard A.	o.	ST	6 Dec. 1918	9	4	
Ross	Lodema	m.	ST	27 Sept. 1918	1	2	
Ross	Mabel E.	m.	PC	29 Nov. 1917	5	6	
Ross	Mervyn	o.	ST	26 July 1918	8	4	
Ross	Mervyn	o.	PD	6 Aug. 1918	6	1	
Ross	Milburn	d.	PD	14 Oct. 1916	8	1	
Ross	Milburn/Melvin	d.	SRR	14 Oct. 1916	7	1	also 16 Oct., 4:4
Ross	Phil	o.	PC	22 Aug. 1917	1	5	
Ross	Viola	m.	SRR	13 June 1916	7	2	
Ross	Walter	o.	PA	17 Dec. 1918	5	3	

(1) Surname	(2) Given Name	(3)	(4)	(5) Date	(6) Pg	(7) Col	(8) Comments
Ross	Walter	o.	PC	17 Dec. 1918	8	2	
Ross	William D.	o.	PA	12 Dec. 1916	4	4	
Ross	William D.	o.	PD	12 Dec. 1916	5	4	
Rosselli	Eivetia A.	m.	PC	19 Mar. 1916	6	1	
Rosselli	Elvus	o.	PC	13 Sept. 1918	1	3	
Rossi	Albert	m.	SIT	13 May 1916	1	6	
Rossi	Albert	m.	PD	18 May 1916	8	7	
Rossi	Amelie	d.	CR	20 Mar. 1917	1	4	
Rossi	Lavinia	d.	PD	22 Nov. 1918	1	4	
Rossi	Pietro	d.	PD	24 Nov. 1917	6	2	also 27 Nov., 6:2
Rossi	Pietro	d.	SRR	24 Nov. 1917	3	1	also 26 Nov., 6:5
Rossi	Pietro	d.	PC	27 Nov. 1917	2	3	
Rossi	Rene	d.	PA	24 Sept. 1918	4	4	Two Rock; also 29 Sept., 5:4&5
Rossi	Rene	d.	PC	24 Sept. 1918	8	3	also 27 Sept., 8:3; 28 Sept., 8:4
Rossi	Rene	d.	PD	25 Sept. 1918	5	4	Petaluma
Roth	Ethel	o.	PD	1 Feb. 1917	6	2	
Roth	Ethel	o.	PD	11 Oct. 1916	7	5	
Roth	Ethel A.	o.	PC	1 Feb. 1917	1	2	
Roth	Ethel A.	o.	SRR	10 Oct. 1916	1	3	
Roth	Ethel A.	o.	SRR	31 Jan. 1917	6	2	
Roth	Harold	o.	PD	1 Feb. 1917	6	2	
Roth	Harold R.	o.	PC	1 Feb. 1917	1	2	
Roth	Harold R.	o.	SRR	10 Oct. 1916	1	3	
Roth	Harold R.	o.	PD	11 Oct. 1916	7	5	
Roth	Harold R.	o.	SRR	31 Jan. 1917	6	2	
Rouse	Elizabeth	d.	SRR	28 Oct. 1916	10	1	Oak Mound Cemetery
Rouse	Elizabeth	d.	HT	3 Nov. 1916	4	1	Oak Mound Cemetery
Rouse	Mabel E.	m.	HT	12 Oct. 1916	1	6	
Roussan	Evelyn I.	d.	PA	2 Feb. 1916	2	3	
Roussan	Evelyn I.	d.	SRR	29 Jan. 1916	1	3	I.O.O.F. Cemetery; also 31 Jan., 5:6
Roussan	Evelyn I.	d.	PD	30 Jan. 1916	1	2	I.O.O.F. Cemetery; also 1 Feb., 3:3
Roussan	Fred	d.	PA	17 Apr. 1916	1	3	
Roussan	Fred	d.	PD	18 Apr. 1916	5	2	
Roussan	Fred	p.	PA	19 Apr. 1916	6	5	
Roussan	Frederick E.	d.	SRR	17 Apr. 1916	5	2	
Roussan	Frederick E.	d.	PC	18 Apr. 1916	4	4	
Roussan	Walter (dau of)	d.	PD	9 Feb. 1917	6	2	
Roux	Annie	m.	PD	20 June 1916	2	3	
Rovai	Joseph, Mrs.	d.	SIT	1 Apr. 1916	4	7	
Rovai	Joseph, Mrs.	d.	PD	31 Mar. 1916	7	2	Calvary Cemetery

(1) Surname	(2) Given Name	(3)	(4)	(5) Date	(6) Pg	(7) Col	(8) Comments
Rovai	Margaret	d.	SRR	28 Mar. 1916	8	5	Sonoma; also 29 Mar., 7:3; 30 Mar., 8:3
Rowe	Gertrude	m.	ST	10 June 1916	1	5	
Rowe	H.	o.	PA	20 Aug. 1918	4	4	Canadian Army
Royal	Nellie	m.	HT	27 Jan. 1916	1	6	also 4 Mar., 2:3
Royal	Nettie	m.	SRR	26 Jan. 1916	5	3	also 4 Mar., 5:1
Rozas	Joseph	b.	SRR	24 Nov. 1917	12	2	
Rubenstein	Bessie	m.	PA	19 May 1916	8	7	also 22 May, 5:1
Rubenstein	Bessie	m.	PC	20 May 1916	4	4	also 22 May, 4:1
Rubin	Bessie	m.	SRR	28 May 1917	3	3	
Rubke	Grover C.	b.	SIT	11 Mar. 1916	4	5	
Rubke	Henry	d.	SIT	1 Jan. 1916	1	7	
Rubke	Henry	d.	PD	2 Jan. 1916	10	1	also 4 Jan., 5:1
Rubke	Henry	d.	SRR	3 Jan. 1916	7	3	
Rubke	Henry	d.	HT	6 Jan. 1916	4	5	
Ruffner	James	d.	SIT	14 Oct. 1916	1	3	
Ruffner	James	d.	PC	15 Oct. 1916	1	5	
Ruffoni	John	b.	PA	6 July 1916	4	6	
Ruggeri	Pete	m.	PD	19 Sept. 1916	8	3	
Rundel	M. S.	b.	PD	30 Jan. 1918	2	1	
Rundel	M. S.	b.	PC	31 Jan. 1918	6	3	
Rundge	Emma	m.	PD	2 Nov. 1917	5	2	
Rundge	Richard	m.	PD	2 Nov. 1917	5	2	
Runge	Ada	m.	PC	10 Mar. 1918	8	2	
Runge	Emma	m.	SRR	1 Nov. 1917	8	2	
Runge	H.	o.	PA	11 Oct. 1918	7	1	
Runge	Richard	m.	SRR	1 Nov. 1917	8	2	
Runyon	Edith	m.	PD	27 Dec. 1917	8	4	
Runyon	Edith	m.	SRR	3 Dec. 1917	8	6	also 27 Dec., 3:5; 29 Dec., 4:2
Rupp	Winnie	m.	PD	17 Apr. 1917	8	5	
Rusden	Nicholas J.	d.	PD	1 Jan. 1916	8	1	
Rusden	Nicholas J.	d.	SRR	1 Jan. 1916	9	4	cremation; also 3 Jan., 1:2
Rush	Eva	m.	PA	1 Aug. 1917	3	4	
Rush	Eva	m.	PD	1 Aug. 1917	2	2	
Rush	Sarah Eva	m.	SRR	31 July 1917	7	3	
Rush	Sarah Eva	m.	PC	1 Aug. 1917	3	4	
Rush	Sarah Eva	m.	ST	17 Aug. 1917	1	3	
Rushen	Amanda	d.	PC	5 Feb. 1918	5	3	
Rushen	Amanda Ellen	d.	PD	5 Feb. 1918	6	4	Masonic Cemetery; also 6 Feb., 4:2
Rushen	Amanda Ellen	d.	PA	6 Feb. 1918	3	3	Masonic Cemetery, Sebastopol
Rushmore	Mattie G.	d.	ST	22 Nov. 1918	1	1	

(1) Surname	(2) Given Name	(3)	(4)	(5) Date	(6) Pg	(7) Col	(8) Comments
Rushmore	Mattie Glynn	d.	PD	19 Nov. 1918	2	1	Sebastopol; also 4:2; 20 Nov., 2:2; 21 Nov., 8:1
Russ	Jene P.	o.	PA	11 Sept. 1918	8	3	
Russ	Joseph B.	o.	PD	26 Oct. 1918	3	2	
Russ	Joseph Ray	o.	PA	11 Sept. 1918	8	3	
Russ	Joseph Ray	o.	PC	27 Oct. 1918	5	3	
Russ	June P.	o.	PD	26 Oct. 1918	3	2	
Russ	Pearl	o.	PC	27 Oct. 1918	5	3	
Russ	Ray	m.	PA	21 Dec. 1917	1	3	
Russ	Ray	m.	PC	21 Dec. 1917	1	3	
Russ	Wilhelmina	d.	PA	2 Apr. 1918	6	5	
Russell	Cora	m.	SRR	23 Apr. 1917	3	1	
Russell	Cora	m.	PD	24 Apr. 1917	5	1	
Russell	Ed	m.	SRR	26 Apr. 1917	5	4	also 1 May, 6:1
Russell	Edwin	d.	PD	20 Aug. 1918	2	4	Fulton Cemetery; also 4:2; 22 Aug., 2:3
Russell	Edwin M.	m.	PD	26 Apr. 1917	8	3	
Russell	Edwin M.	m.	PC	27 Apr. 1917	8	3	
Russell	Lucieanne	b.	PD	17 Feb. 1918	5	5	
Rutherford	B. W.	m.	ST	11 Jan. 1918	1	5	
Rutherford	Ernest S.	m.	ST	12 Feb. 1916	1	2	
Rutledge	Joseph	d.	PD	10 June 1917	6	3	Rockford, IL; also 12 June, 2:2
Rutlidge	Josiah Fanklin	d.	SRR	11 June 1917	3	4	Illinois
Ryan	Violet G.	m.	PD	22 July 1916	8	4	
Ryland	C. T., Mrs.	d.	PD	13 Oct. 1918	6	3	
Ryland	Caius Tacitus	d.	SIT	19 Oct. 1918	1	3	Mountain Cemetery

S

(1) Surname	(2) Given Name	(3)	(4)	(5) Date	(6) Pg	(7) Col	(8) Comments
Sabine	Elizabeth	d.	PA	14 May 1917	3	3	
Sagner	Sarah Josephine	d.	HT	17 May 1917	1	1	
Salaya	(baby)	d.	HT	28 Nov. 1918	1	1	
Sales	John	o.	PC	17 Oct. 1916	5	4	
Saline	Elizabeth	d.	PC	15 May 1917	5	4	
Salisbury	Carrie	d.	SRR	2 Jan. 1917	1	2	I.O.O.F. Cemetery; also 3 Jan, 7:4; 4 Jan., 6:1
Salisbury	Carrie	d.	PD	4 Jan. 1917	3	3	also 5 Jan., 6:3
Salisbury	Margaret Bell	o.	PA	12 Dec. 1918	8	7	also 21 Dec., 1:6
Salisbury	Ralph F.	o.	PA	12 Dec. 1918	8	7	also 21 Dec., 1:6
Salmina	Mamie	m.	PA	14 Nov. 1917	4	3	
Salmon	Edward	m.	PA	12 July 1917	6	6	
Saloman	Edward	m.	SRR	29 May 1916	5	1	
Salomon	Albert	m.	PA	27 May 1916	1	1	
Salomon	Edward	m.	SRR	11 July 1917	4	6	
Salvadori	Anton	o.	PD	16 May 1917	1	3	
Salvadori	Marie	o.	PD	16 May 1917	1	3	
Sampson	Omar	d.	PA	2 Jan. 1918	6	1	
Samson	O.	d.	PC	1 Jan. 1918	1	3	
Samuels	Madeline	b.	PD	9 Sept. 1917	4	3	
Sanborn	H. R.	o.	PA	16 May 1917	1	3	
Sanborn	R. E.	o.	SRR	17 May 1917	1	5	New American Legion Canadian Army
Sancher	Maria	m.	PC	17 Apr. 1917	3	3	
Sanchez	Fred	o.	ST	24 May 1918	8	3	
Sandborn	Elmer	o.	HT	17 Oct. 1918	8	1	
Sandborn	June Hellon	d.	HT	17 Oct. 1918	6	3	
Sanders	Amanda	d.	PD	11 Nov. 1918	4	2	also 5:4; 14 Nov., 4:2
Sandersen	Volna	d.	PC	12 Dec. 1918	4	3	moved from Cypress Hill to Riddles, OR; also 13 Dec., 5:3
Sanderson	Velma	d.	PA	12 Dec. 1918	4	4	moved from Cypress Hill to Riddles, OR
Sanderson	Volna	d.	PA	9 Nov. 1918	5	6	Cypress Hill; also 12 Nov., 5:3
Sanderson	Volna	d.	PC	9 Nov. 1918	8	3	Cypress Hill; also 12 Nov., 8:2; 13 Nov., 4:3
Sanderson	William	d.	PA	7 June 1918	4	4	Riddles, OR; also 8 June, 8:4; 10 June, 5:7
Sanderson	William	d.	PC	9 June 1918	1	3	Riddles, Oregon
Sandvig	Marty	o.	PC	4 Dec. 1917	5	4	
Sanford	Eliza J.	d.	PD	21 Nov. 1918	2	2	Sebastopol; also 22 Nov., 4:2

(1) Surname	(2) Given Name	(3)	(4)	(5) Date	(6) Pg	(7) Col	(8) Comments
Sanford	Fred M.	m.	SRR	29 Dec. 1916	6	3	
Sanger	John	m.	PD	20 Sept. 1917	8	4	
Sanger	Sarah Josephine	d.	SRR	17 May 1917	6	4	
Sani	Adam D.	b.	SRR	29 Sept. 1917	8	6	
Sani	Julius	m.	PD	6 Nov. 1917	2	3	
Sani	Julius H.	m.	SRR	5 Nov. 1917	8	1	
Sani	Julius H.	m.	PC	7 Nov. 1917	2	2	
Sani	Lloyd	d.	PD	5 Apr. 1918	7	3	Calvary Cemetery; also 6 Apr., 4:2, 7:2
Sanpietro	Ben	b.	PC	11 Apr. 1917	8	4	
Santiago	Hurley	d.	PC	5 Nov. 1918	8	5	Bloomfield
Santiago	son	d.	PA	5 Nov. 1918	8	5	
Santich	Matt (dau of)	d.	PD	20 May 1916	7	4	Sebastopol Cemetery
Santich	Matt (dau of)	d.	SRR	20 May 1916	7	2	
Santini	Hazel	m.	PD	29 Oct. 1918	7	2	
Santos	Carlo	m.	PC	9 Jan. 1918	2	2	
Santos	Virginia	d.	PD	15 Nov. 1918	4	2	
Sargent	Myrtle	m.	PA	21 July 1917	8	5	
Sargisson	Cornelius	d.	HT	14 Nov. 1916	1	4	
Sarra	Carmine	o.	PD	26 Feb. 1918	3	3	
Sarra	Rachela	o.	PD	26 Feb. 1918	3	3	
Sartori	Anna	m.	PC	5 Jan. 1918	4	5	
Saul	Bessie	m.	SRR	15 July 1916	12	1	
Saul	Roy	m.	PD	20 Nov. 1917	2	3	
Saul	Roy M.	m.	HT	22 Nov. 1917	5	3	
Saunders	Millard, Mrs.	d.	PD	10 Oct. 1916	8	4	
Saunders	William	d.	SRR	18 Dec. 1916	5	1	
Saunders	William A.	d.	HT	23 Dec. 1916	8	3	
Saunders	William E.	d.	PD	17 Dec. 1916	8	3	also 19 Dec., 6:5
Saunders	William E.	d.	PC	19 Dec. 1916	4	1	
Savior	Fern	m.	SIT	29 Apr. 1916	1	1	
Savory	William	d.	PD	30 Mar. 1918	4	2	I.O.O.F. Cemetery; also 2 Apr., 3:6
Sawtell	Roy	o.	HT	16 May 1918	7	2	
Sawtelle	Winifred	m.	PD	26 May 1917	6	2	
Sawtelle	Winnifred	m.	SRR	25 May 1917	6	5	
Sawyer	Maradan Albert	d.	PD	3 June 1917	5	6	
Sayer	William	m.	PC	22 May 1916	6	2	
Sayers	William	m.	SRR	19 June 1916	1	1	also 28 June, 8:4
Sayers	William A.	m.	PD	28 June 1916	2	3	
Sayers	William G.	m.	PD	2 July 1916	2	2	
Saylor	Fern	m.	PC	2 Apr. 1916	5	3	
Saylor	John, Jr.	d.	PD	5 Feb. 1918	8	1	also 8 Feb., 8:1
Sbarboro	Andrea	d.	PD	7 July 1917	2	1	
Sbarboro	Andrea	d.	HT	12 July 1917	5	3	

(1) Surname	(2) Given Name	(3)	(4)	(5) Date	(6) Pg	(7) Col	(8) Comments
Scalena	Edna	m.	SRR	14 May 1917	6	3	
Scales	Walter	m.	PA	13 Feb. 1917	6	4	
Scandolera	Joseph	d.	PA	30 Mar. 1917	5	1	Tomales; also 2 Apr., 3:5
Scanlon	Jeremiah	m.	PD	1 May 1918	2	3	
Scanlon	Matt	d.	PD	22 Oct. 1918	1	6	
Scanlon	Matthew	d.	CR	18 Oct. 1918	1	3	
Scaten	Walter	m.	PC	10 Feb. 1917	1	6	
Scatena	Daniel	o.	HT	7 Mar. 1918	1	3	adoption
Scatena	Edna	m.	PD	15 May 1917	5	4	
Schackman	P.	m.	PA	10 Dec. 1918	3	4	
Schackman	P.	m.	PC	8 Dec. 1918	4	2	
Schalich	Anton, Mrs.	d.	PD	27 July 1916	3	1	also 30 July, 3:3
Schalich	Marie	d.	SRR	26 July 1916	8	6	
Schapp	George A.	m.	PD	25 Aug. 1918	2	5	
Scharf	Samuel J.	m.	SRR	6 May 1916	10	5	
Scharf	Samuel J.	m.	PD	7 May 1916	3	1	
Schaumberg	George	d.	SRR	2 Jan. 1917	5	2	
Schaumberg	George N.	d.	PD	3 Jan. 1917	3	2	
Scheiffer	Robert	m.	SRR	15 Feb. 1917	1	3	
Scheller	John F.	d.	SIT	25 Aug. 1917	1	7	
Scheller	John F.	d.	PC	27 Aug. 1917	1	4	
Schelling	Geoege C.	m.	PD	18 Aug. 1916	3	4	
Schelling	George	m.	PC	18 Aug. 1916	5	4	
Schelling	George C.	m.	SRR	17 Aug. 1916	8	1	
Schenk	Johann	m.	SRR	20 Dec. 1917	8	3	
Schieck	David	b.	SRR	29 Oct. 1917	3	4	
Schieck	David	b.	PD	30 Oct. 1917	6	2	
Schieck	David	b.	PC	31 Oct. 1917	3	2	
Schieffer	Robert	m.	PA	15 Feb. 1917	8	3	
Schieffer	Robert A.	m.	PC	16 Feb. 1917	8	5	
Schieffer	Robert A.	m.	PD	16 Feb. 1917	8	4	
Schieffer	Robert A.	m.	HT	22 Feb. 1917	3	1	
Schilling	Blanch	m.	SRR	9 Aug. 1917	1	2	
Schindler	Emmie O.	o.	PC	29 Mar. 1916	1	3	portrait
Schindler	T. C.	o.	PD	15 Jan. 1918	1	1	
Schinkel	Otto	d.	PA	19 Feb. 1917	4	5	cremation; also 5:3; 20 Feb., 4:3; 21 Feb., 8:6
Schinkel	Otto	d.	PC	20 Feb. 1917	6	1	also 8:2; 21 Feb., 4:5; 22 Feb., 8:4
Schirmer	Margaret D.	m.	SRR	20 Dec. 1917	8	3	
Schlake	Chris	d.	PA	1 May 1916	4	2	
Schlake	Chris	d.	ST	29 Apr. 1916	1	4	
Schlake	Chris	d.	PC	30 Apr. 1916	5	4	Cypress Hill; also 2 May, 5:4
Schlake	Christian, Sr.	d.	SRR	1 May 1916	5	3	
Schlake	Christian, Sr.	d.	PD	30 Apr. 1916	5	3	also 1 May, 5:3

(1) Surname	(2) Given Name	(3)	(4)	(5) Date	(6) Pg	(7) Col	(8) Comments
Schlanert	William	d.	PC	27 Sept. 1918	1	3	
Schlener	Rose	m.	PC	16 Jan. 1917	1	5	
Schleth	David	b.	PA	9 Mar. 1916	8	6	
Schleth	William F.	d.	PA	20 Aug. 1918	4	3	Cypress Hill; also 22 Aug., 5:7
Schleth	William F.	d.	PC	21 Aug. 1918	8	4	Cypress Hill; also 22 Aug., 3:5; 23 Aug., 5:5
Schleuter	Florence E.	o.	PC	31 Oct. 1918	3	3	
Schleuter	W. E.	o.	PC	13 Mar. 1918	1	2	
Schleuter	William E.	o.	PC	31 Oct. 1918	3	3	
Schlombohm	Eva M.	o.	SRR	16 July 1917	8	2	
Schlombohm	Heinrich F.	o.	SRR	16 July 1917	8	2	
Schlombohn	Eva	o.	PD	17 July 1917	6	3	
Schlombohn	Eva M.	o.	SRR	16 June 1917	10	1	
Schlombohn	Heinrich F.	o.	SRR	16 June 1917	10	1	
Schlombohn	Henrich	o.	PD	17 July 1917	6	3	
Schluckabier	Elsa	m.	PC	16 Mar. 1917	4	5	
Schluckebier	Elsa	m.	PA	15 Mar. 1917	4	4	
Schluckebier	Elsa	m.	SRR	15 Mar. 1917	2	3	
Schluckebier	Elsa	m.	PD	16 Mar. 1917	5	4	
Schluckebier	Henry	d.	PA	3 May 1917	4	3	Cypress Hill; also 5 May, 4:3
Schluckebier	Henry	d.	PC	3 May 1917	1	3	Cypress Hill; also 4 May, 3:1, 8:5; 6 May, 5:3
Schluckebier	Henry	d.	PD	3 May 1917	8	1	also 5 May, 3:3
Schluckebier	Henry	d.	SRR	3 May 1917	4	2	
Schluckebier	Robert	m.	PA	25 June 1917	2	3	
Schlueter	Florence	o.	PA	10 June 1918	4	1	
Schlueter	Florence E.	o.	PA	17 Feb. 1917	5	1	
Schlueter	William E.	o.	PA	10 June 1918	4	1	
Schlueter	William E.	o.	PA	17 Feb. 1917	5	1	
Schlumbarger	C.	b.	PA	11 Nov. 1916	4	4	
Schlumberger	Carl	d.	PA	24 Jan. 1917	5	4	Cypress Hill
Schlumberger	Charles	d.	PA	6 Aug. 1917	5	3	Cypress Hill; also 7 Aug., 4:4
Schlumberger	Christ	d.	PC	7 Aug. 1917	1	5	Cypress Hill; also 8 Aug., 4:2
Schlumberger	Crist	d.	SRR	6 Aug. 1917	1	3	
Schluneger	Robert	m.	PC	26 June 1917	1	5	
Schluster	Florence	o.	PD	12 June 1918	8	2	
Schluster	W. E.	o.	PD	12 June 1918	8	2	
Schluter	Florence E.	o.	SRR	19 Mar. 1917	4	3	
Schluter	Florence E.	o.	PC	20 Mar. 1917	3	2	
Schluter	William E.	o.	SRR	19 Mar. 1917	4	3	
Schluter	William E.	o.	PC	20 Mar. 1917	3	2	
Schmalmenbach	Edward	b.	SRR	18 Jan. 1916	6	3	

(1) Surname	(2) Given Name	(3)	(4)	(5) Date	(6) Pg	(7) Col	(8) Comments
Schmeckpeper	Henry J. D.	d.	PA	26 June 1918	4	2	Cypress Lawn, S. F.; also 28 June, 8:5
Schmeckpeper	Henry J. D.	d.	PC	27 June 1918	5	3	
Schmeiser	Rose Ann	d.	PC	30 Aug. 1916	1	5	Holy Cross, S. F.; also 31 Aug., 1:2; 2 Sept., 8:2
Schmeizer	Rose A.	d.	PA	30 Aug. 1916	5	3	
Schmeltz	Alice	m.	PA	27 May 1916	1	1	
Schmelz	Alice	m.	SRR	29 May 1916	5	1	
Schmelz	Alice	m.	SRR	11 July 1917	4	6	
Schmelz	Alice	m.	PA	12 July 1917	6	6	
Schmidt	Anita	m.	PD	29 Aug. 1918	2	4	
Schmidt	Harry	m.	PC	3 Dec. 1916	5	4	
Schmidt	Harry	m.	PA	4 Dec. 1916	2	5	
Schmidt	Helena	d.	PC	7 June 1918	8	4	
Schmidt	Helena	d.	PD	7 June 1918	3	4	Calvary Cemetery, also 4:2
Schmidt	Helena	d.	ST	7 June 1918	5	4	Calvary Cemetery
Schmidt	Katherine	m.	PD	10 Apr. 1917	8	4	
Schmidt	Katherine	m.	ST	14 Apr. 1917	3	2	
Schmidt	Katherine	m.	SRR	9 Apr. 1917	4	4	
Schmiedecke	Francis M.	m.	SRR	12 June 1916	1	2	
Schmieser	Rose	d.	PA	1 Sept. 1916	4	4	Holy Cross, S. F.
Schnabel	H. I.	m.	ST	29 Mar. 1918	1	1	
Schnabel	H. I.	m.	PC	31 Mar. 1918	2	2	
Schnabel	H. S.	m.	PD	23 Mar. 1918	8	3	
Schneider	Emma	m.	PD	28 Sept. 1917	7	2	
Schneider	George	o.	SRR	23 Feb. 1017	1	4	adoption
Schneider	Georgia	o.	PD	24 Feb. 1917	6	4	
Schneider	Georgia	o.	SIT	3 Mar. 1917	2	5	adoption
Schneider	Herman	m.	SRR	17 June 1916	4	2	
Schneider	Herman	m.	PD	31 Oct. 1916	2	3	
Schneider	John H.	b.	PA	2 Feb. 1917	5	4	
Schneider	John H.	b.	PC	3 Feb. 1917	8	1	
Schneider	William A.	m.	PD	17 Sept. 1916	7	2	
Schoenfeld	M. J.	d.	PA	5 July 1918	6	3	
Schoeningh	Elsie	m.	PA	7 June 1916	4	7	also 24 June, 2:4; 26 June, 3:4
Schoeningh	Elsie	m.	PC	8 June 1916	3	2	also 23 June, 3:3; 27 June, 5:2
Schoeningh	Joseph	o.	PA	8 Nov. 1918	4	4	
Schoeningh	William F.	m.	PC	7 Sept. 1918	4	4	
Schoeningh	William P.	m.	PA	9 Sept. 1918	3	3	
Schoennigh	Elizabeth Ida	m.	PD	28 June 1916	5	2	
Schomp	Meriam	m.	PC	18 Oct. 1918	5	3	
Schoppe	J. C.	b.	PD	2 Dec. 1917	2	1	
Schoppe	John	d.	PD	25 Oct. 1918	6	3	

(1) Surname	(2) Given Name	(3)	(4)	(5) Date	(6) Pg	(7) Col	(8) Comments
Schott	Edgar G.	d.	PA	18 Oct. 1918	4	3	Calvary Cemetery; also 8:4; 19 Oct., 4:4
Schott	Edgar George	d.	PC	18 Oct. 1918	8	3	also 19 Oct., 5:6; 20 Oct., 5:4
Schott	Edward G.	d.	PD	18 Oct. 1918	6	6	
Schourp	C. F.	d.	PC	27 June 1916	2	1	
Schourp	Otto P.	d.	SRR	26 June 1916	5	3	also 27 June, 8:3
Schourp	Otto R.	d.	PD	27 June 1916	2	5	also 28 June, 3:3
Schourp	Roberta	d.	SRR	12 Feb. 1917	7	4	
Schram	Emma	o.	ST	21 Apr. 1917	8	6	also 17 Aug., 7:3
Schram	Emma P.	o.	SRR	13 Aug. 1917	5	5	
Schram	Emma P.	o.	PA	14 Aug. 1917	7	4	
Schram	Emma Peerman	o.	SRR	18 Apr. 1917	8	1	
Schram	Leland W.	o.	SRR	13 Aug. 1917	5	5	
Schram	Leland W.	o.	PA	14 Aug. 1917	7	4	
Schram	Leland W.	o.	SRR	18 Apr. 1917	8	1	
Schram	Leland W.	o.	ST	21 Apr. 1917	8	6	also 17 Aug., 7:3
Schrank	William D.	m.	PC	29 Mar. 1918	3	4	
Schroeder	Anton M.	m.	PC	8 May 1918	5	4	
Schroup	Otto Robert	d.	PA	26 June 1916	5	1	
Schroup	Roberta	d.	PD	13 Feb. 1917	8	3	
Schrowsky	A.	d.	PA	19 Feb. 1917	5	2	
Schuann	Frank	d.	PD	17 Oct. 1918	8	1	
Schuler	C. O.	d.	PA	15 June 1918	5	3	
Schuler	Charles Otto	d.	PC	16 June 1918	5	4	also 19 June, 8:4
Schuler	Will	o.	PA	5 Nov. 1918	4	3	
Schuler	Will	o.	PC	6 Sept. 1917	8	3	
Schuler	Will	o.	PC	7 Nov. 1918	4	3	
Schulte	William A.	m.	PC	2 May 1916	1	2	
Schulter	Florence E.	o.	PA	1 Nov. 1918	7	5	
Schulter	William F.	o.	PA	1 Nov. 1918	7	5	
Schultz	Elizabeth	d.	CR	17 Feb. 1917	1	3	
Schultz	Mrs.	d.	PD	17 Feb. 1917	3	2	Riverside Cemetery
Schulz	Carl	b.	PA	10 Aug. 1916	5	5	
Schulz	Hugo	d.	PD	1 Oct. 1918	6	5	Tacoma, WA
Schulze	Ella Marie	m.	SRR	3 Jan. 1917	1	3	
Schulze	Marie	m.	PD	4 Jan. 1917	7	5	
Schulzs	Carl	b.	PC	11 Aug. 1916	5	2	
Schumacher	Gottfried	m.	PA	21 July 1917	8	5	
Schumacher	Helen Estelle	m.	PA	2 Jan. 1918	5	3	
Schumacher	Stella	m.	PC	3 Jan. 1918	1	4	
Schumann	Frank	d.	PA	14 Oct. 1918	5	5	also 17 Oct., 4:1
Schumann	Frank	d.	PC	16 Oct. 1918	4	3	Liberty Cemetery; also 8:2; 18 Oct., 5:5
Schumara	Naoki	d.	PD	14 Nov. 1918	4	2	
Schumberger	Carl	d.	PC	25 Jan. 1917	6	4	Cypress Hill

(1) Surname	(2) Given Name	(3)	(4)	(5) Date	(6) Pg	(7) Col	(8) Comments
Schurba	Celia A.	m.	CR	27 Sept. 1918	1	1	
Schurba	Peter	d.	PD	6 Oct. 1918	6	2	
Schurz	Ida Elanore	d.	SIT	7 Apr. 1917	1	3	
Schuster	Alvin	d.	PA	3 Dec. 1918	5	4	
Schuster	Alvin	d.	PD	3 Dec. 1918	5	1	also 4 Dec., 7:7
Schuster	Alvin	d.	PC	4 Dec. 1918	3	1	
Schwab	Frank	m.	PA	24 May 1917	5	2	
Schwab	Frank	m.	HT	31 May 1917	1	1	
Schwab	Frank B.	m.	PD	20 May 1917	8	2	also 25 May, 5:2; 27 May, 7:2
Schwab	Frank E	m.	SRR	21 May 1917	4	4	also 24 May, 8:5
Schwan	F.	d.	PC	10 Nov. 1918	8	5	France
Schwan	Frank	d.	ST	15 Nov. 1918	6	2	France
Schwartz	Frank C.	d.	PC	12 Feb. 1918	8	5	also 13 Feb., 4:2
Schwartz	Fred	d.	PC	4 Dec. 1918	2	3	
Schwartz	Hilda	m.	SIT	11 Aug. 1917	1	3	
Schwartz	Hilda	m.	PC	9 Aug. 1917	1	5	
Schwartz	Hilda	m.	PD	9 Aug. 1917	8	3	
Schwartz	Hilda	m.	SRR	9 Aug. 1917	5	1	
Schwartz	Moses	d.	SRR	26 Dec. 1916	8	6	also 27 Dec., 8:3
Schwartz	Moses	d.	PA	27 Dec. 1916	4	3	Salem Cemetery
Schwartz	Moses	d.	PC	27 Dec. 1916	1	3	
Schwartz	Moses	d.	PD	27 Dec. 1916	5	1	also 28 Dec., 3:2
Schwerter	H.	b.	PD	29 Nov. 1916	2	4	
Scideler	Isabella B.	d.	PA	5 July 1917	8	4	Sebastopol; also 6 July, 7:4; 7 July, 8:5
Scofield	S. W.	m.	ST	3 June 1916	5	3	
Scoggan	John	d.	PD	10 Feb. 1918	8	1	
Scole	Lui	m.	PD	30 Jan. 1916	8	7	
Scolling	Samuel Ward	d.	SRR	6 Apr. 1917	6	3	also 7 Apr., 5:5; 9 Apr., 6:2
Scott	Arthur V.	m.	PA	18 Dec. 1917	18	3	
Scott	Arthur V.	m.	PC	18 Dec. 1917	1	2	
Scott	Arthur V.	m.	PD	19 Dec. 1917	6	1	
Scott	Arthur V.	m.	SRR	19 Dec. 1917	5	1	
Scott	Bernice M.	m.	PD	20 June 1916	5	3	
Scott	Bernice M.	m.	HT	22 June 1916	2	3	
Scott	Bessie	m.	SRR	18 Sept. 1916	2	2	
Scott	Charles	m.	PD	23 Nov. 1917	8	2	
Scott	Clarence	d.	PA	27 Apr. 1918	8	3	
Scott	Clarence	d.	PC	27 Apr. 1918	6	2	Cypress Hill; also 28 Apr., 6:2
Scott	Ellen	d.	PA	21 Nov. 1918	1	5	
Scott	Harry E.	b.	ST	12 Feb. 1916	8	3	
Scott	Harry E.	b.	SRR	19 Feb. 1916	1	4	
Scott	James Franklin	d.	SRR	5 May 1917	5	2	

(1) Surname	(2) Given Name	(3)	(4)	(5) Date	(6) Pg	(7) Col	(8) Comments
Scott	James Franklin	d.	PD	6 May 1917	3	3	
Scott	James Franklin	d.	SRR	18 May 1917	1	5	
Scott	John	d.	HT	4 July 1918	4	4	
Scott	John A.	d.	PD	30 June 1918	7	1	Healdsburg
Scott	K.	b.	PA	28 Mar. 1917	1	6	
Scott	K.	b.	PC	29 Mar. 1917	1	4	
Scott	Kreston K.	m.	PC	12 May 1916	6	1	
Scott	Loretta	m.	PA	3 Aug. 1917	8	3	
Scott	Loretta	m.	PC	4 Aug. 1917	4	3	
Scott	M. L.	d.	SIT	20 Oct. 1917	1	2	
Scott	Manson	d.	PA	10 Oct. 1917	2	4	Cypress Hill; also 5:1; 11 Oct., 4:7
Scott	Manson L.	d.	PC	11 Oct. 1917	8	3&5	Cypress Hill; also 12 Oct., 8:4
Scott	Marie E.	d.	PD	22 Nov. 1918	1	5	I.O.O.F. Cemetery, also 4:2
Scott	Marie Ellen	d.	PC	22 Nov. 1918	8	3	
Scott	Ruth	m.	PD	12 Oct. 1916	5	1	
Scott	Ruth	m.	PA	7 Oct. 1916	5	2	also 11 Oct., 4:4
Scott	Ruth	m.	PC	8 Oct. 1916	4	2	also 12 Oct., 1:5
Scott	Ruth	m.	SRR	9 Oct. 1916	4	5	also 12 Oct., 5:4
Scott	Thomas	m.	PA	28 Jan. 1916	5	2	also 29 Jan., 6:4
Scott	Thomas	m.	PD	28 Jan. 1916	5	2	
Scott	Thomas	m.	PC	29 Jan. 1916	4	1	
Scott	Will	b.	SRR	18 July 1917	6	5	
Scott	Will Orin	m.	PC	7 July 1916	4	4	
Scott	Will Orrin	m.	SRR	6 July 1916	8	2	also 8 July, 4:1
Scott	Will, Jr.	b.	PD	19 July 1917	3	2	
Scudder	Jared W.	m.	PA	10 Sept. 1917	5	4	also 11 Sept., 5:3
Scudder	Jared W.	m.	PC	11 Sept. 1917	5	3	also 12 Sept., 3:4
Scudder	Lydia	d.	PC	16 Apr. 1918	4	3	cremation
Scudder	N. W., Mrs.	d.	PA	15 Apr. 1918	8	5	also 17 Apr., 5:2
Scudder	N. W., Mrs.	d.	PD	16 Apr. 1918	1	4	
Sealock	J. T.	m.	PD	21 Mar. 1916	8	2	
Sealock	J. T.	m.	SRR	21 Mar. 1916	5	2	
Seaman	Jesse	d.	HT	24 Feb. 1916	1	3	
Seaman	Jesse Fowler	d.	PD	25 Feb. 1916	6	3	
Searby	D. M.	b.	PD	30 June 1918	6	5	
Sears	Clara	m.	PA	2 Jan. 1918	3	5	
Sears	Clara	m.	PC	3 Jan. 1918	3	3	also 4 Jan., 8:4
Sears	Weltha Amanda	d.	HT	2 May 1918	8	1	
Sears	Weltha Amanda	d.	PD	3 May 1918	2	2	
Seaton	Roland	b.	PD	22 May 1918	3	3	
Seaton	Roland	m.	PD	8 Nov. 1917	5	3	
Seaton	Roland A.	m.	SRR	7 Nov. 1917	8	1	
Seaver	Chris	m.	SIT	17 Mar. 1917	1	6	also 30 June, 1:2

(1) Surname	(2) Given Name	(3)	(4)	(5) Date	(6) Pg	(7) Col	(8) Comments
Seaver	Chris	m.	PC	18 Mar. 1917	3	3	
Seaver	Chris	m.	PD	24 Mar. 1917	3	3	
Seaver	George A.	d.	ST	1 Feb. 1918	4	4	also 7:3
Seaver	George A.	d.	PC	3 Feb. 1918	6	3	
Seavey	Robert	m.	PC	15 July 1917	6	4	
Seavey	Robert	m.	PD	15 July 1917	8	3	
Seavey	Robert	m.	PA	1 Sept. 1917	2	3	
Seavey	Robert	m.	PC	1 Sept. 1917	8	3	also 2 Sept., 8:3
Seavey	Robert T.	m.	PA	14 July 1917	4	4	
Seawell	David	d.	SRR	15 Mar. 1917	8	2	
Seawell	David Rickman	d.	PD	16 Mar. 1917	3	1	Morris Hill Cemetery, Boise, Idaho
Seawell	George	d.	PD	8 Dec. 1918	6	2	also 10 Dec., 1:4
Seawell	George C.	d.	HT	12 Dec. 1918	1	3	
Seawell	George Chancellor	d.	PC	8 Dec. 1918	4	1	
Seawell	L. E.	m.	SIT	11 Aug. 1917	1	4	
Seawell	L. E.	m.	PC	12 Aug. 1917	2	3	
Seawell	Retta Hale	d.	PD	30 Oct. 1918	3	3	
Sebering	Mary J.	m.	PD	2 Nov. 1916	8	1	
Sechooper/ Sechuber	Charles	d.	PC	9 Aug. 1917	1	3	also Aug., 8:3
Seckler	Joseph	d.	PC	25 Aug. 1916	8	5	
Secord	Velma	m.	SIT	8 June 1918	1	7	
Secord	Vilma	m.	PD	30 May 1918	2	3	
Sedgley	W. Frank	o.	CR	4 Oct. 1918	1	5	
Sedley	Frank	o.	PD	2 Mar. 1918	3	1	
Seed	William H.	m.	SRR	2 Oct. 1916	5	2	
Seehooper	Charles	d.	PA	9 Aug. 1917	5	4	
Seehooper	Charles	d.	PD	9 Aug. 1917	5	1	also 10 Aug., 2:1
Segard	Jennie	d.	PA	23 Feb. 1916	4	4	Cypress Hill; also 25 Feb., 10:6
Segard	Jennie	d.	PC	24 Feb. 1916	5	4	also 26 Feb., 2:3; Cypress Hill
Seibel	Charles	b.	PA	11 Jan. 1917	6	4	
Seibel	Charles	b.	PC	11 Jan. 1918	4	6	
Seibel	Clark J.	m.	PC	12 Oct. 1916	5	3	
Seid	Daniel John	b.	PD	13 June 1917	6	3	
Seid	David	b.	SRR	12 June 1917	2	3	
Seipp	Henry	d.	SIT	24 Aug. 1918	1	2	
Seipp	Henry	d.	HT	29 Aug. 1918	7	3	
Seito	Margaret Genevieve	m.	PC	16 Mar. 1918	5	2	
Seito	Margaret Guinevere	m.	ST	8 Mar. 1918	8	3	
Seldner	B.	o.	PA	1 Feb. 1917	5	1	
Seligsburger	Hattie	m.	PA	3 Jan. 1918	8	3	

(1) Surname	(2) Given Name	(3)	(4)	(5) Date	(6) Pg	(7) Col	(8) Comments
Selling	Simon S.	d.	PA	2 Jan. 1918	7	4	
Sellon	Violet O.	m.	SRR	3 Mar. 1916	6	2	
Sellon	Violet Olive	m.	PD	3 Mar. 1917	5	2	
Serzatti	Minnie	m.	PD	24 Nov. 1918	6	3	
Severance	Fred	d.	PD	23 Apr. 1918	4	2	
Seward	Frances	m.	PA	21 Oct. 1916	8	4	
Sewell	Luther E.	m.	PD	19 July 1917	3	1	also 7 Aug., 3:3
Sewell	Luther E.	m.	ST	20 July 1917	4	2	also 10 Aug., 7:3
Sewell	Luther Enloe	m.	SRR	18 July 1917	4	3	also 4 Aug., 8:4; 6 Aug., 8:3
Sexton	R. C.	m.	PC	8 Sept. 1918	5	3	also 10 Sept., 4:1
Sexton	Reg C.	m.	PA	9 Sept. 1918	4	5	also 8 Sept., 8:5
Seymour	Clara	d.	PD	27 May 1917	6	3	
Seymour	Clara E.	d.	SRR	21 May 1917	8	4	Rural Cemetery
Seymour	George Archibald	d.	PD	18 Oct. 1918	4	2	also 7:5; 22 Oct., 2:2
Sgheiza	Theodore	d.	PA	12 June 1916	4	5	
Sgherza	T.	d.	SIT	17 June 1916	1	7	
Shackman	Catherine	d.	PA	29 Mar. 1916	1	3	Cypress Hill; also 31 Mar., 1:3
Shackman	Catherine	d.	PC	29 Mar. 1916	1	4	Cypress Hill; also 31 Mar., 2:2; 1 Apr., 8:1
Shafe	Helen	d.	PA	11 Mar. 1918	8	5	also 13 Mar., 5:2
Shafe	Helen	d.	PC	12 Mar. 1918	3	3	Cypress Hill; also 6:3; 13 Mar., 3:4; 14 Mar., 5:5
Shafer	Fred	b.	PD	10 Aug. 1917	8	3	
Shaffer	Call	o.	PA	12 Feb. 1918	4	6	
Shaffer	Emma Lloyd	d.	PD	24 May 1918	4	2	Healdsburg; also 7:4
Shaffer	Emma Lloyd	d.	PC	25 May 1918	6	5	Healdsburg
Shaffer	S. M.	d.	PC	25 Jan. 1918	4	2	
Shane	Amos M.	d.	PD	21 July 1917	8	2	
Shane	Amos N.	d.	SRR	21 July 1917	6	5	
Shane	Ethel	m.	SIT	17 Mar. 1917	1	6	also 30 June, 1:2
Shane	Ethel	m.	PC	18 Mar. 1917	3	3	
Shane	Ethel	m.	PD	24 Mar. 1917	3	3	
Shannon	Thomas H.	d.	PA	12 Oct. 1916	4	3	
Shapiro	Aaron	m.	PD	17 Aug. 1918	4	2	
Shapiro	Aron D.	m.	PC	16 Aug. 1918	3	4	
Sharboro	Romida	d.	CR	13 July 1917	1	4	
Sharkey	J. H.	m.	PD	18 Jan. 1918	5	1	
Sharp	Ernest	m.	ST	13 Dec. 1918	9	4	
Sharp	H. H.	b.	PA	18 June 1917	8	6	
Sharp	H. H.	b.	PC	19 June 1917	6	3	
Sharp	J. H.	b.	PD	19 Feb. 1916	8	2	
Sharpnack	Roy	m.	PD	8 July 1917	5	4	
Shatto	Francis Elmer Willard	d.	ST	27 Dec. 1918	8	3	Odd Fellows Cem.

(1) Surname	(2) Given Name	(3)	(4)	(5) Date	(6) Pg	(7) Col	(8) Comments
Shattuck	Karl W.	m.	PD	23 Dec. 1916	5	4	
Shaw	Herbert	o.	SIT	25 Aug. 1917	2	4	
Shaw	James A.	d.	SIT	10 Aug. 1918	1	7	
Shaw	James A.	d.	PD	6 Aug. 1918	7	1	
Shaw	Jane	d.	PD	24 Feb. 1917	1	7	
Shaw	Margaret	d.	SIT	11 May 1918	1	5	also 18 May, 1:7
Shea	Thomas	d.	PA	28 Dec. 1918	6	4	
Shea	Thomas Franklin	d.	PD	27 Dec. 1918	4	2	Calvary Cemetery; also 7:1; 28 Dec., 3:2
Shearer	Mathilda	m.	PC	25 Jan. 1917	2	2	
Shearer	Matilda	m.	PA	24 Jan. 1917	8	6	
Shearer	Melville Preston	m.	SRR	29 May 1916	8	1	also 8 June, 1:5
Shee	Joe Moon Jow, Mrs.	d.	SIT	13 Oct. 1917	1	5	San Francisco
Shelford	Erastus M.	m.	PD	23 Oct. 1917	7	4	
Shelford	Lola	m.	SRR	18 Nov. 1916	8	3	also 25 Nov., 8:4
Shelford	Lola Leona	m.	PD	18 Nov. 1916	3	2	also 25 Nov., 3:3; 26 Nov., 3:1
Shelley	A. E.	b.	ST	3 Aug. 1917	8	3	
Shelley	John Leland	d.	PC	28 Dec. 1918	8	4	
Shelley	Lee	d.	ST	27 Dec. 1918	1	6	
Shelley	Louis	m.	SRR	10 July 1916	8	5	also 11 July, 2:3
Shelley	Louis	m.	PD	11 July 1916	3	4	
Shelly	Louis	m.	PC	11 July 1916	5	1	
Shelton	A C.	d.	PC	3 Jan. 1917	8	3	
Shelton	A. C.	p.	PA	11 Jan. 1917	3	3	
Shelton	A. C.	d.	PA	3 Jan. 1917	6	5	
Shelton	A. C.	d.	PD	3 Jan. 1917	2	2	
Shelton	A. C.	d.	PC	30 Dec. 1916	1	4	
Shelton	Abraham Cooper	p.	PC	11 Jan. 1917	1	5	
Shelton	Abram Cooper	d.	SRR	2 Jan. 1917	1	4	
Shelton	Abram Cooper	d.	PA	30 Dec. 1916	3	4	
Shelton	Abram Cooper	d.	PD	30 Dec. 1916	8	1	also 31 Dec., 6:1
Shelton	Abram Cooper	d.	SRR	30 Dec. 1916	7	3	
Shepard	Bert	o.	SIT	1 June, 1918	2	1	
Shepard	Eliza	o.	SRR	13 Sept. 1916	4	3	also 13 Oct., 8:3
Shepard	Eliza	o.	PC	14 Sept. 1916	3	1	
Shepard	Eliza	o.	SRR	28 Apr. 1916	5	3	
Shepard	Irving	o.	SIT	5 May 1917	2	3	also 14 July, 1:1
Shepard	Irving	m.	PD	24 May 1918	2	4	
Shepard	J. H.	o.	SRR	13 Sept. 1916	4	3	also 13 Oct., 8:3
Shepard	J. H.	o.	PC	14 Sept. 1916	3	1	
Shepard	J. H.	d.	SIT	21 Apr. 1917	3	4	
Shepard	J. H.	d.	PC	22 Apr. 1917	1	6	
Shepard	J. H.	o.	SRR	28 Apr. 1916	5	3	
Shepard	J. H.	o.	SIT	5 Feb. 1916	1	6	

(1) Surname	(2) Given Name	(3)	(4)	(5) Date	(6) Pg	(7) Col	(8) Comments
Shephard	Irving	m.	SIT	25 May 1918	1	4	
Sheridan	Anna	d.	PC	16 Jan. 1918	3	5	Duncans Mills
Sherman	Elia	o.	SRR	7 Sept. 1916	4	3	
Sherman	Oscar W.	o.	SRR	7 Sept. 1916	4	3	
Sherrard	Mary Helena	d.	HT	25 Jan. 1917	1	4	Oak Mound Cemetery
Sherwood	Harry	d.	PD	6 Jan. 1918	3	3	
Sherwood	Ivah	m.	PD	28 July 1916	6	2	
Shideler	Isabel	d.	ST	6 July 1917	8	5	I.O.O.F. Cemetery; also 13 July, 1:4
Shideler	Isabella B.	d.	SRR	5 July 1917	8	1	
Shideler	Isabella B.	d.	PC	6 July 1917	1	3	Sebastopol; also 8:5; 8 July, 8:4
Shideler	Isabella K.	d.	PD	6 July 1917	7	4	
Shields	John	d.	PA	30 June 1917	8	3	
Shields	Sarah Anne	d.	PA	10 July 1916	6	3	
Shields	Sarah Anne	d.	PC	11 July 1916	8	4	Tomales; also 13 July, 3:1
Shifflet	Ada Belle	o.	SRR	5 Oct. 1916	8	1	
Shifflet	Wade N.	o.	SRR	5 Oct. 1916	8	1	
Shilling	Blanche	m.	PA	9 Aug. 1917	5	4	
Shoff	Joseph	d.	PC	24 Nov. 1917	1	4	Calvary Cemetery; also 25 Nov., 2:3, 3:5; 27 Nov., 8:4
Shofner	Bud	o.	SIT	14 July 1917	1	1	
Shofner	May	d.	SIT	2 Nov. 1918	1	1	
Shofner	May	d.	PD	3 Nov. 1918	7	1	
Sholden	Mr. & Mrs.	b.	SIT	26 Jan. 1918	3	5	
Shook	Mr. & Mrs.	b.	ST	22 Jan. 1916	8	3	
Short	Walter	m.	PA	20 Jan. 1917	2	2	
Short	Walter	m.	PC	21 Jan. 1917	5	2	
Short	Walter Clyde	m.	PC	24 Dec. 1916	4	5	
Shortridge	Lee	d.	PA	3 June 1916	5	2	Odd Fellows, Forestville; also 5 June, 3:5
Shortridge	Lee Edwin	d.	PC	4 June 1916	5	2	
Shortridge	Lee Edwin	d.	PD	4 June 1916	2	3	also 6 June, 7:2
Shortridge	Leo Edwin	d.	SRR	3 June 1916	10	1	I.O.O.F. Cemetery, Forestville; also 5 June, 1:3
Shott	William	m.	PD	27 Apr. 1918	7	5	
Shott	William	m.	SIT	27 Apr. 1918	1	7	
Showalter	Lucy	m.	PA	24 Dec. 1917	5	3	
Showers	Earl F.	m.	PD	19 June 1917	2	1	
Showers	Earl Franklin	m.	SRR	18 June 1917	8	5	
Shrauleg	Louis	m.	PA	1 Apr. 1918	4	4	
Shriver	R. G.	b.	SRR	27 Apr. 1917	1	4	
Shriver	Thomas J.	d.	PA	24 Jan. 1917	2	3	

(1) Surname	(2) Given Name	(3)	(4)	(5) Date	(6) Pg	(7) Col	(8) Comments
Shriver	Thomas J.	d.	PD	24 Jan. 1917	2	4	also 25 Jan., 5:3
Shriver	Thomas J.	d.	PC	25 Jan. 1917	4	3	
Shriver	Thomas J.	d.	SRR	25 Jan. 1917	6	1	Shiloh Cemetery
Shudy	Frank S.	d.	SRR	4 May 1916	8	5	San Diego
Shuh	Rudolph A.	m.	SRR	28 May 1917	4	4	
Shuhart	Elizabeth	d.	HT	20 Oct. 1916	1	6	
Shuhart	Elizabeth	d.	PD	22 Oct. 1916	6	4	
Shulte	William A.	m.	PA	29 Apr. 1916	5	1	also 1 May, 5:4
Shurtleff	John T.	d.	PD	11 July 1917	5	1	
Shurtleff	John T.	d.	CR	13 July 1917	1	3	
Sibard	M.	d.	SRR	23 Feb. 1916	10	5	
Sibbald	Kent	b.	PD	4 Oct. 1918	3	3	
Siebel	C. J.	m.	PD	12 Oct. 1916	3	1	
Siebel	Charles	m.	SRR	11 Oct. 1916	6	3	
Siegler	L.	b.	PD	2 June 1917	6	5	
Siegler	Louis	m.	PA	8 July 1916	8	2	
Siegler	Louis	m.	PC	9 July 1916	2	2	
Sieversten	George N.	o.	PA	15 Nov. 1918	8	4	
Sights	John M.	d.	SRR	26 Dec. 1917	8	5	Rural Cemetey; also 27 Dec., 8:3
Sights	John M.	d.	PD	27 Dec. 1917	2	4	Rural Cemetery; slso 4:2
Silacci	Dora	m.	PA	4 Sept. 1918	8	2	
Silacci	Dora	m.	PC	5 Sept. 1918	5	4	
Silacci	Q. V.	b.	PA	15 June 1916	8	3	
Silacci	Quinto	b.	PC	1 Dec. 1917	5	5	
Silacci	Quinto	b.	PA	30 Nov. 1917	4	6	
Silva	A. D.	b.	PA	14 Sept. 1917	4	4	also 8:1
Silva	Antone (son of)	b&d	PC	9 May 1916	1	7	
Silva	F. A.	o.	PC	18 Sept. 1918	1	5	
Silva	Frank	m.	SRR	10 Jan. 1916	4	2	
Silva	Frank	m.	PC	11 Jan. 1916	2	2	
Silva	Frank	m.	PD	11 Jan. 1916	2	3	
Silva	Frank	m.	PA	22 Nov. 1916	6	4	
Silva	Frank	m.	PC	5 Jan. 1916	5	2	
Silva	Frank	m.	PA	8 Jan. 1916	4	5	also 10 Jan., 5:6
Silva	Genevieve	d.	PC	18 Feb. 1916	5	5	Calvary Cemetery
Silva	George S.	d.	PA	27 Feb. 1917	3	3	Tomales; also 28 Feb., 4:3
Silva	George S.	d.	PC	27 Feb. 1917	1	5	
Silva	Isabella	d.	PD	15 Nov. 1916	3	3	
Silva	Isabella B.	d.	SRR	15 Nov. 1916	3	6	Sebastopol
Silva	Isabelle B.	d.	PC	16 Nov. 1916	6	5	
Silva	John	o.	PC	19 Sept. 1918	3	4	
Silva	Julia	m.	SRR	4 May 1917	8	6	
Silva	Julia	m.	PD	5 May 1917	5	3	also 27 May, 6:5

(1) Surname	(2) Given Name	(3)	(4)	(5) Date	(6) Pg	(7) Col	(8) Comments
Silva	Julia	m.	SRR	26 May 1917	10	6	
Silva	Louise Dalphine	m.	SRR	14 May 1917	10	3	
Silva	Louise Delphine	m.	PD	15 May 1917	6	3	
Silva	M. G.	d.	PD	1 Sept. 1916	8	2	
Silva	M. G.	d.	SRR	1 Sept. 1916	6	1	
Silva	M. G.	d.	PA	2 Sept. 1916	8	5	Calvary Cemetery
Silva	M. G.	d.	PA	31 Aug. 1916	4	3	
Silva	M. G.	d.	PC	31 Aug. 1916	1	3	Calvary Cemetery; also 3 Sept., 8:3
Silva	Manuel B.	d.	ST	29 Nov. 1918	1	4	
Silva	Manuel G.	m.	PC	30 Mar. 1917	4	5	also 8 Apr., 3:3
Silva	Maria	d.	SIT	12 Feb. 1916	1	5	Catholic Cemetery
Silva	Marie	d.	PD	13 Feb. 1916	8	4	Sonoma Cemetery
Silva	Mary	m.	PA	22 Nov. 1918	4	5	
Silva	Mary	m.	PC	23 Nov. 1918	8	2	also 24 Nov., 4:4
Silva	Mary		PD	23 Nov. 1918	5	1	also 24 Nov., 6:4, 10:2
Silva	Mary	m.	SRR	28 Sept. 1917	7	5	
Silva	Mary	m.	CR	29 Nov. 1918	1	3	
Silva	Mary	m.	SIT	30 Nov. 1918	1	4	
Silva	Mike	b.	PC	11 Aug. 1918	8	2	
Silva	Mike	b.	PC	21 Sept. 1916	5	4	
Silva	Mr. & Mrs.	b.	PC	11 Sept. 1917	3	2	
Silva	Sarah Frances	d.	PA	22 June 1916	7	3	also 24 June, 5:1
Silva	Sarah Frances	d.	PC	22 June 1916	1	1	Calvary Cemetery; also 23 June, 4:5; 25 June, 4:4
Silver	A. D.	m.	PA	30 Sept. 1916	5	1	
Silver	Joseph	m.	SRR	3 Dec. 1917	8	4	
Silveria	Joseph	m.	PC	12 Dec. 1916	3	4	
Silveria	Joseph	m.	PA	19 Feb. 1917	5	4	
Silveria	Joseph	m.	PC	20 Feb. 1917	4	4	
Silveria	Joseph W.	m.	PA	11 Dec. 1916	5	5	
Silvershield	Harold	m.	PD	8 Feb. 1918	7	1	
Silzely	Roy	m.	PD	12 Apr. 1916	2	4	
Silzely	Roy	m.	SRR	12 Apr. 1916	7	5	
Simcoe	James	m.	PD	1 Dec. 1917	6	5	
Simcoe	James J.	m.	SRR	30 Nov. 1917	5	3	
Simcoe	John D.	m.	SRR	24 Apr. 1916	8	2	
Simcoe	John D.	m.	PD	25 Apr. 1916	2	2	
Simeons	Julius	b.	PA	12 Apr. 1917	4	1	
Simi	Annie	d.	SRR	15 Sept. 1917	6	4	Oak Mound Cemetery; also 17 Sept., 8:2
Simi	Annie	p.	SRR	18 Sept. 1917	8	2	
Simi	Annie	p.	PC	20 Sept. 1917	2	3	
Simi	Annie	d.	PC	16 Sept. 1917	7	4	
Simi	George H.	d.	HT	12 Dec. 1918	17	3	
Simi	George R.	d.	PC	13 Dec. 1918	1	3	

(1) Surname	(2) Given Name	(3)	(4)	(5) Date	(6) Pg	(7) Col	(8) Comments
Simi	George R.	d.	PD	13 Dec. 1918	5	1	Calvary Cemetery; also 14 Dec., 8:3; 15 Dec., 4:2; 17 Dec., 5:3; 18 Dec., 3:3; portrait
Simi	George R.	d.	PA	14 Dec. 1918	4	1	
Simi	Louis	d.	HT	28 June 1917	4	1	
Simi	Louis	d.	SRR	28 June 1917	6	5	
Simi	Louis	d.	PC	29 June 1917	5	6	
Simi	P.	d.	PD	31 Mar. 1918	4	2	
Simi	Parisse	d.	PD	2 Apr. 1918	4	2	also 3 Apr., 6:2
Simmons	Clara	m.	SRR	11 Oct. 1916	6	3	
Simmons	Clara	m.	PD	12 Oct. 1916	3	1	
Simmons	Clara E.	m.	PC	12 Oct. 1916	5	3	
Simmons	Gladys	m.	PD	3 Nov. 1916	6	3	
Simmons	Gladys	m.	SRR	3 Nov. 1916	5	4	
Simmons	Gladys	m.	SIT	4 Nov. 1916	1	2	
Simmons	Lindsay	m.	PD	3 May 1918	2	1	
Simoens	Julius	b.	PC	13 Apr. 1917	4	6	
Simon	Elise	d.	PD	9 Jan. 1917	8	4	
Simon	Elizabeth	d.	PC	10 Jan. 1917	2	2	
Simon	Elsie	p.	SIT	3 Mar. 1917	1	5	
Simoni	Angelo	d.	SRR	29 July 1916	10	6	
Simoni	Angelo	d.	PD	1 Aug. 1916	3	4	
Simonini	Batista	d.	PD	5 Oct. 1918	5	1	
Simpson	Bert	b.	PD	27 Jan. 1917	6	5	
Sims	Mabel	m.	PD	1 July 1917	3	2	also 4 July, 5:2
Sims	Mabel Morrison	m.	SRR	30 June 1917	10	3	also 5 July, 3:5
Sinclair	Anita	d.	PD	21 July 1918	2	4	
Sinclair	Elizabeth	m.	PD	12 Apr. 1916	2	3	
Sinclair	Elizabeth	m.	PC	13 Apr. 1916	2	1	
Sinclair	Elizabeth M.	m.	SRR	12 Apr. 1916	7	5	
Singley	Denna Vialta	m.	PC	21 Nov. 1918	4	3	
Singley	Helen	d.	PA	16 July 1917	1	3	Calvary Cemetery; also 2:4&5; 4:5; 17 July, 6:6
Singley	Helen	d.	SRR	16 July 1917	5	3	also 17 July, 6:1
Singley	Helen	d.	PC	17 July 1917	1	3	Calvary Cemetery; also 3:3, 6:2; 19 July, 4:3
Singley	Helen	d.	PD	17 July 1917	2	1	also 19 July, 5:1
Singley	Sarah	d.	PA	7 Aug. 1916	7	3	
Sink	W. Dan	m.	SRR	12 Sept. 1917	4	4	
Sirsher	Riley	o.	HT	24 May 1917	7	4	
Sission	Wade	b.	SRR	25 Sept. 1917	4	3	
Sjorlander	Carl T.	m.	SRR	23 Nov. 1916	8	4	
Sjospen	Jane	d.	PC	17 Oct. 1916	5	3	cremation; also 18 Oct., 8:3; 19 Oct., 4:5; 20 Sept., 1:4

(1) Surname	(2) Given Name	(3)	(4)	(5) Date	(6) Pg	(7) Col	(8) Comments
Sjosten	Jane	d.	PA	17 Oct. 1916	8	5	cremation; also 19 Oct., 8:5
Skabo	R.	b.	PA	8 Mar. 1918	5	2	also 6:5
Skaggs	Alexander	d.	PD	28 Apr. 1918	6	4	Geyserville; also 4 May, 6:3
Skaggs	Amos	d.	PA	27 Dec. 1917	7	4	
Skaggs	Franklin	o.	SRR	6 Mar. 1916	4	6	
Skaggs	Franklin	o.	PD	7 Mar. 1917	6	2	
Skaggs	Margaret	d.	PA	12 June 1916	1	6	
Skaggs	Margaret	d.	SRR	12 June 1916	5	3	
Skaggs	Margaret Eliza	d.	PC	11 June 1916	1	4	
Skaggs	Margaret Elizabeth	d.	PD	11 June 1916	10	4	also 13 June, 8:2
Skaggs	Phoebe	o.	SRR	6 Mar. 1916	4	6	
Skaggs	Phoebe	o.	PD	7 Mar. 1917	6	2	
Skaggs	W. W.	d.	HT	6 Dec. 1917	5	4	
Skaggs	William W.	d.	SRR	3 Dec. 1917	8	3&4	also 5 Dec., 8:1
Skaggs	William W.	d.	PC	4 Dec. 1917	4	1	
Skaggs	William W.	d.	PD	4 Dec. 1917	2	5	also 4:3; 6 Dec., 6:1
Skaggs	William W.	d.	SIT	8 Dec. 1917	3	1	
Skee	Bertha L.	d.	PD	4 Sept. 1918	8	3	
Skee	Bertha L.	d.	HT	5 Sept. 1918	1	3	
Skelly	E.	m.	SRR	15 Oct. 1917	7	4	
Skinner	J. C.	d.	ST	24 June 1916	1	2	
Skinner	J. C., Mrs.	d.	PD	23 June 1916	5	4	also 28 June, 8:3
Skinner	J. E.	d.	PA	22 June 1916	3	3	Sebastopol; also 4:5; 27 June, 8:5; 29 June, 6:4
Skinner	J. E.	d.	SRR	22 June 1916	8	5	
Skinner	J. E.	d.	PC	23 June 1916	3	3	also 28 June, 4:3; 30 June, 6:3
Skinner	Mary	m.	PD	24 Aug. 1916	7	4	
Skoff	Joseph	d.	PD	25 Nov. 1917	7	6	
Skoff	Joseph	d.	SRR	26 Nov. 1917	7	4	
Skov	C. H. (son of)	b&d	PA	16 June 1916	7	4	
Slack	Rose	m.	PA	23 Apr. 1917	5	4	
Slater	Edna E.	d.	PA	8 July 1916	5	4	
Slater	Edna Elite	d.	PD	8 July 1916	8	1	also 9 July, 1:4
Slater	Edna Eliza	d.	SRR	8 July 1916	5	1	also 10 July, 8:5
Slater	Edna Eliza	d.	PC	9 July 1916	6	3	
Slater	William B.	d.	PD	1 Sept. 1918	2	5	Faught Cemetery
Slattery	John	b.	SRR	28 Sept. 1916	6	4	
Slattery	John F.	d.	ST	27 Sept. 1918	1	2	
Slattery	M. D.	d.	PD	22 July 1916	5	4	
Slocum	George	d.	HT	8 Feb. 1917	1	1	
Sluff	Joseph	d.	PA	24 Nov. 1917	4	4	also 26 Nov., 4:6
Slusser	Irma	m.	SRR	5 May 1917	4	1	also 1 June, 1:5; 4 June, 3:2

(1) Surname	(2) Given Name	(3)	(4)	(5) Date	(6) Pg	(7) Col	(8) Comments
Slusser	Irma	m.	SRR	1 Feb. 1917	3	5	
Slusser	Irma Gladys	m.	PD	3 June 1917	7	1	
Smalley	Ina Maye	m.	SRR	1 June 1916	1	2	
Smalley	Ina Maye	m.	PD	2 June 1916	7	3	
Smart	Agnes	o.	PD	10 Aug. 1918	6	3	
Smart	Edna	o.	PA	21 June 1918	3	2	
Smart	Edna	o.	PC	22 June 1918	8	4	
Smart	Edna	o.	PA	9 Aug. 1918	8	5	
Smart	Wayne	o.	PC	22 June 1918	8	4	
Smart	Wayne	o.	PD	10 Aug. 1918	6	3	
Smart	Wayne A.	o.	PA	21 June 1918	3	2	
Smart	Wayne A.	o.	PA	9 Aug. 1918	8	5	
Smeckpeper	Lillian D.	m.	PD	12 Mar. 1918	4	2	
Smith	A. F.	d.	PD	24 Feb. 1918	4	2	also 8:4
Smith	A. L., Mrs.	d.	SRR	21 Sept. 1916	6	1	
Smith	Abraham B.	d.	SRR	5 Sept. 1917	5	5	
Smith	Adah	m.	PC	28 Apr. 1918	5	3	
Smith	Adah	m.	SRR	29 Dec. 1917	4	1	portrait
Smith	Adah	m.	PC	30 Dec. 1917	5	4	
Smith	Andrew	d.	SRR	7 Nov. 1916	5	1	
Smith	Andrew F.	d.	PC	7 Nov. 1916	6	5	
Smith	Andrew F.	d.	PD	7 Nov. 1916	1	6	
Smith	Annie L.	d.	PD	21 Sept. 1916	6	3	San Francisco
Smith	Arthur M.	m.	SRR	29 Nov. 1916	3	4	
Smith	Arthur Melvin	m.	PD	2 Dec. 1916	5	4	also 6:1
Smith	Arthur Melvin	m.	SRR	2 Dec. 1916	9	2	
Smith	Chandler H.	o.	PD	10 Dec. 1918	5	3	
Smith	Charles Frederich	d.	HT	17 Feb. 1916	1	3	
Smith	Chester	o.	ST	12 Oct. 1917	7	2	
Smith	Cleo	o.	SRR	16 June 1916	6	5	
Smith	Cleo	o.	PD	8 Aug. 1916	5	2	
Smith	Dagmar	m.	PA	26 Dec. 1917	5	3	
Smith	Dewey	o.	SIT	28 Apr. 1917	2	5	
Smith	Dorothy E.	m.	PD	23 June 1918	6	1	
Smith	Duncan	o.	ST	24 Aug. 1917	3	5	
Smith	Duncan	o.	SRR	27 Nov. 1916	7	3	English Air Force
Smith	Edson	m.	PC	8 Aug. 1917	4	4	
Smith	Eliza	d.	HT	10 Feb. 1916	5	1	Illinois
Smith	Eliza	d.	SRR	3 Feb. 1916	5	3	
Smith	Eliza Bryan	d.	PD	3 Feb. 1916	2	4	
Smith	Elizabeth Mae Middagh	o.	PC	5 Dec. 1916	8	2	
Smith	Ellen H.	d.	SIT	10 Aug. 1918	1	5	
Smith	Elsie	d.	PA	23 Nov. 1917	2	4	Duluth, MN
Smith	Elsie	d.	PC	23 Nov. 1917	1	2	Duluth, MN

(1) Surname	(2) Given Name	(3)	(4)	(5) Date	(6) Pg	(7) Col	(8) Comments
Smith	Emmaline	d.	PA	21 Mar. 1918	4	3	Cypress Hill; also 23 Mar., 8:3
Smith	Frank	o.	PD	15 Aug. 1917	7	5	
Smith	Frank	o.	PC	29 Feb. 1916	?	4	
Smith	Frank A.	d.	PD	25 Feb. 1916	8	1	Sebastopol Cemetery; also 29 Feb., 3:1
Smith	Frank A.	d.	PA	26 Feb. 1916	3	4	Sebastopol; also 4:6; 29 Feb., 6:1
Smith	Frank A.	d.	PC	26 Feb. 1916	1	6	Sebastopol Cemetery
Smith	Frank A.	d.	SRR	26 Feb. 1916	5	1	Sebastopol; also 28 Feb., 4:1
Smith	Frank W.	d.	PA	6 May 1916	6	2	
Smith	Frank W.	d.	PC	6 May 1916	5	3	
Smith	Frank W.	d.	PD	7 May 1916	8	4	Holy Cross, S. F.
Smith	Frank, Mrs.	d.	PA	24 June 1916	2	2	Sebastopol
Smith	Frank, Mrs.	d.	PD	24 June 1916	7	3	Sebastopol Cemetery; also 27 June, 8:5
Smith	Frank, Mrs.	d.	PC	25 June 1916	5	7	
Smith	Fred (dau of)	d.	HT	29 Sept. 1916	1	4	
Smith	George	o.	SRR	16 June 1916	6	5	
Smith	George	o.	PD	8 Aug. 1916	5	2	
Smith	George B.	m.	PD	31 Aug. 1918	2	5	
Smith	Georgia	m.	PD	18 Nov. 1917	7	5	
Smith	Georgia	m.	SRR	19 Nov. 1917	6	6	
Smith	Guy D.	o.	PD	5 May 1917	1	3	British Army; also 9 May, 2:5
Smith	Guy Duncan	o.	PC	6 May 1917	2	1	British Army; also 9 May, 6:4
Smith	Guy Duncan	o.	SRR	8 May 1917	1	5	
Smith	Harold	o.	ST	24 Aug. 1917	3	5	
Smith	Harold	o.	SRR	27 Nov. 1916	7	3	English Air Force
Smith	Harold	o.	SRR	29 Jan. 1916	10	2	English Flying Corps
Smith	Harry	m.	PA	18 June 1917	4	4	
Smith	Harry B.	m.	PC	10 Apr. 1917	5	2	
Smith	Harry C.	b.	PA	27 Aug. 1918	5	5	
Smith	Harry J.	m.	PC	15 June 1917	5	2	also 19 June, 8:4
Smith	Harry J.	m.	PD	20 June 1917	3	1	
Smith	Harry J.	m.	HT	21 June 1917	7	4	
Smith	Harry J.	m.	SRR	21 June 1917	6	6	
Smith	Hilda Beatrice	m.	PC	7 Sept. 1918	8	5	
Smith	Hoke, Mrs.	d.	PA	18 Oct. 1918	4	4	
Smith	Hoke, Mrs.	d.	PD	18 Oct. 1918	5	1	also 20 Oct., 7:3; 22 Oct., 1:7
Smith	Ida Beatrice	m.	PD	8 Sept. 1918	3	3	
Smith	Isadora	d.	HT	7 Mar. 1918	8	2	
Smith	J. F.	d.	PD	20 Nov. 1917	1	4	

(1) Surname	(2) Given Name	(3)	(4)	(5) Date	(6) Pg	(7) Col	(8) Comments
Smith	J. F.	d.	SRR	20 Nov. 1917	5	4	also 21 Nov., 6:4
Smith	J. G., Mrs.	d.	PC	18 Oct. 1918	5	1	
Smith	J. T.	d.	PC	9 May 1917	3	2	Cypress Hill; also 4:3; 11 May, 4:4
Smith	J. Ward	b.	PD	11 Aug. 1918	12	7	
Smith	James R.	m.	SRR	4 Oct. 1916	4	3	,
Smith	John Tyler	d.	PA	8 May 1917	5	3	Cypress Hill; also 10 May, 5:3
Smith	John Tyler	d.	PD	10 May 1917	7	2	
Smith	Joseph C.	m.	PD	15 Oct. 1916	5	2	also 17 Oct., 3:3
Smith	Joseph C.	m.	SRR	16 Oct. 1916	2	2	
Smith	Laura A.	d.	PC	2 Dec. 1916	3	6	Cypress Hill; also 8:4; 3 Dec., 8:1
Smith	Laura A.	d.	PA	29 Nov. 1916	4	7	Cypress Hill; also 2 Dec., 5:1
Smith	Laura A.	d.	ST	9 Dec. 1916	1	5	
Smith	Lenabelle	m.	PD	15 Nov. 1917	4	2	
Smith	Leon Anthony	d.	PA	11 Aug. 1917	6	3	
Smith	Leon Anthony	d.	PC	11 Aug. 1917	4	3	
Smith	Leslie D.	d.	PD	28 Feb. 1917	6	2	Guerneville
Smith	Leslie D.	d.	SRR	28 Feb. 1917	6	3	
Smith	Lester	d.	PD	13 Dec. 1918	6	2	
Smith	Lester L.	d.	PC	13 Dec. 1918	1	5	
Smith	Lester M.	o.	HT	18 July 1918	1	2	
Smith	Lester Merritt	m.	PD	16 Aug. 1917	6	5	
Smith	Lester Merritt	m.	SRR	16 Aug. 1917	8	3	
Smith	Louisa	d.	SRR	24 June 1916	7	2	
Smith	Madeline	m.	PD	18 Oct. 1918	7	4	
Smith	Manuel Ferrera	d.	PC	22 Sept. 1918	5	3	aka Fereira; also 6:3
Smith	Mary	d.	PD	3 Jan. 1918	2	4	
Smith	Mary Ellen	o.	PD	15 Aug. 1917	7	5	
Smith	Max	o.	PA	24 June 1918	5	4	also 25 June, 5:6; 29 June, 5:4
Smith	Max	o.	PD	25 June 1918	5	1	also 26 June, 8:3; 28 June, 7:4
Smith	May Gibson	d.	PD	20 Oct. 1918	4	2	
Smith	Melvin O.	m.	PD	1 Dec. 1917	5	2	also 2 Dec., 10:6
Smith	Minnie	d.	PD	19 Mar. 1918	3	4	also 4:2
Smith	Minnie Etta	m.	PD	27 June 1916	7	5	
Smith	Minnie/Emiline	d.	PC	19 Mar. 1918	8	2	Cypress Hill; also 23 Mar., 5:5; 24 Mar., 8:3
Smith	Nellie V.	m.	PA	19 Mar. 1918	6	6	
Smith	Nettie	m.	PD	25 Apr. 1916	1	4	
Smith	Peter	m.	PA	7 Feb. 1916	7	5	
Smith	Press	b.	SRR	12 Jan. 1916	3	2	
Smith	R. Press	b.	PD	20 Aug. 1918	3	5	

(1) Surname	(2) Given Name	(3)	(4)	(5) Date	(6) Pg	(7) Col	(8) Comments
Smith	Rowena	m.	PC	21 June 1916	3	4	
Smith	Rowena	m.	SRR	22 June 1916	5	5	
Smith	Sarah Ellen	d.	PC	5 Feb. 1918	4	2	Cypress Hill
Smith	Susanna	d.	PA	15 Oct. 1917	8	3	
Smith	Thomas	d.	PC	2 Nov. 1918	8	4	France
Smith	Thomas	d.	PD	9 Jan. 1918	8	3	
Smith	Thomas J.	d.	SRR	26 Mar. 1917	4	6	also 27 Mar., 4:3
Smith	Thomas Jefferson	d.	PC	27 Mar. 1917	6	2	
Smith	Thomas Jefferson	d.	PD	27 Mar. 1917	4	3	Rural Cemetery; also 6:1; 28 Mar., 2:5
Smith	Thomas P.	d.	PD	24 Dec. 1918	8	3	France
Smith	Thomas R.	o.	PC	7 Dec. 1918	1	3	
Smith	Verna Alta	m.	PD	23 May 1918	7	3	also 25 May, 2:5; 22 June, 3:5
Smith	Volney T.	m.	PA	4 Dec. 1916	4	2	
Smith	Volney T.	m.	PC	5 Dec. 1916	8	2	
Smith	W. H.	o.	HT	18 July 1918	6	4	
Smith	W. S., Mrs.	d.	SRR	20 July 1916	1	4	Guerneville; also 22 July, 9:2
Smith	W. S., Mrs.	d.	PC	21 July 1916	4	3	
Smith	W. S., Mrs.	d.	PD	22 July 1916	2	5	
Smith	W. S., Mrs.	d.	ST	29 July 1916	5	3	
Smith	W. Thomas	o.	SRR	14 Sept. 1916	6	2	
Smith	W. W., Mrs.	d.	PA	20 July 1916	1	4	also 4:3
Smith	Walter	b.	PC	31 Oct. 1916	5	6	
Smith	Walter Frederick	m.	SRR	3 Jan. 1917	8	5	
Smith	Walter Frederick	m.	PC	4 Jan. 1917	5	4	
Smith	Walter Frederick	m.	PD	4 Jan. 1917	3	2	
Smith	William F.	d.	PC	3 Jan. 1918	1	2	
Smith	William F.	d.	PD	3 Jan. 1918	1	2	
Smith	William J.	m.	SRR	5 Jan. 1916	4	6	
Smith	William T.	d.	PD	30 Mar. 1918	5	3	
Smith	William Thomas	d.	HT	4 Apr. 1918	2	3	
Sneed	Roy G.	m.	SRR	23 Sept. 1916	8	3	
Snider	Verlie Eldeen	m.	PA	11 Mar. 1918	1	1	
Snider	Verlie Eldeen	m.	PC	12 Mar. 1918	5	2	
Snider	Verlie Eldeen	m.	PA	3 June 1918	5	5	aka Verlie Marango; also 5 June, 8:5; 17 June, 5:4
Snodgrass	J. F.	o.	PD	28 July 1917	6	2	
Snodgrass	J. F.	o.	SRR	28 July 1917	7	4	
Snodgrass	Lulu E.	o.	PD	28 July 1917	6	2	
Snodgrass	Lulu M.	o.	SRR	28 July 1917	7	4	
Snook	E. B.	d.	SRR	29 Mar. 1917	6	4	
Snook	Edward Birdsey	d.	PD	30 Mar. 1917	4	3	Odd Fellows Cemetery; also 8:4
Snook	Hazel	m.	ST	25 Mar. 1916	1	2	

(1) Surname	(2) Given Name	(3)	(4)	(5) Date	(6) Pg	(7) Col	(8) Comments
Snook	Hazel	m.	PC	26 Mar. 1916	1	6	
Snook	Margaret Adams	d.	PD	22 Dec. 1917	6	1	
Snow	Clyde	m.	ST	25 Mar. 1916	1	2	
Snow	Clyde	m.	PC	26 Mar. 1916	1	6	
Snow	May	d.	ST	14 Apr. 1917	4	2	also 23 Apr., 8:2
Snow	May	d.	SRR	16 Apr. 1917	6	4	
Snowden	Mamie	o.	PA	20 July 1918	8	4	
Snyder	Charles	d.	PA	15 Jan. 1918	4	3	
Snyder	Charles	d.	PC	16 Jan. 1918	1	2	Rural Cemetery; also 18 Jan., 2:2. 8:2; 19 Jan., 8:5
Snyder	Charles M.	d.	PD	18 Jan. 1918	4	2	Stanley's Cemetery
Snyder	Ernest	o.	PD	26 Apr. 1918	2	5	
Snyder	Philip	d.	PA	7 Dec. 1916	2	2	
Snyder	Philip	d.	PD	7 Dec. 1916	3	3	
Snyder	Philip	d.	SRR	7 Dec. 1916	5	3	
Snyder	Philip	d.	PC	8 Dec. 1916	4	3	
Soares	Emily	d.	PD	4 Oct. 1918	8	1	
Soares	Emily	d.	ST	6 Oct. 1918	1	6	
Soares	Emily R.	d.	PA	4 Oct. 1918	6	2	
Soares	Emily R.	d.	PC	4 Oct. 1918	1	4	
Sobbe	Milton	o.	SIT	9 Nov. 1918	3	3	
Sobranes	Thomas	o.	PC	30 July 1918	8	2	
Soderberg	Alice	m.	SIT	1 Apr. 1916	2	5	
Soderberg	Alice	m.	PD	7 Apr. 1916	7	2	
Soderberg	Alice	m.	SRR	7 Apr. 1916	8	6	
Soderberg	Alice	m.	PC	8 Apr. 1916	2	2	
Soderberg	Charles, Mrs.	d.	SIT	14 Sept. 1918	1	2	cremation
Solari	George	d.	SRR	25 Nov. 1916	1	5	
Solari	Linda	m.	SRR	23 Oct. 1917	4	4	
Soldate	Marino	m.	PA	8 Apr. 1918	4	4	
Soldate	Marino	m.	PC	9 Apr. 1918	5	3	
Soldate	Olympia	m.	PA	14 Mar. 1918	6	3	
Soldate	Will	b.	PA	10 Dec. 1918	3	3	
Soldate	Will	b.	PC	10 Dec. 1918	5	3	
Soldati	Effie Olympia	m.	PC	14 Mar. 1918	1	3	also 15 Mar., 4:2
Somerville	Robert	d.	PA	25 Aug. 1916	8	2	
Soracco	Clarence	o.	PC	28 Aug. 1918	5	4	
Sorensen	Camilla	m.	PA	18 Oct. 1916	5	2	also 4 Nov., 4:4
Sorensen	Camilla	m.	PC	18 Oct. 1916	1	5	also 3 Nov., 6:5; 4 Nov., 4:6
Sorensen	Camilla	m.	PD	19 Oct. 1916	6	4	also 4 Nov., 1:5
Sorensen	Rasmus (dau of)	d.	PC	30 July 1916	8	2	cremation
Sorensen	Rasmus D.	b.	PA	29 July 1916	4	3	
Sorensen	Soren N. S.	m.	PA	2 Nov. 1918	8	2	
Sorensen	Soren N. S.	m.	PC	3 Nov. 1918	5	3	

(1) Surname	(2) Given Name	(3)	(4)	(5) Date	(6) Pg	(7) Col	(8) Comments
Sorenson	Samuel	b.	PA	31 Mar. 1916	6	6	
Sorini	J.	b.	SIT	3 Mar. 1917	1	7	
Southard	Emma	m.	SRR	18 Aug. 1916	6	1	
Southard	Emma	m.	PC	20 Aug. 1916	5	2	
Souza	A. J.	b.	PC	18 Sept. 1918	5	5	
Souza	Albert Joseph	m.	PA	1 Feb. 1917	4	5	also 12 Feb., 5:4
Souza	Alfred Joseph	m.	PC	2 Feb. 1917	8	3	
Souza	Bert	b.	PA	9 Aug. 1917	5	5	
Souza	Gertrude	m.	PA	1 Nov. 1916	7	4	
Souza	Gertrude	m.	PC	31 Oct. 1916	6	5	also 26 Nov., 4:3
Souza	J. P.	b.	PA	1 July 1916	8	4	
Souza	Manuel C.	d.	PA	11 Feb. 1918	2	5	also 12 Feb., 8:5
Souza	Manuel C.	d.	PC	12 Feb. 1918	6	4	Calvary Cemetery; also 13 Feb., 5:4
Spaich	Julia	m.	PA	8 Sept. 1918	8	3	
Spaich	Marie	m.	PC	9 Apr. 1918	5	3	
Spalch	Marie	m.	PA	8 Apr. 1918	4	4	
Spaulding	Ambrose Newell	d.	PA	6 Sept. 1916	4	5	Cypress Hill; also 7 Sept., 5:2
Spaulding	Ambrose Newell	d.	PC	6 Sept. 1916	1	5	also 8 Sept., 5:6; Cypress Hill
Spaulding	Walter	m.	PD	7 June 1918	3	5	
Speaker	Charles	d.	PD	24 Aug. 1917	2	3	
Speaker	Charles A.	d.	SRR	23 Aug. 1917	8	5	
Speaks	Chester	d.	PD	17 Feb. 1916	6	3	also 20 Feb., 9:2
Spears	Chester B.	d.	SRR	16 Feb. 1916	10	5	also 17 Feb., 8:6
Spence	David H.	d.	PC	4 Apr. 1916	5	4	
Spence	David H.	d.	SIT	8 Apr. 1916	1	1	
Spence	David S.	d.	PD	4 Apr. 1916	8	3	
Spencer	M. E., Mrs.	d.	PD	6 Sept. 1917	8	3	Sonoma
Spencer	M. E., Mrs.	d.	SRR	7 Sept. 1917	8	2	
Spencer	Mary E.	d.	SIT	8 Sept. 1917	1	5	
Spencer	Mary Shattuck	d.	PC	7 Sept. 1917	8	4	Sonoma; also 8 Sept., 3:4
Spillum	Sigurd	b.	PA	22 July 1916	4	2	
Spillum	Sigurd	b.	PC	23 July 1916	8	3	
Spinder	Belle	o.	PD	23 Oct. 1918	4	2	
Spinder	Charles	o.	PD	23 Oct. 1918	4	2	
Spindler	Matilda	d.	PC	21 Mar. 1916	6	1	also 23 Mar., 5:5
Spindler	Matilda	d.	PD	22 Mar. 1916	1	2	also 23 Mar., 8:2; Odd Fellows Cemetery
Spindler	Matilda	d.	PA	24 Mar. 1916	5	6	
Spindler	Otto	m.	SIT	10 June 1916	1	2	
Spolini	Arturo	d.	PC	3 Dec. 1918	1	3	France
Spolini	Arturo	d.	PD	4 Dec. 1918	5	4	France
Spolini	Ataro	d.	ST	6 Dec. 1918	1	3	France
Spotswood	Addie	d.	PD	1 Dec. 1917	8	1	Potter Valley

(1) Surname	(2) Given Name	(3)	(4)	(5) Date	(6) Pg	(7) Col	(8) Comments
Spotswood	Elva	m.	SRR	6 Mar. 1916	8	1	
Spotswood	Rose	m.	PA	20 Jan. 1917	2	2	
Spotswood	Rose	m.	PC	21 Jan. 1917	5	2	
Spottswood	Elva	m.	PD	7 Mar. 1917	5	3	
Spottswood	Rowenna	m.	PC	24 Dec. 1916	4	5	
Springer	Charles E.	d.	PC	9 Apr. 1918	8	2	
Springer	Charles E.	d.	PD	9 Apr. 1918	2	1	
Sproul	Frank	d.	PD	1 June 1917	3	4	
Sproul	Frank R.	d.	PA	28 May 1917	2	3	Cypress Hill; also 8:7
Sproul	Frank R.	d.	PC	29 May 1917	1	2	Cypress Hill; also 3:4, 5:3; 30 May, 5:2; 1 June, 1:4
Sproule	Allan	m.	PC	13 July 1918	6	5	
Sproule	Allen	m.	PD	12 July 1918	8	2	
Sproule	Frank	d.	SRR	28 May 1917	8	1	
Spruance	Elizabeth A.	d.	PC	2 June 1917	8	1	Cypress Hill
Sprul	George Washington	d.	PA	6 Dec. 1917	6	5	also 8 Dec., 1:3
Squires	Robert Lee	m.	PC	29 Mar. 1917	5	2	
St. Clair	Carolyn Lee	m.	PD	30 May 1918	8	2	portrait
Stables	Jack	o.	SRR	10 Oct. 1917	3	1	
Stables	Joseph	o.	PC	11 Oct. 1917	3	3	
Stacey	William J.	d.	PA	23 July 1918	4	4	Cypress Hill; also 25 July, 8:1
Stacey	William J.	d.	PC	24 July 1918	8	4	Cypress Hill; also 25 July, 8:3; 26 July, 5:5
Stacey	William J.	d.	PD	25 July 1918	6	2	Petaluma
Stack	Anna E.	m.	PA	8 July 1916	8	2	
Stack	Lydia	m.	PD	25 Dec. 1917	8	3	also 27 Dec., 6:3
Stack	Lydia	m.	SRR	26 Dec. 1917	5	4	
Stack	Lydia	m.	HT	3 Jan. 1918	8	4	
Stack	Lydia D.	m.	PC	27 Dec. 1917	1	3	also 29 Dec., 8:2
Stack	Lydia Dorothy	m.	PD	13 Nov. 1917	6	1	
Stack	Lydia Dorothy	m.	PC	14 Nov. 1917	3	4	
Staff	Katherine	m.	SRR	28 May 1917	4	4	
Stafford	Alvin	m.	PD	18 Oct. 1916	6	4	
Stafford	Alvin	m.	HT	19 Oct. 1916	1	6	
Stafford	Alving	m.	SRR	18 Oct. 1916	3	3	
Stafford	Ernest	m.	SRR	3 Jan. 1917	1	3	
Stafford	Ernest	m.	PD	4 Jan. 1917	7	5	
Stafford	Geraldine V.	o.	PC	20 May 1917	6	2	
Stafford	Harry	o.	PC	20 May 1917	6	2	
Stagg	Amos A.	d.	SRR	27 Dec. 1917	5	2	
Stagg	Ann	d.	PD	3 June 1917	4	3	also 8:3
Stagg	Hester Ann	d.	SRR	2 June 1917	1	5	Guerneville; also 7:1
Stagg	Hester Ann	d.	PC	3 June 1917	5	4	
Stahl	Fredericka	d.	PD	15 May 1918	2	3	

(1) Surname	(2) Given Name	(3)	(4)	(5) Date	(6) Pg	(7) Col	(8) Comments
Staley	Clarence	m.	PD	18 Feb. 1917	5	4	
Staley	Clarence	m.	SRR	19 Feb. 1917	5	4	
Standley	Mabel E.	d.	PD	extra 9 Nov. 1918	1	4	also 10 Nov., 7:2
Standt	Albert	m.	PA	3 May 1917	5	2	
Standt	Albert	m.	PC	3 May 1917	6	3	
Standt	Albert	m.	PC	12 June 1917	8	4	
Stanger	Elizabeth	d.	HT	20 Jan. 1916	1	3	
Stanley	J. P.	d.	PC	11 Jan. 1918	8	4	
Stanley	James P.	d.	PD	11 Jan. 1918	8	1	Mt Olivet, San Mateo; also 12 Jan, 4:2; 13 Jan., 5:3; 15 Jan., 3:1
Stanley	James P.	d.	ST	11 Jan. 1918	1	3	also 18 Jan., 1:2
Stanley	John P.	p.	PA	20 Dec. 1916	4	6	
Stanley	John Preston	d.	PA	11 Jan. 1917	6	4	
Stanley	John Purvine	d.	PA	13 Dec. 1916	5	3	Cypress Hill; also 14 Dec., 4:3
Stanley	John Purvine	d.	PC	13 Dec. 1916	8	3	Cypress Hill; also 14 Dec., 3:3; 15 Dec., 3:5
Stanley	John Purvine	d.	PD	14 Dec. 1916	6	3	
Stark	Anna E.	m.	PC	9 July 1916	2	2	
Stark	Georgia	d.	SRR	12 Apr. 1916	1	5	I.O.O.F. Cemetery
Stark	Henry B.	m.	PD	23 Dec. 1917	6	4	
Stark	Henry R.	m.	SRR	22 Dec. 1917	10	6	
Starke	Agatha	m.	PA	2 Sept. 1916	4	3	
Starke	Agatha	m.	PC	2 Sept. 1916	1	2	also 3 Sept., 8:2
Starke	Agatha	m.	PD	2 Sept. 1916	1	6	
Starke	Clarence	o.	PC	4 Dec. 1917	5	4	
Starke	Earle	b.	PA	10 July 1918	2	5	also 8:5
Starkey	H.	o.	PD	18 Dec. 1918	3	1	
Starky	Alfred	m.	SRR	3 Apr. 1916	2	2	
Starling	Rose	m.	PC	12 May 1917	5	5	
Starling	Rose	m.	PD	16 May 1917	3	4	
Starling	Rose	m.	SRR	16 May 1917	5	3	
Starret	Annie	d.	PA	20 May 1918	2	2	
Starret	Enid Helen	m.	PC	19 June 1917	5	3	26 June, 5:3
Starret	Robert, Mrs.	d.	PC	21 May 1918	4	3	
Starrett	Enid	m.	PD	17 June 1917	2	6	also 27 June, 6:3
Starrett	Enid	m.	SRR	18 June 1917	2	3	also 27 June, 8:5
Starrett	Enid	m.	PA	26 June 1917	2	5	
Starrett	Enid	m.	ST	29 June 1917	8	1	
Starrett	Robert, Mrs.	d.	PD	19 May 1918	2	1	
Stateler	Frank M.	d.	PA	20 Dec. 1916	5	2	Cypress Hill; also 21 Dec., 5:7, 6:3; 22 Dec., 7:2
Stateler	Frank M.	d.	PC	21 Dec. 1916	8	3	

(1) Surname	(2) Given Name	(3)	(4)	(5) Date	(6) Pg	(7) Col	(8) Comments
Staup	Fannie	m.	PC	6 Feb. 1917	4	6	also 11 Feb., 5:3; 13 Feb., 5:4
Staup	Fannie B.	m.	PA	22 Jan. 1917	2	5	also 12 Feb., 6:1
Stedham	Albert Henry	d.	SRR	9 May 1917	10	2	also 11 May, 4:6
Steele	Ben	m.	SRR	5 May 1917	4	1	also 1 June, 1:5; 4 June, 3:2
Steele	Ben	b.	PD	20 Apr. 1918	6	1	
Steele	Ben F.	m.	PD	3 June 1917	7	1	
Steele	Ben L.	m.	SRR	1 Feb. 1917	3	5	
Steele	Cora	m.	PC	14 June 1918	5	2	also 25 June, 5:4
Steele	Cora Lovina	m.	PA	13 June 1918	4	3	also 22 June, 5:7; 24 June, 4:1
Steele	Dorothy	m.	SRR	29 May 1916	8	1	also 8 June, 1:5
Steele	Helen Marie	d.	SRR	1 June 1916	8	6	also 2 June, 8:2; 3 June, 10:3
Steele	Helen Marie	d.	PD	2 June 1916	2	2	
Steele	Jack	m.	SRR	6 Apr. 1916	2	4	
Steengrafe	Herman	o.	PD	13 Nov. 1917	5	4	
Steengrafe	Herman	o.	SRR	17 Apr. 1916	2	3	
Steengrafe	Herman	o.	PC	18 Apr. 1916	3	4	
Steengrafe	Herman S.	o.	SRR	22 June 1917	3	5	
Steengrafe	Linette	o.	PC	18 Apr. 1916	3	4	
Steengrafe	Lisette	o.	PD	13 Nov. 1917	5	4	
Steengrafe	Lizetta	o.	SRR	17 Apr. 1916	2	3	
Steengrafe	Lizette	o.	SRR	22 June 1917	3	5	
Stefanoni	Luigi	m.	PA	31 Oct. 1917	5	2	
Stefenoni	Luigi	m.	PC	2 Nov. 1917	6	5	
Steffanoi	Louis	b.	PA	6 Aug. 1918	8	5	
Stegeman	Katheryn	m.	SRR	25 May 1917	3	5	
Stegemann	Katherine	m.	PC	23 May 1917	8	2	also 24 May, 1:3
Stegemann	Katherine R.	m.	SRR	22 May 1917	4	1	
Stegemann	Kathryn	m.	PA	22 May 1917	5	2	also 23 May, 8:3
Steimbaugh	Gail	o.	PA	12 July 1917	2	4	
Steimer	Joseph	o.	PC	18 Feb. 1917	4	6	
Steimer	Joseph	o.	PA	29 Jan. 1917	4	4	
Steimer	Monica	o.	PC	18 Feb. 1917	4	6	
Steimer	Monica	o.	PA	29 Jan. 1917	4	4	
Steinbeck	Eugene H.	m.	PC	15 Aug. 1918	8	4	
Steinberg	Ella H.	m.	PC	26 July 1917	3	5	
Steinberg	Maudie Lee	m.	HT	9 Mar. 1916	1	6	
Steinberger	Lottie Mae	d.	PC	3 May 1916	3	1	also 4 May, 2:2
Steinberger	Lottie May	d.	PA	2 May 1916	5	3	also 3 May, 8:6
Steiner	Joseph	o.	PA	23 Feb. 1917	1	5	also 26 Feb., 5:7
Steiner	Josephine	m.	SIT	7 Sept. 1918	1	7	
Steiner	Josephine A.	m.	PD	5 Sept. 1918	3	3	also 8 Sept., 3:4
Steiner	Minica	o.	PA	23 Feb. 1917	1	5	also 26 Feb., 5:7

(1) Surname	(2) Given Name	(3)	(4)	(5) Date	(6) Pg	(7) Col	(8) Comments
Steingraf	Herman	o.	PA	10 Apr. 1916	1	5	
Steingraf	Lisette	o.	PA	10 Apr. 1916	1	5	
Steinmeyer	Ann I.	m.	PC	22 Apr. 1918	1	6	
Steinmeyer	Anna	m.	PD	23 Apr. 1918	6	4	
Steinweg	Ernest	b.	PC	7 July 1917	4	4	
Stella	Thelma	d.	PC	5 Jan. 1916	1	5	Cypress Hill
Stelliesch	Mr. & Mrs.	o.	SIT	3 Nov. 1917	4	7	
Stelliesch	Mr. & Mrs.	o.	SRR	6 Nov. 1917	3	3	
Stellisch	Nellie	o.	SRR	6 Aug. 1917	1	4	
Stellisch	William	o.	SRR	6 Aug. 1917	1	4	
Stenz	Mary Louise Davis & child	d.	PD	1 Dec. 1918	9	5	Woodlawn Cemetery, S. F.
Stenz	Max E.	m.	SRR	6 Oct. 1916	4	1	
Stephens	Frank B.	m.	PA	22 May 1917	8	3	
Stephens	John & son	o.	SRR	23 July 1917	1	5	also 24 July, 1:4; 25 July, 4:1
Stephens	Mae	m.	SRR	10 Jan. 1916	4	2	
Stephens	Mae	m.	PC	11 Jan. 1916	2	2	
Stephens	Mae	m.	PD	11 Jan. 1916	2	3	
Stephens	Mae	m.	PC	5 Jan. 1916	5	2	
Stephens	Mary H.	m.	PA	8 Jan. 1916	4	5	also 10 Jan., 5:6
Sternlov	E. F.	m.	SRR	4 Feb. 1916	3	3	also 8 Feb., 6:3; 20 Mar., 8:4
Sterwart	William	d.	SRR	1 June 1916	4	1	
Stetson	Mr.	m.	PD	3 Nov. 1916	6	3	
Stetson	Mr.	m.	SRR	3 Nov. 1916	5	4	
Steuart	David E.	m.	PD	5 Sept. 1918	8	3	
Steurmer	Walter	o.	SIT	9 Mar. 1918	1	6	
Stevens	Austin	m.	PD	2 Mar. 1918	2	3	
Stevens	Carrie	d.	PC	28 Dec. 1916	3	1	
Stevens	Carrie	d.	PD	29 Dec. 1916	5	5	
Stevens	Helen	m.	PD	19 June 1917	1	5	
Stevens	Helen	m.	SRR	19 June 1917	3	4	
Stevens	Kate H.	d.	PD	27 Dec. 1918	8	2	also 29 Dec., 4:2
Stevens	Marguerite	m.	HT	14 Nov. 1918	3	4	
Stevens	Marguerite	m.	PC	16 Nov. 1918	5	2	
Stevens	Martha	d.	PD	5 June 1917	7	2	
Stevens	Martha Marian	d.	SRR	4 June 1917	3	3	
Stevens	Paul	b.	PC	16 Feb. 1918	4	2	
Stevens	Paul Wesley	b.	PA	16 Feb. 1918	5	1	
Stewart	Alden	o.	PC	11 May 1918	8	3	
Stewart	Alden	o.	PC	14 Apr. 1918	1	5	
Stewart	Alden	o.	PC	8 Feb. 1918	1	4	also 12 Feb., 2:1; 15 Mar., 6:4
Stewart	Alden	o.	PC	9 Feb. 1918	8	3	
Stewart	Alice A.	d.	PD	16 May 1917	4	3	

(1) Surname	(2) Given Name	(3)	(4)	(5) Date	(6) Pg	(7) Col	(8) Comments
Stewart	Alice Atilda	d.	SRR	15 May 1917	8	1	Rural Cemetery; also 16 May, 6:3
Stewart	Bernice	m.	PA	7 June 1918	8	3	also 15 June, 3:3
Stewart	Bernice	m.	PD	8 June 1918	5	6	
Stewart	Bernice A.	m.	PC	7 June 1918	6	4	also 15 June, 3:1; 16 June, 5:3
Stewart	Charles	d.	PA	3 July 1917	4	3	
Stewart	Charlotte	d.	PD	26 Oct. 1917	2	4	
Stewart	David A.	m.	PD	11 Aug. 1918	9	5	
Stewart	Evan McK.	o.	PD	1 June 1918	2	5	
Stewart	James C.	m.	SRR	7 Sept. 1916	8	5	
Stewart	James C.	m.	PD	8 Sept. 1916	3	4	
Stewart	Lizzie F.	m.	SRR	7 Sept. 1916	8	5	
Stewart	Lizzie F.	m.	PD	8 Sept. 1916	3	4	
Stewart	William	d.	PC	2 June 1916	2	2	
Stewart	William	d.	PD	2 June 1916	8	2	
Stewart	Willie	d.	PD	15 May 1917	1	2	
Stewart	Willis, Mrs.	d.	SRR	14 May 1917	1	4	
Stice	Ivan	b.	PA	20 June 1916	4	1	
Stice	Ivan	b.	PC	21 June 1916	8	6	
Stice	Ivan	b.	PA	1 Feb. 1918	8	2	
Stice	Ivan	b.	PC	4 Feb. 1918	5	6	
Stickel	Ernest	d.	PC	11 Aug. 1918	5	2	
Sticket	Ernest	d.	SIT	10 Aug. 1918	1	1	
Stidham	Albert H.	d.	CR	11 May 1917	1	2	
Stidham	Albert Henry	d.	PD	10 May 1917	4	3	Rural Cemetery; also 6:3; 11 May, 4:3; 12 May, 2:4
Stier	Anna Mary	d.	PC	1 Dec. 1917	3	2	
Stier	Annie M.	d.	PD	1 Dec. 1917	6	4	
Stillings	Lloyd	o.	PC	24 July 1918	3	4	
Stockharm	Hugh Bruce	m.	PD	30 May 1917	6	4	
Stocking	Julia	d.	SRR	7 Feb. 1916	1	4	also 10 Feb., 5:4
Stocking	Julia A.	d.	PD	10 Feb. 1916	5	4	
Stockoff family		o.	SRR	16 May 1916	8	6	also 18 May, 8:4
Stoddard	Harry W.	d.	ST	13 May 1916	1	5	
Stoddard	Henry W.	d.	PD	10 May 1916	2	4	S. F.
Stofen	J. J.	d.	PC	22 Apr. 1917	3	2	
Stoffel	Emma	m.	PC	20 July 1916	6	4	also 26 July, 6:2
Stokes	Janet	m.	SRR	13 Nov. 1916	7	3	
Stolker	Charles	d.	PC	1 Feb. 1917	3	3	Richmond; also 3 Feb., 5:5
Stolker	Charles W.	d.	PA	31 Jan. 1917	1	4	
Stolling	Samuel W.	d.	PD	7 Apr. 1917	3	3	Bloomfield
Stollings	Samuel Ward	d.	PA	6 Apr. 1917	8	2	
Stollings	Samuel Ward	d.	PC	7 Apr. 1917	8	4	Bloomfield; also 10 Apr., 2:1

(1) Surname	(2) Given Name	(3)	(4)	(5) Date	(6) Pg	(7) Col	(8) Comments
Stone	Alfred J.	m.	PA	4 Sept. 1918	4	4	
Stone	Alfred John	m.	PC	5 Sept. 1918	4	4	
Stone	Aro Jane	d.	PC	29 Dec. 1918	8	5	also 31 Dec., 8:2
Stone	C. M.	b.	PD	21 Apr. 1917	8	2	
Stone	C. M.	b.	SRR	21 Apr. 1917	7	2	
Stone	Edward	d.	PD	12 Sept. 1916	3	4	Rural Cemetery; also 14 Sept., 3:3
Stone	Edward E.	d.	SRR	11 Sept. 1916	8	3	Rural Cemetery; also 13 Sept., 8:2
Stone	Elizabeth R.	m.	SRR	17 Aug. 1916	8	1	
Stone	Elizabeth R.	m.	PC	18 Aug. 1916	5	4	
Stone	Elizabeth R.	m.	PD	18 Aug. 1916	3	4	
Stone	Genevieve	m.	SRR	10 June 1916	11	2	also 17 June, 4:1
Stone	Gladys C.	m.	SRR	12 Nov. 1917	8	3	also 14 Nov., 4:3
Stone	Gladys C.	m.	PA	13 Nov. 1917	2	5	
Stone	Gladys C.	m.	PC	13 Nov. 1917	5	2	
Stone	Gladys C.	m.	PD	13 Nov. 1917	2	3	also 15 Nov., 8:3
Stone	Grace E.	m.	SRR	6 Dec. 1917	8	1	
Stone	Grace E.	m.	PD	7 Dec. 1917	5	6	
Stone	Helen A.	m.	PD	10 Nov. 1916	8	4	
Stone	Helen A.	m.	SRR	11 Nov. 1916	8	1	
Stone	Helen C.	m.	PA	10 Nov. 1916	7	5	
Stone	Henry Austin	d.	PA	27 Feb. 1917	4	5	Calvary Cemetery; also 1 Mar., 7:3
Stone	Henry Austin	d.	PC	28 Feb. 1917	4	3&4	Calvary Cemetery; also 1 Mar., 4:6; 2 Mar., 5:5
Stone	Henry Austin	d.	PD	28 Feb. 1917	4	2	
Stone	Marie Genevieve	m.	PC	5 Sept. 1918	4	4	
Stone	Mary Genevieve	m.	PA	4 Sept. 1918	4	4	
Stone	Ore Jane	d.	PA	28 Dec. 1918	4	2	Cypress Hill; also 30 Dec., 1:3
Stone	Stanley	o.	PD	21 Dec. 1918	6	1	
Stone	Thomas W.	d.	HT	12 Apr. 1917	8	4	
Stone	Tom B.	d.	SRR	6 Apr. 1917	6	5	
Stone	Wald	o.	HT	30 Oct. 1918	3	3	
Stone	William S.	d.	PC	11 June 1916	8	4	Cypress Hill; also 13 June, 5:5
Stone	William Searles	d.	PA	10 June 1916	4	3	Cypress Hill; also 12 June, 5:7
Stonier	Clara	d.	SIT	2 Sept. 1916	1	2	
Storch	H. W.	d.	SRR	1 Oct. 1917	8	2	
Storch	Hugo William	d.	PD	30 Sept. 1917	1	4	also 4:2; 2 Oct., 7:1
Storey	Elizabeth	m.	HT	13 June 1918	5	5	
Storey	Nancy	d.	SRR	18 July 1917	5	3	I.O.O.F. Cemetery; also 8:2; 19 July, 4:4
Storm	Theodore	d.	PC	10 Aug. 1917	3	4	

(1) Surname	(2) Given Name	(3)	(4)	(5) Date	(6) Pg	(7) Col	(8) Comments
Stornetta	L.	b.	PC	27 Dec. 1916	4	2	
Story	Nancy A.	d.	PA	19 July 1917	3	3	
Story	Nancy C.	d.	PD	18 July 1917	4	3	Odd Fellows Cemetery; also 5:1; 20 July, 8:3
Story	Nanny A.	d.	PC	19 July 1917	1	5	
Stouder	Charles	d.	PD	25 July 1916	8	3	
Stouder	Charles	d.	PC	26 July 1916	5	2	
Stouder	Charles	d.	ST	29 July 1916	1	3	
Stouder	Helen M.	m.	PD	5 Sept. 1917	7	4	
Stoup	Fannie B.	m.	PC	21 Jan. 1917	5	5	
Stradling	Nora	o.	PC	20 Dec. 1918	6	3	also 29 Dec., 8:2
Stradling	Nora	o.	PC	3 Dec. 1918	3	3	
Stradling	Nora	o.	PA	7 Nov. 1918	3	5	
Strand	Harry	m.	PA	3 Feb. 1916	8	3	
Straub	F. X. (son of)	d.	PC	20 Nov. 1918	4	3	
Straub	Frank (son of)	b&d	PC	16 Nov. 1918	5	3	
Strebel	Minnie	m.	PD	15 Oct. 1916	5	2	also 17 Oct., 3:3
Strebel	Minnie	m.	SRR	16 Oct. 1916	2	2	
Strebel	William	m.	PD	14 Sept. 1918	8	3	
Street	Thomas B.	m.	ST	1 Jan. 1916	1	1	
Streeter	Ben	b.	SIT	1 Sept. 1917	4	5	
Streeter	Benjamin E.	m.	PA	2 Oct. 1916	4	3	
Streeter	Benjamin E.	m.	PC	2 Oct. 1916	8	4	
Streeter	Benjamin E.	m.	SRR	2 Oct. 1916	8	3	
Streeter	G. W., Jr.	m.	SRR	2 July 1917	6	5	
Streeter	George W.	m.	HT	5 July 1917	4	2	
Strickler	Eno E.	d.	SRR	23 Nov. 1916	8	5	also 24 Nov., 10:2
Strickler	Eno E.	d.	PD	24 Nov. 1916	5	4	
Strickler	Eona E.	d.	ST	25 Nov. 1917	1	6	cremation
Strickler	Eona Evelyn	m.	PC	24 Nov. 1916	8	5	
Strickler	Rosa Evelyn	m.	PA	23 Nov. 1916	8	3&5	
Stridde	Carl	d.	SRR	5 Aug. 1916	1	3	also 7 Aug., 5:1; 8 Aug., 6:1
Stridde	Charles	d.	PD	6 Aug. 1916	3	4	also 9 Aug., 5;4
Strock	Emma F.	o.	SRR	4 Dec. 1916	5	5	
Strock	Emma F.	o.	PC	5 Dec. 1916	3	1	
Strock	H. M.	o.	SRR	4 Dec. 1916	5	5	
Strock	H. M.	o.	PC	5 Dec. 1916	3	1	
Strode	Clara Gerogiana	m.	PD	1 Dec. 1917	5	2	also 2 Dec., 10:6
Strong	Ben	b.	SRR	19 Dec. 1916	10	6	
Strong	William G.	d.	PD	26 May 1918	5	1	I.O.O.F. Cemetery; also 28 May, 4:2; 29 May, 7:2
Strout	Wilmar	m.	ST	6 Dec. 1918	2	3	
Strualey	Louis	m.	PC	31 Mar. 1918	1	4	also 1 Apr., 5:3; 2 Apr., 5:2
Struckmeier	Armin	d.	SRR	15 Sept. 1916	6	2	San Francisco

(1) Surname	(2) Given Name	(3)	(4)	(5) Date	(6) Pg	(7) Col	(8) Comments
Struckmeier	Armin	d.	PC	16 Sept. 1916	6	4	Mt. Olivet, S. F.
Strummer	John	d.	PD	20 Dec. 1918	8	1	
Strummer/Rummer	John	d.	PA	20 Dec. 1918	8	3	also 21 Dec., 6:5
Struve	Robert D.	d.	PA	10 Sept. 1917	7	3	Mt. Tamalpais Cemetery; also 11 Sept., 2:3
Stuart	Charles	d.	SRR	3 July 1917	8	4	
Stuart	Charles	d.	PC	4 July 1917	6	3	
Stuart	Charles	d.	PD	4 July 1917	5	3	
Stuart	Charles E.	d.	HT	5 July 1917	4	5	
Stuart	Kenneth	o.	PD	15 Mar. 1918	2	3	
Stuart	William	d.	ST	3 June 1916	1	1	
Stumbaugh	Ann	d.	PD	1 Jan. 1918	6	3	
Stumbaugh	Anna	d.	PA	3 Jan. 1918	5	6	
Stumbaugh	Annie	d.	PC	1 Jan. 1918	1	6	Sebastopol; also 2:2
Stumbaugh	Annie	d.	PA	31 Dec. 1917	5	1	
Stumbaugh	Columbus	d.	ST	1 Feb. 1918	4	4	
Stumbaugh	Gail	o.	PC	5 Feb. 1918	4	4	
Stumbaugh	Gale	o.	PA	13 Aug. 1917	4	1	
Stump	Mae	d.	PA	20 Apr. 1917	8	5	Santa Rosa; also 21 Apr., 8:5
Stump	Mary	d.	PC	20 Apr. 1917	1	3	Rural Cemetery; also 21 Apr., 3:6; 22 Apr., 5:4
Stump	May	d.	SRR	20 Apr. 1917	2	4	
Stump	May/Mae	d.	PD	20 Apr. 1917	1	6	also 22 Apr., 1:3
Stumpf	William A.	m.	PD	27 Sept. 1916	6	1	
Sturlini	Ida	d.	PD	27 Jan. 1917	6	5	
Sturlini	Ida	d.	PC	28 Jan. 1917	3	2	
Sturtevant	Robert S.	d.	PC	10 Nov. 1918	6	2	France
Sucher	Clara V.	o.	SRR	3 May 1917	8	5	
Sucher	Clara V.	o.	PD	4 May 1917	6	5	
Sucher	Clara V.	o.	SRR	30 July 1917	1	4	also 29 Sept., 10:3
Sucher	Clara V.	o.	SRR	1 Oct. 1917	1	1	
Sucher	Victor	o.	PD	4 May 1917	6	5	
Sucher	Victor E.	o.	SRR	3 May 1917	8	5	
Sucher	Victor E.	o.	SRR	30 July 1917	1	4	also 29 Sept., 10:3
Sucher	Victor E.	o.	SRR	1 Oct. 1917	1	1	
Sugker	Eleen	m.	PA	6 June 1916	5	6	
Sugker	Eleen	m.	PC	6 June 1916	5	1	
Sulham	Frank L.	d.	PC	16 June 1918	3	2	Cypress Hill; also 8:3; 18 June, 4:2
Sulham	Frank L.	d.	PA	17 June 1918	4	7	Cypress Hill
Sullivan	Catherine	o.	PA	13 Aug. 1917	4	5	
Sullivan	Catherine	o.	PA	28 Oct. 1918	5	7	
Sullivan	Cathrine	o.	PA	16 Oct. 1917	3	1	
Sullivan	Doris	m.	ST	16 Nov. 1917	1	1	

(1) Surname	(2) Given Name	(3)	(4)	(5) Date	(6) Pg	(7) Col	(8) Comments
Sullivan	Doris	m.	PD	17 Nov. 1917	4	2	
Sullivan	Doris	m.	PC	18 Nov. 1917	6	4	
Sullivan	F.	b.	PC	22 May 1916	5	2	
Sullivan	Frank	d.	PD	7 Aug. 1918	5	4	
Sullivan	J. B.	o.	PA	16 Oct. 1917	3	1	
Sullivan	James	o.	PC	14 Aug. 1917	4	6	
Sullivan	James	d.	PA	8 Aug. 1918	4	7	Cypress Hill
Sullivan	James B.	o.	SRR	16 Oct. 1917	8	6	
Sullivan	James B.	o.	PD	18 Oct. 1917	5	4	
Sullivan	James B.	o.	PA	28 Oct. 1918	5	7	
Sullivan	James H.	d.	PA	28 Apr. 1916	2	5	
Sullivan	James H.	d.	PC	28 Apr. 1916	4	5	
Sullivan	James H.	d.	SRR	28 Apr. 1916	5	4	
Sullivan	James H.	d.	SIT	29 Apr. 1916	3	5	San Francisco
Sullivan	James L.	o.	PA	13 Aug. 1917	4	5	
Sullivan	John P.	b.	PC	29 Aug. 1916	8	4	
Sullivan	Katherine	o.	PC	14 Aug. 1917	4	6	
Sullivan	Katherine	o.	PD	18 Oct. 1917	5	4	
Sullivan	Leo	m.	SRR	28 Dec. 1917	4	1	also 29 Dec., 4:2
Sullivan	Leo	m.	PD	29 Dec. 1917	3	1	
Sullivan	Marian A.	m.	PD	13 Jan. 1918	2	3	
Sullivan	Marian A.	m.	PC	15 Jan. 1918	2	2	
Sullivan	Patrick	b.	PC	28 Apr. 1918	6	5	
Sullivan	Winifred	m.	PD	23 June 1917	2	2	
Sumfleth	Henry	d.	SRR	12 July 1916	8	5	I.O.O.F. Cemeeery
Sumfleth	Henry	d.	PC	13 July 1916	1	6	Odd Fellows, Santa Rosa; also 15 July, 4:1
Sumfleth	Henry	d.	PD	13 July 1916	8	2	also 15 July, 6:4
Summ	Erna G.	m.	PC	13 July 1916	4	2	
Summ	Irma Georgia	m.	PA	12 July 1916	5	1	
Summerfield	Clara	m.	SRR	6 Mar. 1916	8	4	
Sumpfelth	H. J.	d.	PA	14 July 1916	4	1	
Surrhyne	John C.	o.	PD	9 Apr. 1918	2	4	
Surrhyne	Mary E.	o.	PD	9 Apr. 1918	2	4	
Surryhne	Barbara	m.	PD	12 Aug. 1916	8	4	
Sutherland	Elmer M.	m.	PC	18 July 1917	1	4	also 20 July, 7:4
Sutherland	Elmer M.	m.	PA	19 July 1917	7	3	
Sutherland	Elmer M.	m.	PD	19 July 1917	2	3	
Sutherland	Hannah	d.	PD	23 Sept. 1917	8	3	Cypress Lawn, San Francisco
Sutherland	Hannah	d.	SRR	24 Sept. 1917	2	4	Cypress Lawn, S. F.
Sutter	Louis	d.	PC	10 Nov. 1917	4	4	Calvary Cemetery; also 8:2; 13 Nov., 8:5
Sutter	Louis	d.	PA	9 Nov. 1917	5	4	also 12 Nov., 2:4
Sutter	Rose	m.	PD	5 May 1918	5	2	
Sutter	Rose Kempf	m.	SIT	4 May 1918	1	3	

(1) Surname	(2) Given Name	(3)	(4)	(5) Date	(6) Pg	(7) Col	(8) Comments
Sutter	William J.	o.	SIT	25 Aug. 1917	1	5	
Sutton	Ernest	m.	PD	10 Aug. 1917	3	1	
Sutton	Ernest	m.	SRR	8 Aug. 1917	6	3	
Sutton	Ernest	m.	PC	9 Aug. 1917	5	3	
Sutton	Frank	o.	PC	1 Oct. 1918	3	3	
Sutton	Will	o.	PD	11 Aug. 1917	5	4	
Swack	Edna M.	o.	PD	10 Aug. 1918	6	3	
Swack	Wayne A.	o.	PD	10 Aug. 1918	6	3	
Swain	Sarah	d.	PA	14 Apr. 1917	4	7	
Swan	Al	d.	SRR	10 Oct. 1917	4	1	
Swan	Al	d.	PD	11 Oct. 1917	6	5	
Swan	Alfred	d.	HT	11 Oct. 1917	1	3	
Swan	James	d.	PA	3 Jan. 1918	3	5	
Swan	James	d.	PD	3 Jan. 1918	5	4	
Swan	James	d.	PC	4 Jan. 1918	6	1	
Swanets	Clara Josephine	d.	PD	10 May 1918	4	2	also 8:2
Swanson	Andrew	o.	PC	19 May 1917	2	3	
Swanson	Andrew J.	o.	PD	18 May 1917	6	3	
Swanson	Andrew J.	o.	SRR	16 July 1917	8	2	
Swanson	Gertrude I.	o.	PD	18 May 1917	6	3	
Swanson	Gertrude I.	o.	PC	19 May 1917	2	3	
Swanson	Gertrude I.	o.	SRR	16 July 1917	8	2	
Swanson	Vivian B.	m.	PA	1 Mar. 1918	8	6	
Swanson	Vivien	m.	PC	7 Mar. 1918	8	2	
Swanstrom	Ernest	o.	CR	13 Apr. 1917	1	2	
Swedenborg	Axel	d.	SIT	13 July 1918	3	1	Valley Cemetery; also 4:3
Sweem	Harry	m.	PC	7 June 1917	5	2	
Sweeney	James F.	d.	PC	25 July 1918	6	2	Sebastopol
Sweeney	Mrs.	d.	ST	24 Mar. 1917	2	4	Forestville
Sweeney	Walter Thomas	m.	PC	8 Dec. 1918	1	2	
Sweeney	Walter Thomas	m.	PA	9 Dec. 1918	6	1	
Sweeney	William	d.	PA	19 Sept. 1917	7	5	Cypress Hill
Sweeney	William	d.	PC	20 Sept. 1917	1	2	
Sweet	Bryan	m.	PD	21 Dec. 1917	2	3	also 23 Dec., 5:4
Sweet	Bryan A.	m.	SRR	20 Dec. 1917	8	3	
Sweetman	Harold	d.	PA	2 Nov. 1918	4	7	France
Sweetman	Moore	d.	PC	3 Nov. 1918	5	3	France; also 10 Nov., 5:3
Sweetman	Moore	d.	ST	8 Nov. 1918	1	3	
Swift	Mary Jane	d.	SRR	7 Nov. 1917	1	4	
Swift	Mary Jane	d.	HT	8 Nov. 1917	4	3	
Swift	Mary Jane	d.	PD	8 Nov. 1917	2	3	
Swift	Mary Jane	d.	PC	9 Nov. 1917	3	4	
Swift	Robert	b.	PC	21 July 1916	8	1	
Swisher	Kathleen	m.	HT	27 July 1916	1	4	also 17 Aug., 1:5

(1) Surname	(2) Given Name	(3)	(4)	(5) Date	(6) Pg	(7) Col	(8) Comments
Swisher	Kathleen	m.	SIT	29 July 1916	1	1	also 19 Aug., 1:5
Swisher	Kathleen	m	PD	12 Aug. 1916	2	4	also 17 Aug., 8:3
Swisher	Kathleen	m.	PC	13 Aug. 1916	1	5	
Swisher	Kathleen	m.	SRR	14 Aug. 1916	5	5	
Swisher	Kathleen	m.	PA	17 Aug. 1916	4	2	
Switzer	Eugenia Wilson	d.	PC	24 June 1917	4	2	
Switzer	Eugenia Wilson	d.	SIT	30 June 1917	1	6	
Switzer	W. H.	d.	PC	10 Nov. 1916	1	2	
Switzer	William Henry	d.	SIT	11 Nov. 1916	4	4	
Swyers	George	b.	PC	26 June 1917	8	4	
Swyers	George G.	b.	PA	26 June 1917	3	1	
Sychronsky	Adolph A.	d.	PC	20 Feb. 1917	4	4	
Sychrowsky	A.	d.	PD	20 Feb. 1917	5	1	
Sychrowsky	A.	d.	SRR	20 Feb. 1917	2	3	
Sychrowsky	Adolph	d.	SIT	3 Mar. 1917	4	4	
Sylvester	Isabelle	d.	HT	14 June 1917	4	1	Oak Mound Cemetery
Sylvester	Isabelle W.	d.	SRR	9 June 1917	6	5	
Symonds	A., Mrs.	d.	PA	13 July 1918	5	3	Cypress Hill; also 15 July, 5:5
Symonds	A., Mrs.	d.	PC	14 July 1918	4	3	Cypress Hill; also 16 July, 5:1
Symonds	J. L., Mrs.	d.	PA	20 May 1916	5	1	Seattle
Symonds	William	o.	PA	6 June 1917	3	1	

T

(1) Surname	(2) Given Name	(3)	(4)	(5) Date	(6) Pg	(7) Col	(8) Comments
Taber	Garfield	d.	PA	24 Apr. 1918	5	4	
Taber	J. W.	d.	ST	1 Feb. 1918	4	4	Cypress Hill
Taber	James W.	d.	PA	29 Jan. 1918	4	7	Cypress Hill; also 30 Jan., 8:1
Taber	James W.	d.	PC	29 Jan. 1918	8	2	Cypress Hill; also 30 Jan., 6:2; 31 Jan., 8:2
Taber	James W.	d.	PD	29 Jan. 1918	8	1	
Taber	William	m.	SRR	23 Apr. 1917	8	4	
Taber	William	m.	PD	24 Apr. 1917	2	3	
Tabor	Garfield	d.	PD	30 Apr. 1918	2	3	Presidio; also 3 May, 6:2
Tabor	Garfield	d.	SIT	4 May 1918	1	7	
Tabor	Garfield	d.	PC	30 Apr. 1918	1	6	
Tabor	Henderson	d.	PD	1 Oct. 1918	4	2	Rural Cemetery; also 2 Oct., 6:5
Tabor	Henderson	d.	PD	29 Sept. 1918	6	2	
Talamantes	Pat	b.	PC	27 Apr. 1916	8	6	
Talamates	Pat	b.	PA	26 Apr. 1916	1	7	
Talbert	Ernest	m.	HT	30 Mar. 1916	2	3	
Talbot	Joseph R.	m.	SRR	23 Oct. 1917	4	4	
Talley	Hiram	d.	PA	20 Sept. 1916	1	3	
Talley	Hiram	d.	PC	20 Sept. 1916	1	3	also 23 Sept., 4:5
Talmadge	Charles V.	m.	PA	15 May 1917	5	6	
Talmadge	Charles V.	m.	PD	16 May 1917	8	3	
Talmadge	Charles V., Mrs.	d.	PD	16 July 1916	3	4	Oakland for cremation; also 16 Jul, 6:2; 18 July, 5:5
Talmadge	Charles V., Mrs.	d.	PA	15 July 1917	5	2	
Talmadge	Rowena Slusser	d.	SRR	15 July 1916	5	1	cremation; also 17 July, 1:3
Talmage	Charles V.	m.	SRR	15 May 1917	8	3	
Tamagini	Frank	d.	PC	18 Apr. 1916	1	5	Cypress Hill; also 20 Apr., 8:5; 22 Apr., 2:1
Tamagni	Frank	d.	PA	17 Apr. 1916	2	3	Cypress Hill; also 18 Apr., 5:4; 19 Apr., 4:7, 21 Apr., 8:4
Tamagni	Frank	d.	SRR	17 Apr. 1916	8	5	
Tamagni	Frank	d.	PD	22 Apr. 1916	7	1	
Tamaoka	T.	d.	SRR	27 Dec. 1916	3	4	
Tamba	Frank	d.	PA	18 June 1917	4	5	Tomales; also 20 June, 8:7

(1) Surname	(2) Given Name	(3)	(4)	(5) Date	(6) Pg	(7) Col	(8) Comments
Tamba	Frank	d.	SRR	18 June 1917	1	4	Tomales; also 19 June, 8:1
Tamba	Frank	d.	PC	19 June 1917	6	3	Tomales; also 7:3; 21 June, 5:4
Tamba	Tessie	m.	PC	16 Aug. 1917	6	2	
Tann	Charles	d.	PA	28 Nov. 1916	4	6	also 29 Nov., 8:1
Tann	Charles	d.	PC	29 Nov. 1916	5	6	Cypress Hill; also 30 Nov., 4:4
Tanner	Carl	d.	PD	24 Oct. 1918	5	2	
Tanner	Edward	o.	PD	1 Oct. 1918	6	1	
Tanner	L.	b.	ST	16 Aug. 1918	8	4	
Tanner	Ralph	o.	PC	6 Sept. 1918	5	4	
Tanner	Ralph A.	o.	PC	13 Aug. 1918	5	2	
Tanner	Ruth E.	o.	PC	13 Aug. 1918	5	2	
Tanner	Ruth Preshaw	d.	PC	6 Dec. 1918	8	2	
Taplin	William	m.	ST	22 Apr. 1916	1	2	
Tapscott	Robert M.	m.	PD	2 Sept. 1917	7	3	
Tapscott	Robert M.	m.	SRR	4 Sept. 1917	2	3	
Tapscott	Robert M.	m.	PC	5 Sept. 1917	3	3	
Tartar	Fred	d.	PD	28 Aug. 1917	5	2	Oakland
Tauboi	K.	d.	SRR	3 Jan. 1916	1	2	
Taylor	Bayard	d.	PC	6 Apr. 1916	4	1	
Taylor	Bayard	d.	PD	6 Apr. 1916	5	5	Cypress Lawn, S.F.; also 7 Apr., 6:4; 8 Apr., 6:4
Taylor	Bayard	d.	SRR	7 Apr. 1916	4	5	
Taylor	Bill	o.	PC	2 July 1916	4	3	
Taylor	Charles A.	d.	SRR	10 Nov. 1916	3	3	
Taylor	Charles Augustus	d.	SIT	11 Nov. 1916	3	3	Mountain Cemetery
Taylor	Effie	m.	ST	14 Sept. 1917	2	3	
Taylor	Effie	m.	PD	6 Sept. 1917	6	3	also 12 Sept., 3:4
Taylor	Effie J.	m.	SRR	8 Sept. 1917	1	4	also 11 Sept., 10:2
Taylor	Eleanor	m.	PC	5 Jan. 1916	3	1	
Taylor	Eme J.	m.	PA	12 Sept. 1917	4	3	
Taylor	Harry	m.	SRR	24 Apr. 1916	7	5	
Taylor	Ivy	o.	PC	22 May 1918	4	4	
Taylor	Ivy	o.	PD	23 May 1918	7	4	
Taylor	Ivy	o.	PD	18 June 1918	5	5	
Taylor	Ivy B.	o.	PA	11 July 1916	4	3	
Taylor	Ivy R.	o.	PA	20 May 1918	1	4	
Taylor	Ivy R.	o.	ST	24 May 1918	1	3	
Taylor	James	d.	PC	7 Jan. 1916	6	4	
Taylor	Janet	p.	PD	30 Apr. 1918	6	5	
Taylor	Janet/Janette	d.	PD	26 Apr. 1918	3	2	cremation; also 27 Apr., 4:2; 30 Apr., 2:5

(1) Surname	(2) Given Name	(3)	(4)	(5) Date	(6) Pg	(7) Col	(8) Comments
Taylor	Jennette	d.	ST	26 Apr. 1918	1	4	
Taylor	Jimmie	d.	SIT	8 Jan. 1916	1	4	
Taylor	Lucretia Jane	d.	PD	6 July 1918	8	4	
Taylor	Theodore	d.	SRR	28 Feb. 1916	4	3	
Taylor	Theodore	d.	PA	29 Feb. 1916	2	3	
Taylor	Theodore	o.	PC	29 Feb. 1916	4	1	
Taylor	Theodore	d.	PD	29 Feb. 1916	6	1	Sebastopol Cemetery; also 4 Mar., 3:1
Taylor	Theodore	d.	ST	4 Mar. 1916	7	4	
Taylor	W. B.	o.	PD	18 June 1918	5	5	
Taylor	W. R.	o.	PD	23 May 1918	7	4	
Taylor	William	d.	SRR	8 Mar. 1917	6	3	
Taylor	William	d.	PD	9 Mar. 1917	6	1	
Taylor	William A.	d.	PA	8 Mar. 1917	5	3	
Taylor	William Alfred	d.	PC	9 Mar. 1917	5	3	Presidio
Taylor	William D.	o.	PA	20 May 1918	1	4	
Taylor	William D.	o.	PC	22 May 1918	4	4	
Taylor	William D.	o.	ST	24 May 1918	1	3	
Taylor	William D.	o.	PA	11 July 1916	4	3	
Tedford	Bert	o.	HT	7 Feb. 1918	8	4	
Temple	Earl	b.	SRR	27 Mar. 1916	3	4	
Temple	Rosamond	m.	PD	21 May 1916	8	2	also 25 May, 5:2
Temple	Rosamond	m.	SRR	24 May 1916	1	4	
Temple	Rosamond	m.	PC	30 Apr. 1916	8	5	
Templeman	A., Mrs.	d.	PC	9 Dec. 1917	7	5	Sebastopol
Templeman	Lelia Ellen	d.	SRR	3 Dec. 1917	8	4&5	Forestville; also 5 Dec., 8:6
Templeman	Lelia Ellen	d.	PD	4 Dec. 1917	3	4	
Tennant	Edith	m.	SRR	8 Nov. 1917	8	1	
Tennant	Edith	m.	PD	9 Nov. 1917	5	3	
Tenny	Edith	m.	SRR	18 May 1917	6	5	
Tennyson	Martin	m.	PA	16 Dec. 1918	5	4	
Tennyson	Martin	m.	PC	4 Dec. 1918	8	4	
Tenter	John	d.	SRR	11 Aug. 1916	5	4	
Tenter	John Dedrich	d.	PD	11 Aug. 1916	5	4	Odd Fellows Cemetery; also 14 Aug., 1:6
Terrablini	Mr. & Mrs.	b&d	PA	16 Oct. 1916	1	6	also 5:6
Terriblini	Joseph (son of)	d.	PC	17 Oct. 1916	5	6	Tomales
Terry	Victor	d.	PD	17 Sept. 1916	8	3	Fulkerson Cemetery; 8 yrs.
Tesgnia/Teagnia/ Tiscornia	Rachael/Catherine	m.	PC	20 Apr. 1917	5	3	also 28 Apr., 6:3; 2 May, 5:4
Tevendale	Jean	m.	SRR	11 June 1917	8	3	
Thais	John Henry	d.	PC	26 June 1918	1	2	

(1) Surname	(2) Given Name	(3)	(4)	(5) Date	(6) Pg	(7) Col	(8) Comments
Thares	J. S.	b.	PD	23 May 1918	2	3	
Thayer	Albert E.	m.	PD	31 Jan. 1917	3	2	
Thayer	Albert Earnest	m.	SRR	31 Jan. 1917	7	4	
Thayer	Elizabeth	d.	SRR	18 Nov. 1916	3	2	Oak Mound Cemetery
Thayer	Elizabeth	d.	PD	19 Nov. 1916	5	3	
Thayer	Elizabeth	d.	HT	23 Nov. 1916	1	4	
Theiss	W. A.	b.	PC	27 July 1916	8	5	
Thiele	Carl	d.	SIT	17 Nov. 1917	1	6	Mountain Cemetery
Thiele	Carl Alexander	d.	PC	15 Nov. 1917	1	4	
Thiele	Carl Alexander	d	PD	15 Nov. 1917	4	2	
Thiele	Carl Alexander	d.	SRR	15 Nov. 1917	2	4	
Thies	John Henry	d.	PD	26 June 1918	5	4	
Thies	John Henry Frederck	d.	PA	26 June 1918	8	4	
Thiess	W. A.	b.	PA	28 July 1916	5	4	cremation; also 2 Aug., 5:1
Thole	William C.	m.	PD	4 June 1916	5	4	
Thole	William C.	m.	SRR	5 June 1916	5	2	also 15 June, 3:4
Thomas	Carl D.	m.	PA	27 Aug. 1917	1	4	also 2:2
Thomas	Carl D.	m.	PC	28 Aug. 1917	5	6	also 29 Aug., 8:2
Thomas	Carl D.	m.	PD	28 Aug. 1917	8	3	
Thomas	Carrie	o.	PD	9 Apr. 1918	3	1	
Thomas	Cora I.	o.	PD	16 May 1918	2	5	
Thomas	Douglas	d.	ST	26 Apr. 1918	8	4	Bloomfield
Thomas	George	d.	PA	4 Dec. 1917	4	1	
Thomas	George P.	d.	SRR	3 Dec. 1917	5	2	
Thomas	George P.	d.	PC	4 Dec. 1917	4	4	
Thomas	H. B.	b&d	PA	1 Dec. 1916	4	4	
Thomas	H. H.	b.	PA	8 Mar. 1917	5	5	
Thomas	Joseph	m.	PA	2 Feb. 1918	6	2	also 4 Feb., 5:4
Thomas	Joseph	m.	PC	3 Feb. 1918	8	3	
Thomas	Joseph	m.	PD	3 Feb. 1918	8	5	
Thomas	Leonard	o.	SIT	27 Apr. 1918	2	6	
Thomas	Louisa	d.	PC	21 Apr. 1916	2	2	
Thomas	Louisa Agnes	d.	SRR	20 Apr. 1916	5	1	Guerneville
Thomas	Lucinda Agnes	d.	PD	20 Apr. 1916	8	2	Guerneville Cemetery; also 22 Apr., 2:3
Thomas	Manuel	b.	PA	24 June 1918	5	6	
Thomas	Meta	d.	PA	24 Oct. 1918	5	1	cremation; also 25 Oct., 5:3
Thomas	Minnie	m.	SRR	15 July 1916	12	2	
Thomas	Minnie	m.	SRR	28 Aug. 1916	3	3	
Thomas	Minnie	m.	PD	29 Aug. 1916	3	3	
Thomas	Myrtle	m.	SIT	18 May 1918	1	5	

(1) Surname	(2) Given Name	(3)	(4)	(5) Date	(6) Pg	(7) Col	(8) Comments
Thomas	Robert Morris	o.	SRR	24 Sept. 1917	8	3	
Thomas	Robert Morris	d.	PD	25 Sept. 1917	8	4	
Thomas	Roger	m.	PD	5 Sept. 1918	6	2	
Thomas	Samuel	o.	PD	16 May 1918	2	5	
Thomas	Samuel	o.	PD	9 Apr. 1918	3	1	
Thomas	Vera	m.	PD	11 Apr. 1918	7	1	
Thomas	Vera	m.	HT	29 Aug. 1918	8	2	
Thomas	Vera Jewell	m.	PD	27 Aug. 1918	8	3	
Thomason	Richard	b.	SIT	6 Jan. 1917	1	6	
Thompson	Anna	m.	SRR	10 Jan. 1916	8	5	
Thompson	Anna H.	m.	HT	13 Jan. 1916	3	6	
Thompson	Bertha M.	m.	PD	21 Mar. 1916	8	2	
Thompson	C. H.	d.	PC	19 Aug. 1917	6	3	
Thompson	Catherine	m.	SRR	6 Sept. 1916	6	2	
Thompson	Catherine R.	m.	HT	7 Sept. 1916	1	4	
Thompson	Charles	m.	SRR	20 Aug. 1917	3	4	
Thompson	Charles	d.	PA	7 Nov. 1918	3	4	France
Thompson	Charles H.	m.	SRR	15 Aug. 1917	4	4	also 8:3; 17 Aug., 8:3
Thompson	Charles H.	m.	PC	21 Aug. 1917	6	1	
Thompson	Charles Henry	d.	PD	15 Aug. 1917	5	4	Odd Fellows Cemetery; also 16 Aug., 4:2; 18 Aug., 5:3
Thompson	Electa	m.	SRR	4 Dec. 1916	8	4	
Thompson	Electa	m.	PD	5 Dec. 1916	8	2	
Thompson	Fred C.	m.	SRR	17 July 1917	5	3	
Thompson	Fred C.	m.	PC	18 July 1917	5	2	
Thompson	Fred G.	m.	PD	17 July 1917	8	3	
Thompson	Hiram W.	d.	PA	18 Jan. 1917	5	3	Bloomfield; also 19 Jan., 8:4; 20 Jan., 7:4; 22 Jan., 6:2
Thompson	Hiram W.	d.	PC	19 Jan. 1917	8	3	also 20 Jan., 1:6
Thompson	Hugh S.	d.	PD	29 Oct. 1918	8	3	also 30 Oct., 7:2
Thompson	Ivetta	b.	HT	18 Jan. 1917	7	5	
Thompson	James Wilbur	o.	PC	25 Mar. 1917	4	2	adoption
Thompson	John C.	d.	PA	18 Oct. 1917	5	4	Cypress Hill; also 19 Oct., 5:3; 20 Oct., 8:5
Thompson	John C.	d.	PC	19 Oct. 1917	4	4	Cypress Hill; also 20 Oct., 3:3, 5:6; 23 Oct., 6:4
Thompson	John C.	d.	SRR	19 Oct. 1917	4	2	
Thompson	John C.	d.	PD	20 Oct. 1917	6	2	
Thompson	Joseph	m.	SRR	10 Jan. 1916	8	5	
Thompson	Joseph C.	m.	HT	13 Jan. 1916	3	6	
Thompson	K. K.	o.	PC	25 Mar. 1917	4	2	adoption

(1) Surname	(2) Given Name	(3)	(4)	(5) Date	(6) Pg	(7) Col	(8) Comments
Thompson	M., Mrs.	m.	SRR	21 Mar. 1916	5	2	
Thompson	Margaret	o.	SRR	24 Apr. 1916	1	2	
Thompson	Margaret	o.	PD	25 Apr. 1916	5	2	
Thompson	Mildred	m.	PD	8 Apr. 1917	6	1	
Thompson	Pearl	m.	SRR	3 Feb. 1917	3	5	
Thompson	R. J., Mrs.	d.	ST	12 Oct. 1917	1	5	
Thompson	Robert	o.	SRR	24 Apr. 1916	1	2	
Thompson	Robert M.	o.	PD	25 Apr. 1916	5	2	
Thompson	Sallie	d.	PD	15 Nov. 1916	2	1	
Thompson	Sallie	d.	SRR	20 Nov. 1916	8	3	
Thompson	Samuel Granville	d.	PD	6 Jan. 1918	4	2	also 5:3
Thompson	Samuel S.	m.	PD	14 June 1917	5	2	
Thompson	W. A.	d.	PC	11 Oct. 1916	6	3	
Thompson	W. A.	d.	SRR	9 Oct. 1916	3	3	home property; also 10 Oct., 2:2; 11 Oct., 7:4
Thompson	W. H.	d.	SIT	14 Oct. 1916	1	1	
Thompson	Will Arthur	m.	PD	3 June 1916	8	2	
Thompson	Will Arthur	m.	SRR	3 June 1916	5	2	
Thompson	William	d.	SRR	14 Nov. 1916	8	1	also 16 Nov., 8:3
Thompson	William	d.	PC	15 Nov. 1916	5	6	
Thompson	William	d.	PD	15 Nov. 1916	5	4	
Thompson	William A.	d.	PD	10 Oct. 1916	8	1	also 14 Oct., 6:4
Thoren	Gustav	m.	SIT	31 Aug. 1918	1	5	
Thorman	August	d.	PD	5 Feb. 1918	6	4	
Thormann	August	d.	HT	7 Feb. 1918	5	4	
Thornberg	Eula	m.	PA	28 July 1917	5	5	
Thorpe	J.	m.	PA	22 Jan. 1916	3	4	
Thorpe	J.	m.	SRR	22 Jan. 1916	10	4	
Thorpe	J.	m.	PD	23 Jan. 1916	3	3	
Thorpe	J.	m.	SIT	29 Jan. 1916	4	4	
Thorpe	J. T.	m.	PC	23 Jan. 1916	3	1	
Thorpe	J. T.	m.	HT	27 Jan. 1916	6	2	
Tibbets	Mabel	m.	SRR	24 Apr. 1916	7	5	
Tibbetts	Francis A.	m.	SRR	5 Nov. 1917	1	5	
Tice	Ruth	m.	PD	10 Aug. 1917	3	1	
Tice	Ruth	m.	SRR	8 Aug. 1917	6	3	
Tice	Ruth	m.	PC	9 Aug. 1917	5	3	
Tichenor	Leslie	d.	PC	11 July 1916	1	3	also 12 July, 4:1
Tichenor	Leslie Carroll	d.	PA	11 July 1916	1	4	also 8:7; 12 July, 4:4
Tichenor	Leslie Carroll	d.	SRR	12 July 1916	8	6	I.O.O.F. Cemetery; also 14 July, 3:5
Tighe	Genevieve	m.	PC	29 May 1917	4	1	also 1 May, 5:4
Tighe	Genevieve	m.	PA	30 Apr. 1917	5	1	
Timney	Thomas A.	m.	SRR	20 Nov. 1917	8	2	

(1) Surname	(2) Given Name	(3)	(4)	(5) Date	(6) Pg	(7) Col	(8) Comments
Tinsbaugh	Edna	o.	PC	4 Jan. 1916	1	6&7	
Tipton	W. O.	m.	PD	10 Mar. 1916	2	2	
Tobin	Ida	d.	SRR	10 Nov. 1917	7	4	also 12:3; 12 Nov., 8:4
Tobin	Ida	d.	PD	11 Nov. 1917	4	2	also 6:3; 13 Nov., 2:3
Tocchini	Dan	b.	PD	22 Aug. 1916	8	3	
Tocchini	Evelyn	d.	PD	12 Aug. 1917	8	4	
Tochini	Dan	b.	SRR	22 Aug. 1916	6	3	
Todd	Addison	m.	PD	8 Dec. 1917	8	3	also 9 Dec., 7:1
Todd	Addison	m.	PC	9 Dec. 1917	6	3	
Todd	Addison F.	m.	SRR	8 Dec. 1917	4	2	
Todd	Cora	m.	PD	24 Mar. 1917	8	2	
Todd	E. Thayer	o.	PC	10 Mar. 1918	6	4	
Todd	Judith Ann	d.	SRR	31 May 1917	1	2	Rural Cemetery; also 4:6; 2 June, 7:1; 4 June, 10:3
Todd	Judith R.	d.	PD	1 June 1917	8	3	also 2 June, 4:3
Todd	Marion E.	m.	SRR	8 Feb. 1917	4	3	
Todd	R. H.	o.	PC	21 Aug. 1917	5	5	
Todd	Raymond	m.	SRR	26 Nov. 1917	5	3	
Todd	Raymond	m.	ST	30 Nov. 1917	6	3	
Todd	Raymond	m.	PA	6 Nov. 1917	4	2	
Todd	Raymond	m.	PD	7 Nov. 1917	5	4	also 25 Nov., 9:1
Todd	Rodney A.	d.	PC	5 Feb. 1918	1	6	
Todd	Rodney A.	d.	PD	5 Feb. 1918	7	4	
Todd	Rodney A.	d.	PA	6 Feb. 1918	6	6	
Todd	Thayer	o.	PC	2 Dec. 1917	1	2	
Todd	Thayer	o.	PC	21 Aug. 1917	5	5	
Todd	W. Raymond	m.	PA	26 Nov. 1917	3	3	
Todd	W. Raymond	m.	PC	8 Nov. 1917	5	2	also 24 Nov., 1:2; 27 Nov., 6:3
Todenworth	Beatriz	m.	SIT	27 Oct. 1917	1	5	also 17 Nov., 1:7
Tognacca	A.	d.	PA	3 Jan. 1917	5	3	Calvary Cemetery; also 6 Jan., 5:3
Tognacca	A.	d.	PC	4 Jan. 1917	5	5	Calvary Cemetery; also 6 Jan., 3:6; 7 Jan., 3:4
Tognacca	A.	d.	SRR	4 Jan. 1917	7	3	
Tognassa	A.	d.	PD	4 Jan. 1917	8	1	
Tognotti	Carmille	o.	SRR	27 July 1916	3	6	
Tognotti	Guglielmo	o.	SRR	27 July 1916	3	6	
Tollifson	Iver, Mrs.	d.	SRR	11 July 1916	1	4	Rose/Rural Cemetery; also 12 July, 2:1, 3:5
Tollifson	Mrs.	d.	PD	11 July 1916	8	2	also 12 July, 8:3
Tomasetti	Otto	m.	PA	25 Aug. 1917	4	4	also 29 Aug., 2:5

(1) Surname	(2) Given Name	(3)	(4)	(5) Date	(6) Pg	(7) Col	(8) Comments
Tomasi	E.	b.	PA	9 Nov. 1917	5	3	
Tomasi	Linda	m.	PD	4 Jan. 1918	8	4	
Tomasini	A. F.	b.	PA	31 May 1918	5	6	also 8:2
Tomasini	A. F.	m.	PA	12 Sept. 1917	5	4	
Tomasini	A. F.	m.	PC	13 Sept. 1917	5	2	
Tomasini	A. F.	m.	PD	13 Sept. 1917	8	3	
Tomasini	A. F.	m.	SRR	13 Sept. 1917	3	5	
Tomasini	M. C.	b.	PA	7 Jan. 1918	4	6	
Tomblinson	Hazel	m.	SRR	17 Oct. 1917	8	1	
Tomblinson	Hazel L.	m.	PD	18 Oct. 1917	7	2	
Tombs	Logan	d.	PA	19 Mar. 1918	4	4	
Tombs	Logan	d.	PD	20 Mar. 1918	3	4	also 22 Mar., 4:2; 23 Mar., 3:3
Tomini	Bernard Ernest	o.	SRR	4 Oct. 1916	8	5	
Tompkins	Edith	d.	ST	1 Feb. 1918	2	2	
Tompkins	Edith	d.	PC	23 Jan. 1918	1	4	Cypress Hill; also 25 Jan., 6:3; 26 Jan., 8:2
Tompkins	Edith	d.	PD	24 Jan. 1918	3	3	
Tompkins	Edith Ruth	d.	PA	23 Jan. 1918	4	5	Cypress Hill; also 5:3
Tompkins	Erwin	m.	PC	3 Mar. 1917	6	5	
Tonasetti	Otto	m.	PC	27 Aug. 1917	5	4	
Tonelli	Louis	d.	SRR	27 Nov. 1916	3	4	also 28 Nov., 10:2; Calvary Cemetery
Toney	George W.	o.	PD	18 May 1917	6	3	
Toney	George W.	o.	SRR	22 May 1917	10	6	
Toney	Ora	o.	PD	18 May 1917	6	3	
Toney	Ora H.	o.	SRR	22 May 1917	10	6	
Tonini	Bernard E.	o.	PA	4 Oct. 1916	4	4	
Tonini	Bernard Ernst	o.	PC	5 Oct. 1916	1	5	
Tonini	Hattie May	o.	PA	4 Oct. 1916	4	4	
Tonini	Hattie May	o.	SRR	4 Oct. 1916	8	5	
Tonini	Hattie May	o.	PC	5 Oct. 1916	1	5	
Toombs	W. Logan	d.	PC	20 Mar. 1918	4	3	
Tope	Selina	m.	PD	3 Feb. 1918	8	5	
Topete	Mike	d.	PC	8 Feb. 1918	4	4	
Topete	Mike	d.	SIT	9 Feb. 1918	3	4	
Toplin	William, Jr.	m.	PC	19 Apr. 1916	5	3	
Toppete	Mike	p.	PA	31 July 1918	2	6	
Torliatt	Charles	m.	PC	20 Feb. 1917	2	1	
Torliatt	Charles Louis	m.	PA	17 Feb. 1917	4	4	
Torliatt	Peter	m.	PA	7 June 1918	8	3	also 15 June, 3:3
Torliatt	Peter	m.	PC	7 June 1918	6	4	also 15 June, 3:1; 16 June, 5:3
Torliatt	Peter	m.	PD	8 June 1918	5	6	
Torliatt	Peter	d.	PA	24 Jan. 1916	8	6	also 26 Jan., 7:6

(1) Surname	(2) Given Name	(3)	(4)	(5) Date	(6) Pg	(7) Col	(8) Comments
Torliatt	Peter	d.	PD	25 Jan. 1916	2	4	
Torliatt	Peter	d.	PC	27 Jan. 1916	3	3	Mt. Olive Cemetery
Torpey	Hanna	d.	PC	10 Dec. 1916	1	5	Tomales; also 12 Dec., 6:2
Torpey	Hanna	d.	ST	16 Dec. 1916	7	3	
Torpey	Hannah	d.	PD	10 Dec. 1916	7	3	also 12 Dec., 3:1
Torpey	Hannah	d.	PA	11 Dec. 1916	6	6	
Torpey	Hannah	d.	SRR	11 Dec. 1916	3	3	
Totemeier	Clinton Rae	b.	PD	14 Nov. 1918	5	2	
Totten	Arthur	o.	SRR	22 June 1917	8	3	
Totten	Marie Ida	m.	PD	18 Oct. 1916	6	4	
Totten	Marie Ida May	m.	SRR	18 Oct. 1916	3	3	
Totten	Marie May	m.	HT	19 Oct. 1916	1	6	
Totten	Rinda	m.	SRR	22 Dec. 1917	10	6	
Totten	Rinda	m.	PD	23 Dec. 1917	6	4	
Towey	Jack	m.	PC	19 Oct. 1916	8	3	
Towey	John	m.	SRR	1 Dec. 1916	7	3	
Towey	John	m.	PA	19 Oct. 1916	5	4	
Towey	John	m.	PC	2 Dec. 1916	5	4	
Towey	John	m.	SRR	22 Nov. 1916	2	1	
Towey	John	m.	PA	29 Nov. 1916	4	3	
Towey	John	m.	PD	30 Nov. 1916	8	4	
Towey	John L.	m.	PD	20 Oct. 1916	1	4	
Towey	John L.	m.	SRR	20 Oct. 1916	5	1	
Towey	John L.	b.	PA	8 Sept. 1918	5	1&4	
Towne	Helen Louise	o.	PA	29 Dec. 1917	5	7	
Towne	J. L.	o.	PC	2 Oct. 1918	2	1	
Towne	Louis C.	o.	PA	29 Dec. 1917	5	7	
Towner	Austin G.	m.	PA	15 Jan. 1918	8	5	
Townsend	Mary Ellen	d.	PD	4 Apr. 1916	4	2	I.O.O.F. Cemetery; also 7 Apr., 5:1
Townsend	Mary Ellen	d.	SRR	4 Apr. 1916	5	5	also 6 Apr., 8:5
Toy	San	d.	PA	6 Sept. 1917	8	2	
Toy	Sun	d.	SRR	6 Sept. 1917	8	3	
Toy	Sun	d.	PC	7 Sept. 1917	1	3	
Toy	Sun	d.	PD	7 Sept. 1917	7	1	
Tozer	Iva M.	m.	PC	2 Mar. 1917	5	1	
Tozer	Iva M.	m.	PD	2 Mar. 1917	8	3	
Tozier	Iva M.	m.	SRR	2 Mar. 1917	3	2	
Tozler	Iva M.	m.	PA	1 Mar. 1917	8	2	
Tracey	James G.	d.	PC	1 Apr. 1917	1	5	also 3 Apr., 5:5; 5 Apr., 4:5
Tracey	James G.	d.	PD	4 Apr. 1917	6	5	
Trachman	Helen	m.	PC	15 Feb. 1917	8	6	
Trachman	Helen	m.	PD	15 Feb. 1917	5	4	

(1) Surname	(2) Given Name	(3)	(4)	(5) Date	(6) Pg	(7) Col	(8) Comments
Trachmann	Helen	m.	SRR	14 Feb. 1917	8	1	also 17 Feb., 6:3
Tracy	Asa C.	d.	SRR	25 May 1917	4	1	
Tracy	James	d.	SRR	2 Apr. 1917	6	3	
Tracy	James G.	d.	PA	3 Apr. 1917	6	3	also 4 Apr., 8:5
Tracy	John	d.	SIT	13 July 1918	1	6	
Tracy	John A.	d.	PD	12 July 1918	5	2	
Train	E. Swift	m.	PA	20 Apr. 1917	4	3	
Trainor	James F.	d.	PA	5 Nov. 1918	1	3	Tomales
Trantner	Frances	m.	PC	5 Nov. 1916	7	3	
Traub	Herman	m.	PD	23 June 1916	3	5	
Traub	Hermann	m.	HT	22 June 1916	2	3	
Trauter	Frances	m.	PA	4 Nov. 1916	4	3	
Traversi	Josephine E.	d.	PC	11 July 1917	4	3	
Travis	Analy	o.	ST	11 Oct. 1918	5	3	
Travis	Analy	o.	PC	12 Oct. 1918	3	4	
Treanor	Mildred	m.	PD	5 June 1918	3	1	
Treanor	Mildred	m.	HT	13 June 1918	4	4	
Tremblay	Walter	m.	PD	28 Nov. 1917	6	1	also 5 Dec., 5:3
Tremblay	Walter	m.	ST	30 Nov. 1917	1	6	also 7 Dec., 1:2
Triellanes	A. M.	m.	SRR	24 June 1916	12	6	
Trine	Eulalia	d.	PD	26 Feb. 1918	8	2	
Trine	Ione	m.	SRR	4 Oct. 1916	4	3	
Triolzi	John S.	d.	CR	15 Nov. 1918	1	4	
Tripp	H. L.	d.	SRR	30 Jan. 1917	8	6	
Trondsen	Norman A.	m.	PC	27 Aug. 1917	4	3	also 28 Aug., 5:2
Trondsen	Norman L.	m.	PA	27 Aug. 1917	1	4	
Trondsen	Ruth	m.	PA	4 Apr. 1916	5	4	also 12 Apr., 5:3; 15 Apr., 4:2
Trondsen	Ruth	m.	PC	7 Apr. 1916	6	1	also 15 Apr., 4:2; 16 Apr., 5:3
Tronkcous	E. Manuel	d.	SRR	28 Nov. 1916	3	1	
Tronsden	Norman I	m.	PD	28 Aug. 1917	8	3	
Trowbridge	E. George	m.	SRR	6 Mar. 1916	5	3	
Trudgen	Isabel	m.	PD	19 Oct. 1917	7	4	
Trudgen	Isabelle	m.	SIT	20 Oct. 1917	1	7	
True	Jack	o.	PC	11 Sept. 1918	1	5	also 3 Oct., 8:4; 6 Oct. 4:3
True	John E.	o.	PA	10 Sept. 1918	5	1	
Trumbull	John	d.	PA	15 Jan. 1916	3	4	also 17 Jan., 4:3
Trumbull	John William	d.	PC	18 Jan. 1916	4	1	Cypress Hill
Trusty	John	d.	PD	24 Nov. 1918	10	1	
Tsuman	M.	d.	SRR	18 Apr. 1917	2	3	
Tuck	Thelma	o.	PC	6 Apr. 1916	1	2	portrait
Tucksen	Marie	m.	SRR	6 Mar. 1916	5	3	
Tully	Andrew J.	m.	PA	26 Aug. 1916	6	1	

(1) Surname	(2) Given Name	(3)	(4)	(5) Date	(6) Pg	(7) Col	(8) Comments
Tully	Andrew J.	m.	PD	26 Aug. 1916	6	3	
Tully	Andrew J.	m.	PC	29 Aug. 1916	4	6	
Tunri	Emma M.	m.	PC	2 June 1916	3	3	
Tunzi	Emma M.	m.	PA	1 June 1916	6	2	
Tuomey	Catherine Mulcahy	d.	PC	11 June 1918	1	3	
Tuomey	Catherine Mulcahy	d.	PD	11 June 1918	2	3	also 12 June, 2:5
Tuomey	Catherine Mulcahy	d.	ST	14 June 1918	5	3	
Turcotte	Clarence E.	d.	PD	30 Dec. 1916	6	3	
Turner	A. K.	b.	PA	2 July 1917	4	3&5	
Turner	F. F.	b.	PA	2 Apr. 1917	4	5	
Turner	F. F.	b.	SRR	3 Apr. 1917	5	2	
Turner	George	m.	ST	26 Aug. 1916	5	2	
Turner	George	m.	PC	27 Aug. 1916	6	2	
Turner	Lucille	m.	PD	2 Aug. 1916	6	2	
Turner	W. F.	b.	PC	26 Oct. 1916	5	6	
Turner	Wilbur	o.	SRR	4 Oct. 1917	5	1	also 6 Oct., 1:3; 9 Oct., 1:5; 11 Oct., 8:1
Turner	Will	b.	PA	9 Aug. 1916	1	5	also 4:5
Turner	Will F.	b.	PA	25 Oct. 1916	4	5	also 8:4
Turner	William	d.	SRR	21 Dec. 1916	3	2	
Turney	Lillian	m.	PA	4 Dec. 1917	7	4	
Turriciano	Dominick	d.	PC	26 Nov. 1918	2	1	
Tuttle	Cyrus, Mrs.	d.	PC	12 June 1918	3	3	Cypress Hill
Tuttle	Joe	b.	PA	4 Oct. 1918	4	5	
Tuttle	Joseph W.	b.	PA	1 May 1916	4	4	also 8:4
Tuttle	Margaret	d.	PA	7 Feb. 1918	5	6	Cypress Hill; paper filed after 6 Apr. 1918
Tuttle	Margaret Graham	d.	PA	5 Feb. 1918	8	5	also 6 Feb., 5:7
Tuttle	Margaret Graham	d.	PC	6 Feb. 1918	6	3	Cypress Hill; also 7 Feb., 3:6; 8 Feb., 5:3
Tuttle	Oliver M.	d.	PD	20 May 1916	8	1	Odd Fellows Cemetery
Tuttle	Oliver M.	d.	SRR	20 May 1916	7	1	also 22 May, 8:1
Twigg	James	o.	PA	19 Oct. 1916	4	6	
Twigg	Laura E.	o.	PA	19 Oct. 1916	4	6	
Twiggs	James H.	o.	PD	20 Oct. 1916	1	7	
Twiggs	Laura F.	o.	PD	20 Oct. 1916	1	7	
Twiss	Merrick Averill	o.	SRR	19 Jan. 1917	5	3	adoption
Twist	Mary	d.	PA	17 June 1916	4	1	Cypress Hill; also 19 June, 2:2
Twist	Mary	d.	PC	17 June 1916	1	4	also 20 June, 4:1

(1) Surname	(2) Given Name	(3)	(4)	(5) Date	(6) Pg	(7) Col	(8) Comments
Twitchell	Frank	d.	PC	30 Dec. 1917	8	3	
Twitchell	Frank	d.	SIT	5 Jan. 1918	3	4	
Tyler	Eliza H.	d.	PC	30 Oct. 1917	3	1	Cypress Hill; also 31 Oct., 8:2
Tyler	Ella	d.	PA	29 Oct. 1917	7	4	also 30 Oct., 5:1
Tyler	Leath Ruth	m.	PC	10 Feb. 1918	1	4	
Tyler	Leatha Ruth	m.	ST	15 Feb. 1918	1	2	
Tyler	Moses	d.	PA	5 May 1916	9	4	
Tyler	Moses	d.	PD	5 May 1916	1	7	Red Bluff
Tyler	Moses	d.	ST	6 May 1916	1	2	Red Bluff; also 13 May, 8:3
Tyler	Moses	d.	SRR	5 May 1916	4	2	
Tyrell	Harry	m.	PA	24 Dec. 1917	5	1	
Tyrell	Harry	m.	PC	25 Dec. 1917	5	2	

U & V

(1) Surname	(2) Given Name	(3)	(4)	(5) Date	(6) Pg	(7) Col	(8) Comments
Uban	George	d.	PA	21 Aug. 1917	2	3	also 23 Aug., 3:2
Uhlenberg	Katherine	m.	PA	15 Jan. 1918	5	5	
Uhlenberg	Katherine	m.	PC	16 Jan. 1918	8	4	
Uhlenberg	Katherine	m.	PD	16 Jan. 1918	6	1	
Ukena	Ben	m.	SRR	6 Mar. 1916	8	4	
Umino	G.	d.	PD	12 May 1918	6	1	
Umino	G.	d.	PA	13 May 1918	7	3	
Underhill	Ada	d.	PD	19 Jan. 1918	6	2	Willits
Underhill	Hazel	m.	PD	4 June 1918	2	1	also 7 June, 8:5; 8 June, 5:7
Unger	Carl	b.	PA	5 July 1916	8	6	
Unger	Matilda	d.	PA	25 Oct. 1918	4	5	also 26 Oct., 1:7, 5:5; 28 Oct., 4:3
Unger	Matilda	d.	PC	26 Oct. 1918	5	4	also 27 Oct., 4:4; 29 Oct., 5:4
Unti	Lorenzo	d.	PC	1 Sept. 1916	8	2	
Unti	Lorenzo	d.	PD	1 Sept. 1916	3	2	
Unti	Lorenzo	d.	SRR	31 Aug. 1916	8	1	
Upson	Florence M.	m.	PD	28 June 1917	7	4	
Upson	Merritt	m.	SRR	10 Jan. 1916	8	5	
Upson	Merritt Henry	m.	HT	13 Jan. 1916	3	6	
Upton	Eudora	d.	PA	20 June 1916	8	6	also 21 June, 6:5
Upton	Eudora	d.	PC	20 June 1916	5	6	Rural Cemetery; also 21 June, 1:5; 22 June, 4:1
Upton	Eudora	d.	SRR	20 June 1916	4	3	also 21 June, 8:6; 24 June, 6:3
Upton	Eudora	p.	SRR	24 June 1916	7	1	
Upton	Eudora	p.	PC	25 June 1916	8	3	
Upton	Eudora	d.	PA	6 July 1916	10	7	also 7 July, 7:3
Upton	Eudora	d.	SRR	7 July 1916	5	2	
Upton	Eudora Hardin	d.	PD	20 June 1916	2	4	Santa Rosa Cemetery; also 21 June, 5:3, 2:3; 22 June 3:1
Upton	Eudora Hardin	d.	PD	7 July 1916	8	4	
Upton	Will	d.	PD	22 June 1918	4	2	also 8:1; 23 June, 2:3; 25 June, 3:3
Upton	Will	p.	PD	25 June 1918	5	4	
Upton	Will H., Mrs.	p.	PC	7 July 1916	4	1	
Urban	George W.	d.	SRR	21 Aug. 1917	8	5	also 24 Aug., 8:3
Urban	George W.	d.	PD	22 Aug. 1917	6	5	also 25 Aug., 6:4
Urvan	C. W.	d.	PC	23 Aug. 1917	4	3	
Utley	Frederick	d.	PC	30 Oct. 1918	5	1	also 8:4; 31 Oct., 4:1; 2 Nov., 4:3

(1) Surname	(2) Given Name	(3)	(4)	(5) Date	(6) Pg	(7) Col	(8) Comments
Uttley	Frederick V.	d.	PA	29 Oct. 1918	4	1	Cypress Hill; also 30 Oct., 4:2&7; 1 Nov., 8:6
Uttley	Frederick V.	d.	PD	30 Oct. 1918	3	3	
Valente	D.	d.	PC	9 Aug. 1917	1	3	
Valente	D.	d.	PD	9 Aug. 1917	5	1&5	also 10 Aug., 6:3
Valente	Domenico	d.	SIT	11 Aug. 1917	1	4	Mountain Cemetery
Valin	Frank (child of)	d.	PC	30 July 1918	4	2	Calvary Cemetery
Vallandigham	Hazel	d.	PD	29 June 1918	5	3	Bloomfield; also 30 June, 4:2
Vallandingham	Hazel Dodge	d.	PC	30 June 1918	5	4	
Vallandingham	Robert, Mrs.	d.	PD	2 July 1918	1	5	
Vallejo	Martha B.	d.	SIT	17 Nov. 1917	4	2	
Vallerga	John	d.	SRR	11 Feb. 1916	8	5	also 15 Feb., 2:3
Vallier	Joseph B.	m.	PA	15 Jan. 1918	5	6	
Vallindigham	Hazel	d.	PA	29 June 1918	4	3	Bloomfield
Valverde	Frank	m.	SRR	8 Nov. 1916	3	4	
Van Hofen	Caari	m.	PD	30 Dec. 1917	7	2	
Van Pelt	Roy	m.	PD	28 Sept. 1916	6	4	
Van Pelt	Roy	m.	SRR	28 Sept. 1916	5	4	
Van Wormer	Charlotte	m.	SRR	31 May 1916	8	1	also 3 June, 4:1
VanArx	Harry	m.	PA	28 Mar. 1916	5	2	
VanBebber	James A.	d.	PA	13 Dec. 1918	8	3	Cypress Hill; also 14 Dec., 4:3, 6:3
VanBebber	James Wesley	d.	PC	13 Dec. 1918	8	4	also 15 Dec., 4:4
Vanoli	Frank	o.	SRR	18 Sept. 1917	6	2	
Vanolini	Sylvia	b.	PD	20 Aug. 1916	2	3	
VanWinkle	Arthur M.	m.	PD	23 Nov. 1918	1	5	
VanWormer	Charlotte	m.	PA	2 June 1916	2	4	
VanWormer	Charlotte	m.	PD	3 June 1916	5	3	also 4 June, 8:3
VanWyck	A.	d.	PC	20 Dec. 1916	1	5	New York
VanWyck	A.	d.	PD	21 Dec. 1916	5	5	
VanWyck	Abram	d.	PA	20 Dec. 1916	8	3	New York; also 21 Dec., 5:6; 22 Dec., 8:4
Vara	Madame	m.	SIT	6 May 1916	4	5	
Varner	Phil	o.	PD	27 Feb. 1918	5	4	portrait
Varner	Philip	o.	PA	27 Feb. 1918	7	3	portrait
Vascaressa	Ernest V.	o.	PD	23 July 1918	2	4	
Vascaressa	May H.	o.	PD	23 July 1918	2	4	
Vasqueiro	Juan (son of)	d.	SRR	16 Oct. 1917	4	1	
Vaughan	Benjamin W.	m.	PC	5 Feb. 1918	5	4	
Vaughan	Eva	d.	HT	27 June 1918	1	5	
Vaughan	Jessie	m.	PC	15 June 1916	3	1	
Vaughan	Miller	o.	PA	19 Jan. 1918	6	5	
Vaughan	Miller	o.	PD	19 Jan. 1918	3	5	also 20 Jan., 8:3
Vaughan	Miller	o.	ST	25 Jan. 1918	1	5	

(1) Surname	(2) Given Name	(3)	(4)	(5) Date	(6) Pg	(7) Col	(8) Comments
Vaughan	Spruce C.	d.	PD	21 Dec. 1918	6	1	
Vaughan	William	m.	PC	21 June 1916	3	4	
Vaughan	William	m.	SRR	22 June 1916	5	5	
Veale	Flora	d.	PA	5 Nov. 1917	6	3	Cypress Hill; also 6 Nov., 4:6, 6:4
Veale	Flora Walford	d.	PC	6 Nov. 1917	1	2	Cypress Hill; also 8:2; 7 Nov., 5:6
Veale	T. F.	d.	PA	27 Apr. 1916	4	2	
Vedell	Signe	m.	SRR	10 Feb. 1917	6	6	
Veeder	Eliza	d.	ST	1 Jan. 1916	1	5	
Vella	Joseph	m.	SIT	4 May 1918	1	3	
Vella	Joseph	m.	PD	5 May 1918	5	2	
Vellutini	George	m.	HT	5 Dec. 1918	1	2	
Vencigperra	P.	b.	SRR	29 Oct. 1917	3	4	
Venera	Lillian E.	m.	PC	6 May 1916	2	1	
Venezia	John	o.	PC	14 Nov. 1916	6	5	
Venezia	John	o.	PC	16 Jan. 1917	2	3	
Venezia	John	o.	PA	17 Oct. 1916	5	6	
Venezia	John	o.	PC	18 Oct. 1916	1	6	
Venezia	John	o.	SRR	3 Apr. 1917	5	3	also 4 Apr., 8:3; 9 Apr., 5:5
Venezia	John	o.	PA	4 Apr. 1917	5	2	
Venezia	John	o.	PC	5 Apr. 1917	4	1	
Venezia	John	o.	PD	5 Apr. 1917	2	3	
Venezia	Mary	o.	PC	14 Nov. 1916	6	5	
Venezia	Mary	o.	PC	16 Jan. 1917	2	3	
Venezia	Mary	o.	PA	17 Oct. 1916	5	6	
Venezia	Mary	o.	PC	18 Oct. 1916	1	6	
Venezia	Mary	o.	SRR	3 Apr. 1917	5	3	also 4 Apr., 8:3; 9 Apr., 5:5
Venezia	Mary	o.	PA	4 Apr. 1917	5	2	
Venezia	Mary	m.	PC	4 Dec. 1918	5	3	
Venezia	Mary	o.	PC	5 Apr. 1917	4	1	
Venezia	Mary	o.	PD	5 Apr. 1917	2	3	
Venton	Laura	d.	SRR	1 Mar. 1916	5	2	Eureka, NV
Vera	Madame	m.	SRR	8 May 1916	5	1	
Vestal	Lena	m.	PC	10 Nov. 1917	3	5	
Vestal	Lena	m.	PD	10 Nov. 1917	7	2	
Vestal	Lena	m.	SRR	9 Nov. 1917	8	2	
Vicari	Lillie E.	m.	PC	18 July 1917	1	4	also 20 July, 7:4
Vicari	Lillie E.	m.	PD	19 July 1917	2	3	
Vicari/Vicary	Emilia	d.	PD	30 Jan. 1916	5	4	Fulton Cemetery; also 10:2
Vicary	Emilia	d.	SRR	29 Jan. 1916	5	3	Fulton
Vicary	J. G., Mrs.	d.	HT	3 Feb. 1917	5	2	
Vicary	J. G., Mrs.	d.	PA	31 Jan. 1916	7	6	Fulton

(1) Surname	(2) Given Name	(3)	(4)	(5) Date	(6) Pg	(7) Col	(8) Comments
Vier	Clara	m.	SRR	1 Nov. 1917	4	1	
Vier	Clara	m.	PD	2 Nov. 1917	2	3	
Vier	Clara	m.	ST	2 Nov. 1917	4	3	
Vier	Clara Ellen	m.	PC	28 Oct. 1917	8	5	also 2 Nov., 1:2
Vier	George	m.	PC	11 July 1918	6	5	
Vier	W. J.	b.	PC	24 Nov. 1918	6	5	
Viera	William J.	b.	PD	15 Nov. 1918	4	2	
Vietheer	Clarence	d.	PA	10 July 1916	8	5	
Vietheer	Clarence	d.	PC	12 July 1916	5	4	Cypress Hill; also 13 July, 2:1
Viglioni	C.	b.	PC	16 Apr. 1916	8	4	
Vinal	Alice	m.	PA	3 Feb. 1916	8	3	
Vinal	John T., Jr.	d.	PA	21 June 1916	6	1	
Vincent	Reginal	b.	PC	7 Nov. 1917	4	2	
Violetti	Antonio	m.	PD	3 Apr. 1917	8	2	
Violetti	Joseph	o.	PD	20 June 1918	3	5	
Vitale	Charles E.	m.	PD	10 Feb. 1918	7	1	
Vitas	Frank	d.	PA	3 Jan. 1918	5	4	Calvary Cemetery; also 7 Jan., 5:4
Vitas	Frank	d.	PC	3 Jan. 1918	8	4	Calvary Cemetery; also 4 Jan., 8:3; 6 Jan., 8:6; 8 Jan., 5:3
Vito	Mapranajo	m.	PD	15 Feb. 1917	8	3	
Vivari	Lillie	m.	PA	19 July 1917	7	3	
Vivienne	Miss	m.	HT	28 June 1917	1	3	
Vodon	Fred	o.	CR	18 Oct. 1918	1	4	
Voeille	George	d.	PC	7 Aug. 1918	1	5	
Vogel	Charles A.	m.	SRR	31 July 1917	7	4	
Vogel	Olga T.	m.	PC	14 Aug. 1917	5	1	
Vogell	Olga T.	m.	PA	14 Aug. 1917	5	2	
Vogense/Vonsen	George (son of)	b&d	PC	2 Oct. 1918	5	4	also 8:4
Vogensen	Christine M.	d.	PC	6 July 1918	2	1	cremation; also 6:5; 7 July, 6:5; 9 July, 5:4
Vogensen	Christine Marie	d.	PA	5 July 1918	4	4	cremation; also 5:3; 6 July, 5:3; 8 July, 3:4
Vogensen	George	m.	PA	1 Nov. 1917	5	2	
Vogensen	George	m.	PC	1 Nov. 1917	3	4	also 25 Nov., 5:3
Vogensen	George	m.	PA	26 Nov. 1917	5	5	
Vogesen	George (son of)	b&d	PA	30 Sept. 1918	4	7	
Vogt	George	m.	SRR	12 June 1916	1	5	
Voilers	William H.	m.	PD	16 Mar. 1916	3	4	
Voland	Albert	d.	PD	23 July 1918	6	1	
Voland	Albert E.	d.	PA	22 July 1918	5	1	also 24 July, 4:5
Voland	Alebert	d.	PC	23 July 1918	1	2	
Volkerts	Fred	m.	PC	15 Dec. 1917	8	3	also 16 Dec., 5:3
Volkerts	Fred	b.	PA	18 Oct. 1918	1	7	

(1) Surname	(2) Given Name	(3)	(4)	(5) Date	(6) Pg	(7) Col	(8) Comments
Volkerts	Fred Lawrence	m.	PA	15 Dec. 1917	4	3	
Volkerts	Matilda	m.	PA	26 Nov. 1917	4	7	
Volkerts	Matilda	m.	PC	27 Nov. 1917	3	3	
Volkerts	Matilda Christina	m.	PC	15 Dec. 1917	5	4	
Volpe	John	d.	HT	7 Nov. 1916	4	5	
Volquardsen	Leland	o.	SIT	6 Jan. 1917	1	2	also 14 Jan., 1:4; 19 Jan., 1918, 1:5
Volquardson	Leland	m.	SIT	24 Aug. 1918	1	1	
Volquardson	Leland	m.	PD	25 Aug. 1918	7	4	
Volquardson	Leland	m.	PC	27 Aug. 1918	5	2	
Volz	Fred W.	o.	PC	6 Nov. 1917	5	1	
Volz	Frederick W.	o.	PD	21 Aug. 1917	3	4	
Volz	Frederick W.	o.	PC	22 Aug. 1917	3	4	
Volz	Mary	o.	PD	21 Aug. 1917	3	4	
Volz	Mary	o.	PC	22 Aug. 1917	3	4	
Volz	Mary	o.	PC	6 Nov. 1917	5	1	
Von Arx	Emil	m.	PD	13 Jan. 1918	2	3	
Von Grafen	Clara	m.	PD	21 Nov. 1916	5	1	
VonAndel	Mabel Gray	d.	SRR	19 Sept. 1916	3	5	
VonArx	Emil J.	m.	PC	15 Jan. 1918	2	2	
VonBerg	Rachel F.	o.	SRR	19 Mar. 1917	4	3	
VonBerg	Rachel F.	o.	PD	20 Mar. 1917	3	2	
VonBerg	William J.	o.	SRR	19 Mar. 1917	4	3	
VonBerg	William J.	o.	PD	20 Mar. 1917	3	2	
Vonsen	John	d.	PC	20 July 1917	1	5	also 24 July, 8:3
Vonsen	John	d.	SRR	20 July 1917	4	3	
Vonsen	John	d.	PD	21 July 1917	6	3	
Vonson	John	d.	PA	20 July 1917	4	1	
Vossar	Silas D.	d.	PC	16 Dec. 1917	8	4	
Vought	Agnes	m.	SRR	9 July 1917	7	4	
Vought	Agnes	m.	HT	12 July 1917	4	5	
Vringenberg	Henry	b.	PC	15 Mar. 1918	6	3	
Vuori	Franz	b.	PC	6 May 1917	5	5	

W

(1) Surname	(2) Given Name	(3)	(4)	(5) Date	(6) Pg	(7) Col	(8) Comments
Wada	Ono	d.	PA	31 May 1918	5	3	
Wade	Bernice	m.	PD	29 June 1916	6	3	
Wade	Bernice	m.	PD	2 July 1916	2	2	
Wade	Frederick	b.	PA	24 Jan. 1918	8	5	
Wade	Frederick	b.	PC	25 Jan. 1918	5	4	
Wadsworth	Alice	m.	ST	11 Mar. 1916	1	5	
Wadsworth	Alice	m.	ST	18 Mar. 1916	7	3	
Wadsworth	Alice	m.	SRR	2 Feb. 1916	7	3	also 6 Mar., 1:2; 13 Mar., 8:3
Wadsworth	Alice	m.	PA	3 Feb. 1916	3	6	
Wadsworth	Helen Octavia	m.	SRR	10 Apr. 1916	1	4	
Wadsworth	Helen Octavia	m.	PC	11 Apr. 1916	4	3	
Wadsworth	Helen Octavia	m.	ST	15 Apr. 1916	1	2	also 22 Apr., 1:1
Wadsworth	Helen Octavia	m.	PD	18 Apr. 1916	3	1	
Wagers	Dallas	m.	PD	1 Sept. 1916	3	3	
Wagers	Ealias	m.	SRR	25 Aug. 1916	6	1	also 31 Aug., 6:1
Wagers	Marie	m.	HT	14 Nov. 1918	8	2	also 5 Dec., 1:2
Wagers	Marie	m.	PD	30 Nov. 1918	7	2	
Wagers	Mr. & Mrs.	o.	SRR	13 Mar. 1916	8	6	
Wagers	Owen Dallas	m.	HT	31 Aug. 1916	1	6	
Waggoner	Harry	d.	PA	24 Aug. 1916	4	7	
Waggoner	Harry	d.	PD	24 Aug. 1916	3	2	also 25 Aug., 8:6
Waggoner	Harry	d.	PC	25 Aug. 1916	3	4	
Wagner	Albert	d.	PA	8 Feb. 1917	5	3	Liberty Cemetery; also 9 Feb., 5:4, 7:3; 12 Feb., 6:5
Wagner	Albert	d.	SRR	8 Feb. 1917	5	2	
Wagner	Albert	d.	PC	9 Feb. 1917	1	3	Liberty Cemetery; also 13 Feb., 4:4
Wagner	Ella	m.	PC	12 June 1917	2	2	
Wagner	Ella	m.	PA	13 June 1917	5	1	
Wagner	Ella	m.	SRR	14 June 1917	6	4	
Wagner	Funke, Mrs.	d.	PC	20 May 1917	1	5	
Wagner	Jessie	m.	PD	15 Feb. 1916	5	3	
Wagner	Joseph	b.	ST	12 Feb. 1916	5	4	also 8:3
Wagner	Martha	m.	PC	6 Oct. 1916	8	5	
Wagner	Roy	b.	PA	4 Oct. 1916	1	4	also 5:5
Wagner	Rudolph	o.	SIT	11 Aug. 1917	1	1	
Wagner	Rudolph	m.	SIT	30 Mar. 1918	1	6	
Wagner	Rudolph	m.	PC	4 Apr. 1918	3	3	
Wagner	Theodore	d.	PD	26 July 1916	5	1	also 27 July, 6:5; 28 July, 8:3; 29 July, 3:4

(1) Surname	(2) Given Name	(3)	(4)	(5) Date	(6) Pg	(7) Col	(8) Comments
Wagner	Theodore	d.	SRR	26 July 1916	5	1	Oakland; also 27 July, 8:3; 28 July 8:4
Wagner	Theodore	d.	PA	27 July 1916	2	5	
Wagner	Theodore	d.	PC	27 July 1916	6	2	
Wagner	Theodore	d.	SIT	29 July 1916	1	4	
Wagnin	Hamil	m.	PD	28 Dec. 1918	8	3	
Wagnon	Hamil	o.	SIT	28 Apr. 1917	2	5	
Wagnon	Hamil	m.	SIT	28 Dec. 1918	1	3	
Wagoner	Harry	d.	SRR	24 Aug. 1916	5	3	
Waite	Edgar A.	m.	SRR	31 May 1917	4	1	
Waite	Rolla	b.	PA	15 July 1917	8	3	
Wakeland	Elden	d.	SRR	14 Jan. 1916	4	5	
Wakeland	Elden	d.	PD	15 Jan. 1916	2	2	
Walbridge	Charles	o.	CR	8 June 1917	1	4	
Walce	John	m.	SRR	13 Sept. 1916	8	2	also 18 Sept., 2:4
Walce	John	m.	PD	17 Sept. 1916	8	3	
Walce	John	m.	PC	19 Sept. 1916	8	4	
Walce	John J.	m.	SRR	7 Aug. 1916	5	1	
Walce	John J.	m.	PC	8 Aug. 1916	4	2	
Walce	Pauline	m.	SRR	20 Apr. 1916	4	3	
Waldron	Wesley W.	m.	PD	9 Dec. 1917	6	1	also 11 Dec., 6:5
Waldrop	Juanita	m.	SRR	23 Sept. 1916	8	3	
Walgamott	Frank	o.	SRR	16 June 1916	6	5	
Walgamott	Harriet	o.	SRR	16 June 1916	6	5	
Walgren	Cora	d.	PA	8 Jan. 1917	6	5	also 9 Jan., 3:1; 11 Jan., 2:3
Walgren	Cora B.	d.	PC	9 Jan. 1917	5	2	Cypress Hill; also 8:4; 12 Jan., 4:5
Walk	Ed G.	d.	PD	18 Jan. 1916	8	2	
Walk	Edward G.	d.	SRR	14 Jan. 1916	4	3	also 17 Jan., 8:3
Walker	Alfred	m.	PA	8 June 1916	6	2	
Walker	Alfred	m.	PC	8 June 1916	1	5	
Walker	Alfred	m.	SRR	8 June 1916	5	2	
Walker	Alice	o.	SRR	24 Apr. 1916	1	2	
Walker	Alice	o.	PD	25 Apr. 1916	5	2	
Walker	Alice Burris	d.	PC	23 Sept. 1916	5	6	
Walker	Alice Y.	o.	HT	6 Jan. 1916	3	3	
Walker	Ancil	o.	PD	12 July 1918	3	3	
Walker	B. K.	d.	SRR	19 Jan. 1917	2	3	
Walker	Benjamin K.	d.	PD	19 Jan. 1917	6	3	
Walker	Carroll	o.	HT	5 Dec. 1918	1	3	
Walker	Charles	d.	SRR	26 Apr. 1917	5	1	
Walker	Charles A.	o.	PD	23 July 1918	2	4	
Walker	Charles Arthur	o.	PA	23 July 1918	2	7	
Walker	Douglas	m.	PD	1 Jan. 1918	3	4	

(1) Surname	(2) Given Name	(3)	(4)	(5) Date	(6) Pg	(7) Col	(8) Comments
Walker	Eleanor	m.	ST	1 Apr. 1916	1	2	
Walker	Eleanor	m.	PD	26 Mar. 1916	1	2	
Walker	Eleanor	m.	PA	27 Mar. 1916	2	6	
Walker	Eleanor	m.	SRR	27 Mar. 1916	3	2	
Walker	Eleanor	m.	PC	28 Mar. 1916	2	1	
Walker	Hazel L.	m.	PD	27 June 1916	7	5	
Walker	Helen	m.	SRR	3 Aug. 1916	2	6	also 7 Aug., 7:3
Walker	Henry	d.	PC	27 Apr. 1917	1	3	
Walker	Herman	o.	SRR	24 Apr. 1916	1	2	
Walker	Herman	o.	PD	25 Apr. 1916	5	2	
Walker	Herman P.	o.	HT	6 Jan. 1916	3	3	
Walker	John, Mrs.	d.	SRR	9 May 1916	5	5	
Walker	Lena May	o.	PA	23 July 1918	2	7	
Walker	Lena May	o.	PD	23 July 1918	2	4	
Walker	Mary	d.	HT	16 Mar. 1916	1	5	
Walker	William Albert	d.	PA	19 Sept. 1917	3	3	Cypress Hill; also 20 Sept., 8:7
Walker	William Albert	d.	PC	19 Sept. 1917	1	5	Cypress Hill; also 20 Sept., 3:2; 21 Sept., 5:3
Walker	William Albert	d.	PD	23 Sept. 1917	7	4	
Walker	William C.	m.	SRR	29 Mar. 1917	3	3	
Wallace	Delia	d.	PC	8 Sept. 1918	4	3	Bloomfield
Wallace	Delia	d.	PD	8 Sept. 1918	4	2	Bloomfield; also 5:3
Wallace	Delia	d.	PA	9 Sept. 1918	4	4	Bloomfield
Wallace	Florence May	m.	SRR	28 Dec. 1916	3	1	
Wallace	John R.	m.	PD	28 Sept. 1917	7	2	
Wallace	William	d.	PD	26 Feb. 1918	2	2	
Wallerson	Julius Axsel	d.	PC	2 July 1918	8	4	
Walls	Burne, Mrs.	d.	SIT	22 July 1916	1	7	
Walls	Burns, Mrs.	d.	PC	19 July 1916	1	3	cremation; also 20 July, 4:3; 21 July, 5:2
Walls	D. B., Mrs.	d.	SRR	19 July 1916	5	3	
Walls	David Burns	m.	PA	10 Sept. 1917	6	1	
Walls	David Burns	m.	PC	8 Sept. 1917	1	4	also 12 Sept., 5:4
Walls	David Burns	m.	PD	9 Sept. 1917	8	3	
Walls	Irene	d.	PA	19 July 1916	3	3	cremation; also 20 July, 5:4
Walsh	Jack	d.	HT	27 June 1918	7	2	
Walsh	John	o.	SRR	28 Feb. 1916	1	3	
Walsh	Rose	m.	SRR	21 May 1917	1	5	
Walsh	Rose	m.	PD	22 May 1917	7	3	
Walsh	Rose	m.	PA	23 May 1917	2	6	
Walsh	Rose	m.	PC	23 May 1917	4	2	
Walsh	Rose	m.	ST	25 May 1917	2	3	
Walsh	Rose	o.	SRR	28 Feb. 1916	1	3	

(1) Surname	(2) Given Name	(3)	(4)	(5) Date	(6) Pg	(7) Col	(8) Comments
Walt	Benjamin	b.	SRR	24 Feb. 1916	5	5	
Walters	Aubrey	m.	PD	12 June 1917	8	1	
Walters	Aubrey	m.	SRR	12 June 1917	8	3	
Walters	Martin	m.	PA	22 Jan. 1916	4	3	
Walters	Martin	m.	PA	28 Feb. 1916	3	4	
Walters	Martin Edwin	m.	PC	29 Feb. 1916	3	1	
Walters	Marty	b.	PA	27 May 1918	4	6	also 5:5
Walters	Mary	d.	PA	10 Aug. 1916	5	4	cremation; also 11 Aug., 4:4
Walters	Mary	d.	SRR	11 Aug. 1916	5	3	
Walters	William	m.	SRR	3 Oct. 1916	6	2	
Walters	William S.	m.	PD	1 Oct. 1916	6	4	
Walters	William S.	m.	HT	5 Oct. 1916	1	3	
Waltz	Harold	m.	PD	10 Nov. 1916	2	1	
Waltz	Harold S.	m.	PC	11 Nov. 1916	5	1	
Waltz	Henry, Jr.	o.	SIT	23 Mar. 1918	1	2	
Wampley	William	m.	PD	2 Aug. 1916	6	2	
Wann	Emerson R.	m.	HT	17 Jan. 1918	1	2	
Ward	Arthur E., Mrs.	d.	PD	2 Dec. 1916	6	5	
Ward	Captain	d.	SIT	25 May 1918	4	6	cremation
Ward	Edward	d	SRR	8 May 1917	1	2	also 9 May, 4:3
Ward	Edward	d.	PD	9 May 1917	1	2	
Ward	Francis Moore	d.	PD	22 May 1918	4	2	cremation; also 8:4; 24 May, 7:1
Ward	James	d.	PD	26 Aug. 1917	7	6	
Ward	James A.	d.	PA	25 Aug. 1917	4	3	Oak Mound Cemetery
Ward	James A.	d.	SRR	27 Aug. 1917	1	4	Oak Mound Cemetery
Ward	John	d.	SRR	10 May 1917	10	5	
Ward	John	d.	PD	11 May 1917	8	4	Fulton
Ward	John E.	d.	PA	8 May 1917	1	5	also 9 May, 1:5
Ward	Laura	d.	ST	11 Jan. 1918	1	1	
Ward	Laura	d.	PA	7 Jan. 1918	5	3	
Ward	Laura	d.	PC	8 Jan. 1918	8	5	
Ward	Laura	d.	PD	8 Jan. 1918	5	6	
Ward	Lelah B.	d.	SRR	1 Dec. 1916	3	3	
Ward	Thomas A.	d.	SRR	30 June 1917	6	3	also 10:1
Ward	Thomas Alfred	d.	HT	5 July 1917	2	3	
Ward	William W.	m.	SIT	24 Mar. 1916	1	7	
Wardell	Helen	d.	PD	5 May 1916	8	1	
Warden	Mr.	m.	HT	27 Sept. 1917	4	3	
Warden	Robert	m.	PC	12 June 1917	2	2	
Warden	Robert A.	m.	PA	13 June 1917	5	1	
Warden	Robert A.	m.	SRR	14 June 1917	6	4	
Ware	Charles M.	o.	PD	4 July 1918	2	3	
Ware	Charles M.	o.	PD	23 Oct. 1918	5	3	

(1) Surname	(2) Given Name	(3)	(4)	(5) Date	(6) Pg	(7) Col	(8) Comments
Ware	Grace	o.	PD	4 July 1918	2	3	
Ware	Grace E.	o.	PD	23 Oct. 1918	5	3	
Ware	J. B.	o.	HT	3 Oct. 1918	6	4	
Ware	Mabel	m.	PD	2 Aug. 1916	5	6	also 4 Aug., 6:3
Ware	Mabel	m.	SRR	3 Aug. 1916	8	5	
Ware	Mabel	m.	PA	4 Aug. 1916	2	4	
Ware	Maggie	d.	HT	18 Oct. 1917	2	3	
Ware	Wallace	m.	SRR	26 Mar. 1917	5	3	
Ware	Wallace	m.	SRR	7 Aug. 1917	8	4	also 8 Aug., 6:4
Ware	Wallace L.	m.	HT	5 July 1917	3	3	
Ware	Wallace L.	m.	ST	10 Aug. 1917	3	3	
Ware	Wallace L.	m.	PA	7 Aug. 1917	8	2	
Ware	Wallace L.	m.	PC	8 Aug. 1917	1	5	
Warfield	George H., Mrs.	d.	PD	21 Dec. 1917	6	2	also 22 Dec., 2:2
Warfield	George, Mrs.	d.	HT	20 Dec. 1917	1	1	
Warfield	Hattie	d.	SRR	19 Dec. 1917	8	2	Healdsburg; also 21 Dec., 3:6
Warnecke	Carl I.	m.	SRR	30 Oct. 1916	8	5	
Warnecke	Carl Ingomar	m.	SRR	27 June 1916	4	3	
Warnecke	Karl	m.	PD	26 Oct. 1916	2	3	
Warner	Emma	o.	SRR	19 Oct. 1917	6	4	
Warner	Emma	o.	PC	20 Oct. 1917	4	5	
Warner	Emma F.	o.	SRR	27 Aug. 1917	8	6	
Warner	Emma F.	o.	PC	28 Aug. 1917	5	5	
Warner	Ernest	b.	PD	2 Dec. 1917	6	1	
Warner	John	d.	PC	22 July 1917	1	5	Calvary Cemetery; also 25 July, 4:1, 5:6
Warner	John	d.	PD	22 July 1917	8	3	
Warner	John	d.	PA	23 July 1917	8	5	Cypress Hill; also 24 July, 5;4
Warner	John Carl	m.	PC	6 Mar. 1918	4	5	also 7 Mar., 5:3
Warner	L. Verne	o.	PC	20 Oct. 1917	4	5	
Warner	LaVerne	o.	PA	19 Oct. 1917	5	4	
Warner	LaVerne	o.	SRR	19 Oct. 1917	6	4	
Warner	LaVerne A.	o.	SRR	27 Aug. 1917	8	6	
Warner	LaVerne A.	o.	PC	28 Aug. 1917	5	5	
Warner	Susan	o.	PA	19 Oct. 1917	5	4	
Warnock	Flavia	d.	SRR	20 Sept. 1916	4	3	
Warren	Cynthia	d.	HT	3 Mar. 1916	1	2	Oak Mound Cemetery
Warren	George, Mrs.	d.	PD	22 Nov. 1918	1	6	
Warren	George, Mrs.	d.	HT	21 Nov. 1918	3	2	San Francisco
Warren	Gladys	m.	PD	9 Apr. 1918	2	2	
Warren	Maria	p.	PC	21 Mar. 1917	3	3	aka Maria Silva
Warren	Maude Ryall	d.	CR	22 Nov. 1918	1	3	
Warto	Maria	o.	PD	18 Nov. 1917	8	2	adoption

(1) Surname	(2) Given Name	(3)	(4)	(5) Date	(6) Pg	(7) Col	(8) Comments
Wartters	Marty	m.	PC	27 Feb. 1916	3	4	
Wasserman	Milton L.	b.	PD	3 Sept. 1916	7	2	
Watbridge	Charles S.	m.	PD	5 Jan. 1918	3	5	
Waterbury	P. W.	d.	PC	26 Nov. 1918	2	1	
Waterman	Carroll G.	m.	SRR	9 May 1917	6	3	
Waterman	Florence	m.	PA	2 Jan. 1917	8	1	
Waterman	Florence	m.	PC	3 Jan. 1917	3	3	
Waterman	Florence	m.	PC	31 Dec. 1916	4	2	
Waters	Elizabeth	m.	PA	20 Dec. 1916	4	5	also 21 Dec., 4:4; 22 Dec., 3:1
Waters	Elizabeth	m.	SRR	20 Dec. 1916	1	3	portrait; also 21 Dec., 1:3; 23 Dec., 6:1
Waters	Elizabeth	m.	PC	21 Dec. 1916	3	2	
Waters	Elizabeth	m.	PD	21 Dec. 1916	2	1	also 22 Dec., 8:2
Waters	Elizabeth	m.	ST	22 Dec. 1916	3	2	
Waters	Elsie W.	o.	PD	27 Feb. 1917	5	5	
Waters	Herbert J.	b.	PA	11 July 1916	5	7	
Waters	Herbert J.	b.	PD	11 July 1916	8	3	
Waters	Mary	d.	PC	10 Aug. 1916	1	4	cremation; also 13 Aug., 2:3
Waters	William	o.	PD	27 Feb. 1917	5	5	
Watkins	Sarah Francis	d.	PD	16 Nov. 1918	5	2	
Watson	E. H.	d.	HT	29 Aug. 1918	8	5	
Watson	Edward	d.	PC	28 Aug. 1918	4	2	
Watson	Herbert	b.	SRR	22 May 1916	8	5	
Watson	Herbert	b.	PD	23 May 1916	6	4	
Watson	J. S.	o.	PA	19 Dec. 1918	7	3	
Watson	Jacob Albert	o.	PD	12 Oct. 1917	5	2	adoption
Watson	John	d.	PA	23 Mar. 1917	5	3	Cypress Hill; also 24 Mar., 4:3; 26 Mar., 5:4
Watson	John	d.	PD	24 Mar. 1917	8	3	
Watson	John Alexander	d.	PC	24 Mar. 1917	1	3	also 25 Mar., 6:4; 27 Mar., 4:3
Watson	Mamie	m.	PD	7 Sept. 1916	3	2	
Watson	Richard	d.	PA	28 Aug. 1918	8	5	
Watson	Richard	d.	PD	29 Aug. 1918	3	1	
Watson	Susan G.	m.	PD	4 June 1916	5	4	
Watson	Susan G.	m.	SRR	5 June 1916	5	2	also 15 June, 3:4
Watt	Lettie	m.	PC	12 Dec. 1916	6	4	
Watt	Lettie	m.	SIT	9 Dec. 1916	1	3	
Watterson	Irwin	d.	SRR	26 Dec. 1917	8	4	Chico
Watterson	Julius A.	d.	PD	2 July 1918	8	3	also 3 July, 2:2
Watterson	Julius Axsel	d.	PA	1 July 1918	3	4	also 2 July, 1:5
Weatherhead	Bruce, Mrs.	d.	PD	9 July 1916	2	2	
Weatherhead	Bruce, Mrs.	d.	SRR	10 July 1916	5	2	

(1) Surname	(2) Given Name	(3)	(4)	(5) Date	(6) Pg	(7) Col	(8) Comments
Weatherhead	Mary Frances	d.	SIT	8 July 1916	1	4	also 15 July, 1:5
Weatherington	William	d.	SRR	18 Nov. 1916	5	1	
Weatherington	William	d.	PD	19 Nov. 1916	4	2	also 21 Nov., 2:3
Webb	J. P.	m.	PD	16 Oct. 1917	5	5	
Webb	William	b.	PA	2 Sept. 1918	5	2	
Webb	William	b.	PC	4 Sept. 1918	8	5	
Webb	William B.	d.	PA	24 Jan. 1918	4	4	
Webb	William Baker	d.	PC	24 Jan. 1918	3	3	Cypress Hill; also 8:4; 25 Jan., 4:1
Weber	Henry, Mrs.	d.	PC	20 Feb. 1918	6	1	cremation
Weber	Lillian	m.	PA	2 Sept. 1918	5	5	
Weber	Lillian	m.	PC	4 Sept. 1918	3	3	
Weber	Sophie Peter	d.	SIT	23 Feb. 1918	1	3	cremation
Wedel	Katherine Constance	o.	PA	6 June 1918	8	6	surname changed to Williams
Wedel	Katherine Constance Margaret	o.	PC	6 June 1918	1	4	name change to Williams
Wedge	Alice Flora	m.	PC	2 Feb. 1917	8	3	
Wedge	Alice Laura	m.	PA	1 Feb. 1917	4	5	also 12 Feb., 5:4
Wedge	Clara	m.	ST	18 Nov. 1916	1	4	
Wedge	Clara B.	m.	PC	14 Nov. 1916	8	3	also 21 Nov., 2:2
Wedge	Josephine M.	m.	SRR	14 July 1917	4	3	
Wedge	W.	b.	PC	15 Dec. 1917	4	5	
Wedge	William A.	m.	PC	10 Mar. 1917	5	2	
Weeks	Mervyn	m.	SRR	13 Mar. 1917	2	4	
Weeks	Wayne I.	m.	SRR	18 July 1917	8	4	
Weeks	Wayne I.	m.	PC	19 July 1917	8	2	
Weibert	Duvall	m.	HT	12 July 1917	4	5	
Weidemann	George	d.	PD	25 Oct. 1918	5	3	
Weidlich	Chris, Jr.	d.	SRR	5 Sept. 1917	5	2	
Weidlick	Chris	d.	PD	5 Sept. 1917	5	2	
Weigand	Mary	o.	PA	20 Apr. 1917	8	3	
Weigand	Mary	o.	SRR	5 Mar. 1917	8	5	
Weigand	William	o.	PA	20 Apr. 1917	8	3	
Weigand	William	o.	SRR	5 Mar. 1917	8	5	
Weis	Adam	m.	PA	7 June 1916	4	7	also 24 June, 2:4; 26 June, 3:4
Weis	Adam	m.	PC	8 June 1916	3	2	also 23 June, 3:3; 27 June, 5:2
Weis	E. Adam	m.	PD	28 June 1916	5	2	
Weise	Henry	o.	SIT	18 May 1918	1	2	
Weisshand	Carl	p.	PC	24 Feb. 1917	1	6	
Weisshand	Carl F. A.	d.	PA	21 Feb. 1917	4	5	Cypress Hill; also 23 Feb., 4:1

(1) Surname	(2) Given Name	(3)	(4)	(5) Date	(6) Pg	(7) Col	(8) Comments
Weisshand	Carl F. A.	d.	PC	22 Feb. 1917	4	4	Cypress Hill; also 8:2; 24 Feb., 8:6
Weisshand	Carl F. A.	p.	PA	24 Feb. 1917	6	5	will
Weisshand	George W.	o.	PA	9 Dec. 1918	4	3	
Weisshand	George William	o.	PC	8 Dec. 1918	8	2	
Welch	Bertrand	d.	PD	3 Dec. 1918	6	4	
Welch	Bertrand	d.	PC	4 Dec. 1918	2	1	
Welch	Betrand	d.	PA	4 Dec. 1918	3	4	
Welch	Florence	d.	PA	20 Aug. 1917	1	4	also 21 Aug., 3:4
Welch	Florence	d.	SRR	20 Aug. 1917	8	5	
Welch	Florence	d.	PC	21 Aug. 1917	1	6	
Welch	Henry	d.	PC	15 Feb. 1917	4	4	
Welch	Homer	d.	PA	15 Feb. 1917	2	2	Santa Rosa
Welch	James F.	d.	PA	20 Aug. 1917	1	4	also 21 Aug., 3:4
Welch	James F.	d.	SRR	20 Aug. 1917	8	5	
Welch	James F.	d.	PC	21 Aug. 1917	1	6	
Welch	James F., Mr. & Mrs.	d.	HT	16 Aug. 1917	2	3	
Welch	James F., Mr. & Mrs.	d.	PD	21 Aug. 1917	5	4	
Welch	Julia	m.	HT	11 Oct. 1917	1	5	
Welch	Mary	d.	PA	13 Apr. 1917	5	3	Calvary Cemetery; also 14 Apr., 5:2; 16 Apr., 5:4
Welch	Mary	d.	PC	14 Apr. 1917	1	5	Calvary Cemetery; also 8:4; 15 Apr., 8:1; 17 Apr., 2:1
Welch	Mary	d.	PD	14 Apr. 1917	3	3	
Welker	Alice Burris	d.	SRR	22 Sept. 1916	4	4	Cypress Lawn, S. F.; also 26 Sept., 2:1
Weller	Margaret	m.	HT	2 Aug. 1917	1	3	
Weller	Margaret	m.	SRR	2 Aug. 1917	6	3	
Wells	D. P.	m.	SRR	8 Apr. 1916	1	5	
Wells	D. P.	m.	PC	9 Apr. 1916	1	3	
Wells	Elbert	m.	PD	23 May 1918	8	1	
Wells	George	d.	PD	24 Nov. 1916	3	2	
Wells	Guerney	m.	SRR	19 Sept. 1916	6	1	
Wells	Guerney	m.	PC	20 Sept. 1916	5	2	
Wells	Howard	b.	SRR	26 June 1917	2	4	
Wells	John	m.	SRR	29 Sept. 1917	4	4	
Wells	Gurney	m.	PD	19 Sept. 1916	5	3	
Welsh	James	d.	PD	25 June 1918	5	5	
Welsh	John	d.	PC	25 June 1918	1	2	
Welsh	John	d.	PA	26 June 1918	7	4	
Welsh	Viola	m.	PD	29 Sept. 1918	7	3	
Welter	Alfred M.	m.	PD	19 Apr. 1917	2	3	
Welter	Alfred M.	m.	SRR	19 Apr. 1917	3	1	

(1) Surname	(2) Given Name	(3)	(4)	(5) Date	(6) Pg	(7) Col	(8) Comments
Welti	Hazel	d.	PA	24 Oct. 1918	6	3	
Welts	Katherine	m.	HT	10 May 1917	1	5	
Wendt	Madison	m.	PD	5 Dec. 1916	8	2	
Wendt	Milton	m.	SRR	4 Dec. 1916	4	4	
Wengren	Amelia	m.	PC	12 May 1918	8	3	
Wengren	Amelia	m.	PA	13 May 1918	5	1	
Wengren	Amelia	m.	PD	14 May 1918	3	7	
Wengren	Ellen	m.	PA	13 May 1918	5	1	
Wengren	Ellen	m.	PD	14 May 1918	3	7	
Wengren	Ellen V.	m.	PC	14 May 1918	4	4	
Wenscoweski	Julius	d.	PD	5 May 1917	1	7	Rural Cemetery; also 4:3
Went	Jack Thomas	m.	SRR	11 Oct. 1917	8	1	
Wentworth	Ira	d.	PA	31 Mar. 1916	6	5	cremation; also 3 Apr., 8:6
Wentworth	Ira M.	d.	PD	1 Apr. 1916	6	5	
Wentworth	Ira W.	d.	ST	1 Apr. 1916	1	3	
Wentworth	Marie	d.	PC	2 Apr. 1916	6	1	cremation
Wentworth	Mary	o.	SRR	14 Sept. 1917	8	1	
Wentworth	Mary	o.	PD	14 Sept. 1918	3	1	
Wentworth	Mary	o.	PA	23 Oct. 1917	7	4	
Wentworth	Mary	o.	PD	23 Oct. 1917	8	5	
Wentworth	Samuel	o.	SRR	14 Sept. 1917	8	1	
Wentworth	Samuel	o.	PD	14 Sept. 1918	3	1	
Wentworth	Samuel	o.	PA	23 Oct. 1917	7	4	
Wentworth	Samuel	o.	PD	23 Oct. 1917	8	5	
Wenzer	Selma/Sentina	m.	PA	20 July 1916	4	4	also 21 July, 3:6
Wenzer	Sentina	m.	PD	21 July 1916	1	5	
Werden	Carl	m.	PA	5 Mar. 1918	4	5	also 6 Mar., 4:5
Werner	Carl	m.	PA	24 Dec. 1917	5	2	
Werner	Carl	m.	PC	28 Dec. 1917	4	5	
Werth	Anna	d.	PC	17 Sept. 1916	5	2&3	Cypress Hill; also 19 Sept., 3:3
Werth	Anne	d.	PA	16 Sept. 1916	5	4	Cypress Hill; also 18 Sept., 5:5
Wertz	Katherine	m.	SRR	5 May 1917	10	4	
Wescott	Oliver	d.	PD	12 Oct. 1918	5	4	
Wesivell	Hattie	m.	PA	1 May 1917	5	3	also 2 May, 2:5
Wesley	Charles	d.	SIT	7 Sept. 1918	1	3	
West	Charles N.	d.	PD	25 Nov. 1916	6	1	
Westfall	W. H.	d.	PA	18 Dec. 1918	8	3&4	cremation; also 19 Dec., 4:4
Westfall	William Henry	d.	PC	19 Dec. 1918	1	5	also 20 Dec., 4:3
Westof	Oscar	m.	PD	15 Dec. 1916	6	1	
Weston	H. L.	o.	PA	6 Oct. 1916	5	4	
Weston	H. L.	o.	PA	6 Oct. 1917	5	5	

(1) Surname	(2) Given Name	(3)	(4)	(5) Date	(6) Pg	(7) Col	(8) Comments
Weston	Hall	m.	PC	10 Dec. 1918	8	3	
Weston	Hall	m.	PA	9 Dec. 1918	5	5	
Westover	Irma	m.	PD	7 June 1918	5	2	
Westover	Minnie Merle	m.	PD	26 July 1916	2	3	
Wetmore	H. D.	b.	PD	8 Sept. 1917	8	2	
Wetzler	Joseph	m.	PD	4 Feb. 1916	8	3	
Weyhe	Oscar	m.	PD	23 Dec. 1917	3	4	
Weyhe	Oscar	m.	SRR	24 Dec. 1917	9	4	
Weyhe	Roy	d.	PD	27 Dec. 1916	5	2	
Weyhe	Roy	d.	SRR	27 Dec. 1916	2	3	
Weyhe	Roy	d.	PC	28 Dec. 1916	3	2	
Weyler	Rena	d.	PA	18 Oct. 1918	8	5	cremation; also 19 Oct., 2:2
Weyler	Rena Church	d.	PC	18 Oct. 1918	4	3	also 19 Oct., 4:3
Weymouth	George H.	d.	SRR	10 Feb. 1917	6	4	
Weymouth	George H.	d.	PD	11 Feb. 1917	4	2	Oak Mound Cemetery
Weymouth	George H.	d.	HT	8 Feb. 1917	7	3	Oak Mound Cemetery
Whallon	Clinton G.	d.	PC	29 Apr. 1916	2	2	
Wharff	David	d.	PA	16 Sept. 1918	5	5	Cypress Hill; also 18 Sept., 2:5, 4:5
Wharff	David	d.	PC	17 Sept. 1918	4	2	Cypress Hill; also 5:3; 18 Sept. 5:3; 19 Sept., 5:3
Whaton	Daniel	d.	PD	4 July 1917	5	3	Oakland; also 6 July, 2:2
Whaton	Daniel	d.	SRR	5 July 1917	4	3	
Whedon	Augustus	d.	ST	18 Mar. 1916	1	4	
Wheeler	Andrew C.	d.	PA	27 Apr. 1917	8	2	Cypress Hill; also 30 Apr., 8:3
Wheeler	Arthur	m.	ST	10 June 1916	1	5	
Wheeler	Henry C.	d.	PC	27 Apr. 1917	5	3	Cypress Hill; also 28 Apr., 3:3, 5:4; 1 May, 3:6
Wheeler	Madge	m.	SRR	26 Aug. 1916	4	2	
Wheeler	Percy	o.	PA	29 Nov. 1918	5	3	
Wheeler	Robert	b.	SRR	27 Oct. 1916	1	4	
Wheeler	Vera	m.	SRR	9 June 1916	2	3	
Wheeler	Vere	m.	SRR	2 June 1916	6	1	
Whelan	John T.	d.	PC	6 Dec. 1916	1	3	Calvary Cemetery; also 7 Dec., 3:3; 8 Dec., 8:5
Wheldon	Ida	d.	SIT	9 Feb. 1918	3	1	
Whelen	John T.	d.	PA	7 Dec. 1916	5	1	
Wherman	Henry	b.	ST	12 Oct. 1917	2	3	
Whipple	Margaret	m.	HT	1 Feb. 1917	6	4	
Whipple	Margaret	m.	PD	27 Jan. 1917	1	3	
Whipple	Margaret	m.	SRR	27 Jan. 1917	3	5	
Whipple	Margaret	m.	PC	28 Jan. 1917	6	2	
Whitaker	Delilah	d.	PD	30 Dec. 1917	4	2	Petaluma; also 6:1
Whitaker	Herman	d.	PD	21 Oct. 1916	3	3	

(1) Surname	(2) Given Name	(3)	(4)	(5) Date	(6) Pg	(7) Col	(8) Comments
Whitaker	James Carroll	d.	PA	8 Jan. 1917	4	3	
Whitaker	Jane Carroll	d.	SRR	6 Jan. 1917	8	6	
Whitaker	Jane Carroll	d.	PC	7 Jan. 1917	5	3	
Whitaker	Jane Carroll	d.	PD	7 Jan. 1917	3	2	
Whitaker	Lyle Snyder	d.	PC	30 Dec. 1917	5	3	
Whitaker	Mabel A.	m.	PA	15 Jan. 1918	8	5	
Whitaker	Maude E.	m.	PA	5 Apr. 1916	6	1	
Whitaker	Scott	d.	PC	1 Jan. 1918	8	2	
Whitcomb	Daniel H.	d.	ST	6 July 1917	1	1	
Whitcomb	Mr.	d.	PC	4 July 1917	7	4	
Whitcomb	Private	d.	PD	1 July 1917	6	2	
Whitcomb	Private	d.	SRR	2 July 1917	5	1	
Whitcomb	Private	d.	HT	5 July 1917	4	4	
White	Alden	m.	PC	3 May 1916	1	3	
White	Alden P.	m.	PC	9 May 1916	6	3	
White	Alden P.	m.	PA	10 May 1917	4	4	
White	Blanche Mabel	m.	SRR	8 Nov. 1916	3	4	
White	Charles Wesley	d.	PA	28 Oct. 1918	2	5	
White	Charles Wesley	d.	PD	8 Sept. 1918	3	3	
White	Dean D.	m.	SRR	7 July 1917	8	2	
White	Eva	m.	PC	17 Aug. 1917	8	5	
White	Francis A.	d.	PA	22 Aug. 1916	4	1	
White	Francis A.	d.	PC	22 Aug. 1916	1	5	also 23 Aug., 1:4
White	Francis A.	d.	SRR	22 Aug. 1916	5	2	also 25 Aug., 6:2
White	J. L.	b.	PA	9 June 1916	8	6&7	
White	J. L.	b.	PA	7 Aug. 1918	3	6	also 4:2
White	J. L.	b.	PC	8 Aug. 1918	8	3	
White	John	d.	PA	20 May 1918	5	4	
White	John	d.	PC	22 May 1918	5	4	Cypress Hill; also 8:3; 23 May, 5:4; 24 May, 4:4
White	John	d.	PD	25 May 1918	2	2	
White	John C.	o.	PD	28 June 1917	2	5	
White	John C.	o.	PD	7 Aug. 1917	1	5	also 8 Aug., 3:1
White	Lora J.	d.	PA	24 June 1918	4	2	Cypress Hill; also 26 June, 4:5
White	Mary Alice	o.	PD	7 Aug. 1917	1	5	also 8 Aug., 3:1
White	Mary C.	o.	PD	28 June 1917	2	5	
White	Maude	d.	SRR	3 Mar. 1916	5	1	
White	Maude	d.	PD	3 Mar. 1917	8	4	Little River; also 6 Mar., 8:3
White	Maude	d.	PC	4 Mar. 1917	4	4	
White	Myrtle	m.	ST	3 June 1916	5	3	
White	Ramona	m.	PC	6 July 1917	5	1	
White	Ramona	m.	PD	7 July 1917	5	3	
White	Ramona	m.	SIT	7 July 1917	1	3	

(1) Surname	(2) Given Name	(3)	(4)	(5) Date	(6) Pg	(7) Col	(8) Comments
White	Ramona	m.	SRR	7 July 1917	6	5	
White	Sarah J.	d.	ST	15 Nov. 1918	5	3	
Whitlow	Ted	m.	PD	15 July 1917	2	4	
Whitlow	Ted	m.	SRR	16 July 1917	5	1	
Whitmore	C. A.	b.	SIT	1 July 1916	7	3	
Whitmore	J. S.	d.	PD	3 July 1918	7	4	Merced
Whitney	Charles D.	o.	PD	6 June 1916	2	1	
Whitney	Charles P.	o.	PA	7 June 1916	7	5	
Whitney	Charles T.	o.	PA	21 Mar. 1916	6	5	
Whitney	Cora A.	o.	PA	7 June 1916	7	5	
Whitney	Cora A.	o.	PA	21 Mar. 1916	6	5	
Whitney	Cora B.	o.	PD	6 June 1916	2	1	
Whitney	Susan	d.	PA	3 May 1917	3	4	Cypress Hill
Whitney	Susan D.	d.	PA	27 Jan. 1917	4	4	also 29 Jan., 5:4
Whitney	Susan D.	d.	PD	28 Jan. 1917	2	4	
Whitney	Susan E.	d.	PC	27 Jan. 1917	1	5	also 28 Jan., 3:4, 5:2; 30 Jan., 6:4
Whitsen	John A. "Allie"	o.	PC	5 Dec. 1917	6	4	
Whitson	Linda	m.	PA	14 Mar. 1918	5	4	
Whitson	Linda	m.	PC	15 Mar. 1918	4	2	
Whitson	Walter	o.	HT	16 May 1918	7	2	
Whittaker	Delilah	d.	SRR	29 Dec. 1917	8	1&3	Petaluma; also 31 Dec., 8:3
Whittaker	Hazel	m.	PC	28 Oct. 1917	5	1	
Whittaker	Hazel	m.	PD	30 Oct. 1917	7	2	
Whittaker	Hazel Rae	m.	SRR	27 Oct. 1917	10	2	
Whittaker	Herman, Jr.	d.	SRR	21 Oct. 1916	7	3	
Whittaker	James, Mrs.	d.	PC	10 Jan. 1917	6	4	
Whittaker	Scott, Mrs.	d.	PD	1 Jan. 1918	6	4	
Whittingham	James M.	b.	SRR	30 July 1917	8	1	
Whitton	John	o.	PD	10 July 1917	5	4	East Lawn Cemetery, Sacramento; also 12 July, 6:1; 14 July, 5:2; 15 July, 7:2
Wibie	Dean D.	m.	PD	8 July 1917	2	4	
Wieberts	D. C.	m.	SRR	9 July 1917	7	4	
Wieland	Mr. & Mrs.	d.	SIT	24 Aug. 1918	1	6	
Wiggins	Charles	o.	ST	22 June 1918	3	2	
Wightman	Chancey G.	d.	ST	14 June 1918	8	4	cremation; also 26 July, 6:2
Wilber	Frank	o.	PD	11 July 1918	5	2	
Wilber	Helen	o.	PD	11 July 1918	5	2	
Wilbur	Andrew G.	d.	PC	5 Aug. 1917	3	4	
Wilbur	Frank	o.	PA	12 July 1918	3	4	
Wilbur	Helen	o.	PA	12 July 1918	3	4	
Wilcox	Marion S.	m.	PC	16 July 1918	6	2	

(1) Surname	(2) Given Name	(3)	(4)	(5) Date	(6) Pg	(7) Col	(8) Comments
Wilcoxsen	Roy	m.	PD	29 Jan. 1918	5	3	
Wild	John C.	m.	PD	13 Sept. 1917	5	3	
Wild	John C.	m.	SRR	13 Sept. 1917	5	4	
Wilder	William	d.	PA	16 Mar. 1918	3	3	Cypress Hill; also 18 Mar., 2:2
Wilder	William	d.	PC	17 Mar. 1918	5	3&6	Cypress Hill; also 19 Mar., 5:4
Wilen	Alfred	m.	PA	13 May 1918	8	5	also 15 May, 5:7; 17 May, 3:1
Wilen	Alfred John	m.	PD	12 May 1918	7	5	also 16 May, 6:4
Wilen	Alfred John	m.	PC	16 May 1918	5	2	
Wilen	Lillian	m.	PA	2 Nov. 1917	5	1	also 3 Nov., 8:3; 5 Nov., 4:3
Wilen	Lillian C.	m.	PC	3 Nov. 1917	4	3	also 4 Nov., 8:4; 6 Nov., 3:4
Wilford	Sebera	m.	PA	29 Sept. 1918	5	3	
Wilie	Bessie	b.	PD	1 July 1916	2	4	son H. Mel deceased
Wilkie	Annie	m.	PD	19 Sept. 1916	5	3	also 20 Sept., 5:4
Wilkie	Annie	m.	SRR	19 Sept. 1916	6	1	
Wilkie	Annie	m.	PC	20 Sept. 1916	5	2	
Wilkinson	Elizabeth	d.	PC	5 Dec. 1917	1	4	Cypress Hill; also 5:5; 7 Dec., 8:3; 8 Dec., 3:2
Wilkinson	Elizabeth	d.	PD	6 Dec. 1917	3	1	
Wilkinson	Elizabeth	d.	SRR	6 Dec. 1917	5	4	
Will	Leona	m.	SRR	24 Apr. 1917	6	4	
Will	Leona	m.	PD	25 Apr. 1917	2	5	
Will	Leona	m.	HT	26 Apr. 1917	4	3	groom not named
Willard	Alfred J.	o.	PA	21 Mar. 1918	3	3	
Willett	R. C.	m.	SRR	6 May 1916	10	5	
Williams	Alice M.	m.	PC	4 Jan. 1918	3	5	
Williams	Alta	d.	PD	27 Jan. 1916	8	3	
Williams	Alta	d.	SRR	27 Jan. 1916	8	4	Fruitvale; also 29 Jan., 6:3
Williams	Andrew B.	m.	PD	24 Sept. 1916	1	6	
Williams	Andrew B.	m.	SRR	25 Sept. 1916	5	2	
Williams	Cecil Clayton	d.	PD	17 Feb. 1917	8	2	
Williams	Cecil Clayton	d.	SRR	17 Feb. 1917	5	6	
Williams	Clayton (son of)	d.	PC	17 Feb. 1917	5	5	
Williams	Clayton, Mrs.	d.	SRR	16 Mar. 1916	4	3	Riverside Cemetery
Williams	Cora	o.	SRR	9 Aug. 1917	2	4	
Williams	Crayton	d.	PA	15 Mar. 1916	5	1	16 Mar., 10:6
Williams	Crayton A., Mrs.	d.	PD	16 Mar. 1916	2	4	Riverside Cemetery, Cloverdale
Williams	Elsie May	d.	PD	1 Jan. 1916	8	3	Riverside Cematary
Williams	Ernest	m.	PC	31 Mar. 1916	5	3	also 4 Apr., 2:1
Williams	Frank R.	d.	PC	22 Aug. 1918	1	4	

(1) Surname	(2) Given Name	(3)	(4)	(5) Date	(6) Pg	(7) Col	(8) Comments
Williams	Frank R.	d.	PD	22 Aug. 1918	5	4	Calvary Cemetery; also 23 Aug., 8:1; 24 Aug., 2:1; 4:2; 2 Aug., 3:5
Williams	Henry B.	o.	SRR	9 Aug. 1917	2	4	
Williams	Ira	d.	PD	5 Oct. 1916	6	4	
Williams	J. B.	b.	HT	14 Nov. 1918	3	4	
Williams	James	o.	PD	21 Nov. 1918	5	3	
Williams	James	o.	PD	27 Apr. 1918	6	5	
Williams	James	o.	PD	3 Nov. 1918	5	3	
Williams	Jim	o.	PD	18 July 1918	6	4	
Williams	John A.	d.	PD	26 June 1918	6	5	also 28 June, 8:3
Williams	John A.	d.	ST	28 June 1918	1	5	
Williams	Katherine Constance	o.	PA	6 June 1918	8	6	surname changed from Wedel
Williams	Katherine Constance Margaret	o.	PC	6 June 1918	1	4	name change from Wedel
Williams	Lottie	m.	SRR	16 July 1917	6	3	
Williams	Lottie	m.	PD	17 July 1917	3	3	
Williams	Lucile	d.	ST	1 Nov. 1918	1	2	
Williams	Lucille	d.	PA	30 Oct. 1918	4	5	
Williams	Lucille	d.	PD	30 Oct. 1918	8	3	
Williams	Lucy	d.	PC	1 Feb. 1917	1	3	
Williams	Lyle Taylor	d.	ST	14 Sept. 1917	2	5	Odd Fellows Cem.
Williams	Mrs.	d.	PC	16 Mar. 1916	4	3	
Williams	R.	d.	PA	4 Oct. 1916	1	3	
Williams	Ralph	b.	HT	10 Aug. 1916	3	2	
Williams	Robert	d.	SRR	24 May 1916	5	1	
Williams	Steve	o.	SRR	29 Jan. 1916	10	4	
Williams	Wallace W.	m.	PD	22 Nov. 1916	6	2	
Williams	Wallace W.	m.	PC	24 Nov. 1916	2	3	
Williams	Wallace W.	m.	ST	25 Nov. 1917	1	1	
Williams	William	o.	SRR	21 June 1916	1	2	also 4:1
Williams	William	m.	PD	22 June 1916	7	3	
Williamson	Elizabeth	d.	PA	5 Dec. 1917	6	4	
Williamson	F. F.	b.	ST	18 Mar. 1916	8	4	
Williamson	Hilda	m.	PA	11 Sept. 1916	4	5	
Williamson	Hilda	m.	PC	12 Sept. 1916	5	2	
Williamson	J. F.	o.	PC	12 July 1918	1	3	
Williamson	James	d.	PD	25 July 1918	4	2	Sebastopol; also 6:1
Williamson	James A.	d.	PA	25 July 1918	3	6	Sebastopol
Williamson	Joe	o.	ST	18 Oct. 1918	1	1	
Williamson	Joe	o.	PC	20 Oct. 1918	6	3	
Williamson	Joseph	o.	ST	13 Dec. 1918	1	1	
Williamson	Lucy	d.	HT	8 Feb. 1917	1	1	

(1) Surname	(2) Given Name	(3)	(4)	(5) Date	(6) Pg	(7) Col	(8) Comments
Williamson	Mary Lucy	d.	PD	1 Feb. 1917	5	5	also 2 Feb., 8:7; 3 Feb., 6:4
Williamson	Mary Lucy	d.	SRR	31 Jan. 1917	8	6	Rural Cemetery; also 1 Feb., 6:5; 2 Feb., 6:4
Williamson	Roy	o.	ST	26 July 1918	1	3	
Williamson	Roy	o.	PD	3 Aug. 1918	8	3	
Willis	Adah	o.	SRR	13 June 1917	8	2	
Willis	Everett	o.	SRR	13 June 1917	8	2	
Willis	John	o.	PC	2 Nov. 1917	5	3	
Willis	Thomas Augustus	d.	SRR	10 Oct. 1916	8	4	Rural Cemetery; also 11 Oct., 1:6; 12 Oct., 3:2
Willis	William	d.	PA	15 May 1917	5	5	Fresno; also 23 May, 6:5
Willitt	R. V.	m.	PD	7 May 1916	3	1	
Willock	Martin	m.	SRR	21 Feb. 1916	1	6	
Willock	Martin L.	m.	PD	22 Feb. 1916	2	2	
Wilmer	Mabel	m.	PA	24 July 1917	2	2	
Wilsey	Hayes C.	b.	PA	8 Jan. 1917	2	2	
Wilson	Alice	m.	PD	4 Jan. 1918	6	2	
Wilson	Andrew C.	m.	PA	23 Mar. 1918	5	4	
Wilson	Andrew C.	m.	PC	23 Mar. 1918	3	4	also 24 Mar., 5:4
Wilson	C. C.	m.	SRR	14 Feb. 1917	8	6	also 12 Mar., 2:4
Wilson	C. C.	m.	PD	15 Mar. 1917	2	3	
Wilson	Charles	d.	PD	20 Jan. 1916	8	2	
Wilson	Charles E.	d.	SRR	19 Jan. 1916	8	5	also 20 Jan., 1:2
Wilson	Cyrus	o.	PD	7 Nov. 1916	5	2	
Wilson	D. W.	m.	PC	18 Nov. 1916	6	3	
Wilson	Earl	m.	SRR	14 Aug. 1917	8	4	also 15 Aug., 8:3; 16 Aug., 5:3
Wilson	Earl	m.	PC	15 Aug. 1917	8	1	
Wilson	Elizabeth E.	m.	PD	3 Sept. 1916	5	3	
Wilson	Ellen	d.	PA	23 Nov. 1918	4	4	also 5:3; 25 Nov.; 6:3; Cypress Hill
Wilson	Ellen Whitman	d.	PC	24 Nov. 1918	2	2	Cypress Hill; also 6:3; 26 Nov., 5:4, 8:4
Wilson	Elmer	m.	PC	10 July 1917	5	2	also 25 July, 4:3
Wilson	Elmer M.	m.	PA	24 July 1917	2	2	
Wilson	Hardy	m.	PD	8 Oct. 1918	7	2	
Wilson	Helen R.	o.	PD	7 Nov. 1916	5	2	
Wilson	Helen R. Bartram	o.	SRR	7 Nov. 1916	5	1	
Wilson	Iva	m.	SRR	1 Sept. 1917	6	3	
Wilson	Iva	m.	PD	2 Sept. 1917	6	2	
Wilson	J. T.	b.	PD	27 Oct. 1918	2	4	
Wilson	James	d.	PA	23 Nov. 1918	4	4	Cypress Hill
Wilson	James Fisk	d.	PA	15 Nov. 1918	5	1&6	Cypress Hill; also 16 Nov., 4:5

(1) Surname	(2) Given Name	(3)	(4)	(5) Date	(6) Pg	(7) Col	(8) Comments
Wilson	James Fisk	d.	PC	16 Nov. 1918	3	2	Cypress Hill; also 5:3; 17 Nov., 5:3
Wilson	Jesse W.	b.	PD	29 Nov. 1916	3	3	
Wilson	Jesse Webber	b.	SRR	28 Nov. 1916	4	3	
Wilson	John	m.	SRR	10 Feb. 1917	6	6	
Wilson	Josephine	d.	PA	4 Sept. 1917	8	5	
Wilson	Josephine	d.	SRR	4 Sept. 1917	1	6	
Wilson	Josephine	d.	PC	5 Sept. 1917	1	2	
Wilson	Josephine	d.	PD	5 Sept. 1917	7	3	
Wilson	Lafayette	o.	ST	26 July 1918	3	1	
Wilson	Lee	b.	PA	15 Dec. 1917	2	6	
Wilson	M. F., Mrs.	d.	PD	26 Jan. 1918	8	2	
Wilson	M. F., Mrs.	d.	PC	27 Jan. 1918	6	4	
Wilson	M. F., Mrs.	d.	HT	31 Jan. 1918	4	3	
Wilson	Mary Frances	d.	PD	28 Jan. 1917	2	4	
Wilson	Mildred Irma	m.	PD	16 Sept. 1917	7	4	
Wilson	Mildred Irma	m.	SRR	17 Sept. 1917	5	1	
Wilson	Mr.	d.	PA	14 Oct. 1918	5	4	
Wilson	Nellie	d.	PA	14 Mar. 1918	4	3	Cypress Hill; also 16 Mar., 5:6
Wilson	Nellie	d.	PC	15 Mar. 1918	5	4	Cypress Hill; also 17 Mar., 4:4
Wilson	S. G.	o.	PD	5 May 1918	8	1	
Wilson	Stephen H.	d.	PD	22 Aug. 1917	3	4	Calvary Cemetery; also 23 Aug., 4:2
Wilson	Todd	m.	PA	15 May 1917	8	7	
Wilson	Todd	m.	PC	16 May 1917	8	2	
Wilson	Todd	o.	PA	26 Nov. 1918	8	5	
Wilson	Todd	o.	PC	26 Nov. 1918	3	3	
Wilson	William Cyrus	o.	SRR	7 Nov. 1916	5	1	
Wilton	Thomas	d.	SRR	22 Mar. 1916	10	1	also 24 Mar., 8:6
Wilton	Thomas G.	d.	PA	22 Mar. 1916	4	5	
Wilton	Thomas G.	d.	PD	25 Mar. 1916	6	3	Sebastopol Cemetery
Wilton	Thomas G.	d.	ST	25 Mar. 1916	1	1	
Winans	David M.	d.	PC	1 Apr. 1918	3	4	also 5 Apr., 4:2
Winans	David M.	d.	HT	4 Apr. 1918	5	4	
Winans	David Madison	d.	PA	1 Apr. 1918	8	5	Cypress Hill; also 4 Apr., 8:5
Winans	Helen	d.	PA	10 Mar. 1916	4	4	
Winans	Henry I.	o.	PC	29 Aug. 1917	3	4	
Winans	J. L.	d.	PC	13 June 1918	1	4	Cypress Hill; also 8:4
Winans	J. L.	o.	PC	3 Jan. 1918	4	4	
Winans	J. L.	o.	PC	4 Jan. 1916	4	3	
Winans	James L.	d.	PA	12 June 1918	5	3	Cypress Hill; also 13 June, 4:4; 14 June, 4:5
Winans	James L.	d.	ST	14 June 1918	5	2	

(1) Surname	(2) Given Name	(3)	(4)	(5) Date	(6) Pg	(7) Col	(8) Comments
Winans	L. J.	d.	PC	7 Apr. 1916	1	6	Cypress Hill; also 8 Apr., 4:1&3; 11 Apr., 2:1
Winans	Lewis J.	d.	PA	7 Apr. 1916	2	3	also 10 Apr., 5:4
Winans	Lewis J.	d.	PD	8 Apr. 1916	6	1	
Winans	Louis J.	d.	SRR	7 Apr. 1916	4	1	also 10 Apr., 5:3
Winchell	Choyce	m.	PA	16 Feb. 1918	4	2	
Winchester	Giles	o.	PD	27 Nov. 1917	5	4	
Winchester	Giles A.	o.	PD	24 Mar. 1917	6	5	
Winchester	Giles A.	o.	PC	27 Nov. 1917	4	3	
Winchester	Giles A.	o.	SRR	27 Nov. 1917	7	4	
Winchester	Giles A.	o.	PC	7 Dec. 1918	6	3	
Winchester	Leona Anna	o.	PD	24 Mar. 1917	6	5	
Winchester	Leona Anna	o.	PC	7 Dec. 1918	6	3	
Winchester	Leone	o.	PD	27 Nov. 1917	5	4	
Winchester	Leone Anna	o.	PC	27 Nov. 1917	4	3	
Winchester	Leone Anna	o.	SRR	27 Nov. 1917	7	4	
Wing	Wong Dott	m.	PC	16 Mar. 1918	5	2	
Wing	Wong Dott	m.	ST	8 Mar. 1918	8	3	
Winkler	Jess	o.	ST	20 Dec. 1918	1	3	
Winkler	Mable	m.	HT	24 Aug. 1916	1	4	
Winkler	Maybel	m.	SRR	22 Aug. 1916	3	3	
Winn	Elizabeth	d.	PC	27 Oct. 1916	1	3	Tomales; also 8:2; 28 Oct., 8:1; 29 Oct., 1:2
Winsby	J. C., Mrs.	d.	SRR	8 Mar. 1917	8	3	Pleasant Hill Cemetey
Winsby	Philomena	d.	ST	10 Mar. 1917	1	5	Pleasant Hill
Winsby	Robert F.	m.	SRR	20 Feb. 1917	1	2	
Winsby	Robert F.	m.	PC	21 Feb. 1917	1	1	
Winset	Jacob C.	d.	PD	20 July 1918	4	2	I.O.O.F. Cemetery; also 7:1; 24 July, 2:3
Winslow	L. J.	b.	PC	1 May 1917	4	4	
Winters	Sam	b.	PA	18 Feb. 1916	1	3	
Winton	Robert F.	d.	PD	5 May 1917	4	3	also 5:3; 8 May, 2:5
Winton	Robert Frederick	d.	SRR	4 May 1917	8	2	Rural Cemetery; also 5 May, 10:3; 7 May, 8:3
Wintringham	H. B.	o.	PC	15 Nov. 1917	1	5	
Wintringham	H. B.	o.	PA	5 Dec. 1917	4	4	
Wintringham	Henry	o.	SRR	5 Dec. 1917	4	2	
Wintringham	Henry	o.	PC	6 Dec. 1917	8	4	
Wintringham	Leah	o.	PA	5 Dec. 1917	4	4	
Wintringham	Leah	o.	SRR	5 Dec. 1917	4	2	
Wintringham	Leah	o.	PC	6 Dec. 1917	8	4	
Wipner	Antone H.	d.	PA	18 Nov. 1918	4	4	Cypress Hill; also 20 Nov., 5:1
Wipner	Antone H.	d.	PC	19 Nov. 1918	5	3	Cypress Hill; also 20 Nov., 2:2; 21 Nov., 5:1
Wipner	Antone H.	d.	PD	19 Nov. 1918	2	2	

(1) Surname	(2) Given Name	(3)	(4)	(5) Date	(6) Pg	(7) Col	(8) Comments
Wipner	Mabel	m.	PC	10 July 1917	5	2	also 25 July, 4:3
Wirts	John W.	m.	PD	4 Jan. 1918	3	5	
Wirtz	John	m.	SRR	28 Dec. 1917	8	5	
Wisecarver	Lloyd	b.	SRR	1 Sept. 1916	6	2	
Wisecarver	Percy, Mrs.	d.	HT	17 Oct. 1918	8	2	
Wisel	Anna	d.	PD	9 July 1918	5	5	
Wiseman	A W.	d.	PA	15 June 1918	4	4	
Wiseman	William Alexander	d.	PD	15 June 1918	1	5	Rural Cemetery; also 16 June, 4:2; 18 June, 3:3
Wisner	Fred	m.	SRR	1 Feb. 1916	5	4	
Wiswell	Hattie F.	m.	SRR	1 May 1917	8	2	
Wiswell	Hattie F.	m.	PD	2 May 1917	8	5	
Wiswell	Hattie P.	m.	PC	2 May 1917	4	3	
Wiswell	Nelson	d.	PC	6 Aug. 1916	3	1	Cypress Hill; also 5:3; 8 Aug., 5:5; 10 Aug., 4:4
Wiswell	Nelson	d.	PA	7 Aug. 1916	8	5	Cypress Hill; also 9 Aug., 8:3
Wiswell	Nelson	d.	SRR	8 Aug. 1916	6	3	also 10 Aug., 6:2
Wittkopp	John	d.	PA	18 Jan. 1916	5	4	also 21 Jan., 6:5
Wittkopp	John	d.	PC	18 Jan. 1916	1	4	
Wittkopp	John A.	d.	PC	20 Jan. 1916	3	1	Calvary Cemetery; also 22 Jan., 4:2
Woelffel	G. S.	d.	PD	22 Aug. 1917	5	4	also 23 Aug., 5:1
Wolcott	C. H.	b.	SRR	28 Nov. 1917	6	6	
Woldeman	Niels	b.	PC	17 May 1916	8	4	
Woldemar	Claus	d.	PA	20 Apr. 1916	4	5	Cypress Hill; also 21 Apr., 8:5; 22 Apr., 4:1
Woldemar	Claus	d.	PC	21 Apr. 1916	1	6	Cypress Hill; also 23 Apr., 5:6
Woldemar	Neils	b.	PA	17 May 1916	4	6	
Wolf	Anton	o.	ST	12 Oct. 1917	7	2	
Wolf	Madeline	m.	PD	30 Nov. 1916	5	6	
Wolf	Magdalene	m.	SRR	29 Nov. 1916	8	6	
Wolf	Prospea S.	m.	CR	11 May 1917	1	5	
Wolf	Prosper S.	m.	PD	5 May 1917	2	6	
Wolf	Prosper S.	m.	SRR	5 May 1917	3	5	
Wolfe	Mary	m.	PD	27 July 1918	6	1	
Wolff	Isadore	d.	PA	24 Apr. 1918	4	6	also 25 Apr., 4:6
Wolff	Isadore	d.	PC	24 Apr. 1918	4	2	Salem Cemetery; also 5:4; 26 Apr., 5:4
Wolfskill	Katherine A.	d.	PD	27 Dec. 1918	7	2	Rural Cemetery
Wolgamott	Frank	o.	SRR	19 Nov. 1917	8	5	
Wolgamott	Frank	o.	PD	24 Oct. 1916	7	4	
Wolgamott	Frank	o.	SRR	9 Oct. 1916	8	1	also 31 Oct., 5:3
Wolgamott	Hanna	o.	SRR	9 Oct. 1916	8	1	also 31 Oct., 5:3
Wolgamott	Hannah	o.	SRR	19 Nov. 1917	8	5	

(1) Surname	(2) Given Name	(3)	(4)	(5) Date	(6) Pg	(7) Col	(8) Comments
Wolgamott	Hannah	o.	PD	24 Oct. 1916	7	4	
Wolters	Ruth	m.	PD	1 Oct. 1916	6	4	
Wolters	Ruth	m.	SRR	3 Oct. 1916	6	2	
Wolters	Ruth	m.	HT	5 Oct. 1916	1	3	
Wonderley	Ivan	d.	SRR	8 May 1916	8	4	
Wood	Ben S., Jr.	d.	PA	27 June 1918	8	4	Healdsburg
Wood	Ben S., Jr.	d.	PD	27 June 1918	5	3	Healdsburg; also 29 June, 2:3
Wood	Byron F.	d.	PD	14 May 1918	4	2	also 8:4
Wood	Christina S.	d.	HT	29 Aug. 1918	7	3	
Wood	Clara Edith	m.	SRR	25 July 1917	3	1	
Wood	Hazel	d.	PD	21 Nov. 1918	2	3	Guerneville; also 6:2; 22 Nov., 3:3; 23 Nov., 5:4
Wood	Hazel Graham	d.	PA	21 Nov. 1918	3	4	
Wood	Hazel Graham	d.	PC	21 Nov. 1918	8	3	
Wood	Homer W.	b.	PA	30 June 1917	8	3	
Wood	James L.	d.	PD	16 June 1918	8	3	
Wood	Maggie J.	d.	SIT	7 July 1917	1	5	
Wood	Margaret	d.	SRR	5 July 1917	8	4	Sonoma; also 7 July, 8:3; 9 July, 4:5
Wood	Margaret	d.	PD	6 July 1917	6	4	Mountain Cemetery; also 7 July, 4:3; 8 July, 3:4; 10 July, 5:5
Wood	Sarah Ann	d.	PD	6 Jan. 1918	3	4	
Wood	Sarah Ann	d.	PC	8 Jan. 1918	2	3	Olive Hill
Wood	Will	b.	SRR	2 Nov. 1917	6	3	
Woodard	Helen	o.	PD	5 Dec. 1918	5	4	
Woodard	Walter	o.	PD	5 Dec. 1918	5	4	
Wooden	Emma	d.	PD	11 Sept. 1918	8	3	
Woodhams	Charles	m.	PD	19 May 1917	8	1	
Woodhams	Roy C.	m.	HT	24 May 1917	5	2	
Woodhams	Roy Charles	m.	SRR	18 May 1917	1	4	also 21 May, 6:4
Woodhouse	W. J.	m.	PD	30 Oct. 1917	7	2	
Woodhouse	William Johnson	m.	SRR	27 Oct. 1917	10	2	
Woodhouse	William Johnson	m.	PC	28 Oct. 1917	5	1	
Woodrich	Robert J.	m.	SRR	1 Oct. 1917	4	3	
Woodrich	Robert J.	m.	PD	2 Oct. 1917	2	3	
Woods	Arthur C.	d.	PD	26 Feb. 1918	2	4	
Woods	Harry C.	m.	PD	22 May 1918	5	2	
Woods	Henry Albert	d.	ST	20 July 1917	1	6	
Woods	Henry Albert	d.	PC	22 July 1917	6	5	
Woods	Katie	m.	SRR	19 July 1917	8	3	
Woods	Mizima	o.	PD	26 Mar. 1918	3	3	
Woods	Paul C.	o.	PD	26 Mar. 1918	3	3	
Woodsen	Charles Hiram	d.	PC	26 Oct. 1917	4	3	Bloomfield; also 27 Oct., 8:4

(1) Surname	(2) Given Name	(3)	(4)	(5) Date	(6) Pg	(7) Col	(8) Comments
Woodsen	Rebecca	d.	ST	26 July 1918	5	5	
Woodsen	Walter	b.	PC	25 Apr. 1917	8	1	
Woodsen	Walter N.	m.	PC	20 July 1916	6	4	also 26 July, 6:2
Woodsen	Walter N.	b.	PC	8 Nov. 1918	5	1	
Woodson	Charles H.	d.	PA	25 Oct. 1917	4	6	Bloomfield; also 26 Oct., 5:5
Woodson	Charles H.	d.	PD	26 Oct. 1917	5	4	
Woodson	Rebecca	d.	PA	30 July 1918	8	5	Bloomfield; also 31 July, 5:5; 1 Aug., 8:3
Woodson	Rebecca H.	d.	PD	31 July 1918	8	4	
Woodson	Walter	b.	PA	25 Apr. 1917	5	4	
Woodson/Woodsen	Rebecca	d.	PC	31 July 1918	5	1	also 2 Aug., 8:3
Woodward	Bess	m.	PD	3 June 1916	8	3	also 4 June, 8:1
Woodward	Bess	m.	SRR	5 June 1916	8	3	also 10 June, 2:1
Woodward	Bess	m.	PC	25 Apr. 1916	3	3	
Woodward	Bess van Alst	m.	SRR	24 Apr. 1916	4	4	
Woodward	Elizabeth Juanita	d.	SRR	19 July 1917	3	2	
Woodward	Helen	o.	CR	6 Dec. 1918	4	2	
Woodward	Martha	d.	PD	9 Feb. 1917	4	2	I.O.O.F. Cemetery; also 5:1
Woodward	Martha J.	d.	SRR	8 Feb. 1917	8	5	
Woodward	Walter A.	o.	CR	6 Dec. 1918	4	2	
Woodworth	A.	o.	PC	18 Jan. 1918	1	2	
Woodworth	Fred	o.	SRR	14 Mar. 1917	5	1	
Woodworth	Fred	o.	PD	18 Mar. 1917	2	6	
Woodworth	Fred	o.	PA	19 Mar. 1917	8	4	
Woodworth	Mildred	o.	SRR	14 Mar. 1917	5	1	
Woodworth	Mildred Mathes	m.	ST	5 July 1918	1	5	
Woodworth	Miss	d.	PC	7 June 1917	1	3	
Woodworth	Miss	d.	ST	8 June 1917	1	6	
Woodworth	Myrtle	d.	SRR	6 June 1917	1	2	also 8 June, 6:4; 9 June, 5:1
Woodworth	Myrtle	d.	PD	7 June 1917	8	1	also 8 June, 5:2; 8:2; 9 June, 8:4
Woodworth	Myrtle Estelle	d.	PA	6 June 1917	1	1	also 11 June, 7:2
Worms	Alice D.	m.	PD	25 May 1916	3	4	
Worth	Cletus C.	d.	PC	11 July 1917	4	3	
Worth	Louis W.	d.	SIT	19 Feb. 1916	3	4	
Worth	C.	b.	PA	15 Feb. 1918	5	3&4	
Wortherington	William	d.	PC	19 Nov. 1916	8	3	
Worthman	Christian	d.	SRR	3 May 1916	1	4	
Worthman	Christian	d.	PC	4 May 1916	5	3	
Wotring	F. R.	d.	PA	21 Nov. 1918	4	3	portrait; Cypress Hill; also 22 Nov., 4:1; 23 Nov., 5:3; 25 Nov., 5:6; 26 Nov., 2:4

(1) Surname	(2) Given Name	(3)	(4)	(5) Date	(6) Pg	(7) Col	(8) Comments
Wotring	Frederick R.	d.	PC	22 Nov. 1918	3	3	portrait; also 5:1; 26 Nov., 4:3; 27 Nov., 3:3
Wotring	Martha	d.	PC	4 Mar. 1917	1	3	also 6 Mar., 3:3; 8 Mar., 5:3
Wotring	Martha	d.	PA	5 Mar. 1917	6	5	Cypress Hill; also 7 Mar., 5:5
Wotring	Martha	d.	SRR	5 Mar. 1917	1	4	
Wotring	W. T., Mrs.	d.	PD	6 Mar. 1917	3	5	
Wright	Arthur	m.	PA	10 Nov. 1917	8	4	
Wright	Arthur	m.	SRR	10 Nov. 1917	5	1	
Wright	Arthur G.	m.	PD	13 Jan. 1918	7	1	also 19 Jan., 2:4; 20 Jan., 7:1
Wright	Arthur G.	m.	PA	19 Jan. 1918	6	2	
Wright	Arthur Goodman	m.	PD	11 Nov. 1917	10	1	
Wright	Benjamin	d.	SRR	24 July 1917	5	5	
Wright	Benjamin F.	d.	PD	24 July 1917	3	1	
Wright	Benjamin Franklin	d.	HT	26 July 1917	1	5	
Wright	Charles Dana	m.	SRR	4 Jan. 1917	1	3	
Wright	Charles Dana	m.	PC	5 Jan. 1917	5	2	
Wright	Duncan McFarlane	d.	PC	6 Mar. 1917	3	3	
Wright	Elois	m.	PD	19 Apr. 1917	3	4	
Wright	Eloise	m.	SRR	16 Apr. 1917	6	4	
Wright	Frances Allen	d.	SRR	13 Mar. 1917	4	4	
Wright	George, Jr.	o.	ST	25 Jan. 1918	2	3	
Wright	Jarena D.	d.	SRR	15 Nov. 1916	5	3	cremation; also 17 Nov., 9:4
Wright	Jarena D.	p.	PD	23 Apr. 1918	5	2	
Wright	Jarena Dabney	d.	PD	15 Nov. 1916	5	1	also 17 Nov., 8:2; 18 Nov., 8:3
Wright	Jarena Dabney	p.	PD	17 Nov. 1916	8	4	also 21 Nov., 5:1; 22 Nov., 6:1
Wright	John K.	d.	PD	15 Feb. 1918	4	2	also 8:2; 17 Feb., 2:2
Wright	Lee W.	b.	PD	26 Mar. 1916	8	1	
Wright	Lovella	d.	PD	10 Oct. 1916	8	3	
Wright	Mabel Louise	m.	PC	19 June 1918	4	1	
Wright	Ruth	m.	SRR	2 Jan. 1917	10	1	
Wright	Ruth Irene	m.	PD	31 Dec. 1916	6	4	
Wright	Sophia	p.	PD	30 May 1918	5	2	aka Sophie Hess
Wright	Sophie	d.	PA	25 May 1918	1	5	aka Sophie Hess
Wright	Sophie	p.	PA	29 May 1918	8	3	will
Wright	Viola	m.	SRR	31 May 1916	5	3	
Wright	Viola	m.	PA	1 June 1916	8	3	
Wright	Viola May	m.	PC	1 June 1916	5	2	
Wright	Winfield	m.	PA	28 Apr. 1916	8	3	

(1) Surname	(2) Given Name	(3)	(4)	(5) Date	(6) Pg	(7) Col	(8) Comments
Wright	Winfield	m.	PC	28 Apr. 1916	5	3	
Wright	Winfield R.	m.	PD	28 Apr. 1916	6	5	
Wugan	Louis G.	m.	PD	20 July 1918	3	4	
Wugan	Louis G.	m.	ST	26 July 1918	1	3	
Wyatt	Amanda	o.	PD	11 Dec. 1917	8	3	
Wyatt	Amanda	o.	PD	13 Nov. 1917	5	4	
Wyatt	Amanda G.	o.	SIT	15 Dec. 1917	3	2	
Wyatt	Charles	b.	PA	31 May 1918	4	7	also 8:6
Wyatt	Stanley	m.	SRR	1 Jan. 1916	6	1	
Wyatt	William T.	o.	PD	11 Dec. 1917	8	3	
Wyatt	William T.	o.	PD	13 Nov. 1917	5	4	
Wyatt	William T.	o.	SIT	15 Dec. 1917	3	2	
Wyhe	Leroy	d.	ST	30 Dec. 1916	1	2	
Wylie	Melville	d.	PD	1 Jan. 1916	2	5	
Wylie	Melville James	b.	SRR	1 July 1916	3	5	
Wymore	C. C., Mrs.	d.	SRR	14 Sept. 1917	4	1	
Wymore	C. C., Mrs.	d.	PD	14 Sept. 1918	8	1	also 15 Sept., 4:2; 16 Sept., 2:1; 5:2
Wymore	C. C., Mrs.	d.	PC	15 Sept. 1917	3	4	
Wymore	Maria Alameda	d.	SRR	14 Sept. 1917	8	3	also 17 Sept., 3:2

Y & Z

(1) Surname	(2) Given Name	(3)	(4)	(5) Date	(6) Pg	(7) Col	(8) Comments
Yamamoto	Masa	d.	ST	10 Aug. 1917	1	4	
Yamaoka	Tomenburo	d.	PC	28 Dec. 1916	6	1	
Yamaoka	Tomesaburo	d.	HT	28 Dec. 1916	4	2	
Yamasaki	Sumio	o.	SRR	15 Aug. 1916	1	1	
Yamatoto	Harbho	d.	ST	18 Mar. 1916	8	4	
Yantz	Mary A.	m.	PA	17 Aug. 1917	4	2	
Yantz	Mary A.	m.	PC	17 Aug. 1917	1	3	
Yao	Yoshio	o.	SRR	15 Aug. 1916	1	1	
Yasoichi	Tadashi	d.	ST	18 Mar. 1916	8	4	
Yeager	J.	d.	PC	11 June 1916	1	5	
Yeager	Mr.	d.	PA	10 June 1916	8	5	Cypress Hill; also 14 June, 5:4
Yeagley	Frank A.	d.	ST	27 July 1917	1	6	
Yeagley	Sidney, Mrs.	d.	ST	15 Feb. 1918	1	3	Odd Fellows Cem.
Yell	Elizabeth	d.	PC	30 July 1916	1	6	Calvary Cemetery; also 1 Aug., 4:4
Yell	Elizabeth	d.	PA	31 July 1916	5	4	
Yend	William	m.	PC	6 Oct. 1916	8	5	
Yenni	Adam	d.	SIT	8 July 1916	3	5	
Yenni	Jacob	o.	SIT	11 Aug. 1917	1	2	
Yenni	Peter, Jr.	o.	SIT	17 Mar. 1917	3	1	also 4:1
Yocum	Ora Stevens	d.	PD	21 Nov. 1918	2	3	also 22 Nov., 2:4
Yoder	C. M.	b.	PC	25 Jan. 1918	5	4	
Yoder	C. N.	b.	PA	24 Jan. 1918	8	5	
Yoo	Tom	d.	PC	6 Feb. 1916	4	5	
Yordi	Andrew	o.	PC	27 July 1916	4	6	
Yordi	Carl Andrew	o.	PC	29 Aug. 1916	1	6	
Yordi	Carl Andrew	o.	SRR	29 Aug. 1916	8	6	
Yordi	Grace I.	o.	PC	27 July 1916	4	6	
Yordi	Grace I.	o.	PC	29 Aug. 1916	1	6	
Yordi	Grace I.	o.	SRR	29 Aug. 1916	8	6	
York	Albert Taylor	b.	HT	7 Mar. 1918	1	4	
York	Russell	o.	HT	2 May 1918	1	3	
York	W. G.	m.	PD	7 June 1916	5	3	
York	Warren	o.	HT	2 May 1918	1	3	
York	William	o.	HT	2 May 1918	1	3	also 11 July, 7:3
York	Willis	m.	SRR	7 June 1916	8	2	
Yost	Charles	m.	SRR	31 May 1917	3	3	
Yost	Charles	m.	PD	1 June 1917	6	4	
Youker	Malcolm	b.	PA	29 Apr. 1916	6	5	
Youker	Mildred	b.	SRR	27 Apr. 1916	8	4	also 29 Apr., 6:3
Young	Carl	m.	PC	12 May 1918	8	3	

(1) Surname	(2) Given Name	(3)	(4)	(5) Date	(6) Pg	(7) Col	(8) Comments
Young	Carl A.	m.	PA	13 May 1918	5	1	
Young	Carl A.	m.	PD	14 May 1918	3	7	
Young	Cora B.	m.	PA	10 Sept. 1917	6	1	also 11 Sept., 2:3
Young	Cora B.	m.	PC	8 Sept. 1917	1	4	also 12 Sept., 5:4
Young	Cora B.	m.	PD	9 Sept. 1917	8	3	
Young	Dora	d.	PA	1 Apr. 1918	3	5	Cypress Hill; also 4:1; 2 Apr., 4:5
Young	Dora	d.	SIT	6 Apr. 1918	4	7	
Young	Dora H.	d.	PC	31 Mar. 1918	1	5	Cypress Hill; also 5:4; 2 Apr., 4:3; also 29 Mar., 1:5
Young	Fred	o.	HT	2 May 1918	7	1	also 11 July, 3:4
Young	George C., Mrs.	d.	PD	2 Apr. 1918	5	2	also 4 Apr., 8:3
Young	Grace	m.	PD	25 Jan. 1917	8	5	
Young	Harold	o.	SRR	20 Feb. 1917	4	3	adoption
Young	Harold	o.	PD	21 Feb. 1917	3	2	adoption
Young	Ivy M.	m.	PD	18 Aug. 1916	3	5	
Young	James Edward	d.	SIT	7 Sept. 1918	1	2	
Young	John	o.	SRR	24 Nov. 1917	12	2	
Young	John	o.	PD	25 Nov. 1917	10	3	
Young	John S.	d.	PD	27 Dec. 1918	2	1	
Young	John Solomon, Mrs.	d.	PA	15 Feb. 1917	4	3	Cypress Hill; also 16 Feb., 8:5; 17 Feb., 4:5
Young	John Solomon, Mrs.	d.	PC	16 Feb. 1917	4	4	Cypress Hill; also 17 Feb., 8:1; 18 Feb., 4:6
Young	Louise	d.	SRR	22 June 1916	8	5	
Young	Louise Gertrude	d.	PD	23 June 1916	8	2	S. F.
Young	Minnie	o.	SRR	24 Nov. 1917	12	1	
Young	Minnie	o.	PD	25 Nov. 1917	10	3	
Young	Minnie	d.	PA	30 Dec. 1916	6	3	
Young	Minnie	d.	PC	30 Dec. 1916	1	6	
Young	Minnie	d.	PD	30 Dec. 1916	8	3	
Young	Minnie	d.	SRR	30 Dec. 1916	2	4	
Young	Ralph	d.	PA	19 Oct. 1918	5	2	Cypress Hill; also 8:3; 21 Oct., 4:3
Young	Ralph	d.	PC	19 Oct. 1918	5	3	Cypress Hill; also 8:3; 20 Oct., 5:4, 8:4; 22 Oct., 4:3
Young	Ralph	d.	PD	23 Oct. 1918	7	3	Cypress Hill
Young	Silas H.	m.	PD	28 June 1917	7	4	
Zabel	Henry	d.	PA	7 Feb. 1916	5	3	also 9 Feb., 7:3
Zacchi	Angelo	d.	PA	6 June 1916	4	5	also 7 June, 5:5
Zacchi	Angelo	d.	PC	7 June 1916	1	5	
Zacchi	Angelo	d.	SRR	7 June 1916	5	2	
Zalim/Valin	Frank (son of)	d.	PA	27 July 1918	4	5	also 29 July, 8:2
Zamaroni	John	o.	PC	12 Sept. 1918	6	3	

(1) Surname	(2) Given Name	(3)	(4)	(5) Date	(6) Pg	(7) Col	(8) Comments
Zamaroni	John	o.	PA	30 Nov. 1918	8	3	
Zamorini	John	o.	PC	30 Nov. 1918	1	2	
Zane	Neil	m.	SIT	28 July 1917	2	4	
Zanni	Joseph	d.	PD	25 Oct. 1918	4	2	Petaluma
Zanni/Zenni	Joseph	d.	PC	25 Oct. 1918	8	2	also 30 Oct., 1:4
Zanni/Zenni	Joseph	d.	PA	26 Oct. 1918	1	7	Calvary Cemetery; also 29 Oct., 4:5; 30 Oct., 4:1
Zanoin	Elviza F.	m.	PA	29 Aug. 1917	2	1	
Zanolini	Eda	m.	PC	30 Aug. 1916	6	2	
Zanolini	Edna	m.	PA	29 Aug. 1916	8	3	
Zanoni	Elvezia A.	m.	SRR	29 Aug. 1917	4	3	
Zanoni	Elvezzia	m.	PC	29 Aug. 1917	5	5	also 30 Aug., 5:2
Zanzi	Tony	b.	SRR	29 July 1916	4	2	
Zappa	Lillian	m.	SRR	26 June 1917	8	6	
Zenetta	Frank	d.	PA	7 Mar. 1918	6	6	
Zenetta	Frank	d.	PC	8 Mar. 1918	4	1	
Zerga	Jane L.	m.	PD	16 Mar. 1916	3	4	
Ziegler	J. W.	d.	PA	30 Dec. 1918	6	5	
Ziegler	John William	d.	PC	29 Dec. 1918	4	2	
Zietbeer	Clarence	d.	PD	11 July 1916	2	1	
Zietheer/Vietheer	Clarence	d.	SRR	10 July 1916	8	1	also 12 July, 5:3
Zimmerman	Arnold	d.	SRR	13 June 1916	6	5	also 15 June, 8:3
Zimmerman	Ferdinand, Mrs.	d.	PC	1 Oct. 1917	5	3	Cypress Hill; also 9 Oct., 8:5
Zimmerman	Ferdinand, Mrs.	d.	PA	6 Oct. 1917	5	4	
Zimmerman	Frederick W.	d.	PD	20 Apr. 1916	6	3	
Zimmerman	Frederick William	d.	PA	18 Apr. 1916	1	3	Cypress Hill; also 20 Apr., 4:6
Zimmerman	Frederick William	d.	PC	19 Apr. 1916	1	6	Cypress Hill; also 20 Apr., 4:5; 21 Apr., 8:4
Zippa	Annie	m.	PD	1 June 1918	3	1	also 4 June, 3:5
Zittleman	Fred	m.	CR	6 July 1917	1	1	
Zocchi	A.	d.	SIT	10 June 1916	3	6	
Zook	Mary	d.	PA	16 June 1916	5	3	Cypress Hill; also 17 June, 8:5
Zook	Mary Louise	d.	PC	17 June 1916	3	2	Cypress Hill; also 18 June, 4:5
Zoppi	Walter	m.	PA	21 July 1917	4	3	
Zoppi	Walter	m.	PC	21 July 1917	5	2	also 22 July, 5:3
Zoppi	Walter	m.	ST	3 Aug. 1917	3	3	
Zoppi	Walter Amerigo	m.	PD	22 July 1917	7	4	
Zoric	Antone	b.	PA	21 Nov. 1916	5	2	
Zorie	Antone	b.	PC	22 Nov. 1916	4	5	
Zuchetti	Joseph	b.	PA	2 July 1918	5	6	
Zuchetti	Joseph	b.	PC	3 July 1918	5	2	
Zumini	Pete	d.	PA	15 Oct. 1917	5	5	also 16 Oct., 6:6

(1) Surname	(2) Given Name	(3)	(4)	(5) Date	(6) Pg	(7) Col	(8) Comments
Zumini	Pete	d.	PD	16 Oct. 1917	5	3	also 17 Oct., 6:4
Zumini	Peter	d.	SRR	17 Oct. 1917	5	3	
Zumini	Peter	d.	PC	18 Oct. 1917	4	1	
Zumwalt	Alice Viola	m.	PC	18 Nov. 1916	6	3	
Zumwalt	Berenice	m.	PA	24 Apr. 1918	4	5	
Zumwalt	Bernice I.	m.	PC	28 Apr. 1918	6	2	also 30 Apr., 5:4
Zumwalt	Ed	b.	ST	24 Mar. 1917	3	2	
Zunino	Giovanni	o.	SRR	26 Sept. 1917	8	4	
Zunino	Giovanni	o.	PD	27 Sept. 1916	5	2	
Zunino	Maddelina	o.	PD	27 Sept. 1916	5	2	
Zunino	Madelena	m.	SRR	26 Sept. 1917	5	3	
Zunino	Madelena	o.	SRR	26 Sept. 1917	8	4	
Zurcher	Martha	o.	PD	1 Oct. 1916	5	4	
Zurcher	Martha	o.	SRR	10 Jan. 1916	4	2	
Zurcher	Martha	o.	SRR	3 Oct. 1916	2	1	
Zurcher	Martha L.	o.	CR	10 Mar. 1917	1	4	also 20 Sept. 1918, 1:4; 1 Nov. 1918, 1:4
Zurcher	Martha L.	o.	PD	19 Jan. 1917	5	2	
Zurcher	Martha L.	o.	SRR	9 Jan. 1917	5	6	also 18 Jan., 8:4
Zurcher	Ulysses	o.	PD	1 Oct. 1916	5	4	
Zurcher	Ulysses	o.	SRR	10 Jan. 1916	4	2	
Zurcher	Ulysses	o.	CR	10 Mar. 1917	1	4	also 20 Sept. 1918, 1:4; 1 Nov. 1918, 1:4
Zurcher	Ulysses	o.	PD	19 Jan. 1917	5	2	
Zurcher	Ulysses	o.	SRR	3 Oct. 1916	2	1	
Zurcher	Ulysses	o.	SRR	5 Oct. 1917	5	4	
Zurcher	Ulysses	o.	SRR	9 Jan. 1917	5	6	also 18 Jan., 8:4

Other Heritage Books by the Sonoma County Genealogical Society, Inc.:

CD: *Sonoma County [California] Records, Volume 1*

Early School Attendance Records of Sonoma County, California, Beginning 1858

Early School Attendance Records of Sonoma County, California, Volume II: 1874–1932

Homestead Declarations: Amended Index, Sonoma County, California, Second Edition

Index and Abstracts of Wills, Sonoma County, California: 1850–1900

Index to Naturalization Records in Sonoma County, California, Volume 1: 1841–1906

Naturalization Records in Sonoma County, California, Volume II: 1906–1930

Index to The Sonoma Searcher*: Volume 16, No. 1 to Volume 28, No. 3*
(Including Index to The Sonoma Searcher*: Volume 1, No. 1 to Volume 15, No. 4, SCGS, August 1993)*

Index to Vital Data in Local Newspapers of Sonoma County, California, Volume 1: 1855–1875

Index to Vital Data in Local Newspapers of Sonoma County, California, Volume 2: 1876–1880

Index to Vital Data in Local Newspapers of Sonoma County, California, Volume 3: 1881–1885

Index to Vital Data in Local Newspapers of Sonoma County, California, Volume 4: 1886–1890

Index to Vital Data in Local Newspapers of Sonoma County, California, Volume 5: 1891–1899

Index to Vital Data in Local Newspapers of Sonoma County, California, Volume 6: 1900–1903

Index to Vital Data in Local Newspapers of Sonoma County, California, Volume 7: 1904–1906

Index to Vital Data in Local Newspapers of Sonoma County, California, Volume 8: 1907–1909

Index to Vital Data in Local Newspapers of Sonoma County, California, Volume 9: 1910–1912

Index to Vital Data in Local Newspapers of Sonoma County, California, Volume 10: 1913–1915

Index to Vital Data in Local Newspapers of Sonoma County, California, Volume 11: 1916–1918

Indigent Records in Sonoma County, California 1878 to 1926, Volume 1: The Indigents

Indigent Records in Sonoma County, California 1878 to 1926, Volume 2: Taxpayers Who Certified Indigent Need

Militia Lists of Sonoma County, California, 1846 to 1900

Santa Rosa Rural Cemetery, 1853–1997

Sonoma County, California Cemetery Records, 1846–1921, Third Edition

Sonoma County, California Death Records, 1873–1905, Second Edition

Sonoma County California Reconstructed 1890 Census

The 1930 School Census of Sonoma County, California

www.ingramcontent.com/pod-product-compliance
Lightning Source LLC
Chambersburg PA
CBHW081426270326
41932CB00019B/3115